A CATALOG OF MODERN WORLD COINS 1850–1964

15th Edition

R.S. Yeoman

Revised and edited by
Arthur L. Friedberg

Whitman Publishing, LLC
PUBLISHING SINCE 1934

A Catalog of Modern World Coins, 1850–1964

Whitman Publishing, LLC
PUBLISHING SINCE 1934

1974 Chandalar Drive, Suite D, Pelham, AL 35124

Correspondence concerning this book may be directed to the publisher, Attn: Modern World Coins, at the address above.

ISBN: 0794848346
Printed in the United States of America.

Disclaimer: Expert opinion should be sought in any significant numismatic purchase. This book is presented as a guide only. No warranty or representation of any kind is made concerning the accuracy or completeness of the information presented, or its usefulness in numismatic purchases or sales. The opinions of others may vary. The editor, a longtime numismatist, regularly buys, sells, and sometimes holds certain of the items discussed in this book.

Caveat: The price estimates given are subject to variation and differences of opinion. Especially rare coins trade infrequently, and an estimate or past auction price may have little relevance to a future transaction. Before making decisions to buy or sell, consult the latest information. Grading of coins is subject to wide interpretation, and opinions can differ. Past performance of the numismatic market or any coin or series within that market is not necessarily an indication of future performance, as the future is unknown. Such factors as changing demand, popularity, grading interpretations, strength of the overall market, and economic conditions will continue to be influences. The market for a given coin can fall or it can rise.

CONTENTS

PREFACE

Updated from the 14th Edition

"It seems hard to believe that collecting modern world coins could have changed so substantially since the first edition of this book was published in 1957." These were the words of R.S. Yeoman as he introduced the 13th edition of this book in 1984.

"It almost seems incredible," he continued, "that prior to that time, Americans seemed to little more than dabble in the world of collecting the monies of foreign lands, whose exotic jingle has proved to be so fascinating with time."

His words could be published almost verbatim today, almost 40 years later!

"That the book has grown in size and scope is readily apparent," wrote Yeoman, "but perhaps the most important additions are those that changing economic conditions have wrought, together with the dramatic increase in the popularity of collecting type coins of the world."

His analysis of the coin market has a familiar ring to today's collector:

> Back in 1957, when the first edition was issued, and even in 1974, when the 11th edition was published, the prices of gold and silver did not make a substantial difference in the way that coins were valued. Gold, after all, had remained stable at $35 per ounce from 1837 to 1971; even in 1974, when (on December 31) Americans were finally able to own gold legally, prices remained at affordable levels. (In January of 1974, gold opened at $117 per ounce, and by year's end, the price had risen to $194, only to slide again at the start of the following year.) Silver, likewise, remained a pillar of stability. From the high price of 91¢ an ounce in 1957, it did not rise above $1 an ounce until 1961, and even in 1974, prices averaged only $4.70—hardly enough to encourage the melting of coins, let alone have a major effect on their price structure.
>
> By contrast, the 1980s brought major changes in the way we collected coins of foreign lands, and major changes in the way these sought-after collectibles are valued. In the first place, on direct consequence of the gold and silver boom was that the price of silver rose to nearly $50 an ounce, while the price of gold approached the $800 mark. This was an extraordinary development, one that was not predicted (at least initially) by even the most daring of seers. Indeed, it is probably fair to say that if such a change had been forecast in the last edition of the book, no one would have believed it.
>
> What has happened to the precious metals in our coinage is endemic to what has happened to coin collecting; it has risen steadily—in collector interest and in value.

Nearly 40 years later, gold and silver have again seen spikes and dramatic climbs, with no telling where they will plateau. In fact, as this book goes to press, gold is trading near its all-time high, and silver, at close to $23 an ounce, is at a level not seen in years. And—in another mirror image of Yeoman's writing in the early 1980s—collector interest in world coins is continually on the rise.

The famous numismatist had glowing praise for the editors of the 13th edition:

> Two people who have also witnessed this extraordinary increase and chronicled it in *Gold Coins of the World* are Arthur Friedberg and Ira Friedberg, two brothers, who have revised the work of the late Robert Friedberg, their father, through several editions since the book was first published in 1958.
>
> This book and *Gold Coins of the World* are extraordinarily compatible, and they are similar to each other in the descriptive manner in which they catalog coins—by their type, the way most people collect them.
>
> *Gold Coins of the World* starts at the very beginning of coinage, millennia before the first coin listed in this catalog; but for those collecting popular gold coins produced between 1850 and the end of the gold boom marked by World War II, *Modern World Coins* offers an additional invaluable aid.

Finally, R.S. Yeoman offered a bit of philosophy that stands true today; its 13th-edition wording needs no revision:

> In prior volumes, I always offered a word to the beginning collector. You may be young, or you may be retired; you may have consulted this book upon the suggestion of a friend or the reference librarian at your local library. Someone in your family may have returned from overseas or from a tour in foreign lands with a pocketful of strange coins. This book will tell you what those coins are about.
>
> The country of origin, denomination, relative monetary value, and government and geography of the ruling nation are all part of the fascinating and wonderful world of coin collecting. If you examine these coins, and let this book guide the way for you, it is entirely possible for you to start your own personal coin collection and be assured in the process of a richly rewarding experience that may last your entire lifetime.
>
> If you are a collector of American coins, you may have reached the point of a waning interest in your present specialty. By moving into the realm of foreign coins, you can begin an entirely different collection, obtainable at modest cost—and have the entire world to choose from.
>
> It's easy to collect foreign coins, for even today, most are not collected by date and mintmark, the way American coins are, but rather by type. It is for this reason that the numbering systems in this book are so useful. This is how most coins have been collected for years.
>
> There are dozens of different ways that you can collect foreign coins. You can select gold coins of the world; crown-size coins (approximately U.S. silver-dollar size, though actually 39 mm and larger) from various countries; type coins of a particular country; commemorative coins; a single coin from each country; all types of coins from a single country or group of countries; or coins of a different variety or design—for example, coins with fishes on them, or coins with foreign rulers. As you get into it, you can view and consider many other areas.

> After more than half a century of involvement with the coin field, I must confess to having always retained a strong interest in coins of the world, as opposed to those of a particular country. American coins are certainly involved, and in this volume are listed all but the most recent of commemorative issues, of which there are more than 66 different designs and varieties. These, as most of the other coins in this book, can be collected by type, since a complete set of dates and mintmarks becomes more and more difficult and expensive to obtain.

This book, then, as revised by Arthur Friedberg, offers a substantial opportunity to any collector of (or investor in) coins. "Clearly, it is a book that belongs in your library," wrote Yeoman—who might easily write the same words today—"not only for the value, but also for the new information that modern research has disclosed about these wonderful coins."

INTRODUCTION

An Appreciation of R.S. Yeoman

To the collector of coins, be they world coins or American, the name R.S. Yeoman is as synonymous with organization and structure as the name Samuel Johnson is to lexicographers.

An examination of the library catalog of the American Numismatic Association discloses the reason why.

The author of numerous major titles, Yeoman was a prolific author of books and magazine articles. Through the years, he published on a variety of subjects. *Monies of the Bible,* a 1961 work, was an illustrated digest of coins of biblical times complete with scriptural references. His first book, *Handbook of United States Coins With a Premium List,* known as the Blue Book, was first published in 1942. The following year, he authored the *Handbook of United States Type Coins.* Four years later, in 1946, he wrote the classic *Guide Book of United States Coins,* which became known as the Red Book and has long since passed its 60th edition. Having seen distribution of more than 21 million copies, it is among the best-selling nonfiction books of all time.

A little later came *Buying and Selling United States Coins,* with coauthor (and editor of later editions of many of Yeoman's works) Kenneth Bressett, *Current Coins of the World* (first published in 1966), and the present book, *A Catalog of Modern World Coins* (first published in 1957).

In many respects, Yeoman was a consummate Renaissance man. His articles in *The Numismatist* covered such subjects as commemorative coins, emergency coinage of the California gold rush, the American eagle and half eagle, the 1848 quarter eagle with CAL., and even Lincoln cents. He found time, as well, to write for *The Young Numismatist,* and to serve as editor in chief of the *Whitman Numismatic Journal,* which started publication in 1964.

For more than 40 years he led Whitman Publishing Company to leadership in the coin industry, ultimately becoming vice president and general manager of the coin-supply division and a member of the company's board of directors.

Born in Milwaukee in 1904, Yeoman went to the University of Wisconsin and, at the age of 28, became a member of the staff of Whitman in Racine. His initial duties were in sales, sales promotion, and advertising. It was not until two years later, in 1934, that Whitman obtained an order to produce coin boards and then quickly bought the rights to the product and added them to their regular line of books, stationery supplies, and children's games.

Yeoman joined the American Numismatic Association in 1941, and in 1957 was awarded its coveted Farran Zerbe Award, the highest honor the ANA can give a member for distinguished service. He served as a member of the board of governors of the ANA from 1946 to 1951, and probably did more than any other individual in modern times to popularize coin collecting in all its various forms.

I knew Dick Yeo (his real name; Yeoman was a pen name) for more than 40 years, since shortly after I began writing about coins. Unfailingly courteous, always a good source for news or information, he was accessible as well as reliable, and always a good friend. His *Catalog of Modern World Coins* and *Current Coins of the World* were two desk references that I used repeatedly, not only for the valuable information they contained, but also for the convenience of having slim, easy-to-carry volumes that could be used almost as checklists.

The last edition of *Modern World Coins* was published 15 years ago, and without question, huge changes have taken place within what was once called a hobby. Coin collecting has become a growth industry. Millions of dollars are made each year in the buying and selling of coins. Yeoman's numbering system is widely used in the field of foreign coins. Pick up a coin periodical, any of the weekly publications, and the Yeoman numbering system is the shorthand in use for copper and silver coins.

It is a tribute to R.S. Yeoman that this book is now in its 15th edition, more than 65 years after it was first published. It seems obvious that it is a book destined to be revised and remain in print as the true encyclopedia of the field for many years to come.

David L. Ganz
New York, New York
Past President,
American Numismatic Association

How to Use This book

PURPOSE

This is essentially an introductory coin book, intended as an outline or framework for organizing a collection of type coins of the world. As such, it is useful for beginner and advanced collector alike as a handy source of information to supplement more complex books that list all dates, mints, and varieties. A single volume such as this does not illustrate all coins, though every effort is made to show as many as possible. All major or popular varieties a collector will find useful are also listed in this catalog. Medals, patterns, and tokens are generally excluded, but bullion issues are included for some of the popular series.

GENERAL INFORMATION

ARRANGEMENT

A simple alphabetical sequence is employed for finding each country in this book, regardless of geographical location or government affiliation. This arrangement was decided upon to reduce the use of the Index.

Illustrations in every instance are adjacent to corresponding listings and descriptions for easy identification. Unless noted, coins are pictured at actual size.

Historical and geographical data and monetary equivalents are placed at the beginning of each country group.

Minor coinage is listed first in each period or type group, followed by coins struck in precious metals. Commemorative coins are indicated by gray-shaded boxes.

The coin listings cross-reference the Yeoman (Y) numbering system to the Krause-Mishler (KM) numbering system.

SCOPE

Just over a century of coinage of the world—from the mid-19th century to about 1964—is the scope of this book; a logical starting and ending date for each country has been selected.

COMPOSITIONS

The listings hold the various coins' compositions, which are as follows; most are abbreviated in the charts.

anodized aluminum	AAl	clay	Clay	nickel-clad steel	N-CS
aluminum-bronze	A-Bz	copper-nickel	C-N	nickel-plated iron	N-PI
aluminum	Alum	copper-nickel-clad steel	C-NS	nickel-silver	N-S
antimony	Anti	copper-nickel-zinc	CNZ	nickel or copper-nickel	N/C-N
billon	Bill	copper	Cop	nickel	Nick
brass	Br	chromium-plated steel	C-PS	silver or billon	S/B
bronze	Bz	chrome-steel	C S	stainless steel	S S
brass-clad steel	Br-CS	fiber	Fiber	silver	Silv
bronze-clad steel	Bz-CS	gold	Gold	steel	Steel
bronze or brass	Bz/Br	iron	Iron	tin	Tin
card	Card	lead	Lead	zinc-coated steel	Z-CS
copper or brass	C/Br	nickel-brass	N-Br	zinc	Zinc
copper or bronze	C/Bz	nickel-bronze	N-Bz	various	Var

LISTING OF DATE RANGES

In most instances the first and last known dates of issue for each type are shown (e.g., 1898–1911). Coinage during intervening years may not necessarily be continuous. Dates shown are those actually appearing on the coins. For some countries they do not always conform to the year of production. "ND" indicates that no date appears on the coin. See details of unusual dating systems in the following pages.

LISTINGS OF RARE DATES

A substantial number of rare dates are shown separately, just beneath their respective type listings. The usual date span for the type remains unaltered. This listing is not exhaustive; there may be other dates within a series that may sell for a premium over the common type.

PROOF-COIN LISTINGS

Similarly, a number of prices for Proof coins (as a type) are shown separately, beneath their respective type-coin charts.

VALUATIONS

Prices are given opposite each catalog number, in three columns—for coins in Very Fine, Extremely Fine, and Uncirculated conditions. In every instance these values refer to the commonest date and mintmark if coined in several years or at several mints. The omission of a price usually indicates rarity and no recent sales record, but may also mean lack of information about a newly discovered type or variety. "BV" (bullion value) indicates that a coin's precious-metal value is greater than its numismatic value. The values listed were compiled from information received from experts around the world. They are approximate and intended only as a guide. Latest prices may be obtained from established coin dealers.

The opinions of many dealers and collectors are combined to arrive at each value. The values shown are not offers to buy or sell but are included only as general information.

Prices are in U.S. dollars, and reflect the U.S. retail market.

GRADING

Grading standards may vary from dealer to dealer, from collector to collector, and even from country to country. The American Numismatic Association has developed guidelines for the grading of United States coins; relevant portions are summarized here from the *Official American Numismatic Association Grading Standards for United States Coins*:

> PROOF—A specially made coin distinguished by sharpness of detail and usually with a brilliant, mirrorlike surface. *Proof* refers to the method of manufacture and is not a grade. The term implies mint condition.
>
> UNCIRCULATED—The terms *Uncirculated* and *Mint State* are often used interchangeably to describe coins showing no trace of wear. Such coins may vary to some degree because of blemishes, toning, or slight imperfections.
>
> EXTREMELY FINE—Light wear on the design throughout, but all features are sharp and well defined. Traces of the original mint luster may show.
>
> VERY FINE—Moderate wear on high points. All major details are clear.

NUMBERING SYSTEM

When a coin type is inserted in a previously established sequence, a capital letter is placed before a catalog number to avoid the necessity of renumbering all later issues. A lowercase letter following a catalog number indicates a minor difference (e.g., change of metal or size only) of a reissued type.

There are instances throughout this catalog where numbers and their corresponding listings have been removed. The reasons are numerous, but the most likely cause in each case is that the listing has been combined with earlier types that are identical except for date, or that the coin has been discovered to be a pattern, medal, or otherwise unauthorized piece. We regret that since earlier editions, occasional renumbering or rearranging has been necessary. This is done only to make the continuity more natural and useful, and is kept to a minimum.

HOW TO DETERMINE THE ORIGIN OF A COIN

First of all, a magnifying glass will prove useful in reading the legends, symbols, dates, and other interesting details on your coin specimens.

Sort your coins as best you can, grouping them by countries, or at least by similar types for later checking. Start with the easy ones, which might be coins using the familiar Latin alphabet (A, B, C, D. . .), with portraits of monarchs familiar to you and languages you may recognize immediately, such as English, Spanish, German, French, and so on. The spellings of country names are often similar to the Anglicized spelling (e.g., *Nederland* for *Netherlands*, *Liban* for *Lebanon*, etc.). Bear in mind, however, that there are many colonial issues. Thus, a coin with French legends could be issued for such faraway places as French Indo-China (Indo-Chine Française), French West Africa (Afrique Occidentale Française), and the like.

Many countries, especially in Asia, have alphabets strange to Westerners. Until characteristics of such coins become familiar to you, it is best to page through this volume until you locate illustrations that are similar to the designs on the coin. Far from being an arduous task, this phase can be intriguing. If the coin was struck from the 1850s to the 1960s, the chances are it can be located in this book.

The denomination shown on the coin often is a shortcut to identification. Terms such as *shilling*, *centavo*, *franc*, and so on are more or less familiar to us, and it would be natural to conclude that they belong to Great Britain, Mexico, and France, respectively. The table of denominations, however, might reveal that this is not necessarily so. A more careful inspection of the coins may show that the shilling actually was struck for Southern Rhodesia, the centavo for St. Thomas and Prince Islands, and the franc for Guadeloupe, where the same coin denominations are or have been used. That is the romance of collecting world coins. The quest is the thing.

Millimeter Scale

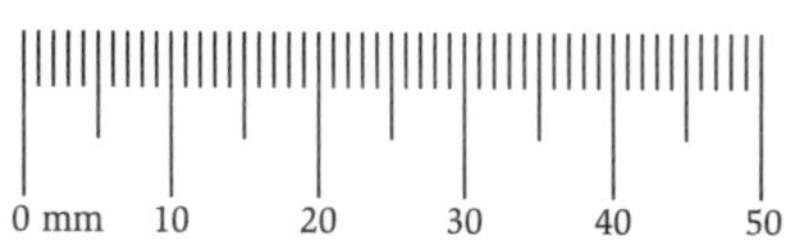

ERAS AND DATING SYSTEMS

Most countries show the dates more or less prominently on their coins. Little difficulty will be encountered with the coins of Europe, parts of Africa, and the Americas. In the Arabic and Asian countries, however, non-Latin symbols and letters pose a difficult problem of translation for both legends and dates. The chart below shows some of the date-numerals now in use throughout the world, while other, less-common systems are shown with their respective countries.

Numerals:

Western	1	2	3	4	5	6	7	8	9	0	10	100	1000
Arabic	١	٢	٣	٤	٥	٦	٧	٨	٩	٠	١٠	١٠٠	١٠٠٠
Arabic variants (Persia, etc.)	۱	۲	۳	۴	۵	۶	۷	۸	۹	٠			
Chinese, Japanese, Korean (ordinary)	一	二	三	四	五	六	七	八	九		十	百	千
Chinese, Japanese, Korean (official)	壹	貳	叄	肆	伍	陸	柒	捌	玖		拾	(半½)	
Devanagari (India, Nepal)	१	२	३	४	५	६	७	८	९	०			

Many countries using Arabic numerals observe the *Mohammedan era,* also known as the Era of the Hegira (A.H. or S.H.), dating from Mohammed's flight from Mecca to Medina in 622 A.D. This era has traditionally been based on a lunar year of 354 days—about 3% fewer days than the 365 in the Gregorian (A.D.) solar year. Mohammedan lunar dates are indicated by the letters "AH" in this volume. The following method may be used for an approximate conversion of A.H. to A.D. dates:

A.D. date = A.H. date – (3% of A.H. date) + 622

Example: A.H. date = 1330
3% of 1330 = 39.90 (closest whole number is 40)
1330 – 40 = 1290
1290 + 622 = 1912 A.D.

A few countries, such as *Afghanistan* and *Iran,* have adopted a modification of the Mohammedan calendar based on a solar year of normal length. Such dates are indicated by the letters "SH," and the corresponding A.D. year is found by simply adding 621.

The coins of *Thailand* use the dating systems of three eras:

The "Buddhist" era (B.E.), which dates from 543 B.C. Subtract 543 for A.D. dates. Four numerals are found on current issues. (Example: 1910 A.D. = 2453 B.E.)

The "Bangkok," or Ratanakosind-sok, era (RS), which dates from 1782. Add 1781 to convert to an A.D. date. Dates will have three numerals. (Example: 1910 A.D. = 129 R.S.)

The "Little," or Chula Sakarat, era (CS), which dates from 638 A.D. Add 638 to convert to A.D. dates. Dates will have four numerals. (Example: 1910 A.D. = 1271 C.S.

Several different eras were observed on the coinage of the *India Princely States:*

The Vikrama era has its initial point in 57 B.C. and is observed mainly in northern India. This is also known as the Samvat Era. Their year 1957 is 1900 A.D.

The Saka era, originating in the southwest corner of Northern India, is the dominant era and the great historical reckoning of Southern India. It dated from 78 A.D. but is based on elapsed years, so that A.D. equivalents are found by adding 78. Thus Saka 1822 began in 1900 A.D.

Chinese dates are correctly read from right to left. Coins of the Republic, when dated, start with the year 1912 A.D. Unlike coins dated by the Gregorian system, some coins of the Chinese Empire are dated according to a 60-year (sexagenary) cycle. Such dates are shown in this book by the abbreviation CD.

Coins with *no date* are indicated by the abbreviation ND, followed by the date of striking in parentheses when known.

AFGHANISTAN

Afghanistan is a mountainous inland country in southwest Asia. An independent kingdom from 1747 to 1973, it was then proclaimed an Islamic republic. A Soviet-backed Marxist regime took control in a 1979 coup and was in turn supplanted in the late 1990s by a Muslim fundamentalist coalition led by the Pakistani-supported Taliban. The republic was reestablished in 2001 by a U.S.-led alliance that ensured free elections. *Languages:* Pushtu, Persian. *Capital:* Kabul.

The traditional reverse design is the national emblem, a mosque with pulpit, generally over crossed arms. Inscriptions have been mostly in Persian; Pushtu was introduced in 1929 and used exclusively after 1950. Islamic-era lunar dating (AH) was used until AH 1337 (1919) and during the period AH 1347–1350 (1929–1931). In 1919, the solar calendar (SH) was introduced, which was about 40 years earlier than the AH calendar at that time. The AH calendar was restored in 1931 and has been retained since then. To figure AD dates from AH and SH dates, see the Introduction at the front of the book.

MONETARY SYSTEM

Before AD 1926	From 1926
10 dinar = 1 paisa	100 pul = 1 afghani
5 paisa = 1 shahi	20 afghani = 1 amani
10 paisa = 1 sanar	10 rupees = 1 tilla, 1 amani, 4 gram
20 paisa = 1 abbasi	30 rupees = 1 habibi
30 paisa = 1 qiran	
60 paisa = 1 kabuli rupee	

PRECIOUS METAL CONTENT

Dates	Denomination	Gross Wt (g)	Fineness	Net Wt (g)	Troy Oz.
		SILVER			
Typical Weights					
1880–1919	1 sanar	1.5500	0.5000	0.7745	0.0249
	1 abbasi	3.1100	0.5000	1.5519	0.0499
	1 qiran	4.6500	0.5000	2.3232	0.0747
	1 rupee	9.2000	0.5000	4.5966	0.1478
	5 rupees	45.6000	0.9000	41.0334	1.3194
1919–33	1 qiran	4.7500	0.5000	2.3730	0.0763
	1 rupee	9.2500	0.9000	8.3224	0.2676
	2-1/2 rupees	22.9200	0.9000	20.6256	0.6632
	1/2 afghani	5.0000	0.5000	2.4974	0.0803
	1 afghani	10.0000	0.9000	8.9973	0.2893
	2-1/2 afghani	25.0000	0.9000	22.4978	0.7234
1933–37	1/2 afghani	4.7500	0.5000	2.3730	0.0763
		GOLD			
Typical Weights					
1880–1919	1 tilla	4.6000	0.9000	4.1400	0.1331
	2 tilla	9.2000	0.9000	8.2800	0.2662
1920	1/2 amani	2.3000	0.9000	2.0700	0.0665
	1 amani	4.6000	0.9000	4.1400	0.1331
	2 amani	9.2000	0.9000	8.2800	0.2662
	5 amani	23.0000	0.9000	20.7000	0.6656
1921–27	1/2 amani	3.0000	0.9000	2.7000	0.0868
	1 amani	6.0000	0.9000	5.4000	0.1736
	2 amani	9.2000	0.9000	8.2800	0.2662
	2-1/2 amani	15.0000	0.9000	13.5000	0.4340
1929–31	1 habibi	4.6000	0.9000	4.1400	0.1331
	20 afghani	6.0000	0.9000	5.4000	0.1736
1934	1 tilla	6.0000	0.9000	5.4000	0.1736
1935–38	4 gram / 1 tilla	4.0000	0.9000	3.6000	0.1157
	8 gram / 2 tilla	8.0000	0.9000	7.2000	0.2314

AMIR ABDUR RAHMAN, *AH 1297–1319 (1880–1901)*

For crude "dump" issues of this reign, which preceded the machine-struck types, see Craig, *Coins of the World*.

Most early issues listed below are extraordinarily difficult to find in Uncirculated condition.

Y#	KM#	Metal	Description	VF	EF	Unc
1	800	C/Br	1 Paisa, AH 1309 (1891) (24 mm)	300	600	—
2	802	C/Br	1 Paisa, AH 1309–17 (20–21 mm)	10	20	—
3	803	Br	1 Shahi, AH 1309 (31 mm)	175	350	—
4	809	C/Br	100 Dinars, AH 1311 (41 mm)	1,000	2,000	—

Y#	KM#	Metal	Description	VF	EF	Unc
5	827	C/Br	1 Paisa, AH 1317, no wreaths (20 mm)	12.50	25	—
6	828	C/Br	1 Paisa, AH 1317, obverse of Y5, reverse of Y2	35.00	70	—

All silver of this reign has a toughra in a wreath on the obverse, and a mosque in a wreath on the reverse, but there are many minor varieties of inscriptions, ornamentation (such as stars and weapons), and date location.

Y#	KM#	Metal	Description	VF	EF	Unc
7	823–24	Silv	1 Sanar, AH 1315 (2 vars) (13 mm)	30.00	45	—
8	Several	Silv	1 Abbasi, AH 1313–14 (3 vars) (15–16 mm)	12.50	25	—
9	804	Silv	1 Qiran, AH 1308–09 (18–20 mm)	12.50	25	—
A10	805	Silv	1 Rupee, AH 1304	50.00	150	300
10	806	Silv	1 Rupee, AH 1308–18 (23–26 mm)	25.00	55	100
11	820	Silv	5 Rupees, AH 1314, thick (39 mm)	85.00	170	350

Y#	KM#	Metal	Description	VF	EF	Unc
12	826	Silv	5 Rupees, AH 1316, thin (45 mm)	60	150	300

Y#	KM#	Metal	Description	VF	EF	Unc
A13	807	Gold	1 Tilla, AH 1309 (22 mm)	400	700	—
13	Several	Gold	1 Tilla, AH 1313–16 (19–21 mm)	400	700	—
14	808	Gold	2 Tilla, AH 1309 (21 mm)	1,500	2,500	—

AMIR HABIBULLAH, *AH 1319–1337 (1901–1919)*

First Coinage, *AH 1319–1321, 1325*

Design: ***Similar to Y8–10, 12–13***
Obverse: ***Toughra in wreath***
Reverse: ***Mosque in wreath***

Y#	KM#	Metal	Description	VF	EF	Unc
15	837	Silv	1 Abbasi, AH 1320 (1902) (16 mm)	100	200	—
16	Several	Silv	1 Qiran, AH 1319–25 (19 mm)	65	125	—
17	Several	Silv	1 Rupee, AH 1319–21, 25 (25 mm)	25	50	—
18	834	Silv	5 Rupees, AH 1319 (46 mm)	125	250	—

Y#	KM#	Metal	Description	VF	EF	Unc
19	835–36	Gold	1 Tilla, AH 1319–20 (21 mm)	400	750	1,200

Second Coinage, *AH 1321–1329*

Design: ***Similar to Y2***

Y#	KM#	Metal	Description	VF	EF	Unc
20	848	Br	1 Paisa, AH 1329 (1911) (20 mm)	30	60	—

Obverse: ***Inscription in wreath***
Reverse: ***Mosque in wreath***

Y#	KM#	Metal	Description	VF	EF	Unc
21	846	Silv	1 Sanar, AH 1324–29 (13 mm)	50	100	200
22	845	Silv	1 Abbasi, AH 1324–29 (17 mm)	100	200	—
23	844	Silv	1 Qiran, AH 1323–29 (19 mm)	15	30	—
24	842/847	Silv	1 Rupee, AH 1321–29 (25 mm)	15	30	—

Y#	KM#	Metal	Description	VF	EF	Unc
25	843	Silv	5 Rupees, AH 1322–29 (45 mm)	75	125	250

Third Coinage, *AH 1329–1337*

Obverse: ***Inscription, no wreath***
Reverse: ***Mosque in sunburst***

Y#	KM#	Metal	Description	VF	EF	Unc
26	Several	C/Br	1 Paisa, AH 1329–37 (19–22 mm)	22.50	45	—

Y#	KM#	Metal	Description	VF	EF	Unc
27	850	Silv	1 Sanar, AH 1329–37 (13 mm)	22.50	45	—

Obverse: ***Inscription in wreath***
Reverse: ***Mosque in sunburst in wreath***

Y#	KM#	Metal	Description	VF	EF	Unc
28	851	Silv	1 Abbasi, AH 1329–37 (17 mm)	15.00	22.50	—
29	852	Silv	1 Qiran, AH 1329–37 (20 mm)	7.50	15.00	—
30	853	Silv	1 Rupee, AH 1329–37 (25 mm)	15.00	22.50	—
31	856	Gold	1 Tilla, AH 1335–37 (21 mm)	500.00	800.00	1,200

Amir Amanullah, *AH 1337, SH 1298–1307 (1919–1929)*

Pre–Decimal System, Through 1925

First Coinage, *AH 1337, SH 1298–1300*

Obverse: ***Inscription in wreath***
Reverse: ***Mosque in sunburst***

Y#	KM#	Metal	Description	VF	EF	Unc
32	857–58	C/Br	1 Paisa, AH 1337, SH 1298 (1919) (20 mm)	15	25	—

Obverse: ***Inscription in stars***
Reverse: ***Mosque in sunburst in stars***

Y#	KM#	Metal	Description	VF	EF	Unc
33	880	C/Br	1 Paisa, SH 1299–1303 (20 mm)	12.00	20	—
34	859–60	C/Br	1 Shahi, AH 1337–38 (25 mm)	30.00	60	—
35	861–62	C/Br	1 Sanar, AH 1337 (29–30 mm)	25.00	45	—
36	872	C/Br	3 Shahi, AH 1337, SH 1298–1300 (33 mm)	7.50	15	—

Y#	KM#	Metal	Description	VF	EF	Unc
37	874	Bill	1 Abbasi, SH 1298 (20 mm)	95	175	—
38	882	Bill	1 Abbasi, SH 1299 (25 mm)	50	100	—

Design: ***Similar to Y28–31***

Y#	KM#	Metal	Description	VF	EF	Unc
39	Several	Silv	1 Qiran, AH 1337, SH 1298–1300 (20 mm)	7.50	15	—
40	867/877	Silv	1 Rupee, AH 1337, SH 1298–99 (25 mm)	15.00	30	—

Design: ***Similar to Y31***

Y#	KM#	Metal	Description	VF	EF	Unc
41	868	Gold	1 Tilla, AH 1337 (21 mm)	235	375	500
42	879	Gold	2 Tilla, SH 1298 (23 mm)	500	1,000	2,000

Second Coinage

Obverse: ***Toughra in stars***
Reverse: ***Mosque in sunburst in stars***

Y#	KM#	Metal	Description	VF	EF	Unc
43	893	Cop	3 Shahi, SH 1300–01 (33 mm)	7.50	15	—

Y#	KM#	Metal	Description	VF	EF	Unc
44	883	Bill	1 Abbasi, SH 1299–1303 (25 mm)	12.50	25	—

Obverse: *Toughra in wreath*
Reverse: *Mosque in sunburst in wreath*

Y#	KM#	Metal	Description	VF	EF	Unc
45	894	Silv	1 Qiran, SH 1300–03 (20 mm)	7.50	15	—
46	885	Silv	1 Rupee, SH 1299–1303 (27 mm)	15.00	25	—
47	878	Silv	2-1/2 Rupee, SH 1298–1303 (34 mm)	30.00	55	—

Y#	KM#	Metal	Description	VF	EF	Unc
48	886	Gold	1/2 Amani, SH 1299 (16 mm)	130	200	350
49	887	Gold	1 Amani, SH 1299 (22 mm)	285	325	550
50	888	Gold	2 Amani, SH 1299–1303 (24 mm)	425	550	750
51	889-90	Gold	5 Amani, SH 1299 (34 mm)	2,000	2,850	—

DECIMAL SYSTEM, 1926–

100 pul = 1 afghani

Third Coinage

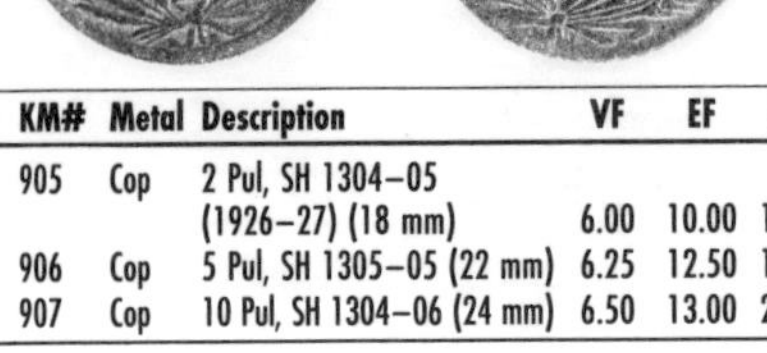

Y#	KM#	Metal	Description	VF	EF	Unc
52	905	Cop	2 Pul, SH 1304–05 (1926–27) (18 mm)	6.00	10.00	15.00
53	906	Cop	5 Pul, SH 1305–05 (22 mm)	6.25	12.50	17.50
54	907	Cop	10 Pul, SH 1304–06 (24 mm)	6.50	13.00	20.00

Y#	KM#	Metal	Description	VF	EF	Unc
55	908	Silv	20 Pul, ND (SH 1304) (19 mm)	75	150	300

Y#	KM#	Metal	Description	VF	EF	Unc
56	909/915	Silv	1/2 Afghani, SH 1304–07 (25 mm)	6	10	20
57	910	Silv	1 Afghani, SH 1304–07 (29 mm)	10	20	45
58	913	Silv	2-1/2 Afghani, SH 1305–06 (38 mm)	35	75	150

Y#	KM#	Metal	Description	VF	EF	Unc
59	911	Gold	1/2 Amani, SH 1304–06 (18 mm)	150	200	350
60	912	Gold	1 Amani, SH 1304–06 (23 mm)	250	375	550
61	914	Gold	2-1/2 Amani, SH 1306 (29 mm)	5,000	7,500	10,000

HABIBULLAH GHAZI (BACHA-I-SAQAO), *AH 1347–1348 (1929)*

LUNAR DATING RESUMED

First Coinage

Obverse: *Horizontal legend*

Y#	KM#	Metal	Description	VF	EF	Unc
62	895	C/Br	20 Paisa, AH 1347 (1929) (25 mm)	10	20	—

Y#	KM#	Metal	Description	VF	EF	Unc
63	896	Silv	1 Qiran, AH 1347 (21 mm)	12.50	25	—
64	897	Silv	1 Rupee, AH 1347 (25 mm)	15.00	30	—

Y#	KM#	Metal	Description	VF	EF	Unc
65	899	Gold	1 Habibi, AH 1347 (21 mm)	325	425	700

Second Coinage

Obverse: ***Circular legend***

Y#	KM#	Metal	Description	VF	EF	Unc
66	901	Cop	10 Paisa, AH 1348 (22 mm)	15	25	75

Y#	KM#	Metal	Description	VF	EF	Unc
67	902	Silv	1 Qiran, AH 1348 (21 mm)	30	60	—
68	898	Silv	1 Rupee, AH 1347 (26 mm)	25	35	—

MUHAMMAD NADIR SHAH, *AH 1348–1350, SH 1310–1312 (1929–1933)*

FIRST COINAGE

Lunar Dating

Obverse: ***Inscription***

Y#	KM#	Metal	Description	VF	EF	Unc
69	A922	C/Br	1 Pul, AH 1349 (1930) (15 mm)	1.50	2	5

Obverse: ***Toughra***

Y#	KM#	Metal	Description	VF	EF	Unc
A69	922	C/Br	1 Pul, AH 1349 (1930) (15 mm)	225	350	500

Y#	KM#	Metal	Description	VF	EF	Unc
70	917	C/Br	2 Pul, AH 1348 (18 mm)	2.50	3.00	25
71	923	C/Br	5 Pul, AH 1349–50 (22 mm)	2.00	3.00	25
72	918	C/Br	10 Pul, AH 1348–49 (25 mm)	4.00	6.00	45
73	919	C/Br	20 Pul, AH 1348–49 (25 mm)	4.50	6.50	50
74	924	C/Br	25 Pul, AH 1349 (25 mm)	4.00	6.00	45

Y#	KM#	Metal	Description	VF	EF	Unc
75	920	Silv	1/2 Afghani, AH 1348–50 (24 mm)	3.75	15	45
76	921	Silv	1 Afghani, AH 1348–50 (30 mm)	10.00	25	75

Y#	KM#	Metal	Description	VF	EF	Unc
78	925	Gold	20 Afghani, AH 1348–50 (22 mm)	425	500	650

SECOND COINAGE SOLAR DATING RESUMED

Y#	KM#	Metal	Description	VF	EF	Unc
80	928	Br	2 Pul, SH 1311–14 (1932–35) (18 mm)	3	4	24
81	929	Br	5 Pul, SH 1311–14 (21 mm)	6	10	30
82	930	Br	10 Pul, SH 1311–14 (23 mm)	6	10	30

Note: Y80–82 do not bear the name of the ruler and were continued into the reign of Muhammad Zahir.

Y#	KM#	Metal	Description	VF	EF	Unc
83	926	Silv	1/2 Afghani, SH 1310–12 (24 mm)	6	15	45
84	927	Silv	1 Afghani, SH 1310–11 (27 mm)	75	150	250

Muhammad Zahir Shah, *SH 1312–1352 (1933–1973)*

First Coinage

Also see Y80–82.

Y#	KM#	Metal	Description	VF	EF	Unc
85	931	C/Br	25 Pul, SH 1312–16 (24–25 mm)	15	30	60

Y#	KM#	Metal	Description	VF	EF	Unc
86	932	Silv	1/2 Afghani, SH 1312–16 (24 mm)	15	35	75
87	933	Gold	1 Tilla, SH 1313 (22 mm)	250	450	650

Y#	KM#	Metal	Description	VF	EF	Unc
88	935	Gold	4 Gram (1 Tilla), SH 1315, 17 (19 mm)	225	300	400
89	934	Gold	8 Gram (2 Tilla), SH 1314–17 (22 mm)	425	500	700

Second Coinage

Y#	KM#	Metal	Description	VF	EF	Unc
90	936	Bz	2 Pul, SH 1316 (1937) (15 mm)	0.65	1.00	3.75
91	937	Bz	3 Pul, SH 1316 (16 mm)	0.75	1.50	2.50
92	938	Bz	5 Pul, SH 1316 (17 mm)	0.90	1.75	3.00

Y#	KM#	Metal	Description	VF	EF	Unc
93	939	C-N	10 Pul, SH 1316 (18 mm)	0.75	2.25	4.50

Y#	KM#	Metal	Description	VF	EF	Unc
94	940	C-N	25 Pul, SH 1316 (20 mm)	1	2.25	4.50

Later Issues

Y#	KM#	Metal	Description	VF	EF	Unc
95	941	Bz	25 Pul, SH 1330–32 (1951–53) (20 mm)	0.30	0.50	1

Y#	KM#	Metal	Description	VF	EF	Unc
96	942	Bz	50 Pul (1/2 Afghani), SH 1330 (22 mm)	2.50	4	7.50
95a	943–44	N-CS	25 Pul, SH 1331–34, edge plain or reeded	1.00	2	4.00
95b	945	Alum	25 Pul, SH 1331 (struck in 1970)	2.00	5	10.00
96a	946	N-CS	50 Pul (1/2 Afghani), SH 1331–34, numeric denomination	1.00	2	4.00

Y#	KM#	Metal	Description	VF	EF	Unc
97	947	N-CS	1/2 Afghani (50 Pul), SH 1331, denomination spelled out	0.50	1	2

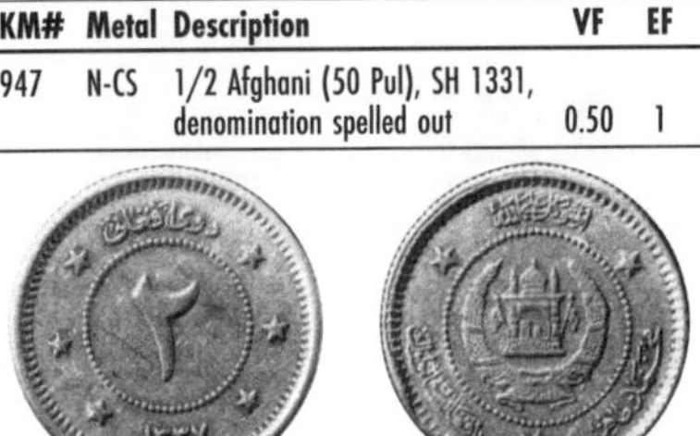

Y#	KM#	Metal	Description	VF	EF	Unc
98	949	Alum	2 Afghani, SH 1337 (1958)	0.75	1.25	2.50

Y#	KM#	Metal	Description	VF	EF	Unc
99	950	Alum	5 Afghani, SH 1337	1	2	4

Y#	KM#	Metal	Description	VF	EF	Unc
100	953	N-CS	1 Afghani, SH 1340 (1961)	0.40	0.75	1.75

Y#	KM#	Metal	Description	VF	EF	Unc
101	954	N-CS	2 Afghani, SH 1340	0.50	0.90	2

Y#	KM#	Metal	Description	VF	EF	Unc
102	955	N-CS	5 Afghani, SH 1340 / AH 1381	0.75	2.25	5

ALBANIA
(SHQIPNI, SHQIPERI)

Albania lies on the Adriatic coast of south-central Europe, just east of Italy's "boot heel." It declared independence from the Ottoman Empire in 1912, existing as a republic and a kingdom before coming under communist control after World War II. An anti-socialist opposition gained strength in the 1990s, setting the nation, Europe's poorest, on an emerging democratic course. *Languages:* Albanian, Greek. *Capital:* Tirana.

MONETARY SYSTEM

1925–1931
100 qindar leku = 1 frang ar
5 lek = 1 frang ar

1939–1941
1 lek = 1 lira

1935–1938
100 qindar ar = 1 frang ar

1947–
100 qindarka = 1 lek

PRECIOUS METAL CONTENT

Dates	Denomination	Gross Wt (g)	Fineness	Net Wt (g)	Troy Oz.
		SILVER			
1925–37	1 frang ar	5.0000	0.8350	4.1750	0.1342
	2 franga ar	10.0000	0.8350	8.3500	0.2685
	5 franga ar	25.0000	0.9000	22.5000	0.7234
1937	5 lek	5.0000	0.8350	4.1750	0.1342
	10 lek	10.0000	0.8350	8.3500	0.2685
		GOLD			
1926–38	10 franga ar	3.2258	0.9000	2.9032	0.0933
	20 franga ar	6.4516	0.9000	5.8064	0.1867
	50 franga ar	16.1290	0.9000	14.5161	0.4667
	100 franga ar	32.2581	0.9000	29.0323	0.9334
	100 franga ar	32.2581	0.9000	29.0323	0.9334

REPUBLIC, *1912–1918*

Y#	KM#	Metal	Description	VF	EF	Unc
1	1	Bz	5 Qindar Leku, 1926	45	90	185

Y#	KM#	Metal	Description	VF	EF	Unc
2	2	Bz	10 Qindar Leku, 1926	25	60	150

Y#	KM#	Metal	Description	VF	EF	Unc
3	3	Nick	1/4 Leku, 1926–27	6.50	20	65

Y#	KM#	Metal	Description	VF	EF	Unc
4	4	Nick	1/2 Lek, 1926	10	25	90

Y#	KM#	Metal	Description	VF	EF	Unc
5	5	Nick	1 Lek, 1926–31	5	15	65

Y#	KM#	Metal	Description	VF	EF	Unc
6	6	Silv	1 Franga Ar, 1927–28	50	115	235

Y#	KM#	Metal	Description	VF	EF	Unc
7	7	Silv	2 Franga Ari, 1926–28	85	175	350

Obverse: ***President Amet Zogu; bust similar to that on Y11–11a, but facing right***

Y#	KM#	Metal	Description	VF	EF	Unc
8	8	Silv	5 Franga Ari, 1926–27	250	400	1,000

Y#	KM#	Metal	Description	VF	EF	Unc
9	9	Gold	10 Franga Ari, 1927	250	350	425
10	10	Gold	20 Franga Ari, 1926–27	300	325	560

Y#	KM#	Metal	Description	VF	EF	Unc
11	11	Gold	100 Franga Ari, 1926, reverse SHQIPNI/ALBANIA	1,475	1,750	2,750
11a	11a	Gold	100 Franga Ari, 1927, reverse ALBANIA–SHQIPNI	1,475	1,750	2,750

Y#	KM#	Metal	Description	VF	EF	Unc
12	12	Gold	20 Franga Ari, 1926–27	300	325	560

KINGDOM, *1928–1939, Amet Zogu, as King Zog I*

First Coinage

Y#	KM#	Metal	Description	VF	EF	Unc
13	13	Nick	1/2 Lek, 1930–31	4	10	30

Note: Y5 was also struck during this period.

Second Coinage

Y#	KM#	Metal	Description	VF	EF	Unc
14	14	Bz	1 Qindar Ar, 1935	35	45	75
15	15	Bz	2 Qindar Ari, 1935	35	45	75

Y#	KM#	Metal	Description	VF	EF	Unc
16	16	Silv	1 Frang Ar, 1935, 37	15.00	25	55
17	17	Silv	2 Franga Ari, 1935	22.50	50	150

25th Anniversary of Independence

Reverse: ***Dated 28 XI [Nov. 28], 1912–1937***

Y#	KM#	Metal	Description	VF	EF	Unc
18	18	Silv	1 Frang Ar, 1937	20	40	100
19	19	Silv	2 Franga Ari, 1937	30	75	165

Y#	KM#	Metal	Description	VF	EF	Unc
20	20	Gold	20 Franga Ari, 1937	300	450	1,000
21	21	Gold	100 Franga Ari, 1937	1,650	1,950	4,000

Marriage of King Zog

Reverse: ***Dated 27 IV [April 27], 1938***

Y#	KM#	Metal	Description	VF	EF	Unc
22	22	Gold	20 Franga Ari, 1938	300	450	900
23	23	Gold	100 Franga Ari, 1938	1,650	1,950	4,000

10th Anniversary of Reign

Reverse: ***Dated 1 IX [Sept. 1], 1928–1938***

Y#	KM#	Metal	Description	VF	EF	Unc
24	24	Gold	20 Franga Ari, 1938	300	450	1,000
25	25	Gold	50 Franga Ari, 1938	1,000	1,500	4,500
26	26	Gold	100 Franga Ari, 1938	1,650	1,950	4,000

VITTORIO EMANUELE III
of Italy, as King of Albania, 1939–1943

MONETARY SYSTEM

1 lek = 1 lira

Y#	KM#	Metal	Description	VF	EF	Unc
27	27	A-Bz	0.05 Lek, 1940–41 *1941, Rare*	12.50	35	110

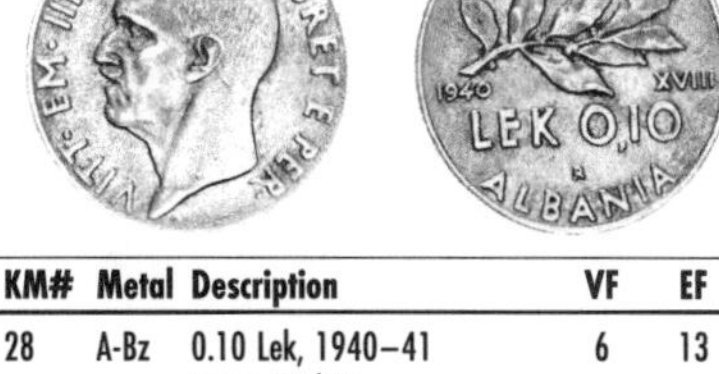

Y#	KM#	Metal	Description	VF	EF	Unc
28	28	A-Bz	0.10 Lek, 1940–41 *1941, VF $40*	6	13	35

Two different alloys were used for Y29–32: non-magnetic in 1939 and part of 1940, and magnetic in the rest of 1940 through 1941.

Y#	KM#	Metal	Description	VF	EF	Unc
29	29	S S	0.20 Lek, 1939–41	3.75	5	20

Y#	KM#	Metal	Description	VF	EF	Unc
30	30	S S	0.50 Lek, 1939–41	3.25	10.00	32.50
31	31	S S	1 Lek, 1939–41, like Y29	3.50	12.50	30.00
32	32	S S	2 Lek, 1939–41, like Y30	4.00	12.50	30.00

Note: Dates after 1939 of Y31–32 not for circulation.

Y#	KM#	Metal	Description	VF	EF	Unc
33	33	Silv	5 Lek, 1939	13	25	50
34	34	Silv	10 Lek, 1939, head right	40	85	150

PEOPLE'S REPUBLIC, *1946–1990*

Y#	KM#	Metal	Description	VF	EF	Unc
35	35	Zinc	1/2 Leku, 1947, 57	1.00	2.00	5.00
36	36	Zinc	1 Lek, 1947, 57	0.75	1.75	3.50
37	37	Zinc	2 Leke 1947, 57	0.75	1.75	3.50
38	38	Zinc	5 Leke 1947, 57	1.00	2.00	5.00

Y#	KM#	Metal	Description	VF	EF	Unc
39	39	Alum	5 Qindarka, 1964	0.50	0.65	1.00
40	40	Alum	10 Qindarka, 1964	0.50	0.65	1.00
41	41	Alum	20 Qindarka, 1964	0.55	0.75	1.25
42	42	Alum	50 Qindarka, 1964	0.60	1.00	3.00
43	43	Alum	1 Lek, 1964	0.65	1.25	3.25

ALGERIA

Situated on the Mediterranean coast of north Africa, Algeria was nominally part of the Ottoman Empire until being colonized by France in the 19th century. After nearly a decade of bloody rebellion begun in the mid-1950s it became an independent republic in 1962. Since then, Islamic fundamentalists and military interests have been engaged in virtually continuous civil unrest. *Languages:* Arabic, French, Berber dialects. *Capital:* Algiers.

MONETARY SYSTEM

100 centimes = 1 franc

FRENCH COLONY, *1830–1962*

France Y89 (2 Francs, 1944) was also issued in Algeria during World War II.

Y#	KM#	Metal	Description	VF	EF	Unc
1	91	C-N	20 Francs, 1949, 56	1	3	10
2	92	C-N	50 Francs, 1949	2	6	20
3	93	C-N	100 Francs, 1950, 52	3	8	25

REPUBLIC, *1962–*

MONETARY SYSTEM

100 centimes = 1 dinar

Y#	KM#	Metal	Description	VF	EF	Unc
4	94	Alum	1 Centime, 1964	0.50	0.75	1.00
5	95	Alum	2 Centimes, 1964	0.50	0.75	1.00
6	96	Alum	5 Centimes, 1964	0.60	0.85	1.25

Y#	KM#	Metal	Description	VF	EF	Unc
7	97	A-Bz	10 Centimes, 1964	0.75	1	2.00
8	98	A-Bz	20 Centimes, 1964	0.75	1	2.00
9	99	A-Bz	50 Centimes, 1964	1.00	2	3.50
10	100	C-N	1 Dinar, 1964	2.00	4	7.50

ANGOLA

On the west coast of Africa, Angola was under Portuguese control from the 1500s until a people's republic was declared in 1975 after 14 years of armed rebellion by Marxist factions. For nearly 30 years thereafter, civil war ensued between anti-communist forces and the socialist government. A ceasefire accord was reached in 2002 when rebels laid down their arms following the death of their leader. *Languages:* Portuguese, Bantu, other dialects. *Capital:* Luanda.

MONETARY SYSTEM

5 centavos = 1 macuta, to 1928
100 centavos = 1 angolar, 1926–1952
100 centavos = 1 escudo, 1914–1926; 1952–1975

Y#	KM#	Metal	Description	VF	EF	Unc
12	60	Bz	1 Centavo, 1921	15.00	45	100
13	61	Bz	2 Centavos, 1921	30.00	75	150
14	62	Bz	5 Centavos, 1921–24	8.00	20	60
15	63	C-N	10 Centavos, 1921–23	7.00	20	60
16	64	C-N	20 Centavos, 1921–22	7.50	15	55

Y#	KM#	Metal	Description	VF	EF	Unc
17	65	Nick	50 Centavos, 1922–23	8	25	65

Value in centavos and macutas.

Y#	KM#	Metal	Description	VF	EF	Unc
18	66	N-Bz	5 Centavos, 1927	5	17.50	50
19	67	N-Bz	10 Centavos, 1927–28	5	20.00	50
20	68	N-Bz	20 Centavos, 1927–28	5	20.00	50
21	69	N-Bz	50 Centavos, 1927–28	7	20.00	65

New Coinage System

Y#	KM#	Metal	Description	VF	EF	Unc
22	70	Bz	10 Centavos, 1948–49	0.50	1	5.00
23	71	Bz	20 Centavos, 1948–49	0.50	1	5.00
24	72	N-Bz	50 Centavos, 1948, 50	1.00	2	7.50

Decree of January 21, 1952

"Colonia De" Omitted

Y#	KM#	Metal	Description	VF	EF	Unc
23a	78	Bz	20 Centavos, 1962	0.20	0.50	2
25	75	Bz	50 Centavos, 1953–61	0.25	1.00	3
26	76	Bz	1 Escudo, 1953–74	0.50	2.00	5

Y#	KM#	Metal	Description	VF	EF	Unc
27	77	C-N	2-1/2 Escudos, 1953–74	0.50	2	5

Design: ***Similar to Y27***

Y#	KM#	Metal	Description	VF	EF	Unc
28	73	Silv	10 Escudos, 1952, 55	2	5	15.00
29	74	Silv	20 Escudos, 1952, 55	4	7	17.50

ANNAM

Annam is now part of Vietnam, formerly one of three protectorates in French Indo-China, located along the coast of the South China Sea. *Language:* Khmer. *Capital:* Hue.

Thanh Thai, *1889–1907*

Cast Coins

Y#	KM#	Metal	Description	VF	EF	Unc
1	626	Br	1 Sapeque (Phan), reverse blank	10.00	25.00	—
2	628	C/Br	10 Sapeque (Van), reverse shows value	3.50	9.50	—
A3	632	Silv	1 Lang	900.00	1,800.00	—
A4	634	Gold	1 Tien	2,500.00	3,500.00	—
B4	636	Gold	1-1/2 Tien	3,500.00	4,500.00	—
A5	638	Gold	3 Tien	4,000.00	5,500.00	—
A6	641	Gold	4 Tien	5,000.00	8,000.00	—
B6	643	Gold	5 Tien	8,000.00	10,000.00	—
C6	645	Gold	6 Tien	12,000.00	17,000.00	—
A7	647	Gold	1 Lang	6,250.00	9,500.00	—
A8	649–650	Gold	1 Lang Bar, *Rare*			

DUY TAN, *1907–1916*

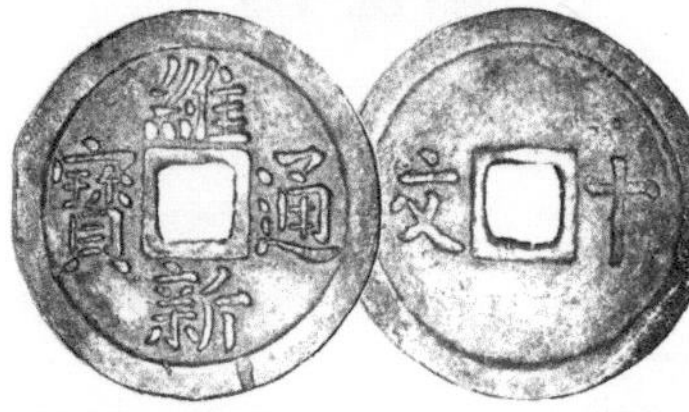

Y#	KM#	Metal	Description	VF	EF	Unc
3	652	Br	10 Sapeque (Van), reverse value	3	9	—

KHAI DINH, *1916–1926*

Y#	KM#	Metal	Description	VF	EF	Unc
4	654	Cop	1 Sapeque (Phan), cast	35	95	—
5	656	Cop	1 Sapeque (Phan), struck	10	55	—

BAO DAI, *1926–1945*

Y#	KM#	Metal	Description	VF	EF	Unc
6	662	Br	1 Sapeque (Phan), reverse blank, small planchet	8.50	20	85

Y#	KM#	Metal	Description	VF	EF	Unc
6a	661	Br	1 Sapeque (Phan), reverse blank, large planchet	12.50	50	150
7	664	Cop	10 Sapeque (Van)	10.00	40	125

ARABIAN SULTANATES
(HADHRAMAUT)

Small, semi-independent sultanates under British control in the former East Aden protectorate, at one time these were sovereign states, extending along the lower coast of the Arabian Peninsula. They are now part of the Republic of Yemen. *Languages:* Arabic, English.

PRECIOUS METAL CONTENT

Dates	Denomination	Gross Wt (g)	Fineness	Net Wt (g)	Troy Oz.
		SILVER			
1897	6 chomsih	0.8500	0.9000	0.7650	0.0246
	12 chomsih	1.5500	0.9000	1.3950	0.0448
	24 chomsih	3.1000	0.9000	2.7900	0.0897
1926	4 chomsih	0.5660	0.9000	0.5094	0.0164
	8 chomsih	1.0333	0.9000	0.9300	0.0299
	15 chomsih	1.9375	0.9000	1.7438	0.0561
	30 chomsih	3.8750	0.9000	3.4875	0.1121
	45 chomsih	5.8125	0.9000	5.2313	0.1682
	60 chomsih	7.7500	0.9000	6.9750	0.2242

GHURFAH *(City)*

A town in Kathiri State, 30 miles southwest of Tarim.

MONETARY SYSTEM

120 chomsih (chamsi) = 1 riyal (Maria Theresa thaler)

Y#	KM#	Metal	Description	VF	EF	Unc
4	101	Silv	4 Chomsih, AH 1344 (1926)	37.50	80	250
6	102	Silv	8 Chomsih, AH 1344	45.00	90	300
8	103	Silv	15 Chomsih, AH 1344	30.00	60	250
10	104	Silv	30 Chomsih, AH 1344	30.00	75	300
11	105	Silv	45 Chomsih, AH 1344	300.00	400	700
12	106	Silv	60 Chomsih, AH 1344	30.00	75	300

QUAITI STATE

SULTAN MONASAR BIN ABDULLAH

Coinage of East Africa, British East India Company, and Maria Theresa thalers counterstamped in Arabic, both copper and silver (dated 1307). The abbreviation "c/s" stands for "counterstamp."

Y#	KM#	Metal	Description	VF	EF	Unc
A1	1	Cop	1/12 Anna size, small c/s	120	—	—
1	Several	Cop	1/4 Anna size, small c/s	90	—	—
1a	5/8	Cop	1/4 Anna size, large c/s	90	—	—
2	15–17	Cop	1/2 Anna size, large c/s	150	—	—
2a	20	Cop	1/2 Anna, size, small c/s	120	—	—
3	25–26	Silv	1/2 Rupee size, small c/s	160	—	—
4	27–28	Silv	1/2 Rupee size, large c/s	180	—	—
5	Several	Silv	1 Rupee size, small c/s	250	—	—
6	33	Silv	1 Rupee size, large c/s	275	—	—
7	35	Silv	1 Ryal (Crown), small c/s	300	—	—
7a	36	Silv	1 Ryal (Crown), large c/s	400	—	—

SULTAN NAWAZ BIN OMER

Y#	KM#	Metal	Description	VF	EF	Unc
8	45	Cop	5 Chomsih, AH 1315 (1897)	65	125	—

Y#	KM#	Metal	Description	VF	EF	Unc
9	48	Cop	5 Chomsih, AH 1318 (1900)	100	150	—

SULTANATE OF MUKALLA

SULTAN AL NAKIB SALAH

Y#	KM#	Metal	Description	VF	EF	Unc
1	1	Cop	1/2 Chomsih, AH 1276 (1859)	150	250	—
2	2	Cop	1 Chomsih, AH 1276	80	125	—

LAHEJ

Small, semi-independent sultanate just north of the city of Aden, in the former West Aden Protectorate.

MONETARY SYSTEM
128 pessa (pice) = 1 Indian rupee

SULTAN ALI MOHASAN, *1849–1863*

Y#	KM#	Metal	Description	VF	EF	Unc
1	1	Cop	1/2 Pessa, ND (1860)	60	80	—

SULTAN FAZAL BIN ALI, *1874–1898*

Date AH 1291 (1874) on coin is accession date.

Y#	KM#	Metal	Description	VF	EF	Unc
2	2	Cop	1/2 Pessa, ND (1896)	70	90	—

TARIM *(City)*

Located in the Hadhramaut in the southern part of Arabia (East Aden Protectorate). This has been a passageway rather than a developed country.

MONETARY SYSTEM
120 chomsih (chamsi) = 1 riyal (Maria Theresa thaler)

Several die varieties exist for YA1–A3.

Y#	KM#	Metal	Description	VF	EF	Unc
A1	N/A	Cop	1 Chomsih, AH 1258 (1842), thin	150	—	—
A2	N/A	Cop	3 Chomsih, AH 1258, thick	180	—	—
A3	N/A	Silv	30 Chomsih, AH 1258, thick	400	—	—
A4	N/A	Silv	4 Chomsih, AH 1270 (1853)	200	—	—
A5	N/A	Silv	8 Chomsih, AH 1270	225	—	—
A6	N/A	Silv	16 Chomish, AH 1270	300	—	—

Y#	KM#	Metal	Description	VF	EF	Unc
1	1	Silv	6 Chomsih, AH 1315 (1897)	20	45	75
2	2	Silv	12 Chomsih, AH 1315	30	35	125
3	3	Silv	24 Chomsih, AH 1315	40	75	150

Note: Y1–3 were occasionally struck to 1926.

ARGENTINA

This republic occupies the major portion of southern South America. Settled by Spain in the 16th century, Argentina's independence was formally declared in 1816. In the last half of the 20th century the nation endured a string of military dictatorships, civil unrest, and economic hardship from which it is slowly emerging. *Language:* Spanish. *Capital:* Buenos Aires.

MONETARY SYSTEM
100 centavos = 1 peso
5 pesos = 1 argentino

PRECIOUS METAL CONTENT

Dates	Denomination	Gross Wt (g)	Fineness	Net Wt (g)	Troy Oz.
		SILVER			
1881–83	10 centavos	2.5000	0.9000	2.2500	0.0723
	20 centavos	5.0000	0.9000	4.5000	0.1447
	50 centavos	12.5000	0.9000	11.2500	0.3617
	1 peso	25.0000	0.9000	22.5000	0.7234
		GOLD			
1881–96	1/2 argentino	4.0322	0.9000	3.6290	0.1167
	1 argentino	8.0645	0.9000	7.2581	0.2333

Y#	KM#	Metal	Description	VF	EF	Unc
1	32	Bz	1 Centavo, 1882–96	2	4	20
			1882, 96, VF $40			
2	33	Bz	2 Centavos, 1882–96	2	6	35
			1882, VF $60; 1887, VF $175; 1888, 96, VF $8			

Y#	KM#	Metal	Description	VF	EF	Unc
3	26	Silv	10 Centavos, 1881–83	10.00	20	100
			1881, Unc $1,000			
4	27	Silv	20 Centavos, 1881–83	17.50	35	115
			1881, Unc $1,250			
5	28	Silv	50 Centavos, 1881–83	25.00	50	135
			1881, Unc $1,500			
6	29	Silv	1 Peso, 1881–83	175.00	300	825

Obverse: ***Similar to Y1–6***
Reverse: ***Liberty head facing right, legend around border***

Y#	KM#	Metal	Description	VF	EF	Unc
10	30	Gold	1/2 Argentino, 1884	3,250	4,500	6,250
11	31	Gold	1 Argentino, 1881–96	375	450	550

Y#	KM#	Metal	Description	VF	EF	Unc
7	34	C-N	5 Centavos, 1896–1942	1.00	4.00	8.50
			1896	6.00	12.50	40.00
			1897–1934	3.50	7.50	17.50

Y#	KM#	Metal	Description	VF	EF	Unc
8	35	C-N	10 Centavos, 1896–192	1.00	4.00	8.50
			1896	12.50	25.00	75.00
			1897–1919	6.50	13.00	35.00
			1920–36	2.00	5.00	10.00
9	36	C-N	20 Centavos, 1896–1942	1.00	3.00	10.00
			1896–1906, 09–10, 16	10.00	25.00	125.00
			1907–08, 11, 14	35.00	65.00	225.00
			1918–30	2.00	6.50	15.00
14	39	Nick	50 Centavos, 1941	0.75	1.50	5.00

Y#	KM#	Metal	Description	VF	EF	Unc
12	37	Bz	1 Centavo, 1939–44	0.25	0.50	2.00
13	38	Bz	2 Centavos, 1939–47	0.35	1.00	4.00
12a	37a	Cop	1 Centavo, 1945–48	0.35	0.65	2.50
13a	38a	Cop	2 Centavos, 1947–50	0.35	0.85	4.00

Y#	KM#	Metal	Description	VF	EF	Unc
15	40	A-Bz	5 Centavos, 1942–50	0.25	0.50	3.00
16	41	A-Bz	10 Centavos, 1942–50	0.25	1.00	4.00
17	42	A-Bz	20 Centavos, 1942–50	0.30	1.25	7.50

Centennial Death of San Martin

Y#	KM#	Metal	Description	VF	EF	Unc
18	43	C-N	5 Centavos, 1950	0.35	0.80	3.50
19	44	C-N	10 Centavos, 1950	0.35	0.80	3.50
20	45	C-N	20 Centavos, 1950	0.40	1.50	4.00

Edge: ***Reeded***

Y#	KM#	Metal	Description	VF	EF	Unc
21	46	C-N	5 Centavos, 1951–53	0.20	0.35	1.00
22	47	C-N	10 Centavos, 1951–52	0.20	0.35	1.00
23	48	C-N	20 Centavos, 1951–52	0.25	0.40	1.50

Edge: ***Plain***
Obverse: ***Smaller bust on Y21a–23a, 1954 and later***

Y#	KM#	Metal	Description	VF	EF	Unc
21a	46a/50	C-NS	5 Centavos, 1953–56	0.15	0.20	0.50
22a	47a/51	C-NS	10 Centavos, 1952–56	0.10	0.15	0.50
23a	48a/52	C-NS	20 Centavos, 1952–56	0.15	0.25	0.50
24	49	C-NS	50 Centavos, 1952–56	0.20	0.35	1.00

Y#	KM#	Metal	Description	VF	EF	Unc
25	53	N-CS	5 Centavos, 1957–59	0.15	0.20	0.35
26	54	N-CS	10 Centavos, 1957–59	0.10	0.15	0.25
27	55	N-CS	20 Centavos, 1957–61	0.15	0.20	0.30
28	56	N-CS	50 Centavos, 1957–61	0.20	0.35	0.75
29	57	N-CS	1 Peso, 1957–62	0.20	0.40	1.00

Sesquicentennial of Provisional Government

Y#	KM#	Metal	Description	VF	EF	Unc
30	58	N-CS	1 Peso, 1960	0.50	0.75	1.50

Y#	KM#	Metal	Description	VF	EF	Unc
31	59	N-CS	5 Pesos, 1961–68, 12-sided	0.25	0.40	1.25

Y#	KM#	Metal	Description	VF	EF	Unc
32	60	N-CS	10 Pesos, 1962–68, 12-sided	0.20	0.35	1.25

Y#	KM#	Metal	Description	VF	EF	Unc
33	61	N-CS	25 Pesos, 1964–68, 12-sided	0.25	0.50	2

AUSTRALIA

An island continent between the Pacific and Indian oceans, Australia is a dominion of the British Commonwealth. Settled by Britain in the late 19th century, the six colonies federated in 1901, incorporating British parliamentary and American federal traditions. *Language:* English. *Capital:* Canberra.

Australian mints at Melbourne, Perth, and Sydney struck sovereigns and half sovereigns from 1871 to 1931 with mintmarks M, P, and S, respectively. The designs are standard British types.

MONETARY SYSTEM

12 pence = 1 shilling
2 shillings = 1 florin
5 shillings = 1 crown
20 shillings = 1 pound (sovereign)

PRECIOUS METAL CONTENT

Dates	Denomination	Gross Wt (g)	Fineness	Net Wt (g)	Troy Oz.
		SILVER			
1910–45	3 pence	1.4100	0.9250	1.3031	0.0419
	6 pence	2.8200	0.9250	2.6062	0.0838
1910–45	1 shilling	5.6500	0.9250	5.2249	0.1689
	1 florin	11.3100	0.9250	10.4603	0.3363
	1 crown	28.2800	0.9250	26.1583	0.8411
1946–64	3 pence	1.4100	0.5000	0.7029	0.0226
	6 pence	2.8200	0.5000	1.4089	0.0453
	1 shilling	5.6500	0.5000	2.8239	0.0908
	1 florin	11.3100	0.5000	5.6540	0.1818
		GOLD			
1871–1918	1/2 sovereign	3.9940	0.9170	3.6612	0.1177
1871–1931	1 sovereign	7.9881	0.9170	7.3224	0.2354

VICTORIA, *1837–1901*

YOUNG HEAD

Designs: ***Like Great Britain Y13–15***

Y#	KM#	Metal	Description	VF	EF	Unc
A1	5	Gold	1/2 Sovereign, 1871–87	400	550	10,500

Y#	KM#	Metal	Description	VF	EF	Unc
B1	6	Gold	1 Sovereign, 1871–87, reverse shield	BV	385	1,100
C1	7	Gold	1 Sovereign, 1871–87, reverse St. George	BV	450	900

JUBILEE HEAD

Designs: ***Like Great Britain Y28–29***

Y#	KM#	Metal	Description	VF	EF	Unc
D1	9	Gold	1/2 Sovereign, 1887–93	275	525	1,500
E1	10	Gold	1 Sovereign, 1887–93	BV	BV	175

OLD HEAD

Designs: *Like Great Britain Y42–43*

Y#	KM#	Metal	Description	VF	EF	Unc
F1	12	Gold	1/2 Sovereign, 1893–1901	275	525	2,800
G1	13	Gold	1 Sovereign, 1893–1901	BV	BV	560

EDWARD VII, *1901–1910*

Y#	KM#	Metal	Description	VF	EF	Unc
1	18	Silv	3 Pence, 1910	6.00	25	95
2	19	Silv	6 Pence, 1910	25.00	70	275
3	20	Silv	1 Shilling, 1910	32.50	85	285
4	21	Silv	1 Florin / 2 Shillings, 1910	225.00	575	2,250

Designs: *Same as Great Britain Y56–57*

Y#	KM#	Metal	Description	VF	EF	Unc
A5	14	Gold	1/2 Sovereign, 1902–10	250	275	1,400
B5	15	Gold	1 Sovereign, 1902–10	BV	BV	425

GEORGE V, *1910–1936*

Y#	KM#	Metal	Description	VF	EF	Unc
5	22	Bz	1/2 Penny, 1911–36 *1911, 16–17, 19, 21–22, VF $7; 1912–13, 25, 30–31, VF $23; 1914, 25, VF $40; 1915, VF $300; 1918, VF $85; 1923, VF $2,600*	4.00	17.50	150
						Proof: $40,000
6	23	Bz	1 Penny, 1911–36 *1911–13, 24, 29, 31, VF $20; 1914–16, 18, 20–23, 26, VF $40; 1925, VF $245; 1930, Rare*	6.75	28.00	175
						Proof: $65,000

Y#	KM#	Metal	Description	VF	EF	Unc
9	24	Silv	3 Pence, 1911–36			
			1936	3.50	19.50	115
			1912, 14	110.00	350.00	1,450
9			1915	200.00	550.00	2,750
			1916, 20	55.00	200.00	1,050
			1917–19, 22, 25–26	15.00	65.00	300
			1923	120.00	400.00	1,750
						Proof: $28,000
10	25	Silv	6 Pence, 1911–36			
			1936	11.00	35.00	210
			1912, 22	135.00	425.00	2,300
			1914, 19, 23	55.00	210.00	1,100
			1916–17, 20, 24	100.00	325.00	1,600
			1918	250.00	650.00	3,150
			1925, 35	38.50	150.00	750
			1921, 26–28, 34	21.00	50.00	250
						Proof: $30,000
11	26	Silv	1 Shilling, 1911–36			
			1936	12.50	42.00	300
			1911, 20, 28	70.00	285.00	1,500
			1912–13, 21	145.00	475.00	2,500
			1914, 34	50.00	140.00	750
			1915, 33	175.00	1,050.00	2,750
			1916–18, 25–27, 35	17.50	67.50	375
			1920, 28	70.00	325.00	1,875
						Proof: $40,000
12	27	Silv	1 Florin, 1911–36			
			1931, 36	14.00	45.00	315
			1911–13, 15, 19, 21, 33	245.00	985.00	4,000
			1914, 18	70.00	425.00	2,000
			1916–17, 25–26	55.00	290.00	1,450
			1922–24	28.00	175.00	2,350
			1927–28, 34–35	25.00	165.00	900
			1932	775.00	2,650.00	9,450
						Proof: $65,000

Establishment of Parliament At Canberra

Y#	KM#	Metal	Description	VF	EF	Unc
7	31	Silv	1 Florin, 1927	14	35	140
						Proof: $22,500

Centennial of Victoria And Melbourne

Y#	KM#	Metal	Description	VF	EF	Unc
8	33	Silv	1 Florin, "1934–35" on coin	200	300	550

Designs: ***Like Great Britain Y77–78***

Y#	KM#	Metal	Description	VF	EF	Unc
A13	28	Gold	1/2 Sovereign, 1911–18 *1918, Unc $6,000*	245	275	725
B13	29	Gold	1 Sovereign, 1911–31	BV	BV	400

GEORGE VI,
1936–1952

Y#	KM#	Metal	Description	VF	EF	Unc
13	35	Bz	1/2 Penny, 1938–39	2.50	13.50	100 *Proof: $5,000*

Y#	KM#	Metal	Description	VF	EF	Unc
14	41	Bz	1/2 Penny, 1939–48 *1939, VF $35; 1940–42P, VF 4; 1942M, 44, VF $13; 1945, VF $7*	2.00	4.75	45 *Proof: $25,000*
15	36	Bz	1 Penny, 1938–48 *1938–38, 41–42, VF $6.50; 1940M, 44M, VF $14; 1940P, VF $28*	2.85	7.50	45 *Proof: $29,500*

Note: In 1946, the silver fineness was reduced from .925 to .500.

Y#	KM#	Metal	Description	VF	EF	Unc
16	37	Silv	3 Pence, 1938–44 *1939–40, VF $8*	2.85	7.00	35
16a	37a	Silv	3 Pence, 1947–48 *1948, EF $17.50*	1.50	3.50	21

Y#	KM#	Metal	Description	VF	EF	Unc
17	38	Silv	6 Pence, 1938–45 *1938–40, VF $8*	3	6.00	40
17a	38a	Silv	6 Pence, 1946, 48	2	8.25	55

Y#	KM#	Metal	Description	VF	EF	Unc
18	39	Silv	1 Shilling, 1938–44	2	7.50	15.00
18a	39a	Silv	1 Shilling, 1946, 48	3	10.00	27.50

Y#	KM#	Metal	Description	VF	EF	Unc
19	40	Silv	1 Florin, 1938–45	5	10.00	55.00
19a	40a	Silv	1 Florin, 1946–47	3	7.50	22.50

Y#	KM#	Metal	Description	VF	EF	Unc
20	34	Silv	1 Crown, 1937–38	15	35	100 *Proof: $9,000*

Obverse: ***IND: IMP: omitted from legend***

Y#	KM#	Metal	Description	VF	EF	Unc
21	42	Bz	1/2 Penny, 1949–52	1.00	2	10 *Proof: $6,000*
22	43	Bz	1 Penny, 1949–52	0.60	3	11 *Proof: $10,000*

Fifty-Year Jubilee

Y#	KM#	Metal	Description	VF	EF	Unc
23	47	Silv	1 Florin, 1951	5	6	20

Designs: ***Like Y16–19***

Y#	KM#	Metal	Description	VF	EF	Unc
24	44	Silv	3 Pence, 1949–52	0.75	2.50	6
					Proof: $5,500	
25	45	Silv	6 Pence, 1950–52	2.50	5.00	15
					Proof: $5,000	
26	46	Silv	1 Shilling, 1950, 52	3.00	6.00	20
					Proof: $2,250	
27	48	Silv	1 Florin, 1951–52	7.00	15.00	55
					Proof: $7,500	

ELIZABETH II, *1952–2022*

Y#	KM#	Metal	Description	VF	EF	Unc
28	49	Bz	1/2 Penny, 1953–55	1	3	15

Y#	KM#	Metal	Description	VF	EF	Unc
29	50	Bz	1 Penny, 1953	1	3	22.50

Y#	KM#	Metal	Description	VF	EF	Unc
30	51	Silv	3 Pence, 1953–54	2.50	9.50	35.00
31	52	Silv	6 Pence, 1953–54	1.50	2.25	6.00
32	53	Silv	1 Shilling, 1953–54	3.00	6.00	22.50

Y#	KM#	Metal	Description	VF	EF	Unc
33	54	Silv	1 Florin, 1953–54	2.75	6.00	27.50

Royal Visit

Y#	KM#	Metal	Description	VF	EF	Unc
34	55	Silv	1 Florin, 1954	3.50	7.00	17.50

Obverse: ***F: D: added to legend***
Reverse: ***Designs like Y28–33***

Y#	KM#	Metal	Description	VF	EF	Unc
35	61	Bz	1/2 Penny, 1959–64	0.30	0.75	2.00
						Proof: $225
36	56	Bz	1 Penny, 1955–64	0.25	0.75	2.50
			1959(m), VF $3			*Proof: $350*
37	57	Silv	3 Pence, 1955–64	0.50	1.00	2.00
						Proof: $60
38	58	Silv	6 Pence, 1955–63	1.00	2.00	3.00
						Proof: $60
39	59	Silv	1 Shilling, 1955–63	1.75	3.50	5.00
						Proof: $100
40	60	Silv	1 Florin, 1956–63	1.75	2.25	12.00
						Proof: $130

AUSTRIA
(OESTERREICH)

A republic in central Europe, Austria was ruled by the Hapsburg dynasty from the late-13th century; dual sovereignty with the kingdom of Hungary was established in 1867. The republic was proclaimed after World War I. After annexation to Nazi Germany in 1938, the second republic was established in 1945. *Language:* German. *Capital:* Vienna.

MONETARY SYSTEM

100 kreuzer = 1 florin (gulden), 1857–92
1-1/2 florin = 1 vereinsthaler
100 heller = 1 krone, 1892–1923
10,000 kronen = 1 schilling, 1923–24
100 groschen = 1 schilling, 1924–

PRECIOUS METAL CONTENT

Dates	Denomination	Gross Wt (g)	Fineness	Net Wt (g)	Troy Oz.
		SILVER			
1780	Maria Theresa thaler	28.0668	0.8333	23.3890	0.7520
1857–68	1 vereinsthaler	18.5186	0.9000	16.6667	0.5358
	2 vereinsthaler	37.0371	0.9000	33.3333	1.0717
1858–67	5 kreuzer	1.3333	0.3750	0.5000	0.0161
	10 kreuzer	2.0000	0.5000	1.0000	0.0322

Dates	Denomination	Gross Wt (g)	Fineness	Net Wt (g)	Troy Oz.
		SILVER			
1868–72	10 kreuzer	1.6667	0.4000	0.6667	0.0214
	20 kreuzer	2.6667	0.5000	1.3333	0.0429
1857–92	1/4 florin	5.3450	0.5208	2.7837	0.0895
	1 florin	12.3457	0.9000	11.1111	0.3572
	2 florin	24.6914	0.9000	22.2222	0.7144
1892–1916	1 krone	5.0000	0.8350	4.1750	0.1342
	2 kronen	10.0000	0.8350	8.3500	0.2685
	5 kronen	24.0000	0.9000	21.6000	0.6944
1924	1 schilling	7.0000	0.8000	5.6000	0.1800
1925–38	1/2 schilling	3.0000	0.6400	1.9200	0.0617
	1 schilling	6.0000	0.6400	3.8400	0.1235
	2 schilling	12.0000	0.6400	7.6800	0.2469
	5 schilling	15.0000	0.8350	12.5250	0.4027
1960–68	5 schilling	5.2000	0.6400	3.3281	0.1070
1957–73	10 schilling	7.5000	0.6400	4.7993	0.1543
1955–73	25 schilling	13.0000	0.8000	10.4012	0.3344
1959–73	50 schilling	20.0000	0.9000	18.0000	0.5787
		GOLD			
1857–1915	1 dukat	3.4909	0.9861	3.4424	0.1107
	4 dukaten	13.9636	0.9861	13.7695	0.4427
1858–66	1/2 krone	5.5555	0.9000	5.0000	0.1608
	1 krone	11.1111	0.9000	10.0000	0.3215
1870–92	4 florin / 10 francs	3.2258	0.9000	2.9032	0.0933
	8 florin / 20 francs	6.4516	0.9000	5.8064	0.1867
1892–1934	10 kronen	[illegible]	0.9000	3.0488	0.0980
	20 kronen	6.7751	0.9000	6.0976	0.1960
	100 kronen	33.8753	0.9000	30.4878	0.9802
1926–38	25 schilling	5.8811	0.9000	5.2930	0.1702
	100 schilling	23.5245	0.9000	21.1721	0.6807

FRANZ JOSEPH I,
1848–1916

VEREINSMUNZEN, 1857–1868

"Convention Money" was struck for circulation throughout the Austrian and German states observing the monetary agreement of 1857.

First Obverse: *Portrait with light sideburns*

Y#	KM#	Metal	Description	VF	EF	Unc
1	2244	Silv	1 Vereinsthaler, 1857–65	60	125	250
2	2249	Silv	2 Vereinsthaler, 1865	1,750	3,500	5,500

Opening of Vienna-Trieste Railway

Y#	KM#	Metal	Description	VF	EF	Unc
3	2246	Silv	2 Vereinsthaler, 1857	1,750	3,500	5,500

Y#	KM#	Metal	Description	VF	EF	Unc
4	2251	Gold	1/2 Krone, 1858–65	1,750	4,250	7,000
5	2253	Gold	1 Krone, 1858–65	2,000	4,500	7,000

Second Obverse: *Portrait with heavier beard*

Y#	KM#	Metal	Description	VF	EF	Unc
1a	2245	Silv	1 Vereinsthaler, 1866–67	100	200	375
2a	2250	Silv	2 Vereinsthaler, 1866–67	500	1,200	2,500

Reverse: ***Similar to Y4–5***

Y#	KM#	Metal	Description	VF	EF	Unc
4a	2252	Gold	1/2 Krone, 1866	4,750	9,500	17,500
5a	2255	Gold	1 Krone, 1866	5,000	11,000	19,500

3rd German Shooting Fest

Y#	KM#	Metal	Description	VF	EF	Unc
A16	N/A	Silv	1 Thaler, 1868	100	175	300
						Proof: $400

Opening of Mt. Raxalpe Inn

Y#	KM#	Metal	Description	VF	EF	Unc
A20	N/A	Silv	1 Thaler, 1877	4,000	6,000	10,000
						Proof: $20,000

Note: YA20 was issued only for presentation, and was struck long after the formal end of the Vereinsthaler system.

LANDESMÜNZEN, 1857–1892

This was subsidiary coinage for circulation within the Austro-Hungarian Empire alone. Note that after 1868 Hungary had a separate coinage, but that the money of the two countries continued interchangeable.

Y#	KM#	Metal	Description	VF	EF	Unc
6	Several	Cop	5/10 Kreuzer, 1858–91	4.00	10.00	30
7	Several	Cop	1 Kreuzer, 1858–91	4.50	12.50	35
8	2194	Cop	4 Kreuzer, 1860–64	17.50	45.00	115

First Obverse: ***Portrait with light sideburns***

Y#	KM#	Metal	Description	VF	EF	Unc
9	2197	Bill	5 Kreuzer, 1858–64	6.00	17.50	35
10	2204	Bill	10 Kreuzer, 1858–65	12.50	40.00	85

Y#	KM#	Metal	Description	VF	EF	Unc
13	2213	Silv	1/4 Florin, 1857–59, large eagle	15	37.50	65

Y#	KM#	Metal	Description	VF	EF	Unc
14	2214	Silv	1/4 Florin, 1859–65, small eagle	15	32.50	55

Y#	KM#	Metal	Description	VF	EF	Unc
15	2219	Silv	1 Florin, 1857–65	12.50	18.50	27.50
16	2230	Silv	2 Florin, 1859–65 *1860A, VF $425*	125.00	245.00	375.00

Y#	KM#	Metal	Description	VF	EF	Unc
23	2264	Gold	1 Dukat, 1860–65	250	375	475
25	2272	Gold	4 Dukaten 1860–65	1,750	4,750	7,500

Note: Similar gold types dated 1852–59 with a younger portrait were issued both before and after the Monetary Convention of 1857.

Second Obverse: ***Portrait with heavier beard***

Y#	KM#	Metal	Description	VF	EF	Unc
9a	2198	Bill	5 Kreuzer, 1867	300	600	975
10a	2205	Bill	10 Kreuzer, 1867	350	825	1,500

Y#	KM#	Metal	Description	VF	EF	Unc
14a	2215	Silv	1/4 Florin, 1866	500	800	1,350
15a	2220	Silv	1 Florin, 1866	60	125	250
16a	2231	Silv	2 Florin, 1866	375	800	1,350
23a	2265	Gold	1 Dukat, 1866	325	475	700
25a	2273	Gold	4 Dukaten, 1866	4,500	13,500	25,000

New Reverse Legend: *LOMB. ET VEN. omitted*

Y#	KM#	Metal	Description	VF	EF	Unc
11	2206	Silv	10 Kreuzer, 1868–72	2.25	9.50	30
12	2212	Silv	20 Kreuzer, 1868–72	2.25	9.50	30

Designs: *Similar to Y14a–25a*

Y#	KM#	Metal	Description	VF	EF	Unc
14b	2216	Silv	1/4 Florin, 1867–71	325	525	950
15b	2221	Silv	1 Florin, 1867–72	40	135	235
16b	2232	Silv	2 Florin, 1867–72	200	350	525

Y#	KM#	Metal	Description	VF	EF	Unc
23b	2266	Gold	1 Dukat, 1867–72	300	475	625
25b	2274	Gold	4 Dukaten, 1867–72	1,650	4,950	13,000

Third Obverse: *Portrait with older head*

Y#	KM#	Metal	Description	VF	EF	Unc
14c	2217	Silv	1/4 Florin, 1872–75	325.00	550	950.00
15c	2222	Silv	1 Florin, 1872–92	9.50	19	37.50
16c	2233	Silv	2 Florin, 1872–92	125.00	225	350.00

Y#	KM#	Metal	Description	VF	EF	Unc
23c	2267	Gold	1 Dukat, 1872–1915	BV	325	425
25c	2276	Gold	4 Dukaten, 1872–1915		375	550

Note: Y23c and Y25c, dated 1915, are official restrikes produced 1920–36. These trade at a slight premium above bullion value. Some 1915 ducats were dated 1951 in error.

Trade Coinage

Y#	KM#	Metal	Description	VF	EF	Unc
21	2260	Gold	4 Florin / 10 Francs, 1870–92	BV	475	750
22	2269	Gold	8 Florin / 20 Francs, 1870–92	BV	375	525

Note: Y21–22 were struck on the Latin Monetary Union standard to facilitate foreign trade. Coins dated 1892 are official restrikes of later years and trade for a slight premium over bullion value.

Pribram Mine

Y#	KM#	Metal	Description	VF	EF	Unc
17	N/A	Silv	1 Florin, 1875	325	525	950

Vienna Shooting Fest

Y#	KM#	Metal	Description	VF	EF	Unc
18	N/A	Silv	2 Florin, 1873	1,200	2,400	4,000
A18	N/A	Gold	4 Dukaten, 1873	7,500	10,500	18,000

Silver Wedding Anniversary

Y#	KM#	Metal	Description	VF	EF	Unc
19	N/A	Silv	2 Gulden (on edge), 1879	45	755	135

Note: Modern restrikes exist.

Reopening of Kuttenberg Mines

Y#	KM#	Metal	Description	VF	EF	Unc
20	N/A	Silv	2 Florin, 1887	2,750	4,500	8,500 *Proof: $10,000*

50th Anniversary of Reign

Y#	KM#	Metal	Description	VF	EF	Unc
24	2268	Gold	1 Dukat, 1848–51, date 1898 below eagle	250	475	750

Krone Standard

Y#	KM#	Metal	Description	VF	EF	Unc
26	2800	Bz	1 Heller, 1892–1916 *1892, VF $325*	2	3.25	10

Y#	KM#	Metal	Description	VF	EF	Unc
28	2801	Bz	2 Heller, 1892–1915 *1892, VF $325*	2	3.25	12

Y#	KM#	Metal	Description	VF	EF	Unc
29	2802	Nick	10 Heller, 1892–1911 *1892, VF $850*	2.50	5.00	15
30	2803	Nick	20 Heller, 1892–1914 *1892, VF $35*	3.75	12.50	30

Obverse: ***Laureate head***

Y#	KM#	Metal	Description	VF	EF	Unc
35	2804	Silv	1 Krone, 1892–1907 *1892, VF $200*	3.75	12	30
39	2807	Silv	5 Kronen, 1900, 07	35.00	75	150

Y#	KM#	Metal	Description	VF	EF	Unc
42	2805	Gold	10 Kronen, 1892–1906 *1892, 1893 Pattern, Rare*	BV	BV	265
43	2806	Gold	20 Kronen, 1892–1905	BV	BV	375

60th Anniversary of Reign

Obverse: ***Small bare head***

Y#	KM#	Metal	Description	VF	EF	Unc
36	2808	Silv	1 Krone, 1908	3.25	6.50	10

Y#	KM#	Metal	Description	VF	EF	Unc
40	2809	Silv	5 Kronen, 1908	30.00	85.00	175
						Proof: $750

Y#	KM#	Metal	Description	VF	EF	Unc
44	2810	Gold	10 Kronen, 1908	BV	175	225
45	2811	Gold	20 Kronen, 1908	BV	475	600

Y#	KM#	Metal	Description	VF	EF	Unc
46	2812	Gold	100 Kronen, 1908	2,500	4,000	9,000
						Proof: $15,000

Y#	KM#	Metal	Description	VF	EF	Unc
41	2814	Silv	5 Kronen, 1909	45	85	350
47	2815	Gold	10 Kronen, 1909	BV	BV	265
48	2817	Gold	20 Kronen, 1909	650	1,750	2,500

Obverse: *Large bare head*

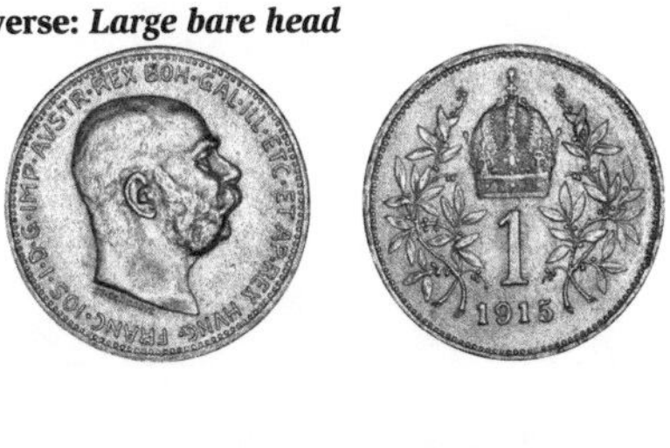

Y#	KM#	Metal	Description	VF	EF	Unc
37	2820	Silv	1 Krone, 1912–16	4.50	6.50	12.50

Y#	KM#	Metal	Description	VF	EF	Unc
38	2821	Silv	2 Kronen, 1912–13	12.50	15	25
A41	2813	Silv	5 Kronen, 1909	40.00	100	200

Y#	KM#	Metal	Description	VF	EF	Unc
49	2816	Gold	10 Kronen, 1909–12	BV	185	200
50	2818	Gold	20 Kronen, 1909–16	BV	365	400
51	2819	Gold	100 Kronen, 1909–15	1,500	4,400	6,500
						Proof: $9,500

Note: Y49 (dated 1912) and Y50–51 (dated 1915) are official restrikes. They trade at slightly over bullion value.

World War I Issues

Y#	KM#	Metal	Description	VF	EF	Unc
31	2822	CNZ	10 Heller, 1915–16	3.50	9	20

Y#	KM#	Metal	Description	VF	EF	Unc
27	2823	Bz	1 Heller, 1916	9	30	60.00
32	2825	CNZ	10 Heller, 1916	4	9	22.50

Y#	KM#	Metal	Description	VF	EF	Unc
33	2824	Iron	2 Heller, 1916–18	4	12.50	35
34	2826	Iron	20 Heller, 1916–18	4	12.50	35

Y#	KM#	Metal	Description	VF	EF	Unc
52	2827	Gold	20 Kronen, 1916	850	1,500	2,500

Trade Coinage

An unofficial "trade dollar," the final date of the famous Maria Theresa thaler has been struck intermittently to modern times at many world mints. It has been used in many areas lacking a firm local coinage, particularly in north and east Africa and the Near East. It is still being struck at the Austrian Mint.

Y#	KM#	Metal	Description	VF	EF	Unc
55	T1	Silv	1 Thaler, 1780	BV	BV	22.50
						Proof: $27.50

Note: This is a modern restrike by the Austrian Mint.

REPUBLIC, *1918–1938*

Monetary Law of December 21, 1923

Y#	KM#	Metal	Description	VF	EF	Unc
56	2832	Bz	100 Kronen, 1923–24	3.50	5	10

Y#	KM#	Metal	Description	VF	EF	Unc
57	2833	Bz	200 Kronen, 1924	4	6	12.50

Y#	KM#	Metal	Description	VF	EF	Unc
58	2834	C-N	1,000 Kronen, 1924	5	7.50	12.50

Bullion Coins

Y#	KM#	Metal	Description	VF	EF	Unc
80	2830	Gold	20 Kronen, 1923–24	875	1,500	2,000
81	2831	Gold	100 Kronen, 1923–24	2,750	4,000	6,000

Coinage Reform of December 20, 1924

Y#	KM#	Metal	Description	VF	EF	Unc
59	2835	Silv	1 Schilling, 1924	11	16.50	35

Y#	KM#	Metal	Description	VF	EF	Unc
60	2836	Bz	1 Groschen, 1925–38 *1932, VF $42*	2.75	4	10

Y#	KM#	Metal	Description	VF	EF	Unc
61	2837	Bz	2 Groschen, 1925–38 *1934, VF $20; 1938, VF $12*	2.75	4	10

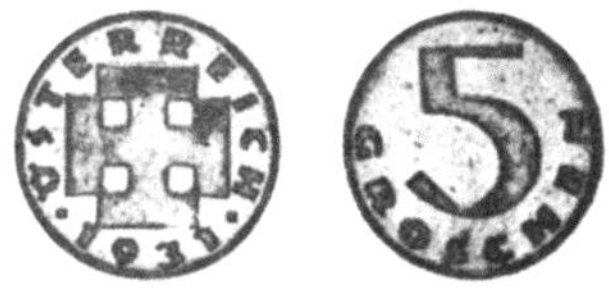

Y#	KM#	Metal	Description	VF	EF	Unc
62	2846	C-N	5 Groschen, 1931–38 *1937, VF $60; 1938, EF $350*	2.75	7	20

Y#	KM#	Metal	Description	VF	EF	Unc
63	2838	C-N	10 Groschen, 1925, 28–29	2.75	9	15

Y#	KM#	Metal	Description	VF	EF	Unc
67	2839	Silv	1/2 Schilling, 1925–26	4	8	17.50

Y#	KM#	Metal	Description	VF	EF	Unc
68	2840	Silv	1 Schilling, 1925–26, 32 *1932, VF $50*	3	5.50	15

Y#	KM#	Metal	Description	VF	EF	Unc
64	2850	C-N	50 Groschen, 1934	15	35	75

Y#	KM#	Metal	Description	VF	EF	Unc
65	2854	C-N	50 Groschen, 1935–36 *1936, VF $50*	6	12.50	22.50

Y#	KM#	Metal	Description	VF	EF	Unc
66	2851	C-N	1 Schilling, 1934–35 *1935, VF $12.50*	4	10	18

Franz Schubert

Y#	KM#	Metal	Description	VF	EF	Unc
69	2843	Silv	2 Schilling, 1928	10	12.50	17.50 *Proof: $425*

Dr. Theodor Billroth

Y#	KM#	Metal	Description	VF	EF	Unc
70	2844	Silv	2 Schilling, 1929	10	20	35 *Proof: $850*

Walther von der Vogelweide

Y#	KM#	Metal	Description	VF	EF	Unc
71	2845	Silv	2 Schilling, 1930	10	12.50	17.50
						Proof: $140

Also see Germany Y71.

Wolfgang Mozart

Y#	KM#	Metal	Description	VF	EF	Unc
72	2847	Silv	2 Schilling, 1931	15	30	40
						Proof: $300

Joseph Haydn

Y#	KM#	Metal	Description	VF	EF	Unc
73	2848	Silv	2 Schilling, 1932	50	90	125
						Proof: $575

Dr. Ignaz Seipel

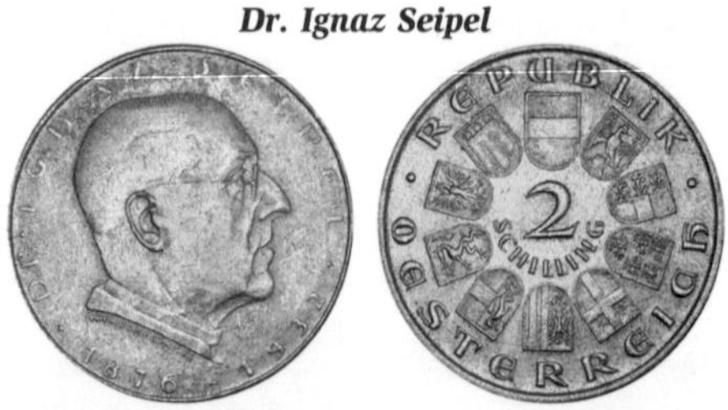

Y#	KM#	Metal	Description	VF	EF	Unc
74	2849	Silv	2 Schilling, 1932	20	35	55
						Proof: $400

Dr. Engelbert Dollfuss

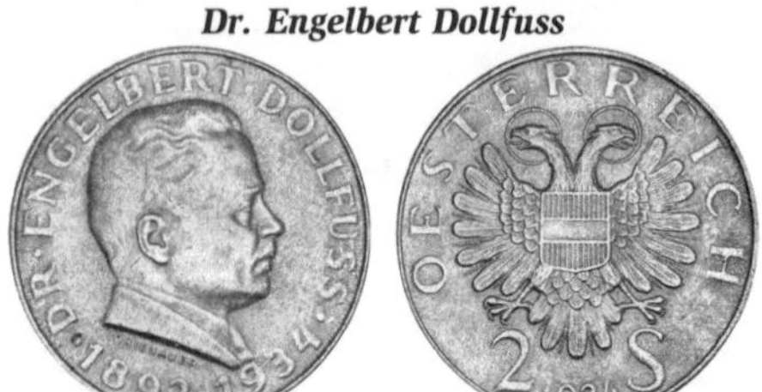

Y#	KM#	Metal	Description	VF	EF	Unc
75	2852	Silv	2 Schilling, 1934	12.50	22.50	35
						Proof: $250

Dr. Karl Lueger

Y#	KM#	Metal	Description	VF	EF	Unc
76	2855	Silv	2 Schilling, 1935	12.50	25	40
						Proof: $250

Prince Eugen of Savoy

Y#	KM#	Metal	Description	VF	EF	Unc
77	2858	Silv	2 Schilling, 1936	10	17.50	32.50
						Proof: $225

Karlskirche in Vienna

Y#	KM#	Metal	Description	VF	EF	Unc
78	2859	Silv	2 Schilling, 1937	10	17.50	27.50
						Proof: $175

Y#	KM#	Metal	Description	VF	EF	Unc
79	2853	Silv	5 Schilling, 1934–36	12.50	27.50	40
			1936, VF $75			*Proof: $250*

Y#	KM#	Metal	Description	VF	EF	Unc
82	2841	Gold	25 Schilling, 1926–34 *1933, EF $2,000*	BV	275	325

Y#	KM#	Metal	Description	VF	EF	Unc
83	2842	Gold	100 Schilling, 1926–34 *1933, EF $2,000*	BV	1,100	1,350

Y#	KM#	Metal	Description	VF	EF	Unc
84	2856	Gold	25 Schilling, 1935–38 *1938, Rare*	750	1,100	1,500

Y#	KM#	Metal	Description	VF	EF	Unc
85	2857	Gold	100 Schilling, 1935–38 *1938, Rare*	1,100	1,750	2,750

REPUBLIC REESTABLISHED, *1945–*

Y#	KM#	Metal	Description	VF	EF	Unc
86	2873	Zinc	1 Groschen, 1947	2.50	5.00	10.00
87	2875	Zinc	5 Groschen, 1948–94	0.35	0.75	2.50
88	2874	Zinc	10 Groschen, 1947–49	3.00	9.50	25.00

Y#	KM#	Metal	Description	VF	EF	Unc
89	2876	Alum	2 Groschen, 1950–94	0.35	0.75	2.25 *Proof: $5*

Y#	KM#	Metal	Description	VF	EF	Unc
90	2878	Alum	10 Groschen, 1951–2001	0.35	1	3 *Proof: $5*

Y#	KM#	Metal	Description	VF	EF	Unc
91	2870	Alum	50 Groschen, 1946–55	2.50	5	11 *Proof: $40*

Y#	KM#	Metal	Description	VF	EF	Unc
92	2871	Alum	1 Schilling, 1946–57	1	5	12.50 *Proof: $45*

Y#	KM#	Metal	Description	VF	EF	Unc
93	2872	Alum	2 Schilling, 1946–52 *1952, VF $200*	6	15	32.50 *Proof: $275*

Y#	KM#	Metal	Description	VF	EF	Unc
94	2879	Alum	5 Schilling, 1952, 57 *1957, VF $375*	7.50	12.50	35 *Proof: $65*

Y#	KM#	Metal	Description	VF	EF	Unc
95	2877	A-Bz	20 Groschen, 1950–54	1	3.50	15 *Proof: $25*

Y#	KM#	Metal	Description	VF	EF	Unc
103	2885	A-Bz	50 Groschen, 1959–2001	0.35	0.75	5 *Proof: $6*

Y#	KM#	Metal	Description	VF	EF	Unc
104	2886	A-Bz	1 Schilling, 1959–2000	0.35	0.75	5 *Proof: $4*

Y#	KM#	Metal	Description	VF	EF	Unc
106	2889	Silv	5 Schilling, 1960–68	4	6.25	7.50 *Proof: $10*

Y#	KM#	Metal	Description	VF	EF	Unc
99	2882	Silv	10 Schilling, 1957–73	6	7.50	12.50 *Proof: $12.50*

Reopening of Bundestheater

Y#	KM#	Metal	Description	VF	EF	Unc
96	2880	Silv	25 Schilling, 1955	8	11	17.50 *Proof: $85*

Bicentennial, Birth of Mozart

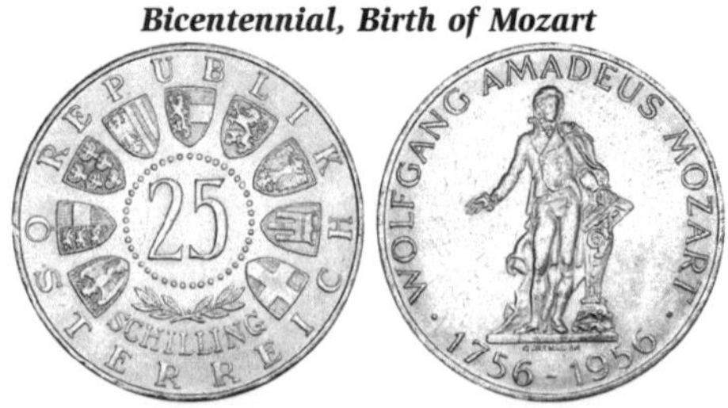

Y#	KM#	Metal	Description	VF	EF	Unc
97	2881	Silv	25 Schilling, 1956	8	11	15 *Proof: $300*

800th Anniversary of Maria Zell Cathedral

Y#	KM#	Metal	Description	VF	EF	Unc
98	2883	Silv	25 Schilling, 1957	8	11	15 *Proof: $300*

Centennial, Birth of Auer von Weisbach

Y#	KM#	Metal	Description	VF	EF	Unc
100	2884	Silv	25 Schilling, 1958	8	11	15 *Proof: $1,350*

Tirol Sesquicentennial

Y#	KM#	Metal	Description	VF	EF	Unc
101	2888	Silv	50 Schilling, 1959	15	17.50	25
						Proof: $300

Centennial, Death of Archduke Johann

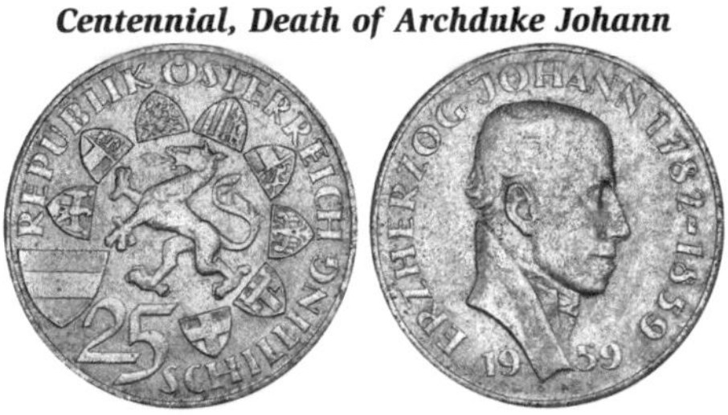

Y#	KM#	Metal	Description	VF	EF	Unc
102	2887	Silv	25 Schilling, 1959	8	11	15
						Proof: $275

40th Anniversary of Carinthian Plebiscite

Y#	KM#	Metal	Description	VF	EF	Unc
105	2890	Silv	25 Schilling, 1960	8	11	15
						Proof: $300

40th Anniversary of Burgenland

Y#	KM#	Metal	Description	VF	EF	Unc
107	2891	Silv	25 Schilling, 1961	8	11	15
						Proof: $250

Anton Bruckner

Y#	KM#	Metal	Description	VF	EF	Unc
108	2892	Silv	25 Schilling, 1962	8	11	15
						Proof: $150

300th Anniversary of Birth of Prince Eugen

Y#	KM#	Metal	Description	VF	EF	Unc
109	2893	Silv	25 Schilling, 1963	8	11	15
						Proof: $75

600th Anniversary of Union With Tirol

Y#	KM#	Metal	Description	VF	EF	Unc
110	2894	Silv	50 Schilling, 1963	15	17.50	25
						Proof: $100

Franz Grillparzer

Y#	KM#	Metal	Description	VF	EF	Unc
112	2895.1	Silv	25 Schilling, 1964	8	11	15
						Proof: $25
112a	2895.2	Silv	25 Schilling, 1964, error, old obverse, nine shields			Proof: $250

Winter Olympic Games

Y#	KM#	Metal	Description	VF	EF	Unc
111	2896	Silv	50 Schilling, 1964	15	17.50	25
						Proof: $25

AZORES

This group of nine islands was colonized in the mid-15th century and is now an autonomous region of the Republic of Portugal. It lies in the North Atlantic about 1,000 miles west of Lisbon. *Language:* Portuguese. *Capital:* Ponta Delgada.

MONETARY SYSTEM
1,000 reis = 1 milreis

LUIS I, *1861–1889*

Y#	KM#	Metal	Description	VF	EF	Unc
1	13	Cop	5 Reis, 1865–66, 80	20	50	90
2	14	Cop	10 Reis, 1865–66 *1866, EF $200*	20	60	100
3	15	Cop	20 Reis, 1865–66	20	70	100

Countermarked Issues

In 1887, various foreign coins were countermarked with a crowned GP ("Governo Portugues") in a circular indent to authorize local circulation. This stamp is found most often on Brazilian coins. Values below are for common varieties.

Y#	KM#	Metal	Description	VF	EF	Unc
C1	N/A	C/Bz	On various issues	160	500	—
C2	N/A	Silv	On small coin	90	300	—
C3	N/A	Silv	On 1/4 dollar size	150	400	—
C4	N/A	Silv	On 1/2 dollar size	100	250	—
C5	N/A	Silv	On 1 dollar size	250	600	—

CARLOS I, *1889–1908*

Y#	KM#	Metal	Description	VF	EF	Unc
4	16	Cop	5 Reis, 1901	12.50	27.50	50
5	17	Cop	10 Reis, 1901	8.00	17.50	40

Note: Bright red Uncirculated specimens of Y1–5 are worth double the Uncirculated prices listed.

BELGIAN CONGO

This former Belgian colony in equatorial Africa became independent in 1960, and is now the Democratic Republic of the Congo. *Languages:* Bantu, French. *Capital:* Leopoldville (now Kinshasa).

MONETARY SYSTEM
100 centimes = 1 franc

PRECIOUS METAL CONTENT

Dates	Denomination	Gross Wt (g)	Fineness	Net Wt (g)	Troy Oz.
		SILVER			
1887–96	50 centimes	2.5000	0.8350	2.0871	0.0671
	1 franc	5.0000	0.8350	4.1750	0.1342
	2 francs	10.0000	0.8350	8.3500	0.2685
	5 francs	25.0000	0.9000	22.5000	0.7234
1944	50 francs	17.5000	0.5000	8.7527	0.2814

CONGO FREE STATE, *1885–1908*

LEOPOLD II OF BELGIUM AS OWNER

Y#	KM#	Metal	Description	VF	EF	Unc
1	1	Cop	1 Centime, 1887–88	7.50	20.00	50.00
2	2	Cop	2 Centimes, 1887–88 *1888, VF $12.50*	5.00	11.00	30.00
3	3	Cop	5 Centimes, 1887–88, 94	6.00	13.50	37.50
4	4	Cop	10 Centimes, 1887–89, 94 *1887, 89 VF $20; 1894, VF $12.50*	7.00	18.00	45.00

Y#	KM#	Metal	Description	VF	EF	Unc
5	5	Silv	50 Centimes, 1887–96	40	90	125
6	6	Silv	1 Franc, 1887–96	45	125	300
7	7	Silv	2 Francs, 1887–96	80	200	500
8	8	Silv	5 Francs, 1887–96	250	575	1,750
			1887, last two letters of legend under neck, Rare			

Y#	KM#	Metal	Description	VF	EF	Unc
9	9	C-N	5 Centimes, 1906, 08	8.00	20	100
10	10	C-N	10 Centimes, 1906, 08	22.50	60	145
11	11	C-N	20 Centimes, 1906, 08	22.50	60	145

BELGIAN CONGO, *1908–1952*

LEOPOLD *II* AS KING, *1908–1909*

New Legend: *CONGO BELGE – BELGISCH CONGO*

Y#	KM#	Metal	Description	VF	EF	Unc
12	12	C-N	5 Centimes, 1909	30	70	200
13	13	C-N	10 Centimes, 1909	30	75	215
14	14	C-N	20 Centimes, 1909	30	75	215

ALBERT I, *1909–1934*

Y#	KM#	Metal	Description	VF	EF	Unc
15	15	Cop	1 Centime, 1910, 19	5	11.00	27.50
16	16	Cop	2 Centimes, 1910, 19	10	22.50	57.50

Y#	KM#	Metal	Description	VF	EF	Unc
17	17	C-N	5 Centimes, 1910–28	5	10	27.50
			1910, VF $8; 1920, 26–28, VF $12			
18	18	C-N	10 Centimes, 1910–28	5	10	27.50
			1910, 19, 24–25, 28, VF $8; 1920, VF $25; 1927, VF $12			
19	19	C-N	20 Centimes, 1910–11	9	20	50.00
			1928, VF $50			

Y#	KM#	Metal	Description	VF	EF	Unc
20	22–23	C-N	50 Centimes, 1921–29	15	35	85
21	20–21	C-N	1 Franc, 1920–30	15	35	85

Note: Y20–21 have either French or Flemish legends.

LEOPOLD III, *1934–1950*

Y#	KM#	Metal	Description	VF	EF	Unc
26	24	N-Bz	5 Francs, 1936–37	37.50	95	350

Y#	KM#	Metal	Description	VF	EF	Unc
24	25	Br	2 Francs, 1943, hexagonal	7.50	22.50	150

Y#	KM#	Metal	Description	VF	EF	Unc
22	26	Br	1 Franc, 1944, 46, 49	4.00	10	55
23	28	Br	2 Francs, 1946–47, round	3.50	11	55
25	29	Br	5 Francs, 1947	10.00	20	115

Y#	KM#	Metal	Description	VF	EF	Unc
27	27	Silv	50 Francs, 1944	45	100	275

BELGIAN CONGO AND RUANDA-URUNDI, *1952–1960*

Baudouin I, *1951–1960*

Y#	KM#	Metal	Description	VF	EF	Unc
28	1	A-Bz	5 Francs, 1952	3.25	11	50

Y#	KM#	Metal	Description	VF	EF	Unc
29	2	Alum	50 Centimes, 1954–55	1.00	2.50	11.50
30	4	Alum	1 Franc, 1957–60	1.00	2.75	12.00
31	3	Alum	5 Francs, 1956–59	1.50	4.50	15.00

Note: For later issues see Katanga; also Rwanda and Burundi.

BELGIUM

This country lies on the North Sea between France and the Netherlands. It was under Spanish rule from the 15th century until 1713, when it was transferred to Austria and later annexed to France. Reunited with the Netherlands and Luxembourg under the king of Holland in 1815, Belgium declared independence in 1830. It is a parliamentary democracy under a constitutional monarchy with ethnic autonomy in three regions. *Languages:* Flemish, French, German. *Capital:* Brussels.

French and Flemish Inscriptions

The population of Belgium is divided into well-defined groups, the Flemings and the Walloons (French). Since 1886 all coins have been minted in approximately equal numbers of French (Belgique) and Flemish (Belgie) specimens; when not, the coin is inscribed with both languages.

MONETARY SYSTEM

100 centimes = 1 franc, frank   5 francs = 1 belga

PRECIOUS METAL CONTENT

Belgium was a member of the Latin Monetary Union, formed by treaties standardizing the silver and gold coinage of Belgium, France, Greece, Italy, and Switzerland. Derived from the French coinage system established in 1803, the union was formed in 1865 and dissolved in 1926. Many other countries, although not union members, struck coinage to these standards.

Dates	Denomination	Gross Wt (g)	Fineness	Net Wt (g)	Troy Oz.
		SILVER			
1865–1918	50 centimes	2.5000	0.8350	2.0871	0.0671
	1 franc	5.0000	0.8350	4.1750	0.1342
	2 francs	10.0000	0.8350	8.3500	0.2685
	5 francs	25.0000	0.9000	22.5000	0.7234
1933–35	20 francs	11.0000	0.6800	7.4800	0.2405
	50 francs	22.0000	0.6800	14.9600	0.4810
1939–40	50 francs	20.0000	0.8350	16.7000	0.5369
1948–60	20 francs	8.0000	0.8350	6.6800	0.2148
	50 francs	12.5000	0.8350	10.4375	0.3356
	100 francs	18.0000	0.8350	15.0300	0.4832
		GOLD			
1867–1914	20 francs	6.4516	0.9000	5.8064	0.1867

Leopold II, *1865–1909*

First Coinage

Y#	KM#	Metal	Description	VF	EF	Unc
1	33–34	Cop	1 Centime, 1869–1907 *1869–70, 73, 76, VF $7.50; 1883, 92, Rare*	2.00	6	10
2	35–36	Cop	2 Centimes, 1869–1909 *1869, VF $65; 1871, VF $35*	2.50	10	25

Y#	KM#	Metal	Description	VF	EF	Unc
3	Several	C-N	5 Centimes, 1894–1901 *1898–1900, VF $12.50*	4	12.00	30
4	42–43	C-N	10 Centimes, 1894–1901 *1895Fr, 1901, VF $50*	5	16.50	50

Y#	KM#	Metal	Description	VF	EF	Unc
5	26	Silv	50 Centimes, 1866–99 *1866, VF $45; 1868, VF $450; 1881, VF $250; 1899, VF $28*	15	55	135
6	28–29	Silv	1 Franc, 1866–87 *1868, Rare; 1869, VF $65; 1881, VF $225*	25	70	175
7	30–31	Silv	2 Francs, 1866–87 *1887, VF $250*	85	225	650
8	24	Silv	5 Francs, 1865–76 *1865–66, VF $250*	25	65	225
19	32/37	Gold	20 Francs, 1867–82	BV	BV	325

50th Anniversary of Independence

Y#	KM#	Metal	Description	VF	EF	Unc
9	38	Silv	1 Franc, 1880	25	65	175
10	39	Silv	2 Francs, 1880	60	200	500

Second Coinage

Y#	KM#	Metal	Description	VF	EF	Unc
12	Several	C-N	5 Centimes, 1901–97 *1901, VF $35; 1907, VF $9*	2	7.00	22.50
13	Several	C-N	10 Centimes, 1901–06 *1901, VF $10*	2	5.00	17.50
14	62–63	C-N	25 Centimes, 1908–09	5	12.50	50.00

Y#	KM#	Metal	Description	VF	EF	Unc
15	50–51	Silv	50 Centimes, 1901	2	25	100

Y#	KM#	Metal	Description	VF	EF	Unc
16	60–61	Silv	50 Centimes, 1907, 09	7	20	50

Y#	KM#	Metal	Description	VF	EF	Unc
17	56–57	Silv	1 Franc, 1904, 09	15	45	100
18	58–59	Silv	2 Francs, 1904, 09	11	35	100

ALBERT I, *1909–1934*

Y#	KM#	Metal	Description	VF	EF	Unc
22	76–77	Cop	1 Centime, 1912, 14	1.50	3.00	9.00
23	64–65	Cop	2 Centimes, 1910–19	1.75	3.75	17.50

Y#	KM#	Metal	Description	VF	EF	Unc
24	Several	C-N	5 Centimes, 1910–32 *1914Fr, VF $5; 1932, VF $225*	0.50	2.50	10
25	85–86	C-N	10 Centimes, 1920–29	0.75	1.50	10
26	68–69	C-N	25 Centimes, 1910–29	1.75	3.75	15

Reverse: ***Star over value for change of alloy***

Y#	KM#	Metal	Description	VF	EF	Unc
24a	93–94	N-Br	5 Centimes, 1930–32	1.50	3.50	10
25a	95–96	N-Br	10 Centimes, 1930–32 *1930Fr, VF $200; 1931Fl; 1932Fr, VF $150*	5.00	15.00	45

Y#	KM#	Metal	Description	VF	EF	Unc
27	87–88	Nick	50 Centimes, 1922–34 *1934Fr, VF $75*	0.50	2.00	7.50
28	89–90	Nick	1 Franc, 1922–35 *1933Fl, VF $900*	0.75	2.00	8.00
29	91–92	Nick	2 Francs, 1923–30 *1924, VF $10; 1930, VF $25*	2.50	5.50	30.00

Y#	KM#	Metal	Description	VF	EF	Unc
30	97–98	Nick	5 Francs / 1 Belga, 1930–34 *1934Fr, VF $40*	4	12.50	50

Centennial of Independence

Y#	KM#	Metal	Description	VF	EF	Unc
31	99–100	Nick	10 Francs / 2 Belgas, 1930	55	175	450

Y#	KM#	Metal	Description	VF	EF	Unc
32	101–02	Nick	20 Francs / 4 Belgas, 1931–32	35	90	250

Y#	KM#	Metal	Description	VF	EF	Unc
33	70–71	Silv	50 Centimes, 1910–14	2.50	8.00	15
34	72–73	Silv	1 Franc, 1910–18 *1917, VF $1,500; 1918, VF $1,000*	3.00	4.50	10
35	74–75	Silv	2 Francs, 1910–12	6.00	12.00	30

Note: Y34 dated 1917–18 was not issued to circulation.

Y#	KM#	Metal	Description	VF	EF	Unc
36	103–04	Silv	20 Francs, 1933–34 *1933, VF $30*	5.00	12.50	32.50

Y#	KM#	Metal	Description	VF	EF	Unc
37	78–79	Gold	20 Francs, 1914	BV	300	335

German Occupation, 1914–1918

Y#	KM#	Metal	Description	VF	EF	Unc
38	80	Zinc	5 Centimes, 1915–16	5.00	12.50	35
39	81	Zinc	10 Centimes, 1915–17 *1917, EF $55*	2.50	8.50	25
40	82	Zinc	25 Centimes, 1915–18	5.00	15.00	40

Y#	KM#	Metal	Description	VF	EF	Unc
41	83	Zinc	50 Centimes, 1918	4	12.50	40

LEOPOLD III, *1934–1950*

All Leopold III coins were minted in both Flemish and French varieties except Y49 and Y56.

Legend: *BELGIE – BELGIQUE or BELGIQUE – BELGIE*

Y#	KM#	Metal	Description	VF	EF	Unc
42	110–11	N-Br	5 Centimes, 1938–40	1.00	3.00	10.00
43	112–13	N-Br	10 Centimes, 1938–39	1.25	3.50	11.00
44	114–15	N-Br	25 Centimes, 1938–39	1.00	2.75	8.50

Y#	KM#	Metal	Description	VF	EF	Unc
45	119–20	Nick	1 Franc, 1939–40	0.75	2.50	7.50
46	116–17	Nick	5 Francs, 1938–39	1.00	3.00	25.00

Y#	KM#	Metal	Description	VF	EF	Unc
47	108–09	Nick	5 Francs, 1936–37	8	20	75

Brussels Exposition / Railway Centennial

Y#	KM#	Metal	Description	VF	EF	Unc
48	106–07	Silv	50 Francs, 1935	85	150	250

Y#	KM#	Metal	Description	VF	EF	Unc
49	105	Silv	20 Francs, 1934–35	5	12.50	27.50

Y#	KM#	Metal	Description	VF	EF	Unc
50	121–22	Silv	50 Francs, 1939–40	12	18	55

GERMAN OCCUPATION, 1940–1945

Y#	KM#	Metal	Description	VF	EF	Unc
51	123–24	Zinc	5 Centimes, 1941–43	1.00	5	15.00
52	125–26	Zinc	10 Centimes, 1941–46	1.00	5	22.50
53	131–32	Zinc	25 Centimes, 1942–47 *1947, Rare, not issued for circulation*	1.00	5	22.50
54	127–28	Zinc	1 Franc, 1941–47 *1947 Belgique/Belgie, Proof only, Rare; 1947 Belgie/Belgique, VF $50*	1.00	5	15.00
55	129–30	Zinc	5 Francs, 1941–47 *1944–46Fr, VF $4; 1945Fl, VF $22.50; 1946Fl, Rare; 1947Fr, VF $90; 1947Fl, VF $900*	1.50	5	15.00

ALLIED ISSUE

Planchet: *U.S. 1943 cent*

Y#	KM#	Metal	Description	VF	EF	Unc
56	133	Z-CS	2 Francs, 1944 *Error on Netherlands 25-cent silver planchet, VF $450*	3	9	25

Postwar Issues

Y#	KM#	Metal	Description	VF	EF	Unc
57	142–43	C-N	1 Franc, 1950–88	0.25	0.50	3.50
58	134–35	C-N	5 Francs, 1948–81	0.25	0.50	3.50

Y#	KM#	Metal	Description	VF	EF	Unc
59	140–41	Silv	20 Francs, 1949–55 *1954, Unc $40; 1955Fr, Unc $800; 1955Fl, Unc $190*	4.50	9	30
60	136–37	Silv	50 Francs, 1948–54	6.50	9	30

Y#	KM#	Metal	Description	VF	EF	Unc
61	138–39	Silv	100 Francs, 1948–54	10	20	50

Baudouin I, *1951–1993*

Y#	KM#	Metal	Description	VF	EF	Unc
62	146–47	Bz	20 Centimes, 1953–63 *1962, EF $4*	0.25	0.75	2.35
63	Several	Bz	50 Centimes, 1952–2001	0.25	0.75	2.75

Brussels Fair

Y#	KM#	Metal	Description	VF	EF	Unc
64	151	Silv	50 Francs, 1958	14	17	35

Marriage Commemorative

Y#	KM#	Metal	Description	VF	EF	Unc
65	152	Silv	50 Francs, MCMLX (1960)	14	17	35

Y#	KM#	Metal	Description	VF	EF	Unc
66	153–54	C-N	25 Centimes, 1964–75	0.10	0.25	0.75

BERMUDA

Explored by the Spanish and English early in the 17th century, this archipelago of more than 350 small islands lies in the Atlantic Ocean about 575 miles east of North Carolina. Settled in 1609, it became a crown colony in 1684, and is the oldest self-governing British overseas territory. *Language:* English. *Capital:* Hamilton.

British coins were used to 1970.

PRECIOUS METAL CONTENT

Dates	Denomination	Gross Wt (g)	Fineness	Net Wt (g)	Troy Oz.
		SILVER			
1959	1 crown	28.2800	0.9250	26.1616	0.8411
1964	1 crown	22.6200	0.5000	11.3094	0.3636

ELIZABETH II, *1952–2022*

350th Anniversary of Founding

Y#	KM#	Metal	Description	VF	EF	Unc
1	13	Silv	1 Crown, 1959	BV	17.50	25
						Proof: $3,500

Obverse: ***Same portrait as Y1***

Y#	KM#	Metal	Description	VF	EF	Unc
2	14	Silv	1 Crown, 1964	BV	BV	15
						Proof: $20

BHUTAN

Bhutan is a semi-independent kingdom in the eastern Himalayas. India controls its external relations. A constitution was drafted in 2005, moving the nation toward a two-party democracy. *Languages:* Dzongkha, plus Tibetan and Nepalese dialects. *Capital:* Thimphu.

Some modern Bhutanese coins use cyclical dates, which appear as the top line in the reverse square as follows:

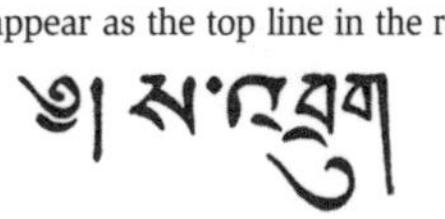

(1928) Year of the Earth-Dragon

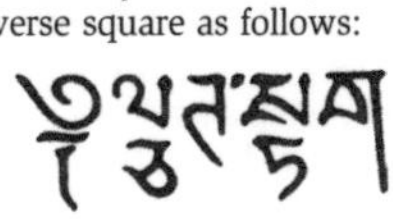

(1950) Year of the Iron-Tiger

MONETARY SYSTEM

100 pice = 1 rupee

MAHARAJAH JIGME WANGCHUK, *1926–1952*

DORJI WANGCHUK, *1952–1972*

Y#	KM#	Metal	Description	VF	EF	Unc
5	N/A	Cop	1 Pice, ND (ca. 1800–1930)	10	20	50
1	23	Bz	1 Pice, CD 1928 (design as Y4)	50	125	300

Y#	KM#	Metal	Description	VF	EF	Unc
4	24–25	Silv	1/2 Rupee, CD 1928	45	100	200

Second Coinage

Y#	KM#	Metal	Description	VF	EF	Unc
3	27	Bz	1 Pice, ND (1951–55)	3	5	10
4a	26	Nick	1/2 Rupee, CD 1928, 50 (5.83 g)	50	125	250
4b	28	Nick	1/2 Rupee, CD 1950 (5.0 g)	4	8	25

Note: Y4a was struck from 1951 to 1955 to the weight standard of the India rupee. Y4b was struck from 1967 to 1968 to the standard of the new (decimal) India rupee. Weights may vary slightly.

BOHEMIA AND MORAVIA

In 1939, Nazi Germany annexed the historical regions of Bohemia and Moravia in Czechoslovakia, declaring them a protectorate of Germany on behalf of their large populations of ethnic Germans. In reality, Germany needed the arms-manufacturing capabilities of the region to prepare for the coming war. From 1939 until 1945, ethnic Germans in the protectorate were subject to German law, while the remainder of the population was ruled by a puppet Czech government. After Germany surrendered to the Allies in 1945, the region returned to Czechoslovakia, and its ethnic Germans were expelled to Austria and Germany. *Languages:* Czech, German. *Capital:* Prague.

MONETARY SYSTEM

100 haleru = 1 koruna

Y#	KM#	Metal	Description	VF	EF	Unc
B29	1	Zinc	10 Haleru, 1940–44	7.50	15	30

Y#	KM#	Metal	Description	VF	EF	Unc
B30	2	Zinc	20 Haleru, 1940–44	8	15	30

Reverse: ***Like Y61***

Y#	KM#	Metal	Description	VF	EF	Unc
B31	3	Zinc	50 Haleru, 1940–44, reverse as Y6	9.50	15	30

Y#	KM#	Metal	Description	VF	EF	Unc
B32	4	Zinc	1 Koruna, 1941–44	9.50	15	30

BOLIVIA

A landlocked country in central South America, this former Spanish colony won its independence in 1825. Large portions of its territory were lost in wars with Chile, Brazil, and Paraguay between 1884 and 1938. A Cuban-backed revolutionary war in the mid-1960s ended in the death of guerrilla leader Ernesto "Che" Guevara. Military rule was the norm thereafter until civilian control was reestablished in 1982. *Languages:* Spanish, Quechua, Aymara. *Capitals:* La Paz (administrative) and Sucre (constitutional).

Pre-Decimal Coinage to *1863*

MONETARY SYSTEM

8 soles = 1 peso
8 soles = 1 Melgarejo
16 soles (sueldos, reales) = 1 escudo

PRECIOUS METAL CONTENT

Dates	Denomination	Gross Wt (g)	Fineness	Net Wt (g)	Troy Oz.
		SILVER			
1852–53	1/4 sol	0.8500	0.6670	0.5661	0.0182
1853–58	1/2 sol	1.5000	0.6670	1.0015	0.0322
1853–59	1 sol	3.0000	0.6670	2.0031	0.0644
1853–56	2 soles	6.2000	0.6670	4.1181	0.1324
1853–59	4 soles	13.5000	0.6670	9.0045	0.2895
1853–59	8 soles	27.0000	0.9030	24.3727	0.7836
1865	1/4 Melgarejo	5.0000	0.6660	3.3312	0.1071
1865, 68	1/2 Melgarejo	10.0000	0.6660	6.6592	0.2141
1865	1 Melgarejo	20.0000	0.6660	13.3186	0.4282
		GOLD			
1852–57	1/2 escudo	1.7000	0.8750	1.4875	0.0478
	1 escudo	3.4000	0.8750	2.9750	0.0956
	8 escudos	27.0000	0.8750	23.6250	0.7596

Potosi Mint

Mintmark: ***PTS monogram in reverse legend***

Reverse: ***Llama in plain field***

Y#	KM#	Metal	Description	VF	EF	Unc
1	111	Silv	(1/4 Sol), 1852	25	50	100

Reverse: ***Llama between branches***

Y#	KM#	Metal	Description	VF	EF	Unc
1a	117	Silv	(1/4 Sol), 1853	175	250	450

Note: Y1a is usually found holed.

Obverse: ***Laureate head, name on neck***
Reverse: ***No value shown***

Y#	KM#	Metal	Description	VF	EF	Unc
2	118.1	Silv	(1/2 Sol), 1853–56 (17 mm)	15	50	100
3	119.1	Silv	(1 Sol), 1853–54 (20 mm)	15	50	175
4	121.1	Silv	(2 Soles), 1853 (25 mm)	35	150	300
5	123.1	Silv	(4 Soles), 1853 (32 mm)	45	125	275
6	112.1	Silv	(8 Soles), 1852–54, 56 (37 mm)	50	100	500

Obverse: ***Like Y2–6***
Reverse: ***Value in legend***

Y#	KM#	Metal	Description	VF	EF	Unc
2a	118.2	Silv	1/2 Sol, 1856–58	15	30	100
3a	119.2	Silv	1 Sol, 1855–58	25	60	250
4a	121.2	Silv	2 Soles, 1854–58	65	175	450

Y#	KM#	Metal	Description	VF	EF	Unc
5a	123.2	Silv	4 Soles, 1853–58	22.50	50	185
6a	112.2	Silv	8 Soles, 1854–55	45.00	95	400

Obverse: ***Name below neck***
Reverse: ***Like Y2a–6a***

Y#	KM#	Metal	Description	VF	EF	Unc
2b	118.3	Silv	1/2 Sol, 1859	55	125	300
3b	119.3	Silv	1 Sol, 1859	60	125	300
4b	121.3	Silv	2 Soles, 1859	75	200	500
5b	123.3	Silv	4 Soles, 1859	60	125	325
6b	137	Silv	8 Soles, 1859	2,500	4,000	7,500

Obverse: ***PESO (weight) in legend***
Reverse: ***Fineness in legend, no value shown***

Y#	KM#	Metal	Description	VF	EF	Unc
7	133.1	Silv	PESO 25 Gs (1/2 Sol), 1859	70	175	300
8	134.1	Silv	PESO 50 Gs (1 Sol), 1859	40	100	250
9	135.1	Silv	PESO 100 Gs (2 Soles), 1859	75	250	500
11	138.3	Silv	PESO 400 Gs (8 Soles), 1859	70	125	425
11a	138.1	Silv	Po 400 Gs, 1859	4,000	6,000	—
11b	138.5	Silv	*Po 400 Gs, 1860, reverse like Y11d (mule)*	—	—	—

Obverse: ***Weight in legend, PESO omitted***
Reverse: ***Fineness above llamas***

Y#	KM#	Metal	Description	VF	EF	Unc
7a	133.2	Silv	25 Gs (1/2 Sol), 1860–63	17.50	35	100
8a	134.2	Silv	50 Gs (1 Sol), 1860–63	20.00	40	110
9a	135.2	Silv	100 Gs (2 Soles), 1860–63	25.00	55	125
10	139	Silv	200 Gs (4 Soles), 1860	75.00	200	500
11c	138.4	Silv	*400 Gs (8 Soles), 1859, reverse like Y11 (mule)*	600.00	1,200	—
11d	138.6	Silv	400 Gs, 1859–63 *1859, VF $600*	50.00	150	300

Y#	KM#	Metal	Description	VF	EF	Unc
12	113	Gold	1/2 Escudo, 1852–56	175	250	400
13	114	Gold	1 Escudo, 1852–56	350	500	300
14	116	Gold	8 Escudos, 1852–57	1,200	2,000	3,000

La Paz Mint

Mintmark: ***PAZ in reverse legend***

Obverse: ***Bare head***
Reverse: ***Value in legend***

Y#	KM#	Metal	Description	VF	EF	Unc
15	122	Silv	2 Soles, 1853	2,750	4,000	12,000
16	124.1	Silv	4 Soles, 1853	750	1,500	—

Obverse: ***"Potosi-style" laureate head (general style of Y2–6)***

Y#	KM#	Metal	Description	VF	EF	Unc
18	120	Silv	1 Sol, 1855	35	90	350
19	126	Silv	2 Soles, 1854	250	475	1,500
20	125	Silv	4 Soles, 1853–55	50	125	400

Obverse: ***Crude, "La Paz"-style head***

Y#	KM#	Metal	Description	VF	EF	Unc
17	127	Silv	1/2 Sol, 1855–56	35	95	350
18a	128	Silv	1 Sol, 1855–56	100	200	500
19a	129	Silv	2 Soles, 1855–56	750	1,500	—
20a	130	Silv	4 Soles, 1855–58	50	100	365

Obverse: ***Crude, so-called Ugly Head***

Y#	KM#	Metal	Description	VF	EF	Unc
17b	132	Silv	1/2 Sol, 1858	45	175	650
18b	131	Silv	1 Sol, 1857, 59	65	130	350
20b	136	Silv	4 Soles, 1859	450	650	1,000

MELGAREJO ISSUES, *1865–1868*

Y#	KM#	Metal	Description	VF	EF	Unc
21	144	Silv	(1/4 Melgarejo), 1865	15	60	200
22	145	Silv	(1/2 Melgarejo), 1865, 68 *1868, Rare*	50	100	250

Y#	KM#	Metal	Description	VF	EF	Unc
23	146	Silv	(1 Melgarejo), 1865	80	145	1,500

DECIMAL COINAGE, *1864–1962*

MONETARY SYSTEM

100 centavos or centecimos = 1 boliviano
2 bolivianos = 1 escudo
8 escudos = 1 onza

PRECIOUS METAL CONTENT

Dates	Denomination	Gross Wt (g)	Fineness	Net Wt (g)	Troy Oz.
		SILVER			
1864–71	1/20 boliviano / 5 centavos	1.2500	0.9000	1.1250	0.0362
	1/10 boliviano / 10 centavos	2.5000	0.9000	2.2500	0.0723
	1/5 boliviano / 20 centavos	5.0000	0.9000	4.5000	0.1447
1873–91	1/2 boliviano / 50 centavos	12.5000	0.9000	11.2500	0.3617
1864–79	1 boliviano	25.0000	0.9000	22.5000	0.7234
1909	20 centavos	4.0000	0.8333	3.3333	0.1072
	50 centavos	10.0000	0.8333	8.3333	0.2679
		GOLD			
1868	1/2 escudo	1.2500	0.9000	1.1250	0.0361
	1 escudo	2.5000	0.9000	2.2500	0.0723
	1 onza	32.4000	0.9000	29.1600	0.9375

First Coinage

Y#	KM#	Metal	Description	VF	EF	Unc
24	147	Cop	1 Centecimo, 1864	175	300	—
25	148	Cop	2 Centecimos, 1864	200	350	—

Y#	KM#	Metal	Description	VF	EF	Unc
26	149	Silv	1/20 Boliviano, 1864–65	20	40	125
27	150	Silv	1/10 Boliviano, 1864–67	15	35	100
28	151	Silv	1/5 Boliviano, 1864–66	20	50	225
29	152.1	Silv	1 Boliviano, 1864–68, obverse 9 stars	25	50	250
29a	152.2	Silv	1 Boliviano, 1866–69, obverse 11 stars	20	40	225

Y#	KM#	Metal	Description	VF	EF	Unc
30	140	Gold	1/2 Escudo, 1868	400	750	2,000
31	141	Gold	1 Escudo, 1868	700	950	3,000
32	142	Gold	1 Onza, 1868	4,500	8,500	15,000

Second Coinage

***Legend:** LA UNION HACE LA FUERZA*

Obverse: ***11 stars at bottom***
Reverse: ***With weight in grams***

Y#	KM#	Metal	Description	VF	EF	Unc
33	156.1	Silv	5 Centavos, 1871	50	100	250
34	153.1	Silv	10 Centavos, 1870–71	12	25	75
35	154.1	Silv	20 Centavos, 1870–71	60	120	—
36	155.1	Silv	1 Boliviano, 1870, large legend and wreath	35	65	115
36a	155.3	Silv	1 Boliviano, 1870–71, small legend and wreath	30	35	100

Obverse: ***11 stars at bottom***
Reverse: ***Without weight***

Y#	KM#	Metal	Description	VF	EF	Unc
33a	156.2	Silv	5 Centavos, 1871–72	20	40	125
34a	153.2	Silv	10 Centavos, 1871	20	40	125
35a	154.2	Silv	20 Centavos, 1871	75	175	—

Obverse: ***9 stars at bottom***

Y#	KM#	Metal	Description	VF	EF	Unc
33b	156.3	Silv	5 Centavos, 1872	15	40	75
34b	158.1	Silv	10 Centavos, 1872	10	20	50
35b	154.3	Silv	20 Centavos, 1871–72	15	40	150
36b	155.4	Silv	1 Boliviano, 1871–72	35	60	110

Third Coinage

Obverse: ***Date at bottom***
Reverse: ***Value in wreath***

Y#	KM#	Metal	Description	VF	EF	Unc
37	162	Cop	1 Centavo, 1878	200	300	—
38	164	Cop	2 Centavos, 1878	225	400	—

Obverse: ***Value at bottom***
Reverse: ***Legend in wreath, date below***

Y#	KM#	Metal	Description	VF	EF	Unc
37a	163	Cop	1 Centavo, 1878	500	900	—
38a	165	Cop	2 Centavos, 1878	550	1,150	—

Y#	KM#	Metal	Description	VF	EF	Unc
39	167	Bz	1 Centavo, 1883	10.00	20	50
40	168	Bz	2 Centavos, 1883	12.50	25	60

Y#	KM#	Metal	Description	VF	EF	Unc
41	169.1	C-N	5 Centavos, 1883	15	30	75
42	170.1	C-N	10 Centavos, 1883	20	45	100

Y#	KM#	Metal	Description	VF	EF	Unc
41a	169.2	C-N	5 Centavos, 1883	7.50	15.00	40
42a	170.2	C-N	10 Centavos, 1883	8.50	17.50	50

Note: Y41a–42a were converted from Y41–42 by officially punching a center hole to prevent confusion with the silver 10 and 20 centavos.

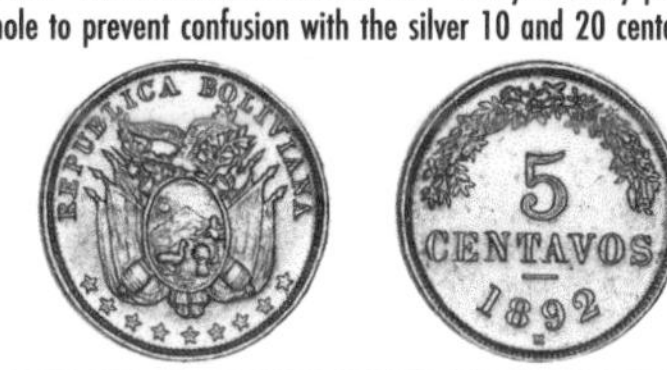

Y#	KM#	Metal	Description	VF	EF	Unc
43	171	C-N	5 Centavos, 1892	5	15	50
44	172	C-N	10 Centavos, 1892	15	40	125

Y#	KM#	Metal	Description	VF	EF	Unc
45	173	C-N	5 Centavos, 1893–1919	3	10	25
46	174	C-N	10 Centavos, 1893–1919	2	10	20

Legend: LA UNION ES LA FUERZA

Reverse: ***Fineness below value***

Y#	KM#	Metal	Description	VF	EF	Unc
47	157.1	Silv	5 Centavos, 1872–84	5	10	25
48	158	Silv	10 Centavos, 1872–84	6	12	30
49	159.1	Silv	20 Centavos, 1872–85	6	12	35
50	161.3	Silv	1/2 Boliviano, 1879	50	100	250

Reverse: ***Weight and fineness below value***

Y#	KM#	Metal	Description	VF	EF	Unc
51	161.1	Silv	1/2 Boliviano / 50 Centavos, 1873	35	70	200
52	160	Silv	1 Boliviano, 1872–93	45	85	300
			1877, VF $175; 1879, VF $400; 1893, VF $1,500			

Dies: ***Slightly modified, both sides***

Y#	KM#	Metal	Description	VF	EF	Unc
47a	157.2	Silv	5 Centavos, 1885–1900	5	10	25
48a	158.3	Silv	10 Centavos, 1885–1900 *1887–88, VF $30*	7	15	30
49a	159.2	Silv	20 Centavos, 1885–1907 *1907, Unc $375*	6	10	30
51a	161.4	Silv	1/2 Boliviano / 50 Centavos, 1891, weight below value	400	640	1,250
51b	161.5	Silv	1/2 Boliviano / 50 Centavos, 1891–1900, weight omitted	15	25	75

Note: Y47a–51a dated 1894 are patterns, as are probably all 1884–93 dates of the 1 boliviano.

Daza Commemorative

Y#	KM#	Metal	Description	VF	EF	Unc
53	166	Silv	20 Centavos, 1879	35	60	200

Obverse: ***Stars above arms***
Reverse: ***Fineness ("9 Ds") in legend***

Y#	KM#	Metal	Description	VF	EF	Unc
54	175.1	Silv	50 Centavos, 1900–08, Potosi	7.50	17.50	40
54a	175.2	Silv	50 Centavos, 1900, Santiago	12.50	25.00	65

Obverse: ***Stars below arms***
Reverse: ***Fineness ("10/12") in legend***

Y#	KM#	Metal	Description	VF	EF	Unc
55	176	Silv	20 Centavos, 1909	6	13	25
56	177	Silv	1/2 Boliviano / 50 Centavos, 1909	15	30	50

Fourth Coinage

Design: ***Like Y45–46, but reduced size***

Y#	KM#	Metal	Description	VF	EF	Unc
57	178	C-N	5 Centavos, 1935	1.50	3.00	12.50
58	179	C-N	10 Centavos, 1935–36, 39	1.00	2.50	10.00
59	182	C-N	50 Centavos, 1939	0.50	1.00	5.00
57a	179a	Zinc	10 Centavos, 1942	1.00	2.00	8.00
58a	183	Zinc	20 Centavos, 1942	1.00	2.00	8.00
59a	182a.1	Bz	50 Centavos, 1942	1.00	2.00	3.50
59b	182a.2	Bz	50 Centavos, 1942, restrike, poor detail	1.00	2.00	3.50

Y#	KM#	Metal	Description	VF	EF	Unc
60	180	C-N	10 Centavos, 1937	1	2	6
61	181	C-N	50 Centavos, 1937	30	45	75

Fifth Coinage

Y#	KM#	Metal	Description	VF	EF	Unc
62	184	Bz	1 Boliviano, 1951	0.50	1	3

Y#	KM#	Metal	Description	VF	EF	Unc
63	185	Bz	5 Bolivianos, 1951	0.50	1	4

Y#	KM#	Metal	Description	VF	EF	Unc
64	186	Bz	10 Bolivianos, 1951	1	2	5

BRAZIL

Brazil, the largest country in South America, covers more than half the continent. From 1549 to 1822 it was a royal colony of Portugal. A republic was proclaimed in 1889, though various military governments have ruled over the years. Civilian administrations in the early 21st century leaned toward socialism. *Language:* Portuguese. *Capital:* Brasilia.

MONETARY SYSTEM

1,000 reis = 1 milreis, to 1942
100 centavos = 1 cruzeiro, 1942–

PRECIOUS METAL CONTENT

Dates	Denomination	Gross Wt (g)	Fineness	Net Wt (g)	Troy Oz.
		Silver			
1867–69	200 reis	2.5000	0.8350	2.0875	0.0671
	500 reis	6.2500	0.8350	5.2188	0.1678
	1,000 reis	12.5000	0.8350	10.4375	0.3356
	2,000 reis	25.0000	0.8350	20.8750	0.6711
1875–1900	400 reis	5.1000	0.9167	4.6750	0.1503
	500 reis	6.3750	0.9167	5.8438	0.1879
	1,000 reis	12.7500	0.9167	11.6875	0.3758
	2,000 reis	25.0000	0.9167	23.3750	0.7515
	4,000 reis	51.0000	0.9167	46.7500	1.5030
1906–13	500 reis	5.0000	0.9000	4.5000	0.1447
	1,000 reis	10.0000	0.9000	9.0000	0.2894
	2,000 reis	20.0000	0.9000	18.0000	0.5787
1922	2,000 reis	8.0000	0.9000	7.2000	0.2315
1922–35	2,000 reis	8.0000	0.5000	4.0000	0.1286
1936–38	5,000 reis	10.0000	0.6000	6.0000	0.1929
		Gold			
1849–1922	5,000 reis	4.4822	0.9170	4.1087	0.1321
	10,000 reis	8.9645	0.9170	8.2175	0.2642
	20,000 reis	17.9290	0.9170	16.4349	0.5284

PEDRO II, *1831–1889*

DECIMAL ISSUES

First Coinage

Y#	KM#	Metal	Description	VF	EF	Unc
A1	458	Silv	500 Reis, 1849–52	6	12.00	40
A2	459	Silv	1,000 Reis, 1849–52 *1849, VF $750*	8	15.00	50
A3	462	Silv	2,000 Reis, 1851–52	14	22.50	65

Note: Dates not shown are either counterfeits or patterns.

Y#	KM#	Metal	Description	VF	EF	Unc
A4	460	Gold	10,000 Reis, 1849–51	390	650	845
A5	461	Gold	20,000 Reis, 1849–51	455	650	975

Second Coinage

Y#	KM#	Metal	Description	VF	EF	Unc
A6	469	Silv	200 Reis, 1854–67	4	8.00	15
A7	464	Silv	500 Reis, 1853–67	4	8.00	15
A8	465	Silv	1,000 Reis, 1853–66	5	9.00	20
A9	466	Silv	2,000 Reis, 1853–67 *1859, 66–67, VF $750*	14	22.50	75

Y#	KM#	Metal	Description	VF	EF	Unc
A10	463	Gold	20,000 Reis, 1851–52	600	650	750

Third Coinage

Y#	KM#	Metal	Description	VF	EF	Unc
A11	473	Bz	10 Reis, 1868–70	0.50	2	20
A12	474	Bz	20 Reis, 1868–70	1.00	4	25
A13	479	Bz	40 Reis, 1873–80	3.00	10	75

Y#	KM#	Metal	Description	VF	EF	Unc
A14	477	C-N	100 Reis, 1871–85 *1872, VF $750*	1	3	25
A15	478	C-N	200 Reis, 1871–84	3	20	70
A16	482	C-N	50 Reis, 1886–88	3	6	50
A17	483	C-N	100 Reis, 1886–89	3	6	70
A18	484	C-N	200 Reis, 1886–89	4	10	60

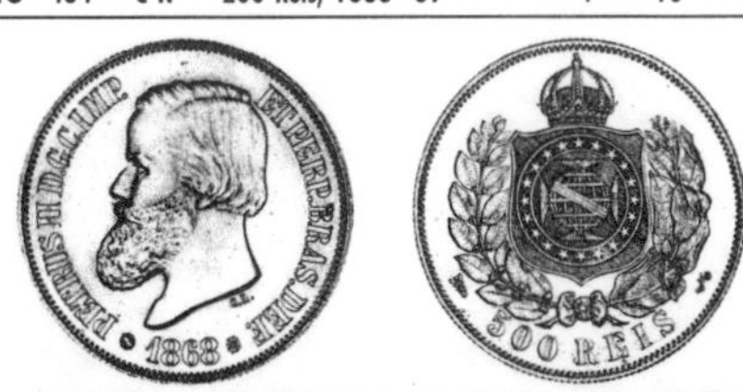

Y#	KM#	Metal	Description	VF	EF	Unc
A19	471	Silv	200 Reis, 1867–69	4.00	8	15
A20	472	Silv	500 Reis, 1867–68	5.00	9	20
A21	476	Silv	1,000 Reis, 1869	17.50	40	125
A22	475	Silv	2,000 Reis, 1868–69, 75–76	20.00	40	125

Reverse: *"Decreto de 1870" added*

Y#	KM#	Metal	Description	VF	EF	Unc
A23	480	Silv	500 Reis, 1876–89	5	9	50
			1887, VF $750			
A24	481	Silv	1,000 Reis, 1876–89	8	20	50
A25	485	Silv	2,000 Reis, 1886–89	14	20	40
			1886, VF $500			

Y#	KM#	Metal	Description	VF	EF	Unc
A26	470	Gold	5,000 Reis, 1854–59	125	200	400
A27	467	Gold	10,000 Reis, 1853–89	BV	250	500
A28	468	Gold	20,000 Reis, 1853–89	BV	400	650

REPUBLIC, *1889–1942*

Y#	KM#	Metal	Description	VF	EF	Unc
1	490	Bz	20 Reis, 1889–1912	1	2	20

Y#	KM#	Metal	Description	VF	EF	Unc
2	491	Bz	40 Reis, 1889–1912	1	2	20

Y#	KM#	Metal	Description	VF	EF	Unc
3	492	C-N	100 Reis, 1889–1900	1	3	25
4	493	C-N	200 Reis, 1889–1900	3	10	40

Y#	KM#	Metal	Description	VF	EF	Unc
5	494	Silv	500 Reis, 1889	4	8	20
6	495	Silv	1,000 Reis, 1889	10	25	80
7	498	Silv	2,000 Reis, 1891–97	500	800	1,200
		Silv	*1891, 96, VF $1,250*			

400th Anniversary of Discovery

Y#	KM#	Metal	Description	VF	EF	Unc
8	499	Silv	400 Reis, 1900	30	45	75

Y#	KM#	Metal	Description	VF	EF	Unc
9	500	Silv	1,000 Reis, 1900	60	90	150

Y#	KM#	Metal	Description	VF	EF	Unc
10	501	Silv	2,000 Reis, 1900	100	175	500

Y#	KM#	Metal	Description	VF	EF	Unc
11	502	Silv	4,000 Reis, 1900	325	500	1,000

Y#	KM#	Metal	Description	VF	EF	Unc
12	503	C-N	100 Reis, MCMI (1901)	1	3	10
13	504	C-N	200 Reis, MCMI	1	5	12
14	505	C-N	400 Reis, MCMI	2	8	25

Y#	KM#	Metal	Description	VF	EF	Unc
B14	515	C-N	400 Reis, 1914	100	150	250

Note: YB14 was not issued to circulation. Some authorities consider it a pattern.

Y#	KM#	Metal	Description	VF	EF	Unc
15	506	Silv	500 Reis, 1906–12 *1912, VF $50*	3	6	15
16	507	Silv	1,000 Reis, 1906–12	5	8	20
17	508	Silv	2,000 Reis, 1906–12	8	15	75

Obverse: ***Dashes between stars***
Reverse: ***Divided legend***

Y#	KM#	Metal	Description	VF	EF	Unc
18	509	Silv	500 Reis, 1912	5	10	50
19	510	Silv	1,000 Reis, 1912–13	5	9	30
20	511	Silv	2,000 Reis, 1912–13	10	25	75

Obverse: ***No dashes between stars***
Reverse: ***Continuous legend***

Y#	KM#	Metal	Description	VF	EF	Unc
21	512	Silv	500 Reis, 1913	3	6	15
22	513	Silv	1,000 Reis, 1913	5	8	20
23	514	Silv	2,000 Reis, 1913	10	20	60

Y#	KM#	Metal	Description	VF	EF	Unc
24	526	Silv	2,000 Reis, 1924–34	3	4	8

Y#	KM#	Metal	Description	VF	EF	Unc
25	496	Gold	10,000 Reis, 1889–1922	600	1,000	1,500

Y#	KM#	Metal	Description	VF	EF	Unc
26	497	Gold	20,000 Reis, 1889–1922	600	1,000	1,500

Y#	KM#	Metal	Description	VF	EF	Unc
27	516	C-N	20 Reis, 1918–35 *1935, Unc $500*	0.15	0.50	2
28	517	C-N	50 Reis, 1918–35 *1935, Unc $500*	0.15	0.50	3
29	518	C-N	100 Reis, 1918–35	0.15	0.50	10
30	519	C-N	200 Reis, 1918–35	0.25	1.00	12
31	520	C-N	400 Reis, 1918–35	0.40	2.00	15

Note: Y27–28 dated 1935 were not issued to circulation.

Y#	KM#	Metal	Description	VF	EF	Unc
32	524	A-Bz	500 Reis, 1924–30	0.50	1.00	20
33	525	A-Bz	1,000 Reis, 1924–31	0.50	1.50	25

Independence Centennial

Y#	KM#	Metal	Description	VF	EF	Unc
34	521.1	A-Bz	500 Reis, 1922	1	2.00	20
35	522.1	A-Bz	1,000 Reis, 1922	1	2.50	25
34a	521.2	A-Bz	500 Reis, 1922 (BBASIL error)	35	60.00	125
35a	522.2	A-Bz	1,000 Reis, 1922 (BBASIL error)	4	8.00	15

Y#	KM#	Metal	Description	VF	EF	Unc
38	523	Silv	2 MilReis, 1922, struck in both .900 and .500 silver	3	4	10

Note: Y38 was struck in both .900 and .500 silver.

400th Anniversary of Colonization

Y#	KM#	Metal	Description	VF	EF	Unc
39	527	Silv	100 Reis, 1932	1	2	6

Y#	KM#	Metal	Description	VF	EF	Unc
40	528	Silv	200 Reis, 1932	1	3	8

Y#	KM#	Metal	Description	VF	EF	Unc
41	529	Silv	400 Reis, 1932	2	4	10

Y#	KM#	Metal	Description	VF	EF	Unc
42	530	A-Bz	500 Reis, 1932	10	50	100

Y#	KM#	Metal	Description	VF	EF	Unc
43	531	A-Bz	1,000 Reis, 1932	4	8	50

Y#	KM#	Metal	Description	VF	EF	Unc
44	532	Silv	2,000 Reis, 1932	3	4	8

National Heroes Series, *1935–1938*

Y#	KM#	Metal	Description	VF	EF	Unc
45	536	C-N	100 Reis, 1936–38	0.50	1	3

Y#	KM#	Metal	Description	VF	EF	Unc
46	537	C-N	200 Reis, 1936–38	0.75	2	4

Y#	KM#	Metal	Description	VF	EF	Unc
47	538	C-N	300 Reis, 1936–38	1	2	4

Y#	KM#	Metal	Description	VF	EF	Unc
48	539	C-N	400 Reis, 1936–38	1	2	6

Y#	KM#	Metal	Description	VF	EF	Unc
49	533	A-Bz	500 Reis, 1935 (4 g)	6	10	50
50	540	A-Bz	500 Reis, 1936–38 (5 g)	1	2	6

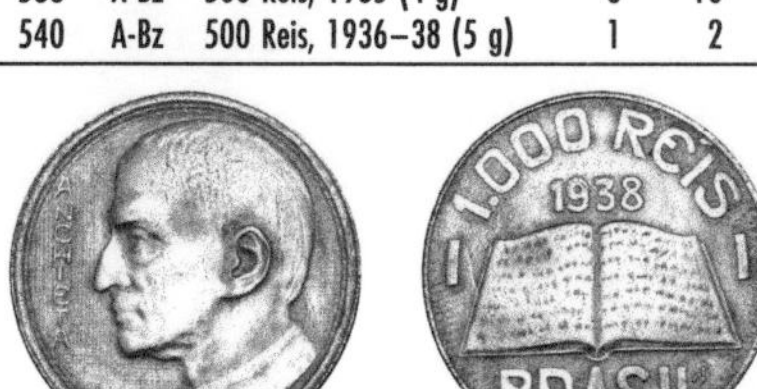

Y#	KM#	Metal	Description	VF	EF	Unc
51	534	A-Bz	1,000 Reis, 1935 (26 mm)	2	4	10
52	541	A-Bz	1,000 Reis, 1936–38 (24 mm)	2	3	8

Y#	KM#	Metal	Description	VF	EF	Unc
53	542	A-Bz	2,000 Reis, 1936–38	2	3	10
54	548	A-Bz	2,000 Reis, 1938, polygonal	2	4	15

Y#	KM#	Metal	Description	VF	EF	Unc
55	535	Silv	2,000 Reis, 1935	3	4	6

Y#	KM#	Metal	Description	VF	EF	Unc
56	543	Silv	5000 Reis, 1936–38	3	4	6

NEW GOVERNMENT

Y#	KM#	Metal	Description	VF	EF	Unc
57	544	C-N	100 Reis, 1938–42	0.35	0.75	2
58	545	C-N	200 Reis, 1938–42	0.35	0.75	2
59	546	C-N	300 Reis, 1938–42	0.35	1.00	3
60	547	C-N	400 Reis, 1938–42	0.35	1.00	4

Note: The 1942 issues have a yellow color due to higher copper content.

Famous Men Series, *1939*

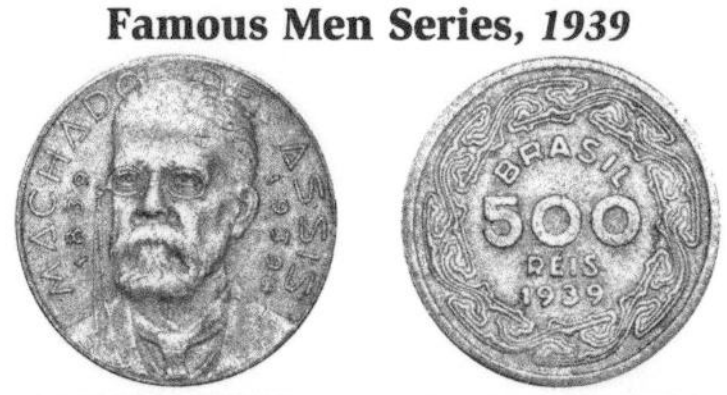

Y#	KM#	Metal	Description	VF	EF	Unc
61	549	A-Bz	500 Reis, 1939	0.50	1	5

Y#	KM#	Metal	Description	VF	EF	Unc
62	550	A-Bz	1,000 Reis, 1939	0.50	1	5

Y#	KM#	Metal	Description	VF	EF	Unc
63	551	A-Bz	2,000 Reis, 1939	0.50	1	5

Currency Reform of 1942

MONETARY SYSTEM
100 centavos = 1 cruzeiro

Y#	KM#	Metal	Description	VF	EF	Unc
64	555	C-N	10 Centavos, 1942–43	0.25	0.50	2
65	556	C-N	20 Centavos, 1942–43	0.25	0.60	3
66	557	C-N	50 Centavos, 1942–43	0.25	0.75	4
64a	555a	A-Bz	10 Centavos, 1943–47	0.25	0.50	2
65a	556a	A-Bz	20 Centavos, 1943–48	0.25	0.60	3
66a	557a	A-Bz	50 Centavos, 1943–47	0.25	0.75	4

Y#	KM#	Metal	Description	VF	EF	Unc
67	558	A-Bz	1 Cruzeiro, 1942–56	0.25	0.65	2
68	559	A-Bz	2 Cruzeiros 1942–56	0.25	0.65	2
69	560	A-Bz	5 Cruzeiros, 1942–43	3.00	5.00	8

Y#	KM#	Metal	Description	VF	EF	Unc
73	561	A-Bz	10 Centavos, 1947–55	0.10	0.25	1

Y#	KM#	Metal	Description	VF	EF	Unc
74	562	A-Bz	20 Centavos, 1948–56	0.10	0.25	1

Y#	KM#	Metal	Description	VF	EF	Unc
75	563	A-Bz	20 Centavos, 1948–56	0.10	0.25	1

Y#	KM#	Metal	Description	VF	EF	Unc
76	564	Alum	10 Centavos, 1956–61	0.10	0.20	1
77	565	Alum	20 Centavos, 1956–61	0.10	0.20	1

Y#	KM#	Metal	Description	VF	EF	Unc
78	566	A-Bz	50 Centavos, 1956	0.10	0.20	1.00
79	567	A-Bz	1 Cruzeiro, 1956	0.20	0.40	0.85
80	568	A-Bz	2 Cruzeiros, 1956	0.15	0.50	1.25

Y#	KM#	Metal	Description	VF	EF	Unc
81	569	Alum	50 Centavos, 1957–61	0.10	0.20	0.30
82	570	Alum	1 Cruzeiro, 1957–61	0.10	0.20	0.30
83	571	Alum	2 Cruzeiros, 1957–61	0.20	0.30	0.60

BRITISH CARIBBEAN TERRITORIES (EASTERN GROUP)

The combined territories of the Leeward Islands, British Guiana, Barbados, Windward Islands, Trinidad, and Tobago made up the Eastern Group of the British Caribbean Territories. The coinage issue was intended to replace regular British coins in these territories.

MONETARY SYSTEM
100 cents = 1 British West Indies dollar

ELIZABETH II, *1952–2022*

Y#	KM#	Metal	Description	VF	EF	Unc
1	1	Bz	1/2 Cent, 1955, 58 *1958 Proof: $225*	0.40	0.80	12.50 *Proof: $7.50*

Y#	KM#	Metal	Description	VF	EF	Unc
2	2	Bz	1 Cent, 1955–65 *1958 Proof: $250*	0.30	0.40	1.00 *Proof: $7.50*
3	3	Bz	2 Cents, 1955–65 *1958 Proof: $225*	0.40	0.75	1.20 *Proof: $7.50*

Y#	KM#	Metal	Description	VF	EF	Unc
4	4	N-Br	5 Cents, 1955–65	0.50	0.85	1.50 *Proof: $7.50*
5	5	C-N	10 Cents, 1955–65	0.50	0.85	1.50 *Proof: $7.50*
6	6	C-N	25 Cents, 1955–65	0.75	1.00	2.00 *Proof: $10.00*

Y#	KM#	Metal	Description	VF	EF	Unc
7	7	C-N	50 Cents, 1955, 65	1.50	2.25	2.75 *Proof: $15*

BRITISH GUIANA

Under Dutch and French influences until 1831, this former British crown colony on the north shore of South America gained independence as the Republic of Guyana in 1966. *Language:* English. *Capital:* Georgetown.

MONETARY SYSTEM

50 pence = 1 British Guiana dollar

PRECIOUS METAL CONTENT

Dates	Denomination	Gross Wt (g)	Fineness	Net Wt (g)	Troy Oz.
		SILVER			
1888–1943	4 pence	1.8851	0.9250	1.7437	0.0561
1944–45	4 pence	1.8851	0.5000	0.9425	0.0303

VICTORIA, *1837–1901*

Y#	KM#	Metal	Description	VF	EF	Unc
A1	731	Silv	4 Pence, 1838–55 *1851–53, VF $75*	20	50	110

Note: YA1 same as Great Britain Y4.

Y#	KM#	Metal	Description	VF	EF	Unc
B2	772	Silv	4 Pence, 1888	20	650	125

Note: YB2 struck for British Guiana and West Indies only.

Legend: ***BRITISH GUIANA AND WEST INDIES***

Y#	KM#	Metal	Description	VF	EF	Unc
1	26	Silv	4 Pence, 1891–1901	15	35	100 *Proof: $550*

EDWARD VII, *1901–1910*

Y#	KM#	Metal	Description	VF	EF	Unc
2	27	Silv	4 Pence, 1903–10	15	50	100 *Proof: $1,000*

GEORGE V, *1910–1936*

Y#	KM#	Metal	Description	VF	EF	Unc
3	28	Silv	4 Pence, 1911, 13, 16	25	60	125

Legend: ***BRITISH GUIANA only***

Y#	KM#	Metal	Description	VF	EF	Unc
4	29	Silv	4 Pence, 1917–36	20	50	100
						Proof: $900

George VI, *1936–1952*

Y#	KM#	Metal	Description	VF	EF	Unc
5	30	Silv	4 Pence, 1938–45	4	7.50	25
						Proof: $800

BRITISH HONDURAS

On the Caribbean coast of Central America, British Honduras was settled in the 1600s. It was administered as part of Jamaica from 1862 to 1884, when it became a separate crown colony. In 1973 it took the name of *Belize* upon attaining independence. In 1981 it became a member of the British Commonwealth. *Languages:* English, Spanish. *Capital:* Belize City.

MONETARY SYSTEM

100 cents = 1 dollar

PRECIOUS METAL CONTENT

Dates	Denomination	Gross Wt (g)	Fineness	Net Wt (g)	Troy Oz.
		SILVER			
1894–1946	5 cents	1.1620	0.9250	1.0749	0.0346
	10 cents	2.3240	0.9250	2.1497	0.0691
	25 cents	5.8100	0.9250	5.3743	0.1728
	50 cents	11.6200	0.9250	10.7485	0.3456

Victoria, *1837–1901*

Y#	KM#	Metal	Description	VF	EF	Unc
1	6	Bz	1 Cent, 1885–94	16	60	175
						Proof: $1,750

Y#	KM#	Metal	Description	VF	EF	Unc
2	7	Silv	5 Cents, 1894	20	40	175
						Proof: $3,750
3	8	Silv	10 Cents, 1894	25	75	325
						Proof: $5,500
4	9	Silv	25 Cents, 1894–1901	30	150	400
						Proof: $5,500
5	10	Silv	50 Cents, 1894–1901	50	250	1,000
						Proof: $8,500

Edward VII, *1901–1910*

Y#	KM#	Metal	Description	VF	EF	Unc
6	11	Bz	1 Cent, 1904–09	20	30	65
			1909, VF $275			*Proof: $5,500*

Y#	KM#	Metal	Description	VF	EF	Unc
7	14	C-N	5 Cents, 1907, 09	55	150	475
						Proof: $7,000

Y#	KM#	Metal	Description	VF	EF	Unc
8	12	Silv	25 Cents, 1906–07	35	100	625
9	13	Silv	50 Cents, 1906–07	75	200	1,250

George V, *1910–1936*

Y#	KM#	Metal	Description	VF	EF	Unc
10	15	Bz	1 Cent, 1911–13	125	325	1,350

Y#	KM#	Metal	Description	VF	EF	Unc
11	19	Bz	1 Cent, 1914–36	3.50	25	75
						Proof: $2,000

Y#	KM#	Metal	Description	VF	EF	Unc
12	16	C-N	5 Cents, 1911–36	12.50	50	150
						Proof: $2,000

Y#	KM#	Metal	Description	VF	EF	Unc
13	20	Silv	10 Cents, 1918–36	7.50	50	250
						Proof: $1,625
14	17	Silv	25 Cents, 1911, 19	10.00	75	400
15	18	Silv	50 Cents, 1911, 19	15.00	100	800
						Proof: $9,750

GEORGE VI, *1936–1952*

Y#	KM#	Metal	Description	VF	EF	Unc
16	21	Bz	1 Cent, 1937–47	2	8	50
						Proof: $1,000

Y#	KM#	Metal	Description	VF	EF	Unc
17	22	C-N	5 Cents, 1939	3	20	100
						Proof: $650
17a	22a	N-Br	5 Cents, 1942–47	5	50	200
						Proof: $750

Y#	KM#	Metal	Description	VF	EF	Unc
18	23	Silv	10 Cents, 1939–46	5	35	125
						Proof: $650

New Legend: *KING GEORGE THE SIXTH*

Y#	KM#	Metal	Description	VF	EF	Unc
19	24	Bz	1 Cent, 1949–51	0.75	2	12.50
						Proof: $155
20	25	N-Br	5 Cents, 1949–52	1.00	2	15.00
						Proof: $250
21	26	C-N	25 Cents, 1952	6.00	55	250.00
						Proof: $1,000

ELIZABETH II, *1952–1973*

Y#	KM#	Metal	Description	VF	EF	Unc
22	27	Bz	1 Cent, 1954	1	2	4.75
						Proof: $350

Y#	KM#	Metal	Description	VF	EF	Unc
23	30	Bz	1 Cent, 1956–73, scalloped	0.10	0.25	0.50
						Proof: $225

Y#	KM#	Metal	Description	VF	EF	Unc
24	31	N-Br	5 Cents, 1956–73	0.10	0.25	0.50
						Proof: $225

Y#	KM#	Metal	Description	VF	EF	Unc
25	32	C-N	10 Cents, 1956–70	0.10	0.25	0.75
						Proof: $250
26	29	C-N	25 Cents, 1955–73	0.25	0.50	1.00
						Proof: $350
27	28	C-N	50 Cents, 1954–71	0.45	1.00	3.00
						Proof: $400

BRITISH NORTH BORNEO

This former protectorate on the northern tip of the island of Borneo, now known as Sabah, is part of the federation of Malaysia. *Languages:* Various. *Capital:* Jesselton (now Kota Kinabalu).

MONETARY SYSTEM

100 cents = 1 Straits dollar

PRECIOUS METAL CONTENT

Dates	Denomination	Gross Wt (g)	Fineness	Net Wt (g)	Troy Oz.
		SILVER			
1929	25 cents	2.8276	0.5000	1.4138	0.0455

Legend: ***BRITISH NORTH BORNEO CO.***

Y#	KM#	Metal	Description	VF	EF	Unc
1	1	Bz	1/2 Cent, 1885–1907 *1907, VF $85*	45	75	150 *Proof: $400*

Y#	KM#	Metal	Description	VF	EF	Unc
2	2	Bz	1 Cent, 1882–1907 *1894–1907, VF $70*	10	25	125 *Proof: $400*

New Legend: ***STATE OF NORTH BORNEO***

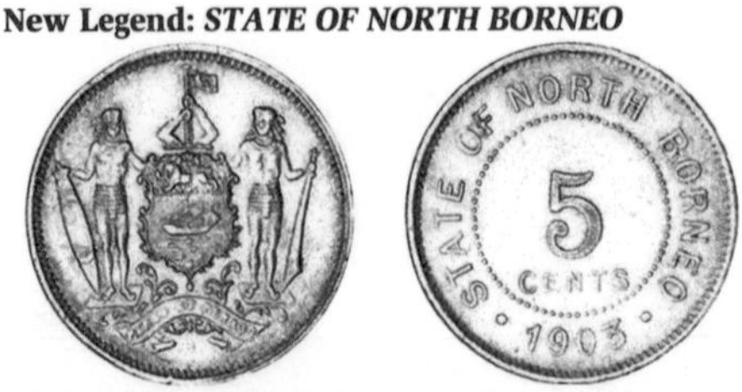

Y#	KM#	Metal	Description	VF	EF	Unc
3	3	C-N	1 Cent, 1904–41	7.50	20	50
4	4	C-N	2-1/2 Cents, 1903, 20	25.00	55	115
5	5	C-N	5 Cents, 1903–41	10.00	20	125

Y#	KM#	Metal	Description	VF	EF	Unc
6	6	Silv	25 Cents, 1929	40	80	250 *Proof: $500*

Note: For later issues, see Malaya.

BRITISH WEST AFRICA

This was an administrative grouping of four separate British colonies on the west coast of Africa: Gambia, Sierra Leone, Gold Coast (now Ghana), and Nigeria. They gained independence between 1957 and 1965. Coins struck for Nigeria (Y1 through Y6) have been moved to the section on Nigeria in the 15th edition.

MONETARY SYSTEM

12 pence = 1 shilling

PRECIOUS METAL CONTENT

Dates	Denomination	Gross Wt (g)	Fineness	Net Wt (g)	Troy Oz.
		SILVER			
1913–20	3 pence	1.4138	0.9250	1.3078	0.0419
	6 pence	2.8276	0.9250	2.6155	0.0838
	1 shilling	5.6552	0.9250	5.2311	0.1689
	2 shillings	11.3104	0.9250	10.4621	0.3364

George V, *1910–1936*

Y#	KM#	Metal	Description	VF	EF	Unc
7	7	C-N	1/10 Penny, 1912–36 *1914, 19KN, VF $45*	1.50	3.00	10
8	8	C-N	1/2 Penny, 1912–36 *1913, Unc $400; 1922, 31, Unc $850*	2.50	7.50	25
9	9	C-N	1 Penny, 1912–36 *1914H, VF $60; 1922, VF $600*	2.00	6.50	15

Y#	KM#	Metal	Description	VF	EF	Unc
14	10	Silv	3 Pence, 1913–20	3	12.50	40
15	11–11a	Silv	6 Pence, 1913–20	5	15.00	60

Y#	KM#	Metal	Description	VF	EF	Unc
16	12	Silv	1 Shilling, 1913–20	9.00	20.00	55
17	13–13a	Silv	2 Shillings, 1913–20	10.00	55.00	100
14a	10b	N-Br	3 Pence, 1920–36 *1927, 36H, Unc $325*	3.00	12.50	50
15a	11b	N-Br	6 Pence, 1920–36 *1928, EF $250*	6.50	25.00	40
16a	12a	N-Br	1 Shilling, 1920–36 *1920G, Rare*	7.50	35.00	65
11a	13b	N-Br	2 Shillings, 1920–36 *1928, Rare*	15.00	50.00	125

EDWARD VIII, *1936*

Y#	KM#	Metal	Description	VF	EF	Unc
18	14	C-N	1/10 Penny, 1936 *1936H, Unc $600*	0.50	1.00	5.00
19	15	C-N	1/2 Penny, 1936	0.75	1.25	5.00
20	16	C-N	1 Penny, 1936	1.00	2.50	7.50
21	17	C-N	10 Cents, 1936, obverse of East Africa Y26 *(mule)*	300.00	450.00	650.00

GEORGE VI, *1936–1952*

Y#	KM#	Metal	Description	VF	EF	Unc
22	20	C-N	1/10 Penny, 1938–47 *1938H, Unc $50; 1947KN, Unc $500*	0.50	1.25	6
23	18	C-N	1/2 Penny, 1937–47	1.00	2.00	15
24	19	C-N	1 Penny, 1937–47 *1946SA, EF $500*	0.75	1.50	15

Y#	KM#	Metal	Description	VF	EF	Unc
25	21	C-N	3 Pence, 1938–47	1.50	5	25
26	22	Br	6 Pence, 1938–47	1.25	5	25

Y#	KM#	Metal	Description	VF	EF	Unc
27	23	Br	1 Shilling, 1938–47 *1946H, EF $750*	2	7.50	32.50
28	24	Br	2 Shillings, 1938–47	4	15.00	45.00

Designs: ***Similar to Y22–28***
New Legend: ***Without IND. IMP***

Y#	KM#	Metal	Description	VF	EF	Unc
29	26	C-N	1/10 Penny, 1949–50	1.00	1.50	5
30	27	C-N	1/2 Penny, 1949–51	4.50	15.00	35
31	30	C-N	1 Penny, 1951	15.00	25.00	60
29a	26a	Bz	1/10 Penny, 1952	1.00	2.00	5
30a	27a	Bz	1/2 Penny, 1952	0.50	1.00	5
31a	30a	Bz	1 Penny, 1952	1.25	3.00	10

Y#	KM#	Metal	Description	VF	EF	Unc
32	31	N-Br	6 Pence, 1952	100	125	250
33	28	N-Br	1 Shilling, 1949–52	1	5	15
34	29	N-Br	2 Shillings, 1949–52	5	25	60

Note: Y31 was not released for circulation. Most were melted.

ELIZABETH II, *1952–1957*

Y#	KM#	Metal	Description	VF	EF	Unc
38	32	Bz	1/10 Penny, 1954–57 *1956, Unc $675; 1957 Unc $250*	1	2	6.50
39	33	Bz	1 Penny, 1956–58	1	3	11.00
A39	34	Bz	1 Penny, 1956, George VI obverse legend *(mule)*	150	250	400.00

Y#	KM#	Metal	Description	VF	EF	Unc
40	35	C-N	3 Pence, 1957	75	200	400

BRUNEI

This constitutional sultanate on the northwest coast of Borneo was under British protection between 1888 and 1984, when it became fully independent. *Languages:* Malay, English. *Capital:* Bandar Seri Begawan (formerly Brunei).

MONETARY SYSTEM

100 cents = 1 Straits dollar

SULTAN HASHIM JELAL, *1885–1906*

Y#	KM#	Metal	Description	VF	EF	Unc
1	3	Bz	1 Cent, AH 1304 (1887)	45	175	350
						Proof: $3,500

BUKHARA

SEE RUSSIAN TURKESTAN

BULGARIA

Bulgaria, on the Balkan peninsula of Europe, gained partial independence from the Ottoman Empire as a principality in 1878, and was proclaimed a kingdom in 1908. Allied with the Central Powers in World War I and the Axis in World War II, it came under communist control as a Soviet-styled people's republic in 1947. Bulgaria adopted a democratic constitution in 1991 and is now a highly centralized parliamentary republic. *Language:* Bulgarian. *Capital:* Sofia.

MONETARY SYSTEM

100 stotinki = 1 lev

PRECIOUS METAL CONTENT

Dates	Denomination	Gross Wt (g)	Fineness	Net Wt (g)	Troy Oz.
		SILVER			
1882–1916	50 stotinki	2.5000	0.8350	2.0871	0.0671
	1 lev	5.0000	0.8350	4.1750	0.1342
	2 leva	10.0000	0.8350	8.3500	0.2685
	5 leva	25.0000	0.9000	22.5000	0.7234
1930–37	20 leva	4.0000	0.5000	2.0000	0.0643
	50 leva	10.0000	0.5000	5.0000	0.1608
	100 leva	20.0000	0.5000	10.0000	0.3215
1963–64	2 leva	8.8889	0.9000	8.0000	0.2572
	5 leva	16.6667	0.9000	15.0000	0.4823
		GOLD			
1894–1912	10 leva	3.2258	0.9000	2.9032	0.0933
	20 leva	6.4516	0.9000	5.8064	0.1867
	100 leva	32.2581	0.9000	29.0323	0.9334
1963–64	10 leva	8.4400	0.9000	7.5960	0.2443
	20 leva	16.8889	0.9000	15.2000	0.4887

PRINCE ALEXANDER I, *1879–1886*

Y#	KM#	Metal	Description	VF	EF	Unc
1	1	Bz	2 Stotinki, 1881	10	25.00	150
2	2	Bz	5 Stotinki, 1881	7	22.50	135
3	3	Bz	10 Stotinki, 1881	6	20.00	135

Y#	KM#	Metal	Description	VF	EF	Unc
4	6	Silv	50 Stotinki, 1883	6	15	50
5	4	Silv	1 Lev, 1882	20	100	250
6	5	Silv	2 Leva, 1882	20	125	500
7	7	Silv	5 Leva, 1884–85	25	65	475

FERDINAND I, AS PRINCE, *1887–1908*

Y#	KM#	Metal	Description	VF	EF	Unc
8	8	C-N	2-1/2 Stotinki, 1888	10.00	20	150
9	9	C-N	5 Stotinki, 1888	10.00	20	175
10	10	C-N	10 Stotinki, 1888	10.00	20	250
11	11	C-N	20 Stotinki, 1888	12.50	30	450

Y#	KM#	Metal	Description	VF	EF	Unc
12	12	Silv	50 Stotinki, 1891	6.00	25	45
13	13	Silv	1 Lev, 1891	5.00	15	60
14	14	Silv	2 Leva, 1891	10.00	30	125
15	15	Silv	5 Leva, 1892	22.50	80	260

Obverse: *Rearranged legend*

Y#	KM#	Metal	Description	VF	EF	Unc
13a	16	Silv	1 Lev, 1894	6.00	22.50	400
14a	17	Silv	2 Leva, 1894	13.50	37.50	500
15a	18	Silv	5 Leva, 1894	35.00	75.00	575

Y#	KM#	Metal	Description	VF	EF	Unc
21	19	Gold	10 Leva, 1894	350	425	850
22	20	Gold	20 Leva, 1894	375	575	975
23	21	Gold	100 Leva, 1894	1,750	2,500	7,500

Y#	KM#	Metal	Description	VF	EF	Unc
16	22	Bz	1 Stotinka, 1901, 12	2.50	9	22
17	23	Bz	2 Stotinki, 1901, 12	2.50	9	15
18	24	C-N	5 Stotinki, 1906–13	1.00	3	7
19	25	C-N	10 Stotinki, 1906–13	1.00	3	7
20	26	C-N	20 Stotinki, 1906–13	2.00	3	10

World War I Issues

Y#	KM#	Metal	Description	VF	EF	Unc
18a	24a	Zinc	5 Stotinki, 1917	1.00	5	60
19a	25a	Zinc	10 Stotinki, 1917	1.00	5	60
20a	26a	Zinc	20 Stotinki, 1917	1.50	7	75

FERDINAND I, AS TSAR, *1908–1918*

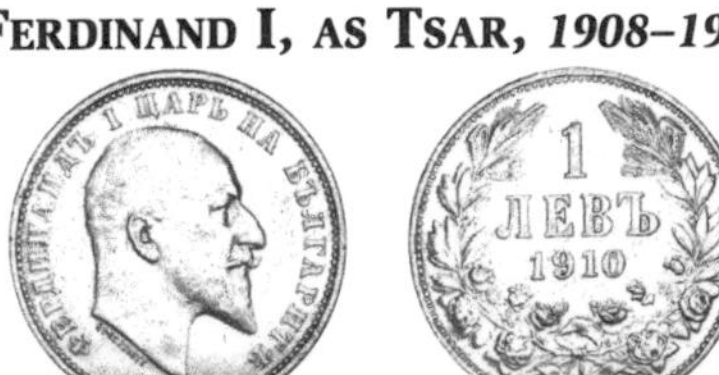

Y#	KM#	Metal	Description	VF	EF	Unc
24	27	Silv	50 Stotinki, 1910	5	20.00	225
25	28	Silv	1 Lev, 1910	10	22.50	225
26	29	Silv	2 Leva, 1910	12	35.00	300

Y#	KM#	Metal	Description	VF	EF	Unc
27	30	Silv	50 Stotinki, 1912–16 *1916, EF $300*	5	12.50	25
28	31	Silv	1 Lev, 1912–16 *1916, EF $1,250*	5	10.00	25
29	32	Silv	2 Leva, 1912–16 *1916, VF $3,500*	12	22.50	75

Establishment of Tsardom / 25th Year of Reign

Y#	KM#	Metal	Description	VF	EF	Unc
30	33	Gold	20 Leva, 1912 *Proof Restrike (1960s): $6,00*	500	600	1,100
31	34	Gold	100 Leva, 1912 *Proof Restrike (1960s): $2,250*	2,000	2,500	3,250

BORIS III, *1918–1943*

Designs: *Like Y34–35*

Y#	KM#	Metal	Description	VF	EF	Unc
32	35	Alum	1 Lev, 1923, LEV in 3 letters	3.00	9	35
32a	N/A	Alum	1 Lev, 1923, LEV in 4 letters	—	—	—
33	36	Alum	2 Leva, 1923	3.50	15	55

Y#	KM#	Metal	Description	VF	EF	Unc
34	37	C-N	1 Lev, 1925	0.75	2	7.50
35	38	C-N	2 Leva, 1925	0.75	2	7.50

Y#	KM#	Metal	Description	VF	EF	Unc
36	39	C-N	5 Leva, 1930	1.50	3	12.50
37	40	C-N	10 Leva, 1930	2.50	5	15.00

Y#	KM#	Metal	Description	VF	EF	Unc
41	46	A-Bz	50 Stotinki, 1937	0.75	1.50	10

Y#	KM#	Metal	Description	VF	EF	Unc
38	41	Silv	20 Leva, 1930	3.00	6	15
39	42	Silv	50 Leva, 1930	8.50	10	20
40	43	Silv	100 Leva, 1930	10.00	20	55

Y#	KM#	Metal	Description	VF	EF	Unc
44	44	Silv	50 Leva, 1934	6.00	12.50	30
45	45	Silv	100 Leva, 1934, 37	8.50	17.50	35

Y#	KM#	Metal	Description	VF	EF	Unc
42	47	C-N	20 Leva, 1940	1.50	3	9
43	48	C-N	50 Leva, 1940	2.00	5	13

World War II Issues

Designs: *Like Y34–37*

Y#	KM#	Metal	Description	VF	EF	Unc
34a	37a	Iron	1 Lev, 1941	7	22.50	100
35a	38a	Iron	2 Leva, 1941	2	10.00	50
36a	39a	Iron	5 Leva, 1941	3	12.50	55
37a	40a	Iron	10 Leva, 1941	15	32.50	100

Y#	KM#	Metal	Description	VF	EF	Unc
A45	49	Iron	2 Leva, 1943	2.50	7.50	100

Y#	KM#	Metal	Description	VF	EF	Unc
36b	39b	N-CS	5 Leva, 1943	1.00	5	20
37b	40b	N-CS	10 Leva, 1943	1.25	4	15
43a	48a	N-CS	50 Leva, 1943	3.00	6	15

PEOPLE'S REPUBLIC, *1946–1991*

Y#	KM#	Metal	Description	VF	EF	Unc
46	50	Br	1 Stotinka, 1951	0.05	0.10	5.50
47	51	Br	3 Stotinki, 1951	0.10	0.25	1.25
48	52	Br	5 Stotinki, 1951	0.10	0.25	1.25

Y#	KM#	Metal	Description	VF	EF	Unc
49	53	C-N	10 Stotinki, 1951	0.10	0.25	1.00
A49	55	C-N	20 Stotinki, 1952, 54	0.30	0.75	1.50
50	54	C-N	25 Stotinki, 1951	0.30	0.75	2.50
51	56	C-N	50 Stotinki, 1959	0.30	0.75	3.00

Y#	KM#	Metal	Description	VF	EF	Unc
52	57	C-N	1 Lev, 1960	0.45	0.75	1

Currency Revision, *1962*

Y#	KM#	Metal	Description	VF	EF	Unc
53	59	Br	1 Stotinka, 1962, 70	0.10	0.15	0.50
54	60	Br	2 Stotinki, 1962	0.10	0.15	0.50
55	61	Br	5 Stotinki, 1962	0.10	0.20	1.50
56	62	N-Br	10 Stotinki, 1962	0.10	0.20	0.50
57	63	N-Br	20 Stotinki, 1962	0.20	0.30	0.75
58	64	N-Br	50 Stotinki, 1962	0.40	0.65	1.50
59	58	N-Br	1 Lev, 1962	0.50	1.00	1.75

1,100th Anniversary of Slavic Literature

Y#	KM#	Metal	Description	VF	EF	Unc
60	65	Silv	*2 Leva, 1963, Proof only, $20*			
61	66	Silv	*5 Leva, 1963, Proof only, $35*			
62	67	Gold	*10 Leva, 1963, Proof only, $400*			
63	68	Gold	*20 Leva, 1963, Proof only, $750*			

15th Anniversary, Death of Georgi Dimitrov 20th Anniversary of People's Power

Y#	KM#	Metal	Description	VF	EF	Unc
64	69	Silv	*2 Leva, 1964, Proof only, $20*			
65	70	Silv	*5 Leva, 1964, Proof only, $35*			
66	71	Gold	*10 Leva, 1964, Proof only, %400*			
67	72	Gold	*20 Leva, 1964, Proof only, $750*			

BURMA

Located on the Bay of Bengal between India and Thailand, modern Burma was unified in the 1700s. The kingdom ended in 1886 with annexation to British India. It became a separate British colony in 1937, was occupied by Japan in World War II, and gained independence as a republic in 1948. A 1962 military coup established a socialist regime. A name change from *Burma* to *Myanmar* in 1989 is disputed by some political factions and not recognized by some nations. *Languages:* Burmese, many others. *Capital:* Mandalay (1957–1885), Rangoon (1886–).

MONETARY SYSTEM

4 pyas = 1 pe or anna
16 annas = 1 kyat (rupee)
16 kyat = 1 mohur

PRECIOUS METAL CONTENT

Dates	Denomination	Gross Wt (g)	Fineness	Net Wt (g)	Troy Oz.
		SILVER			
1853–78	1 anna	0.7300	0.9170	0.6694	0.0215
	1/8 kyat	1.4580	0.9170	1.3340	0.0430
	1/4 kyat	2.9160	0.9170	2.6740	0.0860
	1/2 kyat	5.8319	0.9170	5.3479	0.1718
	1 kyat	11.6638	0.9170	10.6957	0.3436
		GOLD			
1852–80	1 rupee	0.7000	0.900	0.6300	0.0203
	2 rupees	1.4000	0.900	1.2600	0.0405
1852–72	4 rupees	2.8000	0.900	2.5200	0.0812
1880	5 rupees	3.5000	0.900	3.1500	0.1013

BURMESE NUMERALS

1	2	3	4	5
၁	၂	၃	၄	၅
6	**7**	**8**	**9**	**0**
၆	၇	၈	၉	၀

As with Thailand, early coins are dated in the Chula-Sakarat system (see the introduction).

MINDON, *CS 1214–1240 (1853–1878)*

Obverse: ***Hare to left***
Reverse: ***Similar to Y1***

Y#	KM#	Metal	Description	VF	EF	Unc
C1	22	Lead	1/32 Anna (Pe), CS 1231 (1869) (20–21 mm)	90	160	400
D1	23	Lead	1/16 Anna (Pe), CS 1231 (21–22 mm)	85	150	350

Y#	KM#	Metal	Description	VF	EF	Unc
1	17–18	Cop	1/4 Anna (Pe), CS 1227 (1865)	25	65	400
1a	18a	Iron	1/4 Anna (Pe), CS 1227	150	300	—

Y#	KM#	Metal	Description	VF	EF	Unc
2	24	Cop	1/2 Anna (2 Pe), CS 1231 (1869)	150	350	—

Accession Date: ***CS 1214***

Y#	KM#	Metal	Description	VF	EF	Unc
3	6	Silv	1 Anna (Pe), ND (12 mm)	45	50	1,750
4	7	Silv	1/8 Kyat (Mu), ND (15 mm)	30	90	1,500
5	8	Silv	1/4 Kyat (Mat), ND (20 mm)	35	100	1,500
6	9	Silv	1/2 Kyat (5 Mu), ND (25 mm)	75	165	1,500
7	10	Silv	1 Kyat, ND (30 mm)	50	400	2,000

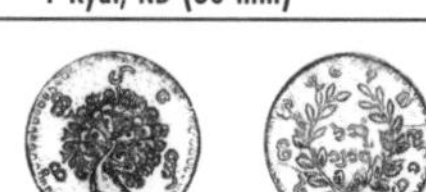

Y#	KM#	Metal	Description	VF	EF	Unc
10	13	Gold	1 Kyat, ND (12 mm)	1,500	2,500	5,000
11	14	Gold	2 Kyat, ND (16 mm)	2,500	3,500	6,000

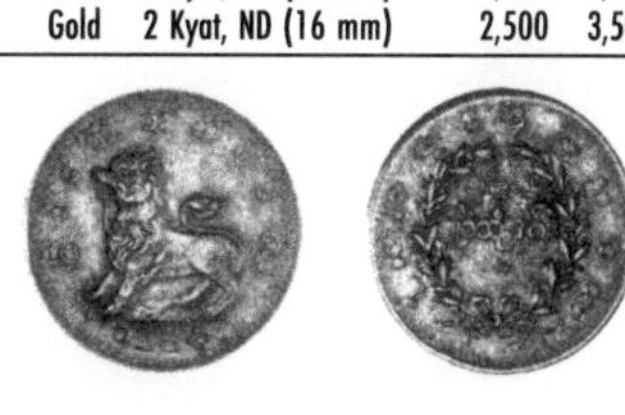

Y#	KM#	Metal	Description	VF	EF	Unc
A8	19	Gold	1 Kyat, CS 1228 (1866) (12 mm)	975	1,250	2,000
8	20	Gold	1/4 Mohur, CS 1228 (18–19 mm)	1,250	1,750	3,000
B8	21	Gold	1 Mohur, CS 1228 (25 mm)			

THIBAW, *CS 1240–1248 (1878–1885)*

Accession Date: *CS 1240 on coins*

Y#	KM#	Metal	Description	VF	EF	Unc
9	25	Cop	1/4 Anna (Pe), ND	65	500	1,350
C8	26	Gold	1/2 Mohur, CS 1240 (21 mm)	—	22,500	30,000

REPUBLIC, *1948–1974*

Y#	KM#	Metal	Description	VF	EF	Unc
13	27	C-N	1/2 Anna (Pe), 1949, square	0.50	1	5.00
14	28	C-N	1 Anna (Pe), 1949–51, scalloped	1.00	2	7.50
15	29	C-N	2 Annas, (Pe), 1949–51, square	1.00	2	8.00

Y#	KM#	Metal	Description	VF	EF	Unc
16	30	Nick	4 Annas, (Pe), 1949–50	4	9	18
17	31	Nick	8 Annas, (Pe), 1949–50	5	11	25

Decimal Coinage System

Y#	KM#	Metal	Description	VF	EF	Unc
18	32	Bz	1 Pya, 1952–65	0.50	1	2

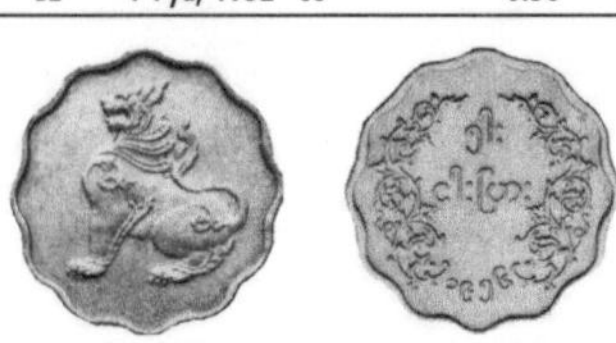

Y#	KM#	Metal	Description	VF	EF	Unc
19	33	C-N	5 Pyas, 1952–66, scalloped	0.50	1	2
20	34	C-N	10 Pyas, 1952–65, square	0.50	1	2
21	35	C-N	25 Pyas, 1952–65, scalloped	0.50	1	2

Y#	KM#	Metal	Description	VF	EF	Unc
22	36	C-N	50 Pyas, 1952–66	0.65	1.25	2.50
23	37	C-N	1 Kyat, 1952–65	2.00	4.00	7.50

1949 Proof Set, $6,500
1952 Proof Set, $5,000
1956 Proof Set, $5,000
1962 Proof Set, $5,000

CAMBODIA

What was then a kingdom on the Southeast Asian peninsula became a French protectorate in 1863, and in 1887 was federated with Annam, Tonkin, and Laos to form French Indo-China. The country regained full independence as a constitutional monarchy in 1953. The monarchy was abolished by a military coup in 1970 and Cambodia became the Khmer Republic. Vietnamese forces installed a communist government in 1979. Free elections since 1993 have established the basis for a multi-party democracy under a constitutional monarchy. *Languages:* Khmer, French. *Capital:* Phnom Penh.

MONETARY SYSTEM

100 centimes = 1 franc
5 francs = 1 piastre
100 centimes (sen) = 1 riel, 1953–

PRECIOUS METAL CONTENT

Dates	Denomination	Gross Wt (g)	Fineness	Net Wt (g)	Troy Oz.
		SILVER			
1860	25 centimes	1.2500	0.9000	1.1250	0.0361
	50 centimes	2.5000	0.9000	2.2500	0.0723
	1 franc	5.0000	0.9000	4.5000	0.1446
	2 francs	10.0000	0.9000	9.0000	0.2893
	4 francs	20.0000	0.9000	18.0000	0.5786
	1 piastre	27.0000	0.9000	24.3000	0.7812

NORODOM I, *1859–1904*

Y#	KM#	Metal	Description	VF	EF	Unc
1	Tn1	Br	1 Centime, ND (1897)	500	700	1,100

Y#	KM#	Metal	Description	VF	EF	Unc
2	42	Bz	5 Centimes, 1860	65	100	300
3	43	Bz	10 Centimes, 1860	75	125	325

Y#	KM#	Metal	Description	VF	EF	Unc
4	44	Silv	25 Centimes, 1860	50	100	250
5	45	Silv	50 Centimes, 1860	50	100	300
6	46	Silv	1 Franc, 1860	75	125	250
7	47	Silv	2 Francs, 1860	100	200	450
8	48	Silv	4 Francs, 1860	125	250	500
9	49	Silv	1 Piastre, 1860	2,000	4,000	11,000

Note: Y2–9 were struck in Phnom Penh circa 1875–89. The date 1860 on coins is the (incorrect) accession date. Coins with E or ESSAI on the obverse are collectors' samples struck in Europe. Y9 was issued for presentation only, as were strikings in gold of this and other denominations.

NORODOM II SIHANOUK, *1941–1955, 1960–1970, 1975–1976*

Y#	KM#	Metal	Description	VF	EF	Unc
11	51	Alum	10 Centimes, 1953	1	2	5

Y#	KM#	Metal	Description	VF	EF	Unc
12	52	Alum	20 Centimes, 1953	0.75	1.50	4.50
13	53	Alum	50 Centimes, 1953	1.00	2.00	6.50

NORODOM SURAMARIT, *1955–1960*

Reverse: ***SEN replaces CENT***

Y#	KM#	Metal	Description	VF	EF	Unc
11a	54	Alum	10 Sen, 1959	0.35	0.50	1.50

Y#	KM#	Metal	Description	VF	EF	Unc
12a	55	Alum	20 Sen, 1959	0.25	0.50	1.75
13a	56	Alum	50 Sen, 1959	0.45	0.75	2.00

CAMEROON

Cameroon became a French territory in 1919 when the former German colony of Kamerun in west-central Africa was divided between Britain and France following World War I. The country attained independence as a republic in 1960. *Languages:* French, English, native dialects. *Capital:* Yaounde.

MONETARY SYSTEM

100 centimes = 1 franc

ISSUES UNDER FRENCH MANDATE

Y#	KM#	Metal	Description	VF	EF	Unc
1	1	A-Bz	50 Centimes, 1924–26	5	15	50
2	2	A-Bz	1 Franc, 1924–26	5	15	175
3	3	A-Bz	2 Francs, 1924–25	10	35	250

Y#	KM#	Metal	Description	VF	EF	Unc
4	4	Bz	50 Centimes, 1943	4	15	50
5	5	Bz	1 Franc, 1943	7	20	40

Obverse: ***LIBRE added to legend***

Y#	KM#	Metal	Description	VF	EF	Unc
6	6	Bz	50 Centimes, 1943	4	15	50
7	7	Bz	1 Franc, 1943	7	20	40

Y#	KM#	Metal	Description	VF	EF	Unc
8	8	Alum	1 Franc, 1948	0.50	1.00	3.00
9	9	Alum	2 Francs, 1948	1.50	2.50	6.50

CANADA

Canada is a member of the British Commonwealth occupying most of northern North America. Control of the vast territory was disputed by England and France from the 17th through the early 19th century; nearly one-third of the nation is of French background. Confederation of southern and eastern provinces created the dominion in 1867, with huge tracts of western and northern lands added through the early 1900s. *Languages:* English, French. *Capital:* Ottawa.

MONETARY SYSTEM

100 cents = 1 dollar

PRECIOUS METAL CONTENT

Dates	Denomination	Gross Wt (g)	Fineness	Net Wt (g)	Troy Oz.
		SILVER			
1858–1910	5 cents	1.1620	0.9250	1.0749	0.0346
	10 cents	2.3240	0.9250	2.1497	0.0691
	20 cents	4.6480	0.9250	4.2994	0.1382
	25 cents	5.8100	0.9250	5.3743	0.1728
	50 cents	11.6200	0.9250	10.7485	0.3456
1910–19	5 cents	1.1664	0.9250	1.0789	0.0347
1910–19	10 cents	2.3328	0.9250	2.1578	0.0694
	25 cents	5.8319	0.9250	5.3945	0.1734
	50 cents	11.6638	0.9250	10.7890	0.3469
1920–67	5 cents	1.1664	0.8000	0.9331	0.0300
	10 cents	2.3328	0.8000	1.8662	0.0600
	25 cents	5.8319	0.8000	4.6655	0.1500
	50 cents	11.6638	0.8000	9.3310	0.3000
	1 dollar	23.3276	0.8000	18.6621	0.6000
		GOLD			
1908–19	1 sovereign	7.9881	0.9170	7.3224	0.2354
1912–14	5 dollars	8.3591	0.9000	7.5232	0.2419
	10 dollars	16.7181	0.9000	15.0463	0.4837

VICTORIA, *1837–1901*

Y#	KM#	Metal	Description	VF	EF	Unc
1	1	Bz	1 Cent, 1858–59 *1858, VF $150*	10	15	75

Y#	KM#	Metal	Description	VF	EF	Unc
2	2	Silv	5 Cents, 1858–1901 *1875, 84, VF $500; 1883, 89, VF $115; 1898, VF $60*	20	40	200
3	3	Silv	10 Cents, 1858–1901 *1872, VF $550; 1875, 84, VF $1,500; 1887, VF $350; 1889, VF $2,350*	50	120	250
4	4	Silv	20 Cents, 1858	150	325	1,350

Y#	KM#	Metal	Description	VF	EF	Unc
5	7	Bz	1 Cent, 1876–1901	7.50	12	50

Y#	KM#	Metal	Description	VF	EF	Unc
8	5	Silv	25 Cents, 1870–1901 *1875, VF $2,500; 1880, VF $375; 1885, 87, 89, 91, VF $450; 1893, VF $825; 1890, 94, VF $200*	75	175	700
9	6	Silv	50 Cents, 1870–1901 *1871, VF $475; 1888, 99, VF $1,100; 1890, VF $5,000; 1894, VF $2,000*	250	500	4,500

EDWARD VII, *1901–1910*

Y#	KM#	Metal	Description	VF	EF	Unc
10	8	Bz	1 Cent, 1902–10	4	6	35

Y#	KM#	Metal	Description	VF	EF	Unc
11a	9	Silv	5 Cents, 1902, royal crown on reverse	5	10	50
11	13	Silv	5 Cents, 1903–10, imperial crown on reverse *1903, 08, VF $85*	5	10	75
12	10	Silv	10 Cents, 1902–10 *1903, VF $85*	20	50	175
13	11	Silv	25 Cents, 1902–10 *1902, 08–09, VF $110; 1904, VF $275; 1905, VF, $175*	55	125	365
14	12	Silv	50 Cents, 1902–10 *1904, VF $850; 1905, VF $1,100*	120	400	1,750

Design: ***Type of Great Britain Y57 with mintmark "C" (Ottawa)***

Y#	KM#	Metal	Description	VF	EF	Unc
A14	14	Gold	1 Sovereign, 1908–10 *1908, Unc $15,000*	BV	BV	500

GEORGE V, *1910–1936*

Obverse: ***Legend omits DEI GRA:***

Y#	KM#	Metal	Description	VF	EF	Unc
15a	15	Bz	1 Cent, 1911	2.50	4	22.50

Y#	KM#	Metal	Description	VF	EF	Unc
17a	16	Silv	5 Cents, 1911	7	12.50	75
18a	17	Silv	10 Cents, 1911	25	55.00	165
19a	18	Silv	25 Cents, 1911	55	125.00	400
20a	19	Silv	50 Cents, 1911	335	725.00	2,250

Obverse: ***DEI GRA: added***

Y#	KM#	Metal	Description	VF	EF	Unc
15	21	Bz	1 Cent, 1912–20	2	3.75	18

Y#	KM#	Metal	Description	VF	EF	Unc
17	22	Silv	5 Cents, 1912–21 *1915, VF $35; 1916, VF $15; 1921, VF $8,000*	4.50	9	40
18	23	Silv	10 Cents, 1912–36 *1915, 33, VF $35; 1921, VF $12; 1935, VF $75*	5.00	10	65
19	24	Silv	25 Cents, 1912–36 *1912–15, 16, 29–35, VF $30; 1915, VF $300; 1921, 27, VF $150*	17.50	40	130
20	25	Silv	50 Cents, 1912–36 *1912–13, VF $200; 1911, 14, VF $325; 1931, 34, 36, VF $125; 1921, Rare; 1932, VF $500*	55.00	145	600

Note: In 1920, silver fineness was reduced from .925 to .800.

25th Anniversary of Reign

Obverse: ***Different bust and legend***
Reverse: ***Like YA22***

Y#	KM#	Metal	Description	VF	EF	Unc
22	30	Silv	1 Dollar, 1935	45	52.50	65

Y#	KM#	Metal	Description	VF	EF	Unc
A22	31	Silv	1 Dollar, 1936	32.50	37.50	55

Y#	KM#	Metal	Description	VF	EF	Unc
23	26	Gold	5 Dollars, 1912–14	575	600	675
24	27	Gold	10 Dollars, 1912–14	1,250	1,350	1,650

Design: ***Type of Great Britain Y78 with mintmark "C"***

Y#	KM#	Metal	Description	VF	EF	Unc
25	20	Gold	1 Sovereign, 1911–19 *1913, VF $1,150; 1916, VF $13,500*	400	425	450

Y#	KM#	Metal	Description	VF	EF	Unc
16	28	Bz	1 Cent, 1920–36 *1922, 25, VF $30; 1923, VF $47.50*	0.85	1.75	15

Y#	KM#	Metal	Description	VF	EF	Unc
21	29	Nick	5 Cents, 1922–36 *1925, VF $125; 1926, Far 6, VF $325*	2	10	55

GEORGE VI, *1936–1952*

Y#	KM#	Metal	Description	VF	EF	Unc
26	32	Bz	1 Cent, 1937–47	0.30	0.60	2.75

Y#	KM#	Metal	Description	VF	EF	Unc
27	33	Nick	5 Cents, 1937–42	0.35	0.60	2.75

Y#	KM#	Metal	Description	VF	EF	Unc
28	39	Br	5 Cents, 1942, 12-sided	2.00	2.75	4.50
29	40	Br	5 Cents, 1943, 12-sided	0.45	0.85	4.50

Y#	KM#	Metal	Description	VF	EF	Unc
29a	40a	C-PS	5 Cents, 1944–45, 12-sided	0.50	0.85	3

Design: ***Like Y28***

Y#	KM#	Metal	Description	VF	EF	Unc
28a	39a	Nick	5 Cents, 1946–47, 12-sided	0.50	1.75	13.50

Y#	KM#	Metal	Description	VF	EF	Unc
30	34	Silv	10 Cents, 1937–47	2.50	3.25	17.50

Y#	KM#	Metal	Description	VF	EF	Unc
31	35	Silv	25 Cents, 1937–47	7.50	8.50	17.50

Y#	KM#	Metal	Description	VF	EF	Unc
32	36	Silv	50 Cents, 1937–47	10	11.50	32.50

Reverse: ***Identical to A22***

Y#	KM#	Metal	Description	VF	EF	Unc
33	37	Silv	1 Dollar, 1937–47 *1945, VF $175*	30	35	50

Royal Visit Commemorative

Y#	KM#	Metal	Description	VF	EF	Unc
34	38	Silv	1 Dollar, 1939	16.50	18.50	30

Designs: ***Like Y26, 28, 30–33***
New Legend: ***Without IND: IMP:***

Y#	KM#	Metal	Description	VF	EF	Unc
35	41	Bz	1 Cent, 1948–52	0.20	0.45	1.75
36	42	Nick	5 Cents, 1948–50, 12-sided	0.40	1.25	10.00
36a	42a	C-PS	5 Cents, 1951–52, 12-sided	0.40	0.75	5.00
38	43	Silv	10 Cents, 1948–52 *1948, VF $10*	2.65	3.25	7.50
39	44	Silv	25 Cents, 1948–52	6.00	7.00	9.75
40	45	Silv	50 Cents, 1948–52 *1948, VF $125*	9.00	10.00	16.00
41	46	Silv	1 Dollar, 1948–52 *1948, VF $1,100*	20.00	22.50	30.00

Commemorating Province of Newfoundland

Y#	KM#	Metal	Description	VF	EF	Unc
42	47	Silv	1 Dollar, 1949	27.50	32.50	40

200th Anniversary of Isolation of Nickel

Y#	KM#	Metal	Description	VF	EF	Unc
37	48	Nick	5 Cents, 1951, 12-sided	0.35	0.50	2.50

ELIZABETH II, *1952–2022*

Reverse: ***Like Y26, 28***

Y#	KM#	Metal	Description	VF	EF	Unc
43	49	Bz	1 Cent, 1953–64	0.10	0.15	0.25
44	50	C-PS	5 Cents, 1953–54, 12-sided	0.60	1.25	4.50
45	50a	Nick	5 Cents, 1955–62, 12-sided	0.50	0.65	1.00

Y#	KM#	Metal	Description	VF	EF	Unc
45a	57	Nick	5 Cents, 1963–64, round	0.10	0.15	0.30

Reverse: ***Like Y30–33***

Y#	KM#	Metal	Description	VF	EF	Unc
46	51	Silv	10 Cents, 1953–64	1.50	1.65	3.00
47	52	Silv	25 Cents, 1953–64	2.25	2.35	4.25
48	53	Silv	50 Cents, 1953–58	5.25	5.35	11.00
49	54	Silv	1 Dollar, 1953–63	10.00	12.00	20.00

Y#	KM#	Metal	Description	VF	EF	Unc
51	56	Silv	50 Cents, 1959–64	5.25	5.35	11

British Columbia Province

Y#	KM#	Metal	Description	VF	EF	Unc
50	55	Silv	1 Dollar, 1958	10	12	20

Centennial of Confederation Meetings

Y#	KM#	Metal	Description	VF	EF	Unc
52	58	Silv	1 Dollar, 1964	10	12	20

CANADA - NEW BRUNSWICK

SEE NEW BRUNSWICK

CANADA - NEWFOUNDLAND

SEE NEWFOUNDLAND

CANADA - NOVA SCOTIA

SEE NOVA SCOTIA

CANADA - PRINCE EDWARD ISLAND

SEE PRINCE EDWARD ISLAND

CAPE VERDE

Until independence in July, 1975, the 10 islands and five islets composing this country were an overseas province of Portugal, lying in the North Atlantic about 600 miles off the west African coast. *Languages:* Portuguese, Crioulo. *Capital:* Praia.

MONETARY SYSTEM

100 centavos = 1 escudo

Y#	KM#	Metal	Description	VF	EF	Unc
1	1	Bz	5 Centavos, 1930	2	3.25	15
2	2	Bz	10 Centavos, 1930	2	3.50	20
3	3	Bz	20 Centavos, 1930	2	4.00	25

Y#	KM#	Metal	Description	VF	EF	Unc
4	4	N-Bz	50 Centavos, 1930	25	75	275
5	5	N-Bz	1 Escudo, 1930	45	85	375

Y#	KM#	Metal	Description	VF	EF	Unc
6	6	N-Bz	50 Centavos, 1949	1.00	2.25	8
7	7	N-Bz	1 Escudo, 1949	1.75	4.50	15

Obverse: ***COLONIA DE omitted in legend***

Y#	KM#	Metal	Description	VF	EF	Unc
8	8	Bz	1 Escudo, 1953, 68	1	2.50	8.50

Y#	KM#	Metal	Description	VF	EF	Unc
9	9	C-N	2-1/2 Escudos, 1953, 67	1	2.50	5
10	10	C-N	10 Escudos, 1953	4	8.00	20

CEYLON

A large island off the southern tip of India, Ceylon came under British control around 1800, after control by the Portuguese and Dutch. Gaining independence within the Commonwealth in 1948, it changed its name to Sri Lanka in 1972. The socialist republic was engaged in civil war between Hindu Tamil rebels and the majority Buddhist Sinhalese from 1983 to 2009. Today Sri Lanka is a presidential republic. *Languages:* Sinhala, Tamil, English. *Capital:* Colombo.

MONETARY SYSTEM

4 farthings = 1 penny
100 cents = 1 rupee

PRECIOUS METAL CONTENT

Dates	Denomination	Gross Wt (g)	Fineness	Net Wt (g)	Troy Oz.
		SILVER			
1838–62	1-1/2 pence	0.7069	0.9250	0.6539	0.0210
1892–1917	10 cents	1.1664	0.8000	0.9331	0.0300
	25 cents	2.9160	0.8000	2.3328	0.0750
	50 cents	5.8319	0.8000	4.6650	0.1500
1919–42	10 cents	1.1664	0.5500	0.6415	0.0206
	25 cents	2.9160	0.5500	1.6038	0.0516
	50 cents	5.8319	0.5500	3.2075	0.1031

VICTORIA, *1837–1901*

Y#	KM#	Metal	Description	VF	EF	Unc
1	737	Cop	1/4 Farthing, 1839–53	55	85	135
2	738	Cop	1/2 Farthing, 1839–56	15	65	165
			1854, Unc $275			

Note: Dates 1839–42 were struck expressly for Ceylon. In 1842, Y2 was changed at the bottom reverse to conform with English coinage, and was declared current in the United Kingdom. For more on Y1–3, see Great Britain.

Y#	KM#	Metal	Description	VF	EF	Unc
3	728	Silv	1-1/2 Pence, 1838–62	20	75	175

Note: Also used in Jamaica.

Decimal System

Y#	KM#	Metal	Description	VF	EF	Unc
4	90	Cop	1/4 Cent, 1870–1901	4	12	20
					Proof: $475	
5	91	Cop	1/2 Cent, 1870–1901	3	5	15
					Proof: $500	
6	92	Cop	1 Cent, 1870–1901	4	10	25
					Proof: $525	
7	93	Cop	5 Cents, 1870–92	15	50	125
					Proof: $600	

Y#	KM#	Metal	Description	VF	EF	Unc
8	94	Silv	10 Cents, 1892–1900	4	15	30
					Proof: $675	
9	95	Silv	25 Cents, 1892–1900	10	25	65
					Proof: $700	
10	96	Silv	50 Cents, 1892–1900	15	35	115
					Proof: $725	

EDWARD VII, *1901–1910*

Y#	KM#	Metal	Description	VF	EF	Unc
11	100	Cop	1/4 Cent, 1904	5	10	25
					Proof: $475	
12	101	Cop	1/2 Cent, 1904–09	4	8	15
					Proof: $500	
13	102	Cop	1 Cent, 1904–10	5	10	25
					Proof: $525	

Y#	KM#	Metal	Description	VF	EF	Unc
14	103	C-N	5 Cents, 1909–10, square	1.75	3	30

Y#	KM#	Metal	Description	VF	EF	Unc
15	97	Silv	10 Cents, 1902–10	3.50	9	30
					Proof: $675	
16	98	Silv	25 Cents, 1902–10	8.50	20	50
					Proof: $750	
17	99	Silv	50 Cents, 1902–10	5.00	10	100
					Proof: $850	

GEORGE V, *1910–1936*

Y#	KM#	Metal	Description	VF	EF	Unc
18	106	Cop	1/2 Cent, 1912–26	2	4	7.50
						Proof: $900
19	107	Cop	1 Cent, 1912–29	1	2	8.00
						Proof: $900

Y#	KM#	Metal	Description	VF	EF	Unc
20	108	C-N	5 Cents, 1912–26, square	1	2	15

Y#	KM#	Metal	Description	VF	EF	Unc
21	104	Silv	10 Cents, 1911–28	1.25	3	20
						Proof: $675
22	105	Silv	25 Cents, 1911–26	2.00	5	30
						Proof: $750
23	109	Silv	50 Cents, 1913–29	4.50	10	40
						Proof: $850

Note: In 1919, silver fineness was reduced from .800 to .525.

GEORGE VI, *1936–1952*

Y#	KM#	Metal	Description	VF	EF	Unc
24	110	Cop	1/2 Cent, 1937–40	1.00	2	5.00
						Proof: $450
25	111	Cop	1 Cent, 1937–42	0.50	1	2.50
						Proof: $525

Obverse: ***Larger head***

Y#	KM#	Metal	Description	VF	EF	Unc
25a	111a	Bz	1 Cent, 1942–45, thin	0.50	1	6
						Proof: $300

Y#	KM#	Metal	Description	VF	EF	Unc
27	117	N-Br	2 Cents, 1944, scalloped	0.25	0.50	4

Y#	KM#	Metal	Description	VF	EF	Unc
28	113.1	N-Br	5 Cents, 1942–43, square, thick	0.50	1.00	10
						Proof: $500
28a	113.2	N-Br	5 Cents, 1944–45, square, thin	0.25	0.50	5
						Proof: $500

Y#	KM#	Metal	Description	VF	EF	Unc
29	118	N-Br	10 Cents, 1944, scalloped	0.35	0.50	10

Obverse: ***Similar to Y24–25***

Y#	KM#	Metal	Description	VF	EF	Unc
30	115	N-Br	25 Cents, 1943	0.35	0.50	10
31	116	N-Br	50 Cents, 1943	0.50	1.00	10

Y#	KM#	Metal	Description	VF	EF	Unc
32	112	Silv	10 Cents, 1941	0.75	2.00	7.50
33	114	Silv	50 Cents, 1942	6.00	12.50	25.00

New Legend: ***KING GEORGE THE SIXTH***

Y#	KM#	Metal	Description	VF	EF	Unc
34	119	N-Br	2 Cents, 1951, scalloped	0.15	0.25	5
						Proof: $45
35	120	N-Br	*5 Cents, 1951, square, Proof only, $60*			
36	121	N-Br	10 Cents, 1951, scalloped	0.10	0.25	5
						Proof: $600

Design: ***Similar to Y30–31***

Y#	KM#	Metal	Description	VF	EF	Unc
37	122	N-Br	25 Cents, 1951	0.20	0.40	5
						Proof: $60
38	123	N-Br	50 Cents, 1951	0.25	0.50	10
						Proof: $75

ELIZABETH II, *1952–1957*

Y#	KM#	Metal	Description	VF	EF	Unc
39	124	N-Br	2 Cents, 1955, 57, scalloped	0.20	0.40	0.75
						Proof: $100

2,500 Years of Buddhism

Y#	KM#	Metal	Description	VF	EF	Unc
40	125	C-N	1 Rupee, 1957	0.50	2	4
						Proof: $52.50

Y#	KM#	Metal	Description	VF	EF	Unc
41	126	Silv	5 Rupees, 1957	15	20	30
						Proof: $225

BRITISH COMMONWEALTH REPUBLIC, *1963–1971*

Y#	KM#	Metal	Description	VF	EF	Unc
43	127	Alum	1 Cent, 1963–71	0.05	0.10	0.25

Y#	KM#	Metal	Description	VF	EF	Unc
44	128	Alum	2 Cents, 1963–71, scalloped	0.05	0.10	0.30

Y#	KM#	Metal	Description	VF	EF	Unc
45	129	N-Br	5 Cents, 1963–71, square	0.10	0.15	0.50

Y#	KM#	Metal	Description	VF	EF	Unc
46	130	N-Br	10 Cents, 1963–71, scalloped	0.10	0.15	0.35
47	131	C-N	25 Cents, 1963–71	0.15	0.40	1.00
48	132	C-N	50 Cents, 1963–71	0.25	0.65	1.25
49	133	C-N	1 Rupee, 1963–71	0.50	1.00	2.50

CHILE

This republic lies on the western coast of South America, between the Andes and the Pacific. The country won independence from Spain in 1818 and was governed by a series of parliamentary dictatorships until a new constitution was adopted in 1925. A military coup in 1973 ended nearly 50 years of democratic government. Free elections were held once again in 1989, and today Chile is a stable democratic republic. *Language:* Spanish. *Capital:* Santiago.

MONETARY SYSTEM

10 centavos = 1 decimo
10 decimos = 1 peso
10 pesos = 1 condor

PRECIOUS METAL CONTENT

Dates	Denomination	Gross Wt (g)	Fineness	Net Wt (g)	Troy Oz.
		SILVER			
1852–59	1/2 decimo	1.2500	0.9000	1.1250	0.0362
	1 decimo	2.5000	0.9000	2.2500	0.0723
	20 centavos	5.0000	0.9000	4.5000	0.1447
	50 centavos	12.5000	0.9000	11.2500	0.3617
	1 peso	25.0000	0.9000	22.5000	0.7234
1853–91	50 centavos	12.5000	0.9000	11.2500	0.3617
	1 peso	25.0000	0.9000	22.5000	0.7234
1860–80	1/2 decimo	1.1500	0.9000	1.0350	0.0333
	1 decimo	2.3000	0.9000	2.0700	0.0666
	20 centavos	4.6000	0.9000	4.1400	0.1331
1879–94	1/2 decimo	1.2500	0.5000	0.6250	0.0201
	1 decimo	2.5000	0.5000	1.2500	0.0402
	20 centavos	5.0000	0.5000	2.5000	0.0804
1891	20 centavos	4.0000	0.5000	2.0000	0.0643
	20 centavos	5.0000	0.2000	1.0000	0.0322

Dates	Denomination	Gross Wt (g)	Fineness	Net Wt (g)	Troy Oz.
		SILVER			
1895–97	5 centavos	1.0000	0.8350	0.8350	0.0268
	10 centavos	2.0000	0.8350	1.6700	0.0537
	20 centavos	4.0000	0.8350	3.3400	0.1074
	1 peso	20.0000	0.8350	16.7000	0.5369
1899–1907	5 centavos	1.0000	0.5000	0.5000	0.0161
	10 centavos	2.0000	0.5000	1.0000	0.0311
	20 centavos	4.0000	0.5000	2.0000	0.0643
	50 centavos	10.0000	0.7000	7.0000	0.2251
	1 peso	20.0000	0.7000	14.0000	0.4501
1907–13	5 centavos	1.0000	0.4000	0.4000	0.0129
	10 centavos	1.5000	0.4000	0.6000	0.0193
	20 centavos	3.0000	0.4000	1.2000	0.0386
	40 centavos	6.0000	0.4000	2.4000	0.0772
	1 peso	12.0000	0.9000	10.7993	0.3472
1915–19	5 centavos	1.0000	0.4500	0.4500	0.0145
	10 centavos	1.5000	0.4500	0.6750	0.0217
	20 centavos	3.0000	0.4500	1.3500	0.0434
	1 peso	9.0000	0.7200	6.4800	0.2083
1919–20	5 centavos	1.0000	0.4000	0.4000	0.0129
	10 centavos	1.5000	0.4000	0.6000	0.0193
	20 centavos	3.0000	0.4000	1.2000	0.0386
1921–27	1 peso	9.0000	0.5000	4.5000	0.1447
	2 pesos	18.0000	0.5000	9.0000	0.2894
	5 pesos	25.0000	0.9000	22.5000	0.7234
1932	1 peso	6.0000	0.4000	2.4000	0.0772
		GOLD			
1851–92	1 peso	1.5253	0.9000	1.3728	0.0441
	2 pesos	3.0506	0.9000	2.7455	0.0883
	5 pesos	7.6265	0.9000	6.8639	0.2207
	10 pesos	15.2520	0.9000	13.7277	0.4413
1895–1917	5 pesos	2.9955	0.9170	2.7459	0.0883
	10 pesos	5.9910	0.9170	5.4918	0.1766
	20 pesos	11.9821	0.9170	10.9836	0.3531
1926–80	20 pesos	4.0679	0.9000	3.6611	0.1177
	50 pesos	10.1698	0.9000	9.1528	0.2943
	100 pesos	20.3397	0.9000	18.3057	0.5885

DECIMAL COINAGE, *1851–*

FIRST COINAGE

Obverse: ***Large flat star, date between stars***

Y#	KM#	Metal	Description	VF	EF	Unc
1	117	Cop	1/2 Centavo, 1851	13	35	275
2	119	Cop	1 Centavo, 1851	16	40	250

Obverse: ***Star in relief, date between dots***

Y#	KM#	Metal	Description	VF	EF	Unc
3	118	Cop	1/2 Centavo, 1851	15	40	250
4	120	Cop	1 Centavo, 1851	20	50	225

Reverse: ***Different wreath***

Y#	KM#	Metal	Description	VF	EF	Unc
3a	126	Cop	1/2 Centavo, 1853	15	25	100
4a	127	Cop	1 Centavo, 1853	20	50	225

Y#	KM#	Metal	Description	VF	EF	Unc
5	121	Silv	1/2 Decimo, 1851–59 (1.25 g) *1851, 59, VF $200*	25	60	200
5a	121a	Silv	1/2 Decimo, 1860–62 (1.15 g)	50	90	400
6	124	Silv	1 Decimo, 1852–59 (2.5 g)	30	60	225
6a	124a	Silv	1 Decimo, 1860–62 (2.3 g)	40	70	250
7	125	Silv	20 Centavos, 1852–59 (5.0 g)	50	90	350
7a	125a	Silv	20 Centavos, 1860–62 (4.6 g)	45	85	300
8	128	Silv	50 Centavos, 1853–62	100	200	600

Y#	KM#	Metal	Description	VF	EF	Unc
9	129	Silv	1 Peso, 1853–62 *1858, VF $350; 1862, VF $450*	125	250	700

SECOND COINAGE

Y#	KM#	Metal	Description	VF	EF	Unc
10	148	CNZ	1/2 Centavo, 1871–73	8	20	40
11	146	CNZ	1 Centavo, 1871–77	6	12	30
12	147	CNZ	2 Centavos, 1871–77	15	40	200

Y#	KM#	Metal	Description	VF	EF	Unc
10a	148a	Bz	1/2 Centavo, 1883–94 *1890, EF $40*	4	10	45
11a	146a	Bz	1 Centavo, 1878–98	10	20	85
12a	147a	Bz	2 Centavos, 1878–94	10	20	95
13	150	Bz	2-1/2 Centavos, 1886–98	15	30	110

.900 Silver

Obverse: *Fineness not shown*

Y#	KM#	Metal	Description	VF	EF	Unc
14	137.1	Silv	1/2 Decimo, 1865–66	40	80	225
15	136.1	Silv	1 Decimo, 1864–66	30	60	200

Y#	KM#	Metal	Description	VF	EF	Unc
16	135	Silv	20 Centavos, 1863–67	40	80	225
17	134	Silv	50 Centavos, 1862–67	35	70	350
18	141	Silv	1 Peso, 1867	2,500	5,000	9,000

Dies: *Slightly modified, both sides*

Y#	KM#	Metal	Description	VF	EF	Unc
14a	137.2	Silv	1/2 Decimo, 1867–78, 80–81	20	50	200
15a	136.2	Silv	1 Decimo, 1867–78, 80	15	40	150

Y#	KM#	Metal	Description	VF	EF	Unc
16a	138.1	Silv	20 Centavos, 1867–79	7	15	75
17a	139	Silv	50 Centavos, 1867–72	25	75	300
18a	142.1	Silv	1 Peso, 1867–91 *1887, Unc $3,500; 1891, Unc $2,000*	20	50	200

.500 Silver

Obverse: *Fineness ("0.5") in legend*

Y#	KM#	Metal	Description	VF	EF	Unc
14b	137.3	Silv	1/2 Decimo, 1879–88, 92–94	20	50	200
15b	136.3	Silv	1 Decimo, 1879–87, 92–94 (0.5 g)	15	40	150
15c	136.3a	Silv	1 Decimo, 1891 (2.0 g)	60	125	350
16b	138.2	Silv	20 Centavos, 1879–81, 92–93 (5.0 g)	7	15	75
16c	138.2a	Silv	20 Centavos, 1891 (4.0 g)	10	25	150

.200 Silver

Obverse: *Fineness ("0.2") in legend*

Y#	KM#	Metal	Description	VF	EF	Unc
16d	138.3	Silv	20 Centavos, 1891	100	200	400

Y#	KM#	Metal	Description	VF	EF	Unc
19	133/140	Gold	1 Peso, 1860–73	125	150	300

Y#	KM#	Metal	Description	VF	EF	Unc
20	132/143	Gold	2 Pesos, 1857–75	BV	225	325
21	Several	Gold	5 Pesos, 1851–73	BV	450	900
22	Several	Gold	10 Pesos, 1851–92	BV	800	1,000

PROVISIONAL COINAGE

CITY OF COPIAPO

REVOLUTION OF 1859

Issues of insurgent leader Pedro Leon Gallo.

Obverse: *Arms/value*
Reverse: *Blank*

Y#	KM#	Metal	Description	VF	EF	Unc
23	1	Silv	50 Centavos, ND	125	250	—
24	2	Silv	1 Peso, ND	225	350	—

Provisional Coinage of 1865

Issued during Spanish blockade of Chilean ports.

Y#	KM#	Metal	Description	VF	EF	Unc
25	3	Silv	50 Centavos, 1865	800	1,000	1,750
26	4	Silv	1 Peso, 1865	150	250	—

Note: It is unknown whether Y25 was issued to circulation. Restrikes were reportedly made later from original dies.

Third Coinage

Y11 and 13 were continued briefly into this period.

Y#	KM#	Metal	Description	VF	EF	Unc
27	161	Bz	1 Centavo, 1904–19	4	10	25
28	164	Bz	2 Centavos, 1919	8	20	40
29	162	Bz	2-1/2 Centavos, 1904–08	10	25	50

.835 Silver

Obverse: ***Fineness not shown***

Y#	KM#	Metal	Description	VF	EF	Unc
30	155.1	Silv	5 Centavos, 1896	7.50	20	75
31	156.1	Silv	10 Centavos, 1896	5.00	10	450
31	151.1	Silv	20 Centavos, 1895	25.00	50	125
35	152.1	Silv	1 Peso, 1895–97	25.00	35	100

.500 Silver

Obverse: ***Fineness ("0.5") in field***

Y#	KM#	Metal	Description	VF	EF	Unc
30a	155.2	Silv	5 Centavos, 1899–1907	5.00	10	25.00
31a	156.2	Silv	10 Centavos, 1899–1907 *1900, EF $300*	4.50	9	17.50
32a	151.2	Silv	20 Centavos, 1899–1907 *1900, EF $300*	3.00	6	12.00

.400 Silver

Obverse: ***Fineness not shown***

Y#	KM#	Metal	Description	VF	EF	Unc
30b	155.2a	Silv	5 Centavos, 1908–13, 19	5	10	25
31b	156.2a	Silv	10 Centavos, 1908–13, 19–20	4	7	15
32b	151.3	Silv	20 Centavos, 1907–13, 19–20	3	6	12
33	163	Silv	40 Centavos, 1907–08 *1908, Unc $200*	20	50	100

.450 Silver

Obverse: ***Fineness ("0.45") in field***

Y#	KM#	Metal	Description	VF	EF	Unc
30c	155.3	Silv	5 Centavos, 1915–19	5	10	25
31c	156.3	Silv	10 Centavos, 1915–18	4	7	12
32c	151.4	Silv	20 Centavos, 1916	5	10	20

.700 Silver

Y#	KM#	Metal	Description	VF	EF	Unc
34	160	Silv	50 Centavos, 1902–05	20	37.50	75
35a	152.2	Silv	1 Peso, 1902–05 (35 mm)	25	50.00	100

.900 Silver

Y#	KM#	Metal	Description	VF	EF	Unc
35b	152.3	Silv	1 Peso, 1910 (31.5 mm)	BV	25	55

.720 Silver

Y#	KM#	Metal	Description	VF	EF	Unc
35c	152.4	Silv	1 Peso, 1915, 17 (28 mm)	BV	10	18

Y#	KM#	Metal	Description	VF	EF	Unc
36	153	Gold	5 Pesos, 1895–96	125	150	250
37	154	Gold	10 Pesos, 1895	BV	300	325

Y#	KM#	Metal	Description	VF	EF	Unc
38	159	Gold	5 Pesos, 1898, 1900	125	175	300
39	157	Gold	10 Pesos, 1896, 98, 1901	BV	300	600
40	158	Gold	20 Pesos, 1896–1917	BV	600	700

FOURTH COINAGE

Y#	KM#	Metal	Description	VF	EF	Unc
41	165	C-N	5 Centavos, 1920–38 *1933, VF $15*	0.50	1.00	4
42	166	C-N	10 Centavos, 1920–41	0.50	1.25	5
43	167	C-N	20 Centavos, 1920–41	0.75	1.50	10

.500 Silver

Y#	KM#	Metal	Description	VF	EF	Unc
35d	152	Silv	1 Peso, 1921–25, value as UN	5	10	20
35e	171	Silv	1 Peso, 1927, value as 1/UN	6	10	20
45	172	Silv	2 Pesos, 1927	6	12	25

.900 Silver

Y#	KM#	Metal	Description	VF	EF	Unc
46	173	Silv	5 Pesos, 1927	15	25	40

.400 Silver

Y#	KM#	Metal	Description	VF	EF	Unc
35f	174	Silv	1 Peso, 1932	2	3.50	10
35g	176	C-N	1 Peso, 1933, 40	1	2.00	5

Y#	KM#	Metal	Description	VF	EF	Unc
47	168	Gold	20 Pesos, 1926, 58–61	BV	BV	90
48	169	Gold	50 Pesos, 1926, 58–74	BV	BV	BV
49	170	Gold	100 Pesos, 1926	BV	BV	1,000

Design: ***Modified lettering, both sides***

Y#	KM#	Metal	Description	VF	EF	Unc
49a	175	Gold	100 Pesos, 1932, 46–80	BV	BV	BV

Note: Coins after 1932 of the 20, 50, and 100 pesos were struck as bullion, and not for circulation.

FIFTH COINAGE

Y#	KM#	Metal	Description	VF	EF	Unc
50	177	Bz	20 Centavos, 1942–53	0.25	0.75	3.00
51	178	Bz	50 Centavos, 1942	2.50	5.00	25.00
52	179	Bz	1 Peso, 1942–54	0.50	1.00	6.00
52a	179a	Alum	1 Peso, 1954–58	0.25	0.50	1.25

Y#	KM#	Metal	Description	VF	EF	Unc
53	180	Alum	5 Pesos, 1956	0.25	0.75	2
54	181	Alum	10 Pesos, 1956–59	0.20	0.50	2

MONETARY REFORM, *1960*

MONETARY SYSTEM

100 centesimos (condores) = 1 escudo

Y#	KM#	Metal	Description	VF	EF	Unc
55	192	Alum	1/2 Centesimo, 1962–63	0.10	0.25	1
56	189	Alum	1 Centesimo, 1960–63	0.50	1.00	2

Y#	KM#	Metal	Description	VF	EF	Unc
57	193	A-Bz	2 Centesimos, 1964–70	0.10	0.20	1.00
58	190	A-Bz	5 Centesimos, 1960–71	0.10	0.20	1.50
59	191	A-Bz	10 Centesimos, 1960–70	0.15	0.25	1.00

CHINA

The second largest of the world's nations, China comprises much of eastern Asia. Before 1911, the land was ruled by a succession of emperors. At that time it became a republic and remained so through several major changes of government. After driving out the Nationalist regime, a people's republic was proclaimed in 1949 by Mao Zedong, with various communist factions vying for power thereafter. *Languages:* Mandarin, Cantonese, minority languages. *Capital:* Beijing.

The listings for China have been considerably reorganized for this edition. Among other changes, East Turkestan and the Uighuristan Republic are now country listings under "E" and "U," respectively.

Coins not listed are probably either fantasies or patterns. Beware of (often clever) forgeries of the rarer coins, including rare dates.

MONETARY SYSTEM

10 li = 1 fen (candareen)
10 fen = 1 ch'ien (mace, Misqal/mithqal)
10 ch'ien - 1 liang (sar, tael)
7 mace and 2 candareens = 1 dollar
10 cash, wen, li = 1 cent, fen, hsien, mei
10 cents = 1 chio, hao
100 cents = 1 dollar, yuan

PRECIOUS METAL CONTENT

Dates	Denomination	Gross Wt (g)	Fineness	Net Wt (g)	Troy Oz.
		SILVER			
Empire, Typical Weights					
1908–11	10 cents	2.7000	0.8200	2.2146	0.0712
	20 cents	5.4000	0.8200	4.5101	0.1450
	50 cents	13.4000	0.8000	10.7215	0.3447
	1 dollar	26.9000	0.9000	24.2145	0.7785
Republic, Typical Weights					
1911–49	1 chio	2.7000	0.7000	1.8880	0.0607
	2 chio	5.4000	0.7000	3.7791	0.1215
	1/2 yuan	13.6000	0.7000	9.5178	0.3060
	1 yuan	26.5000	0.8900	23.4991	0.7555
		GOLD			
Republic					
1919	10 yuan	8.1500	0.8500	6.9275	0.2227
	20 yuan	16.3000	0.8500	13.8550	0.4456

CYCLICAL DATES

Many dated coins use the Chinese sexagenary system as shown below. Coins bearing these cyclical dates are indicated in this guide by the abbreviation CD preceding the date.

戌戊	1898	寅壬	1902	午丙	1906
亥己	1899	卯癸	1903	未丁	1907
子庚	1900	辰甲	1904	申戊	1908
丑辛	1901	巳乙	1905	酉己	1909
戌庚	1910	亥癸	1913	午庚	1930
亥辛	1911	子甲	1924		
子壬	1912	巳己	1929		

MINT NAMES

The first column below shows the abbreviated name used in the center of Tai-Ch'ing-Ti-Kuo coppers. The second column shows the full name as used on most other provincial coins.

皖	安徽	Huan for Anhwei
浙	浙江	Che for Chekiang
直	直隸	Chi for Chihli
淮	清江	Huai for Ching-Kiang
閩	福建	Ming for Fukien
奉	奉天	Fung for Fengtien
汴	河南	Bien for Honan
湘	湖南	Shiang for Hunan
鄂	湖北	Ngau for Hupeh
贛	江西	Kung for Kiangsi
寧	江南	Ning for Kiangnan
蘇	江蘇	Su for Kiangsu
吉	吉林	Chi for Kirin
桂	廣西	Kuei for Kwangsi
粵	廣東	Yuek for Kwantung
黔	貴州	Ch'ien for Kweichow
山	山西	Shan for Shansi
陝	陝西	Shen for Shensi
東	山東	Tung for Shantung
川	四川	Ch'uan for Szechuan
雲	雲南	Yun for Yunnan
滇	雲南	Dien for Yunnan
川滇	雲南	Dien/Ch'uan for Yunnan/Szechuan

EMPIRE

KUANG HSU, *1875–1908*

REIGN SYMBOLS 光緒 *ON COINS*

Legend: ***HU POO***

The Hu Poo (National Board of Revenue) coins were issued about 1903–1905 for general circulation. Y5 was also struck during the early Republican period. Similar silver coins are patterns.

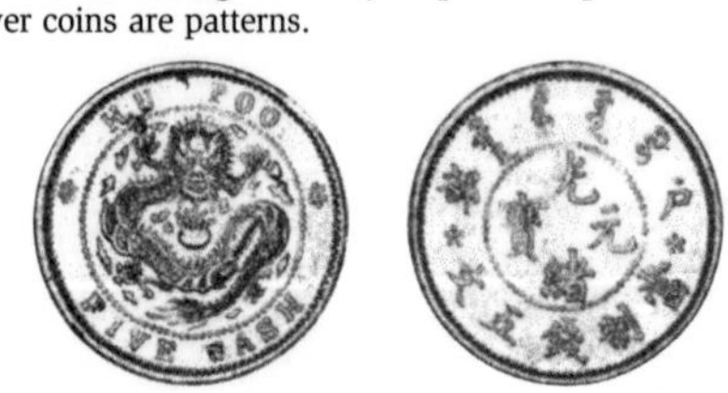

Y#	KM#	Metal	Description	VF	EF	Unc
3	3	C/Br	5 Cash, dragon circled	20	80	225
4	4	C/Br	10 Cash, dragon uncircled	9	15	175
5a	5a	C/Br	20 Cash, dragon circled	50	150	600
5	5	C/Br	20 Cash, dragon uncircled	15	35	150

Legend: *TAI-CH'ING-TI-KUO*

Typical Coin of Tai-Ch'ing-Ti-Kuo Series

The date characters appear at the top as shown below for all coins dated 1905 and 1906, but for some varieties of later dates they appear at the sides in place of the "Hu-Pu" characters (see Y11).

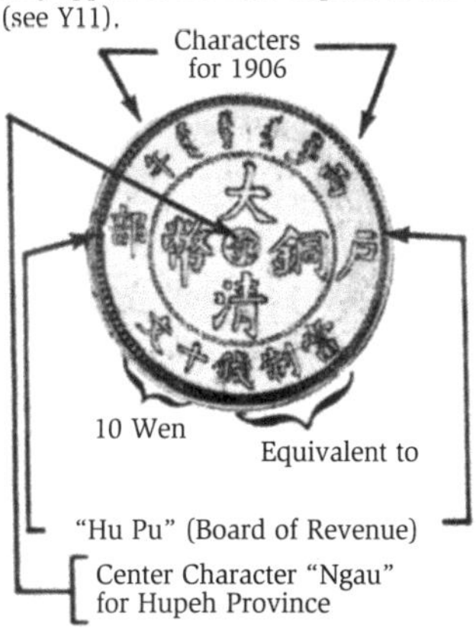

Y#	KM#	Metal	Description	VF	EF	Unc
7	7	Br	1 Wen (Cash), 1908, general	5	8	20
7c	7c	Br	1 Wen, 1908, Chihli	7	10	25
7g	7g	Br	1 Wen, 1908, Honan	40	60	150
7j	7j	Br	1 Wen, 1908, Hupeh	7	10	25
7k	7k	Br	1 Wen, 1908, Kiangnan	7	10	25
7t	7t	Br	1 Wen, 1908, Szechuan	200	250	350

Unless otherwise stated, Y8–11 and Y19–21 in brass rather than copper are generally contemporary counterfeits, usually cast.

Y#	KM#	Metal	Description	VF	EF	Unc
8	8	Cop	2 Wen (Cash), 1905–07, general (blank center)	25	50	175
8b	8b	Cop	2 Wen, 1906, Chekiang	20	45	140
8f	8f	Br	2 Wen, 1906, Fukien	35	95	250
8j	8j	Cop	2 Wen, 1906, Hupeh	35	85	300
8k	Pn3	Cop	2 Wen, 1906, Kiangnan	—	—	70,000
8n	Pn3	Br	2 Wen, 1906, Kiangsu	—	—	2,500
8s	8s	Cop	2 Wen, 1906, Shantung	125	200	600

Y#	KM#	Metal	Description	VF	EF	Unc
9	9	Cop	5 Wen (Cash), 1905–07, general (blank center)	55	100	375
9b	9b	Cop	5 Wen, 1906, Chekiang	55	100	375
9c	9c	Cop	5 Wen, 1906, Chihli	55	100	375
9j	9j	Cop	5 Wen, 1906, Hupeh	55	100	375
9k	9k	Cop	5 Wen, 1906, Kiangnan (vars)	250	450	—
9n	9n	Br	5 Wen, 1906, Kiangsu	225	425	—

Y#	KM#	Metal	Description	VF	EF	Unc
10	10	Cop	10 Wen (Cash), 1905–07, general (blank center)	10.00	15.00	75
10a	10a	Cop	10 Wen, 1906, Anhwei	25.00	45.00	250
10b	10b	Cop	10 Wen, 1906, Chekiang	12.50	25.00	250
10c	10c	Cop	10 Wen, 1906, Chihli	12.50	25.00	200
10d	10d	Cop	10 Wen, 1906, Chingkiang	12.00	25.00	250
10e	10e	Cop	10 Wen, 1905–07, Fengtien	12.00	25.00	250
10f	10f	Cop	10 Wen, 1906, Fukien	12.00	25.00	225
10g	10g	Cop	10 Wen, 1906, Honan	13.00	30.00	275
10h	10h	Cop	10 Wen, 1906, Hunan	6.00	15.00	100
10j	10j	Cop	10 Wen, 1906, Hupeh	6.00	15.00	150
10k	10k	Cop	10 Wen, 1906–08, Kiangnan (vars)	10.00	20.00	175
10m	10m	Cop	10 Wen, 1906, Kiangsi	25.00	50.00	300
10n	10n	Cop	10 Wen, 1906, Kiangsu	20.00	40.00	300
10r	10r	Cop	10 Wen, 1906–08, Kwangtung	12.50	25.00	225
10s	10s	Cop	10 Wen, 1906, Shantung	20.00	50.00	300
10t	10t	Cop	10 Wen, 1906, Szechuan	6.00	17.50	225
10u	10u	Cop	10 Wen, 1906, Yunnan, YUN in center	50.00	150.00	450
10v	10v	Cop	10 Wen, 1906, Yunnan, TIEN in center	40.00	125.00	400
10w	10w	Cop	10 Wen, 1906, Yunnan–Szechuan	75.00	175.00	500

Y#	KM#	Metal	Description	VF	EF	Unc
11	11	Cop	20 Wen (Cash), 1905–07, general (blank center)	10	20	100
11a	11a	Cop	20 Wen, 1906, Anhwei	350	700	—
11b	11b	Cop	20 Wen, 1906, Chekiang	250	350	800
11c	11c	Cop	20 Wen, 1906, Chihli	250	350	—
11d	11d	Cop	20 Wen, 1906, Chingkiang, *Rare*			
11e	11e	Cop	20 Wen, 1905–07, Fengtien	40	150	400
11j	11j	Cop	20 Wen, 1906, Hupeh	750	2,000	10,000
11n	11n	Cop	20 Wen, 1906, Kiangsu	150	400	2,500
11t	11t	Cop	20 Wen, 1906, Szechuan	50	150	300
11u	11u	Cop	20 Wen, 1906, Yunnan, YUN in center	200	400	2,500
11v	11v	Cop	20 Wen, 1906, Yunnan, TIEN in center	400	600	1,500
11v	11w	Cop	20 Wen, 1906, Yunnan–Szechuan	175	400	2,000

Y#	KM#	Metal	Description	VF	EF	Unc
12	12	Silv	10 Cents, ND (1908)	100	500	1,200
13	13	Silv	20 Cents, ND	150	600	1,750
14	14	Silv	1 Dollar, ND	450	975	4,000
15	15	Gold	1 Liang (Tael), ND (1906), *Rare*			

HSUAN T'UNG, *1908–1911*

REIGN SYMBOLS 宣統 *ON COINS*

Designs: ***Like Y7–11***

Y#	KM#	Metal	Description	VF	EF	Unc
18	18	Br	1 Wen, 1909, general	100.00	200.00	750
A18	A18	Br	2 Wen, 1909, *Rare*			
A18g	A18g	Br	2 Wen, 1909, Honan, *Rare*			
19	19	Cop	5 Wen, 1909, general (blank center), *Rare*			
19e	19e	Cop	5 Wen, 1909, Fengtien	225.00	450.00	—
19g	19g	Cop	5 Wen, 1909, Honan, *Rare*			
20	20	Cop	10 Wen, 1909, general (blank center)	10.00	20.00	95
20a	20a	Cop	10 Wen, 1909, Anhwei	125.00	250.00	600
20e	20e	Cop	10 Wen, 1909, Fengtien	35.00	70.00	225
20f	20f	Cop	10 Wen, 1909, Fukien	175.00	300.00	1,500
20g	20g	Cop	10 Wen, 1909, 11, Honan	25.00	50.00	175
20j	20j	Cop	10 Wen, 1909, Hupeh	10.00	20.00	100
20p	20p	Cop	10 Wen, 1909, Kirin	125.00	250.00	500
20r	20r	Cop	10 Wen, 1909, Kwangtung	12.50	20.00	175
20t	20t	Cop	10 Wen, 1909, Szechuan	20.00	45.00	300
20x	20x	Cop	10 Wen, 1909, rosette center (Kirin style dragon)	30.00	75.00	250
21	21	Cop	20 Wen, 1909, general (blank center)	12.50	22.50	175
21e	21e	Cop	20 Wen, 1909, Fengtien	175.00	300.00	600
21g	21g	Cop	20 Wen, 1909 Honan, (wide flan), *Rare*			
21p	21p	Cop	20 Wen, 1909, Kirin	600.00	1,700.00	—
21t	21t	Cop	20 Wen, 1909, Szechuan	75.00	150.00	300

Y#	KM#	Metal	Description	VF	EF	Unc
22	22	Silv	20 Cents, 1909, Kirin	40	75	200

Y#	KM#	Metal	Description	VF	EF	Unc
23	23	Silv	5 Chio / 1/2 Dollar, ND (1910)	2,250	3,500	8,500

Note: Other denominations similar to Y23 are patterns.

Second Coinage

Y#	KM#	Metal	Description	VF	EF	Unc
25	25	Br	1 Wen, ND	4	7.50	15
A26	Pn276	Br	2 Wen, ND (pattern)	1,500	3,500.00	9,500

Note: The origin and date of Y25 are unknown. Some authorities claim it is not a regular issue; others have it assigned to the series of 1905 or 1909.

Y#	KM#	Metal	Description	VF	EF	Unc
26	Pn282	Bz	5 Wen, Yr 3 (1911)	2,000	3,000	5,000
27	27	Bz	10 Wen, Yr 3	50	100	475

Y#	KM#	Metal	Description	VF	EF	Unc
28	28	Silv	1 Chio / 10 Cents, Yr 3 (1911)	500	1,000	3,500
29	29	Silv	2 Chio / 20 Cents, Yr 3	1,250	2,500	6,000
30	30	Silv	5 Chio / 50 Cents, Yr 3	7,500	20,000	50,000

Y#	KM#	Metal	Description	VF	EF	Unc
31	31	Silv	1 Dollar, Yr 3 (1911)	750	1,500	4,500

REPUBLIC, *1911–1949*

GENERAL COINAGE, *1911–1926*

Y#	KM#	Metal	Description	VF	EF	Unc
301	301	C/Br	10 Cash, ND (vars)	5	10	25

Y#	KM#	Metal	Description	VF	EF	Unc
302	302	C/Br	10 Wen (Cash), ND (vars)	4	8	20

Y#	KM#	Metal	Description	VF	EF	Unc
303	303	C/Br	10 Cash, ND	7.50	15	50
304	304	C/Br	10 Wen, ND, obverse of Y303, reverse of Y302	30.00	60	115

Y#	KM#	Metal	Description	VF	EF	Unc
305	305	C/Br	10 Cash, ND	35	75	350

Y#	KM#	Metal	Description	VF	EF	Unc
306	306	C/Br	10 Cash, ND, 4 characters at bottom (3 vars)	3.50	7	35
306a	306a	C/Br	10 Cash, ND, 5 characters at bottom	45.00	90	200

Obverse: ***Striped flag at right***

Y#	KM#	Metal	Description	VF	EF	Unc
307	307	C/Br	1 Mei (10 Cash), ND	8	15.00	75
308	308	C/Br	20 Wen (20 Cash), Yr 8 (1919)	9	17.50	50

Obverse: ***Ornate flag at right***

Y#	KM#	Metal	Description	VF	EF	Unc
307a	307a	C/Br	1 Mei, ND	5	15.00	75
308a	308a	C/Br	20 Wen, Yr 10 (1921)	9	17.50	50

Y#	KM#	Metal	Description	VF	EF	Unc
309	309	C/Br	10 Cash, ND	55	100	300
310	310	C/Br	20 Cash, ND, English at bottom of both sides	60	120	400

Y#	KM#	Metal	Description	VF	EF	Unc
311	311	C/Br	10 Wen, Yr 13 (1924)	500	1,000	3,500
312	312	C/Br	2 Mei (Cents), Yr 13	35	75	—

Note: Some authorities believe Y311 is a pattern.

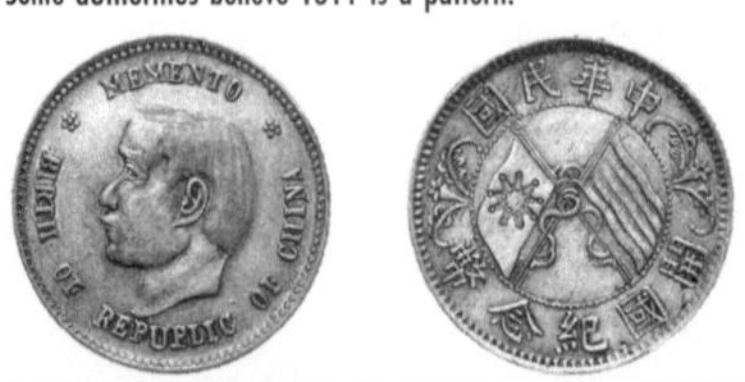

Y#	KM#	Metal	Description	VF	EF	Unc
317	317	Silv	(20 Cents), ND (1912)	200	400	1,100

Obverse: ***Sun Yat-sen***

Y#	KM#	Metal	Description	VF	EF	Unc
318	318	Silv	1 Yuan, ND (1912)	500	1,000	3,500

Note: Y318 has stars on the reverse, near the top. Do not confuse it with the common 1927 issue, Y318a.

Y#	KM#	Metal	Description	VF	EF	Unc
319	319	Silv	1 Dollar, ND, obverse as Y318	500	1,250	4,000

Obverse: ***Li Yuan Yung***

Y#	KM#	Metal	Description	VF	EF	Unc
320	320	Silv	1 Dollar, ND (1912)	2,500	6,500	15,000

Y#	KM#	Metal	Description	VF	EF	Unc
321	321	Silv	1 Dollar, ND (1912)	600	1,500	3,500

Obverse: ***Yuan Shih-kai***

Y#	KM#	Metal	Description	VF	EF	Unc
322	322	Silv	1 Dollar, ND (1914)	500	1,000	7,500

Y#	KM#	Metal	Description	VF	EF	Unc
323	323	Bz	5 Li, Yr 5 (1916)	15	25	75
324	324	Bz	1 Fen, Yr 5	8	15	65

Note: Also see similar 1933 issues, Y324a–325a. The 2-fen Year 5 is a pattern.

Obverse: ***Yuan Shih-kai***

Y#	KM#	Metal	Description	VF	EF	Unc
326	326	Silv	1 Chio (10 Cents), Yrs 3–5 (1914–16)	20	50	200
327	327	Silv	2 Chio (20 Cents), Yrs 3–9 *Yr 9, Rare*	20	50	200
328	328	Silv	1/2 Yuan (50 Cents), Yr 3	200	400	1,250
329	329	Silv	1 Yuan (Dollar), Yrs 3–10	95	135	350

Note: The 5 fen in nickel is a pattern.

Y#	KM#	Metal	Description	VF	EF	Unc
330	330	Gold	10 Yuan (Dollars), Yr 8 (1919)	4,000	6,000	9,000
331	331	Gold	20 Yuan (Dollars), Yr 8	7,000	10,000	20,000

Hung Hsien Reign, 1915–1916

Title assumed by Yuan Shih-kai. Also see Y401.

Y#	KM#	Metal	Description	VF	EF	Unc
332	332	Silv	(1 Yuan), Yr 1 (1912), obverse as Y322, reverse as Y333	2,500	3,500	8,000

Y#	KM#	Metal	Description	VF	EF	Unc
333	333	Gold	10 Yuan (Dollars), Yr 1 (1912)	5,000	7,500	15,000

Republican Issues Resumed

Y#	KM#	Metal	Description	VF	EF	Unc
334	334	Silv	1 Chio (10 Cents), Yr 15 (1926)	85	325	850
335	335	Silv	2 Chio (20 Cents), Yr 15	100	375	1,000
336	336	Silv	1 Yuan (Dollar), Yr 12 (1923)	2,500	5,000	20,000

Nationalist Coinage, *1927–1949*

"Ration" Coins

Reverse: ***Nationalist sun***

Y#	KM#	Metal	Description	VF	EF	Unc
337	Tn1	Br	1 Fen, Yr 17 (1928)	150	250	1,000
338	Tn2	Br	2 Fen, Yr 17	250	450	1,250

Note: Y337–338 always have a small incuse punch mark on both sides. Similar 5 and 10 fen are patterns.

Y#	KM#	Metal	Description	VF	EF	Unc
339	339	Silv	1 Chio (10 Cents), Yr 16 (1927)	100	250	1,250
340	340	Silv	2 Chio (20 Cents), Yr 16	100	250	1,250

Reverse: ***As Y318, but rosettes near top***

Y#	KM#	Metal	Description	VF	EF	Unc
318a	318a	Silv	1 Yuan (Dollar), ND (1927–32)	75	125	225
324a	324a	Bz	1 Fen, Yr 22 (1933)	30	50	135
325a	325a	Bz	2 Fen, Yr 22	65	100	200

Reverse: ***Birds over junk, sun at right***

Y#	KM#	Metal	Description	VF	EF	Unc
344	344	Silv	1 Yuan, Yr 21 (1932)	750	1,500	6,500

Reverse: ***No birds or sun***

Y#	KM#	Metal	Description	VF	EF	Unc
345	345	Silv	1 Yuan, Yrs 22–23 (1933–34)	50	100	375

Note: Other coins of various denominations similar to Y345 are patterns.

Currency Reform, November 1935

First Coinage

Y#	KM#	Metal	Description	VF	EF	Unc
346	346	Bz	1/2 Fen, Yr 25 (1936)	2	4	25
347	347	Bz	1 Fen, Yrs 25–28	8	15	40

Edge: ***Plain***

Y#	KM#	Metal	Description	VF	EF	Unc
348	348	Nick	5 Fen, Yrs 25–28 (1936–39)	7.50	15	40
349	349	Nick	10 Fen, Yrs 25–28	1.00	2	9
350	350	Nick	20 Fen, Yrs 25–28	2.00	4	12

Note: Unlisted denominations, dates, and coins with extra Chinese characters on either side are patterns.

World War II Provisional Issues

Y#	KM#	Metal	Description	VF	EF	Unc
353	353	Br	1 Hsien (Cent), Yr 28 (1939)	70	150	325
354	354	Br	2 Hsien, Yr 28	25	50	150

Y#	KM#	Metal	Description	VF	EF	Unc
355	355	Alum	1 Fen, Yr 29 (1940)	0.30	0.50	1.75

Y#	KM#	Metal	Description	VF	EF	Unc
356	356	Alum	5 Fen, Yr 29 (1940)	1.50	3	6

Note: Coins dated Year 28, and other denominations, are patterns.

Second Coinage

Y#	KM#	Metal	Description	VF	EF	Unc
357	357	Br	1 Fen, Yr 29 (1940)	0.50	0.80	1.25
358	358	Br	2 Fen, Yr 29	0.50	1.00	1.50

Edge: ***Reeded***

Y#	KM#	Metal	Description	VF	EF	Unc
359	359	C-N	5 Fen, Yrs 29–30 (1940–41)	1.50	2.50	5.00
360	360	C-N	10 Fen, Yrs 29–31	1.50	2.50	5.00
361	361	C-N	20 Fen, Yr 31	1.00	2.00	4.50
362	362	C-N	1/2 Yuan, Yrs 31–32	4.50	9.00	20.00

Note: Unlisted dates are patterns.

Third Coinage

Y#	KM#	Metal	Description	VF	EF	Unc
363	363	Bz	1 Fen, Yr 37 (1948)	10	20	40

Note: For Nationalist issues on Taiwan (Formosa), see Y531–536.

COMMUNIST ARMY ISSUES OF 1930–1934

All dated Communist coins bear Western dates, usually expressed in Chinese numerals. Dates are written either right-to-left or left-to-right.

HUPEH-HONAN-ANHWEI SOVIET

Obverse: ***As Y504***
Reverse: ***Similar to Y504, but with garbled Russian legend***

Y#	KM#	Metal	Description	VF	EF	Unc
503	503	Silv	1 Yuan, 1932	10,000	15,000	–

Y#	KM#	Metal	Description	VF	EF	Unc
504	504	Silv	1 Yuan, 1932	7,500	12,000	–

CHINESE SOVIET REPUBLIC (KIANGSI)

Modern copies exist of Y506–507 and Y511–512.

Y#	KM#	Metal	Description	VF	EF	Unc
506	506	Cop	1 Fen, ND (1932)	85	175	–

Y#	KM#	Metal	Description	VF	EF	Unc
507	507	Cop	5 Fen, ND (vars)	80	120	—
506a	506a	Cop	1 Fen	—	—	45
507a	507a	Cop	5 Fen	—	—	55

Note: Y506a and Y507a are modern restrikes.

Y#	KM#	Metal	Description	VF	EF	Unc
508	508	Silv	2 Chio, 1932–33	300	600	1,500

Hsiang-O-Hsi Soviet

Y#	KM#	Metal	Description	VF	EF	Unc
502a	1	Cop	Fen, ND (1931), *Rare*			

Hunan Soviet

Obverse: ***Bust of Lenin***
Reverse: ***Value above hammer and sickle***

Y#	KM#	Metal	Description	VF	EF	Unc
501	N/A	Silv	1 Yuan, ND (ca. 1930)			—

Obverse: ***Hammer and sickle in star***
Reverse: ***Value in wreath***

Y#	KM#	Metal	Description	VF	EF	Unc
502	N/A	Silv	1 Yuan, 1931			—

Note: Y501–502 are controversial. Most authorities consider them bogus.

Y#	KM#	Metal	Description	VF	EF	Unc
502b	1.1	Silv	Dollar, 1931, *Rare*			

Y#	KM#	Metal	Description	VF	EF	Unc
502c	1.2	Silv	Dollar, 1931, *Rare*			

P'ING CHIANG COUNTY SOVIET

Y#	KM#	Metal	Description	VF	EF	Unc
502d	1	Silv	Dollar, 1931, *Rare*			

SHENSI-NORTH SOVIET

Y#	KM#	Metal	Description	VF	EF	Unc
502e	1.1	Silv	Dollar, Yr 5 (1936), *Rare*			
502f	1.2	Silv	Dollar, Yr 5 (1936), *Rare*			
502g	2	Silv	Dollar, Yr 5 (1936), *Rare*			

SZECHUAN-SHENSI SOVIET

Y#	KM#	Metal	Description	VF	EF	Unc
510	510	Cop	200 Wen, 1933 (vars, crude)	450	1,500	—

Y#	KM#	Metal	Description	VF	EF	Unc
511	511	Cop	200 Wen, 1934	250	500	2,500
511a	511a	Cop	200 Wen, modern copy	—	—	75

Y#	KM#	Metal	Description	VF	EF	Unc
512	512	Cop	500 Wen, 1934 (vars)	400	800	3,000
512a	N/A	Cop	500 Wen, modern copy	—	—	75

Y#	KM#	Metal	Description	VF	EF	Unc
513	513	Silv	1 Yuan, 1934 (vars)	3,000	7,500	30,000

Wan-Hsi-Pei Soviet

Y#	KM#	Metal	Description	VF	EF	Unc
513a	1	Br	50 Cash, 1931	8,000	—	—

Reverse: *Value in circle with Chinese legend above, Western legend below*

Y#	KM#	Metal	Description	VF	EF	Unc
513b	2	Cop	50 Cash, ND (1931–32), *Rare*			

"Puppet State" Issues

Japanese-Controlled Regional Governments

Also see Manchukuo.

East Hopei

Y#	KM#	Metal	Description	VF	EF	Unc
516	516	Bz	5 Li (1/2 Cent) Yr 26 (1937)	35.00	75	250
517	517	Bz	1 Fen, Yr 26	17.50	25	150

Y#	KM#	Metal	Description	VF	EF	Unc
518	518	C-N	5 Fen, Yr 26 (1937)	15	30	100

Y#	KM#	Metal	Description	VF	EF	Unc
519	519	C-N	1 Chio, Yr 26 (1937)	15	20	90
520	520	C-N	2 Chio, Yr 26	15	30	100

Meng-Chiang (Inner Mongolia)

Y#	KM#	Metal	Description	VF	EF	Unc
521	521	C-N	5 Chio, Yr 27 (1938)	20	40	100

REFORMED GOVERNMENT OF CHINA

Y#	KM#	Metal	Description	VF	EF	Unc
A521	N/A	Bz	1 Fen, Yr 29 (1940)	150	375	600

Y#	KM#	Metal	Description	VF	EF	Unc
522	522	C-N	10 Fen, Yr 29 (1940)	4	8	20

Note: Other denominations (with different reverse designs) and the 1 fen in cupro-nickel are patterns.

PROVISIONAL GOVERNMENT OF CHINA

Y#	KM#	Metal	Description	VF	EF	Unc
523	523	Alum	1 Fen, Yrs 30–32 (1941–43)	3.00	5	15
524	524	Alum	5 Fen, Yrs 30–32	3.50	6	15
525	525	Alum	1 Chio, Yrs 30–32	3.50	6	15

TAIWAN (FORMOSA), *1949–*

First Coinage

Y#	KM#	Metal	Description	VF	EF	Unc
531	531	Bz	1 Chio, Yr 38 (1949)	0.50	1	4.50

Y#	KM#	Metal	Description	VF	EF	Unc
532	532	Silv	5 Chio, Yr 38 (1949)	3	6	12.50

Second Coinage

Y#	KM#	Metal	Description	VF	EF	Unc
533	533	Alum	1 Chio, Yr 44 (1955)	0.15	0.25	1.25
534	534	Alum	2 Chio, Yr 39	1.00	2.00	5.00

Y#	KM#	Metal	Description	VF	EF	Unc
535	535	Br	5 Chio, Yr 43 (1954)	0.20	0.30	1.25

Y#	KM#	Metal	Description	VF	EF	Unc
536	536	N-S	1 Yuan, Yrs 49–69 (1960–80)	0.15	0.25	0.65

Note: Many patterns of all Republican coins exist, including portrait coins.

CHINA–PROVINCIAL

CHINA–PROVINCIAL: EMPIRE

Provincial coins, especially the copper 10-cash pieces, exist in many varieties; only the major types are listed in this guide. See page 72 for an explanation of the Chinese monetary system, the precious metal content of the coinage, cyclical dates, and Mint names.

ANHWEI

Y#	KM#	Metal	Description	VF	EF	Unc
33	N/A	C/Br	1 Ch'ien, ND, struck	150	225	350

Note: For similar cast pieces, more commonly found, see Craig, *Coins of the World.*

Reverse: ***Side-view dragon***

Y#	KM#	Metal	Description	VF	EF	Unc
34	34	Cop	1 "Cen" (10 Cash), ND	350	950	—
34a	34a	Cop	1 "Sen," ND	375	1,250	—
35	35	Cop	5 Cash, ND	400	750	2,000
36	36	Cop	10 Cash, ND	10	30	120
36a	36a	Cop	(10 Cash), ND, no English value	10	30	120
37	37	Cop	20 Cash, ND	750	1,750	—

Reverse: *Front-view dragon*

Y#	KM#	Metal	Description	VF	EF	Unc
38a	38a	Cop	ToENCash, ND	50	100	500
38b	38b	Cop	(10 Cash), ND, no English value	30	75	200

Note: Coins with a large single Chinese character on the obverse are military award tokens.

Reverse: *Flying dragon (as Y78)*

Y#	KM#	Metal	Description	VF	EF	Unc
39	39	Cop	10 Cash, ND AN–HUI (2 vars), *Rare*			

Y#	KM#	Metal	Description	VF	EF	Unc
41	41	Silv	5 Cents	250	500	2,000
42	42	Silv	10 Cents	275	600	2,300
43	43	Silv	20 Cents	275	850	2,600
44	44	Silv	50 Cents	1,250	2,000	5,000
45	45	Silv	1 Dollar	800	1,750	7,000

Note: Two major varieties exist of Y41–45: with or without the small letters "A-S-T-C" in obverse field. The coins are either undated (1897), or variously dated Years 23–27 (1897–1901) and CD 1898.

Chekiang

Y#	KM#	Metal	Description	VF	EF	Unc
48	N/A	Br	1 Ch'ien, ND, struck	55	80	150

Note: For similar cast pieces, more commonly found, see Craig, *Coins of the World*.

Y#	KM#	Metal	Description	VF	EF	Unc
49	49	C/Br	(10 Cash), ND (vars)	7	17.50	50
49a	49a	C/Br	(10 Cash), ND, 4 characters on bottom row	20	40.00	175
50	50	C/Br	(20 Cash), ND	500	900.00	1,500

Y#	KM#	Metal	Description	VF	EF	Unc
51	51	Silv	5 Cents, ND (1902)	200	450	1,500
52	52	Silv	10 Cents, ND (Yrs 22–23 [1933–34])	250	550	2,000
53	53	Silv	20 Cents, ND (Yrs 22–23)	250	550	2,000
54	54	Silv	50 Cents, ND	35,000	65,000	145,000
55	55	Silv	1 Dollar, ND			

Note: Coins inscribed "Che-Kiang" are Birmingham Mint patterns.

Chihli

Legend: *PEKING*

Y#	KM#	Metal	Description	VF	EF	Unc
58	N/A	Silv	10 Cents, CD 1900	—	—	15,000
59	N/A	Silv	20 Cents, CD 1900	—	—	15,000

Note: Some authorities claim Y58–59 are patterns. Other denominations are strikings made later from unused dies.

Legend: *PEI YANG ARSENAL*

Y#	KM#	Metal	Description	VF	EF	Unc
61	61	Silv	1/2 Chio (5 Cents), Yrs 22–24 (1896–98)	225	550	2,000
62	62	Silv	1 Chio (10 Cents), Yrs 22–24	225	500	1,500
63	63	Silv	2 Chio (20 Cents), Yrs 22–24	250	550	2,000
64	64	Silv	5 Chio (50 Cents), Yrs 22–24	500	1,250	7,000
65	65	Silv	1 Yuan (Dollar), Yrs 22–24	750	1,500	8,500

Note: The Year 22 issue is a major variety without the words "Ta Tsing" in the legend. It is rarer than Years 23–24.

Y#	KM#	Metal	Description	VF	EF	Unc
66	66	Br	1 Wen, ND	20	37.50	100

Y#	KM#	Metal	Description	VF	EF	Unc
A67	N/A	C/Br	1 Ch'ien, ND, struck	25	40	80

Note: For similar cast pieces, more commonly found, see Craig, *Coins of the World.*

Legend: ***PEI YANG***

Y#	KM#	Metal	Description	VF	EF	Unc
67	67	C/Br	10 Cash, ND	6.50	17.50	150
68	68	C/Br	20 Cash, ND	135.00	275.00	975

Y#	KM#	Metal	Description	VF	EF	Unc
69	69	Silv	5 Cents, Yrs 25–26 (1899–1900)	300	600	2,000
70	70	Silv	10 Cents, Yr 25	300	600	2,000
71	71	Silv	20 Cents, Yrs 25–26	250	550	1,750
71a	71a	Silv	20 Cents, Yr 31, dragon circled	250	550	1,750
72	72	Silv	50 Cents, Yr 25	1,750	3,000	9,500
73	73	Silv	1 Dollar, Yrs 25–34	125	550	2,500
74	74	Silv	1 Liang (Tael), Yr 33	20,000	40,000	115,000

FENGTIEN (FUNG-TIEN)

Despite inscriptions on the following coins, Fengtien was not a province, but the capital city of Shengking.

First Coinage

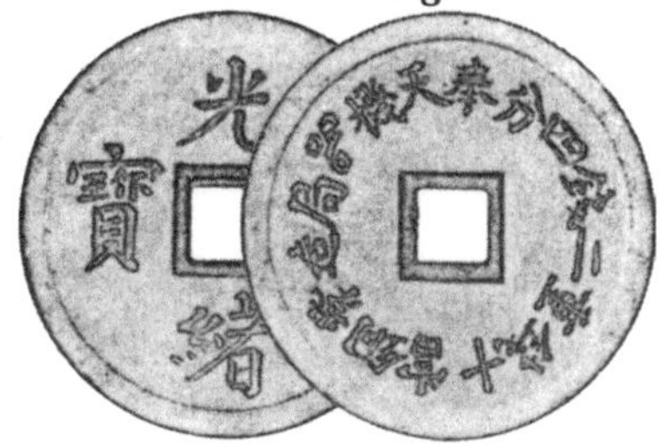

Y#	KM#	Metal	Description	VF	EF	Unc
81	81	Cop	10 Ch'ien (Cash), ND	250	500	—

Y#	KM#	Metal	Description	VF	EF	Unc
83	83	Silv	1/2 Chio (5 Cents), Yr 25 (1899)	200	550	2,000
84	84	Silv	1 Chio (10 Cents), Yr 24	200	550	2,000
85	85	Silv	2 Chio (20 Cents), Yr 24	300	750	3,000
86	86	Silv	5 Chio (50 Cents), Yrs 24–25	3,500	7,500	—
87	87	Silv	1 Yuan (Dollar), Yrs 24–25	2,000	5,000	11,000

Second Coinage

Legend: ***FEN-TIEN PROVINCE***

Y#	KM#	Metal	Description	VF	EF	Unc
88	88	Br	10 Cash, CD 1903	300	600	—

Legend: ***FUNG-TIEN PROVINCE***

Y#	KM#	Metal	Description	VF	EF	Unc
89	89	Br	10 Cash, CD 1903–06	60	125	500
90	90	Br	20 Cash, CD 1903–05	100	200	850

Note: Y88–90 struck in copper are patterns or trial strikes.

Y#	KM#	Metal	Description	VF	EF	Unc
91	91	Silv	20 Cents, CD 1904 (2 vars)	85	350	600
92	92	Silv	1 Dollar, CD 1903 (2 vars)	3,000	4,500	16,000

Note: Undated silver coins, and the 1-liang coin, are patterns. For later Fengtien issues, see Manchurian Provinces.

Formosa – See Taiwan (Formosa)

Fukien

Y#	KM#	Metal	Description	VF	EF	Unc
95	95	Br	1 Wen, ND	25	50	100

Note: Y95 is attributed to Fukien by the Manchu character at right on the reverse. Do not confuse this with Y191 or Y204.

Legend: ***F.K. CUSTOM-HOUSE***

Y#	KM#	Metal	Description	VF	EF	Unc
97	97	C/Br	10 Cash, ND	30	65	265

Legend: ***FOO-KIEN CUSTOM***

Y#	KM#	Metal	Description	VF	EF	Unc
98	98	C/Br	10 Cash, ND	500	1,500	4,750

Legend: ***FOO-KIEN***

Y#	KM#	Metal	Description	VF	EF	Unc
99	99	C/Br	5 Cash, ND	60.00	125	500
100	100	C/Br	10 Cash, ND	7.50	15	125
101	101	C/Br	20 Cash, ND	85.00	200	2,000

Y#	KM#	Metal	Description	VF	EF	Unc
102	102	Silv	5 Cents, ND (1898–1902)	45	100	325
103	103	Silv	10 Cents, ND	25	50	135
104	104	Silv	20 Cents, ND	50	135	400
105	105	Silv	1 Dollar, ND (1898), *Rare*			

Note: The 1898 coins have five characters at the top of the obverse, while the 1902 issues have only four.

Hsuan T'ung Reign

Design: ***Different characters at top-bottom (see illustration above Y18)***

Y#	KM#	Metal	Description	VF	EF	Unc
106	106	Br	1 Wen, ND	100	400	900

Note: See the note below Y95.

Honan

Y#	KM#	Metal	Description	VF	EF	Unc
108	108	C/Br	10 Cash, ND, dragon circled	12.50	25	75
108a	108a	C/Br	10 Cash, ND, dragon uncircled	12.50	25	75

HUNAN

Reverse: *Side-view dragon*

Y#	KM#	Metal	Description	VF	EF	Unc
112	112	C/Br	10 Cash, ND (vars)	5	15	150

Reverse: *Flying dragon*

Y#	KM#	Metal	Description	VF	EF	Unc
113	113	C/Br	10 Cash, ND (vars)	17.50	35	300

Y#	KM#	Metal	Description	VF	EF	Unc
115	115	Silv	10 Cents, CD 1898–99, ND (1902)	200	300	1,250
116	116	Silv	20 Cents, ND	300	800	3,000

Note: Other denominations are patterns.

HUPEH

Y#	KM#	Metal	Description	VF	EF	Unc
119	N/A	Br	1 Ch'ien, ND, struck (vars)	35	50	90

Note: For similar cast pieces, more commonly found, see Craig, *Coins of the World.*

Reverse: *Side-view dragon*

Y#	KM#	Metal	Description	VF	EF	Unc
120	120	Cop	10 Cash, ND, dragon circled	10.00	25	125
120a	120a	Cop	10 Cash, ND, dragon uncircled (vars)	12.50	30	175

Reverse: *Front-view dragon*

Y#	KM#	Metal	Description	VF	EF	Unc
121	121	Cop	1 Cash, ND	30	75	175

Y#	KM#	Metal	Description	VF	EF	Unc
122	122	Cop	10 Cash, ND (vars)	12.50	30	125

Note: Extremely rare patterns exist in brass; these are very heavy, unlike the cast-brass counterfeits.

Y#	KM#	Metal	Description	VF	EF	Unc
122a	122a	Cop	10 Cash, ND, circled front view dragon	35	75	175

Y#	KM#	Metal	Description	VF	EF	Unc
123	123	Silv	5 Cents, ND (1896)	200.00	600	1,800
124	124	Silv	10 Cents, ND (1895–96)	16.50	50	150
125	125	Silv	20 Cents, ND (1895–96)	25.00	60	175
126	126	Silv	50 Cents, ND (1896)	200.00	800	2,700
127	127	Silv	1 Dollar, ND (1895–96)	200.00	550	2,000

Note: The 1895 issue (extremely rare) is an experimental series with two Chinese characters added at the sides of the dragon.

Y#	KM#	Metal	Description	VF	EF	Unc
128	128	Silv	1 Tael, Yr 30 (1904)	2,250	7,500	16,000

Hsuan T'ung Reign

Design: ***Different characters at top-bottom (see illustration above Y18)***

Y#	KM#	Metal	Description	VF	EF	Unc
129	129	Silv	10 Cents, ND (1909)	1,750	3,000	—
130	130	Silv	20 Cents, ND	1,250	3,500	—
131	131	Silv	1 Dollar, ND	150	275	2,250

Kiangnan

A region consisting of Kiangsu, Anhwei, and Kiangsi provinces.

Reverse: ***Flying dragon***

Y#	KM#	Metal	Description	VF	EF	Unc
135	135	C/Br	10 Cash, ND, CD 1902–05	15	35	—

Reverse: ***Front-view dragon***

Y#	KM#	Metal	Description	VF	EF	Unc
138	138	C/Br	10 Cash, CD 1905 (2 vars)	5	15	100
140	140	C/Br	10 Cash, CD 1906, obverse of Y10k, reverse of Y138	10	30	175

Note: Other mules of Kiangnan coppers exist, especially with Kiangsu Y160.

Reverse: ***Dragon circled***

Y#	KM#	Metal	Description	VF	EF	Unc
141	141	Silv	5 Cents, ND (1897)	150	300	900
142	142	Silv	10 Cents, ND, CD 1898	200	400	1,000
143	143	Silv	20 Cents, ND, CD 1898	250	500	1,200
144	144	Silv	50 Cents, ND	18,000	35,000	—
145	145	Silv	1 Dollar, ND	3,000	6,000	—

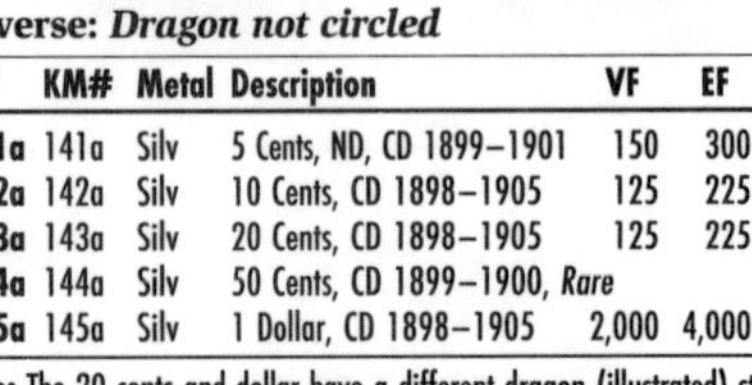

Reverse: ***Dragon not circled***

Y#	KM#	Metal	Description	VF	EF	Unc
141a	141a	Silv	5 Cents, ND, CD 1899–1901	150	300	800
142a	142a	Silv	10 Cents, CD 1898–1905	125	225	500
143a	143a	Silv	20 Cents, CD 1898–1905	125	225	600
144a	144a	Silv	50 Cents, CD 1899–1900, *Rare*			
145a	145a	Silv	1 Dollar, CD 1898–1905	2,000	4,000	6,000

Note: The 20 cents and dollar have a different dragon (illustrated) starting in 1899. Most coins dated 1901–05 have small English initials on the obverse.

Hsuan T'ung Reign

Design: ***Different characters at top-bottom (see illustration above Y18)***

Y#	KM#	Metal	Description	VF	EF	Unc
146	146	Silv	10 Cents, ND (1909)	125	300	900
147	147	Silv	20 Cents, ND	150	350	1,000

KIANGSI

Reverse: ***Side-view dragon***

Y#	KM#	Metal	Description	VF	EF	Unc
149	149	C/Br	10 Cash, KIANG–SEE, dragon circled or uncircled	35	100	400
150	150	C/Br	10 Cash, KIANG–SI	20	45	250

Reverse: ***Front-view dragon***

Y#	KM#	Metal	Description	VF	EF	Unc
152	152	C/Br	10 Cash, KIANG–SI	22.50	35	250
153	153	C/Br	10 Cash, KIANG–SEE PROVINCE	25.00	30	200

Reverse: ***Flying dragon***

Y#	KM#	Metal	Description	VF	EF	Unc
154	154	C/Br	10 Cash, KIANG–SI	70	90	180

KIANGSU

Y#	KM#	Metal	Description	VF	EF	Unc
157	N/A	C/Br	1 Ch'ien, ND, struck	55	125	250

Note: For similar cast pieces, more commonly found, see Craig, *Coins of the World*.

Reverse: ***Side-view dragon***

Y#	KM#	Metal	Description	VF	EF	Unc
158	158	C/Br	EIVE (= 5) Cash, ND	35	75	175

Reverse: ***Front-view dragon***

Y#	KM#	Metal	Description	VF	EF	Unc
160	160	C/Br	10 Cash, ND	27.50	60	150

Reverse: ***Flying dragon***

Y#	KM#	Metal	Description	VF	EF	Unc
159	Pn2	C/Br	2 Cash, ND	1,500	2,000	2,500
161	Pn4/Pn5	C/Br	5 Cash, ND	1,500	2,000	2,500
162	162	C/Br	10 Cash, ND, CD 1903–03, 05	20	40	225
163	163	C/Br	20 Cash, ND	100	200	650

Note: Some authorities consider Y159 and Y161 to be patterns or later strikings from unused dies.

Chingkiang or Tsingkiang

This was a city in Kiangsu Province.

Legend: ***CHING/KIANG***

Y#	KM#	Metal	Description	VF	EF	Unc
77	77	C/Br	(10 Cash), ND	22.50	40	225

Legend: ***TSING/KIANG***

Y#	KM#	Metal	Description	VF	EF	Unc
78	78	C/Br	10 Cash, ND	6	17.50	200

KIRIN
First Coinage

Y#	KM#	Metal	Description	VF	EF	Unc
169	169	Silv	1 Ch'ien (Mace), Yr 10 (1885)	500	700	900
170	170	Silv	3 Ch'ien, Yr 10	800	1,000	1,500
171	171	Silv	5 Ch'ien, Yr 10	800	1,000	1,500
172	172	Silv	7 Ch'ien, Yr 10	1,000	2,000	3,500
173	173	Silv	1 Liang (Tael), Yr 10	10,000	15,000	20,000

Second Coinage

Y#	KM#	Metal	Description	VF	EF	Unc
175	175	Cop	2 Wen, ND	110	150	225
174	174	Cop	10 Wen, ND	400	550	800

Reverse: ***Side-view dragon***

Y#	KM#	Metal	Description	VF	EF	Unc
176	176	C/Br	10 Cashes, ND	80	120	200
A176	A176	C/Br	20 Cashes, ND	300	400	500
B176	B176	C/Br	50 Cashes, CD 1901, *Rare*			

Reverse: ***Flying dragon***

Y#	KM#	Metal	Description	VF	EF	Unc
177	177	C/Br	10 Cashes, ND	60	150	300
178	178	C/Br	20 Cashes, ND	175	400	1,800

Note: Many varieties exist of Y177–178.

Obverse Center: ***Flower vase***

Y#	KM#	Metal	Description	VF	EF	Unc
179	179	Silv	5 Cents, ND (1896–98), CD 1899–1908	100	200	900
180	180	Silv	10 Cents, ND, 1899–1907	100	225	925
181	181	Silv	20 Cents, ND, 1899–1908	125	375	975
182	182	Silv	50 Cents, ND, 1899–1908	225	375	2,000
183	183	Silv	1 Dollar, ND, 1899–1908	1,000	3,000	8,000

Obverse Center: ***Yin-Yang***

Y#	KM#	Metal	Description	VF	EF	Unc
179a	179a	Silv	5 Cents, CD 1900–05	150	300	1,000
180a	180a	Silv	10 Cents, CD 1900–05	75	150	900
181a	181a	Silv	20 Cents, CD 1900–05	75	150	900
182a	182a	Silv	50 Cents, CD 1900–05	300	600	1,200
183a	183a	Silv	1 Dollar, CD 1900–05	1,250	2,500	7,000

Obverse Center: ***Two Manchu characters***

Y#	KM#	Metal	Description	VF	EF	Unc
181b	181b	Silv	20 Cents, CD 1908	375	750	2,500
182b	182b	Silv	50 Cents, CD 1908	4,750	9,500	—
183b	183b	Silv	1 Dollar, CD 1908	6,000	12,000	—

Obverse Center: ***Arabic number***

Y#	KM#	Metal	Description	VF	EF	Unc
180c	180c	Silv	10 Cents, CD 1908, "1" in center	375	750	2,500
181c	181c	Silv	20 Cents, CD 1908, "2" in center	125	250	1,000
183c	183c	Silv	1 Dollar, CD 1908, "11" in center	10,000	25,000	—

Kwangtung

Y189–191 and Y204 are attributed to Kwangtung by the Manchu character on the reverse—at left on Y189, at right on Y190–191.

Y#	KM#	Metal	Description	VF	EF	Unc
189	189	Br	1 Ch'ien, ND (1889–90)	2.25	3.25	40

Y#	KM#	Metal	Description	VF	EF	Unc
190	190	Br	(1 Ch'ien), ND (1892–94)	0.75	2.25	40

Y#	KM#	Metal	Description	VF	EF	Unc
191	191	Br	1 Wen, ND	1.25	2.50	20

Y#	KM#	Metal	Description	VF	EF	Unc
192	192	Cop	1 Cent, ND (1900)	8.00	17.50	100
193	193	Cop	10 Cash, ND	7.50	15.00	85

Obverse: ***English legend***

Y#	KM#	Metal	Description	VF	EF	Unc
194	194	Silv	5 Cents, ND (1889)	3,750	7,500	—
195	195	Silv	10 Cents, ND	3,000	6,000	15,000
196	196	Silv	20 Cents, ND	2,500	5,000	18,000
197	197	Silv	50 Cents, ND	7,500	18,000	35,000
198	198	Silv	1 Dollar, ND	15,000	35,000	75,000

Note: Two varieties exist of Y194–198: the first slightly heavier and inscribed with higher weights, the second of normal weight for provincial silver.

Reverse: ***English legends (regular provincial type)***

Y#	KM#	Metal	Description	VF	EF	Unc
199	199	Silv	5 Cents, ND (1890)	17.50	45	100
200	200	Silv	10 Cents, ND	17.50	45	100
201	201	Silv	20 Cents, ND	15.00	30	85
202	202	Silv	50 Cents, ND	300.00	650	2,000
203	203	Silv	1 Dollar, ND	200.00	450	2,000

Hsuan T'ung Reign

Design: ***Different characters at top-bottom (see illustration above Y18)***

Y#	KM#	Metal	Description	VF	EF	Unc
204	204	Br	1 Wen, ND (as Y191)	3	6	85
205	205	Silv	20 Cents, ND (1909)	15	30	110
206	206	Silv	1 Dollar, ND	225	450	4,000

Manchurian Provinces

Fengtien, Heilungkiang, Kirin

Y#	KM#	Metal	Description	VF	EF	Unc
209	209	Silv	10 Cents, Yr 33 (1907)	65	150	600
210	210	Silv	20 Cents, Yr 33	50	100	200
211	211	Silv	50 Cents, Yr 33	800	2,000	9,500
212	212	Silv	1 Dollar, Yr 33	2,000	4,500	15,000

Hsuan T'ung Reign

Design: ***Different characters in center (see illustration above Y18)***

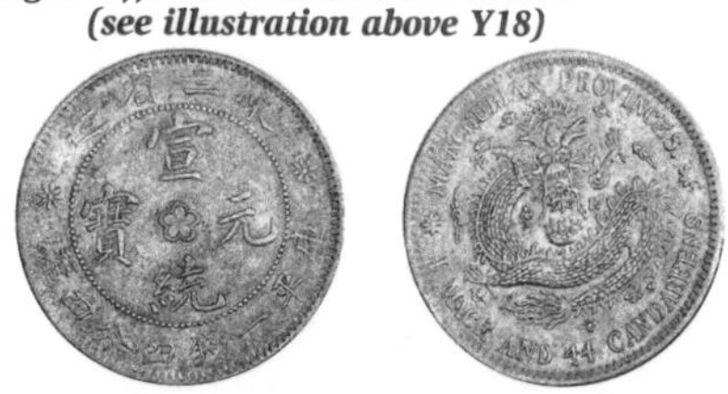

Y#	KM#	Metal	Description	VF	EF	Unc
213	213	Silv	20 Cents, Yr 1 (1909)	25	75	150
213a	213a	Silv	20 Cents, ND (1909–10)	25	75	150

Note: Y213 is inscribed either "1st Year" or "First Year." Do not confuse Y213a with Y217.

Peiyang – See Chihli

Shansi

Y#	KM#	Metal	Description	VF	EF	Unc
217	217	Silv	20 Cents, ND	750	1,500	—

Note: The obverse of Y217 bears Chinese characters for Shansi, but the reverse is a crude copy of Y213a. Several varieties exist, all struck in the early years of the Republic.

Shantung

Reverse: ***Side-view dragon***

Y#	KM#	Metal	Description	.25	EF	Unc
220	220	Cop	10 Cash, ND	70	175	1,500

Reverse: ***Flying dragon***

Y#	KM#	Metal	Description	VF	EF	Unc
221	221	Cop	10 Cash, ND SHANTUNG	45	95	350
221a	221a	Cop	10 Cash, ND SHANGTUNG	18	45	350

Note: Dragon coins of Shensi province are patterns.

Sinkiang or Hsin-Chiang

Chinese Empire

Kuang Hsu, 1875–1908, and Hsuan T'ung, 1908–1912

Struck in China for General Use in Turkestan

Y#	KM#	Metal	Description	VF	EF	Unc
1	1	Cop	1 Fen, 5 Li, ND (Kuang Hsu)	900	1,500	—

Y#	KM#	Metal	Description	VF	EF	Unc
2	2	Cop	10 Wen, ND, CD 1910–11 (Hsuan T'ung legend)	300	600	—

Note: Varieties exist for Y1–2.

Modern Copies

Y#	KM#	Metal	Description	VF	EF	Unc
1a	1a	Cop	1 Fen, 5 Li	—	—	110
2a	2a	Cop	10 Wen	—	—	110

Y#	KM#	Metal	Description	VF	EF	Unc
3	3	Silv	1 Misqal, ND	300	600	1,300
4	4	Silv	2 Misqal, ND	400	1,000	7,000
5	5	Silv	4 Misqal, ND	400	1,000	—
6	6	Silv	5 Misqal, ND	200	400	1,000
7	7	Silv	1 Tael, ND	1,000	2,000	6,500

Note: Many varieties exist, including circled and uncircled dragon, with and without Turkic script, etc.

Y#	KM#	Metal	Description	VF	EF	Unc
A7	A7	Silv	5 Fen, ND, AH 1295 (1878)	50	100	—
B7	B7	Silv	1 Misqal, AH 1292–95	2,500	5,000	—

"Ration Gold"

Y#	KM#	Metal	Description	VF	EF	Unc
8	8	Gold	1 Misqal, ND	15,000	25,000	40,000
9	9	Gold	2 Misqal, ND	17,000	30,000	50,000

Obverse: ***With title SUNGAREI***

Y#	KM#	Metal	Description	VF	EF	Unc
10	10	Silv	1 Mace, ND	1,000	1,500	2,500
11	11	Silv	2 Mace, ND	1,500	3,000	—

Y#	KM#	Metal	Description	VF	EF	Unc
12	46.4	Silv	1 Yuan, Yr 38 (1949), Chinese characters outlined	1,000	2,000	6,000
12a	46	Silv	1 Yuan, Yr 38	200	400	6,000
12b	46.5	Silv	1 Yuan, Yr 38, Different calligraphy	1,000	2,000	2,000

Note: The similarly dated 3, 4, and 5 mace are patterns and/or fantasies.

Struck at Various Mints

Aksu Mint

Legends: ***Kuang Hsu***

Y#	KM#	Metal	Description	VF	EF	Unc
A13	A13	Silv	1 Misqal, AH 1311 (1894) (18 mm), *Rare*			
13	13	Silv	2 Misqal, AH 1311–12 (23 mm)	100	200	—
14	14	Silv	3 Misqal, AH 1311, 13 (26 mm)	100	200	—
15	15	Silv	5 Misqal, AH 1310–12 (31 mm)	200	400	—

Kashghar Mint

Legends: ***Kuang Hsu***

Y#	KM#	Metal	Description	VF	EF	Unc
16	16	Silv	1 Misqal, ND, AH 1309–10	350	750	—
17	17	Silv	2 Misqal, AH 1310–22 (1892–1904) (23 mm)	100	275	—
18	18	Silv	3 Misqal, AH 1310–22	100	275	—
19	19	Silv	5 Misqal, AH 1310–22	75	150	—

Y#	KM#	Metal	Description	VF	EF	Unc
A20	A20	Silv	1 Misqal, AH 1323 (1905)	3,000	7,000	—
B20	B20	Silv	2 Misqal, AH 1323 (23 mm)	3,000	7,000	—
20	20	Silv	3 Misqal, AH 1323 (27 mm)	400	850	—
21	21	Silv	5 Misqal, AH 1323 (32 mm)	225	400	—

Legends: ***Dragon and Ta Ch'ing***

Y#	KM#	Metal	Description	VF	EF	Unc
23	23	Silv	2 Misqal, AH 1325–26 (1907–08) (24 mm)	300	750	—
25	25	Silv	5 Misqal, ND, AH 1325–28	125	250	—
26	26	Silv	1 Liang, AH 1325 (40 mm)	2,000	4,000	8,500

Legends: ***Dragon and Hsuan T'ung***

Y#	KM#	Metal	Description	VF	EF	Unc
27	27	Silv	5 Misqal, AH 1327–29 (1909–11)	125	250	1,000

Legend: ***Dragon and SILVER COIN***

Y#	KM#	Metal	Description	VF	EF	Unc
29	29	Silv	2 Misqal, AH 1329 (2 vars)	350	650	—
30	30	Silv	3 Misqal, AH 1329	4,500	—	—

Legend: ***Dragon and RATION SILVER***

Y#	KM#	Metal	Description	VF	EF	Unc
31	31	Silv	5 Misqal, AH 1329–31 (1911–13)	200	400	—

Urumchi Mint

Legends: ***Kuang Hsu***

Y#	KM#	Metal	Description	VF	EF	Unc
33	33	Silv	2 Misqal, AH 1321–25 (1903–07) (24 mm)	100	185	—
34	34	Silv	3 Misqal, AH 1321–25	125	225	—
35	35	Silv	5 Misqal, AH 1321–25	90	150	—

SZECHUAN

Reverse: ***Side-view dragon***

Y#	KM#	Metal	Description	VF	EF	Unc
225	225	C/Br	5 Cash, ND	200	900	4,000
226	226	C/Br	10 Cash, ND	175	300	—
227	227	C/Br	20 Cash, ND	250	1,000	—

Reverse: ***Flying dragon***

Y#	KM#	Metal	Description	VF	EF	Unc
228	228	C/Br	5 Cash, ND	4,000	9,500	—
229	229	C/Br	10 Cash, ND	30	50	225
230	230	C/Br	20 Cash, ND	55	75	425

Reverse: ***Front-view dragon***

Y#	KM#	Metal	Description	VF	EF	Unc
231	231	C/Br	10 Cash, ND	500	1,500	—
233	Pn4/Pn5	C/Br	30 Cash, ND, *Rare*			

Note: Some authorities believe Y231–233 are patterns.

Y#	KM#	Metal	Description	VF	EF	Unc
234	234	Silv	5 Cents, ND (1897)	125	400	950
235	235	Silv	10 Cents, ND	175	450	1,000
236	236	Silv	20 Cents, ND	175	450	1,000
237	237	Silv	50 Cents, ND	625	1,750	4,000
238	238	Silv	1 Dollar, ND	450	975	8,500

Hsuan T'ung Reign

Design: ***Different characters at top-bottom (see illustration above Y18)***

Y#	KM#	Metal	Description	VF	EF	Unc
239	239	Silv	5 Cents, ND (1909)	200	500	1,500
240	240	Silv	10 Cents, ND	150	450	1,500
242	242	Silv	50 Cents, ND	3,000	5,500	—
243	243	Silv	1 Dollar, ND	375	750	7,500

TAIWAN (FORMOSA)

Y#	KM#	Metal	Description	VF	EF	Unc
246	246	Silv	5 Cents, ND (ca. 1890)	1,000	2,250	5,000
247	247	Silv	10 Cents, ND (2 vars)	575	1,150	2,500
248	248	Silv	20 Cents, ND (2 vars), *Rare*			

TSINGKIANG – SEE KIANGSU

TURKESTAN – SEE SINKIANG

YUNNAN

Design: ***Regular provincial type***

Y#	KM#	Metal	Description	VF	EF	Unc
252	252	Silv	20 Cents, ND (1907)	150	250	650
253	253	Silv	50 Cents, ND	100	200	400
254	254	Silv	1 Dollar, ND	450	900	3,000

Design: ***No English legends***

Y#	KM#	Metal	Description	VF	EF	Unc
255	255	Silv	10 Cents, ND (1908)	50.00	125	300
256	256	Silv	20 Cents, ND	35.00	75	175
257	257	Silv	50 Cents, ND	22.50	45	150
258	258	Silv	1 Dollar, ND	100.00	400	1,500

Hsuan T'ung Reign

Design: ***Different characters in obverse center (see illustration above Y18); regular provincial type***

Y#	KM#	Metal	Description	VF	EF	Unc
259	259	Silv	50 Cents, ND (1909)	175	400	1,500
260	260	Silv	1 Dollar, ND, CD 1910 *CD 1910, Rare*	475	1,500	3,500

CHINA–PROVINCIAL: REPUBLIC

See page 72 for an explanation of the Chinese monetary system, the precious metal content of the coinage, cyclical dates, and Mint names.

CHEKIANG

Y#	KM#	Metal	Description	VF	EF	Unc
371	371	Silv	10 Cents, Yr 13 (1924)	12.50	50	150
372	372	Silv	20 Cents, Yr 13, similar	600.00	1,000	2,500
373	373	Silv	20 Cents, Yr 13, large 20	600.00	1,000	2,500

FUKIEN

Cast

Y#	KM#	Metal	Description	VF	EF	Unc
374	374	Br	1 Wen (Cash), ND (1911)	150	300	—
375	375	Br	2 Wen (Cash), ND (2 vars)	75	150	—

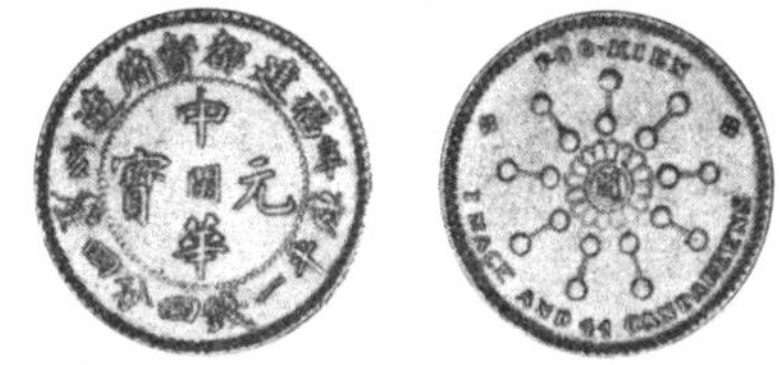

Y#	KM#	Metal	Description	VF	EF	Unc
377	377	Silv	20 Cents, CD 1911	90	200	800

Y#	KM#	Metal	Description	VF	EF	Unc
379	379	Cop	10 Cash, ND (1912)	25	75	200

Y#	KM#	Metal	Description	VF	EF	Unc
380	380	Silv	10 Cents, ND (1912), CD 1924	200	400	4,000
381	381	Silv	20 Cents, ND, CD 1923–24	15	35	175

Y#	KM#	Metal	Description	VF	EF	Unc
382	382	Silv	10 Cents, ND (1913)	20	50	200
383	383	Silv	20 Cents, ND	20	50	200
383a	383a	Silv	20 Cents, Yr 13 (1924)	100	200	700

Northern Expedition Commemoratives

Y#	KM#	Metal	Description	VF	EF	Unc
384	384	Silv	2 Hao (20 Cents), Yr 16 (1927)	750	1,750	4,000
385	385	Silv	2 Hao, Yr 16, obverse center 4 characters		2,000	4,000	—

Canton Martyrs Commemoratives

Y#	KM#	Metal	Description	VF	EF	Unc
388	388	Silv	10 Cents, Yrs 17, 20 (1928, 31)	65	150	600
389	389	Silv	20 Cents, Yrs 17, 20	15	30	75
390	390	Silv	10 Cents, Yr 21 (1932) obverse flags	750	1,500	3,500
391	391	Silv	20 Cents, Yr 21, similar	125	375	900

HONAN

Obverse: ***Value in center***

Y#	KM#	Metal	Description	VF	EF	Unc
A392	A392	C/Br	10 Cash, ND	7.50	17.50	100

Obverse: ***Flower in center***

Y#	KM#	Metal	Description	VF	EF	Unc
392	392	C/Br	10 Cash, ND (1912) (2 vars)	10	20	45
393	393	C/Br	20 Cash, ND (2 vars)	15	30	60
394	394	C/Br	50 Cash, ND (38 mm)	45	125	375
395	395	C/Br	100 Cash, ND (40 mm)	50	135	450
396	396	C/Br	200 Cash, ND (42 mm)	50	135	450

New Legend: ***CHINA replaces HO-NAN***

Y#	KM#	Metal	Description	VF	EF	Unc
393a	393.2	C/Br	20 Cash, ND	70	150	300
394a	394a	C/Br	50 Cash, ND	100	350	600
A397	A397	C/Br	20 Cash, Yr 20 (1931), star replaces China, *Rare*			

Y#	KM#	Metal	Description	VF	EF	Unc
397	397	C/Br	50 Wen, Yr 20 (1931)	200	300	3,500
398	398	C/Br	100 Wen, Yr 20	225	350	3,500

HUNAN

Y#	KM#	Metal	Description	VF	EF	Unc
399	399	Cop	10 Cash, ND (2 vars)	10	22.50	135

Y#	KM#	Metal	Description	VF	EF	Unc
400	400	C/Br	20 Cash, ND, value TWENTY (vars)	7.50	15	75
400a	400a	C/Br	20 Cash, ND, value "20"	175.00	400	—

Hung Hsien Reign

Y#	KM#	Metal	Description	VF	EF	Unc
401	401	C/Br	10 Cash, Yr 1 (1911)	175	250	600

Note: Also see Y332–333 for this reign.

Provincial Constitution Commemoratives

Y#	KM#	Metal	Description	VF	EF	Unc
402	402	Cop	10 Cash, Yr 11 (1922) (2 vars)	60	125	300
403	403	Cop	20 Cash, Yr 11	100	200	1,000

Y#	KM#	Metal	Description	VF	EF	Unc
404	404	Silv	1 Dollar, Yr 11 (1922)	1,750	4,500	15,000

HUPEH

Y#	KM#	Metal	Description	VF	EF	Unc
A405	A405	C/Br	20 Ch'ien (Cash), ND	300	500	1,700

Note: Attribution to Hupeh is uncertain.

Design: ***Similar to Y449***

Y#	KM#	Metal	Description	VF	EF	Unc
405	405	C/Br	50 Wen, Yrs 3, 7 (1914, 18)	800	1,500	—

Note: Two varieties exist of the 1918 issue, one crude, the other as Y449.

Y#	KM#	Metal	Description	VF	EF	Unc
406	406	Silv	2 Chio (20 Cents), Yr 9 (1920)	2,000	3,000	12,000

Note: As Y327, but two characters for Hupeh added at sides of head.

KANSU

Y#	KM#	Metal	Description	VF	EF	Unc
407	407	Silv	1 Yuan, Yr 3 (1914)	10,000	15,000	45,000

Note: As Y329, but two characters for Kansu added at sides of head.

Y#	KM#	Metal	Description	VF	EF	Unc
408	408	Cop	50 Wen, Yr 15 (1926)	350	700	—
409	409	Cop	100 Wen, Yr 15	150	400	1,000

Y#	KM#	Metal	Description	VF	EF	Unc
410	410	Silv	1 Yuan, Yr 17 (1928)	6,500	15,000	35,000

KIANGSI

Obverse: ***Similar to Y10m***
Reverse: ***Stylized Republican star (design of balls and arcs)***

Y#	KM#	Metal	Description	VF	EF	Unc
411	411	Cop	10 Wen, CD 1911, *Rare*			

Y#	KM#	Metal	Description	VF	EF	Unc
412	412	Cop	10 Cash, CD 1912	250	400	—
412a	412a	Cop	10 Cash, CD 1912, different obverse legends	30	55	200

Kwangsi (Kwangsea)

Legend: ***KWANG SEA***

Y#	KM#	Metal	Description	VF	EF	Unc
413	413	Br	1 Cent, Yr 8 (1919)	325	650	2,500

Y#	KM#	Metal	Description	VF	EF	Unc
415	415	Silv	20 Cents, Yrs 8–13 (1919–24)	250	650	1,750

Legend: ***KWANG-SI***

Y#	KM#	Metal	Description	VF	EF	Unc
413a	413a	Br	1 Cent, Yr 8 (1919)	165	325	1,000

Y#	KM#	Metal	Description	VF	EF	Unc
414	414	Silv	10 Cents, Yr 9 (1920)	200	500	1,350
415a	415a	Silv	20 Cents, Yrs 8–14	65	100	225

Reverse: ***Wreath added***

Y#	KM#	Metal	Description	VF	EF	Unc
415b	415b	Silv	20 Cents, Yrs 15–16 (1926–27)	17.50	35	115

Y#	KM#	Metal	Description	VF	EF	Unc
416	416	Silv	2 Chio, Yr 38 (1949)	2,000	4,000	10,000

Kwangtung

Y#	KM#	Metal	Description	VF	EF	Unc
417	417	C/Br	1 Cent, Yrs 1–7 (1912–18)	15	40	115
418	418	C/Br	2 Cents, Yr 7	200	500	2,000

Y#	KM#	Metal	Description	VF	EF	Unc
420	420	C-N	5 Hsien / 5 Cents, Yr 8 (1919)	2.50	5	20
420a	420a	C-N	1/2 Hao / 5 Cents, Yr 12	2.50	5	20

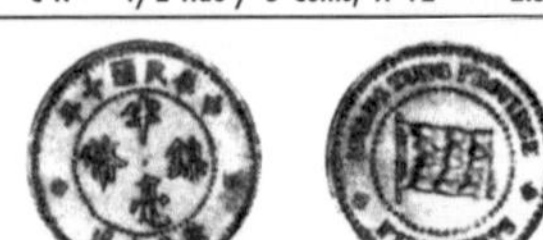

Y#	KM#	Metal	Description	VF	EF	Unc
421	421	C-N	5 Cents, Yr 10 (1921)	4.50	10	25

Y#	KM#	Metal	Description	VF	EF	Unc
422	422	Silv	10 Cents, Yrs 2–11 (1913–22)	10.00	20	45
423	423	Silv	20 Cents, Yrs 1–13	4.50	10	25

Y#	KM#	Metal	Description	VF	EF	Unc
424	424	Silv	2 Hao (20 Cents), Yr 13 (1924)	225	550	1,200

Y#	KM#	Metal	Description	VF	EF	Unc
425	425	Silv	1 Hao (10 Cents), Yr 18 (1929)	17.50	30	60
426	426	Silv	2 Hao, Yrs 17–18	25.00	35	60

Note: Coins dated Year 19 are patterns.

Y#	KM#	Metal	Description	VF	EF	Unc
427	Pn28	Cop	1 Hsien (Cent), Yr 25 (1936)	3,500	7,500	15,000

Note: Some authorities claim Y427 is a pattern.

KWEICHOW

First Road in Kweichow

Y#	KM#	Metal	Description	VF	EF	Unc
428	428	Silv	1 Yuan, Yr 17 (1928)	5,000	9,500	60,000

Y#	KM#	Metal	Description	VF	EF	Unc
429	429	Anti	10 Fen, Yr 20 (1931)	600	950	4,000

Y#	KM#	Metal	Description	VF	EF	Unc
A429	A429	Cop	1/2 Cent, Yr 38 (1949)	950	2,000	—
A429a	A429a	Br	1/2 Cent, Yr 38	750	1,600	—

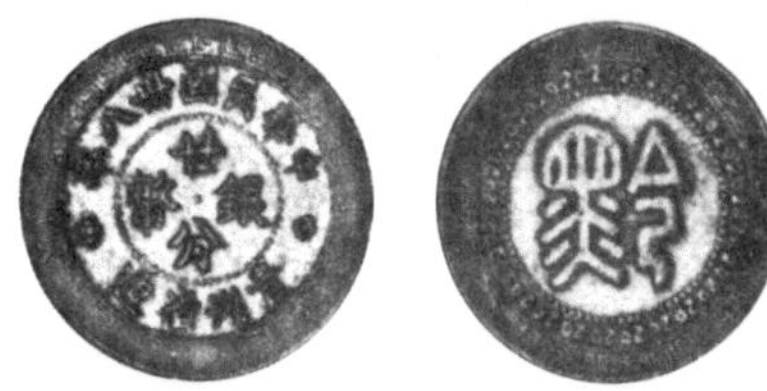

Obverse: ***Similar to Y429, ornate border***

Y#	KM#	Metal	Description	VF	EF	Unc
430	430	Silv	20 Fen, Yr 38 (1949), reverse 3 seal characters	1,500	3,000	8,000

Y#	KM#	Metal	Description	VF	EF	Unc
431	431	Silv	20 Fen, Yr 38 (1949), 20 on reverse, *Rare*			
432	432	Silv	1/2 Yuan, Yr 38, 50 on reverse, *Rare*			

Note: Some authorities consider Y431–432 to be patterns.

Y#	KM#	Metal	Description	VF	EF	Unc
433	433	Silv	1 Yuan, Yr 38 (1949), reverse 3 bamboo stems	15,000	40,000	—

Manchurian Provinces

Y#	KM#	Metal	Description	VF	EF	Unc
434	434	Cop	1 Fen, Yr 18 (1929)	2	4	12

Shansi

Y#	KM#	Metal	Description	VF	EF	Unc
A435	A435	Cop	1 Mei (10 Cash), ND	1,500	2,000	—

Note: As Y307, but two characters for Shansi replace stars on obverse. Some authorities consider this coin a pattern, but most known pieces are well circulated.

Shensi

Y#	KM#	Metal	Description	VF	EF	Unc
435	435	Cop	1 Fen, ND (ca. 1924), IM–TYPIF	180	250	750
436	436	Cop	2 Fen, ND, IMTYPEF (vars)	30	60	250

Sinkiang

Struck at Various Mints

No Mint Name

Y#	KM#	Metal	Description	VF	EF	Unc
A39	A39	Cop	10 Wen, CD 1912 (2 vars)	100	175	—

Reverse: ***Crossed five-striped flags***

Y#	KM#	Metal	Description	VF	EF	Unc
41	41	Silv	5 Misqal, CD 1912, reverse 2 stripes have arabesques	175	350	2,250
42	42	Silv	1 Tael, CD 1912, similar	225	450	2,500
41a	41a	Silv	5 Misqal, CD 1912, reverse 4 stripes have arabesques	225	450	2,500
42a	42a	Silv	1 Tael, CD 1912, similar	225	450	2,500

Y#	KM#	Metal	Description	VF	EF	Unc
B39	B39	Cop	10 Wen, ND (vars)	70	145	350
39	39	Cop	20 Wen, ND, similar	85	175	400

Obverse: ***Similar to YB38***
Reverse: ***Nationalist flags***

Y#	KM#	Metal	Description	VF	EF	Unc
40	40	Cop	10 Wen, CD 1929–30 (vars)	45	90	—

Aksu Mint

Cast

Y#	KM#	Metal	Description	VF	EF	Unc
37	37	Cop	10 Wen, ND	75	150	—

Kashghar Mint

Y#	KM#	Metal	Description	VF	EF	Unc
A36	A36	Cop	5 Wen, ND	750	1,500	—
B36	B36	Cop	10 Wen, ND	150	300	—

Y#	KM#	Metal	Description	VF	EF	Unc
36	36	Cop	5 Wen, AH 1331 (1913)	600	1,250	—
38	38	Cop	10 Wen, ND, AH 1331–32 (vars)	50	100	—

Y#	KM#	Metal	Description	VF	EF	Unc
43	43	Silv	5 Misqal, AH 1331–34	75	150	500

Hung Hsien Reign, 1915–1916

Y#	KM#	Metal	Description	VF	EF	Unc
A38	N/A	Cop	10 Wen, AH 1334 (1916)	150	300	1,100

Republican Issues Resumed

Design: ***Similar to Y38***

Y#	KM#	Metal	Description	VF	EF	Unc
38a	38a	Cop	10 Wen, Yrs 10–11 (1921–22) rearranged obverse legend (vars)	40	80	—

Y#	KM#	Metal	Description	VF	EF	Unc
B38	B38	Cop	10 Wen, CD 1928, reverse Chinese legend	75	150	300
B38a	B38a	Cop	10 Wen, CD 1929, reverse Uighur legend	300	600	1,000

Y#	KM#	Metal	Description	VF	EF	Unc
C38	N/A	Cop	20 Wen, ND (42 mm)	80	150	—

Tihwa (Urumchi) Mint

Y#	KM#	Metal	Description	VF	EF	Unc
45	45	Silv	1 Liang (Tael), Yrs 6–7 (1917–18)	100	200	1,500

SUIYUAN

Y#	KM#	Metal	Description	VF	EF	Unc
45a	3	Br	Fen, Yr 38 (1949)	2,500	5,000	—

Y#	KM#	Metal	Description	VF	EF	Unc
45a	5	Br	5 Fen, Yr 38 (1949)	3,000	6,000	—

SZECHUAN

Y#	KM#	Metal	Description	VF	EF	Unc
441	441	C/Br	(5 Wen), Yr 1 (1912)	375	950	2,000

Y#	KM#	Metal	Description	VF	EF	Unc
443	443	C/Br	5 Wen, Yr 1	150	300	900

Y#	KM#	Metal	Description	VF	EF	Unc
446	446	C/Br	5 Wen, Yr 1, *Rare*			
447	447	C/Br	10 Wen, Yrs 1–2	15.00	25	75
448	448	C/Br	20 Wen, Yrs 1–3 (32 mm)	20.00	40	150
449	449	C/Br	50 Wen, Yrs 1–3 (36 mm)	17.50	30	150
450	450	C/Br	100 Wen, Yrs 2–3 (39 mm)	25.00	45	250

Y#	KM#	Metal	Description	VF	EF	Unc
453	453	Silv	1 Chio (10 Cents), Yr 1	300	600	3,000
454	454	Silv	2 Chio (20 Cents), Yr 1	600	1,500	7,000
455	455	Silv	5 Chio (50 Cents), Yrs 1–2	100	450	1,500
456	456	Silv	1 Yuan (Dollar), Yrs 1, 3	100	250	1,250
457	N/A	C-N	5 Fen, Yr 14, *Rare*			

Y#	KM#	Metal	Description	VF	EF	Unc
459	459	C/Br	200 Cash, Yr 2 (vars)	50	85	250

Y#	KM#	Metal	Description	VF	EF	Unc
462	462	C/Br	50 Wen, Yr 15 (1926)	125	250	600
463	463	C/Br	100 Wen, Yr 15	50	100	350
464	464	C/Br	200 Wen, Yr 15	50	100	350

Y#	KM#	Metal	Description	VF	EF	Unc
466	N/A	Br	100 Wen, Yrs 15, 19 (1926, 30)	350	600	2,000

Y#	KM#	Metal	Description	VF	EF	Unc
468	468	Various	1 Chio (10 Cents), ND (ca. 1926)	50	100	350

Note: Y468 exists in silver, brass, and several other minor metals.

Y#	KM#	Metal	Description	VF	EF	Unc
473	473	Silv	5 Chio, Yr 17 (1928), *Rare*			
474	474	Silv	1 Yuan, Yr 17, *Rare*			

Note: Many other legitimate coins in silver and minor metals were circulated widely; often these coins lack provincial designations. Warlords (or Chinese communists) copied Yuan Shih-kai and Sun Yat-sen dollars, the latter with spelling errors in the English inscription. Crudely struck or cast copies of Y446–450 are not necessarily counterfeit, but often are warlord issues.

Y#	KM#	Metal	Description	VF	EF	Unc
476	476	C/Br	2 Cents, Yr 19 (1930), *Rare*			

YUNNAN

Y#	KM#	Metal	Description	VF	EF	Unc
478	478	C/Br	50 Wen, ND (ca. 1916)	100	500	1,800

Y#	KM#	Metal	Description	VF	EF	Unc
479	479	Silv	50 Cents, ND (1916)	75	175	550

Y#	KM#	Metal	Description	VF	EF	Unc
480	480	Silv	50 Cents, ND (1917)	300	850	3,250

Y#	KM#	Metal	Description	VF	EF	Unc
481	481	Gold	5 Dollars, ND (1919)	2,000	3,500	7,500
482	482	Gold	10 Dollars, ND (2 vars)	2,000	3,500	5,000

Note: There are two other sets of Yunnan gold 5 and 10 dollars, struck about 1917 and 1925, bearing Chinese inscriptions only, but their authenticity is uncertain; see Friedberg, *Gold Coins of the World*, F8–9 and F13–14.

Y#	KM#	Metal	Description	VF	EF	Unc
485	485	C-N	5 Cents, Yr 12 (1923)	100	225	—
486	486	C-N	10 Cents, Yr 12	10	20	100

Y#	KM#	Metal	Description	VF	EF	Unc
488	488	Br	1 Hsien (Cent), Yr 21 (1932), *Rare*			
489	489	Br	2 Hsien (2 Cents), Yr 21	1,000	2,000	—
490	490	Br	5 Hsien (5 Cents), Yr 21	350	750	3,500

Y#	KM#	Metal	Description	VF	EF	Unc
491	491	Silv	2 Chio (20 Cents), Yr 21	25	35	95
492	492	Silv	1/2 Yuan (1/2 Dollar), Yr 21	30	60	125

Y#	KM#	Metal	Description	VF	EF	Unc
493	493	Silv	2 Chio (20 Cents), Yr 38 (1949)	45	100	350

World War II Issues

Y#	KM#	Metal	Description	VF	EF	Unc
495	A1	Silv	1/2 Liang (Tael), ND (1942–43)	475	950	1,750
496	A2	Silv	1 Liang, ND	750	1,500	3,000

Y#	KM#	Metal	Description	VF	EF	Unc
497	A3	Silv	1 Liang, ND	750	1,500	3,000

Note: The exact origin of these so-called Yunnan-Burma taels is uncertain. They are said to have been paid to Chinese troops in southern Yunnan, eastern Burma, or the Laotian area of northern Indo-China.

CHINA, PEOPLE'S REPUBLIC OF

The second largest of the world's nations, China comprises much of eastern Asia. Before 1911, the land was ruled by a succession of emperors. At that time it became a republic and remained so through several major changes of government. After driving out the Nationalist regime, a People's Republic was proclaimed in 1949 by Mao Zedong, with various communist factions vying for power thereafter. *Languages:* Mandarin, Cantonese, minority languages. *Capital:* Beijing.

MONETARY SYSTEM
100 fen = 1 yuan

Y#	KM#	Metal	Description	VF	EF	Unc
1	1	Alum	1 Fen, 1955–97	0.25	0.50	3.50
2	2	Alum	2 Fen, 1956–96	0.25	0.50	3.50
3	3	Alum	5 Fen, 1955–96	0.25	0.50	3.50

COLOMBIA

This mountainous republic, northernmost of the South American countries, is where the Spanish established the first mainland New World settlement, in 1510. Known as New Granada until 1861, it attained independence in 1824. The Liberal and Conservative parties ruled along with occasional military juntas through the 1950s. Today Colombia is a presidential republic with relatively strong democratic institutions. *Language:* Spanish. *Capital:* Bogota.

PRECIOUS METAL CONTENT

Dates	Denomination	Gross Wt (g)	Fineness	Net Wt (g)	Troy Oz.
		SILVER			
1837–38	8 Reales	24.2000	0.6660	16.1172	0.5182
1839–46	8 Reales	23.0000	0.6660	15.3180	0.4925
1837–48	1/4 Real	0.6800	0.6660	0.4529	0.0146
	1/2 Real	1.2600	0.6660	0.8392	0.0270
	1 Real	2.7000	0.6660	1.7982	0.0578
	2 Reales	5.5000	0.6660	3.6630	0.1178
1847	1 Real	2.7000	0.9000	2.4300	0.0781
1847–53	2 Reales	5.0000	0.9000	4.5000	0.1447
	8 Reales	20.0000	0.9000	18.0000	0.5787
	10 Reales	25.0000	0.9000	22.5000	0.7234
1849–58	1/4 Real	0.9000	0.9000	0.8100	0.0260
	1/2 Real	1.4000	0.9000	1.2600	0.0405
	1/2 Decimo	1.5000	0.9000	1.3500	0.0434
	1 Decimo	2.5000	0.9000	2.2500	0.0723
	2 Decimos	5.0000	0.9000	4.5000	0.1447
	1 Real	2.5000	0.9000	2.2500	0.0723
	1 Peso	25.0000	0.9000	22.5000	0.7234
1859–62	1/4 Decimo	0.9000	0.6660	0.5994	0.0193
	1/2 Decimo	1.2500	0.9000	1.1250	0.0362
	1 Decimo	2.5000	0.9000	2.2500	0.0723
	1 Peso	25.0000	0.9000	22.5000	0.7234
	1/2 Real	1.4000	0.9000	1.2600	0.0405
	2 Reales	5.0000	0.9000	4.5000	0.1447
1872–86	5 centavos	1.2500	0.6667	0.8333	0.0268
	10 centavos	2.5000	0.8350	2.0875	0.0671
	20 centavos	5.0000	0.8350	4.1750	0.1342
	50 centavos / 5 decimos	12.5000	0.8350	10.4375	0.3356
1885–89	10 centavos	2.5000	0.5000	1.2500	0.0402
	20 centavos	5.0000	0.5000	2.5000	0.0804
	50 centavos / 5 decimos	12.5000	0.5000	6.2500	0.2009
1889–1908	5 centavos	1.2500	0.6667	0.8333	0.0286
	10 centavos	2.5000	0.6667	1.6667	0.0536
	20 centavos	5.0000	0.6667	3.3333	0.1072
	50 centavos	12.5000	0.8350	10.4375	0.3356
1911–42	10 centavos	2.5000	0.9000	2.2500	0.0723
	20 centavos	5.0000	0.9000	4.5000	0.1447
	50 centavos	12.5000	0.9000	11.2500	0.3617
1945–52	10 centavos	2.5000	0.5000	1.2500	0.0402
	20 centavos	5.0000	0.5000	2.5000	0.0804
	50 centavos	12.5000	0.5000	6.2500	0.2009
1953	20 centavos	5.0000	0.3000	1.5000	0.0482
1956	1 peso	25.0000	0.9000	22.5000	0.7234
		GOLD			
1837–46	1 Peso	1.6875	0.8750	1.4766	0.0475
	2 Pesos	3.3750	0.8750	2.9531	0.0949
1849–53	2 Pesos	3.2300	0.9000	2.9070	0.0935
	16 pesos	27.0000	0.8750	23.6250	0.7596
1853–57	10 pesos	16.4000	0.9000	14.7600	0.4745
1857–62	1 Peso	1.6100	0.9000	1.4490	0.0466
	2 Pesos	3.2300	0.9000	2.9070	0.0935
	5 Pesos	8.0600	0.9000	7.2540	0.2332
	10 Pesos	16.1300	0.9000	14.5170	0.4667
	20 Pesos	32.2600	0.9000	29.0340	0.9335
1862–78	1 peso	1.6129	0.9000	1.4516	0.0467
	2 pesos	3.2258	0.9000	2.9032	0.0933
	5 pesos	6.4516	0.9000	5.8064	0.1867
	10 pesos	16.1290	0.9000	14.5161	0.4667
	20 pesos	32.2581	0.9000	20.0323	0.9334
1885–86	5 pesos	8.0645	0.6660	5.3710	0.1728
	10 pesos	16.1290	0.6660	10.7419	0.3453
1913–30	2-1/2 pesos	3.9940	0.9170	3.6612	0.1177
	5 pesos	7.9881	0.9170	7.3224	0.2354
	10 pesos	15.9761	0.9170	14.6448	0.4708

Note: Most silver and gold coins of 1862–1908 bear mint names BOGOTA, POPAYAN, or MEDELLIN.

REPUBLICA DE NUEVA GRANADA, *1837–1858*

MONETARY SYSTEM

8 reales = 1 peso

Y#	KM#	Metal	Description	VF	EF	Unc
Cr-141	90.1	Silv	1/4 Real, 1837–48, Bogota *1837, 45, 48, Scarce*	125	200	500
Cr-141a	90.2	Silv	1/4 Real, 1838–46, Popayan, *Rare*			
Cr-142	96.1	Silv	1/2 Real, 1838–47, Bogota *1838, Rare; 1843, Scarce*	125	200	500
Cr-142a	96.2	Silv	1/2 Real, 1838–48, Popayan *1840, 41, 42, 44, 45, 48, Rare; 1843, Scarce*	125	200	500
Cr-143	91.1	Silv	1 Real, 1837–46, Bogota *1841, Rare; 1840, Scarce*	75	150	350
Cr-143a	91.2	Silv	1 Real, 1844–46, Popayan	60	125	300
Cr-144	97.1	Silv	2 Reales, 1839–46, Bogota *1839, 46, Rare; 1841, 45, 46, Scarce*	125	250	750
Cr-144a	97.2	Silv	2 Reales, 1840–44, Popayan *1841, 44/3, Rare; 1842, Scarce; 1849, does not exist in this type*	125	250	750
Cr-147	98	Silv	8 Reales, 1839–46, Bogota (condor/cornucopia obverse) *1840/39, 41/0, 41, 46/4, 46/5, Scarce*	150	300	900
Cr-145	92	Silv	8 Reales, 1837–38, Bogota (shield obverse), *Very Scarce* *1838, Rare*	750	1,500	3,000

Y#	KM#	Metal	Description	VF	EF	Unc
Cr-148	93	Gold	1 Peso, 1837–46, Bogota	100	200	400
Cr-149	95	Gold	2 Pesos, 1838–46, Popayan *1842UM, 1845UE, Rare*	400	750	1,500
Cr-150	94.1	Gold	16 Pesos, 1837–49, Bogota	BV	1,500	2,500
Cr-150	94.2	Gold	16 Pesos, 1837–46, Popayan	BV	1,500	2,500

MONETARY SYSTEM

10 reales = 1 peso

Y#	KM#	Metal	Description	VF	EF	Unc
Cr-151	101	Cop	1/2 Decimo de Real, 1847–48	10	25	50
Cr-152	102	Cop	1 Decimo de Real, 1847–48	10	25	50
Cr-153	108.1	Silv	1/4 Real, 1850–55, Bogota, pomegranate, stars flanking bottom of denomination *1851, Rare; 1852, Very Rare; 1855, 3 known; 1853–54, unknown*	30	60	150

Y#	KM#	Metal	Description	VF	EF	Unc
Cr-153	113	Silv	1/4 Real, 1852, 55, Bogota, pomegranate, caducei flanking bottom of denomination *1852, 3–4 known; 1855, 2 known*	—	—	—
Cr-153	108.2	Silv	1/4 Real, 1849–58, Popayan, pomegranate *1853–54, Rare; 1856, 2–3 known; 1858, 2–3 known*	120	200	400
Cr-154	110	Silv	1/2 Real, 1850–53, Bogota	120	250	500
Cr-154a	133	Silv	1/2 Real, 1862/48, Popayan (anachronistic issue)	120	250	500
Cr-155	103	Silv	1 Real, 1847, Bogota	40	100	200
Cr-155a	112	Silv	1 Real, 1851–53, Bogota *1852, Scarce*	40	100	200
Cr-156a	105	Silv	2 Reales, 1847–49, Bogota, rosettes flanking wreath on reverse	15	30	150
Cr-156b	109	Silv	2 Reales, 1849–53, Bogota, caducei flanking wreath on reverse *1849, Very Rare; 1852–53, Scarce*	10	20	50
Cr-158	106	Silv	8 Reales, 1847, Bogota	200	400	800
Cr-159	107	Silv	10 Reales, 1847–49, Bogota, arms on trophies, condor above *1849, Rare*	70	150	300
Cr-160	111	Silv	10 Reales, 1850–51, Bogota, large condor with spread wings	250	500	1,000

MONETARY SYSTEM

10 decimos = 1 peso

Y#	KM#	Metal	Description	VF	EF	Unc
Cr-161	114	Silv	1/2 Decimo, 1853–58, Bogota	125	250	500
Cr-162	115	Silv	1 Decimo, 1853–58, Bogota	40	75	150
Cr-163	117	Silv	2 Decimos, 1854–58, Bogota	150	400	800
Cr-165	118	Silv	1 Peso, 1855–58, Bogota	100	200	400

Y#	KM#	Metal	Description	VF	EF	Unc
Cr-170	99	Gold	(2 Pesos) PESO 3.2258, 1849, 51, Bogota *1851, 2 known*	400	750	1,500
Cr-171	116.1	Gold	(10 Pesos) PESO 16.400, 1853–57, Bogota *1853, 57, Scarce*	900	1,500	3,000
Cr-171a	116.2	Gold	(10 Pesos) PESO 16.400, 1853, 56–57, Popayan, medal axis	1,200	2,000	4,000
Cr-172	100	Gold	(16 Pesos) PESO 25.8064, 1849–53, Bogota	3,000	4,500	—

Y#	KM#	Metal	Description	VF	EF	Unc
Cr-174	121	Gold	2 Pesos, 1857–58, Popayan	400	750	1,500
Cr-175	120	Gold	5 Pesos, 1857–58, Bogota *1858, 2 known*	850	1,250	2,500
Cr-176	122	Gold	10 Pesos, 1857–58, Bogota	1,200	2,000	4,000
			10 Pesos, 1857–58, Popayan	1,200	2,000	4,000

CONFEDERACION GRANADINA, *1858–1862*

Y#	KM#	Metal	Description	VF	EF	Unc
Cr-181	131	Silv	1/4 Decimo, 1860, Bogota, caducei flanking denomination	150	250	500
Cr-181a	132	Silv	1/4 Decimo, 1859–62, Popayan, three stars on reverse	175	300	600
Cr-182	124	Silv	1/2 Decimo, 1859–61, Bogota	100	200	400
Cr-183	125	Silv	1 Decimo, 1859–60, Bogota	60	125	250
Cr-184	134	Silv	2 Reales, 1862, Popayan	70	150	300
Cr-186	126	Silv	1 Peso, 1859–61, Bogota, condor above shield	100	200	500
Cr-191a	—	Silv	1 Peso, 1862, Popayan, restruck on 10 reales, *1 known*			

Y#	KM#	Metal	Description	VF	EF	Unc
Cr-187	135	Gold	1 Peso, 1862, Medellin, *3 known*			
Cr-188	127	Gold	2 Pesos, 1859, Popayan *1860, 2 known*	300	500	1,000
Cr-189	128	Gold	5 Pesos, 1859, Popayan, *2 known*			
Cr-190	136	Gold	5 Pesos, 1862, Medellin, *1 known*			
—	—	Gold	10 Pesos, 1859–61, Bogota	1,200	1,500	3,000
Cr-191	129	Gold	10 Pesos, 1858–62, Popayan	1,200	1,500	3,000
Cr-192	130	Gold	20 Pesos, 1859, Bogota, *8 known*	5,000	10,000	20,000

ESTADOS UNIDOS DE NUEVA GRANADA, *1860–1861*

Y#	KM#	Metal	Description	VF	EF	Unc
Cr-193	—	Silv	1/4 Decimo, 1861, Bogota, 9 stars on reverse	175	350	750
Cr-194	—	Silv	1/4 Decimo, 1860, Popayan, 9 stars on reverse (backdated issue)	275	550	1,000
Cr-195	137	Silv	1 Decimo, 1861, Bogota	125	250	500
Cr-197	138	Silv	1 Peso, 1861, Bogota	500	750	1,500

ESTADOS UNIDOS DE COLOMBIA, *1863–1886*

MONETARY SYSTEM

10 decimos or reales = 1 peso 100 centavos = 1 peso

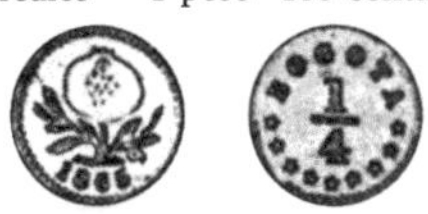

Obverse: *Pomegranate*
Reverse: *Denomination*

Y#	KM#	Metal	Description	VF	EF	Unc
1	143	Silv	1/4 Decimo, 1862–71, Bogota *1881, contemporary fakes*	75	150	300
1	143	Silv	1/4 Decimo, 1862–81, Popayan *1883, 84, contemporary fakes*	75	150	300
1a	143.3	Silv	1/4 Decimo, 1874, Medellin	40	75	150
12	169	Silv	2-1/2 Centavos, 1872–81, Bogota	20	40	80

Obverse: *Cornucopia*
Reverse: *Wreath*

Y#	KM#	Metal	Description	VF	EF	Unc
2	144	Silv	1/2 Decimo, 1863–65, Bogota (.900 fine)	125	250	500
2a	144a	Silv	1/2 Decimo, 1867, Bogota (.666 fine)	60	120	—
3	145	Silv	1 Decimo, 1863–66, Bogota (.900 fine) *1865, 3 known*	75	150	300
3a	145.1a	Silv	1 Decimo, 1866, Bogota (.835 fine)	30	60	120
3	145.1		1 Decimo, 1863–64, Popayan (.900 fine)	100	200	400
3	145.2a		1 Decimo, 1866, Popayan (.835 fine)	200	400	800

Obverse: *Liberty*
Reverse: *Arms*

Y#	KM#	Metal	Description	VF	EF	Unc
6	150.1	Silv	1/2 Decimo, 1868–71, Bogota (.666 fine)	100	200	400
6	150.2	Silv	1/2 Decimo, 1868–70, Medellin (.666 fine) *1870, 3 known*	125	250	500
6	150.3	Silv	1/2 Decimo, 1868–78, Popayan (.666 fine) *1876, 78, Scarce*	100	200	400
6a	150.2a	Silv	1/2 Decimo, 1870–72, Medellin (.835 fine) *1870, 1 known*	60	150	300
6a	150.4	Silv	1/2 Decimo, 1873–74, Medellin (.835 fine), AB below bust	200	400	800
6a	150.3a	Silv	1/2 Decimo, 1875, Popayan (.835 fine)	350	700	1,500
A12	170	Silv	5 Centavos, 1872–74, Bogota (.666 fine)	35	75	150
7	151.1	Silv	1 Decimo, 1868–72, Bogota (.835 fine)	75	150	300
7	151.2	Silv	1 Decimo, 1874, Medellin (.835 fine)	100	200	400
B12	171	Silv	10 Centavos, 1872–74, Bogota (.835 fine)	75	150	300
8	155.1	Silv	2 Decimos, 1872, Bogota (.835 fine)	300	600	1,200
8	155.2	Silv	2 Decimos, 1870–72, Medellin (.835 fine), crude head	150	300	600
8	—	Silv	2 Decimos, 1872, Medellin (.835 fine), fine head, *Rare*			
8	—	Silv	2 Decimos, 1872, Medellin (.835 fine), Wyon head	30	75	150
A9	152	Silv	1/2 Peso, 1868, Medellin, *6 known*			
9	153/161	Silv	5 Decimos, 1868–86 (.835 fine) *Popayan, Rare*			
9	153.1	Silv	5 Decimos, 1868–71, Bogota (.835 fine)	150	300	600
9	153.2, 153.3	Silv	5 Decimos, 1868–69; 1872–73, Medellin (.835 fine), standard bust *1868, 2 known; 1869, Very Scarce*	100	200	400
9	153.6	Silv	5 Decimos, 1869–80, Popayan (.835 fine), *All Rare*			
		Silv	5 Decimos, 1873–77, Medellin (.835 fine), Barre head *1873, 74, Scarce; 1877, 5 known*	100	200	400
9	161.1	Silv	5 Decimos, 1877–86, Medellin (.835 fine), Wyon head *1877, 4 known; various overdates and varieties of other dates, Scarce to Rare*	30	60	120
9a	Several	Silv	5 Decimos, 1886, Medellin (.500 fine), Wyon head *Many varieties, some Scarce*	200	400	800
9a	—	Silv	5 Decimos, 1886, Medellin (.500 fine), long head, *Rare*			
16	172	Silv	50 Centavos, 1872–74, Bogota (.835 fine), denomination 50, standard head *1872, Scarce*	70	150	300
17	177.1	Silv	50 Centavos, 1874–85, Bogota (.835 fine), value CINCUENTA, Wyon head *1874–77, double value; 1885, Scarce*	30	60	120
17	177.2	Silv	50 Centavos, 1880, Popayan (.835 fine), value CINCUENTA, Wyon head	400	800	—
17a	177a.1	Silv	50 Centavos, 1885–86, Bogota (.500 fine), value CINCUENTA, Wyon head *Several Scarce varieties known*	30	60	120

Y#	KM#	Metal	Description	VF	EF	Unc
17a	—	Silv	50 Centavos, 1886, Medellin (.500 fine), value CINCUENTA, Bogota head	300	600	1,200
			Variant with Medellin head, Rare			
10	154.1	Silv	1 Peso, 1868–71, Bogota	75	150	300
			1868, Scarce; 1870, not confirmed			
10	154.2	Silv	1 Peso, 1869–71, Medellin	125	250	500

Obverse: ***Arms***
Reverse: ***Wreath***

Y#	KM#	Metal	Description	VF	EF	Unc
5	139.1	Silv	1 Peso, 1862–67, Bogota	75	150	300
5	139.2	Silv	1 Peso, 1863, Popayan, *Very Rare*			

Obverse: ***Liberty***
Reverse: ***Cornucopia***

Y#	KM#	Metal	Description	VF	EF	Unc
13a	174a.1	Silv	5 Centavos, 1875–85, Bogota (.666 fine)	25	50	100
13	174	Silv	5 Centavos, 1874, Medellin (.835 fine)	100	200	400
13a	174a.2	Silv	5 Centavos, 1875, Medellin (.666 fine)	250	500	1,000
14	175.1	Silv	10 Centavos, 1874–84, Bogota (.835 fine)	35	75	150
14	175.2	Silv	10 Centavos, 1885, Medellin (.835 fine)	100	200	400
14a	175.2a	Silv	10 Centavos, 1885–86, Medellin (.500 fine)	125	250	500
			1886, Scarce (2 vars)			
15	176.1	Silv	20 Centavos, 1874, Medellin, GRAM, 5 (.835 fine), Wyon head	50	100	200
15b	176.2	Silv	20 Centavos, 1874; 1882, Medellin, GRAMOS 5 (.835 fine), Wyon head, *Scarce*	300	700	1,500
			1874, Rare			
15	178.1/ 178.2	Silv	20 Centavos, 1875–82, Medellin, GRAM. 5 (.835 fine), Barre head	25	60	125
			Several varieties; 1882, Scarce (double value)			
15b	178.3	Silv	20 Centavos, 1882–85, Medellin, GRAMOS 5 (.835 fine), Barre head	25	60	125
			1885, Scarce (double value)			
15b	176.3	Silv	20 Centavos, 1884, Bogota	25	60	125
15a	178.3a	Silv	20 Centavos, 1886, Medellin, GRAM. 5 (.500 fine), *Very Rare*	2,500	5,000	—

Obverse: ***Shield in wreath***

Y#	KM#	Metal	Description	VF	EF	Unc
4	149	Silv	2 Decimos, 1865, Bogota (.900 fine)	400	1,000	—
4a	149a.1, 149a.2	Silv	2 Decimos, 1866–67, Bogota (.835 fine)	25	60	120
4a	149b	Silv	2 Decimos, 1867, Popayan (.835 fine)	30	75	150
A4	162	Silv	2 Reales, 1880, Popayan (.835 fine), anachronistic denomination	400	1,000	—

Obverse: ***Phrygian cap***
Reverse: ***Denomination***

Y#	KM#	Metal	Description	VF	EF	Unc
18	173	C-N	1-1/4 Centavos, 1874 (Heaton)	10	30	60
19	179	C-N	2-1/2 Centavos, 1881 (14 mm) (Waterbury)	15	40	80
20	180	C-N	2-1/2 Centavos, 1881 (18 mm) (Heaton)	40	80	160
22	181	Cop	2-1/2 Centavos, 1885, Bogota	50	100	200
21	182	C-N	2-1/2 Centavos, 1886 (Waterbury)	15	40	80

Obverse: ***Liberty***
Reverse: ***Wreath***

Y#	KM#	Metal	Description	VF	EF	Unc
A37	146.1	Gold	1 Peso, 1863, Medellin, legend ESTADOS UNIDOS DE COLOMBIA	250	500	1,000
A37	146.2	Gold	1 Peso, 1864, Medellin, legend COLOMBIA, *Very Rare*			
B37	147	Gold	2 Pesos, 1863, Medellin	400	750	1,500
C37	140, A148	Gold	5 Pesos, 1863–64, Medellin, legend ESTADOS UNIDOS DE COLOMBIA, *Rare*			
			1864, 1 known			
C37	148	Gold	5 Pesos, 1864, Medellin, legend COLOMBIA, *Very Rare*			

Obverse: ***Liberty***
Reverse: ***Condor***

Y#	KM#	Metal	Description	VF	EF	Unc
32	157.2	Gold	1 Peso, 1871–75, Bogota	125	250	500
			1871, 3 known			
32a	157.1	Gold	1 Peso, 1872–73, Medellin	125	250	500
			1873/2, Scarce; 1873, Clean 3, 3 known			

Obverse: ***Liberty***
Reverse: ***Arms***

Y#	KM#	Metal	Description	VF	EF	Unc
37	156	Gold	1 Peso, 1872, Medellin	125	250	500
38	A154	Gold	2 Pesos, 1871–72, Medellin *1876, reported, probably fake*	250	500	1,000
39	A154a	Gold	2 Pesos, 1885/74, Medellin (.666/.900 fine), *5 known*			
39	163	Gold	5 Pesos, 1885/74, Medellin (.666/.900 fine), *Rare*			
40	141.1	Gold	10 Pesos, 1862–66, Bogota *1862, 64, Scarce; 1863, 66, with larger heads, believed to be contemporary fakes*	1,250	2,000	4,000
40	141.3	Gold	10 Pesos, 1863–70, Popayan *1865, 67, Scarce; 1869, contemporary fake; 1870, 2–3 known*	900	1,500	3,000
40	141.2	Gold	10 Pesos, 1864–73, Medellin *1863, 70, 71, Scarce; 1873, Rare*	900	1,500	3,000
40	141.4	Gold	10 Pesos, 1873–76, Medellin, Barre head *1873, Scarce; 1874, 1 known; 1875, 1 known*	900	1,500	3,000
40a	141.2a	Gold	10 Pesos, 1886/74, Medellin (.666/.900 fine), *4 known*			
41	142.1	Gold	20 Pesos, 1862–77, Bogota *1867, 76, Rare; 1871, Scarce; 1877, 2 known*	2,000	3,000	5,000
41	142.3	Gold	20 Pesos, 1863–78, Popayan *1877, 1–2 known; 1878, 1–2 known*	2,000	2,500	4,000
41	142.2	Gold	20 Pesos, 1867–71, Medellin *1867, known only as pattern; 1871, Scarce*	2,000	2,500	3,750

REPUBLICA DE COLOMBIA, *1886–*

Obverse: ***Liberty left***
Reverse: ***Denomination in wreath (Waterbury design)***

Y#	KM#	Metal	Description	VF	EF	Unc
24	183	C-N	5 Centavos, 1886 (5 with short or long bar), 88	1	5	30
25	184	C-N	5 Centavos, 1886 (large 5), 1902 *1902, Rare*	1	5	30

Obverse: ***"Cocobola" head left***
Reverse: ***Arms***

Y#	KM#	Metal	Description	VF	EF	Unc
27	185	Silv	50 Centavos, 1887–88 *1888, 6 known*	50	100	350

Obverse: ***Liberty left***
Reverse: ***Arms***

Y#	KM#	Metal	Description	VF	EF	Unc
26	165	Silv	5 Decimos, 1887–88, Medellin, various head varieties, some *Very Rare* *1888, Scarce*	100	200	600
26a	166	Silv	5 Decimos, 1888–89, Medellin, large mulatto head *1889, Rare; variety with flower and star, 3 known*	100	200	600
28	186.1	Silv	50 Centavos, 1888, Bogota (.500 fine) *0.500/0.835 fine, Rare*	200	400	800
28a	176.1a	Silv	50 Centavos, 1889, 98–99 (.835 fine) (Wyon) *1898, double value; 1899, Very Scarce*	70	150	500
28a	186.2	Silv	50 Centavos, 1906–08 (.835 fine) (Heaton)	5	15	60

Fourth Centennial, Discovery of America

Obverse: ***Columbus head left***
Reverse: ***Arms***

Y#	KM#	Metal	Description	VF	EF	Unc
29	187	Silv	50 Centavos, 1892 (1.5x values for larger head size)	10	25	100

Obverse: ***Liberty right***
Reverse: ***Arms***

Y#	KM#	Metal	Description	VF	EF	Unc
30	188	Silv	10 Centavos, 1897	1.50	3	10
31	189	Silv	20 Centavos, 1897	2.50	5	10

Obverse: ***Denomination***
Reverse: ***Lazareto***

Y#	KM#	Metal	Description	VF	EF	Unc
L1	L1	Bz	*2-1/2 Centavos, 1901, 12 known*			
L2	L2	Bz	5 Centavos, 1901	1	3	30
L3	L3	Bz	10 Centavos, 1901	1	3	30
L4	L4	Bz	20 Centavos, 1901	1	3	30
L5	L5	Bz	50 Centavos, 1901	1	3	30

Obverse: ***Liberty left***
Reverse: ***Denomination (5c) or Arms (50c)***

Y#	KM#	Metal	Description	VF	EF	Unc
45	191	Silv	5 Centavos, 1902 (Philadelphia) (0.666 fine)	1	5	35
46	192	Silv	50 Centavos, 1902 (Philadelphia) (0.835 fine)	20	50	200

Obverse: ***Phrygian cap***
Reverse: ***Arms***

Y#	KM#	Metal	Description	VF	EF	Unc
23	190	C-N	2-1/2 Centavos, 1900, 02 (Waterbury), *Rare* *1900, probably a pattern (value 1.25x)*	300	800	—

SANTANDER

Revolutionary issues by General Ramon Gonzales Valencia. Struck in thin brass on one side only. Impression shows through on reverse (incuse).

Uniface design: ***SANTANDER around denomination***

Y#	KM#	Metal	Description	VF	EF	Unc
S1	A1	Br	10 Centavos, (1902), struck on rifle-cartridge casings	200	400	800
S2	A2	Br	20 Centavos, 1902, struck on rifle-cartridge casings	200	400	800
S3	A3	Br	50 Centavos, 1902, struck on rifle-cartridge casings	50	100	200

MONETARY SYSTEM

1 peso p/m (*papel moneda*, or paper money) = 1 centavo

Obverse: ***Lazareto***
Reverse: ***Denomination in wreath***

Y#	KM#	Metal	Description	VF	EF	Unc
L6	L6	C-N	1 Peso p/m, 1907	10	100	—
L7	L7	C-N	5 Pesos p/m, 1907, *Scarce*	100	400	—
L8	L8	C-N	10 Pesos p/m, 1907, round bow, *Scarce* *Wide bow variety, Rare, EF $1,000*	350	800	—
L9	L9	C-N	1 Centavo, 1921	5	15	150
L10	L10	C-N	2 Centavos, 1921	5	15	150
L11	L11	C-N	5 Centavos, 1921	5	15	150
L12	L12	C-N	10 Centavos, 1921	5	15	150
L13	L13	C-N	50 Centavos, 1921	5	15	150
L14	L14	Bz	50 Centavos, 1928, reeded edge	5	15	150

Obverse: ***Liberty right***
Reverse: ***Denomination in wreath***

Y#	KM#	Metal	Description	VF	EF	Unc
42	A279	C-N	1 Peso p/m, 1907, 10–14, 16 *1912–13, Unc $150; 1914, 16, Scarce, Unc $500*	3.00	10	70
43	B279	C-N	2 Pesos p/m, 1907, 1910, 1914	8.00	15	100
44	279	C-N	5 Pesos p/m, 1907, 09, 12–14 *1913, 14, Scarce, Unc $300*	6.00	12	80
57	275	C-N	1 Centavo, 1918–21, 33, 35–36, 38, 41, 46–48 *1918–21, 36, EF $35; 1941, no B, Rare*	3.00	5	10
59	198	C-N	2 Centavos, 1918–22, 33, 35, 38, 41–42, 46–47 *1918, 20, 21, EF $40; 1919, EF $125; 1942, EF $100*	3.50	7	30
60	199	C-N	5 Centavos, 1918–22, 24, 33, 35–36, 38–39, 41, 46, 49–50 *1918–22, 24, EF $50; some varieties Rare*	3.50	7	30
57a	275a	N-CS	1 Centavo, 1952, 54, 56–58	0.25	2	6

Obverse: ***Bolivar (narrow head)***
Reverse: ***Denomination in wreath***

Y#	KM#	Metal	Description	VF	EF	Unc
47	196	Silv	10 Centavos, 1911, 13–14, 20, 34, 37–38, 40–42, Bogota (Birmingham)	BV	1.00	10
			1920, EF $10; some varieties Scarce			
48	197	Silv	20 Centavos, 1911, 13–14, 20–22, 33, 38, 41–42, Bogota (Birmingham)	5.00	10.00	30
			Some dates Scarce in EF or better			
49	193.1	Silv	50 Centavos, 1912–19, 22–23, 31–33, Bogota (Birmingham)	10.00	20.00	75
			Some varieties Scarce or Very Scarce			
49	193.2	Silv	50 Centavos, 1914–15, 18–19, 21–22, 32–33, Medellin	10.00	20.00	75
			Some varieties Scarce to Very Rare			
70	215	C-N	20 Centavos, 1956, 59, 63–66	0.15	0.30	5

Obverse: ***Bolivar (rounded head) right***
Reverse: ***Arms***

Y#	KM#	Metal	Description	VF	EF	Unc
49a	274	Silv	50 Centavos, 1916–17, 21–22 (Philadelphia), 34 (San Francisco)	10	20	30
			1916, EF $40; 1917, EF $60			

Obverse: ***Santander right***
Reverse: ***Denomination in continuous wreath***

Y#	KM#	Metal	Description	VF	EF	Unc
64	207	Silv	10 Centavos, 1945–52 (0.500 fine)	2.00	3.00	15
65	208	Silv	20 Centavos, 1945–51 (0.500 fine)	3.00	7.00	30
			1945, EF $25			
A65	228	N-CS	50 Centavos, 1967–69	0.25	0.50	2

Obverse: ***Santander left***
Reverse: ***Denomination in continuous wreath***

Y#	KM#	Metal	Description	VF	EF	Unc
66	209	Silv	50 Centavos, 1947–48	10	20	75

Obverse: ***Phrygian cap in wreath***
Reverse: ***Denomination within sprigs***

Y#	KM#	Metal	Description	VF	EF	Unc
61	205	Bz	1 Centavo, 1942–45, 48–51, 57–66	0.50	2	6
62	210	Bz	2 Centavos, 1948–50	1.00	7	20
63	206	Bz	5 Centavos, 1942–46, 52–66	0.25	1	10
			Some varieties Scarce			
61a	205a	C-CS	1 Centavo, 1967–78	0.50	2	6
63a	206a	C-CS	5 Centavos, 1967–78	0.25	1	4
			1977, Scarce, Unc $15			

Obverse: ***Mercury head left***
Reverse: ***Denomination in wreath***

Y#	KM#	Metal	Description	VF	EF	Unc
67	211	A-Bz	2 Centavos, 1952, 65, divided legend	0.50	3	10
67a	214	A-Bz	2 Centavos, 1955, 59, continuous legend	0.50	3	10

Obverse: ***Arms***
Reverse: ***Indian Head right***

Y#	KM#	Metal	Description	VF	EF	Unc
68	212.1	C-N	10 Centavos, 1952–53 (18 mm)	0.25	1	6
68a	212.2	C-N	10 Centavos, 1954–56, 59–66 (18.5 mm)	0.25	1	6

Obverse: ***Arms***
Reverse: ***Bolivar left***

Y#	KM#	Metal	Description	VF	EF	Unc
69	213	Bill	20 Centavos, 1953 (0.300 fine)	1	3	10

Obverse: *Arms*
Reverse: *Bolivar right*

Y#	KM#	Metal	Description	VF	EF	Unc
71	217	C-N	50 Centavos, 1958–66 *1960, Rare, Unc $30*	0.50	1	5

Obverse: *Miner*
Reverse: *Arms*

Y#	KM#	Metal	Description	VF	EF	Unc
50	194	Gold	2-1/2 Pesos, 1913	BV	BV	250
51	195	Gold	5 Pesos, 1913, 1917–19 *1917, Scarce, Unc $650*	BV	BV	500

Obverse: *Bolivar (rounded head)*
Reverse: *Arms*

Y#	KM#	Metal	Description	VF	EF	Unc
52	200	Gold	2-1/2 Pesos, 1919–20	BV	BV	250
53	201	Gold	5 Pesos, 1919–24 *1921, Very Scarce, Unc $2,000*	BV	BV	500
54	202	Gold	10 Pesos, 1919, 24	BV	BV	1,000

Obverse: *Bolivar (narrow head)*
Reverse: *Arms*

Y#	KM#	Metal	Description	VF	EF	Unc
55	203	Gold	2-1/2 Pesos, 1924, 27–28 *1928, Rare, Unc $1,000*	BV	BV	250
56	204	Gold	5 Pesos, 1924–30	BV	BV	500

200th Anniversary of Milled Coinage

Y#	KM#	Metal	Description	VF	EF	Unc
72	216	Silv	1 Peso, 1956	17.50	25	35

Uprising Commemoratives, 1810–1960

Design: *Same as Y61, 63, 67a, 70–71 with dates "1810–1960"*

Y#	KM#	Metal	Description	VF	EF	Unc
73	218	Bz	1 Centavo, 1960	1	3	10

Y#	KM#	Metal	Description	VF	EF	Unc
74	219	A-Bz	2 Centavos, 1960	2	10	40
A74	220	Bz	5 Centavos, 1960	1	20	70

Y#	KM#	Metal	Description	VF	EF	Unc
75	221	C-N	10 Centavos, 1960	1.00	3	20
76	222	C-N	20 Centavos, 1960	0.25	1	20
77	223	C-N	50 Centavos, 1960	0.50	1	5

COMOROS

This former French territory is located in the Mozambique Channel off the east coast of Africa. It achieved autonomy in 1961 and proclaimed independence unilaterally in 1975. After a period of coups and attempted secessions, Comoros over the course of the early 21st century has developed into a more peaceful federal presidential republic. *Languages:* French, Swahili. *Capital:* Moroni.

MONETARY SYSTEM

100 centimes = 1 franc

PRECIOUS METAL CONTENT

Dates	Denomination	Gross Wt (g)	Fineness	Net Wt (g)	Troy Oz.
		SILVER			
1890	5 francs	25.0000	0.9000	22.5000	0.7234

Y#	KM#	Metal	Description	VF	EF	Unc
1	1	Bz	5 Centimes, AH 1308 (1890)	30	50	125
2	2	Bz	10 Centimes, AH 1308	35	60	225

Y#	KM#	Metal	Description	VF	EF	Unc
3	3	Silv	5 Francs, AH 1308	650	1,125	3,000

Y#	KM#	Metal	Description	VF	EF	Unc
4	4	Alum	1 Franc, 1964	0.20	0.40	4.50
5	5	Alum	2 Francs, 1964	0.25	0.50	6.00
6	6	Alum	5 Francs, 1964	0.30	0.55	7.50

Y#	KM#	Metal	Description	VF	EF	Unc
7	7	A-Bz	10 Francs, 1964	0.35	0.65	9.00
8	8	A-Bz	20 Francs, 1964	0.45	0.95	12.50

CONGO FREE STATE

SEE BELGIAN CONGO

COSTA RICA

A Spanish province in southern Central America between 1524 and 1821 (when it achieved independence), Costa Rica became a republic in 1848. Since then it has been one of the most democratic nations in Latin America. *Language:* Spanish. *Capital:* San Jose.

MONETARY SYSTEM

8 reales = 1 peso
2 pesos = 1 escudo
8 escudos = 1 onza, to 1864
100 centavos = 1 peso, 1865–1896
100 centimos = 1 colon, 1896–

PRECIOUS METAL CONTENT

Dates	Denomination	Gross Wt (g)	Fineness	Net Wt (g)	Troy Oz.
		SILVER			
1864–93	5 centavos	1.2680	0.7500	0.9510	0.0306
	10 centavos	2.5361	0.7500	1.9021	0.0612
	25 centavos	6.3402	0.7500	4.7552	0.1529
	50 centavos	12.6804	0.7500	9.5103	0.3058
1902–14	5 centavos	1.0000	0.9000	9.0000	0.0289
	10 centavos	2.0000	0.9000	1.8000	0.0579
	50 centavos	10.0000	0.9000	9.0000	0.2894
1917–24	10 centavos	2.0000	0.5000	1.0000	0.0322
	25 centavos	3.4500	0.6500	2.2425	0.0721
	50 centavos	10.0000	0.5000	5.0000	0.1608
		GOLD			
1850–64	1/2 escudo	1.6000	0.8750	1.4000	0.0450
	1 escudo	3.1000	0.8750	2.7125	0.0872
	2 escudos	6.3000	0.8750	5.5125	0.1772
	1/2 onza	12.6000	0.8750	11.0250	0.3545
1864–76	1 peso	1.4677	0.8750	1.2843	0.0413
	2 pesos	2.9355	0.8750	2.5685	0.0826
	5 pesos	7.3387	0.8750	6.4213	0.2064
	10 pesos	14.6774	0.8750	12.8427	0.4129
1873	5 pesos	8.0645	0.9000	7.2581	0.2333
	20 pesos	32.2581	0.9000	29.0323	0.9334
1897–1928	2 colones	1.5560	0.9000	1.4004	0.0450
	5 colones	3.8900	0.9000	3.5010	0.1126
	10 colones	7.7800	0.9000	7.0020	0.2251
	20 colones	15.5600	0.9000	14.0040	0.4502

Y#	KM#	Metal	Description	VF	EF	Unc
5	101	Silv	1/16 Peso, 1850–55, 62 *1862, EF $1,300*	150	300	950
6	102	Silv	1/8 Peso, 1850–55	500	1,000	3,000
7	103	Silv	1/4 Peso, 1850–55	75	175	550

Y#	KM#	Metal	Description	VF	EF	Unc
22	97	Gold	1/2 Escudo, 1850–64	200	400	—
23	98	Gold	1 Escudo, 1850–55	250	750	—
24	99	Gold	2 Escudos, 1850–63	450	1,200	—
25	100	Gold	1/2 Onza, 1850	900	2,000	—

Decimal System, *1864–1896*

Y#	KM#	Metal	Description	VF	EF	Unc
32	108	C-N	1/4 Centavo, ND (1865)	250	500	—

Note: There are many counterfeits of Y32.

Y#	KM#	Metal	Description	VF	EF	Unc
30	109	C-N	1 Centavo, 1865–68	30	100	—

Y#	KM#	Metal	Description	VF	EF	Unc
31	120	C-N	1 Centavo, 1874	15	30	—

Y#	KM#	Metal	Description	VF	EF	Unc
9	110	Silv	5 Centavos, 1865–75	25	65	400
10	111	Silv	10 Centavos, 1865–72 (19.5 mm) *1868, 72, VF $200*	50	125	600
10a	121	Silv	10 Centavos, 1875 (18 mm)	75	300	900
11	105	Silv	25 Centavos, 1864, small 25Cs	200	700	—
11a	106	Silv	25 Centavos, 1864–75, large 25Cs	75	200	700
12	112	Silv	50 Centavos, 1865–75	150	1,000	—

Y#	KM#	Metal	Description	VF	EF	Unc
26	107/116	Gold	1 Peso, 1864–72	50	100	150
27	113	Gold	2 Pesos, 1866–68	75	125	200
27a	122	Gold	2 Pesos, 1876	500	700	1,000

Y#	KM#	Metal	Description	VF	EF	Unc
28	114	Gold	5 Pesos, 1867–70	150	250	450
28a	117	Gold	5 Pesos, 1873–75	600	1,000	1,200
29	115	Gold	10 Pesos, 1870–72	BV	275	500
29a	123	Gold	10 Pesos, 1876	1,500	2,200	3,000

Designs: *As Y26–29*
Reverse: *LEI 0.00 G.W. added to legend*

Y#	KM#	Metal	Description	VF	EF	Unc
33	118	Gold	5 Pesos, 1873	1,500	2,500	4,500
34	119	Gold	20 Pesos, 1873	6,000	12,000	20,000

Y#	KM#	Metal	Description	VF	EF	Unc
13	125	Silv	5 Centavos, 1885–87	15	40	150
14	126	Silv	10 Centavos, 1886–87	15	40	150
15	127	Silv	25 Centavos, 1886–87	25	60	175
16	124	Silv	50 Centavos, 1880–90	12	30	75

Reverse: ***HEATON BIRMn***

Y#	KM#	Metal	Description	VF	EF	Unc
17	128	Silv	5 Centavos, 1889–92	5.00	25	100
18	129	Silv	10 Centavos, 1889–92	7.50	45	125
19	130	Silv	25 Centavos, 1889–93	7.50	40	100

Y#	KM#	Metal	Description	VF	EF	Unc
20	133–136	Silv	50 Centavos of Colombia countermarked on both sides (1889)	200	400	—

NEW COINAGE SYSTEM, *1896–*

Y#	KM#	Metal	Description	VF	EF	Unc
46	144	C-N	2 Centimos, 1903	1	3	15

.900 Silver

Y#	KM#	Metal	Description	VF	EF	Unc
39	145	Silv	5 Centimos, 1905–14	3	7.50	20
40	146	Silv	10 Centimos, 1905–14	5	15.00	30
41	143	Silv	50 Centimos, 1902–14 *1914, Unc $5,000*	85	175.00	375

.500 Silver

Y#	KM#	Metal	Description	VF	EF	Unc
42	148	Silv	10 Centavos, 1917	2	5	15
A42	150	Silv	50 Centavos, 1917–18	—	2,500	4,000

Note: All YA42 were counterstamped as Y44 except for 10 presentation pieces.

.650 Silver

Y#	KM#	Metal	Description	VF	EF	Unc
45	168	Silv	25 Centimos, 1924	7.50	15	30

REVALUATION, 1923

Y#	KM#	Metal	Description	VF	EF	Unc
43	Several	Silv	50 Centimos, 1923 stamped on various 25c pieces	10	20	75
44	162–165	Silv	UN COLON, 1923 stamped on 50c pieces of various dates	20	40	150

Y#	KM#	Metal	Description	VF	EF	Unc
35	139	Gold	2 Colones, 1900–28	BV	100	150
36	142	Gold	5 Colones, 1899–1900	BV	BV	250
37	140	Gold	10 Colones, 1897–1900	BV	425	500
38	141	Gold	20 Colones, 1897–1900	BV	850	1,000

Y#	KM#	Metal	Description	VF	EF	Unc
47	147	Br	5 Centavos, 1917–19 *1917, Unc $1,250*	17.50	35	150

Y#	KM#	Metal	Description	VF	EF	Unc
48	148–149	Br	10 Centavos, 1917–19	20	50	175
49	151	Br	5 Centimos, 1920–41	2	5	85
50	152	Br	10 Centimos, 1920–22, reverse GCR at lower right	5	15	150
54	174	Br	10 Centimos, 1936–41, reverse GCR below wreath	2	5	70
51	169	Bz	5 Centimos, 1929	2	5	70
52	170	Bz	10 Centimos, 1929	2	5	70

BANCO INTERNACIONAL DE COSTA RICA

Reverse: ***Initials B.I.C.R.***

Y#	KM#	Metal	Description	VF	EF	Unc
55	171	C-N	25 Centimos, 1935	2	5	15
56	172	C-N	50 Centimos, 1935	3	8	35
57	173	C-N	1 Colon, 1935	5	10	50

Banco Nacional de Costa Rica

Reverse: ***Initials B.N.C.R.***

Y#	KM#	Metal	Description	VF	EF	Unc
58	178	C-N	5 Centimos, 1942, struck over 2c, Y46	1.00	3.00	15.00
A58	179	Br	5 Centimos, 1942–47	1.00	3.00	15.00
B58	180	Br	10 Centimos, 1942–47	1.50	4.50	17.50

Y#	KM#	Metal	Description	VF	EF	Unc
59	175	C-N	25 Centimos, 1937–48	1.00	2.00	5
60	176	C-N	50 Centimos, 1937	2.00	5.00	30
60a	182	C-N	50 Centimos, 1948, larger	0.25	0.50	5
61	177	C-N	1 Colon, 1937–48	0.75	2.00	5
62	183	C-N	2 Colones, 1948	1.00	4.00	10

Y#	KM#	Metal	Description	VF	EF	Unc
63	181	Br	25 Centimos, 1944–46	1.25	5	17.50

Banco Central de Costa Rica

Reverse: ***Initials B.C.C.R.***

Y#	KM#	Metal	Description	VF	EF	Unc
A64	A184	C-N	5 Centimos, 1951, reverse B.C. / C.R. divided	0.25	1	4

Y#	KM#	Metal	Description	VF	EF	Unc
64	184	C-N	5 Centimos, 1951, 69–78, reverse B.C.C.R. undivided	0.05	0.10	0.40
65	185	C-N	10 Centimos, 1951, 69–76	0.05	0.15	0.75

Y#	KM#	Metal	Description	VF	EF	Unc
66	184.1a	S S	5 Centimos, 1953–67	0.05	0.10	0.35
67	185.1a	S S	10 Centimos, 1953–79	0.05	0.10	0.50
68	186.1	S S	1 Colon, 1954	0.50	2.00	10.00
69	187.1	S S	2 Colones, 1954	0.50	2.00	15.00
68a	186.1a	C-N	1 Colon, 1961–78	0.25	0.50	2.00
69a	187.1a	C-N	2 Colones, 1961–78	30.00	60.00	2.25

CRETE

The largest of the Greek islands, Crete became part of the Turkish Empire in the late 17th century. It was ceded to Egypt after the Greek revolution of the 1820s, and returned to Turkey in 1840. After the second Balkan War, Crete was ceded to Greece in 1913. *Language:* Greek. *Capital:* Canea.

MONETARY SYSTEM

100 lepta = 1 drachma

PRECIOUS METAL CONTENT

Dates	Denomination	Gross Wt (g)	Fineness	Net Wt (g)	Troy Oz.
		SILVER			
1901	50 lepta	2.5000	0.8350	2.0871	0.0671
	1 drachma	5.0000	0.8350	4.1750	0.1342
	2 drachmai	10.0000	0.8350	8.3500	0.2685
	5 drachmai	25.0000	0.9000	22.5000	0.7234

Under Greek Administration, *1898–1906*

Y#	KM#	Metal	Description	VF	EF	Unc
1	1	Bz	1 Lepton, 1900–01	20.00	40	125
2	2	Bz	2 Lepta, 1900–01	22.50	50	145

Y#	KM#	Metal	Description	VF	EF	Unc
3	3	C-N	5 Lepta, 1900	20	50	275
4	4	C-N	10 Lepta, 1900	20	65	400
5	5	C-N	20 Lepta, 1900	25	75	600

Note: For similar coins dated 1894–95, see Greece Y16–18.

Y#	KM#	Metal	Description	VF	EF	Unc
6	6	Silv	50 Lepta, 1901	60	150	1,000
7	7	Silv	1 Drachma, 1901	150	650	1,250
8	8	Silv	2 Drachmai, 1901	275	900	3,500
9	9	Silv	5 Drachmai, 1901	300	2,000	9,000

CUBA

The largest and westernmost of the Caribbean islands, Cuba was discovered by Columbus in 1492 and Spanish settlements were in place by 1511. With U.S. military aid, independence was achieved in 1899. The republic came under the rule of a military junta between 1933 and 1959, when guerrillas ousted the government and installed Fidel Castro as president of the now avowedly communist state. *Language:* Spanish. *Capital:* Havana.

MONETARY SYSTEM
100 centavos = 1 peso

PRECIOUS METAL CONTENT

Dates	Denomination	Gross Wt (g)	Fineness	Net Wt (g)	Troy Oz.
		SILVER			
1897–98	1 peso	22.5500	0.9000	20.2985	0.6526
1915–53	10 centavos	2.5000	0.9000	2.2488	0.0723
	20 centavos	5.0000	0.9000	4.4976	0.1446
	25 centavos	6.2500	0.9000	5.6236	0.1808
	40 centavos	10.0000	0.9000	8.9984	0.2893
	50 centavos	12.5000	0.9000	11.2503	0.3617
	1 peso	26.7295	0.9000	24.0589	0.7735
		GOLD			
1915–16	1 peso	1.6718	0.9000	1.5046	0.0484
	2 pesos	3.3436	0.9000	3.0092	0.0967
	4 pesos	6.6872	0.9000	6.0185	0.1935
	5 pesos	8.3591	0.9000	7.5232	0.2419
	10 pesos	16.7181	0.9000	15.0463	0.4837
	20 pesos	33.4363	0.9000	30.0926	0.9675

Y#	KM#	Metal	Description	VF	EF	Unc
1	N/A	Silv	Souvenir Peso, 1897 (3 vars)	125	200	1,000

Y#	KM#	Metal	Description	VF	EF	Unc
2	A8	Silv	1 Peso, 1898	850	1,250	3,500

Y#	KM#	Metal	Description	VF	EF	Unc
3	9.1	C-N	1 Centavo, 1915–38 ("2.5 G.")	1.00	3.00	25
					Proof: $800	
4	A10	C-N	2 Centavos, 1915–16	1.25	4.50	35
					Proof: $825	
5	11.1	C-N	5 Centavos, 1915–20 ("5.0 G")	1.50	5.50	40
					Proof: $850	

Y#	KM#	Metal	Description	VF	EF	Unc
3a	9.2a	Br	1 Centavo, 1943	0.50	1.50	30
5a	11.2	Br	5 Centavos, 1943	1.00	3.00	35

Y#	KM#	Metal	Description	VF	EF	Unc
3b	9.2	C-N	1 Centavo, 1946, 61	0.50	1	3.00
5b	11.3	C-N	5 Centavos, 1946, 60, 61	0.50	1	5.50

Y#	KM#	Metal	Description	VF	EF	Unc
6	A12	Silv	10 Centavos, 1915–49	2.00	5	20
			1916, 20, EF $12.50			*Proof: $1,250*
7	13	Silv	20 Centavos, 1915–49	3.50	7	25
			1932, VF $1,350			*Proof: $2,250*
8	14	Silv	40 Centavos, 1915–20	15.00	30	500
			1916, 20, VF $55			*Proof: $2,250*
9	15	Silv	1 Peso, 1915–34	25.00	50	175
						Proof: $3,500

Y#	KM#	Metal	Description	VF	EF	Unc
10	16	Gold	1 Peso, 1915–16	100	150	550
						Proof: $2,500
11	17	Gold	2 Pesos, 1915–16	BV	225	325
						Proof: $3,000
12	18	Gold	4 Pesos, 1915–16	BV	350	750
						Proof: $4,000
13	19	Gold	5 Pesos, 1915–16	BV	475	625
						Proof: $4,500
14	20	Gold	10 Pesos, 1915–16	BV	BV	950
						Proof: $15,000
15	21	Gold	20 Pesos, 1915–16	BV	1,850	2,250
			1915 Proof: $40,000; 1916 Proof: Rare			

Y#	KM#	Metal	Description	VF	EF	Unc
16	22	Silv	1 Peso, 1934–39	35	60	300
			1937, EF $850			

50th Anniversary of Republic

Y#	KM#	Metal	Description	VF	EF	Unc
17	23	Silv	10 Centavos, 1952	3	6.00	20
18	24	Silv	20 Centavos, 1952	5	9.00	20
19	25	Silv	40 Centavos, 1952	10	17.50	50

Jose Marti Centennial

Y#	KM#	Metal	Description	VF	EF	Unc
20	26	Br	1 Centavo, 1953	1	4	15
						Proof: $1,500

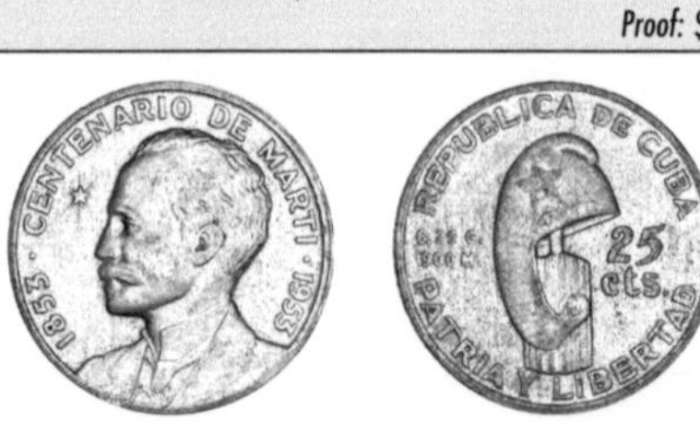

Y#	KM#	Metal	Description	VF	EF	Unc
21	27	Silv	25 Centavos, 1953	5	8	20

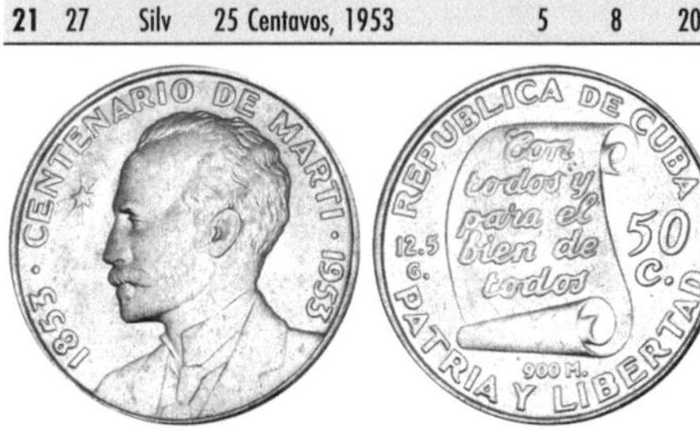

Y#	KM#	Metal	Description	VF	EF	Unc
22	28	Silv	50 Centavos, 1953	BV	12.50	25

Y#	KM#	Metal	Description	VF	EF	Unc
23	29	Silv	1 Peso, 1953	25	40	75

Y#	KM#	Metal	Description	VF	EF	Unc
24	30	C-N	1 Centavo, 1958	0.75	2	17.50

SECOND REPUBLIC, *1962–*

CURRENCY REFORM, AUGUST 1961

Y#	KM#	Metal	Description	VF	EF	Unc
25	31	C-N	20 Centavos, 1962, 68	1.00	2.50	8.50
26	32	C-N	40 Centavos, 1962	3.00	5.00	15.00
27	33.1	Alum	1 Centavo, 1963–82	0.25	0.50	2.00
28	34	Alum	5 Centavos, 1963–72	0.25	0.50	2.00

CURAÇAO

One of the Leeward Islands in the West Indies, off the coast of Venezuela, Curaçao was discovered by Spain in 1499. It passed to the Dutch in 1624, and was a colony until becoming part of the Netherlands Antilles in 1954. The country ratified its federation with the Netherlands in 1994. *Languages:* Dutch, Papiamento, English, Spanish. *Capital:* Willemstad.

MONETARY SYSTEM
100 cents = 1 gulden

PRECIOUS METAL CONTENT

Dates	Denomination	Gross Wt (g)	Fineness	Net Wt (g)	Troy Oz.
		SILVER			
1900–48	1/10 gulden / 10 cents	1.4000	0.6400	0.8958	0.0288
	1/4 gulden / 25 cents	3.5800	0.6400	2.2893	0.0736
	1 gulden	10.0000	0.7200	7.2000	0.2315
	2-1/2 gulden	25.0000	0.7200	19.0000	0.5787

WILHELMINA, *1890–1948*

First Coinage

Y#	KM#	Metal	Description	VF	EF	Unc
1	36	Silv	1/10 Gulden, 1901	40	90	175
2	35	Silv	1/4 Gulden, 1900	45	100	200

Second Coinage

Y#	KM#	Metal	Description	VF	EF	Unc
3	41	Bz	1 Cent, 1944, 47	3.00	7.00	15.00
4	42	Bz	2-1/2 Cents, 1944–48	3.25	7.50	17.50

Y#	KM#	Metal	Description	VF	EF	Unc
5	43	Silv	1/10 Gulden, 1944, 47	3.00	7.50	12.50
6	44	Silv	1/4 Gulden, 1944, 47	4.50	12.50	30.00

Y#	KM#	Metal	Description	VF	EF	Unc
7	45	Silv	1 Gulden, 1944	15	30.00	65
10	46	Silv	2-1/2 Gulden, 1944	15	18.50	30

For other World War II issues, see Netherlands Y34a, 36b, 43a, and 44a.

Third Coinage

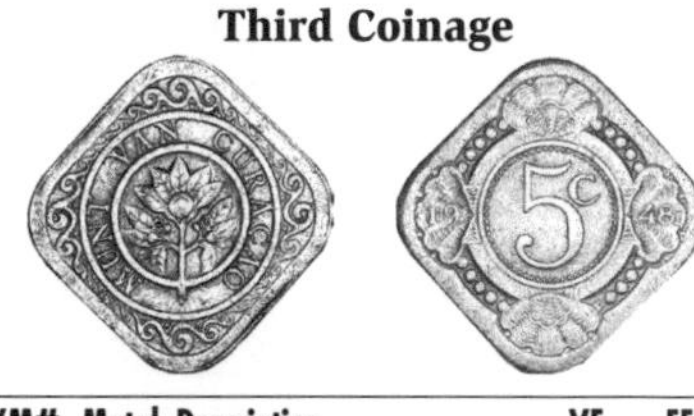

Y#	KM#	Metal	Description	VF	EF	Unc
9	47	C-N	5 Cents, 1948, square	4	6	12.50

Y#	KM#	Metal	Description	VF	EF	Unc
8	48	Silv	1/10 Gulden, 1948	3	7.50	12.50

For issues since 1952, see Netherlands Antilles.

CYPRUS

The Turks wrested this eastern Mediterranean Sea island from the Greeks in 1571. The British annexed it in 1878 and it became a crown colony until 1960 when it became an independent republic within the British Commonwealth. Since 1974 the nation has been effectively divided into Greek (southern) and Turkish (northern) regions. *Languages:* Greek, Turkish, English. *Capital:* Lefkosia (Nicosia).

MONETARY SYSTEM

9 piastres = 1 shilling, to 1955
1,000 mils = 1 pound, 1955–

PRECIOUS METAL CONTENT

Dates	Denomination	Gross Wt (g)	Fineness	Net Wt (g)	Troy Oz.
		SILVER			
1901–40	3 piastres	1.8851	0.9250	1.7437	0.0561
	4-1/2 piastres	2.8276	0.9250	2.6155	0.0841
	9 piastres	5.6552	0.9250	5.2311	0.1682
	18 piastres	11.3104	0.9250	10.4621	0.3364
	45 piastres	28.2759	0.9250	26.1552	0.8409

VICTORIA, *1837–1901*

Y#	KM#	Metal	Description	VF	EF	Unc
1	1	Bz	1/4 Piastre, 1879–1901	45	75	200
						Proof: $1,650
2	2	Bz	1/2 Piastre, 1879–1900	45	75	200
						Proof: $1,650
3	3	Bz	1 Piastre, 1879–1900	75	125	300
						Proof: $1,650

Y#	KM#	Metal	Description	VF	EF	Unc
4	4	Silv	3 Piastres, 1901	25	75	1,000
						Proof: $1,750

Y#	KM#	Metal	Description	VF	EF	Unc
5	5	Silv	4 1/2 Piastres, 1901	40	150	800
						Proof: $2,250
6	6	Silv	9 Piastres, 1901	60	165	1,000
						Proof: $2,750
7	7	Silv	18 Piastres, 1901	150	250	2,500
						Proof: $3,000

EDWARD VII, *1901–1910*

Y#	KM#	Metal	Description	VF	EF	Unc
8	8	Bz	1/4 Piastre, 1902–08	25	90	300
			1902, VF $100; 1908, VF $350			
9	11	Bz	1/2 Piastre, 1908	350	750	5,500
10	12	Bz	1 Piastre, 1908	375	750	6,000

Y#	KM#	Metal	Description	VF	EF	Unc
11	9	Silv	9 Piastres, 1907	125	700	2,000
12	10	Silv	18 Piastres, 1907	125	750	6,000

GEORGE V, *1910–1936*

Y#	KM#	Metal	Description	VF	EF	Unc
13	16	Bz	1/4 Piastre, 1922, 26	25	45	175
						Proof: $2,750
14	17	Bz	1/2 Piastre, 1922–31	30	60	250
						Proof: $2,000
15	18	Bz	1 Piastre, 1922–31	45	150	650
						Proof: $4,000

Y#	KM#	Metal	Description	VF	EF	Unc
16	20	C-N	1/2 Piastre, 1934, scalloped	3.50	10	75
						Proof: $2,000
17	21	C-N	1 Piastre, 1934, scalloped	3.50	10	75
						Proof: $2,000

Reverse: ***Design like Y5–7***

Y#	KM#	Metal	Description	VF	EF	Unc
18	15	Silv	4-1/2 Piastres, 1921	35	60	350
19	13	Silv	9 Piastres, 1913–21	30	100	350
20	14	Silv	18 Piastres, 1913, 21	85	200	1,500

50th Anniversary of British Rule

Y#	KM#	Metal	Description	VF	EF	Unc
21	19	Silv	45 Piastres, 1928	50	100	250
						Proof: $1,500

GEORGE VI,
1936–1952

Y#	KM#	Metal	Description	VF	EF	Unc
22	22	C-N	1/2 Piastre, 1938, scalloped	3.50	10	30
						Proof: $250
23	23	C-N	1 Piastre, 1938, scalloped	3.50	10	25
						Proof: $300
22a	22a	Bz	1/2 Piastre, 1942–45, scalloped	3.50	10	30
						Proof: $350
23a	23a	Bz	1 Piastre, 1942–46, scalloped	3.50	10	30
						Proof: $350

Y#	KM#	Metal	Description	VF	EF	Unc
28	24	Silv	4-1/2 Piastres, 1938	10.00	250	100
						Proof: $450
29	25	Silv	9 Piastres, 1938, 40	12.50	30	70
						Proof: $400
30	26	Silv	18 Piastres, 1938, 40	20.00	45	75
			1938 Proof Set: $6,500			*Proof: $450*

Y#	KM#	Metal	Description	VF	EF	Unc
26	27	C-N	1 Shilling, 1947	6	12.50	125
						Proof: $3,500
27	28	C-N	2 Shillings, 1947	10	20.00	200
						Proof: $4,000

New Legend: ***GEORGIUS SEXTUS DEI GRATIA REX***

Y#	KM#	Metal	Description	VF	EF	Unc
31	29	Bz	1/2 Piastre, 1949	1.50	3	60
						Proof: $250
32	30	Bz	1 Piastre, 1949, scalloped	3.00	6	60
						Proof: $300

Y#	KM#	Metal	Description	VF	EF	Unc
33	31	C-N	1 Shilling, 1949	6	12.50	125
						Proof: $350
34	32	C-N	2 Shillings, 1949	10	20.00	200
			1949 Proof Set: $6,500			*Proof: $400*

ELIZABETH II,
1952–1960
DECIMAL CURRENCY,
1955–2022

Y#	KM#	Metal	Description	VF	EF	Unc
35	33	Bz	3 Mils, 1955	0.35	0.75	4
						Proof: $50

Y#	KM#	Metal	Description	VF	EF	Unc
36	34	Bz	5 Mils, 1955–56	0.50	1	7.50
						Proof: $70

Y#	KM#	Metal	Description	VF	EF	Unc
37	35	C-N	25 Mils, 1955	0.60	1.25	20
						Proof: $85

Y#	KM#	Metal	Description	VF	EF	Unc
38	36	C-N	50 Mils, 1955	1	2	25
						Proof: $85

Y#	KM#	Metal	Description	VF	EF	Unc
39	37	C-N	100 Mils, 1955, 57	1	2.50	30
			1957, VF $100; 1957 Proof, Rare			*Proof: $85*

REPUBLIC, *1960–*

Y#	KM#	Metal	Description	VF	EF	Unc
41	38	Alum	1 Mil, 1963–72, 12-sided	0.05	0.10	1.25

Y#	KM#	Metal	Description	VF	EF	Unc
42	39	Bz	5 Mils, 1963–80	0.10	0.15	1.50

Y#	KM#	Metal	Description	VF	EF	Unc
43	40	C-N	25 Mils, 1963–82	0.15	0.20	1.50

Y#	KM#	Metal	Description	VF	EF	Unc
44	41	C-N	50 Mils, 1963–82	0.25	0.50	1.50

Y#	KM#	Metal	Description	VF	EF	Unc
45	42	C-N	100 Mils, 1963–82	0.35	0.65	3

CZECHOSLOVAKIA

This Central European republic was created in 1918 through the dissolution of the Austro-Hungarian Empire following World War I. The communists won control in the 1946 elections. The federation was dissolved in 1993, resulting in the creation of the Czech Republic and Slovakia. *Languages:* Czech, Slovak. *Capital:* Prague.

MONETARY SYSTEM

100 haleru = 1 koruna

PRECIOUS METAL CONTENT

Dates	Denomination	Gross Wt (g)	Fineness	Net Wt (g)	Troy Oz.
		SILVER			
1928–37	5 korun	7.0000	0.5000	3.5000	0.1125
	10 korun	10.0000	0.7000	7.0000	0.2251
	20 korun	12.0000	0.7000	8.4000	0.2701
1939–44	10 korun	7.0000	0.5000	3.5000	0.1125
	20 korun	15.0000	0.5000	7.5000	0.2411
	50 korun	16.5000	0.7000	11.5500	0.3713
1947–51	50 korun	10.0000	0.5000	5.0000	0.1608
	100 korun	14.0000	0.5000	7.0000	0.2251
1954–64	10 korun	12.0000	0.5000	6.0000	0.1929
	25 korun	16.0000	0.5000	8.0000	0.2572
	50 korun	20.0000	0.9000	18.0000	0.5787
	100 korun	24.0000	0.9000	21.6021	0.6945

Dates	Denomination	Gross Wt (g)	Fineness	Net Wt (g)	Troy Oz.
		GOLD			
1923–51	1 dukat	3.4909	0.9861	3.4424	0.1107
	2 dukaty	6.9818	0.9861	6.8848	0.2213
	5 dukatu	17.4545	0.9861	17.2119	0.5534
	10 dukatu	34.9089	0.9861	34.4237	1.1067

Y#	KM#	Metal	Description	VF	EF	Unc
1	5	Zinc	2 Halere, 1923–25 *1923, EF $12.50*	3.50	5	35

Y#	KM#	Metal	Description	VF	EF	Unc
2	6	Bz	5 Haleru, 1923–38 *1924, Rare; 1926, EF $45; 1930, 32, EF $20*	1.00	2.25	6.50
3	3	Bz	10 Haleru, 1922–38	1.25	2.50	7.50

Y#	KM#	Metal	Description	VF	EF	Unc
4	1	C-N	20 Haleru, 1921–38 *1925,30, V4; 1933, VF $25*	0.35	0.60	3

Y#	KM#	Metal	Description	VF	EF	Unc
5	16	C-N	25 Haleru, 1932–33 *1923, EF $5,500*	1.25	2.25	4.50

Y#	KM#	Metal	Description	VF	EF	Unc
6	2	C-N	50 Haleru, 1921–31 *1926, VF $20; 1930, Rare*	0.45	0.75	2.25

Y#	KM#	Metal	Description	VF	EF	Unc
7	4	C-N	1 Koruna, 1922–38	0.50	0.75	3

Y#	KM#	Metal	Description	VF	EF	Unc
8	10	C-N	5 Korun, 1925–27 (30 mm) *1927, EF $150*	3.00	6.00	22.50
8a	11	Silv	5 Korun, 1928–32 (27 mm)	2.50	7.50	25.00
8b	11a	Nick	5 Korun, 1937–38 (27 mm) *1937, EF $4,400*	3.00	4.50	12.50

10th Anniversary of Independence

Y#	KM#	Metal	Description	VF	EF	Unc
11	12	Silv	10 Korun, 1928	7.50	10	17.50

Y#	KM#	Metal	Description	VF	EF	Unc
12	15	Silv	10 Korun, 1930–33	5	10	15

Y#	KM#	Metal	Description	VF	EF	Unc
13	17	Silv	20 Korun, 1933–34	7.50	10	15

Death of President Masaryk

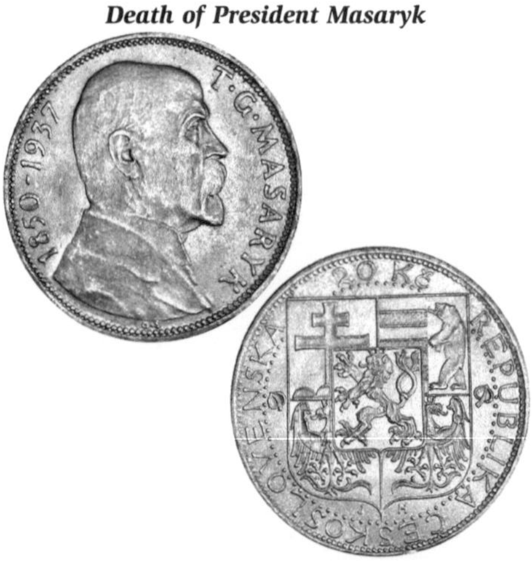

Y#	KM#	Metal	Description	VF	EF	Unc
14	18	Silv	20 Korun, 1937	7.50	10	20

Trade Coins (YA15–18)

Fifth Anniversary of the Republic

Design: *As Y15*

Y#	KM#	Metal	Description	VF	EF	Unc
A15	7	Gold	1 Dukat, 1923	3,000	4,000	5,000

Note: All pieces of YA15 were serially numbered (from 1 to 1,000) below the figure on reverse.

Y#	KM#	Metal	Description	VF	EF	Unc
15	8	Gold	1 Dukat, 1923–39, 51	200	400	550
16	9	Gold	2 Dukaty, 1923–38, 51	425	1,500	2,250

Y#	KM#	Metal	Description	VF	EF	Unc
17	13	Gold	5 Dukatu, 1929–38, 51	2,500	3,500	5,500
18	14	Gold	10 Dukatu, 1929–38, 51	3,500	7,500	10,000

CZECHOSLOVAKIA–SLOVAKIA, GERMAN PROTECTORATE

SEE SLOVAKIA

CZECHOSLOVAKIA–BOHEMIA AND MORAVIA, GERMAN PROTECTORATE

SEE BOHEMIA AND MORAVIA

REPUBLIC, *1945–1960*

Y#	KM#	Metal	Description	VF	EF	Unc
33	20	Bz	20 Haleru, 1947–50 *1947, Unc $450*	0.20	0.45	1.50

Y#	KM#	Metal	Description	VF	EF	Unc
35	21	Bz	50 Haleru, 1947–50	0.25	0.40	1

Y#	KM#	Metal	Description	VF	EF	Unc
37	19	C-N	1 Koruna, 1946–47	0.40	0.65	1.25

Y#	KM#	Metal	Description	VF	EF	Unc
39	23	C-N	2 Koruny, 1947–48	0.45	0.80	1.75

Y#	KM#	Metal	Description	VF	EF	Unc
34	31	Alum	20 Haleru, 1951–52	0.20	0.30	1.25
36	32	Alum	50 Haleru, 1951–53	0.45	0.65	1.25
38	22	Alum	1 Koruna, 1947–53 *1947, EF $1,500*	0.35	0.60	1.25

Y#	KM#	Metal	Description	VF	EF	Unc
A39	34	Alum	5 Korun, 1952	40	80	185

Note: YA39 was not released for circulation because of the 1953 currency reform.

Third Anniversary of Slovak National Uprising

Y#	KM#	Metal	Description	VF	EF	Unc
40	24	Silv	50 Korun, 1947	7.50	10	17.50

Third Anniversary of Prague Uprising

Y#	KM#	Metal	Description	VF	EF	Unc
41	25	Silv	50 Korun, 1948	7.50	10	17.50

600th Anniversary of Kerlovy University at Prague

Y#	KM#	Metal	Description	VF	EF	Unc
42	26	Silv	100 Korun, 1948	7.50	10	17.50

30th Anniversary of Independence

Y#	KM#	Metal	Description	VF	EF	Unc
43	27	Silv	100 Korun, 1948	7.50	10	17.50

700th Anniversary of Mining Privileges of Jihlava

Y#	KM#	Metal	Description	VF	EF	Unc
44	29	Silv	100 Korun, 1949	7.50	10	17.50

70th Birthday of Stalin

Y#	KM#	Metal	Description	VF	EF	Unc
45	28	Silv	50 Korun, 1949	5.00	7.50	12.50
46	30	Silv	100 Korun, 1949	7.50	10.00	17.50

30th Anniversary of Communist Party

Y#	KM#	Metal	Description	VF	EF	Unc
47	33	Silv	100 Korun, 1951	7.50	10	17.50

CURRENCY REFORM, *1953*

Y#	KM#	Metal	Description	VF	EF	Unc
48	35	Alum	1 Haler, 1953–60	0.10	0.15	0.54
49	36	Alum	3 Halere, 1953–54	0.10	0.15	0.50
50	37	Alum	5 Haleru, 1953–55	0.15	0.25	0.75
51	38	Alum	10 Haleru, 1953–58 *1955, Unc $65; 1958, Unc $55*	0.20	1.25	8.50
52	39	Alum	25 Haleru, 1953–54 *1954, Unc $25*	0.35	0.75	7.50

Y#	KM#	Metal	Description	VF	EF	Unc
61	46	A-Bz	1 Koruna, 1957–60	0.30	0.45	5

10th Anniversary of Slovak National Uprising

Y#	KM#	Metal	Description	VF	EF	Unc
53	40	Silv	10 Korun, 1954	3.50	5	9
					Proof: $27.50	
54	41	Silv	25 Korun, 1954	8.00	10	25
					Proof: $35	

10th Anniversary of Liberation From Nazis, May 9, 1945

Y#	KM#	Metal	Description	VF	EF	Unc
55	42	Silv	10 Korun, 1955	5	10	25
					Proof: $30	

Y#	KM#	Metal	Description	VF	EF	Unc
56	43	Silv	25 Korun, 1955	5	7.50	15
					Proof: $27.50	

Y#	KM#	Metal	Description	VF	EF	Unc
57	44	Silv	50 Korun, 1955	10	15	25

Y#	KM#	Metal	Description	VF	EF	Unc
58	45	Silv	100 Korun, 1955	15	20	55

250th Anniversary of Technical High Schools in Prague

Y#	KM#	Metal	Description	VF	EF	Unc
59	47	Silv	10 Korun, 1957	3	5.50	10 *Proof: $30*

Bishop Komensky Commemorative

Y#	KM#	Metal	Description	VF	EF	Unc
60	48	Silv	10 Korun, 1957	3	5.50	10 *Proof: $30*

SOCIALIST REPUBLIC, *1960–1990*

New Legend: ***CESKOSLOVENSKA SOCIALISTICKA REPUBLIKA***

Y#	KM#	Metal	Description	VF	EF	Unc
62	51	Alum	1 Haler, 1962–63	0.10	0.15	0.25
63	52	Alum	3 Halere, 1962–63	0.10	0.15	0.25
64	53	Alum	5 Haleru, 1962–76	0.10	0.15	0.25
65	49.1	Alum	10 Haleru, 1961–71	0.10	0.20	0.55
A65	49.2	Alum	10 Haleru, 1963, obverse of Y67 (flat-top 3)	30.00	60.00	150.00
66	54	Alum	25 Haleru, 1962–64	0.15	0.20	0.55

Y#	KM#	Metal	Description	VF	EF	Unc
67	55.1	Bz	50 Haleru, 1963–71	0.20	0.30	0.65

Y#	KM#	Metal	Description	VF	EF	Unc
68	50	A-Bz	1 Koruna, 1961–90	0.15	0.30	0.75

20th Anniversary of Slovak National Uprising

Y#	KM#	Metal	Description	VF	EF	Unc
69	56	Silv	10 Korun, 1964	3	4.50	8.50

DANISH WEST INDIES

This group of about 50 islands lies in the Caribbean, southeast of Puerto Rico. They were purchased from Denmark by the United States in 1917 and became the U.S. Virgin Islands, a territory of the United States with local self-government, *Language:* English. *Capital:* Charlotte Amalie.

MONETARY SYSTEM

5 bits = 1 cent
20 cents = 1 franc
5 francs = 1 daler

PRECIOUS METAL CONTENT

Dates	Denomination	Gross Wt (g)	Fineness	Net Wt (g)	Troy Oz.
		SILVER			
1878–79	5 cents	1.7400	0.6250	1.0875	0.0350
	10 cents	3.4800	0.6250	2.1750	0.0699
	20 cents	6.9600	0.6250	4.3500	0.1399
1905–07	10 cents / 50 bit	2.5000	0.8000	2.0000	0.0643
	20 cents / 1 franc	5.0000	0.8000	4.0000	0.1286
	40 cents / 2 francs	10.0000	0.8000	8.0000	0.2572
		GOLD			
1904–05	4 daler / 20 francs	6.4516	0.9000	5.8064	0.1867
	10 daler / 50 francs	16.1290	0.9000	14.5161	0.4667

CHRISTIAN IX, *1863–1906*

Y#	KM#	Metal	Description	VF	EF	Unc
1	68	Bz	1 Cent, 1868–83 *1879, $250*	20	50	400 *Proof: $350*

Y#	KM#	Metal	Description	VF	EF	Unc
2	69	Silv	5 Cents, 1878–79	50	125	425
					Proof: $950	
3	70	Silv	10 Cents, 1878–79	60	135	400
			1879, VF $150		*Proof: $950*	

Y#	KM#	Metal	Description	VF	EF	Unc
4	71	Silv	20 Cents, 1878–79	95	200	475
			1879, VF $350		*Proof: $1,200*	

Y#	KM#	Metal	Description	VF	EF	Unc
5	74	Bz	1/2 Cent / 2-1/2 Bit, 1905	20	40	75
6	75	Bz	1 Cent / 5 Bit, 1905	20	45	100
7	76	Bz	2 Cents / 10 Bit, 1905	35	85	500

Y#	KM#	Metal	Description	VF	EF	Unc
8	77	Nick	5 Cents / 25 Bit, 1905	25	65	400

Y#	KM#	Metal	Description	VF	EF	Unc
9	78	Silv	10 Cents / 50 Bit, 1905	35	65	125

Y#	KM#	Metal	Description	VF	EF	Unc
10	79	Silv	20 Cents / 1 Franc, 1905	80	225	650
11	80	Silv	40 Cents / 2 Francs, 1905	300	600	1,250

Note: All Proofs of 1905 (Y5–11) are rare.

Y#	KM#	Metal	Description	VF	EF	Unc
12	72	Gold	4 Daler / 20 Francs, 1904–05	950	1,200	2,000
13	73	Gold	10 Daler / 50 Francs, 1904	4,000	5,500	12,500

FREDERIK VIII, *1906–1912*

Y#	KM#	Metal	Description	VF	EF	Unc
14	81	Silv	20 Cents / 1 Franc, 1907	100	275	600
15	82	Silv	40 Cents / 2 Francs, 1907	150	375	1,400

Note: Proofs of Y14–15 are rare.

CHRISTIAN X, *1912–1917*

Y#	KM#	Metal	Description	VF	EF	Unc
16	83	Bz	1 Cent / 5 Bit, 1913	65	125	250

DANZIG

A major port on the Baltic Sea, Danzig was created a free city under the administration of the League of Nations by the Treaty of Versailles in 1919. Danzig struck its own coinage until it was proclaimed part of the German Reich in 1939. It is now under Polish administration as the city of Gdansk.

MONETARY SYSTEM

100 pfennig = 1 mark, to 1923
100 pfennige = 1 gulden, 1923–1939

PRECIOUS METAL CONTENT

Dates	Denomination	Gross Wt (g)	Fineness	Net Wt (g)	Troy Oz.
		SILVER			
1923–27	1/2 gulden	2.5000	0.7500	1.8750	0.0603
	1 gulden	5.0000	0.7500	3.7500	0.1206
	2 gulden	10.0000	0.7500	7.5000	0.2411
	5 gulden	25.0000	0.7500	18.7500	0.6028
1932	2 gulden	10.0000	0.5000	5.0000	0.1608
	5 gulden	15.0000	0.5000	7.5000	0.2411

Dates	Denomination	Gross Wt (g)	Fineness	Net Wt (g)	Troy Oz.
		GOLD			
1923–30	25 gulden	7.9881	0.9170	7.3224	0.2354

EMERGENCY ISSUES (NOTGELD)

Y#	KM#	Metal	Description	VF	EF	Unc
1	Tn1	Zinc	10 Pfennig, 1920	20	35	50
2	Tn2	Zinc	10 Pfennig, 1920, reverse large 10	350	500	800

REGULAR ISSUES

FIRST COINAGE

Y#	KM#	Metal	Description	VF	EF	Unc
3	140	Bz	1 Pfennig, 1923–37	5.00	17.50	30.00
						Proof: $325
4	141	Bz	2 Pfennige, 1923–37	7.50	20.00	37.50
						Proof: $650

Y#	KM#	Metal	Description	VF	EF	Unc
5	142	C-N	5 Pfennige, 1923, 28	17.50	35	70
						Proof: $650

Y#	KM#	Metal	Description	VF	EF	Unc
6	143	C-N	10 Pfennige, 1923	17.50	25	40
						Proof: $650

Y#	KM#	Metal	Description	VF	EF	Unc
7	144	Silv	1/2 Gulden, 1923, 27	50	75	135
						Proof: $1,200

Y#	KM#	Metal	Description	VF	EF	Unc
8	145	Silv	1 Gulden, 1923	55	100	175
						Proof: $1,000
9	146	Silv	2 Gulden, 1923	100	150	400
						Proof: $1,250

Y#	KM#	Metal	Description	VF	EF	Unc
10	147	Silv	5 Gulden, 1923, 27	300	500	1,000
						Proof: $2,500

Y#	KM#	Metal	Description	VF	EF	Unc
11	148	Gold	*25 Gulden, 1923, Proof only, $7,500*			
12	150	Gold	*25 Gulden, 1930, different reverse arms, Proof only, $2,750*			

Note: Y12 was not issued to circulation. In 1999 a hoard of 1,000 pieces was sold into the market.

SECOND COINAGE

Y#	KM#	Metal	Description	VF	EF	Unc
13	151	A-Bz	5 Pfennig, 1932	6	12.50	35

Y#	KM#	Metal	Description	VF	EF	Unc
14	152	A-Bz	10 Pfennig, 1932	5.75	10	35

Y#	KM#	Metal	Description	VF	EF	Unc
15	153	Nick	1/2 Gulden, 1932	35	50	125

Y#	KM#	Metal	Description	VF	EF	Unc
16	154	Nick	1 Gulden, 1932	35	45	85

Y#	KM#	Metal	Description	VF	EF	Unc
17	155	Silv	2 Gulden, 1932	300	625	1,200

Y#	KM#	Metal	Description	VF	EF	Unc
18	156	Silv	5 Gulden, 1932	825	1,700	2,875

Y#	KM#	Metal	Description	VF	EF	Unc
19	157	Silv	5 Gulden, 1932	1,200	2,500	4,000

THIRD COINAGE

Y#	KM#	Metal	Description	VF	EF	Unc
20	158	Nick	5 Gulden, 1935	375	700	1,600

Y#	KM#	Metal	Description	VF	EF	Unc
21	159	Nick	10 Gulden, 1935	1,500	2,750	4,500

DENMARK

This constitutional monarchy occupies the Jutland peninsula and about 500 islands between the Baltic and the North Seas. The Viking homeland was Christianized in the 10th century. In past centuries the country has lost the areas that now comprise Sweden, Norway, Finland, and Greenland. *Language:* Danish. *Capital:* Copenhagen.

MONETARY SYSTEM

96 skilling = 1 rigsdaler
10 rigsdaler = 1 christian d'or, to 1873
100 ore = 1 krone, 1873–

PRECIOUS METAL CONTENT

Denmark was a member of the Scandinavian Monetary Union; see appendix A.

Dates	Denomination	Gross Wt (g)	Fineness	Net Wt (g)	Troy Oz.
		SILVER			
1874–1958	10 ore	1.4500	0.4000	0.5800	0.0186
	25 ore	2.4200	0.6000	1.4520	0.0467
	50 ore	5.0000	0.6000	3.0000	0.0965
	1 krone	7.5000	0.8000	6.0000	0.1929
	2 kroner	15.0000	0.8000	12.0000	0.3858
1960, 64	5 kroner	17.0000	0.8000	13.6000	0.4372

PRECIOUS METAL CONTENT

Dates	Denomination	Gross Wt (g)	Fineness	Net Wt (g)	Troy Oz.
		GOLD			
1866–70	1 Christian d'Or	6.6420	0.8960	5.9512	0.1913
	2 Christian d'Or	13.2840	0.8960	11.9025	0.3827
1873–1931	10 kroner	4.4803	0.9000	4.0323	0.1296
	20 kroner	8.9606	0.9000	8.0645	0.2593

CHRISTIAN IX, *1863–1906*

Y#	KM#	Metal	Description	VF	EF	Unc
1	776	Bz	1/2 Skilling, 1868	12	22.50	45
2	774	Bz	1 Skilling, 1867–72 *1871, VF $30*	12	22.50	50

Death of Frederik VII Accession of Christian IX

Y#	KM#	Metal	Description	VF	EF	Unc
3	770	Silv	2 Rigsdaler, 1863	175	275	750

Y#	KM#	Metal	Description	VF	EF	Unc
4	775	Silv	4 Skilling, 1867–74 *1874, EF $90*	20	40	100

Y#	KM#	Metal	Description	VF	EF	Unc
5	772	Silv	2 Rigsdaler, 1864–72	400	700	1,500

Y#	KM#	Metal	Description	VF	EF	Unc
6	778	Gold	1 Christian d'Or, 1869	4,000	7,000	14,000
7	773	Gold	2 Christian d'Or, 1866–70	3,500	5,500	12,000

DECIMAL SYSTEM, 1873–

Y#	KM#	Metal	Description	VF	EF	Unc
8	792	Bz	1 Ore, 1874–1904 *1876, VF $925; 1878, VF $150; 1881,VF $3,000; 1886, VF $135; 1892, VF $325*	4.75	10.00	25
9	793	Bz	2 Ore, 1874–1906 *1876, VF $300; 1887, VF $250; 1892, VF $100*	6.50	12.50	55
10	794	Bz	5 Ore, 1874–1906 *1875, VF $145; 1884, 91, VF $60; 1890, VF $245*	45.00	95.00	300

Y#	KM#	Metal	Description	VF	EF	Unc
11	795	Silv	10 Ore, 1874–1905 *1874–75, VF $60; 1882, 84, VF $150; 1886, 88, VF $245*	12	25	50
12	796	Silv	25 Ore, 1874–1905	35	75	150

Y#	KM#	Metal	Description	VF	EF	Unc
13	797	Silv	1 Krone, 1875–98 *1876, VF $125; 1898, VF $100*	80	150	300
14	798	Silv	2 Kroner, 1875–99 *1897, VF $175*	80	175	425

25th Anniversary of Reign

Y#	KM#	Metal	Description	VF	EF	Unc
15	799	Silv	2 Kroner, 1888	35	55	95

Golden Wedding

Y#	KM#	Metal	Description	VF	EF	Unc
1	162	Silv	2 Reales, 1880	250	400	—

40th Anniversary of Reign

Y#	KM#	Metal	Description	VF	EF	Unc
17	802	Silv	2 Kroner, 1903	35	55	95

Y#	KM#	Metal	Description	VF	EF	Unc
18	790	Gold	10 Kroner, 1873–1900	BV	250	300
19	791	Gold	20 Kroner, 1873–1900 *1874, EF $3,000*	BV	500	250

FREDERIK VIII, *1906–1912*

Y#	KM#	Metal	Description	VF	EF	Unc
20	804	Bz	1 Ore, 1907–12	6.50	12.50	35
21	805	Bz	2 Ore, 1907–12	7.50	22.00	70
22	806	Bz	5 Ore, 1907–12	25.00	75.00	175

Y#	KM#	Metal	Description	VF	EF	Unc
23	807	Silv	10 Ore, 1907–12 *1911, VF $55*	10	20	50
24	808	Silv	25 Ore, 1907, 11	20	40	90

Death of Christian IX Accession of Frederik VIII

Y#	KM#	Metal	Description	VF	EF	Unc
25	803	Silv	2 Kroner, 1906	35	45	70

Y#	KM#	Metal	Description	VF	EF	Unc
26	809	Gold	10 Kroner, 1908–09	BV	250	475
27	810	Gold	20 Kroner, 1908–12	BV	475	600

CHRISTIAN X, *1912–1947*

Y#	KM#	Metal	Description	VF	EF	Unc
28	812	Bz	1 Ore, 1913–23 *1913, 15–16, 19, 21–23, VF $2.50; 1917, VF $45; 1920, VF $20; 1927, VF $15*	2.00	4.00	8
29	813	Bz	2 Ore, 1913–23 *1913, VF $55; 1917, EF $17*	7.50	12.50	45
30	814	Bz	5 Ore, 1913–23 *1913, VF $225; 1914–17, VF; 1923, $95*	22.50	35.00	75
28a	812	Iron	1 Ore, 1918–19 *1919, VF $30*	11.00	40.00	115
29a	813	Iron	2 Ore, 1918–19 *1919, VF $80*	10.00	45.00	175
30a	814	Iron	5 Ore, 1918–19 *1919, VF $80*	20.00	65.00	225

Y#	KM#	Metal	Description	VF	EF	Unc
31	818.2a	C-N	10 Ore, 1920–23 *1922 VF $45; 1923, Unc $800*	6.50	135	60
32	815.2a	C-N	*25 Ore, 1920–22* *1922, VF $35*	15.00	30	75

Y#	KM#	Metal	Description	VF	EF	Unc
33	831	A-Bz	1/2 Krone, 1924–40 *1939, EF $125*	12.00	27.50	100
34	824	A-Bz	1 Krone, 1924–41 *1924, 30, 38, VF $60; 1925–29, 31, 36, 38, 41, 43, VF $32.50*	6.50	15.00	50
35	825	A-Bz	2 Kroner, 1924–41 *1924, EF $450; 1925–38, VF $40; 1940, VF $25; 1941, VF $100*	8.00	17.50	80

Y#	KM#	Metal	Description	VF	EF	Unc
36	818	Silv	10 Ore, 1914–19	4.50	7	15
37	815	Silv	25 Ore, 1913–19* *1914, EF $150; 1917, EF $75*	17.50	25	50

*Coins dated 1919 are worth about half the above prices.

Y#	KM#	Metal	Description	VF	EF	Unc
38	819	Silv	1 Krone, 1915–16	14.50	23	45
39	820	Silv	2 Kroner, 1915–16	35.00	70	115

Death of Frederik VIII / Accession of Christian X

Y#	KM#	Metal	Description	VF	EF	Unc
40	811	Silv	2 Kroner, 1912	27.50	40	75

Silver Wedding Anniversary

Y#	KM#	Metal	Description	VF	EF	Unc
41	821	Silv	2 Kroner, 1923	15	25	37.50

King's 60th Birthday

Y#	KM#	Metal	Description	VF	EF	Unc
42	829	Silv	2 Kroner, 1930	12.50	17.50	25

25th Year of Reign

Y#	KM#	Metal	Description	VF	EF	Unc
43	830	Silv	2 Kroner, 1937	12.50	17.50	28.50

Y#	KM#	Metal	Description	VF	EF	Unc
44	816	Gold	10 Kroner, 1913–17	BV	250	300
45	817	Gold	20 Kroner, 1913–31 *1926–27, 30–31, EF $12,500*	BV	425	475

Y#	KM#	Metal	Description	VF	EF	Unc
46	826	Bz	1 Ore, 1926–40 *1926, 27N, VF $20; 1928, 1929–33, EF $7.50*	0.20	1.00	7.50
47	827	Bz	2 Ore, 1926–40 *1926, VF $75; 1930, 32, VF $9; 1934, VF $2.50*	0.40	1.50	10.00
48	828	Bz	5 Ore, 1927–40 *1928, VF $15; 1929–34, VF $2; 1935, VF $9.50*	0.80	1.75	12.00

Note: For similar coins dated 1941, see Faeroe Islands.

Y#	KM#	Metal	Description	VF	EF	Unc
49	822	C-N	10 Ore, 1924–47* *1933, VF $20; 1945, VF $100; 1947, VF $125*	4.00	8.00	35
50	823	C-N	25 Ore, 1924–47* *1932, VF $27.50; 1933, VF $60; 1935, 39, VF $35*	7.50	17.50	55

*Coins dated 1940 are worth about half the above prices.
Note: For similar coins dated 1941 without mintmark and initials, see Faeroe Islands.

Y#	KM#	Metal	Description	VF	EF	Unc
52	833	Alum	2 Ore, 1941	1.50	5.00	25
53	834	Alum	5 Ore, 1941	2.25	7.50	35
51	832	Zinc	1 Ore, 1941–46 *1945, VF $5; 1946, $12.50*	0.75	15.00	60
52a	833a	Zinc	2 Ore, 1942–47 *1945, VF $15; 1947, $5*	1.50	15.00	80
53a	834a	Zinc	5 Ore, 1942–45 *1945, VF $15*	5.00	45.00	150
49a	822.2a	Zinc	10 Ore, 1941–45 *1945, VF $100*	5.00	25.00	65
50a	823.2a	Zinc	25 Ore, 1941–45 *1941, 45, VF $15*	7.50	26.50	75

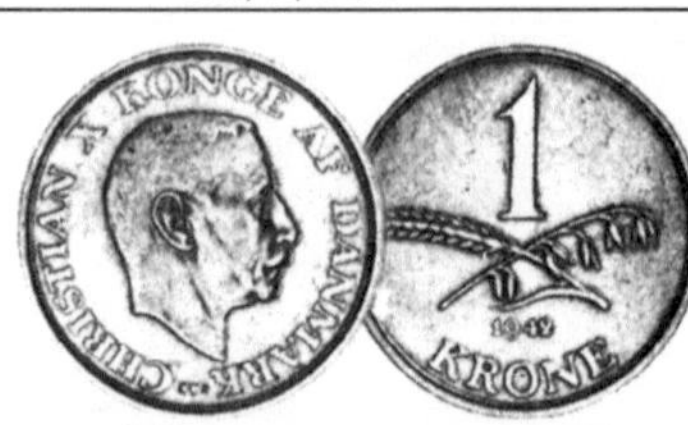

Y#	KM#	Metal	Description	VF	EF	Unc
54	835	A-Bz	1 Krone, 1942–47 *1943, VF $25*	3.25	6	20

75th Birthday

Y#	KM#	Metal	Description	VF	EF	Unc
55	836	Silv	2 Kroner, 1945	17.50	30	50

FREDERIK IX, *1947–1972*

Y#	KM#	Metal	Description	VF	EF	Unc
56	839	Zinc	1 Ore, 1948–72 *1948, VF $5; 1949–51, VF $1.50*	0.25	0.50	1.50
57	840	Zinc	2 Ore, 1948–72 *1948, 53–54, VF $6; 1949, VF $30; 1950–54, VF $8; 1960–62, VF $1.5*	0.25	0.50	1.50
58	843	Zinc	5 Ore, 1950–64 *1950, VF $20, 1951, VF $7; 1952–55, VF $3.75*	0.35	1.50	6.50

Y#	KM#	Metal	Description	VF	EF	Unc
59	841	C-N	10 Ore, 1948–60 *1959, $45*	0.35	3.00	11.00
60	842	C-N	25 Ore, 1948–60 *1948, VF $5; 1952, VF $4; 1959, VF $6*	0.75	1.50	9.50

Y#	KM#	Metal	Description	VF	EF	Unc
61	837	A-Bz	1 Krone, 1947–60 *1947, 53, VF $7.50; 1948, 56, 58, VF $3.75; 1949, 55, VF $11; 1954, 59, VF $25; 1960, Rare*	1.75	4	7.50
62	838	A-Bz	2 Kroner, 1947–59 *1851, 59 VF $22.50*	3.00	5	10.00

Greenland Commemorative

Y#	KM#	Metal	Description	VF	EF	Unc
63	844	Silv	2 Kroner, 1953	25	35	55

18th Birthday of Princess Margrethe

Y#	KM#	Metal	Description	VF	EF	Unc
64	845	Silv	2 Kroner, 1958	12.50	15	25

Silver Wedding

Y#	KM#	Metal	Description	VF	EF	Unc
65	852	Silv	5 Kroner, 1960	12.50	15	25

Y#	KM#	Metal	Description	VF	EF	Unc
66	846	Bz	1 Ore, 1960–64	0.25	1.00	2.25
67	847	Bz	2 Ore, 1960–66	0.25	1.00	2.25
68	848	Bz	5 Ore, 1960–72 *1962, VF $1.50*	0.25	0.75	1.00

Y#	KM#	Metal	Description	VF	EF	Unc
69	849	C-N	10 Ore, 1960–72	0.25	0.50	1
70	850	C-N	25 Ore, 1960–72	0.20	0.75	3

Y#	KM#	Metal	Description	VF	EF	Unc
71	851	C-N	1 Krone, 1960–72	0.50	1.00	2.25
72	853	C-N	5 Kroner, 1960–72	1.00	2.25	3.50

Wedding of Princess Anne-Marie

Y#	KM#	Metal	Description	VF	EF	Unc
73	854	Silv	5 Kroner, 1964	12.50	17.50	27.50

DOMINICAN REPUBLIC

The Dominican Republic occupies the eastern two-thirds of the Caribbean island of Hispaniola, between Cuba and Puerto Rico. Explored by Columbus in 1492 and settled by Spain, the country was ceded to France in 1795 and alternated between Haitian occupation and Spanish colonial rule for the next 175 years, with brief periods of independence as a republic intervening. A century of mainly non-representative rule, including the Trujillo military dictatorship of 1930 to 1961, ended with the resumption of free elections in 1966. *Language:* Spanish. *Capital:* Santo Domingo.

MONETARY SYSTEM

100 centesimos = 1 franco   100 centavos = 1 peso

PRECIOUS METAL CONTENT

Dates	Denomination	Gross Wt (g)	Fineness	Net Wt (g)	Troy Oz.
		SILVER			
1891	50 centesimos	2.5000	0.8350	2.0871	0.0671
	1 franco	5.0000	0.8350	4.1742	0.1342
	5 francos	25.0000	0.9000	22.5001	0.7234
1897	10 centavos	2.5000	0.3500	0.8750	0.0281
	20 centavos	5.0000	0.3500	1.7500	0.0563
	1/2 peso	12.5000	0.3500	4.3750	0.1407
	1 peso	25.0000	0.3500	8.7500	0.2813
1937–61	10 centavos	2.5000	0.9000	2.2500	0.0723
	25 centavos	6.2500	0.9000	5.6250	0.1808
	1/2 peso	12.5000	0.9000	11.2500	0.3617
	1 peso	26.7000	0.9000	24.0300	0.7725
1963	10 centavos	2.5000	0.6500	1.6250	0.0522
	25 centavos	6.2500	0.6500	4.0625	0.1306
	1/2 peso	12.5000	0.6500	8.1250	0.2612
	1 peso	26.7000	0.6500	17.3550	0.5579

Dates	Denomination	Gross Wt (g)	Fineness	Net Wt (g)	Troy Oz.
		GOLD			
1955	30 pesos	29.6220	0.9000	26.6598	0.8572

Y#	KM#	Metal	Description	VF	EF	Unc
A1	1/2	Bz/Br	1/4 Real, 1844,48	25	90	600

Y#	KM#	Metal	Description	VF	EF	Unc
1	3	Br	1 Centavo, 1877	2.25	9.50	30

Y#	KM#	Metal	Description	VF	EF	Unc
4	4	C-N	2-1/2 Centavos, 1877	60	140	650

Y#	KM#	Metal	Description	VF	EF	Unc
5	5	C-N	5 Centavos, 1877	35	90	375

Y#	KM#	Metal	Description	VF	EF	Unc
6	6	C-N	1-1/4 Centavos, 1882, 88	15	30	450
				1882 Proof: $650		
7	7	C-N	2-1/2 Centavos, 1882, 88	3	10	175
				1882 Proof: $750		

Y#	KM#	Metal	Description	VF	EF	Unc
2	8	Bz	5 Centesimos, 1891	5.50	20	125
3	9	Bz	10 Centesimos, 1891	6.00	25	150

Y#	KM#	Metal	Description	VF	EF	Unc
8	10	Silv	50 Centesimos, 1891	15	50	200
9	11	Silv	1 Franco, 1891	18	55	300
10	12	Silv	5 Francos, 1891	125	250	1,000

Y#	KM#	Metal	Description	VF	EF	Unc
11	13	Bill	10 Centavos, 1897	12.50	30	400
12	14	Bill	20 Centavos, 1897	10.00	25	400
13	15	Bill	1/2 Peso, 1897	20.00	50	1,000
14	16	Bill	1 Peso, 1897	75.00	325	2,000

Y#	KM#	Metal	Description	VF	EF	Unc
15	17	Bz	1 Centavo, 1937–61	0.50	1	3
				1937 Proof: $200		

Y#	KM#	Metal	Description	VF	EF	Unc
16	18	C-N	5 Centavos, 1937–74 *1939, EF $65*	0.25	0.50	2
				1937 Proof: $900		
16a	18a	Bill	5 Centavos, 1944	4.50	9.00	150

Y#	KM#	Metal	Description	VF	EF	Unc
17	19	Silv	10 Centavos, 1937–61 *1939, EF $60*	3.00	6.00	20
				1937 Proof: $600		
18	20	Silv	25 Centavos, 1937–61 *1937,42–51, EF $30; 1939, EF $115*	2.75	4.00	8
				1937 Proof: $750		
19	21	Silv	1/2 Peso, 1937–61	15.00	22.50	45
				1937 Proof: $1,600		

Y#	KM#	Metal	Description	VF	EF	Unc
20	22	Silv	1 Peso, 1952	20	25	50
20a	22	Silv	1 Peso, 1939	20	35	700

25th Year of Trujillo Government

Reverse: ***Like Y20***

Y#	KM#	Metal	Description	VF	EF	Unc
21	23	Silv	1 Peso, 1955	17.50	25	45

Y#	KM#	Metal	Description	VF	EF	Unc
22	24	Gold	30 Pesos, 1955	BV	BV	1,500

Centennial, Restoration of the Republic

Y#	KM#	Metal	Description	VF	EF	Unc
23	25	Bz	1 Centavo, 1963	0.20	0.45	0.75

Y#	KM#	Metal	Description	VF	EF	Unc
24	26	C-N	5 Centavos, 1963	0.25	0.50	1

Y#	KM#	Metal	Description	VF	EF	Unc
25	27	Silv	10 Centavos, 1963	1.00	2	4.00
26	28	Silv	25 Centavos, 1963	2.50	5	10.00
27	29	Silv	1/2 Peso, 1963	5.00	9	17.50
28	30	Silv	1 Peso, 1963	10.00	15	35.00

Note: Y28 was not released to circulation.

EAST AFRICA

East Africa was an administrative grouping of five British territories. These territories—Kenya, Uganda, Tanganyika (now Tanzania), British Somaliland (now part of Somalia), and the Sultanate of Zanzibar and Pemba (now part of Tanzania)—all became independent between 1960 and 1963. The East African coinage was also legal tender in Ethiopia and Aden (now in Yemen).

MONETARY SYSTEM

64 pice = 1 India rupee, to 1905
100 cents = 1 rupee, 1905–1920
100 cents = 1 florin, 1920–1921
100 cents = 1 shilling, 1921–1963

PRECIOUS METAL CONTENT

Dates	Denomination	Gross Wt (g)	Fineness	Net Wt (g)	Troy Oz.
		SILVER			
1906–19	25 cents	2.9160	0.8000	2.3328	0.0750
	50 cents	5.8319	0.8000	4.6650	0.1500
1920	25 cents	2.9160	0.5000	1.4580	0.0469
	50 cents / 1 shilling	5.8319	0.5000	2.9160	0.0937
	1 florin	11.6638	0.5000	5.8319	0.1875
1921–46	50 cents	3.8879	0.2500	0.9720	0.0312
	1 shilling	7.7759	0.2500	1.9440	0.0625

Victoria, *1837–1901*

Legend: ***EAST AFRICA PROTECTORATE***

Y#	KM#	Metal	Description	VF	EF	Unc
1	1	Bz	1 Pice, 1897–99	15	60	125
						Proof: $300

Edward VII, *1901–1910*

Legend: ***EAST AFRICA & UGANDA PROTECTORATES***

Y#	KM#	Metal	Description	VF	EF	Unc
2	6	Alum	1/2 Cent, 1908	15.00	40	250
3	5	Alum	1 Cent, 1907–08	10.00	35	110
2a	6a	C-N	1/2 Cent, 1909	15.00	35	200
3a	5a	C-N	1 Cent, 1909–10	1.25	4	15
6	2	C-N	10 Cents, 1907, 10	5.00	20	45

Note: The similar 1908 5 cents is a pattern.

Y#	KM#	Metal	Description	VF	EF	Unc
7	3	Silv	25 Cents, 1906, 10	10	45	85
8	4	Silv	50 Cents, 1906–10	35	90	200

GEORGE V, *1910–1936*

First Coinage

Y#	KM#	Metal	Description	VF	EF	Unc
9	7	C-N	1 Cent, 1911–18	1.50	4.00	42.50
10	11	C-N	5 Cents, 1913–19 *1919, EF $50*	3.50	15.00	45.00
11	8	C-N	10 Cents, 1911–18 *1913, VF $150*	5.00	27.50	75.00

Y#	KM#	Metal	Description	VF	EF	Unc
12	10	Silv	25 Cents, 1912–18 *1918, VF $250*	12.50	440	90
13	9	Silv	50 Cents, 1911–19 *1918H, VF $200; 1919, VF $350*	40.00	85	200

Second Coinage

Legend: ***EAST AFRICA***

Y#	KM#	Metal	Description	VF	EF	Unc
14	12	C-N	1 Cent, 1920–21 *1921, Rare*	50	150	300
15	13	C-N	5 Cents, 1920	125	350	600
16	14	C-N	10 Cents, 1920	175	275	550

Y#	KM#	Metal	Description	VF	EF	Unc
17	15	Silv	25 Cents, 1920	40	100	250
18	16	Silv	50 Cents / 1 Shilling, 1920, *Rare*	3,500	5,000	—
19	17	Silv	1 Florin, 1920	65	150	300

Note: Y18 was not issued to circulation.

Third Coinage

Y#	KM#	Metal	Description	VF	EF	Unc
20	22	Bz	1 Cent, 1922–35 *1925, No mintmark, VF $60*	0.50	2.00	10
21	18	Bz	5 Cents, 1921–36	1.00	5.00	15
22	19	Bz	10 Cents, 1921–36	2.50	9.50	30

Y#	KM#	Metal	Description	VF	EF	Unc
23	20	Bill	50 Cents / 1/2 Shilling, 1921–24	3	10	40
24	21	Bill	1 Shilling, 1921–25	4	15	25

EDWARD VIII, *1936*

Y#	KM#	Metal	Description	VF	EF	Unc
25	23	Bz	5 Cents, 1936	1.00	3	10
26	24	Bz	10 Cents, 1936	1.50	4	15

GEORGE VI, *1936–1952*

Y#	KM#	Metal	Description	VF	EF	Unc
27	29	Bz	1 Cent, 1942	1	2	6
28	25	Bz	5 Cents, 1937–43	1	2	9
29	26	Bz	10 Cents, 1937–45	1	3	10

Note: Y28–29 dated 1942 or later are reduced in weight about 15%.

Y#	KM#	Metal	Description	VF	EF	Unc
30	27	Bill	50 Cents, 1937–44	2	7.50	30
31	28	Bill	1 Shilling, 1937–46 *1943, EF $1,000*	4	8.00	40

Legend: ***GEORGIUS SEXTUS REX***

Y#	KM#	Metal	Description	VF	EF	Unc
32	32	Bz	1 Cent, 1949–52	0.50	1.25	4.00
33	33	Bz	5 Cents, 1949–52	0.50	2.00	5.00
34	34	Bz	10 Cents, 1949–52	0.50	2.00	7.50

Y#	KM#	Metal	Description	VF	EF	Unc
35	30	C-N	50 Cents, 1948–52	0.50	2.50	8.00
36	31	C-N	1 Shilling, 1948–52	1.00	2.00	7.50

ELIZABETH II, *1952–1963*

Y#	KM#	Metal	Description	VF	EF	Unc
37	35	Bz	1 Cent, 1954–62	0.25	0.75	3.00
38	37	Bz	5 Cents, 1955–63	0.30	0.85	1.50
39	38	Bz	10 Cents, 1956	1.00	3.00	10.00

Y#	KM#	Metal	Description	VF	EF	Unc
40	36	C-N	50 Cents, 1954–63	0.25	1	5

INDEPENDENT COINAGE

Y#	KM#	Metal	Description	VF	EF	Unc
41	39	Bz	5 Cents, 1964	0.20	0.40	1
42	40	Bz	10 Cents, 1964	0.25	0.50	2

EAST TURKESTAN

A largely Muslim region of Asia to the northwest of China, East Turkestan is bounded by Mongolia to the north and Tibet to the south, and by six nations from Kazakhstan to India along its western side. The region comprises 706,000 square miles (roughly four times the size of state of California). Its population is about 46 percent Uighur and 40 percent Han Chinese. The area was first annexed by the Manchu Empire in 1884 and renamed Xinjiang. Repeated uprisings finally resulted in a short-lived independent republic (the First East Turkestan Republic) from 1933 to 1934; then another in 1944 (the Second East Turkestan Republic), which lasted until the People's Liberation Army retook control in October 1949. Since that time it has been under Chinese rule as the Xinjiang Uighur Autonomous Region. In September 2004, a group of Uighurs, Kazakhs, and others from the region formed the East Turkestan Government-in-Exile in Washington, D.C. Although China maintains that it annexed Xinjiang peacefully, its mistreatment of ethnic Uighurs led the United States in 2021 to designate its activities genocide. *Languages:* Uighur, Chinese. *Capital:* Urumchi.

Y#	KM#	Metal	Description	VF	EF	Unc
1	E38	Cop	20 Cash, AH 1352	200	350	—

ECUADOR

Part of the Inca Empire that had existed for centuries, Ecuador was conquered by Spain in 1532. Early in the 19th century, Ecuador joined Venezuela, Colombia, and Panama to form the Gran Colombia confederacy. When that association dissolved in 1830, Ecuador became independent, though the republic was beset with revolutions, dictatorships, and border wars with Peru. Military rule through the 1970s and early 2000s temporarily stabilized the country during periods of near economic collapse. *Language:* Spanish. *Capital:* Quito.

MONETARY SYSTEM

16 reales = 1 escudo, to 1856
10 centavos = 1 decimo
10 decimos = 1 sucre
25 sucres = 1 condor

PRECIOUS METAL CONTENT

Dates	Denomination	Gross Wt (g)	Fineness	Net Wt (g)	Troy Oz.
		SILVER			
1884–1916	1/2 decimo	1.2500	0.9000	1.1250	0.0362
	1 decimo	2.5000	0.9000	2.2500	0.0723
	2 decimos	5.0000	0.9000	4.5000	0.1447
	1/2 sucre	12.5000	0.9000	11.2500	0.3617
	1 sucre	25.0000	0.9000	22.5000	0.7234
1928–44	50 centavos	2.5000	0.7200	1.8000	0.0579
	1 sucre	5.0000	0.7200	3.6000	0.1157
	2 sucres	10.0000	0.7200	7.2000	0.2315
	5 sucres	25.0000	0.7200	18.0000	0.5787
		GOLD			
1899–1900	10 sucres	8.1360	0.9000	7.3224	0.2354
1928	1 condor	8.3592	0.9000	7.5233	0.2419

PRE–DECIMAL SYSTEM

DRAPED BUST OF LIBERTY

Obverse: *Fineness ("8Ds") in legend*

Y#	KM#	Metal	Description	VF	EF	Unc
8	36	Silv	1/4 Real, 1849–62 (vars) *1862, VF $500*	150	300	600
9	35	Silv	1/2 Real, 1848–49	150	300	600
10	33	Silv	2 Reales, 1847–52	200	500	1,000
10a	38	Silv	2 Reales, 1857, *Rare*	8,000	—	—
11	37	Silv	4 Reales, 1855, 57	200	500	1,750
12	32	Silv	8 Reales, 1846	2,000	3,000	6,000

Obverse: *Fineness ("0,666") in legend*

Y#	KM#	Metal	Description	VF	EF	Unc
11a	37a	Silv	4 Reales, 1862, *Rare*	—	—	—

Obverse: *Fineness ("0,900") in legend*

Y#	KM#	Metal	Description	VF	EF	Unc
13	39	Silv	5 Francos, 1858	400	900	2,000

UNDRAPED LIBERTY

Obverse: *Barre head; fineness "0666" in legend*

Y#	KM#	Metal	Description	VF	EF	Unc
14	40	Silv	2 Reales, 1862, *Rare*	4,000	—	—
						Proof: $17,500
15	41	Silv	4 Reales, 1862	300	1,000	3,000
						Proof: $25,000

Note: Y14 probably was not issued to circulation.

Y#	KM#	Metal	Description	VF	EF	Unc
19	34.1	Gold	8 Escudos, 1847–55, *Rare*	—	—	—
19a	34.2	Gold	8 Escudos, 1856	3,000	4,500	—

DECIMAL SYSTEM

Y#	KM#	Metal	Description	VF	EF	Unc
20	54	Cop	1/2 Centavo, 1890H	20	45	150
					Proof: $400	
21	45	Cop	1 Centavo, 1872 HEATON, 1890H	25	65	225
					Proof: $400	
23	46	Cop	2 Centavos, 1872 HEATON	40	100	475
					Proof: $800	

Reverse: ***Mintmark "HEATON BIRMINGHAM"***

Y#	KM#	Metal	Description	VF	EF	Unc
24	47	C-N	1/2 Centavo, 1884	20.00	45	150
					Proof: $400	
25	48	C-N	1 Centavo, 1884, 86	17.50	40	135
					Proof: $375	
26	49	C-N	1/2 Decimo, 1884, 86	20.00	45	150
					Proof: $750	

Y#	KM#	Metal	Description	VF	EF	Unc
27	55.1	Silv	1/2 Decimo, 1893–1912 LIMA	3.00	10	50
27a	55.2	Silv	1/2 Decimo 1915 BIRMM	2.00	5	10
					Proof: $200	
28	50.1	Silv	1 Decimo, 1884–90 HEATON BIRMINGHAM	20.00	45	150
			1884, VF $40		*Proof: $500*	
28a	50.2	Silv	1 Decimo, 1889 D.T. SANTIAGO CHILE	10.00	30	100
28b	50.3	Silv	1 Decimo, 1892–1912 LIMA	7.50	15	40
28c	50.4	Silv	1 Decimo 1915 BIRMM	2.50	5	10
					Proof: $300	
28d	50.5	Silv	1 Decimo 1916 PHILA.	2.50	5	10
29	51.1	Silv	2 Decimos, 1884–90 HEATON BIRMINGHAM	17.50	35	100
					Proof: $500	
29a	51.2	Silv	2 Decimos, 1889, 91 D.T. SANTIAGO CHILE	15.00	25	75
29b	51.3	Silv	2 Decimos, 1889–1915 LIMA	15.00	25	75
29c	51.4	Silv	2 Decimos, 1895–1916 PHILADELPHIA	5.00	10	25
					Proof: $500	
30	52	Silv	1/2 Sucre, 1884 HEATON BIRMINGHAM	100.00	250	500
					Proof: $2,500	
31	53.1	Silv	1 Sucre, 1884–95 HEATON BIRMINGHAM	50.00	85	300
					Proof: $3,000	
31a	53.2	Silv	1 Sucre, 1888–89 SANTIAGO CHILE	17.50	25	200
31b	53.3	Silv	1 Sucre, 1890–97, LIMA	17.50	25	200

Y#	KM#	Metal	Description	VF	EF	Unc
32	56	Gold	10 Sucres, 1899–1900 J.M. BIRMINGHAM	BV	475	750

Y#	KM#	Metal	Description	VF	EF	Unc
33	57	C-N	1/2 Centavo, 1909H	8	20	125
34	58	C-N	1 Centavo, 1909H	8	20	125
35	59	C-N	2 Centavos, 1909H	8	20	150
					Proof: $200	
37	60.1	C-N	5 Centavos, 1909H	10	35	200

Reverse: ***Value spelled out***

Y#	KM#	Metal	Description	VF	EF	Unc
36	61	C-N	2-1/2 Centavos, 1917	20.00	50	250
37a	60.2	C-N	5 Centavos, 1917–18	10.00	20	100
39	62	C-N	10 Centavos, 1918	12.50	40	200

Reverse: ***Value in numerals***

Y#	KM#	Metal	Description	VF	EF	Unc
38	63	C-N	5 Centavos, 1919	2	8	50
40	64	C-N	10 Centavos, 1919	2	8	50
						Proof: $300

Y#	KM#	Metal	Description	VF	EF	Unc
41	65	C-N	5 Centavos, 1924H	2	8	40
42	66	C-N	10 Centavos, 1924H	2	5	20
						Proof: $250

New Coinage

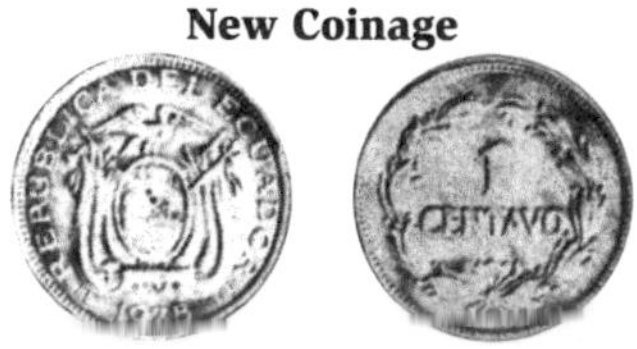

Y#	KM#	Metal	Description	VF	EF	Unc
44	67	Bz	1 Centavo, 1928	1	2	17.50
45	68	Nick	2-1/2 Centavos, 1928	2	8	50.00

Y#	KM#	Metal	Description	VF	EF	Unc
46	69	Nick	5 Centavos, 1928	2	5	25
47	70	Nick	10 Centavos, 1928	2	8	50

Y#	KM#	Metal	Description	VF	EF	Unc
48	71	Silv	50 Centavos, 1928, 30 PHILA U S A	3.50	15	50
49	72	Silv	1 Sucre, 1928–34 PHILA U S A	3.50	15	50
50	73	Silv	2 Sucres, 1928, 30 PHILA U S A	12.50	35	125

Y#	KM#	Metal	Description	VF	EF	Unc
43	74	Gold	1 Condor, 1928 BIRMINGHAM	600	750	1,000

Y#	KM#	Metal	Description	VF	EF	Unc
51	75	Nick	5 Centavos, 1937HF	0.25	0.60	3
52	76	Nick	10 Centavos, 1937	0.50	1.00	3
53	77.1	Nick	20 Centavos, 1937HF	0.50	1.00	3

Y#	KM#	Metal	Description	VF	EF	Unc
54	78.1	Nick	1 Sucre, 1937HF	1	3	6

Y#	KM#	Metal	Description	VF	EF	Unc
51a	75a	Br	5 Centavos, 1942, 44D	2	5	15.00
52a	76a	Br	10 Centavos, 1942	1	5	15.00
53a	77.1a	Br	20 Centavos, 1942, 44D	1	3	12.50

Y#	KM#	Metal	Description	VF	EF	Unc
55	80	Silv	2 Sucres, 1944M MEXICO	10	15	35
56	79	Silv	5 Sucres, 1943–44M MEXICO	10	20	40

Y#	KM#	Metal	Description	VF	EF	Unc
51b	75b	C-N	5 Centavos, 1946	0.25	0.50	2
52b	76b	C-N	10 Centavos, 1946	0.25	0.50	2
53b	77.1b	C-N	20 Centavos, 1946	0.50	1.00	4

Y#	KM#	Metal	Description	VF	EF	Unc
54a	78.2	Nick	1 Sucre, 1946	0.25	0.50	2

Y#	KM#	Metal	Description	VF	EF	Unc
54b	78a	C-N	1 Sucre, 1959	0.30	0.60	1.50
					Proof: $250	
54c	78b	N-CS	1 Sucre, 1964–81	0.15	0.35	0.90

Y#	KM#	Metal	Description	VF	EF	Unc
52c	76c	N-CS	10 Centavos, 1964–72	0.10	0.20	0.80
53c	77.1c	N-CS	20 Centavos, 1959–72	0.10	0.20	0.50
57	81	N-CS	50 Centavos, 1963–82	0.20	0.30	0.50

EGYPT

One of the world's oldest civilized lands, Egypt occupies the northeast corner of Africa. It was a province of the Ottoman (Turkish) Empire from 1517 to 1914, when it became a British protectorate. It became an independent kingdom in 1922 and a republic in 1953. In 1958 it joined Syria to form the United Arab Republic. That union was dissolved in 1961, but Egypt retained the UAR name until 1971. (See under "United Arab Republic" for coins of that era.) *Languages:* Arabic, English, French. *Capital:* Cairo.

MONETARY SYSTEM

To 1916:
40 para = 1 ghirsh (piastre)

Since 1916:
10 milliemes (millim) = 1 ghirsh (piastre)
100 ghirsh = 1 jiniah (pound)

PRECIOUS METAL CONTENT

Dates	Denomination	Gross Wt (g)	Fineness	Net Wt (g)	Troy Oz.
		SILVER			
1885–1942	1 ghirsh	1.4000	0.8333	1.1667	0.0375
	2 ghirsh	2.8000	0.8333	2.3333	0.0750
	5 ghirsh	7.0000	0.8333	5.8333	0.1875
	10 ghirsh	14.0000	0.8333	11.6667	0.3751
	20 ghirsh	28.0000	0.8333	23.3333	0.7502
1944	2 ghirsh	2.8000	0.5000	1.4000	0.0450
1955–57	5 ghirsh	3.5000	0.7200	2.5200	0.0810
	10 ghirsh	7.0000	0.6250	4.3750	0.1406
	10 ghirsh	7.0000	0.7200	5.0400	0.1620
	20 ghirsh	14.0000	0.7200	10.0800	0.3241
	25 ghirsh	17.5000	0.7200	12.6000	0.4051
	50 ghirsh	28.0000	0.9000	25.2000	0.8102
		GOLD			
1861–76	5 ghirsh	0.4272	0.8750	0.3738	0.0120
	10 ghirsh	0.8554	0.8750	0.7485	0.0240
	25 ghirsh	2.1360	0.8750	1.8690	0.0601
	50 ghirsh	4.2740	0.8750	3.7398	0.1202
	100 ghirsh	8.5440	0.8750	7.4760	0.2404
	500 ghirsh	42.7200	0.8750	37.3800	1.2018
1876–1909	5 ghirsh	0.4200	0.8750	0.3675	0.0120
	10 ghirsh	0.8554	0.8750	0.7485	0.0240
	25 ghirsh	2.1360	0.8750	1.8690	0.0601
	50 ghirsh	4.2720	0.8750	3.7380	0.1202
	100 ghirsh	8.5440	0.8750	7.4760	0.2404
	500 ghirsh	42.7400	0.8750	37.3975	1.2024
1916–38	20 ghirsh	1.7000	0.8750	1.4875	0.0478
	50 ghirsh	4.2500	0.8750	3.7188	0.1195
	100 ghirsh	8.5000	0.8750	7.4375	0.2391
	500 ghirsh	42.5000	0.8750	37.1875	1.1957
1955, 57	1 pound	8.5000	0.8750	7.4375	0.2391
	5 pounds	42.5000	0.8750	37.1875	1.1957

Note: For coins issued from 1958 to 1971, see "United Arab Republic—Egypt."

OTTOMAN PROVINCE, *to 1914*

MISR (in Arabic)

Most coins issued before 1916 are similar to Turkish types but are distinguished by the Arabic word "Misr" (Egypt) on the reverse.

Abdul Aziz, *1861–1876*

Accession Date AH 1277 on Coins

Locally Struck Issues

Obverse: ***Like Y5–11, having toughra (a stylized calligraphic design containing the sultan's name and titles) and flower, value below***

Y#	KM#	Metal	Description	VF	EF	Unc
2a	242	Cop	10 Para, Yrs 8–11	750	1,500	—
			Yr 11, EF $4,000			
3a	246	Cop	20 Para, Yrs 8–11	35	60	175
			Yr 11, Rare			
4a	249	Cop	40 Para, Yrs 9–11	1,000	1,850	3,250
			Yrs 9, 11, Rare			

Y#	KM#	Metal	Description	VF	EF	Unc
5	243	Silv	10 Para, Yrs 2–16	15	25	50
6	247	Silv	20 Para, Yrs 1–15 *Yr 1, Rare*	15	25	60
7	250	Silv	1 Ghirsh, Yrs 1–16	10	20	60
8a	252	Silv	2-1/2 Ghirsh, Yrs 8–15	400	800	1,500
9a	254	Silv	5 Ghirsh, Yrs 1–10	500	900	1,650
10a	256/258	Silv	10 Ghirsh, Yrs 2–11 *Yr 11, Rare*	600	1,200	2,000
11	260	Silv	20 Ghirsh, Yrs 1–2 *Yr 1, Rare*	1,100	1,600	—

Y#	KM#	Metal	Description	VF	EF	Unc
A11	255	Gold	5 Ghirsh, Yrs 2–16	125	165	225
B11	259	Gold	10 Ghirsh, Yrs 10–14	150	200	350
C11	261	Gold	25 Ghirsh, Yrs 8–15	175	300	550
D11	262	Gold	50 Ghirsh, Yrs 11–16	200	400	600
E11	263	Gold	100 Ghirsh, Yrs 1–16	375	750	1,500
F11	265	Gold	500 Ghirsh, Yrs 8–15	15,000	23,500	—

Issues Struck in Europe

Y#	KM#	Metal	Description	VF	EF	Unc
1	240	Bz	4 Para, Yr 4	15	25.00	50
2	241	Bz	10 Para, Yrs 4–10 (29 mm)	3	15.00	40
3	244	Bz	20 Para, Yrs 3–10 (32 mm)	5	17.50	45
3b	245	Bz	20 Para, Yr 7 (29 mm, thick)	350	600.00	1,200
4	248	Bz	40 Para, Yr 10	15	45.00	125

Note: Y3b may have been struck in Egypt.

Obverse: *No flower at right of toughra*

Y#	KM#	Metal	Description	VF	EF	Unc
8	251	Silv	2-1/2 Ghirsh, Yr 4	100	200	450
9	253	Silv	5 Ghirsh, Yr 4	175	400	1,200
10	257	Silv	10 Ghirsh, Yr 4	200	450	1,300

Y#	KM#	Metal	Description	VF	EF	Unc
A10	264	Gold	100 Ghirsh, Yr 4	750	1,250	2,500

Note: Other gold coins dated Year 4, without flower, are thought to be patterns.

MURAD V,
1876
ACCESSION DATE AH 1293 ON COINS

Y#	KM#	Metal	Description	VF	EF	Unc
G11	270	Silv	1 Ghirsh, Yr 1	225	350	700

Note: YG11 can be distinguished from Y18a dated Year 1 only by details of the toughra.

Obverse: *Like YC22–D22, but toughra without flower*

Y#	KM#	Metal	Description	VF	EF	Unc
H11	271	Gold	50 Ghirsh, Yr 1	1,500	2,750	6,000
J11	272	Gold	100 Ghirsh, Yr 1	1,250	2,500	5,000

ABDUL HAMID II,
1876–1909
ACCESSION DATE AH 1293 ON COINS

First Coinage (Locally Struck)

Obverse: *Toughra and flower, value below*

Y#	KM#	Metal	Description	VF	EF	Unc
A17	275	Silv	10 Para, Yrs 1–3	75.00	150	225
B17	276	Silv	20 Para, Yrs 1–3	100.00	175	275
18a	277	Silv	1 Ghirsh, Yrs 1–5	7.50	15	50
20a	279	Silv	5 Ghirsh, Yr 2	1,750.00	2,500	—
22a	283	Silv	20 Ghirsh, Yrs 1, 5	2,000.00	4,000	—

Obverse: *Like that for silver coins*

Y#	KM#	Metal	Description	VF	EF	Unc
A22	280	Gold	5 Ghirsh, Yrs 2–7	115	145	200
D22	285	Gold	100 Ghirsh, Yrs 1–8	485	600	1,200
E22	286	Gold	500 Ghirsh, Yrs 1, 6	9,500	15,000	20,000

Obverse: *Phrase "al-Ghazi" (the Victorious) to right of toughra*

Y#	KM#	Metal	Description	VF	EF	Unc
A22a	298	Gold	5 Ghirsh, Yrs 15–34	115	135	175
B22	282	Gold	10 Ghirsh, Yrs 17–34	135	175	350

Second Coinage (Struck in Europe)

Y#	KM#	Metal	Description	VF	EF	Unc
12	287	Bz	1/40 Ghirsh, Yrs 10–35 *Yr 18, VF $45*	7.50	15	40
13	288	Bz	1/20 Ghirsh, Yrs 10–35 *Yr 18, VF $25*	7.50	15	40

Y#	KM#	Metal	Description	VF	EF	Unc
14	289	C-N	1/10 Ghirsh, Yrs 10–35 *Yr 18, VF $15*	7.50	15.00	60
15	290	C-N	2/10 Ghirsh, Yrs 10–35	7.50	17.50	70
16	291	C-N	5/10 Ghirsh, Yrs 10–33	7.50	17.50	70

Y#	KM#	Metal	Description	VF	EF	Unc
17	299	C-N	1 Ghirsh, Yrs 22–33 *Yr 22, VF $15*	7.50	15	60

Y#	KM#	Metal	Description	VF	EF	Unc
18	292	Silv	1 Ghirsh, Yrs 10–33	7.50	12.50	50
19	293	Silv	2 Ghirsh, Yrs 10–33	7.50	12.50	50
20	294	Silv	5 Ghirsh, Yrs 10–33	15.00	30.00	100
21	295	Silv	10 Ghirsh, Yrs 10–33	25.00	90.00	150
22	296	Silv	20 Ghirsh, Yrs 10–33	50.00	150.00	400

Design: ***Floral border both sides***

Y#	KM#	Metal	Description	VF	EF	Unc
F22	297	Gold	100 Ghirsh, Yr 12	BV	650	950

Mohammed V,
1901–1914
Accession Date AH 1327 on Coins

Designs: ***Similar to Y17–22***

Y#	KM#	Metal	Description	VF	EF	Unc
23	300	Bz	1/40 Ghirsh, Yrs 2–6	6.50	15	30
24	301	Bz	1/20 Ghirsh, Yrs 2–6	6.50	15	30

Y#	KM#	Metal	Description	VF	EF	Unc
25	302	C-N	1/10 Ghirsh, Yrs 2–6 *Yr 3, VF $20*	2.50	5.50	20
26	303	C-N	2/10 Ghirsh, Yrs 2–6	5.00	10.00	40
27	304	C-N	5/10 Ghirsh, Yrs 2–6	5.00	10.00	40
28	305	C-N	1 Ghirsh, Yrs 2–6	7.50	15.00	60

Y#	KM#	Metal	Description	VF	EF	Unc
29	306	Silv	1 Ghirsh, Yrs 2–3 *Year 3, Unc $150*	6.00	20	45
30	307	Silv	2 Ghirsh, Yrs 2–3	15.00	50	100
31	308	Silv	5 Ghirsh, Yrs 2–6	12.50	30	90
32	309	Silv	10 Ghirsh, Yrs 2–6	35.00	60	150
33	310	Silv	20 Ghirsh, Yrs 2–6	70.00	175	400

British Protectorate,
1914–1922
Sultan Hussein Kamil,
1915–1917

Y#	KM#	Metal	Description	VF	EF	Unc
34	312	Bz	1/2 Millieme, 1917	4.50	12.50	40

Y#	KM#	Metal	Description	VF	EF	Unc
35	313	C-N	1 Millieme, 1917	3	6.50	25.00
36	314	C-N	2 Milliemes, 1916–17	4	8.00	22.50
37	315	C-N	5 Milliemes, 1916–17 *1916, VF $6*	3	6.00	12.50
38	316	C-N	10 Milliemes, 1916–17 *1916, VF $10*	5	11.00	20.00

Y#	KM#	Metal	Description	VF	EF	Unc
39	317	Silv	2 Piastres, 1916–17	5.00	12	25
40	318	Silv	5 Piastres, 1916–17	7.50	20	50
41	319–320	Silv	10 Piastres, 1916–17	15.00	30	100
42	321–322	Silv	20 Piastres, 1916–17	30.00	55	275
						Proof: $2,500

Y#	KM#	Metal	Description	VF	EF	Unc
43	324	Gold	100 Piastres, 1916	550	700	1,000

FAUD, AS SULTAN,
1917–1922

Y#	KM#	Metal	Description	VF	EF	Unc
44	325	Silv	2 Piastres, 1920	45	125	650
45	326	Silv	5 Piastres, 1920	30	100	700
46	327	Silv	10 Piastres, 1920	45	125	625

Note: All Proofs of Y44–46 are rare.

INDEPENDENT KINGDOM,
1922–1952

FAUD, AS KING FAUD I,
1922–1936

First Coinage

Y#	KM#	Metal	Description	VF	EF	Unc
47	330	Bz	1/2 Millieme, 1924	2.50	6	25
48	331	Bz	1 Millieme, 1924	2.00	5	20

Y#	KM#	Metal	Description	VF	EF	Unc
49	332	C-N	2 Milliemes, 1924	2.00	5.00	20
50	333	C-N	5 Milliemes, 1924	2.50	7.50	30
51	334	C-N	10 Milliemes, 1924	3.50	17.50	65

Y#	KM#	Metal	Description	VF	EF	Unc
52	335	Silv	2 Ghirsh, 1923	5	10	25
53	336	Silv	5 Ghirsh, 1923	10	35	75
54	337	Silv	10 Ghirsh, 1923	25	60	125
55	338	Silv	20 Ghirsh, 1923	50	125	350

Y#	KM#	Metal	Description	VF	EF	Unc
56	339	Gold	20 Ghirsh, 1923	125	150	250
57	340	Gold	50 Ghirsh, 1923	BV	90	150
58	341	Gold	100 Ghirsh, 1922	BV	475	1,100
59	342	Gold	500 Ghirsh, 1922	BV	2,250	3,250
						Proof: $8,000

Second Coinage

Y#	KM#	Metal	Description	VF	EF	Unc
60	343	Bz	1/2 Millieme, 1929, 32	5	17.50	35
61	344	Bz	1 Millieme, 1929–35	1	3.00	10

Y#	KM#	Metal	Description	VF	EF	Unc
62	345	C-N	2 Milliemes, 1929	1.00	2.75	10
64	346	C-N	5 Milliemes, 1929–35	1.50	3.50	10
65	347	C-N	10 Milliemes, 1929–35	1.25	4.50	13

Y#	KM#	Metal	Description	VF	EF	Unc
63	356	C-N	2-1/2 Milliemes, 1933, octagonal	2.50	7.50	25

Reverse: ***Circle around central design***

Y#	KM#	Metal	Description	VF	EF	Unc
66	348	Silv	2 Ghirsh, 1929	5	10	25
67	349	Silv	5 Ghirsh, 1929, 33	10	30	65
68	350	Silv	10 Ghirsh, 1929, 33	25	50	100
69	352	Silv	20 Ghirsh, 1929, 33	50	100	400

Reverse: ***No circle around central design***

Y#	KM#	Metal	Description	VF	EF	Unc
70	351	Gold	20 Ghirsh, 1929–30	100	150	250
71	353	Gold	50 Ghirsh, 1929–30	250	350	500
72	354	Gold	100 Ghirsh, 1929–30	BV	650	1,100
73	355	Gold	500 Ghirsh, 1929–32	BV	3,750	5,750
						Proof: $6,000

FAROUK I,
1936–1952

First Coinage

Y#	KM#	Metal	Description	VF	EF	Unc
74	357	Bz	1/2 Millieme, 1938	3.50	6.50	15

Y#	KM#	Metal	Description	VF	EF	Unc
79	362	C-N	1 Millieme, 1938	2	7.50	20
80	359	C-N	2 Milliemes, 1938	5	15.00	30

Y#	KM#	Metal	Description	VF	EF	Unc
81	363	C-N	5 Milliemes, 1938, 41	1	3.50	10.00
82	364	C-N	10 Milliemes, 1938, 41	1	3.50	12.50

Y#	KM#	Metal	Description	VF	EF	Unc
83	365	Silv	2 Ghirsh, 1937–42	1.50	3.75	15
84	366	Silv	5 Ghirsh, 1937, 39	7.50	15.00	30
85	367	Silv	10 Ghirsh, 1937, 39	15.00	30.00	60
86	368	Silv	20 Ghirsh, 1937, 39	22.00	60.00	225

Royal Wedding

Y#	KM#	Metal	Description	VF	EF	Unc
88	370	Gold	20 Ghirsh, 1938	150	200	300
89	371	Gold	50 Ghirsh, 1938	250	350	500
90	372	Gold	100 Ghirsh, 1938	BV	600	1,000
91	373	Gold	*500 Ghirsh, 1938, Proof only, $7,500*			

Second Coinage

Y#	KM#	Metal	Description	VF	EF	Unc
75	358	Bz	1 Millieme, 1938–50	0.30	0.75	5

Y#	KM#	Metal	Description	VF	EF	Unc
77	360	Bz	5 Milliemes, 1938, 43, scalloped	0.50	1.50	10
						Proof: $55
78	361	Bz	10 Milliemes, 1938, 43, scalloped	0.50	1.50	10
						Proof: $55

Note: Y77–78 dated 1938 were struck in 1942.

Y#	KM#	Metal	Description	VF	EF	Unc
87	369	Silv	2 Ghirsh, 1944, hexagonal	1.25	4	15

REPUBLIC,
1953–1958

Obverse: ***Small bust of Sphinx***

Y#	KM#	Metal	Description	VF	EF	Unc
92	375	A-Bz	1 Millieme, 1954–56	4	9.50	12.50
93	378	A-Bz	5 Milliemes, 1954–56	6	12.00	30.00
94	380	A-Bz	10 Milliemes, 1954–55	6	10.00	35.00

Obverse: ***Large bust of Sphinx***

Y#	KM#	Metal	Description	VF	EF	Unc
92a	377	A-Bz	1 Millieme, 1956–58	0.25	0.50	2
93a	379	A-Bz	5 Milliemes, 1957–58	1.75	3.50	10
94a	381	A-Bz	10 Milliemes, 1955–58	1.75	3.50	10

Y#	KM#	Metal	Description	VF	EF	Unc
95	382	Silv	5 Ghirsh, 1956–57	2.00	4.50	10
96	383	Silv	10 Ghirsh, 1955–57	4.50	10.00	20
97	384	Silv	20 Ghirsh, 1956	12.50	20.00	35

Nationalization of Suez Canal

Y#	KM#	Metal	Description	VF	EF	Unc
98	385	Silv	25 Ghirsh, 1956	10	15	25

Evacuation of the British

Y#	KM#	Metal	Description	VF	EF	Unc
99	386	Silv	50 Ghirsh, 1956	20	30	55

Inauguration of National Assembly

Y#	KM#	Metal	Description	VF	EF	Unc
102	389	Silv	25 Ghirsh, 1957	10	15	25

3rd and 5th Anniversaries of the Revolution

Y#	KM#	Metal	Description	VF	EF	Unc
103	387	Gold	1 Pound, 1955, 57	BV	BV	600
104	388	Gold	5 Pounds, 1955, 57	BV	BV	2,750

EGYPT–UNITED ARAB REPUBLIC

SEE UNDER UNITED ARAB REPUBLIC

EL SALVADOR

Conquered by Spain in 1525, El Salvador is the smallest Central American country. It declared independence in 1821, but was plagued with revolutions and wars for the next century. Military dictatorships held sway from 1931–1979, when civil war erupted. A peace treaty was signed between the government and leftist rebels in 1992 and free elections have been held since 1994. *Language:* Spanish. *Capital:* San Salvador.

MONETARY SYSTEM

100 centavos = 1 peso, to 1940
100 centavos = 1 colon, 1941–

PRECIOUS METAL CONTENT

Dates	Denomination	Gross Wt (g)	Fineness	Net Wt (g)	Troy Oz.
		SILVER			
1892–1914	5 centavos	1.2500	0.8350	1.0438	0.0336
	10 centavos	2.5000	0.8350	2.0875	0.0671
	20 centavos	5.0000	0.8350	4.1750	0.1342
	25 centavos	6.2500	0.8350	5.2188	0.1678
	50 centavos	12.5000	0.9000	11.2500	0.3617
	1 peso	25.0000	0.9000	22.5000	0.7234
1943–44	25 centavos	7.5000	0.9000	6.7500	0.2170
		GOLD			
1892	2-1/2 pesos	4.0323	0.9000	3.6291	0.1167
	5 pesos	8.0645	0.9000	7.2581	0.2333
	10 pesos	16.1290	0.9000	14.5161	0.4667
	20 pesos	32.2581	0.9000	29.0323	0.9334
1925	20 colones	15.5600	0.9000	14.0040	0.4502

Y#	KM#	Metal	Description	VF	EF	Unc
1	106	C-N	1 Centavo, 1889, 1913	2	5	35
2	107	C-N	3 Centavos, 1889, 1913	5	15	70

Y#	KM#	Metal	Description	VF	EF	Unc
3	108	Cop	1 Centavo, 1892–93 *1893, VF $500*	75	150	400

Y#	KM#	Metal	Description	VF	EF	Unc
8	109	Silv	5 Centavos, 1892–93	15	30	60
9	110	Silv	10 Centavos, 1892	40	75	225
10	111	Silv	20 Centavos, 1892	20	50	150

Y#	KM#	Metal	Description	VF	EF	Unc
4	112	Silv	50 Centavos, 1892	50	175	500
5	114	Silv	1 Peso, 1892	150	300	950

Y#	KM#	Metal	Description	VF	EF	Unc
6	113	Silv	50 Centavos, 1892–94	30	90	250
7	115.1	Silv	1 Peso, 1892–1911	45	65	175
7a	115.2	Silv	1 Peso, 1904–14, heavier portrait	40	60	225

Y#	KM#	Metal	Description	VF	EF	Unc
11	116	Gold	2-1/2 Pesos, 1892	700	1,500	2,500
12	117	Gold	5 Pesos, 1892	1,000	2,000	3,500
13	118	Gold	10 Pesos, 1892	2,500	4,000	9,500
14	119	Gold	20 Pesos, 1892	5,000	9,000	15,000

Y#	KM#	Metal	Description	VF	EF	Unc
15	120	Cop	1/4 Real, 1909	25	65	175

Y#	KM#	Metal	Description	VF	EF	Unc
22	121	Silv	5 Centavos, 1911	5	12	55
23	122	Silv	10 Centavos, 1911	6	15	65
24	123	Silv	25 Centavos, 1911	6	15	65

Legend: ***DEL SALVADOR***

Y#	KM#	Metal	Description	VF	EF	Unc
16	127	C-N	1 Centavo, 1915–36	2	7.50	40
17	128	C-N	3 Centavos, 1915	3	20.00	80
18	129	C-N	5 Centavos, 1915–25	3	15.00	60

Legend: ***DE EL SALVADOR***

Y#	KM#	Metal	Description	VF	EF	Unc
19	133	C-N	1 Centavo, 1940	2.00	5.00	25
20	134	C-N	5 Centavos, 1940–74	0.20	0.50	1
21	130	C-N	10 Centavos, 1921–72	0.20	0.50	1

Y#	KM#	Metal	Description	VF	EF	Unc
19a	135	Bz	1 Centavo, 1942–72	0.10	0.20	0.50
20a	134a	CNZ	5 Centavos, 1944–52	0.25	1.00	5.00
21a	130a	CNZ	10 Centavos, 1952	0.25	1.00	3.00

Y#	KM#	Metal	Description	VF	EF	Unc
25	124	Silv	5 Centavos, 1914	4.50	9	40.00
26	125	Silv	10 Centavos, 1914	4.00	10	40.00
27	126	Silv	25 Centavos, 1914	8.00	15	50.00
28	136	Silv	25 Centavos, 1943–44, similar to Y21	5.00	8	17.50

400th Anniversary of San Salvador

Y#	KM#	Metal	Description	VF	EF	Unc
30	131	Silv	1 Colon, 1925	100	150	250

Y#	KM#	Metal	Description	VF	EF	Unc
29	132	Gold	20 Colones, 1925	2,500	3,500	5,000

Y#	KM#	Metal	Description	VF	EF	Unc
31	137	Silv	25 Centavos, 1953	1.25	2.50	4.50
32	138	Silv	50 Centavos, 1953	2.00	3.00	6.00

EQUATORIAL AFRICAN STATES

In 1961 the newly independent republics (former French colonies) of Cameroon, Central Africa, Chad, Congo, and Gabon formed an economic union with a common currency tied to the French franc. The name "Central African States" was adopted in 1974.

MONETARY SYSTEM
100 centimes = 1 franc

DECIMAL COINAGE

Y#	KM#	Metal	Description	VF	EF	Unc
1	1	A-Bz	5 Francs, 1961–62	1.00	1.50	3.00
2	2	A-Bz	10 Francs, 1961–62	1.25	1.75	3.25
3	4	A-Bz	25 Francs, 1962	1.50	2.25	5.00

Y#	KM#	Metal	Description	VF	EF	Unc
4	3	C-N	50 Francs, 1961, 63	3	5	7.50

ERITREA

A former Italian colony on the Red Sea, Eritrea became federated with Ethiopia in 1952 and was annexed as a province in 1962. After three decades of civil war, sovereignty was restored in 1993, though border demarcation questions have fueled fighting since then. *Languages:* Afar, Arabic. *Capital:* Asmara.

MONETARY SYSTEM
100 centesimi = 1 lira
5 lire = 1 tallero

PRECIOUS METAL CONTENT

Dates	Denomination	Gross Wt (g)	Fineness	Net Wt (g)	Troy Oz.
		SILVER			
1890–96	50 centesimi	2.5000	0.8350	2.0875	0.0671
	1 lira	5.0000	0.8350	4.1750	0.1342
	2 lire	10.0000	0.8350	8.3500	0.2685
	5 lire	28.1250	0.8000	22.5000	0.7234
1918	1 tallero	28.0668	0.8350	23.4358	0.7535

UMBERTO I, *1878–1900*

Y#	KM#	Metal	Description	VF	EF	Unc
1	1	Silv	50 Centesimi, 1890	60	150	325
2	2	Silv	1 Lira, 1890–96	50	100	250
3	3	Silv	2 Lire, 1890, 96	75	150	450
4	4	Silv	5 Lire / 1 Tallero, 1891, 96	225	500	1,500

Note: Many counterfeits exist.

VITTORIO EMANUELE III, *1900–1946*

Y#	KM#	Metal	Description	VF	EF	Unc
5	5	Silv	1 Tallero, 1918	125	225	650

Note: Diameter varies because coins were struck without a collar. The average diameter is 40 mm.

ESTONIA

Historically held by Germany, Sweden, and Russia, Estonia was a short-lived republic between 1920 and World War II. It declared independence from the USSR in 1990, and a parliamentary republic was established. *Languages:* Estonian, Russian. *Capital:* Tallinn.

MONETARY SYSTEM

100 penni = 1 mark, 1918–1927
100 senti = 1 kroon, 1928–1941

PRECIOUS METAL CONTENT

Dates	Denomination	Gross Wt (g)	Fineness	Net Wt (g)	Troy Oz.
		SILVER			
1930–33	1 kroon	6.0000	0.5000	3.0000	0.0965
	2 krooni	12.0000	0.5000	6.0000	0.1929

Y#	KM#	Metal	Description	VF	EF	Unc
1	10	Bz	1 Sent, 1929	2	3	6

Y#	KM#	Metal	Description	VF	EF	Unc
1a	19	Bz	1 Sent, 1939	12	17	35
2	15	Bz	2 Senti, 1934	3	5	10
3	11	Bz	5 Senti, 1931	3	6	15

Y#	KM#	Metal	Description	VF	EF	Unc
4	1	C-N	1 Mark, 1922	5	7.50	12
5	2	C-N	3 Marka, 1922	6	8.50	15
6	3	C-N	5 Marka, 1922	7	12.00	25

Y#	KM#	Metal	Description	VF	EF	Unc
4a	1a	N-Bz	1 Mark, 1924	6.00	9	17
5a	2a	N-Bz	3 Marka, 1925	7.50	12	32
6a	3a	N-Bz	5 Marka, 1924	7.50	12	32
7	4	N-Bz	10 Marka, 1925	10.00	17	40

Y#	KM#	Metal	Description	VF	EF	Unc
8	5	N-Bz	1 Mark, 1926	7.50	12	30
9	6	N-Bz	3 Marka, 1926	40.00	50	100
10	7	N-Bz	5 Marka, 1926	200.00	275	400
A10	8	N-Bz	10 Marka, 1926	750.00	1,000	—

Note: YA10 was not issued to circulation.

Y#	KM#	Metal	Description	VF	EF	Unc
11	12	N-Bz	10 Senti, 1931	4.00	7.50	15
12	17	N-Bz	20 Senti, 1935	3.50	6.50	15

Y#	KM#	Metal	Description	VF	EF	Unc
13	9	N-Bz	25 Senti, 1928	12	20	40

Y#	KM#	Metal	Description	VF	EF	Unc
14	18	N-Bz	50 Senti, 1936	15	22	45

Y#	KM#	Metal	Description	VF	EF	Unc
15	16	A-Bz	1 Kroon, 1934	10	15	32

Y#	KM#	Metal	Description	VF	EF	Unc
16	20	Silv	2 Krooni, 1930	15	20	35

Tercentenary, University of Tartu

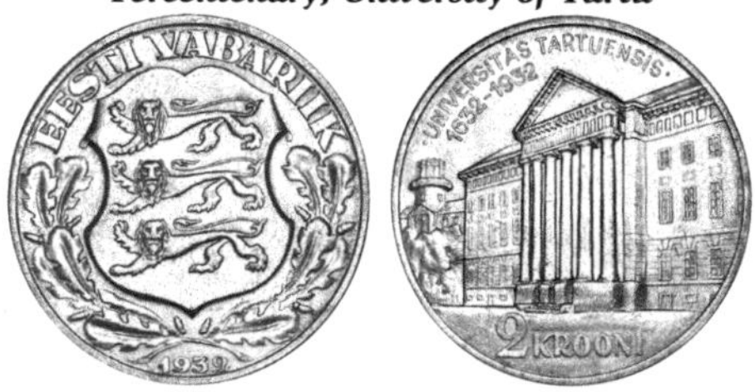

Y#	KM#	Metal	Description	VF	EF	Unc
17	13	Silv	2 Krooni, 1932	20	40	80

Tenth Singing Festival

Y#	KM#	Metal	Description	VF	EF	Unc
18	14	Silv	1 Kroon, 1933	20	37	75

ETHIOPIA

Located in northeast Africa, Ethiopia is one of the world's oldest Christian nations (since 330 AD). Modern Ethiopia established its independence by repelling an Italian invasion in 1896. A constitutional monarchy was created in 1931. In 1974 the emperor was deposed by a leftist military junta and the parliament dissolved; the nation was declared a socialist federal republic. Later it became a federal parliamentary republic. *Language:* Amharic. *Capital:* Addis Ababa.

MONETARY SYSTEM

To 1897
16 mahalek or gersh = 1 birr

1897
100 matona = 20 gersh (mahalek, piastres) = 1 birr (talari, taler)

1898–1933
32 besa = 16 gersh = 1 birr

1933–1945
100 matona = 1 birr

1945–
100 santeem = 1 birr

PRECIOUS METAL CONTENT

Dates	Denomination	Gross Wt (g)	Fineness	Net Wt (g)	Troy Oz.
		SILVER			
1897–1903	1 gersh	1.4038	0.8350	1.1721	0.0377
	1/8 birr	3.5094	0.8350	2.9303	0.0942
	1/4 birr	7.0188	0.8350	5.8607	0.1884
	1/2 birr	14.0375	0.8350	11.7213	0.3768
	1 birr	28.0750	0.8350	23.4426	0.7537
1944–45	50 santeem	7.0307	0.8000	5.6246	0.1808
1947	50 santeem	7.0307	0.7000	4.9215	0.1582
		GOLD			
1897–1931	1/4 wark	1.7500	0.9000	1.5750	0.0506
	1/2 wark	3.5000	0.9000	3.1500	0.1012
	1 wark	7.0000	0.9000	6.3000	0.2025

DATING SYSTEM

Dates on coins are in the Ethiopian Era (EE), which commenced in September of the year 7 AD. To convert from EE to AD dates, add 7 years and 8 months to the EE date.

Numeral Chart

1	2	3	4	5
፩	፪	፫	፬	፭
6	7	8	9	0
፮	፯	፰	፱	•
10	20	30	40	50
፲	፳	፴	፵	፶
60	70	80	90	100
፷	፸	፹	፺	፻

MENELIK II, *EE 1881–1906 (1889–1913)*

First Coinage

Y#	KM#	Metal	Description	VF	EF	Unc
A1	1	Silv	1 Mahalek, EE 1885	225	500	1,800

Second Coinage

Y1–10 were struck in Paris, all with the usual Paris Mint privy marks and (except for Y10) an "A" mintmark on reverse.

Y#	KM#	Metal	Description	VF	EF	Unc
1	9	Cop	1/100 Birr, EE 1889 (1897)	15	45	85
2	6	Br	1/4 Gersh, EE 1888 (1896) (26 mm)	1,000	1,500	2,500
3	7	Br	1/2 Gersh, EE 1888 (30 mm)	600	1,200	2,000
4	8	Br	1 Gersh, EE 1888 (38 mm)	1,000	1,500	2,500

Note: Y2–4 appear to have been struck only for presentation sets.

Reverse: *Lion's left foreleg raised*

Y#	KM#	Metal	Description	VF	EF	Unc
5	12	Silv	1 Gersh, EE 1889–95 (16 mm)	7.50	22.50	50
6	2	Silv	1/8 Birr, EE 1887–88 (20 mm)	45.00	100.00	300
7	3	Silv	1/4 Birr, EE 1887–95 (24 mm)	25.00	85.00	225
8	4	Silv	1/2 Birr, EE 1887–89 (30 mm)	20.00	50.00	200
			EE 1888, EF $525			
9	5	Silv	1 Birr, EE 1887–89 (40 mm)	55.00	150.00	450

Note: Coins dated EE 1888 were struck only for presentation. Final dates of Y5, 7, and 8 were occasionally restruck to 1928.

Obverse: *Slightly modified portrait*
Reverse: *Lion's right foreleg raised*

Y#	KM#	Metal	Description	VF	EF	Unc
10	19	Silv	1 Birr, EE 1892, 95 (1889, 1903)	125	225	950

Third Coinage

Y17-20 and Y11-13 were struck in Addis Ababa circa 1903-1933, all with the frozen date EE 1889. Dies, although made in Paris, lack the mintmarks and privy marks used on Y1-10.

Y#	KM#	Metal	Description	VF	EF	Unc
17	10	Cop	(1/32 Birr), EE 1889 (1897)	15	32.50	65

Note: Y17 was struck from dies intended for a silver 1/8 bir as Y18–20, and the incorrect value below the lion was defaced or removed. Edges may be reeded or plain.

Y#	KM#	Metal	Description	VF	EF	Unc
17a	11	Cop	1/32 Birr, EE 1889 (1897)	20	40	80

Note: Y17a is identical in design to Y17, but the correct value appears at the bottom. Edges may be reeded or plain.

Reverse: *No mintmarks*

Y#	KM#	Metal	Description	VF	EF	Unc
18	13	Silv	1 Gersh, EE 1889 (17 mm)	85	150	400
19	14	Silv	1/4 Birr, EE 1889 (25 mm)	25	75	250
20	15	Silv	1/2 Birr, EE 1889 (30 mm)	150	275	650

Y#	KM#	Metal	Description	VF	EF	Unc
11	16	Gold	1/4 Wark, EE 1889 (16 mm)	300	600	900
12	17	Gold	1/2 Wark, EE 1889 (18 mm)	500	650	950
13	18	Gold	1 Wark, EE 1889 (20 mm)	600	950	1,250

Note: Y11–13 were issued for presentation rather than circulation. Their weights vary widely, with no relationship to the values shown on the coins. Y18–20 were also struck in gold for presentation, usually with value defaced on reverse.

EMPRESS ZAUDITU, *EE 1909–1923 (1916–1930)*

Y#	KM#	Metal	Description	VF	EF	Unc
21	N/A	Gold	1 Wark, EE 1917 (1925)	700	1,400	2,500
A21	N/A	Gold	2 Warks, EE 1917	1,000	2,000	6,500
22	N/A	Gold	4 Warks, EE 1917	3,000	6,000	8,000

Note: These issues were presentation strikings from dies intended for silver coins. Values were usually defaced after striking. Weights of all are very irregular.

HAILE SELASSIE,
EE 1923–1966 (1930–1974)

First Coinage

Y#	KM#	Metal	Description	VF	EF	Unc
28	20	Gold	1/2 Wark, EE 1933 (1931) (18 mm)	500	1,000	3,000
29	21	Gold	1 Wark, EE 1933 (20 mm)	750	1,750	1,750

Note: Y28–29 were issued for presentation in varying weights. Similar silver coins with lion reverse are patterns, as are silver and gold coins dated EE 1921 (1928).

Second Coinage

Y#	KM#	Metal	Description	VF	EF	Unc
23	27	Cop	1 Matona, EE 1923 (1931)	3	7.50	20
24	28	Cop	5 Matonas, EE 1923	4	8.00	30

Y#	KM#	Metal	Description	VF	EF	Unc
25	29	Nick	10 Matonas, EE 1923 (1931)	2.50	5	15
26	30	Nick	25 Matonas, EE 1923	2.50	5	15
27	31	Nick	50 Matonas, EE 1923	4.00	8	20

Third Coinage

Y#	KM#	Metal	Description	VF	EF	Unc
30	32	Bz	1 Santeem (Cent), EE 1936 (1944) (17 mm)	0.25	0.75	3.75
31	33	Bz	5 Santeem, EE 1936 (20 mm)	0.20	0.40	1.00
32	34	Bz	10 Santeem, EE 1936 (23 mm)	0.20	0.40	1.00
33	35	Bz	25 Santeem, EE 1936 (26 mm)	15.00	30.00	55.00

Note: Most specimens of Y33 were converted to Y35 by crimping the edge so as to avoid confusion with Y34. Y30–32 were struck with date unchanged for many years.

Y#	KM#	Metal	Description	VF	EF	Unc
35	36	Bz	25 Santeem, EE 1936 (1944), scalloped	0.50	1	7.50

Note: Like Y30–32, Y35 was struck with date unchanged for many years.

Y#	KM#	Metal	Description	VF	EF	Unc
34	37	Silv	50 Santeem, EE 1936 (1944)	3	12.50	30

FAEROE ISLANDS

In the sixth century, Irish monks settled in this group of 18 islands located about 200 miles northwest of the Shetlands in the North Atlantic. By the ninth century, emigrants escaping tyranny in Norway settled there. Though the Faeroe Islands have been a Danish possession since 1386, they have had extensive home rule since 1948. *Language:* Danish. *Capital:* Thorshavn.

MONETARY SYSTEM

100 ore = 1 krone

CHRISTIAN X,
1912–1947

Y#	KM#	Metal	Description	VF	EF	Unc
1	1	Bz	1 Ore, 1941	27	50	115
2	2	Bz	2 Ore, 1941	20	45	90
3	3	Bz	5 Ore, 1941	20	35	90

Y#	KM#	Metal	Description	VF	EF	Unc
4	4	C-N	10 Ore, 1941	25	50	100
5	5	C-N	25 Ore, 1941	25	50	130

Note: Y1–5 are identical to Denmark Y46–50 except they do not bear a mintmark or mintmaster's initials.

FIJI

A group of about 330 islands in the South Pacific, Fiji was a British colony from 1874 to 1970, when it became an independent nation within the British Commonwealth. For many years ethnic tensions and political turmoil delayed effective parliamentary government. More recently the nation's elections have been deemed fair and free. *Languages:* English, Fijian, Hindustani. *Capital:* Suva.

MONETARY SYSTEM
12 pence = 1 shilling
2 shillings = 1 florin
20 shillings = 1 pound

PRECIOUS METAL CONTENT

Dates	Denomination	Gross Wt (g)	Fineness	Net Wt (g)	Troy Oz.
		Silver			
1934–45	6 pence	2.8276	0.5000	1.4138	0.0455
	1 shilling	5.6552	0.5000	2.8276	0.0909
	1 florin	11.3104	0.5000	5.6552	0.1818
1942–43	6 pence	2.8276	0.9000	2.5448	0.0818
	1 shilling	5.6552	0.9000	5.0897	0.1636
	1 florin	11.3104	0.9000	10.1794	0.3273

George V, *1910–1936*

Y#	KM#	Metal	Description	VF	EF	Unc
1	1	C-N	1/2 Penny, 1934	2.00	6	20
						Proof: $1,250
2	2	C-N	1 Penny, 1934–36	1.50	6	25
						Proof: $1,450

Y#	KM#	Metal	Description	VF	EF	Unc
3	3	Silv	6 Pence, 1934–36	3	15	60
						Proof: $600

Y#	KM#	Metal	Description	VF	EF	Unc
4	4	Silv	1 Shilling, 1934–36	7	20	100
						Proof: $700

Y#	KM#	Metal	Description	VF	EF	Unc
5	5	Silv	1 Florin, 1934–36	10	30	225
						Proof: $900

Edward VIII, *1936*

Y#	KM#	Metal	Description	VF	EF	Unc
6	6	C-N	1 Penny, 1936	1.50	4	10

George VI, *1936–1952*

Y#	KM#	Metal	Description	VF	EF	Unc
7	14	C-N	1/2 Penny, 1940–41	3.00	7	20
8	7	C-N	1 Penny, 1937–41, 45	2.00	4	10
7a	14a	Br	1/2 Penny, 1942–43	1.00	4	15
8a	7a	Br	1 Penny, 1942–43	1.50	5	20

Legend: ***EMPEROR to right of head***

Reverse: ***Designs like Y3–5***

Y#	KM#	Metal	Description	VF	EF	Unc
11	8	Silv	6 Pence, 1937	15	30	100
						Proof: $1,250
12	9	Silv	1 Shilling, 1937	17	50	120
						Proof: $1,550
13	10	Silv	1 Florin, 1937	15	70	300
						Proof: $1,750

Note: Y11–13 issued in both .500 fine (1938–1941, 1945) and .900 fine (1942–1943) silver.

Legend: ***KING EMPEROR to right of head***

Reverse: ***Designs like Y3–5***

Y#	KM#	Metal	Description	VF	EF	Unc
11a	11	Silv	6 Pence, 1938–41	6.00	17.50	85
12a	12	Silv	1 Shilling, 1938–41	7.50	20.00	100
13a	13	Silv	1 Florin, 1938–45	15.00	30.00	275

Y#	KM#	Metal	Description	VF	EF	Unc
17	15	N-Br	3 Pence, 1947, 12-sided	3	10	60 *Proof: $850*

Legend: ***KING GEORGE THE SIXTH***

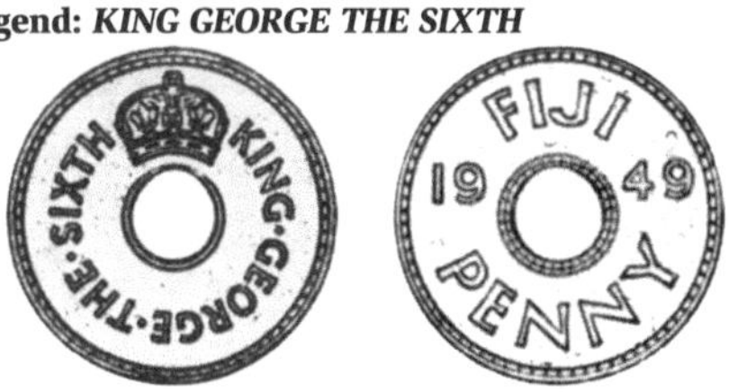

Y#	KM#	Metal	Description	VF	EF	Unc
18	16	C-N	1/2 Penny, 1949–52 *1949–50, Unc $11; 1952, Unc $8*	0.50	1.75	3 *Proof: $550*
19	17	C-N	1 Penny, 1949–52 *1950, Unc $11*	0.75	2.00	6 *Proof: $650*

Design: ***Similar to Y17, but with new legend on obverse***

Y#	KM#	Metal	Description	VF	EF	Unc
20	18	C-N	3 Pence, 1950, 52, 12-sided	3	10	25 *Proof: $900*

ELIZABETH II, *1952–1970*

Y#	KM#	Metal	Description	VF	EF	Unc
21	20	C-N	1/2 Penny, 1954	0.25	0.75	2 *Proof: $650*
22	21	C-N	1 Penny, 1954–68	0.25	0.75	5 *Proof: $550*

Y#	KM#	Metal	Description	VF	EF	Unc
23	22	N-Br	3 Pence, 1955–67, 12-sided	0.25	0.50	3.50 *Proof: $425*

Reverse: ***Designs like Y3–5***

Y#	KM#	Metal	Description	VF	EF	Unc
24	19	C-N	6 Pence, 1953–67	0.50	1.00	3.50 *Proof: $750*
25	23	C-N	1 Shilling, 1957–65	0.75	1.50	3.50 *Proof: $475*
26	24	C-N	1 Florin, 1957–65	0.75	1.25	5.00 *Proof: $950*

FINLAND (SUOMI)

What is now Finland was conquered by Sweden in 1157 and Christianized. In 1809 Russia seized the land and made it a grand duchy. It declared itself an independent republic in 1917, during the Russian revolution. Following a Russian invasion in 1939 and a disastrous alliance with Nazi Germany, Finland was forced to cede significant territory to Russia. After World War II, Finland entered a treaty of friendship and mutual aid with the USSR, but maintained a foreign policy of non-alignment during the Cold War era. *Languages:* Finnish, Swedish. *Capital:* Helsinki.

MONETARY SYSTEM

100 pennia = 1 markka

PRECIOUS METAL CONTENT

Dates	Denomination	Gross Wt (g)	Fineness	Net Wt (g)	Troy Oz.
		SILVER			
1864–1917	25 pennia	1.2747	0.7500	0.9560	0.0307
	50 pennia	2.5494	0.7500	1.9121	0.0615
	1 markka	5.1828	0.8680	4.4987	0.1446
	2 markkaa	10.3657	0.8680	8.9974	0.2893
1951–52	500 markkaa	12.0000	0.5000	6.0000	0.1929
1956–60	100 markkaa	5.2000	0.5000	2.6000	0.0836
	200 markkaa	8.3000	0.5000	4.1500	0.1334
	1000 markkaa	14.0000	0.8750	12.2500	0.3938
		GOLD			
1878–1913	10 markkaa	3.2258	0.9000	2.9032	0.0933
	20 markkaa	6.4516	0.9000	5.8064	0.1867
1926	100 markkaa	4.2105	0.9000	3.7895	0.1218
	200 markkaa	8.4211	0.9000	7.5789	0.2437

UNDER RUSSIAN EMPIRE, *1809–1917*

GENERAL COINAGE

Y1–6 do not bear the name of the ruler and were struck without change through three reigns.

Y#	KM#	Metal	Description	VF	EF	Unc
1	6.1	Silv	25 Pennia, 1865–71 *1867–68, VF $200*	25	55	125
2	2.1	Silv	50 Pennia, 1864–71 *1868, VF $100*	20	50	150

Y#	KM#	Metal	Description	VF	EF	Unc
3	3.1	Silv	1 Markka, 1864–67	12	35	100
4	7.1	Silv	2 Markkaa, 1865–70 *1867, Rare*	20	50	175

Modified Dies

Y#	KM#	Metal	Description	VF	EF	Unc
1a	6.2	Silv	25 Pennia, 1872–1917 *1876, VF $1,500*	10	20	40
2a	2.2	Silv	50 Pennia, 1872–1917 *1876, VF $1,500*	10	20	40
3a	3.2	Silv	1 Markka, 1872–1915	10	20	40
4a	7.2	Silv	2 Markkaa, 1872–1908	15	27	75

Y#	KM#	Metal	Description	VF	EF	Unc
5	8	Gold	10 Markkaa, 1878–1913 *1905, VF $1,500*	110	150	200
6	9	Gold	20 Markkaa, 1878–1913	145	225	275

ALEXANDER II,
1855–1881

Y#	KM#	Metal	Description	VF	EF	Unc
7	1.1	Cop	1 Penni, 1864–71 *1864, VF $2,000*	10	25	60
8	4.1	Cop	5 Pennia, 1865–70	10	35	70
9	5.1	Cop	10 Pennia, 1865–67	15	40	125

Modified Dies

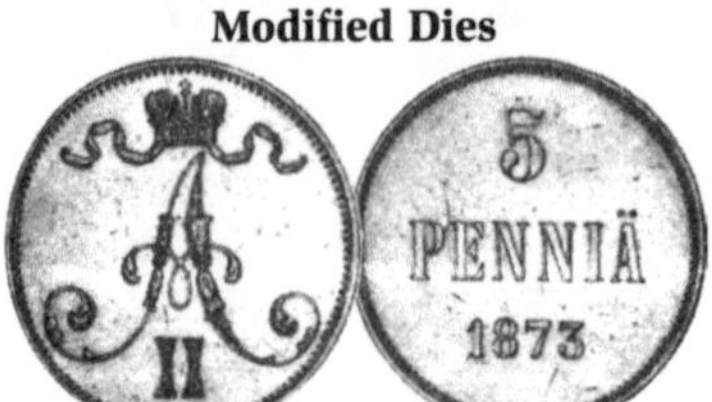

Y#	KM#	Metal	Description	VF	EF	Unc
7a	1.2	Cop	1 Penni, 1872–76	7.50	22	45
8a	4.2	Cop	5 Pennia, 1872–75	7.50	32	100
9a	5.2	Cop	10 Pennia, 1875–76 *1875, VF $200*	22.00	125	300

ALEXANDER III,
1881–1894

Y#	KM#	Metal	Description	VF	EF	Unc
10	10	Cop	1 Penni, 1881–94 *1882, 84, VF $75*	3.00	7.00	17.50
11	11	Cop	5 Pennia, 1888–92	6.00	17.50	70.00
12	12	Cop	10 Pennia, 1889–91	22.50	75.00	200.00

NIKOLAI II,
1894–1917

Y#	KM#	Metal	Description	VF	EF	Unc
13	13	Cop	1 Penni, 1895–1916	3	6.00	13
14	15	Cop	5 Pennia, 1896–1917 *1910, VF $50*	3	6.50	22
15	14	Cop	10 Pennia, 1895–1917 *1898, VF $100*	5	15.00	55

REPUBLIC,
1918–

First Coinage

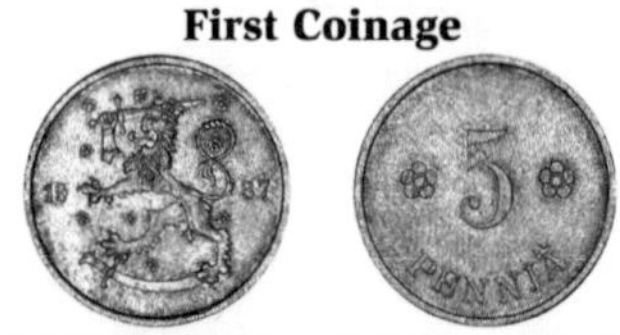

Y#	KM#	Metal	Description	VF	EF	Unc
22	23	Bz	1 Penni, 1919–24	0.60	1.25	2.50
23	22	Bz	5 Pennia, 1918–40	0.40	0.90	2.50
24	24	Bz	10 Pennia, 1919–40	0.40	0.90	2.50

Y#	KM#	Metal	Description	VF	EF	Unc
23a	TS6	Iron	5 Pennia, 1918	500	900	1,500

Y#	KM#	Metal	Description	VF	EF	Unc
25	25	C-N	25 Pennia, 1921–40	0.40	1.00	3.00
26	26	C-N	50 Pennia, 1921–40	0.40	1.50	4.00
27	27	C-N	1 Markka, 1921–24 (24 mm)	1.50	3.75	7.50

Y#	KM#	Metal	Description	VF	EF	Unc
27a	30	C-N	1 Markka, 1928–40 (21 mm)	0.75	2.50	7

Y#	KM#	Metal	Description	VF	EF	Unc
28	31	A-Bz	5 Markkaa, 1928–46 *1928–29, VF $75*	3.00	10.00	27.00
28a	31a	A-Bz	5 Markkaa, 1946–52	0.75	1.75	4.50
29	63	A-Bz	10 Markkaa, 1928–39	4.00	12.00	50.00
30	32	A-Bz	20 Markkaa, 1931–39 *1931–32, VF $40*	3.50	13.50	35.00

Note: Dates after 1946 of Y28a vary in composition.

Y#	KM#	Metal	Description	VF	EF	Unc
31	28	Gold	100 Markkaa, 1926	600	825	1,100
32	29	Gold	200 Markkaa, 1926	850	1,200	1,500

Second Coinage

Y#	KM#	Metal	Description	VF	EF	Unc
33	64	Bz	5 Pennia, 1941–43	0.60	1.25	3.50
34	33	Bz	10 Pennia, 1941–43	0.60	1.25	3.50

Designs: *Like Y25–27*

Y#	KM#	Metal	Description	VF	EF	Unc
25a	25a	Bz	25 Pennia, 1940–43	0.45	2.00	5.00
26a	26a	Bz	50 Pennia, 1940–43	0.45	2.00	5.00
27b	30a	Bz	1 Markka, 1940–51 *1949, VF $2,500*	0.50	1.50	5.50

Y#	KM#	Metal	Description	VF	EF	Unc
34b	34	Iron	10 Pennia, 1943–45	2.00	3.00	6
25b	25b	Iron	25 Pennia, 1943–45	0.75	1.75	6
26b	26b	Iron	50 Pennia, 1943–48	0.75	2.00	8
27c	30b	Iron	1 Markka, 1943–52	0.40	1.00	5

15th Olympic Games

Y#	KM#	Metal	Description	VF	EF	Unc
35	35	Silv	500 Markkaa, 1951–52 *1951, Unc $450*	32	42	55

Third Coinage

Y#	KM#	Metal	Description	VF	EF	Unc
36	36	Iron	1 Markka, 1952–53	0.45	1.00	4.00
37	37	Iron	5 Markkaa, 1952–53	0.45	1.50	5.00
36a	36a	N-Pl	1 Markka, 1953–62 *1953, VF $10*	0.20	0.40	0.75
37a	37a	N-Pl	5 Markkaa, 1953–62 *1953, VF $40*	0.30	0.45	1.25

Y#	KM#	Metal	Description	VF	EF	Unc
38	38	A-Bz	10 Markkaa, 1952–62	0.30	0.75	3
39	39	A-Bz	20 Markkaa, 1952–62 *1952, VF $15*	0.50	15.00	5
40	40	A-Bz	50 Markkaa, 1952–62 *1958, 60, VF $40*	0.75	2.50	6

Y#	KM#	Metal	Description	VF	EF	Unc
41	41	Silv	100 Markkaa, 1956–60	2.00	3.25	5.00
42	42	Silv	200 Markkaa, 1956–59 *1958S, VF $400*	3.50	4.50	7.50

Centennial of Markkaa Currency System

Y#	KM#	Metal	Description	VF	EF	Unc
43	43	Silv	1,000 Markkaa, 1960	12	20	28

Y#	KM#	Metal	Description	VF	EF	Unc
44	44	Bz	1 Penni, 1963–69	0.15	0.50	2
45	45	Bz	5 Pennia, 1963–77	0.10	0.25	1

Y#	KM#	Metal	Description	VF	EF	Unc
46	46	A-Bz	10 Pennia, 1963–82	0.10	0.20	0.50
47	47	A-Bz	20 Pennia, 1963–90	0.10	0.25	0.50
48	48	A-Bz	50 Pennia, 1963–90	0.20	0.50	1.00

Y#	KM#	Metal	Description	VF	EF	Unc
49	49	Bill	1 Markkaa, 1964–68	1	1.50	3

CIVIL WAR, *1917–1918*

OFFICIAL GOVERNMENT ISSUES

Y#	KM#	Metal	Description	VF	EF	Unc
16	16	Cop	1 Penni, 1917	3	7	15
17	17	Cop	5 Pennia, 1917	3	7	15
18	18	Cop	10 Pennia, 1917	3	7	15

Y#	KM#	Metal	Description	VF	EF	Unc
19	19	Silv	25 Pennia, 1917	3.00	6.50	12
20	20	Silv	50 Pennia, 1917	3.50	7.00	13

COMMUNIST GOVERNMENT ISSUE, *1918*

Y#	KM#	Metal	Description	VF	EF	Unc
21	21	Cop	5 Pennia, 1918	27	45	65

FRANCE

That portion of western Europe that roughly comprises today's France was granted by a ninth-century treaty to a grandson of Charlemagne. By the mid-14th century it was the most powerful nation in Europe. The absolute monarchy was dissolved with the creation of the First Republic in the 1789 revolution. Periods of Napoleonic, royal, and republican rule alternated for a century and a half, until World War II. Post-war governments strengthened the executive branch. Today France plays an influential global role as a permanent member of the United Nations Security Council, NATO, the G-7, the G-20, the EU, and other multilateral organizations. *Language:* French. *Capital:* Paris.

MONETARY SYSTEM

100 centimes = 1 franc

PRECIOUS METAL CONTENT

France was a member of the Latin Monetary Union; see appendix A.

Dates	Denomination	Gross Wt (g)	Fineness	Net Wt (g)	Troy Oz.
		SILVER			
1848–66	20 centimes	1.0000	0.9000	0.9000	0.0289
	50 centimes	2.5000	0.9000	2.2500	0.0723
	1 franc	5.0000	0.9000	4.5000	0.1446
	2 francs	10.0000	0.9000	9.0000	0.2893
	5 francs	25.0000	0.9000	22.5000	0.7234
1866–1920	20 centimes	1.0000	0.9000	0.9000	0.0289
	50 centimes	2.5000	0.8350	2.0875	0.0671
	1 franc	5.0000	0.8350	4.1750	0.1342
	2 francs	10.0000	0.9000	9.0000	0.2893
	5 francs	25.0000	0.9000	22.5000	0.7234
1929–39	10 francs	10.0000	0.6800	6.8000	0.2186
	20 francs	20.0000	0.6800	13.6000	0.4372
1960–69	5 francs	12.0000	0.8350	10.0200	0.3221
		GOLD			
1848–1914	5 francs	1.6129	0.9000	1.4516	0.0467
	10 francs	3.2258	0.9000	2.9032	0.0933
	20 francs	6.4516	0.9000	5.8064	0.1867
	50 francs	16.1290	0.9000	14.5161	0.4667
	100 francs	32.2581	0.9000	29.0323	0.9334
1929–36	100 francs	6.5500	0.9000	5.8950	0.1895

Except where noted, prices are for the most common dates and mints. Usually coins bearing other than "A" (Paris) or "BB" (Strasbourg) mintmarks sell for more than the prices stated.

REPUBLIC, *1848–1852*

First Coinage

Y#	KM#	Metal	Description	VF	EF	Unc
1	754	Cop	1 Centime, 1848–51	4	10	35

Y#	KM#	Metal	Description	VF	EF	Unc
7	756	Silv	5 Francs, 1848–49 *1848D, VF $350; 1849D, Rare*	20	40	275 *Proof: $15,000*

Y#	KM#	Metal	Description	VF	EF	Unc
8	757	Gold	20 Francs, 1848–49	BV	300	600

Second Coinage

Y#	KM#	Metal	Description	VF	EF	Unc
2	758	Silv	20 Centimes, 1849–51 *1849A, VF $175*	17.50	40	100
3	769	Silv	50 Centimes, 1849–51 *1849A, VF $400*	60.00	135	300
4	759	Silv	1 Franc, 1849–51	75.00	130	450
5	760	Silv	2 Francs, 1849–51	100.00	300	1,000
6	761	Silv	5 Francs, 1849–51 *1850K, VF $175*	20.00	40	300

Y#	KM#	Metal	Description	VF	EF	Unc
9	770	Gold	10 Francs, 1850–51	175	225	850
10	762	Gold	20 Francs, 1849–51	BV	325	400

Third Coinage

Y#	KM#	Metal	Description	VF	EF	Unc
11	793	Silv	50 Centimes, 1852	90.00	160	400
12	772	Silv	1 Franc, 1852	100.00	175	500
13	773	Silv	5 Francs, 1852 *1852BB, VF $750*	27.50	45	400

Obverse: ***Head to right***

Y#	KM#	Metal	Description	VF	EF	Unc
A13	774	Gold	20 Francs, 1852	BV	285	500

SECOND EMPIRE

BONAPARTE, AS EMPEROR NAPOLEON III, *1852–1870*

First Coinage

Y#	KM#	Metal	Description	VF	EF	Unc
14	775	Bz	1 Centime, 1853–57 *1853B,D,K, 54K, 55MA,W, 56A,BB,K,W, VF $18; 1854D, 55B,D,K, VF $28; 1854B, VF $150; 1856 D,K, VF $275*	7.00	15.00	40
15	776	Bz	2 Centimes, 1853–57 *1853B,BB, 54D,K,MA, 1855K, MA,W, VF $11; 1853K, 55B, 57MA, VF $20; 1853MA, 1857D,K, VF 35*	3.00	9.00	30
16	777	Bz	5 Centimes, 1853–57 *1853BB,D,W, 55BB,D,K,W, 1856D,1857A, VF $12; 1853B, VF $18; 1853K,MA, 57K,MA, VF $37; 1857B,D, VF $95; 1857BB, VF $200*	4.75	17.50	60
17	771	Bz	10 Centimes, 1852–57 *1852A, 53D, 54K,MA,W, 55D,K,MA,W, 57D-W, VF $8; 1853K,MA, 57BB,K,MA, VF $45; 1857W, VF $65*	5.00	15.00	90

Visit of Royal Couple to Lille Bourse

Y#	KM#	Metal	Description	VF	EF	Unc
A16	N/A	Bz	(5 Centimes), 1853	25	75	125
A17	N/A	Bz	(10 Centimes), 1853	25	75	125

Emperor's Visit to Bourse

Y#	KM#	Metal	Description	VF	EF	Unc
B17	N/A	Bz	(10 Centimes), 1854	25	75	125

Dedication of Napoleon I Monument

Y#	KM#	Metal	Description	VF	EF	Unc
C17	N/A	Bz	(10 Centimes), 1854	25	75	145

Note: YA16–C17 were struck on 5- and 10-centime flans using the normal obverse with special reverse legends. Although bearing no denominations, they circulated with regular issues.

Y#	KM#	Metal	Description	VF	EF	Unc
22	778	Silv	20 Centimes, 1853–63 *1856A, 63BB, VF $335; 1857A, VF $90; 1862A, VF $150*	17.50	40	100
23	794	Silv	50 Centimes, 1853–63 *1853A,VF $95; 1863BB, VF $500*	35.00	65	225
24	779	Silv	1 Franc, 1853–64 *1853A, 56D, 60BB, VF $110; 1863A, VF $500; 1863BB, VF $1,250*	40.00	80	300
25	780	Silv	2 Francs, 1853–59 *1858A, VF $1,100; 1859A, VF $3,000*	350.00	650	2,000
26	782	Silv	5 Francs, 1854–59, reverse like Y30 *1854, 57–58, VF $575; 1859, VF $1,250*	80.00	175	900

Y#	KM#	Metal	Description	VF	EF	Unc
33	783	Gold	5 Francs, 1854–55 (14.5 mm) *1855A, Rare*	150	225	425
33A	787	Gold	5 Francs, 1856–60 (16.5 mm) *1855A, VF $3,000; 1858BB, VF $750*	80	135	350
34	784	Gold	10 Francs, 1854–55 (17 mm) *1855A, Rare*	300	525	1,250
34A	784	Gold	10 Francs, 1855–60 (19 mm)	175	200	400

Y#	KM#	Metal	Description	VF	EF	Unc
35	781	Gold	20 Francs, 1853–60	BV	BV	375
36	785	Gold	50 Francs, 1855–60	BV	850	1,350
37	786	Gold	100 Francs, 1855–60	BV	1,500	2,000

Second Coinage

Y#	KM#	Metal	Description	VF	EF	Unc
18	795	Bz	1 Centime, 1861–70 *1870A, VF $35*	3	8	25
19	796	Bz	2 Centimes, 1861–62	3	8	**25**
20	797	Bz	5 Centimes, 1861–65	3	8	**25**
21	798	Bz	10 Centimes, 1861–65 *1863K, 65A, VF $22*	6	20	60

Y#	KM#	Metal	Description	VF	EF	Unc
27	805	Silv	20 Centimes, 1864, 66 (15 mm) *1864A, 66K, VF $20; 1864BB,K, VF $90*	10	20	65
28	808	Silv	20 Centimes, 1867–69 (16 mm) *1855A, VF $3,000; 1858BB, VF $750*	10	20	65
29	814	Silv	50 Centimes, 1864–69 *1868BB, 69BB, VF $100*	10	20	85

Y#	KM#	Metal	Description	VF	EF	Unc
30	806	Silv	1 Franc, 1866–70 *1867K, 69–70, VF $22.50*	11	27.50	100
31	807	Silv	2 Francs, 1866–70 *1866K, 68BB, VF $55; 1867K, 69A,BB, VF $35*	15	55.00	300
32	799	Silv	5 Francs, 1861–70 *1861–66, VF, $500*	20	30.00	225

Obverse: ***Laureate head to right***
Reverse: ***Value in wreath***

Y#	KM#	Metal	Description	VF	EF	Unc
38	803	Gold	5 Francs, 1862–69	85	150	350
39	800	Gold	10 Francs, 1861–69	170	225	350

Y#	KM#	Metal	Description	VF	EF	Unc
40	801	Gold	20 Francs, 1861–70	BV	BV	400
A40	804	Gold	*50 Francs, 1862–69*	BV	650	1,250
B40	802	Gold	100 Francs, 1862–70 *1870A, VF $35,000*	1,650	1,950	2,450
					Proof: $50,000	

REPUBLIC,
1870–1940
First Coinage

Y#	KM#	Metal	Description	VF	EF	Unc
41	826	Bz	1 Centime, 1872–97	1.50	4	10.00
42	827	Bz	2 Centimes, 1877–97 *1894A, VF $13*	2.00	5	12.50
43	821	Bz	5 Centimes, 1871–98 *1871K, 78K, VF $275; 1877–79, VF $30*	8.00	15	50.00
44	815	Bz	10 Centimes, 1870–98 *1871K, VF $160; 1877A, VF $100; 1878K, VF $250*	4.00	8	40.00

Reverse: ***Without motto***

Y#	KM#	Metal	Description	VF	EF	Unc
45	816	Silv	2 Francs, 1870–71 *1870A, VF $50*	25	85	350
46	818	Silv	5 Francs, 1870–71	60	150	700

Reverse: ***With motto***

Y#	KM#	Metal	Description	VF	EF	Unc
47	828	Silv	*20 Centimes, 1878 (30 pcs), 1889 (100 pcs), Proof only, Rare*			
48	834	Silv	50 Centimes, 1871–95 *1872K, 74A, VF $70; 1873K, VF $750; 1886A; VF $100; 1878, 89, Rare*	3	15	50
				Proof: $3,500		
49	822	Silv	1 Franc, 1871–95 *1878, 89, Rare; 1872A,K, VF $10*	6	10	75
				Proof: $5,000		
50	817	Silv	2 Francs, 1870–95 *1878, 89, Rare*	15	30	200
				Proof: $9,500		
51	819	Silv	5 Francs, 1870	50	85	500

Note: Proofs of Y47–57 dated 1878 and 1889 are very rare.

Y#	KM#	Metal	Description	VF	EF	Unc
52	820	Silv	5 Francs, 1870–78 *1872K, VF $950; 1878A, 89, Rare*	20	27.50	75
52a	823	Silv	5 Francs, 1871, reverse small trident symbol (Commune issue)	300	600.00	1,400

Design: ***Like Y9***

Y#	KM#	Metal	Description	VF	EF	Unc
54	830	Gold	10 Francs, 1895–99	185	200	385

Y#	KM#	Metal	Description	VF	EF	Unc
55	825	Gold	20 Francs, 1871–98	BV	BV	400
56	831	Gold	50 Francs, 1878–1904 *1887, 89, 1900, Rare*	1,000	1,500	2,200
57	832	Gold	100 Francs, 1878–1906 *1887, 94, 96, Rare; 1878, 89, Proof only, Rare*	BV	1,850	2,250

Second Coinage

From 1898 to 1920, all Proofs were struck with matte surfaces.

Y#	KM#	Metal	Description	VF	EF	Unc
58	840	Bz	1 Centime, 1898–1920 *1898–99, VF $9; 1901, VF $12; 1902–04, 13, VF $3.50; 1910, VF $55; 1898, 1900, Proof: $350*	1.50	2	6
59	841	Bz	2 Centimes, 1898–1920 *1900, VF $175; 1907, VF $45; 1910, VF $20; 1898, 1900, Proof: $600*	2.00	4	12
60	842	Bz	5 Centimes, 1898–1921 *1921, VF $2,000; 1898, 1900, Proof: $350*	1.00	4	15
61	843	Bz	10 Centimes, 1898–1921 *1905, VF $50; 1898, 1900, Proof: $350*	2.00	4	20

Y#	KM#	Metal	Description	VF	EF	Unc
69	855	Nick	25 Centimes, 1903	2	4	25

Y#	KM#	Metal	Description	VF	EF	Unc
70	856	Nick	25 Centimes, 1904–05	2.50	9	70

Y#	KM#	Metal	Description	VF	EF	Unc
62	854	Silv	50 Centimes, 1897–1920 *1897, VF $75; 1902, 04, 06, VF $9; 1903, 11, VF $30*	1.50	3	15 *Proof: $275*

Note: All dates before 1911 are scarcer.

Y#	KM#	Metal	Description	VF	EF	Unc
63	844	Silv	1 Franc, 1898–1920 *1900, VF $325; 1903, VF $100; 1914C, VF $375*	3	5	20 *Proof: $250*

Note: All dates before 1915 are scarcer.

Y#	KM#	Metal	Description	VF	EF	Unc
64	845	Silv	2 Francs, 1898–1920 *1900, VF $100; 1898–1914, VF $12.50*	10	15	50 *Proof: $650*

Note: All dates before 1915 are scarcer.

Y#	KM#	Metal	Description	VF	EF	Unc
65	846	Gold	10 Francs, 1899–1914	BV	65	275
					Proof: $2,500	
66	847	Gold	20 Francs, 1899–1906, edge DIEU PROTEGE LA FRANCE	BV	BV	365
					Proof: $3,500	
66a	857	Gold	20 Francs, 1907–1914, edge LIBERTE EGALITE FRATERNITE	BV	BV	365

Note: Y66a was officially restruck late in the 20th century.

Third Coinage

Y#	KM#	Metal	Description	VF	EF	Unc
73	866	Nick	10 Centimes, 1914	1,000.00	1,500	2,500
76	867	Nick	25 Centimes, 1914–17 *1916–17, VF $45*	4.50	8	25

Y#	KM#	Metal	Description	VF	EF	Unc
71	865	C-N	5 Centimes, 1914, 17–20 (19 mm) *1914, Rare*	2.50	15.00	20
72	875	C-N	5 Centimes, 1920–38 (17 mm) *1920, VF $20*	0.50	2.00	15
73a	866a	C-N	10 Centimes, 1917–38	0.50	1.00	5
76a	867a	C-N	25 Centimes, 1917–37	1.00	1.50	10

Y#	KM#	Metal	Description	VF	EF	Unc
72a	875a	N-Bz	5 Centimes, 1938–39	0.50	1	4.75
73c	889	N-Bz	10 Centimes, 1938–39	0.50	1	3.00
76b	867b	N-Bz	25 Centimes, 1938–40 *1940, VF $12.50*	0.75	1	3.75

Y#	KM#	Metal	Description	VF	EF	Unc
77	884	A-Bz	50 Centimes, 1921–29 *1929, VF $9.50*	1.00	3	13.00
78	876	A-Bz	1 Franc, 1920–27 *1920, VF $6.50; 1926, VF $8.50*	1.00	2	12.50
79	877	A-Bz	2 Francs, 1920–27 *1920, VF $25; 1927, VF $175*	1.50	3	20.00

Y#	KM#	Metal	Description	VF	EF	Unc
80	894.1	A-Bz	50 Centimes, 1931–41, 47 *1947, VF $75*	0.50	1	4
81	885	A-Bz	1 Franc, 1931–41 *1935, VF $17.50*	1.00	2	7
82	886	A-Bz	2 Francs, 1931–41 *1935, VF $35*	1.00	3	15

Note: For similar aluminum-bronze coins dated 1944, see French West Africa.

Y#	KM#	Metal	Description	VF	EF	Unc
83	887	Nick	5 Francs, 1933	4	8	25

Y#	KM#	Metal	Description	VF	EF	Unc
84	888	Nick	5 Francs, 1933–39 *1936, EF $950; 1938, EF $20, VF $35; 1939, EF $5,000*	2	4.50	55

Y#	KM#	Metal	Description	VF	EF	Unc
84a	888a	A-Bz	5 Francs, 1938–40, 45–47 *1947, VF $400*	3.50	6	50

Y#	KM#	Metal	Description	VF	EF	Unc
86	878	Silv	10 Francs, 1929–39 *1936, 3 known; 1937, VF $125*	3	7.00	20
87	879	Silv	20 Francs, 1929–39 *1932, Unique; 1936, VF $300; 1939, Unc $6,500*	10	12.50	40

Y#	KM#	Metal	Description	VF	EF	Unc
88	880	Gold	100 Francs, 1929–36 *1929, 33, VF $2,000; 1932, 34, Rare*	975	1,250	1,500

WORLD WAR II ISSUES

German Occupation (Vichy) Government, *1940–1944*

First Coinage

Y#	KM#	Metal	Description	VF	EF	Unc
73b	895–897	Zinc	10 Centimes, 1941	1	1.50	7

Y#	KM#	Metal	Description	VF	EF	Unc
80a	894.1a	Alum	50 Centimes, 1941, 44–47	0.50	1.00	7
81a	885a.1	Alum	1 Franc, 1941, 43–59 *1943, Rare*	1.00	3.50	10
82a	886a.1	Alum	2 Francs, 1941, 44–59	0.50	1.00	10

Note: Y80a–82a were struck under the Vichy government in 1941, then were resumed by the de Gaulle government after German withdrawal in 1944.

Second Coinage

Reverse: *Value written out*

Y#	KM#	Metal	Description	VF	EF	Unc
V90	899	Zinc	VINGT (20) Centimes, 1941	3.00	7	27.50
V91	898	Zinc	10 Centimes, 1941–43 (21 mm)	0.50	1	9.00

Reverse: *Value in numerals*

Y#	KM#	Metal	Description	VF	EF	Unc
V93	903	Zinc	10 Centimes, 1943–44 (17 mm)	1	2	13.00
V92	900	Zinc	20 Centimes, 1941–44 *1944, VF $35*	1	3	17.50

Y#	KM#	Metal	Description	VF	EF	Unc
V92a	900.2a	Iron	20 Centimes, 1944	60	100	200

Y#	KM#	Metal	Description	VF	EF	Unc
V94	914	Alum	50 Centimes, 1942–44	0.50	1.00	6.50
V95	902	Alum	1 Franc, 1942–44	2.00	8.50	25.00
V96	904	Alum	2 Francs, 1943–44	0.75	2.00	15.00

Y#	KM#	Metal	Description	VF	EF	Unc
V97	901	C-N	5 Francs, 1941	200	325	600

Note: YV97 was not issued to circulation.

Allied Provisional Issues

Y#	KM#	Metal	Description	VF	EF	Unc
81b	885b	Zinc	1 Franc, 1943	3,000	6,000	12,000

Note: Y81b was struck for use in North Africa, but probably was never issued to circulation.

Y#	KM#	Metal	Description	VF	EF	Unc
89	905	Br	2 Francs, 1944	5	15	150

Note: Y89 is said to have circulated in Algeria and Southern France.

POSTWAR ISSUES

Y#	KM#	Metal	Description	VF	EF	Unc
74	906	Zinc	10 Centimes, 1945–46 (17 mm) *1946, VF $6.50*	2.00	5	15
75	907	Zinc	20 Centimes, 1945–46 *1945B, 46B, VF $150; 1945C, VF $75; 1946, VF $25*	7.50	15	35

Y#	KM#	Metal	Description	VF	EF	Unc
84b	888b.1	Alum	5 Francs, 1945–52	0.50	1	7

Note: Y80a–82a were resumed in this period.

Obverse: ***Large head***

Y#	KM#	Metal	Description			
86a	908	C-N	10 Francs, large head, 1945–47 *1946, long laurel, VF $50*	1	4	12

Obverse: ***Small head***

Y#	KM#	Metal	Description	VF	EF	Unc
86b	909	C-N	10 Francs, 1947–49, small head	0.50	1	3.50

Y#	KM#	Metal	Description	VF	EF	Unc
98	915	A-Bz	10 Francs, 1950–58	0.50	1	7.00
99	916	A-Bz	20 Francs, 1950, designer GEORGES GUIRAUD *4 feathers on tail, Unc $500*	1.00	3	15.00
99a	917	A-Bz	20 Francs, 1950–54, designer G. GUIRAUD *1954, Unc $1,500*	0.50	1	7.50
100	918	A-Bz	50 Francs, 1950–58 *1950, VF $125; 1954, VF $20; 1958, VF $75*	1.00	2	12.50

Y#	KM#	Metal	Description	VF	EF	Unc
101	919	C-N	100 Francs, 1954–58 *1958, owl privy mark, EF $75*	0.75	2	10

MONETARY REFORM, *1960*

MONETARY SYSTEM
1 old franc = 1 new centime
100 old francs = 1 new franc

Y#	KM#	Metal	Description	VF	EF	Unc
102	928	C S	1 Centime, 1962–2001	0.25	0.75	1
103	927	C S	5 Centimes, 1961–64	0.25	0.75	1

Y#	KM#	Metal	Description	VF	EF	Unc
104	929	A-Bz	10 Centimes, 1962–2001	0.25	0.50	0.75
105	930	A-Bz	20 Centimes, 1962–2001	0.25	0.75	1.00
106	939	A-Bz	50 Centimes, 1962–64	1.00	3.50	17.50

Y#	KM#	Metal	Description	VF	EF	Unc
108	925	Nick	1 Franc 1960–2001	0.25	0.75	1

Y#	KM#	Metal	Description	VF	EF	Unc
110	926	Silv	5 Francs, 1960–69	BV	6.75	12.50

FRENCH COCHIN CHINA

Southernmost of the French Indo-China colonial states of the mid-19th century, Cochin China corresponded generally to the former South Vietnam. After World War II the federation of Indo-China was an autonomous region of France. It was incorporated into Vietnam in 1948.

MONETARY SYSTEM
5 sapeque (cash) = 1 centime
100 centimes = 1 piastre

PRECIOUS METAL CONTENT

Dates	Denomination	Gross Wt (g)	Fineness	Net Wt (g)	Troy Oz.
		SILVER			
1879–85	10 centimes	2.7216	0.9000	2.4494	0.0787
	20 centimes	5.4431	0.9000	4.8988	0.1575
	50 centimes	13.6078	0.9000	12.2470	0.3937
	1 piastre	27.2156	0.9000	24.4940	0.7875

Y#	KM#	Metal	Description	VF	EF	Unc
A1	1	Bz	(1 Sapeque), 1875	20	35	125

Note: YA1 is a France 1 centime 1875K (Y41) punched with a center hole.

Y#	KM#	Metal	Description	VF	EF	Unc
1	2	Bz	2 Sapeque, 1879, 85	22.50	45	90
				1885 Proof: $6,000		

Y#	KM#	Metal	Description	VF	EF	Unc
2	3	Bz	1 Centime, 1879, 84–85	22.50	125	350
				1885 Proof: $6,000		

Y#	KM#	Metal	Description	VF	EF	Unc
3	4	Silv	10 Centimes, 1879, 84–85	50	150	400
				1885 Proof: $7,000		
4	5	Silv	20 Centimes, 1879, 84–85	70	200	500
				1885 Proof: $7,500		
5	6	Silv	50 Centimes, 1879, 84–85	150	400	1,250
				1885 Proof: $9,500		
6	7	Silv	1 Piastre	*1885 Proof: $37,500*		

Note: Y6 dated 1879, and all coins dated 1885 except Y2, were issued only in specimen sets. For later issues see French Indo-China.

FRENCH EQUATORIAL AFRICA

This area consisted of the territories of Gabon, Middle Congo, Chad and Ubangi-Shari, altogether nearly one and one-half the size of Alaska. It was held by France from the mid-19th century until 1960, when each territory was given independence. *Languages:* French, native tongues. *Capital:* Brazzaville.

MONETARY SYSTEM
100 centimes = 1 franc

Semi-Official Tokens

5 francs = 1 unit

Reverses: ***Each is identical to its obverse***

Y#	KM#	Metal	Description	VF	EF	Unc
A6	N/A	Br	1 Unit, 1883	250	500	850
A7	N/A	Br	5 Units, 1883	275	550	875
A8	N/A	Br	10 Units, 1883	300	575	900

Regular Issues

Y#	KM#	Metal	Description	VF	EF	Unc
1	1	Br	50 Centimes, 1942	4	8	30
2	2	Br	1 Franc, 1942	3	10	35

Y#	KM#	Metal	Description	VF	EF	Unc
1a	1a	Bz	50 Centimes, 1943	3	7.00	25
2a	2a	Bz	1 Franc, 1943	5	7.50	30

Y#	KM#	Metal	Description	VF	EF	Unc
3	6	Alum	1 Franc, 1948	0.25	1	12.50
4	7	Alum	2 Francs, 1948	1.00	2	15.00

FRENCH EQUATORIAL AFRICA: CAMEROON

INTEGRATED COINAGE

In the 1950s, the neighboring French territory of Cameroon was added to the monetary union of the Equatorial African possessions. The following pieces were formerly listed as Cameroon Y10–12.

Y#	KM#	Metal	Description	VF	EF	Unc
5	10	A-Bz	5 Francs, 1958	0.50	1	6.00
6	11	A-Bz	10 Francs, 1958	1.00	2	7.50
7	12	A-Bz	25 Francs, 1958	2.00	3	10.00

FRENCH INDO-CHINA

This southeast Asian federation was formed in 1887 from the colony of Cochin China and protectorates of Annam, Cambodia, and Tongking (Tonkin). Laos was added in 1898. When the Japanese conquerors were driven out at the end of World War II, communists under Ho Chi Minh controlled much of the area and the returning French regime was unable to regain its hold. In 1953 Indochina was partitioned into North and South Vietnam, Cambodia, and Laos.

MONETARY SYSTEM

5 sapeque (cash) = 1 centime
100 centimes = 1 piastre

PRECIOUS METAL CONTENT

Dates	Denomination	Gross Wt (g)	Fineness	Net Wt (g)	Troy Oz.
		SILVER			
1885–95	10 centimes	2.7216	0.9000	2.4494	0.0787
	20 centimes	5.4431	0.9000	4.8988	0.1575
	50 centimes	13.6078	0.9000	12.2470	0.3937
	1 piastre	27.2156	0.9000	24.4940	0.7875
1895–96	10 centimes	2.7000	0.9000	2.4300	0.0781
	20 centimes	5.4000	0.9000	4.8600	0.1562
1898–1919	10 centimes	2.7000	0.8350	2.2545	0.0725
	20 centimes	5.4000	0.8350	4.5090	0.1450
1920	10 centimes	3.0000	0.4000	1.2000	0.0386
	20 centimes	6.0000	0.4000	2.4000	0.0772
1921–37	10 centimes	2.7000	0.6800	1.8360	0.0590
	20 centimes	5.4000	0.6800	3.6720	0.1181
1896–1936	50 centimes	13.5000	0.9000	12.1500	0.3906
1895–1928	1 piastre	27.0000	0.9000	24.3000	0.7812
1931	1 piastre	20.0000	0.9000	18.0000	0.5787

Y#	KM#	Metal	Description	VF	EF	Unc
1	1	Bz	1 Sapeque, 1887–1902	13	25	125

Y#	KM#	Metal	Description	VF	EF	Unc
2	2	Bz	1 Centime, 1885–94	10	35	100

Y#	KM#	Metal	Description	VF	EF	Unc
2a	7	Bz	1 Centieme, 1895	175	275	550

Y#	KM#	Metal	Description	VF	EF	Unc
3	8	Bz	1 Centime, 1896–1906 *1900, 06, VF $10*	5	10	60 *Proof: Rare*

Y#	KM#	Metal	Description	VF	EF	Unc
4	12	Bz	1 Centime, 1908–39	5	10	20

Note: All dates before 1921 are worth more.

Y#	KM#	Metal	Description	VF	EF	Unc
5	18	C-N	5 Centimes, 1923–38 (24 mm) *1937, VF $6, EF $13, Unc $25*	12	26	50
5a	18.1a	N-Br	5 Centimes, 1938–39 (19.9 mm)	2	5	12

.900 Silver

Reverse: *Weight in legend, 27.215 grams to piastre*

Y#	KM#	Metal	Description	VF	EF	Unc
6	2	Silv	10 Centimes, 1885–95	20	60	200
				1889 Proof: $2,000		
7	3	Silv	20 Centimes, 1885–95	50	200	500
				1889 Proof: $3,250		
8	4	Silv	50 Centimes, 1885–95	150	350	2,250
				1889 Proof: $4,500		
9	5	Silv	1 Piastre, 1885–95	125	250	1,500
			1890, VF $2,500	*1889 Proof: $6,000*		

Note: The only common date is 1885.

Reverse: *Slightly reduced weight, 27.0 grams to piastre, in legend*

Y#	KM#	Metal	Description	VF	EF	Unc
6a	2a	Silv	10 Centimes, 1895–97	75	150	550
			1895, Unc $1,500			
7a	3a	Silv	20 Centimes, 1895–97	150	300	625
8a	4a	Silv	50 Centimes, 1896–1936	5	10	75
			1896, EF $250	*1900 Proof: $8,500*		
9a	5a	Silv	1 Piastre, 1895–1928	40	55	250
				1900 Proof: $8,500		

.835 Silver

Y#	KM#	Metal	Description	VF	EF	Unc
14	9	Silv	10 Centimes, 1898–1919	15	45	200
			1898, 1908–09, 19, EF $75	*1900 Proof: $4,000*		
15	10	Silv	20 Centimes, 1898–1916	20	50	150
			1898, EF $225; 1902–03, 13, 16 EF $60; 1908–09, 19, EF $125	*1900 Proof: $4,000*		

.400 Silver *(Not Shown on Coins)*

Y#	KM#	Metal	Description	VF	EF	Unc
14a	14	Bill	10 Centimes, 1920	25	50	350
15a	15	Bill	20 Centimes, 1920	40	75	375

.680 Silver

Y#	KM#	Metal	Description	VF	EF	Unc
16	16	Silv	10 Centimes, 1921–37	4	8	45
			1928, Unc $375			
17	17	Silv	20 Centimes, 1921–37	7	15	55
			1928, VF $350			

.900 Silver

Y#	KM#	Metal	Description	VF	EF	Unc
18	19	Silv	1 Piastre, 1931	45	75	135

Y#	KM#	Metal	Description	VF	EF	Unc
20	20	Bz	1/2 Centime, 1935–40	0.75	3	17.50
20a	20a	Zinc	1/2 Centime, 1939, 40	225.00	425	4,000.00

Y#	KM#	Metal	Description	VF	EF	Unc
21	21.1	Nick	10 Centimes, 1939–40, reeded edge	3	4.50	15
22	23	Nick	20 Centimes, 1939, security edge	10	20.00	100

Note: These coins are magnetic.

Edge: *Reeded*

Y#	KM#	Metal	Description	VF	EF	Unc
21a	21	C-N	10 Centimes, 1939, 41	1.50	3.00	20
			1939, Unc $350			
22a	23a	C-N	20 Centimes, 1939, 41	1.50	2.50	20

Note: These coins are nonmagnetic.

Vichy Government

Y#	KM#	Metal	Description	VF	EF	Unc
V30	24	Zinc	1 Centime, 1940–41	18	35	100
V31	25	Zinc	1/4 Centime, 1942–44	20	45	120
			1944, VF $200			

Y#	KM#	Metal	Description	VF	EF	Unc
V32	26	Alum	1 Centime, 1943	1.75	4	15
V33	27	Alum	5 Centimes, 1943	1.75	4	15

Postwar Issues

Y#	KM#	Metal	Description	VF	EF	Unc
26	30	Alum	5 Centimes, 1946	1.50	3.50	15
27	28	Alum	10 Centimes, 1945	1.50	3.50	15
28	29	Alum	20 Centimes, 1945	1.75	4.50	20

Y#	KM#	Metal	Description	VF	EF	Unc
23	31	C-N	50 Centimes, 1946	5	10	55

Y#	KM#	Metal	Description	VF	EF	Unc
24	32.1	C-N	1 Piastre, 1946–47, security edge	10	20	125
24a	32.2	C-N	1 Piastre, 1947, reeded edge	2	5	20

Note: For later issues, see Cambodia, Laos, and Vietnam.

FRENCH OCEANIA

This assembly of 125 widely scattered islands in the South Pacific was claimed by France in 1768 and organized into a colony in 1903. It is now known as French Polynesia and was reorganized in 2004 from an Overseas Territory to an Overseas Country. *Languages:* French, Tahitian. *Capital:* Papeete.

MONETARY SYSTEM
100 centimes = 1 franc

Y#	KM#	Metal	Description	VF	EF	Unc
1	1	Alum	50 Centimes, 1949	0.75	1.50	15
2	2	Alum	1 Franc, 1949	0.50	1.00	15
3	3	Alum	2 Francs, 1949	1.00	2.00	15
4	4	Alum	5 Francs, 1952	1.25	3.00	15

FRENCH SOMALILAND

This area of northeast Africa between the Red Sea and Indian Ocean came under French influence in 1839, became a colony in 1896 and a territory within the French Union in 1946. It became the Territory of the Afars and Issas in 1967 and gained independence as the Republic of Djibouti in 1977.

MONETARY SYSTEM
100 centimes = 1 franc

Y#	KM#	Metal	Description	VF	EF	Unc
1	4	Alum	1 Franc, 1948–49	10	20	100
2	5	Alum	2 Francs, 1948–49	10	20	100
3	6	Alum	5 Francs, 1948	10	20	100

Y#	KM#	Metal	Description	VF	EF	Unc
4	7	A-Bz	20 Francs, 1952	3	6	30

Obverse: ***UNION FRANCAISE omitted***

Y#	KM#	Metal	Description	VF	EF	Unc
5	8	Alum	1 Franc, 1959, 65	1	2	8
6	9	Alum	2 Francs, 1959, 65	1	2	8
7	10	Alum	5 Francs, 1959, 65	1	2	8

FRENCH WEST AFRICA

This former federation of colonial territories on the northwestern coast of Africa was formed in 1895 as a union of Senegal, French Sudan, French Guinea, and the Ivory Coast (Côte d'Ivoire). The federation ceased to exist after a 1958 referendum on the future French Community in which the constituent territories voted to became autonomous republics, except for Guinea, which voted for independence.

MONETARY SYSTEM

100 centimes = 1 franc

Y#	KM#	Metal	Description	VF	EF	Unc
1	1	A-Bz	50 Centimes, 1944	5	10	30
2	2	A-Bz	1 Franc, 1944	7	15	40

Y#	KM#	Metal	Description	VF	EF	Unc
3	3	Alum	1 Franc, 1948, 55	0.30	1.00	7.50
4	4	Alum	2 Francs, 1948, 55	0.50	1.25	8.50

Y#	KM#	Metal	Description	VF	EF	Unc
5	5	A-Bz	5 Francs, 1956	0.50	1	7.50
6	6	A-Bz	10 Francs, 1956	1.00	2	10.00
7	7	A-Bz	25 Francs, 1956	1.00	2	12.50

FRENCH WEST AFRICA: TOGO

Integrated Coinage

Y#	KM#	Metal	Description	VF	EF	Unc
8	8	A-Bz	10 Francs, 1957	1	1.50	7.50
9	9	A-Bz	25 Francs, 1957	1	2.00	9.00

GERMAN EAST AFRICA

In 1884, Germany gained control of this east African territory and retained it until after World War I. At that time the colony was divided between Britain (administering Tanganyika), Belgium (Ruanda-Urundi), and Portugal. *Capital:* Dar-es-Salaam.

MONETARY SYSTEM

64 pesa (pica) = 1 rupie, to 1902
100 heller = 1 rupie, 1902–1917

PRECIOUS METAL CONTENT

Dates	Denomination	Gross Wt (g)	Fineness	Net Wt (g)	Troy Oz.
		SILVER			
1890–1914	1/4 rupie	2.9160	0.9170	2.6740	0.0859
	1/2 rupie	5.8319	0.9170	5.3479	0.1719
	1 rupie	11.6638	0.9170	10.6957	0.3437
	2 rupien	23.3200	0.9170	21.3844	0.6872
		GOLD			
1916	15 rupien	7.1680	0.7500	5.3760	0.1728

Wilhelm II, *1888–1918*

German East Africa Co.

Y#	KM#	Metal	Description	VF	EF	Unc
1	1	Cop	1 Pesa, 1890–92	20	30	100
						Proof: $300

Y#	KM#	Metal	Description	VF	EF	Unc
2	3	Silv	1/4 Rupie, 1891–1901	55	135	300
						Proof: $500
3	4	Silv	1/2 Rupie, 1891–1901	125	225	600
						Proof: $675
4	2	Silv	1 Rupie, 1890–1902 *1894, VF $500*	50	125	400
						Proof: $750
5	5	Silv	2 Rupien, 1893–94	625	1,650	4,000
						Proof: $9,750

New Legend: *DEUTSCH OSTAFRIKA only*

Y#	KM#	Metal	Description	VF	EF	Unc
6	6	Bz	1/2 Heller, 1904–06	17.50	37.50	90
						Proof: $850
7	7	Bz	1 Heller, 1904–13	8.00	20.00	90
						Proof: $550
8	11	Bz	5 Heller, 1908–09	65.00	150.00	600
						Proof: $1,200

Y#	KM#	Metal	Description	VF	EF	Unc
11	13	C-N	5 Heller, 1912–14 *1912J Proof: Possibly unique*	10	25	75
						Proof: $800
12	12	C-N	10 Heller, 1908–14	35	60	285
						Proof: $500

Y#	KM#	Metal	Description	VF	EF	Unc
13	8	Silv	1/4 Rupie, 1904–14	65	95	300
						Proof: $650
14	9	Silv	1/2 Rupie, 1904–14	100	200	550
						Proof: $750
15	10	Silv	1 Rupie, 1904–14	60	200	350
						Proof: $650

WORLD WAR I, PROVISIONAL ISSUES

Y#	KM#	Metal	Description	VF	EF	Unc
9	14	Br	5 Heller, 1916	15.00	125	250
10	15	Cop	20 Heller, 1916	22.50	55	275
10a	15a	Br	20 Heller, 1916	25.00	70	375

Note: Four varieties each exist of Y10 and 10a (differences in the size and shape of the lettering and crown).

Y#	KM#	Metal	Description	VF	EF	Unc
16	16	Gold	15 Rupien 1916	4,000	5,500	7,500

Note: Y9, 10, 10a, and 16 were struck at Tabora.

GERMAN NEW GUINEA

German New Guinea comprised the northern part of eastern New Guinea. The territory was annexed by Germany in 1884. After World War I it was mandated to Australia by the League of Nations. In 1973 it became part of Papua New Guinea, which is now independent. *Capital:* Herbertshohe (now Kokopo).

MONETARY SYSTEM

100 pfennig = 1 mark

PRECIOUS METAL CONTENT

Dates	Denomination	Gross Wt (g)	Fineness	Net Wt (g)	Troy Oz.
		SILVER			
1894	1/2 mark	2.7780	0.9000	2.5000	0.0804
	1 mark	5.5560	0.9000	5.0000	0.1608
	2 mark	11.1110	0.9000	10.0000	0.3215
	5 mark	27.7780	0.9000	25.0000	0.8038
		GOLD			
1895	10 mark	3.9825	0.9000	3.5843	0.1152
	20 mark	7.9650	0.9000	7.1685	0.2305

Y#	KM#	Metal	Description	VF	EF	Unc
1	1	Cop	1 Pfennig, 1894	150	225	350
						Proof: $300
2	2	Cop	2 Pfennig, 1894	185	265	385
						Proof: $450

Y#	KM#	Metal	Description	VF	EF	Unc
3	3	Cop	10 Pfennig, 1894	200	300	600
						Proof: $900

Y#	KM#	Metal	Description	VF	EF	Unc
4	4	Silv	1/2 Mark, 1894	350	525	950
						Proof: $500
5	5	Silv	1 Mark, 1894	375	550	1,250
						Proof: $750
6	6	Silv	2 Mark, 1894	600	975	1,850
						Proof: $1,500
7	7	Silv	5 Mark, 1894	2,000	3,000	5,000
						Proof: $3,500

Note: Modern restrikes of Y7 exist.

Y#	KM#	Metal	Description	VF	EF	Unc
8	8	Gold	10 Mark, 1895	25,000	47,500	60,000
						Proof: $65,000
9	9	Gold	20 Mark, 1895	25,000	52,500	62,500
						Proof: $65,000

Note: Modern restrikes of Y9 with the date 2003 above the mintmark exist.

GERMAN STATES

When the states of Germany were unified into an empire in 1871, a new decimal coinage system was established. Coins of 1 pfennig through 1 mark were issued for the empire as a whole (see Germany), while the individual states were permitted to issue their own types of 2 through 20 Mark. These states are included in this section.

During the 1871–1873 transition to the new unified coinage, some states continued to issue coins using older monetary systems. Such older series will be found in Craig, *Coins of the World.*

PRECIOUS METAL CONTENT

Dates	Denomination	Gross Wt (g)	Fineness	Net Wt (g)	Troy Oz.
		SILVER			
1874–1918	2 mark	11.1111	0.9000	10.0000	0.3215
	3 mark	16.6666	0.9000	15.0000	0.4823
	5 mark	27.7777	0.9000	25.0000	0.8038
		GOLD			
1871–1915	5 mark	1.9913	0.9000	1.7922	0.0576
	10 mark	3.9825	0.9000	3.5843	0.1152
	20 mark	7.9650	0.9000	7.1685	0.2305

Through the period 1871–1918 covered in this section, three standard reverse designs were used. They are identified in the listings as follows:

Reverse Style A:
Small eagle; date and value at bottom (1871–1873)

Reverse Style B:
Small eagle; date and value in legend (1874–1889)

Reverse Style C:
Large eagle; date and value in legend (1890–1918)

Exceptions: A few commemoratives from 1910 to 1915 used special reverses. See Y98–99, 130–133, 136, and 177.

GERMAN STATE S:
ANHALT
(DUCHY)

FRIEDRICH I,
1871–1904
First Coinage

Y#	KM#	Metal	Description	VF	EF	Unc
1	22	Silv	2 Mark, 1876	300	1,500	3,000

Y#	KM#	Metal	Description	VF	EF	Unc
2	21	Gold	20 Mark, 1875	3,000	4,000	6,000

Second Coinage

Y#	KM#	Metal	Description	VF	EF	Unc
3	23	Silv	2 Mark, 1896	375	625	1,500
4	24	Silv	5 Mark, 1896	1,500	2,250	3,500
5	25	Gold	10 Mark, 1896, 1901	2,100	3,000	4,000
6	26	Gold	20 Mark, 1896, 1901	2,500	3,250	5,000

FRIEDRICH II,
1904–1918

Y#	KM#	Metal	Description	VF	EF	Unc
7	27	Silv	2 Mark, 1904	400	700	1,500
8	29	Silv	3 Mark, 1909, 11	125	175	325
9	28	Gold	20 Mark, 1904	2,000	2,500	4,000

Silver Wedding Anniversary

Y#	KM#	Metal	Description	VF	EF	Unc
10	30	Silv	3 Mark, 1914	50	85	125
11	31	Silv	5 Mark, 1914	165	265	4,000

GERMAN STATES:
BADEN
(GRAND DUCHY)

FRIEDRICH I,
1852–1907

First Coinage

Reverse: ***Style B***

Y#	KM#	Metal	Description	VF	EF	Unc
12	265	Silv	2 Mark, 1876–88	110	800	3,000
13	263	Silv	5 Mark, 1874–88 *1874, 2 known*	100	1,250	6,000

Note: Varieties exist with and without a crossbar in the "A" of BADEN.

Reverse: ***Style C***

Y#	KM#	Metal	Description	VF	EF	Unc
12a	269	Silv	2 Mark, 1892–1902	95	350	1,150
13a	268	Silv	5 Mark, 1891–1902	95	400	2,650

Reverse: ***Style A***

Y#	KM#	Metal	Description	VF	EF	Unc
15	260	Gold	10 Mark, 1872–73	300	750	2,500
16	261	Gold	20 Mark, 1872–73	365	700	2,250

Reverse: ***Style B***

Y#	KM#	Metal	Description	VF	EF	Unc
14	266	Gold	5 Mark, 1877	625	950	1,850
15a	264	Gold	10 Mark, 1875–88 *1880, Rare*	250	550	1,800
16a	262	Gold	20 Mark, 1874	700	1,500	2,500

Reverse: ***Style C***

Y#	KM#	Metal	Description	VF	EF	Unc
15b	267	Gold	10 Mark, 1890–1901	285	375	700
16b	270	Gold	20 Mark, 1894–95	350	475	800

Second Coinage

Y#	KM#	Metal	Description	VF	EF	Unc
17	272	Silv	2 Mark, 1902–07	50	80	300
18	274	Silv	5 Mark, 1902–07	60	200	850
19	275	Gold	10 Mark, 1902–07	275	475	825

50th Year of Reign

Y#	KM#	Metal	Description	VF	EF	Unc
20	271	Silv	2 Mark, 1902	30	40	65
21	273	Silv	5 Mark, 1902	100	175	375

Golden Wedding Anniversary

Y#	KM#	Metal	Description	VF	EF	Unc
22	276	Silv	2 Mark, 1906	30	40	65
23	277	Silv	5 Mark, 1906	125	200	325

Death of Friedrich I

Y#	KM#	Metal	Description	VF	EF	Unc
24	278	Silv	2 Mark, 1907	60	80	135
25	279	Silv	5 Mark, 1907	125	200	350

Friedrich II, *1907–1918*

Y#	KM#	Metal	Description	VF	EF	Unc
26	283	Silv	2 Mark, 1911, 13	235	400.00	800
27	280	Silv	3 Mark, 1908–15	25	47.50	135
28	281	Silv	5 Mark, 1908, 13	70	115.00	450
29	282	Gold	10 Mark, 1909–13	675	1,100.00	1,500
30	284	Gold	20 Mark, 1911–14	BV	525.00	700

German States: Bavaria (Bayern) (Kingdom)

Ludwig II, *1864–1886*

Reverse: ***Style B***

Y#	KM#	Metal	Description	VF	EF	Unc
31	505	Silv	2 Mark, 1876–83	75	275	800
32	502	Silv	5 Mark, 1874–76	60	250	1,350

Reverse: ***Style A***

Y#	KM#	Metal	Description	VF	EF	Unc
34	500	Gold	10 Mark, 1872–73	350	575	1,350
35	501	Gold	20 Mark, 1872–73	400	575	1,200

Reverse: ***Style B***

Y#	KM#	Metal	Description	VF	EF	Unc
33	506	Gold	5 Mark, 1877–78 *1878, VF $1500*	500	750	1,250
34a	503	Gold	10 Mark, 1874–81	215	550	1,200
35a	504	Gold	20 Mark, 1874–78 *1875, VF $1,750; 1878, VF $1,250*	400	575	1,250

Otto III, *1886–1913* *(Under Regency of Prince Luitpold)*

Reverse: ***Style B***

Y#	KM#	Metal	Description	VF	EF	Unc
36	507	Silv	2 Mark, 1888	500	825	2,000
38	508	Silv	5 Mark, 1888	385	975	3,000

Reverse: *Style C*

Y#	KM#	Metal	Description	VF	EF	Unc
36a	511	Silv	2 Mark, 1891–1913	25	45	125
37	515	Silv	3 Mark, 1908–13	20	25	95
38a	512	Silv	5 Mark, 1891–1913	40	65	200

Reverse: *Style B*

Y#	KM#	Metal	Description	VF	EF	Unc
39	509	Gold	10 Mark, 1888	475	750	1,750

Reverse: *Style C*

Y#	KM#	Metal	Description	VF	EF	Unc
39a	510	Gold	10 Mark, 1890–1900	225	385	730
39b	514	Gold	10 Mark, 1900–12, rearranged obverse legend	235	325	550
40	513	Gold	20 Mark, 1895–1913 *1913, Rare*	365	450	575

90th Birthday of Regent

Y#	KM#	Metal	Description	VF	EF	Unc
41	516	Silv	2 Mark, 1911	20	30	85
42	517	Silv	3 Mark, 1911	25	35	85
43	518	Silv	5 Mark, 1911	65	100	185

LUDWIG III, *1913–1918*

Y#	KM#	Metal	Description	VF	EF	Unc
44	519	Silv	2 Mark, 1914	60	100	200
45	520	Silv	3 Mark, 1914	30	50	95
46	521	Silv	5 Mark, 1914	80	165	300

Y#	KM#	Metal	Description	VF	EF	Unc
47	522	Gold	20 Mark, 1914	4,000	7,000	9,500

Golden Wedding Anniversary

Y#	KM#	Metal	Description	VF	EF	Unc
48	523	Silv	*3 Mark, 1918, EF $25,000*			

GERMAN STATES: BREMEN (FREE CITY)

Y#	KM#	Metal	Description	VF	EF	Unc
49	250	Silv	2 Mark, 1904	67.50	125	225
50	251	Silv	5 Mark, 1906	200.00	325	465
51	253	Gold	10 Mark, 1907	1,250.00	2,400	5,000
52	252	Gold	20 Mark, 1906	1,500.00	3,000	4,500

GERMAN STATES: BRUNSWICK (BRAUNSCHWEIG-WOLFENBUTTEL) (DUCHY)

WILHELM, *1831–1884*

Y#	KM#	Metal	Description	VF	EF	Unc
53	1160	Gold	20 Mark, 1875	1,375	2,450	4,000

ERNST AUGUST, *1913–1918*

Wedding of Ernst August

Obverse: *Legend ends BRAUNSCHWEIG*

Y#	KM#	Metal	Description	VF	EF	Unc
54	1161	Silv	3 Mark, 1915	1,250	2,450	3,500
55	1163	Silv	5 Mark, 1915	2,000	3,000	5,000

Obverse: *U. LUNEB. added*

Y#	KM#	Metal	Description	VF	EF	Unc
54a	1162	Silv	3 Mark, 1915	125	200	350
55a	1164	Silv	5 Mark, 1915	450	800	1,400

GERMAN STATES: HAMBURG (FREE CITY)

First Coinage

Obverse: *Arms not supported*

Y#	KM#	Metal	Description	VF	EF	Unc
56	285	Gold	10 Mark, 1873, reverse A	3,500	4,250	8,000
56a	286	Gold	10 Mark, 1874, reverse B	2,400	3,500	6,250

Second Coinage

Obverse: *Arms supported by lions*

Reverse: *Style B*

Y#	KM#	Metal	Description	VF	EF	Unc
57	290	Silv	2 Mark, 1876–88	45	250	825
59	287	Silv	5 Mark, 1875–76, 88	60	825	2,500

Reverse: *Style C*

Y#	KM#	Metal	Description	VF	EF	Unc
57a	294	Silv	2 Mark, 1892–1914	40	60	175
58	296	Silv	3 Mark, 1908–14	25	35	95
59a	293	Silv	5 Mark, 1891–1913	40	110	300

Reverse: *Style B*

Y#	KM#	Metal	Description	VF	EF	Unc
60	291	Gold	5 Mark, 1877	700	950	1,475
61	288	Gold	10 Mark, 1875–88	225	425	700
62	289	Gold	20 Mark, 1875–89 *1881, Rare*	BV	500	585

Reverse: *Style C*

Y#	KM#	Metal	Description	VF	EF	Unc
61a	292	Gold	10 Mark, 1890–1913	250	325	585
62a	295	Gold	20 Mark, 1893–1913	BV	475	585

GERMAN STATES: HESSE (HESSEN-DARMSTADT) (GRAND DUCHY)

Ludwig III, *1848–1877*

Reverse: *Style B*

Y#	KM#	Metal	Description	VF	EF	Unc
63	355	Silv	2 Mark, 1876–77	625	5,500	14,500
64	353	Silv	5 Mark, 1875–76	200	2,150	9,000

Reverse: *Style A*

Y#	KM#	Metal	Description	VF	EF	Unc
66	350	Gold	10 Mark, 1872–73	400	800	2,450
67	351	Gold	20 Mark, 1872–73	475	750	3,000

Reverse: *Style B*

Y#	KM#	Metal	Description	VF	EF	Unc
65	356	Gold	5 Mark, 1877	1,500	2,450	3,500
66a	354	Gold	10 Mark, 1875–77	375	750	2,150
67a	352	Gold	20 Mark, 1874	825	1,800	4,000

Ludwig IV, *1877–1892*

Reverse: *Style B*

Y#	KM#	Metal	Description	VF	EF	Unc
68	359	Silv	2 Mark, 1888	1,750	4,000	7,500
69	360	Silv	5 Mark, 1888	1,750	4,000	7,500

Reverse: *Style C*

Y#	KM#	Metal	Description	VF	EF	Unc
68a	363	Silv	2 Mark, 1891	800	1,650	3,750
69a	364	Silv	5 Mark, 1891	750	2,800	7,500

Reverse: *Style B*

Y#	KM#	Metal	Description	VF	EF	Unc
70	356	Gold	5 Mark, 1877	1,400	2,500	3,500
71	358/361	Gold	10 Mark, 1878–88	550	1,250	3,000

Reverse: *Style C*

Y#	KM#	Metal	Description	VF	EF	Unc
71a	362	Gold	10 Mark, 1890	1,750	2,750	3,750
72	365	Gold	20 Mark, 1892	2,750	5,250	7,000

Ernst Ludwig,
1892–1918

First Coinage

Y#	KM#	Metal	Description	VF	EF	Unc
73	366	Gold	10 Mark, 1893	1,750	2,750	3,750
74	367	Gold	20 Mark, 1893	2,500	3,500	5,500

Second Coinage

Y#	KM#	Metal	Description	VF	EF	Unc
75	368	Silv	2 Mark, 1895–1900	400	750	2,250
76	369	Silv	5 Mark, 1895–1900	265	1,250	2,750

Y#	KM#	Metal	Description	VF	EF	Unc
77	370	Gold	10 Mark, 1896, 98	950	1,250	2,250
78	371	Gold	20 Mark, 1896–1903, obverse GROSHERZOG	500	625	1,750
78a	374	Gold	20 Mark, 1905–11, obverse GROSSHERZOG	400	600	1,250

Third Coinage

Y#	KM#	Metal	Description	VF	EF	Unc
79	375	Silv	3 Mark, 1910	80	135	275

400th Anniversary, Birth of Philip the Generous

Y#	KM#	Metal	Description	VF	EF	Unc
80	372	Silv	2 Mark, 1904	40	70	125
81	373	Silv	5 Mark, 1904	120	175	300

25th Anniversary of Reign

Y#	KM#	Metal	Description	VF	EF	Unc
82	376	Silv	3 Mark, 1917	2,250	3,750	7,500

German States: LIPPE (Lippe-Detmold) (Principality)

Leopold IV,
1905–1918

Y#	KM#	Metal	Description	VF	EF	Unc
83	270	Silv	2 Mark, 1906	325	425	700
84	275	Silv	3 Mark, 1913	375	575	825

German States: LUBECK (Free City)

Obverse: ***Small eagle***

Y#	KM#	Metal	Description	VF	EF	Unc
85	210	Silv	2 Mark, 1901	225	350	575

Obverse: ***Large eagle***

Y#	KM#	Metal	Description	VF	EF	Unc
85a	212	Silv	2 Mark, 1904–12	135	185	350
86	215	Silv	3 Mark, 1908–14	125	185	250
87	213	Silv	5 Mark, 1904–13	375	575	1,100

Obverse: ***Small eagle***

Y#	KM#	Metal	Description	VF	EF	Unc
88	211	Gold	10 Mark, 1901, 04	1,500	2,750	4,500

Obverse: ***Large eagle***

Y#	KM#	Metal	Description	VF	EF	Unc
88a	214	Gold	10 Mark, 1905–10	1,400	2,650	3,500

GERMAN STATES: MECKLENBURG-SCHWERIN (GRAND DUCHY)

FRIEDRICH FRANZ II, *1842–1883*

Reverse: ***Style B***

Y#	KM#	Metal	Description	VF	EF	Unc
89	320	Silv	2 Mark, 1876	375	1,250	4,000

Reverse: ***Style A***

Y#	KM#	Metal	Description	VF	EF	Unc
90	318	Gold	10 Mark, 1872	5,500	7,500	18,500
91	319	Gold	20 Mark, 1872	2,000	4,000	7,500

Reverse: ***Style B***

Y#	KM#	Metal	Description	VF	EF	Unc
90a	321	Gold	10 Mark, 1878	1,850	3,250	5,250

FRIEDRICH FRANZ III, *1883–1897*

Y#	KM#	Metal	Description	VF	EF	Unc
92	325	Gold	10 Mark, 1890	1,500	2,200	4,200

FRIEDRICH FRANZ IV, *1897–1918*

Y#	KM#	Metal	Description	VF	EF	Unc
93	330	Silv	2 Mark, 1901	350	950	1,450
94	331	Gold	10 Mark, 1901	3,250	4,750	7,000
95	332	Gold	20 Mark, 1901	4,500	7,500	12,000

Wedding of Grand Duke

Y#	KM#	Metal	Description	VF	EF	Unc
96	333	Silv	2 Mark, 1904	50	75	125
97	334	Silv	5 Mark, 1904	215	300	400

Centennial, Elevation to Grand Duchy

Y#	KM#	Metal	Description	VF	EF	Unc
98	340	Silv	3 Mark, 1915	125	225	325
99	341	Silv	5 Mark, 1915	475	750	1,350

GERMAN STATES: MECKLENBURG-STRELITZ (GRAND DUCHY)

FRIEDRICH WILHELM, *1860–1904*

Reverse: ***Style B***

Y#	KM#	Metal	Description	VF	EF	Unc
100	108	Silv	2 Mark, 1877	425	2,500	5,500

Reverse: ***Style A***

Y#	KM#	Metal	Description	VF	EF	Unc
101	104	Gold	*10 Mark, 1873*	25,000	35,000	*Rare*
102	105	Gold	20 Mark, 1873	9,000	15,000	30,000

Reverse: ***Style B***

Y#	KM#	Metal	Description	VF	EF	Unc
101a	106	Gold	10 Mark, 1874, 80	7,500	12,500	27,500
102a	107	Gold	20 Mark, 1874	7,500	12,500	27,500

ADOLF FRIEDRICH V, *1904–1914*

First Coinage

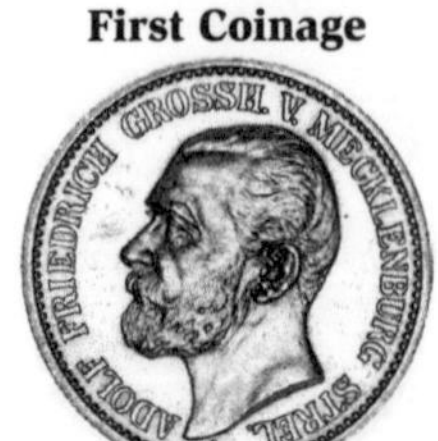

Y#	KM#	Metal	Description	VF	EF	Unc
103	115	Silv	2 Mark, 1905	450	875	1,750

Y#	KM#	Metal	Description	VF	EF	Unc
104	116	Gold	10 Mark, 1905	7,500	10,000	19,500
105	117	Gold	20 Mark, 1905	7,500	10,000	19,500

Second Coinage

Y#	KM#	Metal	Description	VF	EF	Unc
106	120	Silv	3 Mark, 1913	1,000	1,750	2,650

German States: OLDENBURG (Grand Duchy)

Nicolaus Friedrich Peter, *1853–1900*

First Coinage

Y#	KM#	Metal	Description	VF	EF	Unc
107	200	Gold	10 Mark, 1874	6,000	10,500	18,500

Second Coinage

Y#	KM#	Metal	Description	VF	EF	Unc
108	201	Silv	2 Mark, 1891	350	700	1,250

Friedrich August, *1900–1918*

Y#	KM#	Metal	Description	VF	EF	Unc
109	202	Silv	2 Mark, 1900–01	300	500	1,450
110	203	Silv	5 Mark, 1900–01	600	2,000	5,000

German States: PRUSSIA (Preussen) (Kingdom)

Wilhelm I, *1861–1888*

Reverse: ***Style B***

Y#	KM#	Metal	Description	VF	EF	Unc
111	506	Silv	2 Mark, 1876–84 *1879, VF $400*	40	275	800
112	503	Silv	5 Mark, 1874–76	45	300	1,250

Reverse: ***Style A***

Y#	KM#	Metal	Description	VF	EF	Unc
114	502	Gold	10 Mark, 1872–73	200	235	400
115	501	Gold	20 Mark, 1871–73	BV	BV	500

Reverse: ***Style B***

Y#	KM#	Metal	Description	VF	EF	Unc
113	507	Gold	5 Mark, 1877–78	350	500	850
114a	504	Gold	10 Mark, 1874–88	250	300	500
115a	505	Gold	20 Mark, 1874–88	BV	BV	585

Friedrich III, *1888*

Y#	KM#	Metal	Description	VF	EF	Unc
116	510	Silv	2 Mark, 1888	50	95	150
117	512	Silv	5 Mark, 1888	100	150	400
118	514	Gold	10 Mark, 1888	200	250	400

Wilhelm II, *1888–1918*

First Coinage

Reverse: ***Style B***

Y#	KM#	Metal	Description	VF	EF	Unc
119	516	Gold	20 Mark, 1888	BV	BV	585
120	511	Silv	2 Mark, 1888	350	475	750
122	513	Silv	5 Mark, 1888	500	950	2,350

Reverse: ***Style C***

Y#	KM#	Metal	Description	VF	EF	Unc
120a	522	Silv	2 Mark, 1891–1912 *1892, 1901, VF $115*	25	35	125
121	527	Silv	3 Mark, 1908–12	25	30	55
122a	523	Silv	5 Mark, 1891–1908	35	60	300

Reverse: ***Style B***

Y#	KM#	Metal	Description	VF	EF	Unc
123	517	Gold	10 Mark, 1889	6,500	9,500	15,000
124	516	Gold	20 Mark, 1888–89	BV	BV	650

Reverse: ***Style C***

Y#	KM#	Metal	Description	VF	EF	Unc
123a	520	Gold	10 Mark, 1890–1912	275	350	525
124a	521	Gold	20 Mark, 1890–1913	BV	BV	525

Second Coinage

Y#	KM#	Metal	Description	VF	EF	Unc
125	538	Silv	3 Mark, 1914	25	35	90
126	536	Silv	5 Mark, 1913–14	35	50	165
127	537	Gold	20 Mark, 1913–15 *1915, VF $6,000*	BV	BV	575

Bicentennial of Kingdom

Y#	KM#	Metal	Description	VF	EF	Unc
128	525	Silv	2 Mark, 1901	15	25	45
129	526	Silv	5 Mark, 1901	50	85	150

Centennial, Founding of Berlin University

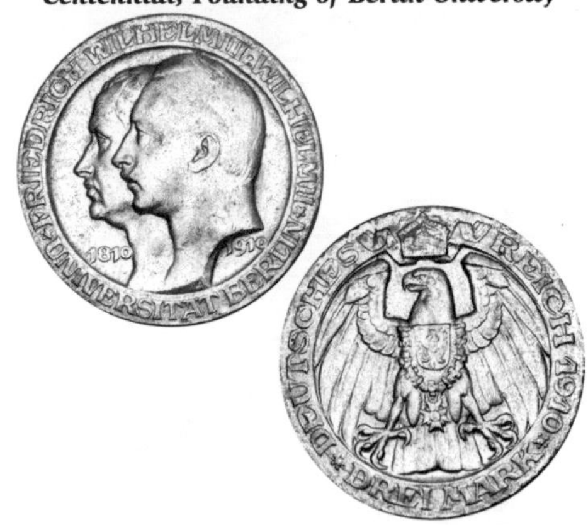

Y#	KM#	Metal	Description	VF	EF	Unc
130	530	Silv	3 Mark, 1910	50	95	140

Centennial, Founding of Breslau University

Y#	KM#	Metal	Description	VF	EF	Unc
131	531	Silv	3 Mark, 1911	45	60	120

Centennial, Defeat of Napoleon

Y#	KM#	Metal	Description	VF	EF	Unc
132	532	Silv	2 Mark, 1913	15.00	25.00	40.00
133	534	Silv	3 Mark, 1913	22.50	27.50	42.50

25th Year of Reign

Y#	KM#	Metal	Description	VF	EF	Unc
134	533	Silv	2 Mark, 1913	15.00	22.50	40
135	535	Silv	3 Mark, 1913	22.50	30.00	75

Centennial, Absorption of Mansfeld

Y#	KM#	Metal	Description	VF	EF	Unc
136	539	Silv	3 Mark, 1915	500	850	1,300

GERMAN STATES: REUSS-GREIZ (REUSS ALTERER LINIE) (PRINCIPALITY)

Heinrich XXII, *1859–1902*

First Coinage

Reverse: ***Style B***

Y#	KM#	Metal	Description	VF	EF	Unc
137	126	Silv	2 Mark, 1877	625	1,500	4,000

Reverse: ***Style C***

Y#	KM#	Metal	Description	VF	EF	Unc
137a	127	Silv	2 Mark, 1892	500	1,000	2,200

Reverse: ***Style B***

Y#	KM#	Metal	Description	VF	EF	Unc
138	125	Gold	*20 Mark, 1875, EF $45,000*			

Second Coinage

Y#	KM#	Metal	Description	VF	EF	Unc
139	128	Silv	2 Mark, 1899, 1901	300	500	950

Heinrich XXIV, *1902–1918*

Y#	KM#	Metal	Description	VF	EF	Unc
140	130	Silv	3 Mark, 1909	400	600	1,000

GERMAN STATES: REUSS-SCHLEIZ (REUSS JUNGERER LINIE) (PRINCIPALITY)

Heinrich XIV, *1867–1913*

Y#	KM#	Metal	Description	VF	EF	Unc
141	82	Silv	2 Mark, 1884	400	1,000	3,250
142	81	Gold	10 Mark, 1882	7,000	10,000	17,500
143	80	Gold	20 Mark, 1881	6,000	9,000	13,000

GERMAN STATES: SAXE-ALTENBURG (DUCHY)

Ernst, *1853–1908*

Reverse: ***Style C***

Y#	KM#	Metal	Description	VF	EF	Unc
144	144	Silv	2 Mark, 1901	450	550	1,250
145	145	Silv	5 Mark, 1901	600	1,350	3,750

Reverse: ***Style B***

Y#	KM#	Metal	Description	VF	EF	Unc
146	146	Gold	20 Mark, 1887	3,500	6,000	8,250

50th Year of Reign

Y#	KM#	Metal	Description	VF	EF	Unc
147	147	Silv	5 Mark, 1903	225	375	600

GERMAN STATES: SAXE-COBURG-GOTHA (DUCHY)

Ernst II, *1844–1893*

Reverse: ***Style A***

Y#	KM#	Metal	Description	VF	EF	Unc
148	148	Gold	20 Mark, 1872	70,000	85,000	165,000

Reverse: ***Style B***

Y#	KM#	Metal	Description	VF	EF	Unc
148a	148a	Gold	20 Mark, 1886	3,500	6,000	12,000

Alfred, *1893–1900*

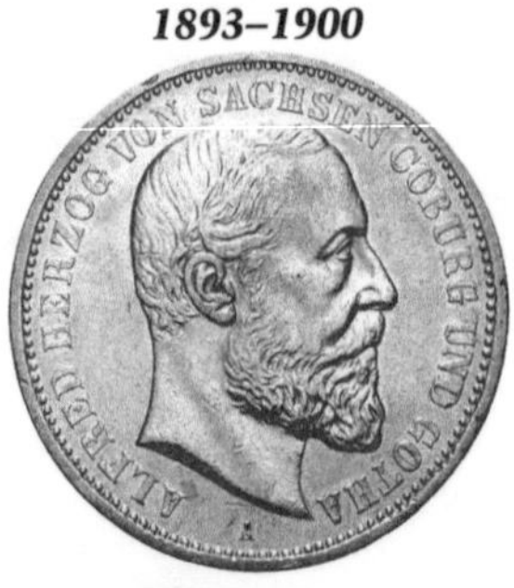

Y#	KM#	Metal	Description	VF	EF	Unc
149	149	Silv	2 Mark, 1895	700	1,200	2,500
150	150	Silv	5 Mark, 1895	2,750	4,000	7,000

Y#	KM#	Metal	Description	VF	EF	Unc
151	151	Gold	20 Mark, 1895	3,500	6,000	12,000

Carl Eduard, *1900–1918*

Y#	KM#	Metal	Description	VF	EF	Unc
152	152	Silv	2 Mark, 1905, 11	1,200	1,500	2,000
			1911, 100 struck	6,000	10,000	17,000
153	153	Silv	5 Mark, 1907	1,000	1,600	3,000
154	154	Gold	10 Mark, 1905	2,500	3,500	6,000
155	155	Gold	20 Mark, 1905	3,000	4,750	6,500

GERMAN STATES: SAXE-MEININGEN (DUCHY)

Georg II, *1866–1914*

First Coinage

Reverse: ***Style A***

Y#	KM#	Metal	Description	VF	EF	Unc
156	180	Gold	20 Mark, 1872	10,000	20,000	45,000

Reverse: ***Style B***

Y#	KM#	Metal	Description	VF	EF	Unc
156a	185	Gold	20 Mark, 1882	10,500	14,000	30,000

Second Coinage

Reverse: ***Style B***

Y#	KM#	Metal	Description	VF	EF	Unc
158	186	Gold	20 Mark, 1889	7,500	11,000	16,000

Reverse: ***Style C***

Y#	KM#	Metal	Description	VF	EF	Unc
157	190	Gold	10 Mark, 1890, 98	4,500	8,500	12,000
158a	195	Gold	20 Mark, 1900, 05	7,500	12,000	20,000

Third Coinage

Y#	KM#	Metal	Description	VF	EF	Unc
159	196	Silv	2 Mark, 1901	325	525	1,000
160	197	Silv	5 Mark, 1901	400	700	1,750

Note: Y159 and 160 celebrate the duke's 75th birthday but are not marked as commemoratives.

Fourth Coinage

Y#	KM#	Metal	Description	VF	EF	Unc
161	199	Silv	2 Mark, 1902, 13 *1902, long beard touching outer border, VF $1,000*	300	450	900
162	203	Silv	3 Mark, 1908, 13	125	185	475
163	201	Silv	5 Mark, 1902, 08 *1902, long beard touching outer border, VF $400*	200	400	1,100
164	202	Gold	10 Mark, 1902, 09, 14	4,000	6,500	9,500
165	205	Gold	20 Mark, 1910, 14	6,500	9,500	15,000

Death of Georg

Y#	KM#	Metal	Description	VF	EF	Unc
166	206	Silv	2 Mark, 1915	125	200	315
167	207	Silv	3 Mark, 1915	135	215	375

GERMAN STATES: SAXE-WEIMAR (GRAND DUCHY)

CARL ALEXANDER, *1853–1901*

Y#	KM#	Metal	Description	VF	EF	Unc
168	168	Silv	2 Mark, 1892, 98	265	475	850

Y#	KM#	Metal	Description	VF	EF	Unc
169	169	Gold	20 Mark, 1892, 96	3,000	4,750	6,000

WILHELM ERNST, *1901–1918*

Y#	KM#	Metal	Description	VF	EF	Unc
170	170	Silv	2 Mark, 1901	375	625	1,450

Y#	KM#	Metal	Description	VF	EF	Unc
171	171	Gold	20 Mark, 1901	3,500	6,500	9,500

First Marriage

Y#	KM#	Metal	Description	VF	EF	Unc
172	172	Silv	2 Mark, 1903	85	120	175
173	173	Silv	5 Mark, 1903	150	175	365

350th Anniversary, Founding of Jena University

Y#	KM#	Metal	Description	VF	EF	Unc
174	174	Silv	2 Mark, 1908	85	150	215
175	175	Silv	5 Mark, 1908	140	225	375

Second Marriage

Y#	KM#	Metal	Description	VF	EF	Unc
176	176	Silv	3 Mark, 1910	35	75	115

Centennial, Elevation to Grand Duchy

Y#	KM#	Metal	Description	VF	EF	Unc
177	177	Silv	3 Mark, 1915	80	175	250

GERMAN STATES: SAXONY (SACHSEN) (KINGDOM)

Johann, *1854–1873*

Y#	KM#	Metal	Description	VF	EF	Unc
178	1232	Gold	10 Mark, 1872–73	400	675	1,850
179	Several	Gold	20 Mark, 1872–73	425	750	1,500

Albert, *1873–1902*

Reverse: ***Style B***

Y#	KM#	Metal	Description	VF	EF	Unc
180	1238	Silv	2 Mark, 1876–88	115	725	2,000
181	1237	Silv	5 Mark, 1875, 76, 89	75	1,200	4,500

Reverse: ***Style C***

Y#	KM#	Metal	Description	VF	EF	Unc
180a	1245	Silv	2 Mark, 1891–1902	55	125	400
181a	1246	Silv	5 Mark, 1891–1902	65	265	1,650

Reverse: ***Style B***

Y#	KM#	Metal	Description	VF	EF	Unc
182	1239	Gold	5 Mark, 1877	700	925	1,750
183	1235	Gold	10 Mark, 1874–88	325	625	1,100
184	1236	Gold	20 Mark, 1874–78	375	575	1,650
			1877–78, Rare			

Reverse: ***Style C***

Y#	KM#	Metal	Description	VF	EF	Unc
183a	1247	Gold	10 Mark, 1891–1902	315	475	1,100
184a	1248	Gold	20 Mark, 1894–95	400	700	1,000

Death of Albert

Y#	KM#	Metal	Description	VF	EF	Unc
185	1255	Silv	2 Mark, 1902	45	85	165
186	1256	Silv	5 Mark, 1902	110	200	325

Georg, *1902–1904*

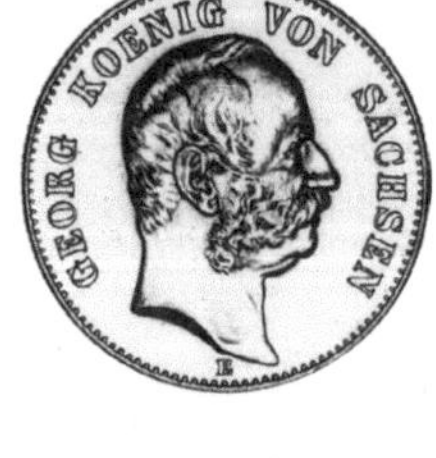

Y#	KM#	Metal	Description	VF	EF	Unc
187	1257	Silv	2 Mark, 1903–04	60	110	400
188	1258	Silv	5 Mark, 1903–04	85	250	1,150
189	1259	Gold	10 Mark, 1903–04	400	750	1,150
190	1260	Gold	20 Mark, 1903	400	700	1,400

Death of Georg

Y#	KM#	Metal	Description	VF	EF	Unc
191	1261	Silv	2 Mark, 1904	50	85	175
192	1262	Silv	5 Mark, 1904	175	300	450

FRIEDRICH AUGUST III, *1904–1918*

Y#	KM#	Metal	Description	VF	EF	Unc
193	1263	Silv	2 Mark, 1905–14	47.50	95	265
194	1267	Silv	3 Mark, 1908–13	22.50	35	125
195	1266	Silv	5 Mark, 1907–14	60.00	110	400
196	1264	Gold	10 Mark, 1905–12	350.00	575	875
197	1265	Gold	20 Mark, 1905, 13, 14	350.00	525	800

500th Anniversary, Founding of Leipzig University

Y#	KM#	Metal	Description	VF	EF	Unc
198	1268	Silv	2 Mark, 1909	47.50	70	125
199	1269	Silv	5 Mark, 1909	145.00	200	350

Centennial, Battle of Leipzig

Y#	KM#	Metal	Description	VF	EF	Unc
200	1275	Silv	3 Mark, 1913	18	30	60

400th Anniversary of Protestant Reformation

Y#	KM#	Metal	Description	VF	EF	Unc
201	1276	Silv	*3 Mark, 1917, Proof only, 100 struck: $85,000*			

GERMAN STATES: SCHAUMBURG-LIPPE (PRINCIPALITY)

ADOLF GEORG, *1860–1893*

Y#	KM#	Metal	Description	VF	EF	Unc
202	202	Gold	20 Mark, 1874	7,000	9,750	15,000

ALBRECHT GEORG, *1893–1911*

Y#	KM#	Metal	Description	VF	EF	Unc
203	203	Silv	2 Mark, 1898, 1904	650	975	1,375
204	204	Silv	5 Mark, 1898, 1904	1,250	1,650	3,000
205	205	Gold	20 Mark, 1898, 1904	3,000	5,000	7,500

Death of Georg

Y#	KM#	Metal	Description	VF	EF	Unc
206	206	Silv	3 Mark, 1911	85	185	300

GERMAN STATES: SCHWARZBURG-RUDOLSTADT (PRINCIPALITY)

Gunther, *1890–1918*

Y#	KM#	Metal	Description	VF	EF	Unc
207	207	Silv	2 Mark, 1898	300	525	1,100

Y#	KM#	Metal	Description	VF	EF	Unc
208	208	Gold	10 Mark, 1898	3,750	6,000	9,000

GERMAN STATES: SCHWARZBURG-SONDERSDHAUSEN (PRINCIPALITY)

Karl Gunther, *1880–1909*

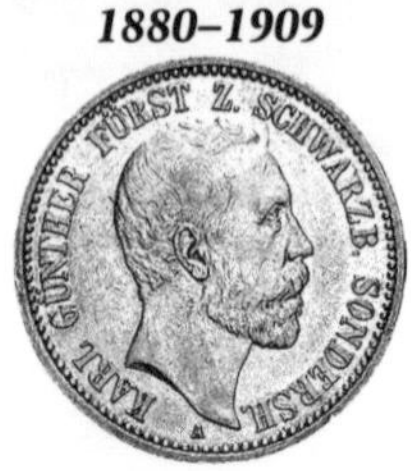

Y#	KM#	Metal	Description	VF	EF	Unc
209	209	Silv	2 Mark, 1896	300	600	1,200
210	210	Gold	20 Mark, 1896	6,000	8,500	12,000

25th Year of Reign

Y#	KM#	Metal	Description	VF	EF	Unc
211	211	Silv	2 Mark, 1905 (2 vars)	115	175	225

Death of Karl Gunther

Y#	KM#	Metal	Description	VF	EF	Unc
212	212	Silv	3 Mark, 1909	85	120	225

GERMAN STATES: WALDECK-PYRMONT (PRINCIPALITY)

Friedrich, *1893–1918*

Y#	KM#	Metal	Description	VF	EF	Unc
213	213	Silv	5 Mark, 1903	2,650	4,250	6,000
214	214	Gold	20 Mark, 1903	6,250	9,000	14,500

GERMAN STATES: WURTTEMBERG (KINGDOM)

KARL, *1864–1891*

Reverse: ***Style B***

Y#	KM#	Metal	Description	VF	EF	Unc
215	626	Silv	2 Mark, 1876–88	80	350	1,800
216	623	Silv	5 Mark, 1874–88	75	800	3,750

Reverse: ***Style A***

Y#	KM#	Metal	Description	VF	EF	Unc
218	621	Gold	10 Mark, 1872–73	225	475	1,500
219	622	Gold	20 Mark, 1872–73	BV	475	1,100

Reverse: ***Style B***

Y#	KM#	Metal	Description	VF	EF	Unc
217	627	Gold	5 Mark, 1877–78 *1878, VF $975*	375	575	950
218a	624	Gold	10 Mark, 1874–88	245	425	850
219a	625	Gold	20 Mark, 1874, 76	375	525	1,400

Reverse: ***Style C***

Y#	KM#	Metal	Description	VF	EF	Unc
218b	630	Gold	10 Mark, 1890–91	525	725	1,350

WILHELM II, *1891–1918*

Y#	KM#	Metal	Description	VF	EF	Unc
220	631	Silv	2 Mark, 1892–1914	27.50	35.00	135
221	635	Silv	3 Mark, 1908–14	25.00	32.50	95
222	632	Silv	5 Mark, 1892–1913	28.00	55.00	325
223	633	Gold	10 Mark, 1893–1913	235.00	325.00	550
224	634	Gold	20 Mark, 1894–1914 *1913, Rare; 1914, VF $11,000*	BV	475.00	600

Silver Wedding Anniversary

Y#	KM#	Metal	Description	VF	EF	Unc
225	636–37	Silv	3 Mark, 1911	325	525	700

25th Year of Reign

Y#	KM#	Metal	Description	VF	EF	Unc
226	638	Silv	*3 Mark, 1916, Matte Proof only: $8,250*			

GERMANY (DEUTSCHES REICH)

The German Empire was formed in 1871, finally unifying the various states of this north-central European country. After World War I it became a republic prior to Adolph Hitler's formation of the totalitarian Third Reich in 1933. Following World War II, Germany was divided into western (Federal Republic) and eastern (Democratic Republic) areas, each becoming autonomous in 1949, and reunifying in 1990. *Language:* German. *Capital:* Berlin.

MONETARY SYSTEM

100 pfennig = 1 mark

PRECIOUS METAL CONTENT

Dates	Denomination	Gross Wt (g)	Fineness	Net Wt (g)	Troy Oz.
		SILVER			
1873–1919	20 pfennig	1.1111	0.9000	1.0000	0.0322
	50 pfennig	2.7777	0.9000	2.5000	0.0804
	1 mark	5.5555	0.9000	5.0000	0.1608
1924–33	1 mark	5.0000	0.5000	2.5000	0.0804
	2 mark	10.0000	0.5000	5.0000	0.1608
	3 mark	15.0000	0.5000	7.5000	0.2411
	5 mark	25.0000	0.5000	12.5000	0.4019
1933–39	2 mark	8.0000	0.6250	5.0000	0.1608
	5 mark	13.8888	0.9000	12.5000	0.4019

EMPIRE, *1871–1918*

First Coinage

Reverse: ***Small eagle***

Y#	KM#	Metal	Description	VF	EF	Unc
1	1	Cop	1 Pfennig, 1873–89 *1873, VF $325; 1874G, VF $40; 1874H, VF $150; 1875H, 76H, 85E, VF $90; 1886G, VF $125; 1876J, 77A, VF $150*	6	13	60

Y#	KM#	Metal	Description	VF	EF	Unc
2	2	Cop	2 Pfennig, 1873–77 *1873A, 73D, 74B–G, VF $25; 1873B, VF $75; 1873C VF $100; 1873F, 77B, VF $350; 1876J, VF $15*	2.50	13	47.50

Y#	KM#	Metal	Description	VF	EF	Unc
5	3	C-N	5 Pfennig, 1874–89 *1875H, VF $55*	6.00	15	60
6	4	C-N	10 Pfennig, 1873–89 *1873H, VF $300*	7.50	25	50

Y#	KM#	Metal	Description	VF	EF	Unc
7	9	C-N	20 Pfennig, 1887–88	25	38	85

Reverse: ***Small eagle in plain field***

Y#	KM#	Metal	Description	VF	EF	Unc
12	5	Silv	20 Pfennig, 1873–77 *1873E, VF $600; 1873H, VF $350; 1877H, VF $225*	9.50	18	42.50
13	6	Silv	50 Pfennig, 1875–77 *1875E, 75H, VF $425; 1877H, VF $160; 1877J, VF $100*	13.00	28	85.00
17	7	Silv	1 Mark, 1873–87, obverse like Y18 *1877B, 79A, VF $165*	8.50	38	125.00

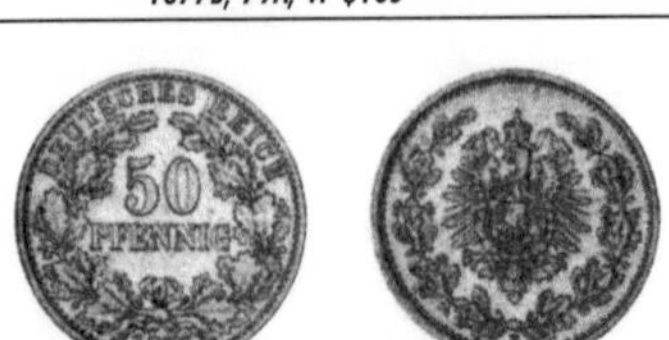

Obverse: ***Like Y18***
Reverse: ***Small eagle in wreath***

Y#	KM#	Metal	Description	VF	EF	Unc
14	8	Silv	50 Pfennig, 1877–78 *1878E, VF $400*	65	125	250

Second Coinage

Reverse: ***Large eagle***

Y#	KM#	Metal	Description	VF	EF	Unc
3	10	Cop	1 Pfennig, 1890–1916 *1891D–E, 93G, 95D–E, 97G, VF $65; 1891G, VF $135*	1.50	3.50	15
4	16	Cop	2 Pfennig, 1904–16	4.00	5.50	22

Y#	KM#	Metal	Description	VF	EF	Unc
8	11	C-N	5 Pfennig, 1890–1915 *1896G, Rare*	1.50	3.50	15

Note: Pre-1905 dates are worth more.

Y#	KM#	Metal	Description	VF	EF	Unc
9	12	C-N	10 Pfennig, 1890–1916 *1892J, Rare*	1.50	3.50	23

Y#	KM#	Metal	Description	VF	EF	Unc
10	13	C-N	20 Pfennig, 1890–92	40	75	200

Y#	KM#	Metal	Description	VF	EF	Unc
11	18	Nick	25 Pfennig, 1909–12 *1909J, Rare*	8.50	13.50	25

Y#	KM#	Metal	Description	VF	EF	Unc
15	15	Silv	50 Pfennig, 1896–1903	275.00	375	575
16	17	Silv	1/2 Mark, 1905–19 *1908F, Rare*	2.50	4	15

Note: Part of the 1917 and all of the 1918–1919 issues were artificially blackened to discourage hoarding.

Y#	KM#	Metal	Description	VF	EF	Unc
18	14	Silv	1 Mark, 1891–1916 *1891D, 1905F, Rare; 1892G, 94G, VF $225; 1909J, VF $250*	5	7	15

Higher Denominations

The right to issue coins larger than 1 mark belonged to the individual states of the German Empire. See German States for these 1871–1918 coins of 2-, 3-, and 5-mark silver and 5-, 10-, and 20-mark gold.

WORLD WAR I AND INFLATION, *1915–1923*

This period marks the end of the German Empire and the rise of the Weimar Republic in 1919. Silver coins were retained unchanged until stopped, while the lower denominations were made in aluminum, zinc, and iron.

Occupation Issue

Struck for use in German-occupied territories of eastern Europe (Baltic states, eastern Poland, northwest Russia).

Y#	KM#	Metal	Description	VF	EF	Unc
A18	21	Iron	1 Kopek, 1916	18.50	35	85
B18	22	Iron	2 Kopeks, 1916	18.50	35	85
C18	23	Iron	3 Kopeks, 1916	18.50	35	85

Regular Issues

Y#	KM#	Metal	Description	VF	EF	Unc
19	24	Alum	1 Pfennig, 1916–18 *1916G, VF $325; 1918A, 18F, Rare; 1918D, VF $20*	2	4	7.50

Y#	KM#	Metal	Description	VF	EF	Unc
21	19	Iron	5 Pfennig, 1915–22	1.25	2.65	11.50

Y#	KM#	Metal	Description	VF	EF	Unc
22	20	Iron	10 Pfennig, 1916–22 *1918D, VF $1,750; 1922E, VF $55; 1922G, VF $75; 1922J, VF $25*	1.75	4	12

Y#	KM#	Metal	Description	VF	EF	Unc
22a	25	Zinc	10 Pfennig, 1917, reverse like Y22	180.00	400.00	—
25	26	Zinc	10 Pfennig, 1917–22, reverse like Y21	0.75	1.50	9

WEIMAR REPUBLIC, *1919–1923*

Y21, 22, and 25 were continued into this period.

Y#	KM#	Metal	Description	VF	EF	Unc
26	27	Alum	50 Pfennig, 1919–22 *1919D, 19J, VF $15; 1919F, VF $40*	1.50	3	6

Third Anniversary, Weimar Constitution

Y#	KM#	Metal	Description	VF	EF	Unc
28	29	Alum	3 Mark, 1922–23 *1922D, VF $350; 1923F, VF $1,250*	2	5	13

Y#	KM#	Metal	Description	VF	EF	Unc
29	28	Alum	3 Mark, 1922, no obverse legend *1922E, VF $300; 1922F, VF $2,500*	3	5	15

Y#	KM#	Metal	Description	VF	EF	Unc
30	35	Alum	200 Mark, 1923	0.50	1.50	3.50
31	36	Alum	500 Mark, 1923 *1923J, VF $38*	0.75	2.00	6.00

Coinage Law of November 1923

Y#	KM#	Metal	Description	VF	EF	Unc
32	30	Bz	1 Rentenpfennig, 1923–24, 29 *1925, Rare; 1929, VF $250*	1.25	3.00	13
33	31	Bz	2 Rentenpfennig, 1923–24	1.25	2.50	10

Y#	KM#	Metal	Description	VF	EF	Unc
34	32	A-Bz	5 Rentenpfennig, 1923–25 *1923F, VF $30; 1923G, VF $20*	1.50	3	18.00
35	33	A-Bz	10 Rentenpfennig, 1923–25 *1923F, VF $175; 1925F, Rare*	2.00	4	17.50
36	34	A-Bz	50 Rentenpfennig, 1923–24 *1923F, VF $150; 1923J, Rare*	15.00	20	65.00

Coinage Reform of 1924

Designs: *Like Y32–33*

Y#	KM#	Metal	Description	VF	EF	Unc
37	37	Bz	1 Reichspfennig, 1924–36 *1924E, VF $325; 1925D, 30E, VF $40*	1.25	1.50	10.00
38	38	Bz	2 Reichspfennig, 1924–36	1.25	2.50	12.50

Y#	KM#	Metal	Description	VF	EF	Unc
39	75	Bz	4 Reichspfennig, 1932	13	18	33

Designs: *Like Y34–36*

Y#	KM#	Metal	Description	VF	EF	Unc
40	39	A-Bz	5 Reichspfennig, 1924–36 *1926E, VF $45*	1.50	2.50	15.00
41	40	A-Bz	10 Reichspfennig, 1924–36 *1928G, VF $165; 1931D, 33A, 34A, 34G, VF $45; 1931G, VF $275; 1932G, VF $900; 1934G, VF $50*	1.50	3.00	12.50
42	41	A-Bz	50 Reichspfennig, 1924–25, *Rare*			

Y#	KM#	Metal	Description	VF	EF	Unc
43	49	A-Bz	50 Reichspfennig, 1927–38 *1930E, 30G–J, VF $45; 1930F, 31J, 32E, 33G, 37J, VF $100; 1931G, VF $425 1932G, Rare*	3.75	9	20

Y#	KM#	Metal	Description	VF	EF	Unc
44	42	Silv	1 Mark, 1924–25	15	28	70
47	43	Silv	3 Mark, 1924–25	50	70	150

Y#	KM#	Metal	Description	VF	EF	Unc
45	44	Silv	1 Reichsmark, 1925–27 *1926J, VF $125; 1927A, VF $450*	18	25	45
46	45	Silv	2 Reichsmark, 1925–31 *1927D, VF $1,400; 1927E, VF $375; 1927F, VF $225; 1927J, VF $115 1931G, VF $85*	15	35	65
48	74	Silv	3 Reichsmark, 1931–33 *1932F, VF $500; 1932G, VF $1,650; 1933G, VF $2,500*	275	450	625

Y#	KM#	Metal	Description	VF	EF	Unc
49	56	Silv	5 Reichsmark, 1927–33 *1929E, VF $450; 1930A, VF $145; 1930F, 30G, VF $1,425; 1933J, VF $3,000*	100	185	315

Millennium, Unification of Rhineland

Y#	KM#	Metal	Description	VF	EF	Unc
50	46	Silv	3 Reichsmark, 1925	40	50	100 *Proof: $750*
51	47	Silv	5 Reichsmark, 1925 *1925J, VF $225*	95	125	225 *Proof: $950*

700th Anniversary, Freedom of Lubeck

Y#	KM#	Metal	Description	VF	EF	Unc
52	48	Silv	3 Reichsmark, 1926	110	150	250 *Proof: $450*

Centennial, City of Bremerhaven

Y#	KM#	Metal	Description	VF	EF	Unc
53	50	Silv	3 Reichsmark, 1927	120	150	250 *Proof: $600*
54	55	Silv	5 Reichsmark, 1927	425	550	750 *Proof: $1,000*

Millennium, City of Nordhausen

Y#	KM#	Metal	Description	VF	EF	Unc
55	52	Silv	3 Reichsmark, 1927	100	150	225 *Proof: $375*

400th Anniversary, University of Marburg

Y#	KM#	Metal	Description	VF	EF	Unc
56	53	Silv	3 Reichsmark, 1927	100	135	195 *Proof: $375*

450th Anniversary, University of Tubingen

Y#	KM#	Metal	Description	VF	EF	Unc
57	54	Silv	3 Reichsmark, 1927	325	450	500
						Proof: $600
58	55	Silv	5 Reichsmark, 1927	350	500	500
						Proof: $600

400th Anniversary, Death of Dürer

Y#	KM#	Metal	Description	VF	EF	Unc
59	58	Silv	3 Reichsmark, 1928	285	450	600
						Proof: $750

900th Anniversary, City of Naumberg

Y#	KM#	Metal	Description	VF	EF	Unc
60	57	Silv	3 Reichsmark, 1928	125	175	275
						Proof: $450

Millennium, City of Dinkelsbuhl

Y#	KM#	Metal	Description	VF	EF	Unc
61	59	Silv	3 Reichsmark, 1928	275	450	725
						Proof: $800

Bicentennial, Birth of Lessing

Y#	KM#	Metal	Description	VF	EF	Unc
62	60	Silv	3 Reichsmark, 1929	45	70	125
						Proof: $175
63	61	Silv	5 Reichsmark, 1929	125	160	255
						Proof: $275

Waldeck-Prussia Union

Y#	KM#	Metal	Description	VF	EF	Unc
64	62	Silv	3 Reichsmark, 1929	115	150	225
						Proof: $875

10th Anniversary of Constitution

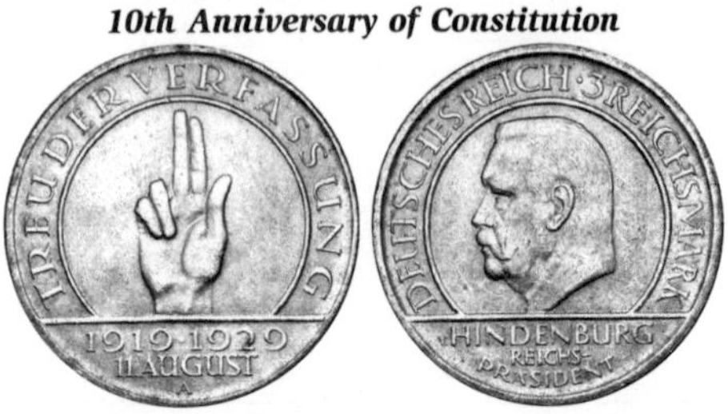

Y#	KM#	Metal	Description	VF	EF	Unc
65	63	Silv	3 Reichsmark, 1929	35	50	85
						Proof: $300
66	64	Silv	5 Reichsmark, 1929	115	150	235
						Proof: $650

Millennium, City of Meissen

Y#	KM#	Metal	Description	VF	EF	Unc
67	65	Silv	3 Reichsmark, 1929	35	55	110
						Proof: $350
68	66	Silv	5 Reichsmark, 1929	400	500	650
						Proof: $1,100

World Flight of Graf Zeppelin

Y#	KM#	Metal	Description	VF	EF	Unc
69	67	Silv	3 Reichsmark, 1930	60	90	150
						Proof: $200
70	68	Silv	5 Reichsmark, 1930	155	190	300
						Proof: $750

700th Anniversary, Death of Vogelweide

Y#	KM#	Metal	Description	VF	EF	Unc
71	69	Silv	3 Reichsmark, 1930	70	95	145
						Proof: $350

Note: Also see Austria Y71.

End of Occupation of Rhineland

Y#	KM#	Metal	Description	VF	EF	Unc
72	70	Silv	3 Reichsmark, 1930	45	57.50	115
						Proof: $375
73	71	Silv	5 Reichsmark, 1930	145	200.00	375
						Proof: $750

300th Anniversary, Rebuilding of Magdeburg

Y#	KM#	Metal	Description	VF	EF	Unc
74	72	Silv	3 Reichsmark, 1931	185	285	425
						Proof: $500

Centennial, Death of Stein

Y#	KM#	Metal	Description	VF	EF	Unc
75	73	Silv	3 Reichsmark, 1931	120	150	225
						Proof: $400

Centennial, Death of Goethe

Y#	KM#	Metal	Description	VF	EF	Unc
76	76	Silv	3 Reichsmark, 1932	85	110	215
						Proof: $325
77	77	Silv	5 Reichsmark, 1932	2,000	2,750	3,500
						Proof: $3,750

THIRD REICH *(NAZI STATE), 1933–1945*

450th Anniversary, Birth of Martin Luther

Y#	KM#	Metal	Description	VF	EF	Unc
78	79	Silv	2 Reichsmark, 1933	25	35	75
						Proof: $300
79	80	Silv	5 Reichsmark, 1933	125	175	300
						Proof: $375

First Anniversary of Nazi Rule

Obverse: ***With date "21 Marz 1933"***

Y#	KM#	Metal	Description	VF	EF	Unc
83	81	Silv	2 Reichsmark, 1934	12.50	35	110
						Proof: $350
84	82	Silv	5 Reichsmark, 1934	20.00	50	150
						Proof: $425

175th Anniversary, Birth of Schiller

Y#	KM#	Metal	Description	VF	EF	Unc
86	84	Silv	2 Reichsmark, 1934	52.50	70	120
						Proof: $200
87	85	Silv	5 Reichsmark, 1934	200.00	325	550
						Proof: $600

First Coinage

Y37-38, 40-41, and 43 were continued into this period.

Y#	KM#	Metal	Description	VF	EF	Unc
81	78	Nick	1 Reichsmark, 1933–39 *1936G, 38J, VF $150; 1937E, 38E–G, 39A, 39D, VF $75; 1939E, VF $150; 1939F, 39J, VF $95*	5	9.50	20

Obverse: ***Like Y84 but commemorative date omitted***

Y#	KM#	Metal	Description	VF	EF	Unc
85	83	Silv	5 Reichsmark, 1934–35	13	20	50

Y#	KM#	Metal	Description	VF	EF	Unc
82	86	Silv	5 Reichsmark, 1935–36	15	18.50	35

Second Coinage

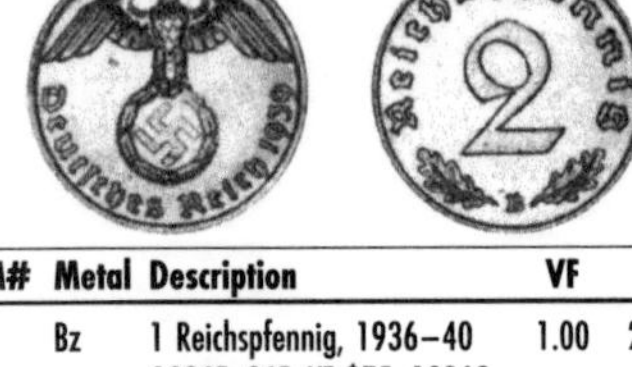

Y#	KM#	Metal	Description	VF	EF	Unc
88	89	Bz	1 Reichspfennig, 1936–40 *1936E, 36F, VF $75; 1936G, 36J, VF $45*	1.00	2.00	10.00
89	90	Bz	2 Reichspfennig, 1936–40 *1936F, 37E, VF $37.50; 1940G, VF $75*	1.25	2.75	7.50

Y#	KM#	Metal	Description	VF	EF	Unc
90	91	A-Bz	5 Reichspfennig, 1936–39 *1936A, VF $95; 1936D,G, VF $110*	1	2.50	13
91	92	A-Bz	10 Reichspfennig, 1936–39 *1936A, VF $50; 1936E, VF $185; 1936G, VF $375*	1	2.50	10

Y#	KM#	Metal	Description	VF	EF	Unc
93	95	Nick	50 Reichspfennig, 1938–39	35	50	85

Y#	KM#	Metal	Description	VF	EF	Unc
96	93	Silv	2 Reichsmark, 1936–39 *1939E,F, VF $30*	5.00	8.00	18
97	94	Silv	5 Reichsmark, 1936–39	12.50	17.50	35

Third Coinage

Y#	KM#	Metal	Description	VF	EF	Unc
A92	97	Zinc	1 Reichspfennig, 1940–45	0.75	1.25	10.00
B92	100	Zinc	5 Reichspfennig, 1940–44 *1942E, 44A, VF $15; 1943B, VF $70; 1944G, VF $275*	1.00	2.00	8.50
C92	101	Zinc	10 Reichspfennig, 1940–45 *1943G, 45E, VF $25; 1943J, VF $50*	1.00	3.00	18.00

Y#	KM#	Metal	Description	VF	EF	Unc
80	87	Alum	50 Reichspfennig, 1935	2.50	12	95

Note: Y80 was coined in 1935 but withheld from circulation until 1939.

Y#	KM#	Metal	Description	VF	EF	Unc
92	96	Alum	50 Reichspfennig, 1939–44 *1944G, VF $150*	4	13	50

German Army Issues

Y#	KM#	Metal	Description	VF	EF	Unc
94	98	Zinc	5 Reichspfennig, 1940–41	35	50	115
95	99	Zinc	10 Reichspfennig, 1940–41	40	75	135

ALLIED OCCUPATION, *1945–1950*

First Coinage

Reverse: ***Swastika omitted***

Y#	KM#	Metal	Description	VF	EF	Unc
98	Several	Zinc	1 Reichspfennig, 1944–46 *1944, Rare*	40.00	50	95.00
99	A105	Zinc	5 Reichspfennig, 1945, 47–48 *1945, Rare; 1948E, VF $375*	12.50	20	40.00
100	A104	Zinc	10 Reichspfennig, 1945–48 *1946G, VF $120; 1947E, VF $300*	10.00	18	37.50

Second Coinage

Legend: ***BANK DEUTSCHER LANDER***

Y#	KM#	Metal	Description	VF	EF	Unc
101	A101	Bz-CS	1 Pfennig, 1948–49	2	10	35
102	102	Br-CS	5 Pfennig, 1949	2	18	90
103	103	Br-CS	10 Pfennig, 1949	2	18	90

Y#	KM#	Metal	Description	VF	EF	Unc
104	104	C-N	50 Pfennig, 1949–50 *1950, VF $200*	3.50	20	65

GERMANY–FEDERAL REPUBLIC
(WEST GERMANY)

In 1949 the three western zones of occupied Germany had their civil government restored and united as a federal republic. In 1990 the country reunified with East Germany. *Capital:* Bern.

MONETARY SYSTEM

100 pfennig = 1 deutsche mark (DM)

PRECIOUS METAL CONTENT

Dates	Denomination	Gross Wt (g)	Fineness	Net Wt (g)	Troy Oz.
		SILVER			
1951–74	5 deutsche mark	11.2000	0.6250	7.0000	0.2250

New Legend: *BUNDESREPUBLIK DEUTSCHLAND*
Designs: *Similar to Y101–104*

Y#	KM#	Metal	Description	VF	EF	Unc
105	105	Bz-CS	1 Pfennig, 1950–2001	0.25	0.40	1.25
106	106	Bz	2 Pfennig, 1950–69 *1969, Rare*	1.00	2.50	10.00
107	107	Br-CS	5 Pfennig, 1950–2001	0.40	0.80	1.75
108	108	Br-CS	10 Pfennig, 1950–2001	0.40	0.80	1.75

Y#	KM#	Metal	Description	VF	EF	Unc
109	109	C-N	50 Pfennig, 1949–71 *1949, Rare*	1.25	3	6

Y#	KM#	Metal	Description	VF	EF	Unc
110	110	C-N	1 Deutsche Mark, 1950–2001	2	3	5

Y#	KM#	Metal	Description	VF	EF	Unc
111	111	C-N	2 Deutsche Mark, 1951	20	40	175

Y#	KM#	Metal	Description	VF	EF	Unc
117	116	C-N	2 Deutsche Mark, 1957–71	2.75	4	13

Y#	KM#	Metal	Description	VF	EF	Unc
112	112	Silv	5 Deutsche Mark, 1951–74	7.50	11	23 *Proof: $275*

Nürnberg Museum Centennial

Y#	KM#	Metal	Description	VF	EF	Unc
113	113	Silv	5 Deutsche Mark, 1952	250	350	700 *Proof: $2,750*

150th Anniversary, Death of Friedrich von Schiller

Y#	KM#	Metal	Description	VF	EF	Unc
114	114	Silv	5 Deutsche Mark, 1955	225	300	550 *Proof: $650*

300th Anniversary, Birth of Ludwig von Baden

Y#	KM#	Metal	Description	VF	EF	Unc
115	115	Silv	5 Deutsche Mark, 1955	225	300	500
						Proof: $650

Centennial, Death of von Eichendorff

Y#	KM#	Metal	Description	VF	EF	Unc
116	117	Silv	5 Deutsche Mark, 1957	225	250	475
						Proof: $650

150th Anniversary, Death of Johann Fichte

Y#	KM#	Metal	Description	VF	EF	Unc
118	118	Silv	5 Deutsche Mark, 1964	35	50	125
						Proof: $425

GERMAN DEMOCRATIC REPUBLIC (EAST GERMANY)

East Germany was proclaimed a democratic republic in 1949 and became sovereign as such in 1954. It was reunified with West Germany in 1990. *Capital:* East Berlin.

MONETARY SYSTEM
100 pfennig = 1 mark

First Coinage

Y#	KM#	Metal	Description	VF	EF	Unc
1	1	Alum	1 Pfennig, 1948–50	1	3	40
2	2	Alum	5 Pfennig, 1948–50	1	3	75
3	3	Alum	10 Pfennig, 1948–50	1	6	150

Y#	KM#	Metal	Description	VF	EF	Unc
4	4	A-Bz	50 Pfennig, 1949–50 *1949, Rare*	3	10	75

Second Coinage

Y#	KM#	Metal	Description	VF	EF	Unc
5	5	Alum	1 Pfennig, 1952–53	1.00	5	15.00
6	6	Alum	5 Pfennig, 1952–53	1.50	5	18.50
7	7	Alum	10 Pfennig, 1952–53	4.50	5	125.00

Third Coinage

Y#	KM#	Metal	Description	VF	EF	Unc
8	8	Alum	1 Pfennig, 1960–75	0.75	2.50	5
10	10	Alum	10 Pfennig, 1963–90 *1963, VF $10*	1.00	3.00	5

Y#	KM#	Metal	Description	VF	EF	Unc
11	12	Alum	50 Pfenning 1958–90	1.50	4.00	6
12	13	Alum	1 Mark, 1956, 62–63	2.00	7.50	55
13	14	Alum	2 Mark, 1957	2.75	5.00	10

GHANA

Situated in West Africa on the Gulf of Guinea, this former British colony was taken over in 1820 from the British merchant company that had developed the Gold Coast. Ghana was given its independence in 1957, and became a republic within the British Commonwealth in 1960. A series of coups in the mid-1960s through the early 1990s kept the nation under autocratic military rule. Free, multi-party elections and a stable democracy returned in 1992. *Languages:* English, African tongues. *Capital:* Accra.

For earlier issues, see British West Africa.

MONETARY SYSTEM
12 pence = 1 shilling

Y#	KM#	Metal	Description	VF	EF	Unc
1	1	Bz	1/2 Penny, 1958	0.75	3	9
2	2	Bz	1 Penny, 1958	1.00	3	9

Y#	KM#	Metal	Description	VF	EF	Unc
3	3	C-N	3 Pence, 1958, scalloped	1.00	3.00	5.00
4	4	C-N	6 Pence, 1958	1.25	3.25	5.00
5	5	C-N	1 Shilling, 1958	1.50	3.50	6.50
6	6	C-N	2 Shillings, 1958	1.75	3.75	7.50

Y#	KM#	Metal	Description	VF	EF	Unc
7	7	Silv	*10 Shillings, 1958, Proof only: $50*			

GREAT BRITAIN

The United Kingdom of Great Britain and Northern Ireland is separated from the European mainland by the North Sea and the English Channel. England has existed as a kingdom since the 10th century. Unification with Wales (1536), Scotland (1707), and Northern Ireland (1921) gave the nation its current composition. It is a constitutional monarchy and parliamentary democracy. *Capital:* London.

MONETARY SYSTEM:

4 farthings = 1 penny
12 pence = 1 shilling
2 shillings = 1 florin
5 shillings = 1 crown
20 shillings = 1 pound
20 shillings = 1 sovereign (gold)

PRECIOUS METAL CONTENT

Dates	Denomination	Gross Wt (g)	Fineness	Net Wt (g)	Troy Oz.
		SILVER			
1837–1920	3 pence	1.4138	0.9250	1.3078	0.0420
	4 pence	1.8851	0.9250	1.7437	0.0561
	6 pence	2.8276	0.9250	2.6155	0.0841
	1 shilling	5.6552	0.9250	5.2311	0.1682
	1 florin	11.3104	0.9250	10.4621	0.3364
	1/2 crown	14.1380	0.9250	13.0777	0.4204
	2 florins	22.6207	0.9250	20.9241	0.6727
	1 crown	28.2759	0.9250	26.1552	0.8409
1895–1935	trade dollar	26.9568	0.9000	24.2611	0.7800
1920–46	3 pence	1.1438	0.5000	0.7069	0.0227
	6 pence	2.8276	0.5000	1.4138	0.0455
	1 shilling	5.6552	0.5000	2.8276	0.0909
	2 shillings / 1 florin	11.3104	0.5000	5.6552	0.1818
	1/2 crown	14.1380	0.5000	7.0690	0.2273
	1 crown	28.2759	0.5000	14.1380	0.4545
		GOLD			
1838–1968	1/2 sovereign	3.9940	0.9170	3.6612	0.1177
	1 sovereign	7.9881	0.9170	7.3224	0.2354
	2 pounds	15.9761	0.9170	14.6448	0.4708
	5 pounds	39.9403	0.9170	36.6119	1.1711

Trade Coin

Y#	KM#	Metal	Description	VF	EF	Unc
T1	T5	Silv	1 Dollar, 1895–1935	55	100	195
			1921B, Rare; 1935, VF $1,600			*Proof: $1,000*

The British trade dollar was legal tender in Hong Kong and the Straits Settlements, but was created primarily to facilitate British commerce throughout Asia. The value ONE DOLLAR appears in English, Chinese, and Malay.

Special Issues for Colonial Use

During the 19th century, several new denominations were created to help adapt the British monetary system to the local systems used in various colonies. They resemble regular British issues and do not bear the names of the colonies, but are easily distinguishable by their unusual denominations. The following guide indicates the location of such pieces in this catalog:

Denomination	Location
Copper 1/4 farthing, 1839–1853	Ceylon, Y1
Copper 1/3 farthing, 1844	Malta, Y1
Copper 1/2 farthing, 1839–1856	Great Britain, YC2; Ceylon, Y2
Bronze 1/3 farthing, 1866–1913	Malta, Y2–4
Silver 1-1/2 pence, 1838–1862	Great Britain, YA5; Ceylon, Y3; Jamaica, YA3
Silver 4 pence, 1838–1855	Great Britain, Y4; British Guiana, YA1
Silver 4 pence, 1888	British Guiana, YB2

Maundy Money

Maundy money is the term for a special set of silver coins ceremonially distributed by the monarch to representative needy persons on Maundy Thursday (the Thursday before Easter). The set consists of one-, two-, three-, and fourpence coins.

The threepence used in the sets was of the regular type until 1927; regular issues after this date use different reverse designs.

VICTORIA, *1837–1901*

Obverse: ***Young portrait***

Y#	KM#	Metal	Description	VF	EF	Unc
C2	738	Cop	1/2 Farthing, 1839–56 (2 var)	11	22	70

Y#	KM#	Metal	Description	VF	EF	Unc
1	725	Cop	1 Farthing, 1838–60 (22 mm) *1860, VF $4,000*	11	40	85
2	726	Cop	1/2 Penny, 1838–59 (28 mm) *1845, VF $550; 1860, VF $4,000*	15	45	145
3	739	Cop	1 Penny, 1841–60 (34 mm) *1849, VF $125; 1860, VF $400*	20	85	250

Y#	KM#	Metal	Description	VF	EF	Unc
16	747/753	Bz	1 Farthing, 1860–95	5.00	25	60
17	748/754	Bz	1/2 Penny, 1860–94	12.50	40	150
18	749/755	Bz	1 Penny, 1860–94 *1882, without H mintmark, Rare*	20.00	70	250

Y#	KM#	Metal	Description	VF	EF	Unc
A5	728	Silv	1-1/2 Pence, 1838–62	20	75	175

Note: YA5 was issued for use only in Ceylon, Jamaica, and other colonies.

Y#	KM#	Metal	Description	VF	EF	Unc
A3	730	Silv	3 Pence, 1838–87	15	60	120

Y#	KM#	Metal	Description	VF	EF	Unc
4	731	Silv	4 Pence (Groat), 1838–62	20	50	110

Y#	KM#	Metal	Description	VF	EF	Unc
5	Several	Silv	6 Pence, 1838–87 *1854, VF $250*	25	90	250
6	734	Silv	1 Shilling, 1838–87 *1850, VF $2,000; 1854, VF $750; 1862, VF $200*	35	125	300

Y#	KM#	Metal	Description	VF	EF	Unc
9	740/756	Silv	1/2 Crown, 1839–87 (32 mm) *1840, VF $2,500*	75	300	575
10	741	Silv	1 Crown, 1839–47 (39 mm) *1839 Proof: $6,000*	300	1,500	3,750

Maundy Coins

Y#	KM#	Metal	Description	VF	EF	Unc
A12	727	Silv	1 Penny, 1838–87	20	50	65
B12	729	Silv	2 Pence, 1838–87	20	50	70
C12	730	Silv	3 Pence, 1838–87	30	50	80
D12	732	Silv	4 Pence, 1838–87	30	50	80

Regular Issues

Y#	KM#	Metal	Description	VF	EF	Unc
13	735	Gold	1/2 Sovereign, 1838–85, reverse arms *1862, VF $2,500*	250	600	1,150 *1839 Proof: $6,500*
14	736	Gold	1 Sovereign, 1838–74, reverse arms in wreath *1839, VF $3,000; 1841, VF Rare; 1874, VF $5,000*	BV	BV	1,500

Reverse: ***St. George and dragon***

Y#	KM#	Metal	Description	VF	EF	Unc
15	752	Gold	1 Sovereign, 1871–85 *1879, VF Rare*	BV	BV	1,250

Obverse: ***Gothic portrait***

Y#	KM#	Metal	Description	VF	EF	Unc
7	745	Silv	1 Florin, 1849	70	250	500

Note: Y7 omits DEI GRATIA from the legend, and is popularly known as the "Godless" florin.

Reverse: ***Date in Roman numerals***

Y#	KM#	Metal	Description	VF	EF	Unc
8	746	Silv	1 Florin, 1851–87 *1854, VF $1,500*	70	250	500 *1851, Proof: Rare*
11	744	Silv	1 Crown, 1847, 53 *1853, Unc $6,500*	2,000	3,250	5,500

Obverse: ***Golden Jubilee portrait***

Y#	KM#	Metal	Description	VF	EF	Unc
A18	758	Silv	3 Pence, 1887–93	6	20	35

Note: For fourpence 1888 with reverse like Y4, see British Guiana.

Y#	KM#	Metal	Description	VF	EF	Unc
19	759	Silv	6 Pence, 1887	12.50	20.00	35
20	761	Silv	1 Shilling, 1887–89, small bust *1889, VF $125*	10.00	22.50	50
21	774	Silv	1 Shilling, 1889–92, large bust	15.00	52.50	95

Y#	KM#	Metal	Description	VF	EF	Unc
22	760	Silv	6 Pence, 1887–93 *1893, VF $500*	10	20	45

Y#	KM#	Metal	Description	VF	EF	Unc
23	762	Silv	1 Florin, 1887–92 (29 mm)	20	40	75
25	763	Silv	2 Florins, 1887–90 (36 mm)	30	60	130

Y#	KM#	Metal	Description	VF	EF	Unc
24	764	Silv	1/2 Crown, 1887–92 (32 mm)	20	37.50	95 *Proof: $500*

Y#	KM#	Metal	Description	VF	EF	Unc
26	765	Silv	1 Crown, 1887–92	40	70	185
						Proof: $1,750

Maundy Coins

Y#	KM#	Metal	Description	VF	EF	Unc
A27	770	Silv	1 Penny, 1888–92	20	35	65
B27	771	Silv	2 Pence, 1888–92	25	35	70
C27	758	Silv	3 Pence, 1888–92	30	60	125
D27	773	Silv	4 Pence, 1888–92	25	45	75

Note: Proofs were struck only in 1887.

Regular Issues

Y#	KM#	Metal	Description	VF	EF	Unc
28	766	Gold	1/2 Sovereign, 1887–93, reverse arms (19 mm)	BV	300	450
29	767	Gold	1 Sovereign, 1887–92 (22 mm)	BV	BV	625
30	768	Gold	2 Pounds, 1887 (28 mm)	BV	1,350	1,750
31	769	Gold	5 Pounds, 1887 (36 mm)	BV	2,250	3,250

Obverse: ***Aged portrait***

Y#	KM#	Metal	Description	VF	EF	Unc
32	788	Bz	1 Farthing, 1895–1901	2.50	12.50	25.00
33	789	Bz	1/2 Penny, 1895–1901	3.50	10.00	30.00
34	790	Bz	1 Penny, 1895–1901	4.00	12.00	37.50

Reverse: ***Value in wreath***

Y#	KM#	Metal	Description	VF	EF	Unc
35	777	Silv	3 Pence, 1893–1901	6.00	17.50	37.50
36	779	Silv	6 Pence, 1893–1901	17.50	40.00	65.00

Y#	KM#	Metal	Description	VF	EF	Unc
37	780	Silv	1 Shilling, 1893–1901	15	40	80
38	781	Silv	1 Florin, 1893–1901	20	50	130

Y#	KM#	Metal	Description	VF	EF	Unc
39	782	Silv	1/2 Crown, 1893–1901	25	75	225
40	783	Silv	1 Crown, 1893–1900	55	200	475

Maundy Coins

Y#	KM#	Metal	Description	VF	EF	Unc
A41	775	Silv	1 Penny, 1893–1901	15	30	50
B41	776	Silv	2 Pence, 1893–1901	15	30	50
C41	777	Silv	3 Pence, 1893–1901	25	50	75
D41	778	Silv	4 Pence, 1893–1901	20	40	60

Note: Proofs were struck only in 1893.

Regular Issues

Y#	KM#	Metal	Description	VF	EF	Unc
42	784	Gold	1/2 Sovereign, 1893–1901	BV	225	325
43	785	Gold	1 Sovereign, 1893–1901	BV	385	4,250
44	786	Gold	2 Pounds, 1893	BV	1,750	2,500
					Proof: $8,000	
45	787	Gold	5 Pounds, 1893	BV	2,500	4,000
					Proof: $17,000	

Edward VII, *1901–1910*

Y#	KM#	Metal	Description	VF	EF	Unc
46	792	Bz	1 Farthing, 1902–10	2	12.50	25
47	793	Bz	1/2 Penny, 1902–10	5	10.00	40
48	794	Bz	1 Penny, 1902–10	2	9.50	35

Y#	KM#	Metal	Description	VF	EF	Unc
49	797	Silv	3 Pence, 1902–10	5	10	20
50	799	Silv	6 Pence, 1902–10	10	30	60

Y#	KM#	Metal	Description	VF	EF	Unc
51	800	Silv	1 Shilling, 1902–10	15	50	100

Y#	KM#	Metal	Description	VF	EF	Unc
52	801	Silv	1 Florin, 1902–10	25	75	160

Y#	KM#	Metal	Description	VF	EF	Unc
53	802	Silv	1/2 Crown, 1902–10 *1905, VF $1,500*	37.50	95	200

Y#	KM#	Metal	Description	VF	EF	Unc
54	803	Silv	1 Crown, 1902	100	250	400
					Matte Proof: $650	

Maundy Coins

Y#	KM#	Metal	Description	VF	EF	Unc
A55	795	Silv	1 Penny, 1902–10	15	25	45
B55	796	Silv	2 Pence, 1902–10	15	25	45
C55	797	Silv	3 Pence, 1902–10	20	40	60
D55	798	Silv	4 Pence, 1902–10	20	40	60

Regular Issues

Y#	KM#	Metal	Description	VF	EF	Unc
56	804	Gold	1/2 Sovereign, 1902–10	200	250	325
				Matte Proof: $800		
57	805	Gold	1 Sovereign, 1902–10	BV	375	450
				Matte Proof: $950		
58	806	Gold	2 Pounds, 1902	1,000	1,500	2,750
				Matte Proof: 3,200		
59	807	Gold	5 Pounds, 1902	BV	850	1,200
				Matte Proof: $6,000		

GEORGE V, *1910–1936*

Y#	KM#	Metal	Description	VF	EF	Unc
60	808/825	Bz	1 Farthing, 1911–36	0.75	5.00	10
61	809/824	Bz	1/2 Penny, 1911–27	2.50	12.50	35
62	837	Bz	1/2 Penny, 1928–36	1.50	6.00	20
63	Several	Bz	1 Penny, 1911–27	2.50	12.50	40
64	838	Bz	1 Penny, 1928–36	1.00	2.50	15
			1933, Rare			

Note: During the period 1925–1927 the portrait was reduced in size. The difference is greatest on Y62 and 64. The silver coins were debased to .500 fine during 1920, but this change was not denoted on the coins.

Y#	KM#	Metal	Description	VF	EF	Unc
65	813	Silv	3 Pence, 1911–26	1.00	2.50	10
					Proof: $125	

Y#	KM#	Metal	Description	VF	EF	Unc
66	815/828	Silv	6 Pence, 1911–27	2.25	12	60
					Proof: $70	

Y#	KM#	Metal	Description	VF	EF	Unc
67	816/829	Silv	1 Shilling, 1911–27	5	30	60
					Proof: $75	

Y#	KM#	Metal	Description	VF	EF	Unc
68	817	Silv	1 Florin, 1911–26	10	35	80
			1925, VF $100		*Proof: $150*	

Y#	KM#	Metal	Description	VF	EF	Unc
69	818/830	Silv	1/2 Crown, 1911–27	10	27.50	50
					Proof: $125	

Y#	KM#	Metal	Description	VF	EF	Unc
70	831	Silv	3 Pence, 1927–36	0.75	3	10
					Proof: $150	

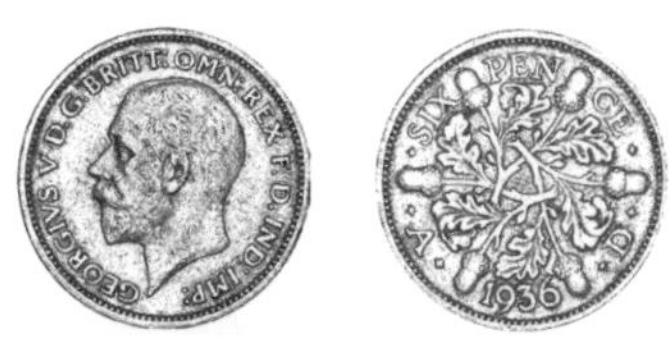

Y#	KM#	Metal	Description	VF	EF	Unc
71	832	Silv	6 Pence, 1927–36	2.25	7	17.50
					Proof: $75	

Y#	KM#	Metal	Description	VF	EF	Unc
72	833	Silv	1 Shilling, 1927–36	5	10	25
					Proof: $75	

Y#	KM#	Metal	Description	VF	EF	Unc
73	834	Silv	1 Florin, 1927–36 *1932, VF $45*	7.50	15	35 *Proof: $150*

Y#	KM#	Metal	Description	VF	EF	Unc
74	835	Silv	1/2 Crown, 1927–36	9	20	30 *Proof: $125*

Y#	KM#	Metal	Description	VF	EF	Unc
75	836	Silv	1 Crown, 1927–36 *1932, 36, VF $400; 1934, VF $1,750*	175	300	375 *Proof: $450*

Silver Jubilee

Y#	KM#	Metal	Description	VF	EF	Unc
76	842	Silv	1 Crown, 1935	25	35	55 *Proof: $450*

Maundy Coins

First Issue (.925 Silver)

Y#	KM#	Metal	Description	VF	EF	Unc
A81	811	Silv	1 Penny, 1911–20	25	50	100
B81	812	Silv	2 Pence, 1911–20	20	45	75
C81	813	Silv	3 Pence, 1911–20	25	50	100
D81	814	Silv	4 Pence, 1911–20	30	60	100

Second Issue (.500 Silver)

Y#	KM#	Metal	Description	VF	EF	Unc
E81	811/839	Silv	1 Penny, 1921–36	25	50	100
F81	812/840	Silv	2 Pence, 1921–36	20	45	75
G81	813/827	Silv	3 Pence, 1921–36	25	50	100
H81	814/841	Silv	4 Pence, 1921–26	30	60	100

Y#	KM#	Metal	Description	VF	EF	Unc
77	819	Gold	1/2 Sovereign, 1911–15	BV	BV	275
78	820	Gold	1 Sovereign, 1911–25	BV	BV	475
79	821	Gold	*2 Pounds, 1911, Proof only: $4,000*			
80	822	Gold	*5 Pounds, 1911, Proof only: $8,000*			

EDWARD VIII, *1936*

Some threepence pieces were minted as patterns and a few escaped into circulation. These are very rare.

GEORGE VI, *1936–1952*

FIRST COINAGE

Y#	KM#	Metal	Description	VF	EF	Unc
82	843	Bz	1 Farthing, 1937–48	0.15	0.75	1.50
						Proof: $10

Y#	KM#	Metal	Description	VF	EF	Unc
83	844	Bz	1/2 Penny, 1937–48	0.15	1	50
						Proof: $18

Y#	KM#	Metal	Description	VF	EF	Unc
84	845	Bz	1 Penny, 1937–48	0.15	0.50	6
						Proof: $18

Y#	KM#	Metal	Description	VF	EF	Unc
85	849	N-Br	3 Pence, 1937–48, 12-sided *1946, VF $30*	0.25	2	5
						Proof: $15

Y#	KM#	Metal	Description	VF	EF	Unc
86	850	Silv	3 Pence, 1937–44	0.50	1	3
						Proof: $20

Y#	KM#	Metal	Description	VF	EF	Unc
87	852	Silv	6 Pence, 1937–46	0.50	1.50	4
						Proof: $15

Reverse A: *English crest* **Reverse B:** *Scottish crest*

Y#	KM#	Metal	Description	VF	EF	Unc
88	853	Silv	1 Shilling, 1937–46, reverse A	2	5	10
						Proof: $25
89	854	Silv	1 Shilling, 1937–46, reverse B	2	5	10
						Proof: $25

Y#	KM#	Metal	Description	VF	EF	Unc
90	855	Silv	2 Shillings, 1937–46	5	8	15
						Proof: $25

Y#	KM#	Metal	Description	VF	EF	Unc
91	856	Silv	1/2 Crown, 1937–46	6.50	10	15
						Proof: $25

Y#	KM#	Metal	Description	VF	EF	Unc
92	857	Silv	1 Crown, 1937	30	45	75 *Proof: $75*

Maundy Coins

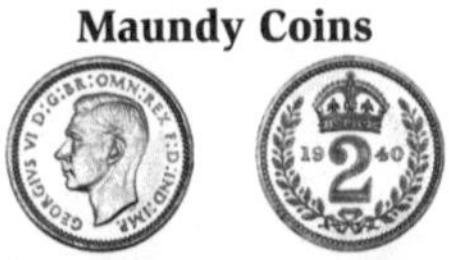

Y#	KM#	Metal	Description	VF	EF	Unc
A93	846	Silv	1 Penny, 1937–48	20	55	100
B93	847	Silv	2 Pence, 1937–48	20	55	100
C93	850	Silv	3 Pence, 1937–48	20	55	100
D93	851	Silv	4 Pence, 1937–48	20	55	100

Regular Issues

Y#	KM#	Metal	Description	VF	EF	Unc
95	862	C-N	6 Pence, 1947–48	0.15	1.00	40
96	863	C-N	1 Shilling, 1947–48, reverse A	0.15	0.50	2
97	864	C-N	1 Shilling, 1947–48, reverse B	0.15	0.50	2
98	865	C-N	2 Shillings, 1947–48	0.25	1.00	4
99	866	C-N	1/2 Crown, 1947–48	1.00	2.00	5

Note: In 1947 the composition of Britain's circulating sixpence through half-crown coins was changed to cupro-nickel. Designs remained as Y87–91.

Y#	KM#	Metal	Description	VF	EF	Unc
100	858	Gold	*1/2 Sovereign, 1937, Proof only: $950*			
101	859	Gold	*1 Sovereign, 1937, Proof only: $3,500*			
102	860	Gold	*2 Pounds, 1937, Proof only: $2,850*			
103	861	Gold	*5 Pounds, 1937, Proof only: $5,500*			

Second Coinage

Obverse: ***IND. IMP. omitted***
Reverse: ***Like Y82–85***

Y#	KM#	Metal	Description	VF	EF	Unc
104	867	Bz	1 Farthing, 1949–52	0.15	0.50	2.00 *Proof: $9.50*
105	868	Bz	1/2 Penny, 1949–52	0.15	0.50	1.50 *Proof: $50*
106	869	Bz	1 Penny, 1949–51 *1950–51, VF $10*	0.15	0.25	6.00 *Proof: $25*

Y#	KM#	Metal	Description	VF	EF	Unc
107	873	N-Br	3 Pence, 1949–52, 12-sided *1949, VF $35*	2	10	20 *Proof: $25*

Reverse: ***IND. IMP. omitted***

Y#	KM#	Metal	Description	VF	EF	Unc
108	875	C-N	6 Pence, 1949–52	0.25	1.25	40 *Proof: $10*
109	876	C-N	1 Shilling, 1949–51, reverse A	0.25	0.50	7 *Proof: $25*

Y#	KM#	Metal	Description	VF	EF	Unc
110	877	C-N	1 Shilling, 1949–51, reverse B	0.25	0.50	7 *Proof: $25*
111	878	C-N	2 Shillings, 1949–51	0.50	2.00	5 *Proof: $12*
112	879	C-N	1/2 Crown, 1949–52 *1952, Rare*	0.50	2.00	9 *Proof: $12*

Maundy Coins

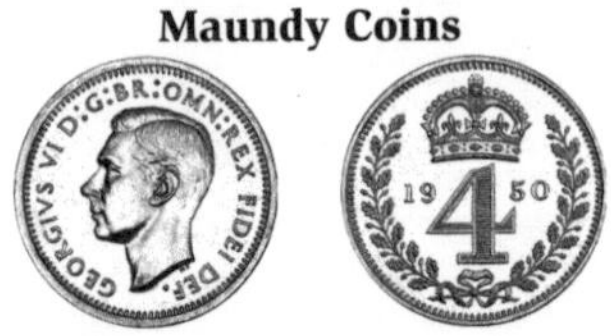

Y#	KM#	Metal	Description	VF	EF	Unc
A113	870	Silv	1 Penny, 1949–52	20	55	100
B113	871	Silv	2 Pence, 1949–52	20	55	100
C113	872	Silv	3 Pence, 1949–52	20	55	100
D113	873	Silv	4 Pence, 1949–52	20	55	100

Centennial of Great Exhibition of 1851 / Festival of Britain of 1951

Y#	KM#	Metal	Description	VF	EF	Unc
114	880	C-N	*5 Shillings, 1951, Prooflike, $15*			

ELIZABETH II, *1952–2022*

FIRST COINAGE

1953 Coronation

Y#	KM#	Metal	Description	VF	EF	Unc
116	881	Bz	1 Farthing, 1953	0.10	0.20	1.50
						Proof: $10
117	882	Bz	1/2 Penny, 1953	0.15	0.25	2.00
						Proof: $10
118	883	Bz	1 Penny, 1953	2.00	3.00	5.00
						Proof: $15

Y#	KM#	Metal	Description	VF	EF	Unc
119	886	N-Br	3 Pence, 1953, 12-sided	0.25	0.50	2
						Proof: $10

Y#	KM#	Metal	Description	VF	EF	Unc
120	889	C-N	6 Pence, 1953	0.10	0.25	1
						Proof: $10

Reverse A: ***English shield*** **Reverse B:** ***Scottish shield***

Y#	KM#	Metal	Description	VF	EF	Unc
121	890	C-N	1 Shilling, 1953, reverse A	0.10	0.25	2
						Proof: $10
122	891	C-N	1 Shilling, 1953, reverse B	0.50	1.00	3
						Proof: $10

Y#	KM#	Metal	Description	VF	EF	Unc
123	892	C-N	2 Shillings, 1953	0.25	0.50	3
						Proof: $15
124	893	C-N	1/2 Crown, 1953	0.25	0.50	3
						Proof: $20

Y#	KM#	Metal	Description	VF	EF	Unc
125	894	C-N	5 Shillings, 1953	0.75	2.00	10
						Proof: $30

Maundy Coins

Y#	KM#	Metal	Description	VF	EF	Unc
A126	884	Silv	1 Penny, 1953	—	—	225
B126	885	Silv	2 Pence, 1953	—	—	225
C126	887	Silv	3 Pence, 1953	—	—	225
D126	888	Silv	4 Pence, 1953	—	—	225

SECOND COINAGE

Obverse: ***BRITT: OMN: omitted***

Y#	KM#	Metal	Description	VF	EF	Unc
127	895	Bz	1 Farthing, 1954–56	0.25	0.50	2.50
128	896	Bz	1/2 Penny, 1954–70	0.10	0.15	1.00
						Proof: $10
A128	897	Bz	1 Penny, 1954–70 *1954, Unique*	0.10	0.15	1.00 *Proof: $10*

Y#	KM#	Metal	Description	VF	EF	Unc
129	900	N-Br	3 Pence, 1954–70, 12-sided	0.10	0.20	1.25
						Proof: $10

Y#	KM#	Metal	Description	VF	EF	Unc
130	903	C-N	6 Pence, 1954–70	0.10	0.20	1.25
						Proof: $10
131	904	C-N	1 Shilling, 1954–70, reverse A	0.10	0.20	1.00
						Proof: $12.50
132	905	C-N	1 Shilling, 1954–70, reverse B	0.10	0.20	1.00
						Proof: $12.50
133	906	C-N	2 Shillings, 1954–70	0.15	0.25	2.00
						Proof: $12.50
134	907	C-N	1/2 Crown, 1954–70	0.25	0.50	2.00
						Proof: $12.50
136	909	C-N	5 Shillings, 1960 *Prooflike, $15*	0.50	2.00	10.00

Note: Coins dated 1970 were struck in Proof only.

Maundy Coins

Y#	KM#	Metal	Description	VF	EF	Unc
A135	898	Silv	1 Penny, 1954–2000	—	—	100
B135	899	Silv	2 Pence, 1954–2000	—	—	100
C135	901	Silv	3 Pence, 1954–2000	—	—	100
D135	902	Silv	4 Pence, 1954–2000	—	—	100

Regular Issues

Y#	KM#	Metal	Description	VF	EF	Unc
137	908	Gold	1 Sovereign, 1957–68	BV	BV	BV

Note: Y137 was issued for overseas distribution only.

GREECE

Southernmost of the Balkan states in eastern Europe, extending down into the Mediterranean Sea. A Roman province by the Christian Era, the Turks added it to the Ottoman Empire by 1460. Independence was won in 1827. The monarchy collapsed after war with Turkey following World War I and a republic was created in 1923. Greece endured several military coups and dictatorships, saw two restorations of the monarchy and a post-WWII rebellion by communist guerrillas. Since 1967 the nation has enjoyed free elections and a parliamentary civilian government. *Language:* Greek. *Capital:* Athens.

MONETARY SYSTEM:

100 lepta = 1 drachma

PRECIOUS METAL CONTENT

Greece was a member of the Latin Monetary Union; see appendix A.

Dates	Denomination	Gross Wt (g)	Fineness	Net Wt (g)	Troy Oz.
		SILVER			
1868–1911	50 lepta	2.5000	0.8350	2.0871	0.0671
	1 drachma	5.0000	0.8350	4.1750	0.1342
	2 drachmai	10.0000	0.8350	8.3500	0.2685
	5 drachmai	25.0000	0.9000	22.5000	0.7234
1930	10 drachmai	7.0000	0.5000	3.5000	0.1125
	20 drachmai	11.3333	0.5000	5.6667	0.1822
1960, 65	20 drachmai	7.5000	0.8350	6.2625	0.2013
1963	30 drachmai	18.0000	0.8350	15.0300	0.4832
1964	30 drachmai	12.0000	0.8350	10.0200	0.3221
		GOLD			
1876–1935	5 drachmai	1.6129	0.9000	1.4516	0.0467
	10 drachmai	3.2258	0.9000	2.9032	0.0933
	20 drachmai	6.4516	0.9000	5.8064	0.1867
	50 drachmai	16.1290	0.9000	14.5161	0.4667
	100 drachmai	32.2581	0.9000	29.0323	0.9334

GEORGIOS I, *1863–1913*

First Coinage

Obverse: ***Young head***

Y#	KM#	Metal	Description	VF	EF	Unc
1	40	Cop	1 Lepton, 1869–70	10	40	125
2	41	Cop	2 Lepta, 1869	7	35	325
3	42	Cop	5 Lepta, 1869–70	10	45	375
4	43	Cop	10 Lepta, 1869–70	10	45	425

Y#	KM#	Metal	Description	VF	EF	Unc
5	44	Silv	20 Lepta, 1874, 83	12.50	30	150
6	37	Silv	50 Lepta, 1868–83 *1868, Rare*	15.00	60	175

Y#	KM#	Metal	Description	VF	EF	Unc
7	38	Silv	1 Drachma, 1868–83	55	150	850
8	39	Silv	2 Drachmai, 1868–83	175	600	3,000

Y#	KM#	Metal	Description	VF	EF	Unc
24	47	Gold	5 Drachmai, 1876	450	850	1,500
25	48	Gold	10 Drachmai, 1876	450	775	1,000

Y#	KM#	Metal	Description	VF	EF	Unc
A25	49	Gold	20 Drachmai, 1876	325	400	750

Second Coinage

Obverse: ***Older head***

Y#	KM#	Metal	Description	VF	EF	Unc
10	52	Cop	1 Lepton, 1878–79	5	10	80
11	53	Cop	2 Lepta, 1878	12	20	250
12	54	Cop	5 Lepta, 1878–82	12	20	350
13	55	Cop	10 Lepta, 1878–82	20	50	125

Y#	KM#	Metal	Description	VF	EF	Unc
14	46	Silv	5 Drachmai, 1875–76	95	300	1,250

Y#	KM#	Metal	Description	VF	EF	Unc
26	56	Gold	20 Drachmai, 1884	325	375	450
27	50	Gold	50 Drachmai, 1876	4,500	7,000	10,000
28	51	Gold	100 Drachmai, 1876	7,500	15,000	20,000

Third Coinage

Y#	KM#	Metal	Description	VF	EF	Unc
16	58	C-N	5 Lepta, 1894–95	7.50	30	300
17	59	C-N	10 Lepta, 1894–95	7.50	30	300
18	57	C-N	20 Lepta, 1893–95	7.50	30	300

Note: For similar coins dated 1900, see Crete.

Y#	KM#	Metal	Description	VF	EF	Unc
19	62	Nick	5 Lepta, 1912	2	10	90
20	63	Nick	10 Lepta, 1912	2	10	90

Y#	KM#	Metal	Description	VF	EF	Unc
21	64	Nick	20 Lepta, 1912	2	10	125

Y#	KM#	Metal	Description	VF	EF	Unc
22	60	Silv	1 Drachma, 1910–11	12.50	50	300
23	61	Silv	2 Drachmai, 1911	20.00	80	400

Konstantinos I
(Second Reign, 1920–1922)

Y#	KM#	Metal	Description	VF	EF	Unc
29	66	Alum	10 Lepta, 1922	5	15	35

Y#	KM#	Metal	Description	VF	EF	Unc
30	65	C-N	50 Lepta, 1921	1,250	2,250	3,750

Note: Y30 was not issued to circulation.

Republic,
1924–1935

Y#	KM#	Metal	Description	VF	EF	Unc
31	67	C-N	20 Lepta, 1926	2	30	60
32	68	C-N	50 Lepta, 1926	2	5	25
33	69	C-N	1 Drachma, 1926	2	50	100
34	70	C-N	2 Drachmai, 1926	2	7	50

Y#	KM#	Metal	Description	VF	EF	Unc
35	71	Nick	5 Drachmai, 1930	1	5	35

Y#	KM#	Metal	Description	VF	EF	Unc
36	72	Silv	10 Drachmai, 1930	15	50	175

Y#	KM#	Metal	Description	VF	EF	Unc
37	73	Silv	20 Drachmai, 1930	25	65	225

Georgios II
(Second Reign, 1935–1947)
Restoration Commemoratives

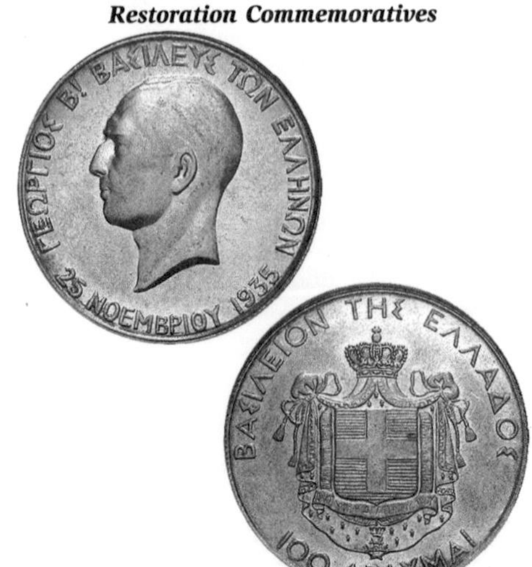

Y#	KM#	Metal	Description	VF	EF	Unc
A37	75	Silv	*100 Drachmai, 1935, Proof only: $2,000*			

Note: 500 struck, all as Proofs.

Y#	KM#	Metal	Description	VF	EF	Unc
B37	74	Gold	*20 Drachmai, 1935, Proof only: $12,500*			
C37	76	Gold	*100 Drachmai, 1935, Proof only: $27,500*			

Note: YA37, B37, and C37 were struck in 1939 and were not issued to circulation.

Y#	KM#	Metal	Description	VF	EF	Unc
38	77	Alum	5 Lepta, 1954, 71	0.10	0.25	2

Y#	KM#	Metal	Description	VF	EF	Unc
39	78	Alum	10 Lepta, 1954–71	0.10	0.25	2.25
40	79	Alum	20 Lepta, 1954–71	0.25	0.75	3.00

Paulos I, *1947–1964*

Y#	KM#	Metal	Description	VF	EF	Unc
41	80	C-N	50 Lepta, 1954–65 *1957, VF $10*	0.25	1.00	10
42	81	C-N	1 Drachma, 1954–65	0.25	1.00	10
43	82	C-N	2 Drachma, 1954–65	0.50	1.50	15
44	83	C-N	5 Drachma, 1954, 65	1.00	2.50	20

Y#	KM#	Metal	Description	VF	EF	Unc
45	84	Nick	10 Drachmai, 1959, 65	3	5	17.50

Y#	KM#	Metal	Description	VF	EF	Unc
46	85	Silv	20 Drachmai, 1960, 65	3	5	10

Centennial of Greek Dynasty

Y#	KM#	Metal	Description	VF	EF	Unc
47	86	Silv	30 Drachmai, 1963	8	15	30

Constantine II, *1964–1973*

Wedding Commemorative

Y#	KM#	Metal	Description	VF	EF	Unc
48	87	Silv	30 Drachmai, 1964	7	13	22.50

GREENLAND

An integral and autonomous part of Denmark, Greenland is the world's largest island, lying between the North Atlantic and the Polar Sea. The land was colonized by Norsemen in the 10th century, but they abandoned it as its climate cooled in the next 500 years. The island was re-colonized by Danish traders in the 1700s, becoming a part of Denmark in 1953 and gaining home rule with its own parliament in 1979. *Languages:* Greenlandic, Danish. *Capital:* Godthaab.

MONETARY SYSTEM

100 ore = 1 krone

Y#	KM#	Metal	Description	VF	EF	Unc
1	Tn46	C-N	10 Ore, 1922	50	100	225
2	Tn47	C-N	50 Ore, 1922	125	175	350
3	Tn48	C-N	2 Kroner, 1922	100	135	275
4	Tn49	C-N	10 Kroner, 1922. Reeded edge	100	150	300
4a	Tn49a	A-Bz	10 Kroner, 1922. Plain edge	450	750	1,500

Note: Y1–4a are tokens struck at the Copenhagen Mint for use in the city of Ivigut under the auspices of the Cryolite Mining and Trading Company. They circulated in Greenland until 1957.

Y#	KM#	Metal	Description	VF	EF	Unc
5	5	C-N	25 Ore, 1926	17.50	35	60
6	6	C-N	25 Ore, 1926 (center hole)	65.00	95	500
7	7	A-Bz	50 Ore, 1926	35.00	50	85
8	8	A-Bz	1 Krone, 1926	30.00	60	100

Y#	KM#	Metal	Description	VF	EF	Unc
9	9	Br	5 Kroner, 1944	90	150	200

Y#	KM#	Metal	Description	VF	EF	Unc
10	10	A-Bz	1 Krone, 1957	25	45	80
10a	10a	C-N	1 Krone, 1960, 64	20	35	65

GUADELOUPE

Comprising two large islands and a handful of smaller dependencies in the West Indies, about 300 miles southeast of Puerto Rico, Guadeloupe was explored by Columbus in 1493. It has been a French possession since 1635, and an overseas department of France since 1946. *Language:* French. *Capital:* Basse-Terre.

MONETARY SYSTEM

100 centimes = 1 franc

Y#	KM#	Metal	Description	VF	EF	Unc
1	45	C-N	50 Centimes, 1903, 21	35	60	125
2	46	C-N	1 Franc, 1903, 21	40	65	165

GUATEMALA

Bounded by Mexico to the north, Guatemala is Central America's northernmost nation. It was part of the Mayan Empire conquered by Spain in 1624 and established itself as an independent republic in 1839. The nation has seen frequent repressive civilian and military dictatorships since 1898 and endured civil war among military governments, leftist rebels and right-wing vigilante groups between 1960 and 1996. With the signing of a peace agreement among the parties, free elections have returned and economic and social stabilization has begun. *Languages:* Spanish, native tongues. *Capital:* Guatemala City.

MONETARY SYSTEM

8 reales = 1 peso

100 centavos = 1 peso, to 1924

100 centavos = 1 quetzal, 1924–

PRECIOUS METAL CONTENT

Dates	Denomination	Gross Wt (g)	Fineness	Net Wt (g)	Troy Oz.
		SILVER			
Typical Weights					
1859–69	1/4 real	0.7600	0.9030	0.6863	0.0220
	1/2 real	1.5500	0.9030	1.3997	0.0449
	1 real	3.0000	0.9030	2.7090	0.0870
	2 reales	6.2000	0.9030	5.5986	1.8000
	4 reales	12.5000	0.9030	11.2875	0.3629
	1 peso	26.0000	0.9030	23.4780	0.7549
1869–71	25 centimos	6.2500	0.9000	5.6250	0.1808
	1 peso	25.0000	0.9000	22.5000	0.7234
1870	50 centavos	12.5000	0.8350	10.4375	0.3356
1872–78	1/4 real	0.7700	0.9000	0.6930	0.0222
	1/2 real	1.5000	0.9000	1.3500	0.0435
	1 real	3.1500	0.9000	2.8350	0.0911
	2 reales	6.1000	0.9000	5.4900	0.1765
1878–93	1/4 real	0.7700	0.8350	0.6430	0.0206
	1/2 real	1.5000	0.8350	1.2525	0.0402
	1 real	3.2500	0.8350	2.7138	0.0872
	2 reales	6.1000	0.8350	5.0935	0.1664
	4 reales	12.5000	0.8350	10.4375	0.3356
1873–93	1 real	3.1500	0.9000	2.8350	0.0911
	2 reales	6.1000	0.9000	5.4900	0.1765
	4 reales	12.5000	0.9000	11.2500	0.3617
	1 peso	25.0000	0.9000	22.5000	0.7234
1881–93	5 centavos	1.2500	0.8350	1.0438	0.0335
	10 centavos	2.5000	0.8350	2.0875	0.0671
	25 centavos	6.2500	0.8350	5.4150	0.1677
	1 peso	25.0000	0.9000	22.5000	0.7234
1894–1900	1/4 real	0.7700	0.8350	0.6430	0.0206
	1/2 real	1.5000	0.8350	1.2525	0.0402
	1/2 real	1.5500	0.6000	0.9300	0.0299
	1 real	3.2500	0.8350	2.7138	0.0872
	1 real	3.1500	0.7500	2.3625	0.0759
	1 real	3.1000	0.6000	1.8600	0.0598
	1 real	3.1500	0.5000	1.5750	0.0506
	2 reales	6.2000	0.8350	5.1770	0.1664
	4 reales	12.5000	0.9000	11.2500	0.3617
	1 peso	25.0000	0.9000	22.5000	0.7234
1925–64	5 centavos	1.6667	0.7200	1.2000	0.0386
	10 centavos	3.3333	0.7200	2.4000	0.0772
	25 centavos / 1/4 quetzal	8.3333	0.7200	6.0000	0.1929
	50 centavos	11.9444	0.7200	8.6000	0.2777
	1/2 quetzal	16.6667	0.7200	12.0000	0.3858
	1 quetzal	33.3333	0.7200	24.0000	0.7716

Dates	Denomination	Gross Wt (g)	Fineness	Net Wt (g)	Troy Oz.
		GOLD			
1859–69	4 reales	0.8459	0.8750	0.7402	0.0238
	1 peso	1.6917	0.8750	1.4802	0.0476
	2 pesos	3.3834	0.8750	2.9605	0.0952
	4 pesos	6.7669	0.8750	5.9210	0.1904
	8 pesos	13.5337	0.8750	11.8420	0.3807
	16 pesos	27.0296	0.8750	23.6509	0.7604
1869–78	5 pesos	8.0645	0.9000	7.2581	0.2333
	10 pesos	16.1290	0.9000	14.5161	0.4667
	20 pesos	32.2581	0.9000	29.0323	0.9334
1926	5 quetzales	8.3591	0.9000	7.5232	0.2419
	10 quetzales	16.7181	0.9000	15.0463	0.4837
	20 quetzales	33.4363	0.9000	30.0926	0.9675

REPUBLIC,
1839–

FIRST COINAGE

Y#	KM#	Metal	Description	VF	EF	Unc
1	130	Silv	1/4 Real, 1859–69 *1859, VF $750*	20	35	100

Y#	KM#	Metal	Description	VF	EF	Unc
2	131	Silv	1/2 Real, 1859–61	12.50	25	75
3	132	Silv	1 Real, 1859–60	15.00	30	100
4	133	Silv	2 Reales, 1859	375.00	750	3,750
5	134	Silv	2 Reales, 1860–61, modified dies	30.00	60	150
6	136	Silv	4 Reales, 1860–61	50.00	100	600
7	178	Silv	1 Peso, 1859	350.00	850	4,500

Design: ***Modified dies both sides***

Y#	KM#	Metal	Description	VF	EF	Unc
8	138	Silv	1/2 Real, 1862–65	12.50	25	75
9	137	Silv	1 Real, 1861–65	15.00	30	100
10	139	Silv	2 Reales, 1862–65	25.00	50	150
11	140	Silv	4 Reales, 1863, 65	20.00	40	275
12	182	Silv	1 Peso, 1862–65	45.00	90	750

Y#	KM#	Metal	Description	VF	EF	Unc
13	135	Gold	4 Reales, 1860–64	60	85	150
14	179	Gold	1 Peso, 1859–60	110	200	400

Y#	KM#	Metal	Description	VF	EF	Unc
15	180	Gold	2 Pesos, 1859	150	275	575
16	181	Gold	4 Pesos, 1861–62	600	900	1,500
17	184	Gold	8 Pesos, 1864	750	1,500	3,000
18	183	Gold	16 Pesos, 1863 (36 mm)	4,500	8,000	12,000
19	185	Gold	16 Pesos, 1865 (33 mm)	4,500	8,000	12,000

SECOND COINAGE

New Legend: ***R. CARRERA FUNDADOR***
Designs: ***Similar to Y8–19***

Y#	KM#	Metal	Description	VF	EF	Unc
20	143	Silv	1/2 Real, 1867–69	15	30	60
21	141	Silv	1 Real, 1866–67	15	30	80
22	145	Silv	1 Real, 1868–69, modified arms	20	40	90
23	142	Silv	2 Reales, 1866–69	15	30	100
24	144	Silv	4 Reales, 1867–68	40	100	400
25	186	Silv	1 Peso, 1866–69, fineness "10D 20G"	50	100	500

Y#	KM#	Metal	Description	VF	EF	Unc
26	187	Gold	4 Pesos, 1866–69	400	500	800
28	188	Gold	16 Pesos, 1867, 69	1,900	2,200	4,000

Note: The coin previously cataloged as Y27 does not exist.

THIRD COINAGE

100 centimos = 1 peso, 1869–1870
100 centavos = 1 peso, 1870–1871

Designs: ***Like Y23–24***

Y#	KM#	Metal	Description	VF	EF	Unc
29	189	Silv	25 Centimos, 1869–70	15	30	100
30	190	Silv	1 Peso, 1869–71, fineness "0900"	50	75	475

Y#	KM#	Metal	Description	VF	EF	Unc
34	196	Bz	1 Centavo, 1871	10	20	50

Y#	KM#	Metal	Description	VF	EF	Unc
35	195	Silv	50 Centavos, 1870	30	75	200

Y#	KM#	Metal	Description	VF	EF	Unc
31	191	Gold	5 Pesos, 1869	BV	550	650
32	193	Gold	10 Pesos, 1869	900	1,000	1,300
33	194	Gold	20 Pesos, 1869	2,000	2,250	2,650

FOURTH COINAGE

After 1871, the silver coinage returned to the *real* system, while gold was struck in the decimal system.

8 reales = 1 peso

.900 Fine

Obverse: ***Short-rayed sun***

Y#	KM#	Metal	Description	VF	EF	Unc
36	146	Silv	1/4 Real, 1872–78	5	10	30

Y#	KM#	Metal	Description	VF	EF	Unc
37	147	Silv	1/2 Real, 1872–73	12.50	25	75
38	148.1	Silv	1 Real, 1872–78	15.00	30	100
39	149	Silv	2 Reales, 1872–73	15.00	30	125

Obverse: ***Fineness not shown***

Y#	KM#	Metal	Description	VF	EF	Unc
36a	146a.2	Silv	1/4 Real, 1878, G on reverse	5	10	30

Note: Y36a has three minor varieties: large, medium, or small G.

Y#	KM#	Metal	Description	VF	EF	Unc
37a	147a.2	Silv	1/2 Real, 1878, 93	5	15	40
38a	148.2	Silv	1 Real, 1878	15	35	125

.835 Fine

Obverse: ***Like Y36***

Y#	KM#	Metal	Description	VF	EF	Unc
36b	146a.1	Silv	1/4 Real, 1878, reverse as Y36	5	10	30
36c	146a.3	Silv	1/4 Real, 1878–79, reverse as Y42	5	10	30

Y#	KM#	Metal	Description	VF	EF	Unc
37b	147a.1	Silv	1/2 Real, 1878–79	7.50	15	40

Obverse: *Long-rayed sun*
Reverse: *Modified wreath*

Y#	KM#	Metal	Description	VF	EF	Unc
42	151	Silv	1/4 Real, 1879–86	3	5	15

Obverse: *Like Y36, but fineness not shown*

Y#	KM#	Metal	Description	VF	EF	Unc
45	156	Silv	1/4 Real, 1887–88, reverse lion	3	5	15
46	157	Silv	1/4 Real, 1889, G below mountains, date below wreath	6	10	30
47	158	Silv	1/4 Real, 1889–91, 5 stars below wreath	3	5	15

Obverse: *Like Y42*

Y#	KM#	Metal	Description	VF	EF	Unc
48	159	Silv	1/4 Real, 1892–93, reverse lion *1892, VF $100*	3	5	15
49	161	Silv	1/4 Real, 1893–94, 3 stars below wreath	3	5	15

.900 Fine

Reverse: *Seated Liberty*

Obverse: *Arms with small wreath*

Y#	KM#	Metal	Description	VF	EF	Unc
54	150	Silv	4 Reales, 1873–93 *1872, VF $1,250; 1893, VF $500*	50	100	250
56	197	Silv	1 Peso, 1872–73, date at bottom	60	100	475
57	200	Silv	1 Peso, 1878–79, date at top	350	700	1,250

Obverse: *Arms with large wreath*

Y#	KM#	Metal	Description	VF	EF	Unc
52	153	Silv	1 Real, 1879	25	55	175
53	154	Silv	2 Reales, 1879	25	55	275

Y#	KM#	Metal	Description	VF	EF	Unc
58	201	Silv	1 Peso, 1879–93	400	800	1,500
58a	207	Silv	1 Peso, 1888–93, modified Liberty *1879, Rare; 1893, EF $3,000*	650	1,100	2,500

.835 Fine

Y#	KM#	Metal	Description	VF	EF	Unc
59	152	Silv	1/2 Real, 1879–80, "1/2 RL"	3	7	20
60	155	Silv	1/2 Real, 1880–90, MEDIO REAL	3	5	10
52a	153a	Silv	1 Real, 1883–93	3	5	10
53a	154a,b	Silv	2 Reales, 1881, 92–93 *1892, VF $150; 1893, Rare*	15	20	50
54a	160	Silv	4 Reales, 1892	1,000	1,750	3,500

Obverse: *Fineness not shown*

Y#	KM#	Metal	Description	VF	EF	Unc
64	163	Silv	1/2 Real, 1893, small wreath	35	75	175
65	164	Silv	1/2 Real, 1893, large wreath	15	40	85

Y#	KM#	Metal	Description	VF	EF	Unc
66	198	Gold	5 Pesos, 1872–78	500	650	1,000
67	199	Gold	20 Pesos, 1877–78	10,000	18,000	25,000

SECOND DECIMAL COINAGE

Y#	KM#	Metal	Description	VF	EF	Unc
68	202	Bz	1 Centavo, 1881 (struck over Y34)	10	20	80

Reverse: *Denomination in wreath*

Y#	KM#	Metal	Description	VF	EF	Unc
69	205	Silv	25 Centavos, 1881–91	10.00	20	75
69a	209	Silv	25 Centavos, 1890–93, larger reverse lettering	7.50	10	25

Y#	KM#	Metal	Description	VF	EF	Unc
70	203	Silv	5 Centavos, 1881	20	40	175
71	204	Silv	10 Centavos, 1881	25	50	200

Y#	KM#	Metal	Description	VF	EF	Unc
72	206	Silv	25 Centavos, 1882	225	400	—

Y#	KM#	Metal	Description	VF	EF	Unc
73	208	Silv	1 Peso, 1882, 89 *1889, EF $750*	100	200	500

Real Coinage Resumed

New dies 1894

Y#	KM#	Metal	Description	VF	EF	Unc
74	162	Silv	1/4 Real, 1894–99	7	12.50	30

Note: Coins dated 1893 are patterns.

Y#	KM#	Metal	Description	VF	EF	Unc
75	165	Silv	1/2 Real, 1894–97, .835 fine	3	5	12
76	170	Silv	1/2 Real, 1899, .600 fine	2	4	10
77	166	Silv	1 Real, 1894–98, .835 fine	5	9	30
78	171	Silv	1 Real, 1899, no fineness	3	7	15
79	172	Silv	1 Real, 1899, .750 fine	150	250	600
80	173	Silv	1 Real, 1899, .600 fine	3	5	15
81	174	Silv	1 Real, 1899–1900, .500 fine	3	6	25
82	167	Silv	2 Reales, 1894–99, .835 fine *1899, VF $40*	10	25	100
83	168	Silv	4 Reales, 1894, .900 fine	40	75	125
84	210	Silv	1 Peso, 1894–97, .900 fine	30	55	150

Designs: ***Similar to Y74–75, 77***

Y#	KM#	Metal	Description	VF	EF	Unc
85	175	C-N	1/4 Real, 1900–01	3	5	20.00
86	176	C-N	1/2 Real, 1900–01	3	5	15.00
87	177	C-N	1 Real, 1900–12	3	5	17.50

Counterstamped Issues

Dies of Y75 (1/2 real) dated 1894 stamped on pesos of Chile, soles of Peru, and others.

Y#	KM#	Metal	Description	VF	EF	Unc
88	224	Silv	(1 Peso) on Peru Sol, 1864–94	50	75	250
88a	216	Silv	(1 Peso) on Chile Peso, 1867–91	65	100	400
88b	225	Silv	(1 Peso) on Peru 5 Pesetas, 1880	150	250	600

This counterstamp is known on several other Latin American crowns. All are very rare.

Provisional Decimal Coinage

Y#	KM#	Metal	Description	VF	EF	Unc
89	230	Bz	12-1/2 Centavos, 1915	2	8	20
90	231	Bz	25 Centavos, 1915	2	8	20

Y#	KM#	Metal	Description	VF	EF	Unc
91	232	A-Bz	50 Centavos, 1922	4	10	20

Y#	KM#	Metal	Description	VF	EF	Unc
92	233	A-Bz	1 Peso, 1923	5	12.50	35

Y#	KM#	Metal	Description	VF	EF	Unc
93	234	A-Bz	5 Pesos, 1923	15	30	75

Coinage Reform, November 26, 1924

Y#	KM#	Metal	Description	VF	EF	Unc
95	237	Bz	1 Centavo, 1925	5.00	15.00	40
96	247	Bz	1 Centavo, 1929, larger arms	4.00	12.00	25
94	248	Br	1/2 Centavo, 1932, 46	1.00	2.00	5
97	249	Br	1 Centavo, 1932–49	0.35	1.00	5
98	250	Br	2 Centavos, 1932	2.00	7.50	30

Obverse: ***Long-tailed quetzal on scroll***

Y#	KM#	Metal	Description	VF	EF	Unc
99	238.1	Silv	5 Centavos, 1925, 44–49	2	5	25
100	239.1	Silv	10 Centavos, 1925, 44–49	2	5	15

Obverse: ***Short-tailed quetzal on scroll***

Y#	KM#	Metal	Description	VF	EF	Unc
99a	238.2	Silv	5 Centavos, 1928–43	2	5	17.50
100a	239.2	Silv	10 Centavos, 1928–43, 47	2	6	25.00
101	240	Silv	1/4 Quetzal, 1925, lettered edge	15	30	150.00
102	243.1	Silv	1/4 Quetzal, 1926–29, different dies	10	20	55.00
102a	243.2	Silv	1/4 Quetzal, 1946–49, reeded edge	10	20	50.00

Y#	KM#	Metal	Description	VF	EF	Unc
103	241	Silv	1/2 Quetzal, 1925	55	75	200
104	242	Silv	1 Quetzal, 1925	1,000	2,000	5,000

Y#	KM#	Metal	Description	VF	EF	Unc
105	244	Gold	5 Quetzales, 1926	500	650	800
106	245	Gold	10 Quetzales, 1926	BV	1,200	1,500
107	246	Gold	20 Quetzales, 1926	BV	2,250	2,800

Wartime Issues

Y#	KM#	Metal	Description	VF	EF	Unc
108	251	Br	1 Centavo, 1943–44	3	10	25
109	252	Br	2 Centavos, 1943–44	3	10	35

Y#	KM#	Metal	Description	VF	EF	Unc
110	253	Silv	25 Centavos, 1943	5	10	50

New Designs

Y#	KM#	Metal	Description	VF	EF	Unc
111	254	Br	1 Centavo, 1949–54, small head	0.15	0.50	5

Y#	KM#	Metal	Description	VF	EF	Unc
112	259	Br	1 Centavo, 1954–58, large head	0.15	0.30	2

Y#	KM#	Metal	Description	VF	EF	Unc
113	260	Br	1 Centavo, 1958–64, modified dies	0.15	0.50	1

Obverse: ***Short-tailed quetzal on scroll***

Y#	KM#	Metal	Description	VF	EF	Unc
114	255	Silv	5 Centavos, 1949, small tree	3	8	30
115	257	Silv	5 Centavos, 1950–58, large tree	1	2	5

Obverse: ***Short-tailed quetzal on scroll***

Y#	KM#	Metal	Description	VF	EF	Unc
117	256.1	Silv	10 Centavos, 1949–58, small monolith	2	4	10
117a	256.2	Silv	10 Centavos, 1957–58, large monolith	2	4	10

Obverse: ***Long-tailed quetzal on scroll***

Y#	KM#	Metal	Description	VF	EF	Unc
115a	257.2	Silv	5 Centavos, 1958–59, reverse like Y115	1	2	3.50
117b	256.3	Silv	10 Centavos, 1958–59, reverse like Y117	2	4	7.50

Y#	KM#	Metal	Description	VF	EF	Unc
119	258	Silv	25 Centavos, 1950–59	6	8	17.50

Modified Dies

Y#	KM#	Metal	Description	VF	EF	Unc
116	261	Silv	5 Centavos, 1960–64	1	1.50	3.00
118	262	Silv	10 Centavos, 1960–64	3	4.00	7.50

Y#	KM#	Metal	Description	VF	EF	Unc
120	263	Silv	25 Centavos, 1960–64	4	6.50	15

Y#	KM#	Metal	Description	VF	EF	Unc
121	264	Silv	50 Centavos, 1962–63	6	8.50	20

GUERNSEY

The Bailiwick of Guernsey is one of the Channel Islands, 30 miles off the coast of France. Though a dependency of the British monarch, Guernsey is administered by its own laws. *Languages:* English, French. *Capital:* St. Peter Port.

MONETARY SYSTEM

8 doubles = 1 penny
12 pence = 1 shilling
5 shillings = 1 crown
20 shillings = 1 pound

Y#	KM#	Metal	Description	VF	EF	Unc
A1	1	Cop	1 Double, 1830	5	25	60
						Proof: $600
B1	4	Cop	2 Doubles, 1858	15	60	250
C1	2	Cop	*4 Doubles, 1830, 58*	12	55	150
						Proof: $600

Y#	KM#	Metal	Description	VF	EF	Unc
D1	3	Cop	8 Doubles, 1834, 58	20	60	250
						Proof: $600

Obverse: ***Three leaves above shield***

Y#	KM#	Metal	Description	VF	EF	Unc
1	10	Bz	1 Double, 1868–1911	2.50	7.50	25
						Proof: $450
2	9	Bz	2 Doubles, 1868–1911	6.00	25.00	45
						Proof: $450
3	5	Bz	4 Doubles, 1864–1911	4.50	11.00	35
						Proof: $500

Y#	KM#	Metal	Description	VF	EF	Unc
4	7	Bz	8 Doubles, 1864–1911	4	20	50
						Proof: $550

Obverse: ***Leaf cluster above shield***

Y#	KM#	Metal	Description	VF	EF	Unc
1a	11	Bz	1 Double, 1911–38	3.00	7.50	25
2a	12	Bz	2 Doubles, 1914–29	4.00	7.50	35
			1917, VF $25			
3a	13	Bz	4 Doubles, 1914–49	4.50	12.50	35
5	14	Bz	8 Doubles, 1914–49	4.00	10.00	20
						Proof $225

Y#	KM#	Metal	Description	VF	EF	Unc
6	15	Bz	4 Doubles, 1956–66	2.50	10	20
						Proof: $25

Y#	KM#	Metal	Description	VF	EF	Unc
7	16	Bz	8 Doubles, 1956, 59, 66	1.50	6	20
						Proof: $45

Y#	KM#	Metal	Description	VF	EF	Unc
8	17	C-N	3 Pence, 1956, thin, scalloped	5	10	15
						Proof: $35
8a	18	C-N	3 Pence, 1959, 66, thick, scalloped	5	10	20
						Proof: $35

GUINEA

The former Fulani Empire territory on the west coast of Africa was claimed as a French overseas territory in 1849 and became part of French West Africa in 1895. Independence as a republic was established in 1958, and the country became the first openly Marxist state in Africa. In recent years its elections and political dialogue have grown more open. *Languages:* French, native tongues. *Capital:* Conakry.

MONETARY SYSTEM
100 centimes = 1 franc

Y#	KM#	Metal	Description	VF	EF	Unc
1	1	A-Bz	5 Francs, 1959	10	20	45

Y#	KM#	Metal	Description	VF	EF	Unc
2	2	A-Bz	10 Francs, 1959	25	50	95

Y#	KM#	Metal	Description	VF	EF	Unc
3	3	A-Bz	25 Francs, 1959	60	120	225

Y#	KM#	Metal	Description	VF	EF	Unc
4	4	C-N	1 Franc, 1962	2.50	4.25	10

Y#	KM#	Metal	Description	VF	EF	Unc
5	5	C-N	5 Francs, 1962	2.50	4.25	10

Y#	KM#	Metal	Description	VF	EF	Unc
6	6	C-N	10 Francs, 1962	3.50	6	20

Y#	KM#	Metal	Description	VF	EF	Unc
7	7	C-N	25 Francs, 1962	3.25	6.50	27.50

HAITI

Located west of the Dominican Republic on the Caribbean island of Hispaniola, Haiti was a prosperous French colony in the 17th century. The lengthy war that gained its independence in 1804 disrupted its agricultural economy to a point from which it never fully recovered. After a series of dictatorships, U.S. forces invaded in 1915 and continued to occupy the small nation until 1934. Dictatorial regimes returned from 1949 to 1986, and the country has struggled to re-establish democracy since free, though widely suspect, elections returned in the 1990s. *Languages:* French, Creole. *Capital:* Port-au-Prince.

MONETARY SYSTEM
100 centimes = 1 gourde

PRECIOUS METAL CONTENT

Dates	Denomination	Gross Wt (g)	Fineness	Net Wt (g)	Troy Oz.
		SILVER			
1881–95	10 centimes	2.5000	0.8350	2.0875	0.0671
	20 centimes	5.0000	0.8350	4.1750	0.1342
	50 centimes	12.5000	0.8350	10.4375	0.3356
	1 gourde	25.0000	0.9000	22.5000	0.0734

Y#	KM#	Metal	Description	VF	EF	Unc
A1	39	Bz	5 Centimes, 1863	7.50	15.00	75
B1	40	Bz	10 Centimes, 1863	7.00	15.00	75
C1	41	Bz	20 Centimes, 1863	10.00	17.50	95

Y#	KM#	Metal	Description	VF	EF	Unc
1	42	Bz	1 Centime, 1881	8	12	45
2	43	Bz	2 Centimes, 1881	8	12	45

Y#	KM#	Metal	Description	VF	EF	Unc
3	48	Bz	1 Centime, 1886, 94, 95	5.00	10	20
4	49	Bz	2 Centimes, 1886, 94	7.50	15	35

Y#	KM#	Metal	Description	VF	EF	Unc
6	44	Silv	10 Centimes, 1881–94	5.00	10	50
7	45	Silv	20 Centimes, 1881–95	10.00	20	80
8	47	Silv	50 Centimes, 1882–95	12.50	25	100
9	46	Silv	1 Gourde 1881–95	50.00	100	450

Insurrection, *1889*

Y#	KM#	Metal	Description	VF	EF	Unc
A5	50	C-N	5 Centimes, 1889	50	100	250

Reverse: ***Blank***

Y#	KM#	Metal	Description	VF	EF	Unc
5	51	Bz	1 Gourde, ND	450	750	1,350

Note: Counterstamped B.P. 1G/GLH (Bon Pour 1 Gourde / General Hippolyte).

Post-Insurrection Regular Issues

Y#	KM#	Metal	Description	VF	EF	Unc
10	53	C-N	5 Centimes, 1904–05 *1904, VF $17.50*	7.50	17.50	50
11	54	C-N	10 Centimes, 1906	7.50	10.00	30
12	55	C-N	20 Centimes, 1907	15.00	40.00	100
13	56	C-N	50 Centimes, 1907–08	15.00	40.00	100

Y#	KM#	Metal	Description	VF	EF	Unc
14	52	C-N	5 Centimes, 1904	10	30	75

Y#	KM#	Metal	Description	VF	EF	Unc
15	57	C-N	5 Centimes, 1949	1.00	2.50	12.50
16	58	C-N	10 Centimes, 1949	2.50	7.50	17.50

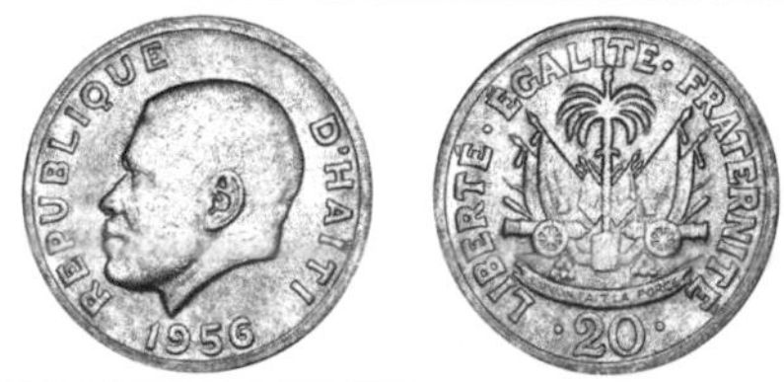

Y#	KM#	Metal	Description	VF	EF	Unc
17	59	CNZ	5 Centimes, 1953	0.20	0.50	3.00
18	60	CNZ	10 Centimes, 1953	0.50	1.00	7.50
19	61	CNZ	20 Centimes, 1956	1.00	2.00	5.00

Y#	KM#	Metal	Description	VF	EF	Unc
20	62	CNZ	5 Centimes, 1958, 70	0.10	0.20	0.75
21	63	CNZ	10 Centimes, 1958, 70	0.10	0.20	0.75

HAWAII

Located 2,400 miles west of San Francisco, the archipelago became the 50th of the United States in 1959. The land was visited by Britain's Captain Cook in 1778, who called it the Sandwich Islands. The eight main islands and countless smaller volcanic peaks stretching for 1,523 miles was ruled as a kingdom under Polynesian-descended royalty from 1791 until 1894 when a republic was proclaimed. Expansionist policies brought about its annexation to the United States in 1898, and it was granted territorial status in 1900. *Languages:* Hawaiian, English. *Capital:* Honolulu.

MONETARY SYSTEM

10 cents = 1 dime 100 cents = 1 dollar (dala)

PRECIOUS METAL CONTENT

Dates	Denomination	Gross Wt (g)	Fineness	Net Wt (g)	Troy Oz.
		SILVER			
1883	1 dime	2.5000	0.9000	2.2488	0.0723
	1/4 dollar	6.2500	0.9000	5.6236	0.1808
	1/2 dollar	12.5000	0.9000	11.2503	0.3617
	1 dollar	26.7295	0.9000	24.0589	0.7735

KAMEHAMEHA III, *1825–1854*

Y#	KM#	Metal	Description	VF	EF	Unc
1	1	Cop	1 Cent, 1847	500	750	1,250

Note: Many souvenir replicas exist of Y1.

KALAKAUA I, *1874–1891*

Y#	KM#	Metal	Description	VF	EF	Unc
2	3	Silv	1 Dime, 1883	120	300	1,500

Y#	KM#	Metal	Description	VF	EF	Unc
3	5	Silv	1/4 Dollar, 1883	90	150	300
4	6	Silv	1/2 Dollar, 1883	150	300	2,000
5	7	Silv	1 Dollar, 1883	500	750	4,500

Note: Proofs exist of Y2–5. All are very rare.

HEJAZ

The Hejaz, meaning "barrier," is the district of the rugged mountain range on the northern Red Sea coast of the Arabian peninsula. It contains the Islamic holy cities of Mecca and Medina. In 1916 it gained independence from the Ottoman Empire, but was conquered by Nejd in 1925. The two countries were united in 1932 to form Saudi Arabia. *Language:* Arabic. *Capital:* Mecca.

MONETARY SYSTEM

40 para = 1 ghirsh
20 ghirsh = 1 ryal
100 ghirsh = 1 dinar

PRECIOUS METAL CONTENT

Dates	Denomination	Gross Wt (g)	Fineness	Net Wt (g)	Troy Oz.
		SILVER			
1916	5 ghirsh	6.1000	0.9170	5.5937	0.1798
	10 ghirsh	12.0500	0.9170	11.0500	0.3552
	20 ghirsh	24.1000	0.9170	22.1000	0.7105

HUSAIN IBN ALI, *1916–1924*

ACCESSION DATE AH 1334 ON COINS

COUNTERSTAMPED COINAGE

Counterstamped with incuse "al-Hejaz" in Arabic.

Y#	KM#	Metal	Description	VF	EF	Unc
1	2	N/C-N	On Turkish 10 Para	125	—	—
2	3	N/C-N	On Turkish 20 Para	30	60	—
3	4–6	N/C-N	On Turkish 40 Para	40	80	—
9	10–12	Silv	On Turkish or Egyptian 5 Ghirsh	500	—	—
10	13–15	Silv	On similar 10 Ghirsh	500	—	—
11	16–17	Silv	On similar 20 Ghirsh	450	—	—
12	18	Silv	On Austria Y55	400	—	—

Note: Copies of the Hejaz counterstamps on some or all of the above silver types are believed to have been produced in recent years.

REGULAR ISSUES

Y#	KM#	Metal	Description	VF	EF	Unc
16	21	Cop	1/8 Ghirsh, Yr 5 (1920) (12–13 mm)	100	200	—
17	22	Cop	1/4 Ghirsh, Yrs 5–6 (16 mm)	18	35	100
18	23	Cop	1/2 Ghirsh, Yr 5 (18–19 mm)	20	40	100
19	24	Cop	1 Ghirsh, Yr 5 (21–22 mm)	25	55	125

Note: Y16–19 are of variable thickness. They are sometimes found with light silver wash.

Y#	KM#	Metal	Description	VF	EF	Unc
20	25	Cop	1/4 Ghirsh, Yr 8 (1923) (17 mm)	40	80	—
21	26	Cop	1/2 Ghirsh, Yr 8 (19 mm), *Rare*			
22	27	Cop	1 Ghirsh, Yr 8 (21 mm)	95	185	—

Y#	KM#	Metal	Description	VF	EF	Unc
23	28	Silv	5 Ghirsh, Yr 8 (24 mm)	200	325	800
24	29	Silv	10 Ghirsh, Yr 8 (28 mm)	600	1,000	1,500
25	30	Silv	20 Ghirsh, Yrs 8–9 (37 mm)	150	200	350

Y#	KM#	Metal	Description	VF	EF	Unc
26	31	Gold	1 Dinar, Yr 8	650	900	1,500

Note: For later issues, see Saudi Arabia.

HONDURAS

After 300 years of Spanish rule, Honduras declared its independence in 1821 to form a federation of Central American states, which it left in 1838. Continuing political unrest in the early 1900s (detrimental to American business interests there) resulted in occupation by the U.S. Marines. In 1932 a military dictatorship seized control and such regimes alternated with short-lived civilian governments until free elections in 1982 returned the nation to a parliamentary democracy. *Language:* Spanish. *Capital:* Tegucigalpa.

MONETARY SYSTEM

8 reales = 1 peso, to 1871
100 centavos = 1 peso, 1871–1926
100 centavos = 1 lempira, 1926–

PRECIOUS METAL CONTENT

Dates	Denomination	Gross Wt (g)	Fineness	Net Wt (g)	Troy Oz.
		SILVER			
1871	5 centavos	1.2500	0.8350	1.0438	0.0336
	10 centavos	2.5000	0.8350	2.0875	0.0671
	25 centavos	6.2500	0.9000	5.6250	0.1808
	50 centavos	12.5000	0.9000	11.2500	0.3617
1884–1913	5 centavos	1.2500	0.8350	1.0438	0.0336
	10 centavos	2.5000	0.8350	2.0875	0.0671
	25 centavos	6.2500	0.8350	5.2188	0.1678
	50 centavos	12.5000	0.8350	10.4375	0.3355
1883–1914	25 centavos	6.2500	0.9000	5.6250	0.1808
	50 centavos	12.5000	0.9000	11.2500	0.3617
	1 peso	25.0000	0.9000	22.5000	0.7234
1931–58	20 centavos	2.5000	0.9000	2.2500	0.0723
	50 centavos	6.2500	0.9000	5.6250	0.1808
	1 lempira	12.5000	0.9000	11.2500	0.3617
		GOLD			
1871–1922	1 peso	1.6129	0.9000	1.4516	0.0467
	5 pesos	8.0645	0.9000	7.2581	0.2333
	10 pesos	16.1290	0.9000	14.5161	0.4667
	20 pesos	32.2581	0.9000	29.0323	0.9334

PROVISIONAL ISSUES

Y#	KM#	Metal	Description	VF	EF	Unc
P1	24	Bz	1 Peso, 1862	15	40	100
P2	25	Bz	2 Pesos, 1862	15	45	150
P3	26	Bz	4 Pesos, 1862	20	50	300
P4	27	Bz	8 Pesos, 1862	60	100	500

REGULAR ISSUES

Y#	KM#	Metal	Description	VF	EF	Unc
1	30	C-N	1/8 Real, 1869–70	6	15	50
2	31	C-N	1/4 Real, 1869–70	10	20	60
3	32	C-N	1/2 Real, 1869–71 *1871, Unc $300*	5	12	50
4	33	C-N	1 Real, 1869–70	15	25	75

DECIMAL ISSUES

FIRST COINAGE

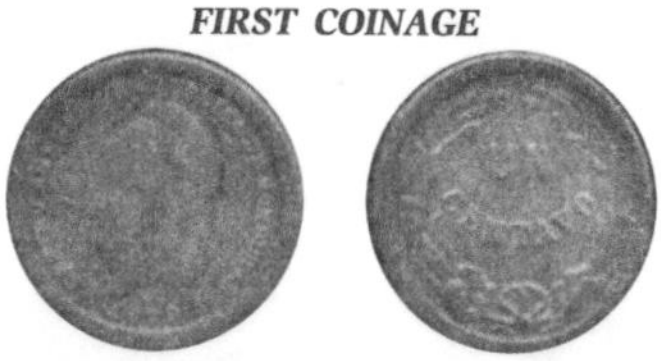

Y#	KM#	Metal	Description	VF	EF	Unc
9	40	Bz	1 Centavo, 1878–80 *1878, VF $400*	150	300	—

Y#	KM#	Metal	Description	VF	EF	Unc
10	43	Silv	5 Centavos, 1879	4,000	6,000	8,000
11	42	Silv	10 Centavos, 1878	10,000	—	—
12	44	Silv	50 Centavos, 1879	600	1,200	—

Note: The 1878 peso is a pattern; two are known.

SECOND COINAGE

Y#	KM#	Metal	Description	VF	EF	Unc
5	34	Silv	5 Centavos, 1871	400	800	2,000
6	35	Silv	10 Centavos, 1871	125	250	600
7	36	Silv	25 Centavos, 1871	15	50	150
8	37	Silv	50 Centavos, 1871	45	75	350

Note: Y5–8 were struck circa 1879–1882.

THIRD COINAGE

Y#	KM#	Metal	Description	VF	EF	Unc
13	45	Bz	1/2 Centavo, 1881–91 *1891, VF $300*	40	80	300

Y#	KM#	Metal	Description	VF	EF	Unc
14	46	Bz	1 Centavo, 1881–1907	35	70	250

Obverse: ***Die of Y14***

Y#	KM#	Metal	Description	VF	EF	Unc
15	59	Bz	1 Centavo, 1890–1908, reverse altered from Y21	6	10	30

Obverse: ***Die of Y14***

Y#	KM#	Metal	Description	VF	EF	Unc
16	60	Bz	1 Centavo, ND, reverse of Y9	400	800	—

Obverse: ***Arms in wreath (die of Y21)***

Y#	KM#	Metal	Description	VF	EF	Unc
17	61	Bz	1 Centavo, 1890–1908, reverse altered from Y21	30	75	150

Obverse: ***Die of Y6***

Y#	KM#	Metal	Description	VF	EF	Unc
18	63	Bz	1 Centavo, 1895, reverse of Y9	1,000	2,000	—

Obverse: ***Arms in wreath***

Y#	KM#	Metal	Description	VF	EF	Unc
19	48	Silv	5 Centavos, 1884–1902 *1902, VF $200*	20	50	150
21	49	Silv	10 Centavos, 1884–1900 *1900, VF $200*	45	125	500

Obverse: ***Die of Y13***

Y#	KM#	Metal	Description	VF	EF	Unc
20	54	Silv	5 Centavos, 1886, 95–96 *1895, VF $150*	15	35	150

Obverse: ***Die of Y6***

Y#	KM#	Metal	Description	VF	EF	Unc
22	55.1	Silv	10 Centavos, 1886, 95, ND, reverse like Y21 (vars)	200	400	—

.900 Silver

Y#	KM#	Metal	Description	VF	EF	Unc
23	50	Silv	25 Centavos, 1883–1912	20	60	300
24	51	Silv	50 Centavos, 1883–1910 *1896, VF $500; 1910, VF $1,250*	20	40	250

Obverse: ***Without weight***
Reverse: ***Small lettering***

Y#	KM#	Metal	Description	VF	EF	Unc
25	47	Silv	1 Peso, 1881–83	50	75	—

Obverse: ***Weight above UN PESO***
Reverse: ***Large lettering***

Y#	KM#	Metal	Description	VF	EF	Unc
25a	52	Silv	1 Peso, 1883–1914 *1899, VF $2,000; 1914, VF $900*	50	75	—
25b	62	Silv	1 Peso, 1894–96, obverse of Y25, reverse of Y25a	50	75	—

.835 Silver

Y#	KM#	Metal	Description	VF	EF	Unc
23a	50a	Silv	25 Centavos, 1899–1913	10	30	225
24a	51a	Silv	50 Centavos, 1908	125	250	500

Y#	KM#	Metal	Description	VF	EF	Unc
26	39	Gold	1 Peso, 1871, obverse of Y5	1,000	1,400	3,500
27	56	Gold	1 Peso, 1888–1922	350	750	1,200
28	53	Gold	5 Pesos, 1888–1913	1,500	3,000	5,000
29	58	Gold	10 Pesos, 1883, 89, *Rare*	20,000	30,000	50,000
30	57	Gold	20 Pesos, 1888–1908 *1908 (overdates), VF $65,000*	20,000	30,000	60,000

Bronze, Reduced Size

Obverse: ***Dies of Y13–14***
Reverse: ***Altered from Y19–20***

Y#	KM#	Metal	Description	VF	EF	Unc
36	68	Bz	1 Centavo, 1910	60	150	300
31	64	Bz	2 Centavos, 1908	250	500	—

Obverse: ***Dies of Y13–14***
Reverse: ***Altered from Y13–14***

Y#	KM#	Metal	Description	VF	EF	Unc
32	65	Bz	1 Centavo, 1910–11	25	60	—
33	69	Bz	2 Centavos, 1910–13	10	25	75

Obverse: ***Die of Y19***

Y#	KM#	Metal	Description	VF	EF	Unc
34	66	Bz	1 Centavo, 1910, reverse altered from Y13	50	120	400
35	67	Bz	1 Centavo, 1910–11, reverse altered from Y19	20	50	175

Obverse and Reverse: ***Dies of Y13–14***

Y#	KM#	Metal	Description	VF	EF	Unc
37	70	Bz	1 (Centavo), 1919–20	10	40	125
38	71	Bz	2 (Centavos), 1919–20	10	40	75

NEW COINAGE SYSTEM

Y#	KM#	Metal	Description	VF	EF	Unc
39	77	Bz	1 Centavo, 1935–57	0.15	0.25	1
40	78	Bz	2 Centavos, 1939–56	0.25	0.50	2
41	72	C-N	5 Centavos, 1931–56, 72	0.25	0.50	2
42	76	C-N	10 Centavos, 1932–93	0.50	1.50	5

Y#	KM#	Metal	Description	VF	EF	Unc
43	73	Silv	20 Centavos, 1931–58	4	8	30
44	74	Silv	50 Centavos, 1931–51	10	20	60
45	75	Silv	1 Lempira, 1931–37	12	20	50

HONG KONG

Often called the "Gateway Between East and West," the city encompassing more than 200 islands at the mouth of the Canton River was ceded by China to Great Britain in 1842 and became a crown colony. By treaty, in mid-1997 it reverted to the People's Republic of China as a Special Administrative Region, with its non-Communist economic system intact and a great deal of autonomy guaranteed for the next 50 years. *Languages:* Cantonese, English.

MONETARY SYSTEM

10 mils = 1 cent
100 cents = 1 dollar

PRECIOUS METAL CONTENT

Dates	Denomination	Gross Wt (g)	Fineness	Net Wt (g)	Troy Oz.
		SILVER			
1863–1993	5 cents	1.3577	0.8000	1.0862	0.0349
	10 cents	2.7154	0.8000	2.1723	0.0698
	20 cents	5.4308	0.8000	4.3446	0.1397
1866–68	1/2 dollar	13.4784	0.9000	12.1306	0.3900
	1 dollar	26.9568	0.9000	24.2611	0.7800
1890–1905	50 cents	13.5769	0.8000	10.8615	0.3492

Victoria,
1837–1901

Y#	KM#	Metal	Description	VF	EF	Unc
1	1–2	Bz	1 Mil (1 Wen in Chinese), 1863–65	20	45	125
			1864, Unc $5,000			*Proof: $1,000*
1a	3	Bz	1 Mil (1 Ch'ien in Chinese), 1866	20	45	150

Y#	KM#	Metal	Description	VF	EF	Unc
2	4	Bz	1 Cent, 1863–1901	15	30	200

Note: There are several minor die varieties of Y2. Dates before 1900 are worth approximately twice the listed prices.

Y#	KM#	Metal	Description	VF	EF	Unc
3	5	Silv	5 Cents, 1866–1901	10	20	100
						Proof: $3,500
4	6	Silv	10 Cents, 1863–1901	10	20	60
			1864, VF $1,500			*Proof: $4,000*

Y#	KM#	Metal	Description	VF	EF	Unc
5	7	Silv	20 Cents, 1866–98	30	90	600
			1879, VF $700; 1880, VF $550; 1881, VF $1,400			*Proof: $4,200*

Y#	KM#	Metal	Description	VF	EF	Unc
6	8	Silv	1/2 Dollar, 1866–68	950	2,000	7,000
			1867, VF $2,500			*Proof: $20,000*
8	10	Silv	1 Dollar, 1866–68	550	1,000	4,700
						Proof: $20,000

Y#	KM#	Metal	Description	VF	EF	Unc
7	9	Silv	50 Cents, 1890–94	225	400	3,000
						Proof: $18,000

Note: Y7 of 1891–92 with H mintmark has a slightly larger diameter than the other dates.

Edward VII,
1901–1910

Y#	KM#	Metal	Description	VF	EF	Unc
9	11	Bz	1 Cent, 1902–05	5	15	100

Y#	KM#	Metal	Description	VF	EF	Unc
10	12	Silv	5 Cents, 1903–05	2	5	40
						Proof: $500
11	13	Silv	10 Cents, 1902–05	4	10	20
			1905, VF $2,000			*Proof: $700*
12	14	Silv	20 Cents, 1902–05	50	145	950
			1905, VF $1,650			*Proof: $2,750*

Y#	KM#	Metal	Description	VF	EF	Unc
13	15	Silv	50 Cents, 1902–05	50	145	475
						Proof: $3,000

GEORGE V, *1910–1936*

Y#	KM#	Metal	Description	VF	EF	Unc
14	16	Bz	1 Cent, 1919–26 (28 mm)	4.00	7.50	45
					Proof: $1,500	
15	17	Bz	1 Cent, 1931–34 (22 mm)	1.25	2.50	20
					Proof: $1,000	
18	18	Silv	5 Cents, 1932–33	2.00	5.00	25
					Proof: $1,750	
16	18a	C-N	5 Cents, 1935	3.00	6.00	35
					Proof: $2,500	
17	19	C-N	10 Cents, 1935–36	1.50	5.00	25
					Proof: $2,750	

GEORGE VI, *1936–1952*

Y#	KM#	Metal	Description	VF	EF	Unc
20	20	Nick	5 Cents, 1937	1.00	1.50	25
					Proof: $300	
21	21	Nick	10 Cents, 1937	0.75	1.25	20
					Proof: $300	

Obverse: ***Larger head***

Y#	KM#	Metal	Description	VF	EF	Unc
19	24	Bz	1 Cent, 1941	2,500	5,250	13,000
					Proof: $18,000	

Note: Y19 was not issued to circulation.

Y#	KM#	Metal	Description	VF	EF	Unc
22	22	Nick	5 Cents, 1938–41 *1941H, EF $6,000; 1941KN, Unc $1,250*	1	2	8
					Proof: $250	
23	23	Nick	10 Cents, 1938–39	1	2	8
					Proof: $425	

New Legend: ***KING GEORGE THE SIXTH***

Y#	KM#	Metal	Description	VF	EF	Unc
24	26	N-Br	5 Cents, 1949–50	0.75	1.50	5.00
					Proof: $550	
25	25	N-Br	10 Cents, 1948–51	1.00	2.50	7.50
					Proof: $500	

Y#	KM#	Metal	Description	VF	EF	Unc
26	27	C-N	50 Cents, 1951	5	15	85
					Proof: $1,375	

ELIZABETH II, *1952–1997*

Y#	KM#	Metal	Description	VF	EF	Unc
27	29	N-Br	5 Cents, 1958–68 *1964, EF $250*	0.20	0.50	5
					Proof: $350	
28	28	N-Br	10 Cents, 1955–68	0.20	0.50	5
					Proof: $350	

Y#	KM#	Metal	Description	VF	EF	Unc
29	30	C-N	50 Cents, 1958–70	0.50	1	5

Y#	KM#	Metal	Description	VF	EF	Unc
30	31	C-N	1 Dollar, 1960, 70	0.75	1.50	7.50

HUNGARY

This Central European nation was part of the Austro-Hungarian Empire from 1867 to 1918. Allied with the Central Powers in World War I, reparations cost the nation nearly 70 percent of its territory. Allied with the Axis in World War II, it was captured by the Russians in 1945 and declared a republic in 1946. Soviet-backed communists seized control in 1948 and declared a single-party people's republic. A 1989 constitution created a parliamentary democracy. *Language:* Magyar (Hungarian). *Capital:* Budapest.

MONETARY SYSTEM

100 krajczar = 1 forint, 1857–1892
100 filler = 1 korona, 1892–1921
100 filler = 1 pengo, 1925–1945
100 filler = 1 forint, 1946–

PRECIOUS METAL CONTENT

Dates	Denomination	Gross Wt (g)	Fineness	Net Wt (g)	Troy Oz.
		SILVER			
1868–92	10 krajczar	1.6667	0.4000	0.6667	0.0214
	20 krajczar	2.6667	0.5000	1.3333	0.0429
	1 forint	12.3457	0.9000	11.1111	0.3572
1892–1916	1 korona	5.0000	0.8350	4.1750	0.1342
	2 korona	10.0000	0.8350	8.3500	0.2685
	5 korona	24.0000	0.9000	21.6000	0.6944
1926–39	1 pengo	5.0000	0.6400	3.2000	0.1029
	2 pengo	10.0000	0.6400	6.4000	0.2058
	5 pengo	25.0000	0.6400	16.0000	0.5144
1946	5 forint	20.0000	0.8330	16.6600	0.5356
1947–48	5 forint	12.0000	0.5000	6.0000	0.1929
	10 forint	20.0000	0.5000	10.0000	0.3215
	20 forint	28.0000	0.5000	14.0000	0.4501
1956	10 forint	12.5000	0.8000	10.0000	0.3215
	20 forint	17.5000	0.8000	14.0000	0.4501
	25 forint	20.0000	0.8000	16.0000	0.5144
1961	25 forint	17.5000	0.7500	13.1250	0.4220
	50 forint	20.0000	0.7500	15.0000	0.4823
		GOLD			
1868–1916	1 dukat	3.4909	0.9861	3.4424	0.1107
	4 forint / 10 francs	3.2258	0.9000	2.9032	0.0933
	8 forint / 20 francs	6.4516	0.9000	5.8064	0.1867
	10 korona	3.3875	0.9000	3.0488	0.0980
	20 korona	6.7751	0.9000	6.0976	0.1960
	100 korona	33.8753	0.9000	30.4878	0.9802
1961	50 forint	3.8380	0.9860	3.7843	0.1217
	100 forint	7.6760	0.9860	7.5685	0.2431
	500 forint	38.3800	0.9860	37.8427	1.2168

Ferencz Jozsef I
(Franz Joseph of Austria), as King of Hungary, 1867–1916

Y#	KM#	Metal	Description	VF	EF	Unc
1	441	C/Bz	1 Krajczar, 1868–73 *1873, VF $60*	5	20	85
2	442	C/Bz	4 Krajczar, 1868	15	50	100

Y#	KM#	Metal	Description	VF	EF	Unc
3	468	C/Bz	5/10 Krajczar, 1882	10.00	18.50	50
4	458	C/Bz	1 Krajczar, 1878–88	12.50	30.00	75
4a	478	C/Bz	1 Krajczar, 1891–92, modified arms	10.00	25.00	80

Obverse: *Legend ends KIRALYA*
Reverse: *Legend VALTO PENZ only*

Y#	KM#	Metal	Description	VF	EF	Unc
6	440	Bill	10 Krajczar, 1868	425	900	1,750
8	445	Bill	20 Krajczar, 1868	400	800	1,350

Obverse: *As Y6, 8*
Reverse: *MAGYAR KIRALYA added*

Y#	KM#	Metal	Description	VF	EF	Unc
7	443	Bill	10 Krajczar, 1868–69	30	60	125
9	446	Bill	20 Krajczar, 1868–69	30	85	200

Y#	KM#	Metal	Description	VF	EF	Unc
12	449	Silv	1 Forint, 1868–69	17.50	50	95

Obverse: *Emperor standing*
Reverse: *Like Y12*

Y#	KM#	Metal	Description	VF	EF	Unc
21	448	Gold	1 Dukat, 1868–70	300	650	950

Obverse: *Legend ends KIR.*
Reverse: *As Y6, 8*

Y#	KM#	Metal	Description	VF	EF	Unc
10	451	Bill	10 Krajczar, 1870–88	20	40	100
11	452	Bill	20 Krajczar, 1870–72	40	135	250

Note: Y10–11 dated 1868 are modern restrikes using reverses of Y6 and 8.

Y#	KM#	Metal	Description	VF	EF	Unc
13	453	Silv	1 Forint, 1870–81 (2 vars)	15	25	50

Y#	KM#	Metal	Description	VF	EF	Unc
14	469	Silv	1 Forint, 1882–90	15	37.50	20

Y#	KM#	Metal	Description	VF	EF	Unc
22	457	Gold	1 Dukat, 1877–81	*Rare*	—	—
22a	457	Gold	1 Dukat, 1870 restrike, *Proof: $1,000*			
17	454/466	Gold	4 Forint / 10 Francs, 1870–90	175	275	475
18	455/467	Gold	8 Forint / 20 Francs, 1870–90	275	325	500

Reverse: *Modified arms*

Y#	KM#	Metal	Description	VF	EF	Unc
15	475	Silv	1 Forint 1890–92	15	30	65

Y#	KM#	Metal	Description	VF	EF	Unc
19	476	Gold	4 Forint / 10 Francs, 1890–92 *1892, EF $18,500*	325	525	1,100
20	477	Gold	8 Forint / 20 Francs, 1890–92	BV	375	475

KORONA SYSTEM, *1892–1921*

Y#	KM#	Metal	Description	VF	EF	Unc
23	480	Bz	1 Filler, 1892–1914 *1892, VF $30; 1906, 14, VF $225*	2.50	5	20
24	481	Bz	2 Filler, 1892–1915 *1900, VF $325*	2.00	5	15

Y#	KM#	Metal	Description	VF	EF	Unc
25	482	Nick	10 Filler, 1892–1914	1.50	5	15
27	483	Nick	20 Filler, 1892–1914	4.00	10	25

Y#	KM#	Metal	Description	VF	EF	Unc
32	484	Silv	1 Korona, 1892–1906, large head *1906, VF $850*	7.50	22.50	45
32a	492	Silv	1 Korona, 1912–16, small head *1913, VF $200*	7.50	12.50	20
33	493	Silv	2 Korona, 1912–14	12.50	17.50	30
34	488	Silv	5 Korona, 1900–09	35.00	75.00	175

Y#	KM#	Metal	Description	VF	EF	Unc
36	485	Gold	10 Korona, 1892–1915 *1895, Rare; 1915, VF $5,000*	145	175	250
A36	486	Gold	20 Korona, 1892–1915	BV	BV	325
B36	495	Gold	20 Korona, 1914, 16, Bosnian arms added to reverse	300	400	650
D36	491	Gold	100 Korona, 1907–08	2,200	3,250	9,750

Notes: All but YB36 exist as restrikes. Modern restrikes of Y36 (dated 1895 and 1915) and YD36 (dated 1908) exist.

Millennium, Founding of Kingdom

Y#	KM#	Metal	Description	VF	EF	Unc
31	487	Silv	1 Korona, 1896	10	15	30

40th Anniversary of Coronation

Y#	KM#	Metal	Description	VF	EF	Unc
35	489	Silv	5 Korona, 1907	35	60	125
C36	490	Gold	100 Korona, 1907 *Restrike, $2,750*	2,250	3,750	5,000

Note: Prooflike silver restrikes of YC36 are commonly found.

WORLD WAR I ISSUES

Y#	KM#	Metal	Description	VF	EF	Unc
26	494	CNZ	10 Filler, 1914–16 *1914, VF $400*	2.00	5.00	15.00
28	497	Iron	2 Filler, 1916–18	5.50	15.00	35.00
29	496	Iron	10 Filler, 1915–20	22.50	50.00	95.00
30	498	Iron	20 Filler, 1916–21 *1921, EF $25*	4.00	12.50	32.50

Note: The Proof 20 Filler 1922 struck in brass is a modern restrike. If in Uncirculated, it is a trial strike worth about $15.00.

REGENCY, *1920–1945*

Y#	KM#	Metal	Description	VF	EF	Unc
37	505	Bz	1 Filler, 1926–39	0.40	0.60	2.00
38	506	Bz	2 Filler, 1926–40	0.40	0.60	2.00

Y#	KM#	Metal	Description	VF	EF	Unc
39	507	C-N	10 Filler, 1926–40	2.25	5.00	12.50
40	508	C-N	20 Filler, 1926–40 *1927, VF $60; 1939–40, EF $25*	3.00	6.00	15.00

Obverse: *Like Y37 and 38*

Y#	KM#	Metal	Description	VF	EF	Unc
41	509	C-N	50 Filler, 1926–40 *1939, EF $25*	1.00	1.75	6.00

Y#	KM#	Metal	Description	VF	EF	Unc
42	510	Silv	1 Pengo, 1926–39	2.50	6	16

Y#	KM#	Metal	Description	VF	EF	Unc
43	511	Silv	2 Pengo, 1929–39 *1931, Unc $200*	5.50	12	25

10th Year of Regency

Reverse: *Like Y57*

Y#	KM#	Metal	Description	VF	EF	Unc
44	512	Silv	5 Pengo, 1930	15	20	35

300th Anniversary, Founding of Pazmany University

Y#	KM#	Metal	Description	VF	EF	Unc
45	513	Silv	2 Pengo, 1935	10	15	25

Bicentennial, Death of Ferenc Rakoczi

Y#	KM#	Metal	Description	VF	EF	Unc
46	514	Silv	2 Pengo, 1935	10	15	25

50th Anniversary, Death of Liszt

Y#	KM#	Metal	Description	VF	EF	Unc
47	515	Silv	2 Pengo, 1936	10	15	25

900th Anniversary, Death of St. Stephan

Y#	KM#	Metal	Description	VF	EF	Unc
48	516	Silv	5 Pengo, 1938	20	25	50

Horthy Government Commemorative

Y#	KM#	Metal	Description	VF	EF	Unc
49	517	Silv	5 Pengo, 1939	17.50	22	47.50

WORLD WAR II COINAGE

Y#	KM#	Metal	Description	VF	EF	Unc
50	518.1	Steel	2 Filler, 1940, plain rim	100.00	200.00	—
50a	518.2	Steel	2 Filler, 1940–42, toothed rim	0.30	0.75	3

Y#	KM#	Metal	Description	VF	EF	Unc
51	519	Zinc	2 Filler, 1943–44	0.40	0.80	15

Y#	KM#	Metal	Description	VF	EF	Unc
52	507a	Steel	10 Filler, 1940–42	0.40	0.80	15

Y#	KM#	Metal	Description	VF	EF	Unc
53	520	Steel	20 Filler, 1941–44	0.50	1	17.50

Y#	KM#	Metal	Description	VF	EF	Unc
54	521	Alum	1 Pengo, 1941–44	0.50	1	12.50
55	522	Alum	2 Pengo, 1941–43	0.50	1	12.50

75th Birthday of Regent

Y#	KM#	Metal	Description	VF	EF	Unc
57	523	Alum	5 Pengo, 1943	1	2.50	15

PROVISIONAL GOVERNMENT, *1944–1946*

Y#	KM#	Metal	Description	VF	EF	Unc
56	525	Alum	5 Pengo, 1945	2	3.50	8.50

Republic,
1946–1949

Legends: ***MAGYAR ALLAMI VALTOPENZ or MAGYAR KOZTARSASAG***

Y#	KM#	Metal	Description	VF	EF	Unc
58	529	Bz	2 Filler, 1946–47	0.50	0.75	4

Y#	KM#	Metal	Description	VF	EF	Unc
59	535	Alum	5 Filler, 1948–51	0.60	0.80	2.50

Y#	KM#	Metal	Description	VF	EF	Unc
60	530	A-Bz	10 Filler, 1946–50	0.80	1	2.75

Note: In the 10 Filler 1946 issue, 50 in aluminum were trial strikes.

Y#	KM#	Metal	Description	VF	EF	Unc
61	531	A-Bz	20 Filler, 1946–50	0.80	1	2.75

Y#	KM#	Metal	Description	VF	EF	Unc
62	536	Alum	50 Filler, 1948	20	40	85

Y#	KM#	Metal	Description	VF	EF	Unc
63	532	Alum	1 Forint, 1946–49	4	6.50	15
64	533	Alum	2 Forint, 1946–47	6	9.00	25

Y#	KM#	Metal	Description	VF	EF	Unc
65	534	Silv	5 Forint, 1946, thick	10.00	17.50	35
66	535	Silv	5 Forint, 1947, thin	2.25	3.50	10

Centennial, 1848 Revolution

Y#	KM#	Metal	Description	VF	EF	Unc
67	537	Silv	5 Forint, 1948	8	10	17.50

Y#	KM#	Metal	Description	VF	EF	Unc
68	538	Silv	10 Forint, 1948	10	15	28

Y#	KM#	Metal	Description	VF	EF	Unc
69	539	Silv	20 Forint, 1948	20	25	45

PEOPLE'S REPUBLIC, *1949–1989*

Legend: ***MAGYAR NEPKOZTARSASAG***

Y#	KM#	Metal	Description	VF	EF	Unc
70	546	Alum	2 Filler, 1950–89	0.10	0.15	0.75

Designs: ***Similar to Y59–62***

Y#	KM#	Metal	Description	VF	EF	Unc
71	549	Alum	5 Filler, 1953–89	0.20	0.30	0.85
72	547	Alum	10 Filler, 1950–66 *1950, Unc $75*	1.00	3.50	10.00
73	550	Alum	20 Filler, 1953–66	2.00	4.50	12.00
74	551	Alum	50 Filler, 1953–66	2.50	5.00	15.00

Y#	KM#	Metal	Description	VF	EF	Unc
75	545	Alum	1 Forint, 1949–52	1	3	13

Y#	KM#	Metal	Description	VF	EF	Unc
76	548	C-N	2 Forint, 1950–52	3	5	15

10th Anniversary of Forint

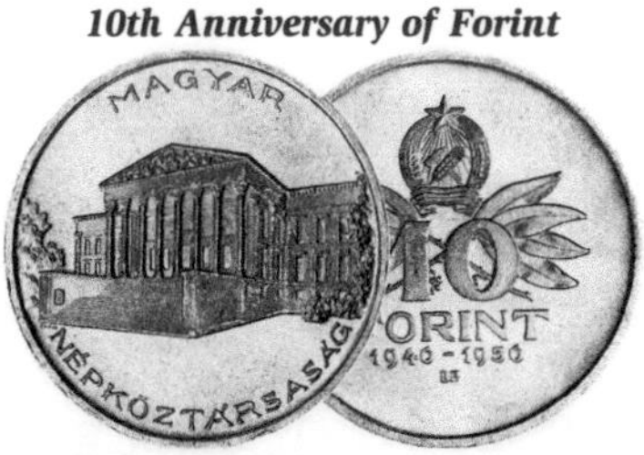

Y#	KM#	Metal	Description	VF	EF	Unc
77	552	Silv	10 Forint, 1956	15	20	25

Y#	KM#	Metal	Description	VF	EF	Unc
78	553	Silv	20 Forint, 1956	6.50	9	17.50

Y#	KM#	Metal	Description	VF	EF	Unc
79	554	Silv	25 Forint, 1956	6.50	10	30

Y#	KM#	Metal	Description	VF	EF	Unc
80	555	Alum	1 Forint, 1957–66	0.75	1.50	7.50
81	556	C-N	2 Forint, 1957–62	0.75	1.50	7.50
81a	556a	CNZ	2 Forint, 1962–66	0.75	1.50	7.50

150th Anniversary, Birth of Liszt

Y#	KM#	Metal	Description	VF	EF	Unc
82	557	Silv	*25 Forint, 1961, Proof only: $25*			
83	559	Silv	*50 Forint, 1961, Proof only: $35*			
84	560	Gold	*50 Forint, 1961, Proof only: $225*			
85	563	Gold	*100 Forint, 1961, Proof only: $475*			
86	565	Gold	*500 Forint, 1961, Proof only: $2,100*			

80th Anniversary, Birth of Bartok

Y#	KM#	Metal	Description	VF	EF	Unc
87	558	Silv	*25 Forint, 1961, Proof only: $25*			
88	561	Silv	*50 Forint, 1961, Proof only: $35*			
89	562	Gold	*50 Forint, 1961, Proof only: $225*			
90	564	Gold	*100 Forint, 1961, Proof only: $475*			
91	566	Gold	*500 Forint, 1961, Proof only: $2,100*			

ICELAND

The island nation in the North Atlantic near the Arctic Circle was under Norwegian rule in the 13th century and later passed to Danish control with the unification of Norway, Sweden, and Denmark in 1397. It was granted sovereign state status in 1918, and in 1944 it was proclaimed an independent republic. Iceland is governed by the Althing, the world's oldest parliamentary assembly, created under a 10th century constitution. *Language:* Icelandic. *Capital:* Reykjavik.

MONETARY SYSTEM

100 aurar = 1 krona

PRECIOUS METAL CONTENT

Dates	Denomination	Gross Wt (g)	Fineness	Net Wt (g)	Troy Oz.
		GOLD			
1961	500 kronur	8.9604	0.9000	8.0644	0.2593

CHRISTIAN X, *1912–1944*

Some coins of 1940 and all of 1942 were struck in Great Britain without the customary Copenhagen mintmarks.

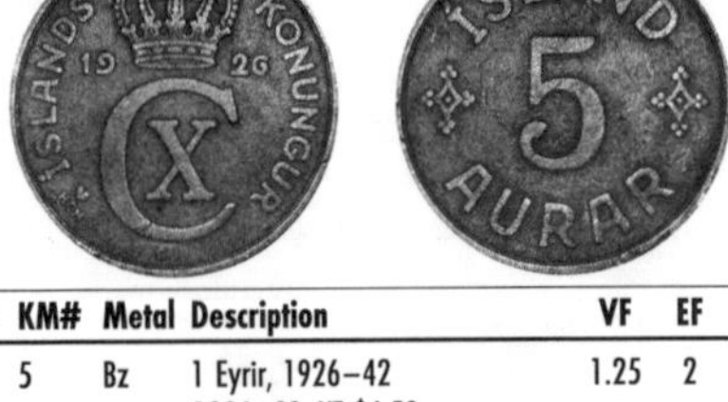

Y#	KM#	Metal	Description	VF	EF	Unc
1	5	Bz	1 Eyrir, 1926–42 *1926–39, VF $4.50*	1.25	2	3.50
2	6	Bz	2 Aurar, 1926–42 *1926, 31, VF $5; 1938, 40, VF $15*	1.25	2	3.50
3	7	Bz	5 Aurar, 1926–42 *1926, 31, VF $15*	1.25	2	4.50

Y#	KM#	Metal	Description	VF	EF	Unc
4	1	C-N	10 Aurar, 1922–40 *1925–33, VF $45; 1936, 39, VF $15*	8	16	40
5	2	C-N	25 Aurar, 1922–40 *1925, VF $15; 1933, $10; 1937, VF $12*	4	8	35

Note: Y4–5 dated 1940 are very common, and worth $10 each in Uncirculated condition.

Y#	KM#	Metal	Description	VF	EF	Unc
6	3	A-Bz	1 Krona, 1925–40 *1925, VF $12; 1929, VF $20*	3.25	8	27.50
7	4	A-Bz	2 Kronur, 1925–40 *1925, VF $40; 1929, VF $55*	2.50	15	37.50

1,000th Anniversary of Iceland Parliament

Y#	KM#	Metal	Description	VF	EF	Unc
8	N/A	Bz	2 Kronur, 1930	45	75	100
9	N/A	Silv	5 Kronur, 1930	100	200	250
10	N/A	Silv	10 Kronur, 1930	125	250	700

Note: The 1930 commemorative issues (Y8–10) are considered by some authorities to be medals. They were struck for the 1,000th anniversary of the Icelandic Parliament. Denominations are on the edge.

World War II Issues

Y#	KM#	Metal	Description	VF	EF	Unc
4a	1a	Zinc	10 Aurar, 1942	6.50	25	—
5a	2a	Zinc	25 Aurar, 1942	3.00	15	—

Republic, *1944–*

Y#	KM#	Metal	Description	VF	EF	Unc
11	8	Bz	1 Eyrir, 1946–66	0.80	1.25	2.50
12	9	Bz	5 Aurar, 1946–66 *1958–59, VF $3.75*	0.60	1.00	3.25
13	10	C-N	10 Aurar, 1946–69 *1957, 59, VF $3.25; 1958, VF $1.25*	0.15	0.35	0.75
14	11	C-N	25 Aurar, 1946–67 *1946–54, 59, Unc $1.75; 1958, 60, VF $1.75*	0.20	0.50	0.85

Y#	KM#	Metal	Description	VF	EF	Unc
15	12	A-Bz	1 Krona, 1946	0.65	1.65	3.50
16	13	A-Bz	2 Kronur, 1946	0.65	1.50	7.00

Y#	KM#	Metal	Description	VF	EF	Unc
15a	12a	N-Br	1 Krona, 1957–75	0.50	0.75	1.00
16a	13a.1	N-Br	2 Kronur, 1958–66 *1958, 62, EF $2.75*	0.50	1.00	3.25

Jon Sigurdsson Sesquicentennial

Y#	KM#	Metal	Description	VF	EF	Unc
17	14	Gold	500 Kronur, 1961	BV	425	700

INDIA

The largest country of the south Asian subcontinent, India extends from the Himalayan Mountains to the Indian Ocean. British influence began in 1612 with the formation of the East India Company. After nearly a century and a half of war with Indian rulers and French, Dutch, and Portuguese traders, the area was fully incorporated into the British Empire by the mid-18th century. A measure of self-rule was restored in 1935 and in 1947 it attained independence, separating from Muslim Pakistan, and joining the Commonwealth of Nations in 1950 as a republic. *Languages:* Hindi, English, Urdu, many others. *Capital:* New Delhi.

MONETARY SYSTEM

3 pies = 1 pice (paisa)
4 pice = 1 anna
16 annas = 1 rupee
15 rupees = 1 mohur (gold)

PRECIOUS METAL CONTENT

Dates	Denomination	Gross Wt (g)	Fineness	Net Wt (g)	Troy Oz.
		SILVER			
1841–1917	2 annas	1.4580	0.9170	1.3365	0.0430
1835–1943	1/4 rupee	2.9160	0.9170	2.6730	0.0859
	1/2 rupee	5.8319	0.9170	5.3459	0.1719
	1 rupee	11.6638	0.9170	10.6918	0.3437
1940–45	1/4 rupee	2.9160	0.5000	1.4800	0.0469
	1/2 rupee	5.8319	0.5000	2.9160	0.0937
	1 rupee	11.6638	0.5000	5.8319	0.1875
		GOLD			
1841–1918	5 rupees	3.8879	0.9170	3.5639	0.1146
	10 rupees	7.7759	0.9170	7.1279	0.2292
	1 mohur / 15 rupees	11.6638	0.9170	10.6918	0.3437
1918	1 sovereign	7.9881	0.9170	7.3224	0.2354

Proof restrikes of the British India coins that follow also exist and, for the most part, are as highly valued as the regular issues.

Victoria, *1837–1901*

British East India Company, to 1858

Legend: *EAST INDIA COMPANY*

For similar copper coinage 1845–1862, see Straits Settlements. Proof restrikes exist for most of these issues.

Obverse: *Continuous legend*

Y#	KM#	Metal	Description	VF	EF	Unc
1	459	Silv	2 Annas, 1841	30	60	150
2	453	Silv	1/4 Rupee, 1840	15	25	100
3	455	Silv	1/2 Rupee, 1840	30	60	350
4	457	Silv	1 Rupee, 1840	25	50	150
A4	461	Gold	1 Mohur, 1841	550	700	1,000

Obverse: ***Divided legend***

Y#	KM#	Metal	Description	VF	EF	Unc
1a	460	Silv	2 Annas, 1841	15	30	100
2a	454	Silv	1/4 Rupee, 1840	12	20	75
3a	456	Silv	1/2 Rupee, 1840	20	40	200
4a	458	Silv	1 Rupee, 1840	30	55	180

Y#	KM#	Metal	Description	VF	EF	Unc
A4a	462	Gold	1 Mohur, 1841	2,500	3,500	5,500

BRITISH INDIA, 1857–1947

New Legend: ***INDIA***

Y#	KM#	Metal	Description	VF	EF	Unc
5	465	Cop	1/12 Anna, 1862, 74–76	3	6	12.50
6	466	Cop	1/2 Pice, 1862, 75	5	10	85.00
7	467	Cop	1/4 Anna, 1862, 74–76	10	20	125.00
8	468	Cop	1/2 Anna, 1862, 75–76	35	100	500.00

Y#	KM#	Metal	Description	VF	EF	Unc
9	469	Silv	2 Annas, 1862, 74–76	15.00	25	75
10	470	Silv	1/4 Rupee, 1862, 74–76	17.50	40	90
11	472	Silv	1/2 Rupee, 1862, 74–76	20.00	50	110
12	473	Silv	1 Rupee, 1862–76	25.00	60	150

Obverse: ***Young portrait, thin face***

Y#	KM#	Metal	Description	VF	EF	Unc
13	474–475	Gold	5 Rupees, 1870, 75	4,000	5,000	6,000
14	477–478	Gold	10 Rupees, 1870, 75	4,500	6,000	7,500
15	480	Gold	1 Mohur, 1862, 70, 75	1,250	1,650	2,500

Note: Y13–14 were not issued to circulation.

Obverse: ***Mature portrait, plump face***

Y#	KM#	Metal	Description	VF	EF	Unc
13a	476	Gold	5 Rupees, 1870	3,500	5,000	6,000
14a	479	Gold	10 Rupees, 1870	4,500	6,000	7,500
15a	481	Gold	*1 Mohur, 1870, Proof only, Rare Restrike, $7,000*			

Note: Y15a was not issued to circulation.

Designs: ***Similar to Y5–12, 13a–15a***
New Obverse Legend: ***VICTORIA EMPRESS***

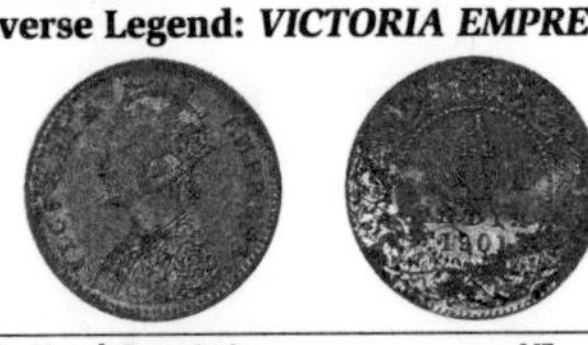

Y#	KM#	Metal	Description	VF	EF	Unc
16	483	Cop	1/12 Anna, 1877–1901	5	10	30
17	484	Cop	1/2 Pice, 1877–1901	6	12	50
18	486	Cop	1/4 Anna, 1877–1901	3	6	10
19	487	Cop	1/2 Anna, 1877	20	50	175

Y#	KM#	Metal	Description	VF	EF	Unc
20	488	Silv	2 Annas, 1877–1901	10	20	125
21	490	Silv	1/4 Rupee, 1877–1901	25	50	150
22	491	Silv	1/2 Rupee, 1877–1900	30	60	175
23	492	Silv	1 Rupee, 1877–1901	15	35	85
24	494	Gold	*5 Rupees, 1879, Proof only, restrike*			3,000
25	495	Gold	*10 Rupees, 1878–79, Proof only, restrike*			4,000
26	496	Gold	1 Mohur (15 Rupees), 1877–91	3,500	4,500	6,000

Note: Y24 was not issued to circulation.

EDWARD VII, *1901–1910*

Planchet: ***Thick***

Y#	KM#	Metal	Description	VF	EF	Unc
27	497	Cop	1/12 Anna, 1903–06	5	10	30
28	499	Cop	1/2 Pice, 1903–06	5	10	40
29	501	Cop	1/4 Anna, 1903–06	5	10	45

Planchet: ***Thin***

Y#	KM#	Metal	Description	VF	EF	Unc
27a	498	Bz	1/12 Anna, 1906–10	5	10	30
28a	500	Bz	1/2 Pice, 1906–10	5	10	40
29a	502	Bz	1/4 Anna, 1906–10	5	10	45

Y#	KM#	Metal	Description	VF	EF	Unc
30	504	C-N	1 Anna, 1906–10, scalloped	25	50	150

Y#	KM#	Metal	Description	VF	EF	Unc
31	505	Silv	2 Annas, 1903–10	12.50	20.00	45
32	506	Silv	1/4 Rupee, 1903–10	15.00	22.50	80
33	507	Silv	1/2 Rupee, 1904–10	50.00	100.00	300
34	508	Silv	1 Rupee, 1903–10	25.00	50.00	120

George V, *1910–1936*

Y#	KM#	Metal	Description	VF	EF	Unc
35	509	Bz	1/12 Anna, 1912–36	2	5	20
36	510	Bz	1/2 Pice, 1912–36	2	5	25
37	511–512	Bz	1/4 Anna, 1911–36 *1911, 16, EF $70*	2	5	40

Y#	KM#	Metal	Description	VF	EF	Unc
38	513	C-N	1 Anna, 1912–36, scalloped	6	10	35

Y#	KM#	Metal	Description	VF	EF	Unc
39	516	C-N	2 Annas, 1918–36, square	10	25	90

Y#	KM#	Metal	Description	VF	EF	Unc
40	519	C-N	4 Annas, 1919–21, scalloped	20	45	160

Y#	KM#	Metal	Description	VF	EF	Unc
41	520	C-N	8 Annas, 1919–20	40	75	475

Y#	KM#	Metal	Description	VF	EF	Unc
42	514–515	Silv	2 Annas, 1911–17 *1911, Unc $225*	2.50	5	10
43	517–518	Silv	1/4 Rupee, 1911–36 *1911, Unc $1,750*	10.00	15	40
44	521–522	Silv	1/2 Rupee, 1911–36 *1911, Unc $6,750*	15.00	25	55
45	523–524	Silv	1 Rupee, 1911–36 *1911, Unc $350*	20.00	30	60

Note: 1935–1936, Proof only.

Y#	KM#	Metal	Description	VF	EF	Unc
46	525	Gold	15 Rupees, 1918	2,000	2,500	3,000

Obverse: *Large uncrowned portrait*
Reverse: *St. George and the Dragon*

Y#	KM#	Metal	Description	VF	EF	Unc
A46	A525	Gold	1 Sovereign, 1918	BV	BV	550

Note: YA46 is identical to Great Britain Y78 but has I mintmark above date.

George VI, *1936–1947*

First Coinage

Obverse: ***First portrait (high relief)***

Y#	KM#	Metal	Description	VF	EF	Unc
47	526	Bz	1/12 Anna, 1938–39	2	4.00	15.00
49	528	Bz	1/2 Pice, 1938–40 *1938, EF $500*	2	4.50	12.00
50	530	Bz	1/4 Anna, 1938–40	1	2.50	7.50

Y#	KM#	Metal	Description	VF	EF	Unc
53	536	C-N	1 Anna, 1938–40, scalloped *1938, Unc $150*	1.50	2.25	15

Y#	KM#	Metal	Description	VF	EF	Unc
54	540	C-N	2 Annas, 1939–40, square *1940, VF $150*	1.50	2.25	15

Y#	KM#	Metal	Description	VF	EF	Unc
55	544	Silv	1/4 Rupee, 1938–40 *1938, Rare, Proof restrike: $400*	12.50	17.50	25.00
56	549	Silv	1/2 Rupee, 1938–39	15.00	20.00	27.50

SECOND COINAGE

Obverse: ***Second portrait (low relief)***

Y#	KM#	Metal	Description	VF	EF	Unc
47a	527	Bz	1/12 Anna, 1939–42	1.00	3.00	6.50
49a	529	Bz	*1/2 Pice, 1942, Proof only: $650*			
50a	531	Bz	1/4 Anna, 1940–42	0.75	1.25	5.00

Y#	KM#	Metal	Description	VF	EF	Unc
51	532	Bz	1 Pice, 1943, small legend	0.60	1.00	5
51a	533	Bz	1 Pice, 1943–47, large legend	0.40	0.75	2

Y#	KM#	Metal	Description	VF	EF	Unc
52a	535	C-N	1/2 Anna, 1946–47, square	1.50	4	8

Y#	KM#	Metal	Description	VF	EF	Unc
53b	537–539	C-N	1 Anna, 1940–41, 45–47, scalloped	1.25	2.25	7.50

Y#	KM#	Metal	Description	VF	EF	Unc
54b	541–542	C-N	2 Annas, 1939–41, 46–47, square *1939, Unc $75; 1940–41, EF $7.50*	1.25	2.25	7.50

Y#	KM#	Metal	Description	VF	EF	Unc
52	534b.1	N-Br	1/2 Anna, 1942–45, square *1942, Unc $25*	1	3	8.50

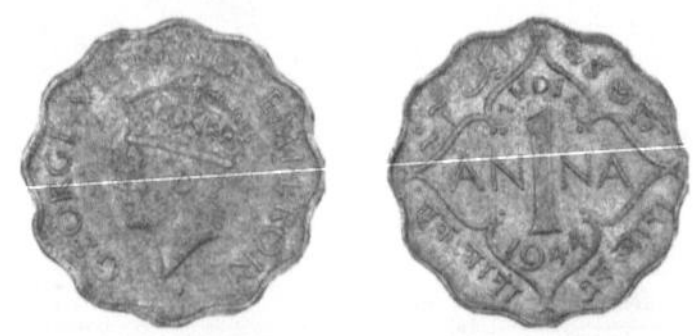

Y#	KM#	Metal	Description	VF	EF	Unc
53a	537a	N-Br	1 Anna, 1942–45, scalloped	1.50	2.50	5

Y#	KM#	Metal	Description	VF	EF	Unc
54a	Several	N-Br	2 Annas, 1942–45, square	1.50	2.50	9

Edge: ***Reeded***

Y#	KM#	Metal	Description	VF	EF	Unc
55a	546	Silv	1/4 Rupee, 1940–43	5.00	6.00	15
56a	550	Silv	1/2 Rupee, 1939–40 *1939, Unc $70*	7.50	7.50	25
57	555	Silv	1 Rupee, 1938–39	115.00	150.00	350

Edge: ***With security groove***

Y#	KM#	Metal	Description	VF	EF	Unc
55b	547	Silv	1/4 Rupee, 1943–45	6	12	25
56b	551–552	Silv	1/2 Rupee, 1941–45	10	15	30
57b	556–557	Silv	1 Rupee, 1939–45 *1939, Rare*	15	20	40

Y#	KM#	Metal	Description	VF	EF	Unc
58	548	Nick	1/4 Rupee, 1946–47	2.00	5	10.00
59	553	Nick	1/2 Rupee, 1946–47	3.50	6	12.50
60	559	Nick	1 Rupee, 1947	5.00	7	20.00

REPUBLIC, *1950–*

Y#	KM#	Metal	Description	VF	EF	Unc
61	1.1–1.2	Bz	1 Pice, 1950, thick (388 gm)	2	4	10
61a	1.3–1.4	Bz	1 Pice, 1951–55, thin (292 gm)	1	2	5

Y#	KM#	Metal	Description	VF	EF	Unc
62	2	C-N	1/2 Anna, 1950, 54–55, square	2.50	4.50	15

Y#	KM#	Metal	Description	VF	EF	Unc
63	3	C-N	1 Anna, 1950, 54, scalloped	6	12	20

Y#	KM#	Metal	Description	VF	EF	Unc
64	4	C-N	2 Annas, 1950, 54, square	10	20	40

Y#	KM#	Metal	Description	VF	EF	Unc
65	5.1–5.2	Nick	1/4 Rupee, 1950–55, large lion	1.50	3.00	6
65a	5.3	Nick	1/4 Rupee, 1954–56, small lion	1.50	3.00	6
66	6	Nick	1/2 Rupee, 1950–56	2.00	4.00	8
67	7	Nick	1 Rupee, 1950, 54 *1954, Unc $45*	4.00	12.50	30

DECIMAL SYSTEM, *1957*

100 naye (new) paise = 1 rupee 1957-1963
100 paise = 1 rupee 1963–

FIRST COINAGE

Y#	KM#	Metal	Description	VF	EF	Unc
68	8	Bz	1 Naya Paisa, 1957–62	0.50	1	3
68a	8a	N-Br	1 Naya Paisa, 1962–63	0.50	1	3

Y#	KM#	Metal	Description	VF	EF	Unc
69	11	C-N	2 Naye Paise, 1957–63, scalloped	0.50	1	3

Y#	KM#	Metal	Description	VF	EF	Unc
70	16	C-N	5 Naye Paise, 1957–63, square	0.50	1	3

Y#	KM#	Metal	Description	VF	EF	Unc
71	24	C-N	10 Naye Paise, 1957–63, scalloped	0.50	1	3

Y#	KM#	Metal	Description	VF	EF	Unc
72	47	Nick	25 Naye Paise, 1957–63	1.00	2.00	4
73	55	Nick	50 Naye Paise, 1960–63	1.00	2.50	6
74	75	Nick	1 Rupee, 1962, 70 *1970, Unc $75*	1.25	4.00	10

SECOND COINAGE

Y#	KM#	Metal	Description	VF	EF	Unc
75	9	N-Br	1 Paisa, 1964	0.50	1	3

Y#	KM#	Metal	Description	VF	EF	Unc
76	12	C-N	2 Paise, 1964, scalloped	0.50	1	3

Y#	KM#	Metal	Description	VF	EF	Unc
77	14	C-N	3 Paise, 1964–68, hexagonal	0.50	1	3

Y#	KM#	Metal	Description	VF	EF	Unc
78	17	C-N	5 Paise, 1964–66, square	0.50	1	3

Y#	KM#	Metal	Description	VF	EF	Unc
79	25	C-N	10 Paise, 1964–67, scalloped	0.50	1	3

Y#	KM#	Metal	Description	VF	EF	Unc
80	48	Nick	25 Paise, 1964–68	0.75	1.50	3
81	58	Nick	50 Paise, 1964–71	1.00	2.00	4

Nehru Commemoratives

Y#	KM#	Metal	Description	VF	EF	Unc
82	56	Nick	50 Paise, 1964	2	3	6
83	76	Nick	1 Rupee, 1964	2	5	12

Y#	KM#	Metal	Description	VF	EF	Unc
82a	57	Nick	50 Paise, 1964, Nagari script on obverse	1	3	5

INDIA–PRINCELY STATES

INDIA–PRINCELY STATES: ALWAR

SHEODAN SINGH, *1857–1874*

Obverse: ***Queen Victoria legend***
Reverse: ***Sheodan Singh legend***
Planchets: ***Dump***

Y#	KM#	Metal	Description	VF	EF	Unc
1	35	Cop	1 Takka, 1859–74 (19–23 mm)	13.50	45	—

Planchet: ***Broad and thin***

Y#	KM#	Metal	Description	VF	EF	Unc
1a	35a	Cop	1 Takka, 1865 / Yr 9, 1866 / Yr 9, 1871 / Yr 15 (25–33 mm)	—	—	—

Planchets: ***Dump***

Y#	KM#	Metal	Description	VF	EF	Unc
2	37	Silv	1 Rupee, 1859–65 (20–24 mm)	35	65	—

Planchets: ***Broad and thin***

Y#	KM#	Metal	Description	VF	EF	Unc
2a	37a	Silv	1 Rupee, 1865, 67, 70 (28–33 mm)	450	950	—

MANGAL SINGH, *1874–1892*

Obverse: ***Like Y1***
Reverse: ***Mangal Singh legend***
Planchets: ***Broad and thin***

Y#	KM#	Metal	Description	VF	EF	Unc
3	40	Cop	1 Takka, 1874–91	125	—	—

Design: *Like Y3*
Planchets: *Broad and thin*

Y#	KM#	Metal	Description	VF	EF	Unc
4	41	Silv	1 Rupee, 1876–77	400	—	—

Reverse: *With title Raja*

Y#	KM#	Metal	Description	VF	EF	Unc
5	45	Silv	1 Rupee, 1788 (error), 1877–82	35	75	300

Reverse: *With title Maharajah*

Y#	KM#	Metal	Description	VF	EF	Unc
5a	46	Silv	1 Rupee, 1891	35	75	300

INDIA–PRINCELY STATES: BAHAWALPUR

ANONYMOUS ISSUES

Planchets: *Round or square*

Y#	KM#	Metal	Description	VF	EF	Unc
1	1	Cop	1 Falus, AH 1205–81 (1790–1864) (14–16 mm)	15	—	—

Y#	KM#	Metal	Description	VF	EF	Unc
2	2.1	Cop	1 Paisa, AH 1301–25, ND, (1884–1907)	15	30	—

Reverse: *Ahmadpur Mint legend*

Y#	KM#	Metal	Description	VF	EF	Unc
3	3.3–3.4	Silv	1 Rupee, AH 1275–86 (7–8 g)	40	75	—

Reverse: *Bahawalpur Mint legend*

Y#	KM#	Metal	Description	VF	EF	Unc
4	4.3	Silv	1 Rupee, AH 1272–75 (115 g)	40	75	—
4a	4.4	Silv	1 Rupee, AH 1276–84 (7 g)	40	75	—

Reverse: *Khanpur Mint legend*

Y#	KM#	Metal	Description	VF	EF	Unc
5	5.3	Silv	1 Rupee, AH 1280	45	85	—
5a	5.1–5.2	Silv	1 Rupee, AH 1255–83 (8.5–10 g)	45	85	—

MUHAMMED BAHAWAL KHAN V, *AH 1317–1325 (1899–1907)*

Obverse: *Ruler's legend*
Reverse: *Date-mint legend*

Y#	KM#	Metal	Description	VF	EF	Unc
6	N/A	Cop	1 Paisa, AH 1324–25 (1906–07)	15	30	—

SADIQ MUHAMMAD KHAN V, *AH 1325–1366 (1907–1947)*

Design: *Similar to Y6*

Y#	KM#	Metal	Description	VF	EF	Unc
7	7.1–7.2	Cop	1 Paisa, AH 1326–27, ND (1908–09)	20	35	—

Y#	KM#	Metal	Description	VF	EF	Unc
8	8	Cop	1 Paisa, AH 1342–43	10	15	25

Y#	KM#	Metal	Description	VF	EF	Unc
9	9	Cop	1 Paisa, AH 1343 (1925)	25	40	—

Obverse: *Bust of Muhammad Bahawal Khan V*
Reverse: *Ornate arms*

Y#	KM#	Metal	Description	VF	EF	Unc
10	10	Silv	1 Rupee, AH 1343 (1925)	225	275	400

Obverse: *Toughra*
Reverse: *Star and crescent with inscription*

Y#	KM#	Metal	Description	VF	EF	Unc
A11	14	Silv	1 Rupee, AH 1343 (1925)	60	85	125

Y#	KM#	Metal	Description	VF	EF	Unc
11	11	Gold	1 Ashrafi, AH 1343	—	—	1,750

Note: Y10–11 were probably struck for presentation only.

Y#	KM#	Metal	Description	VF	EF	Unc
12	12	Cop	1/2 Pice, 1940	7.50	15	35
13	13	Cop	1/4 Anna, 1940	12.50	20	40

Third Coinage

Obverse and Reverse: *More complex symbol in circular legend*

Y#	KM#	Metal	Description	VF	EF	Unc
5	Several	Cop	1 Paisa, ND (18–20 mm)	10	—	—

Obverse and Reverse: *More complex symbol in stylized legend*

Y#	KM#	Metal	Description	VF	EF	Unc
6	20	Silv	1/8 Rupee, ND (10 mm)	15	—	—
7	21	Silv	1/4 Rupee, ND (13 mm)	25	—	—
8	22	Silv	1/2 Rupee, ND (17 mm)	35	—	—
9	23	Silv	1 Rupee, ND (21 mm)	15	—	65

Y#	KM#	Metal	Description	VF	EF	Unc
10	18	Gold	1 Mohur, ND	1,750	2,500	—

India–Princely States: Banswara

Anonymous Issues

First Coinage

Obverse and Reverse: *State symbol in circles*

Y#	KM#	Metal	Description	VF	EF	Unc
1	4-Mar	Cop	1/2 Paisa, ND (18–19 mm)	15	—	—
2	8-Jul	Cop	1 Paisa, ND (21 mm)	15	—	—

Second Coinage

Obverse and Reverse: *State symbol in stylized legend*

Y#	KM#	Metal	Description	VF	EF	Unc
3	6-May	Cop	1/2 Paisa, ND (17–19 mm)	10	—	—
4	Several	Cop	1 Paisa, ND (22–25 mm)	10	—	—

India–Princely States: Baroda

Khande Rao, *AH 1273–1287 (1856–1870)*

First Coinage

Obverse: *Muhammad Akbar II legend*
Reverse: *Mint-date legend, pomegranate, Nagari "Kha"*

Y#	KM#	Metal	Description	VF	EF	Unc
1	1.2	Cop	1/2 Paisa, ND (4 g)	7.50	15	—
2	2	Cop	1 Paisa, Yr 52 (8 g)	7.50	15	—

Obverse: *Muhammad Akbar II legend*
Reverse: *Like Y11*

Y#	KM#	Metal	Description	VF	EF	Unc
3	3	Silv	1/4 Rupee, AH 1273, 78 (13–14 mm)	9	18	—
4	4	Silv	1/2 Rupee, AH 1267–82 (16–17 mm)	10	20	—
5	5	Silv	1 Rupee, AH 1273–8x / Yr 53 (21–22 mm)	15	25	—

Second Coinage

Obverse: *Gaekwar's titles*
Reverse: *Mint-date legend, scimitar, "Kha Ga"*

Y#	KM#	Metal	Description	VF	EF	Unc
6	6	Cop	1/2 Paisa, AH 1275–77 (1857–59) (3.5 g)	4	—	—
7	7.7	Cop	1 Paisa, AH 1274–77 (7–8 g)	5	—	—

Obverse: *Like Y7*
Reverse: *Similar, horse hoof added*

Y#	KM#	Metal	Description	VF	EF	Unc
6a	6a	Cop	1/2 Paisa, AH 1281, 85	13	—	—
7a	7.8	Cop	1 Paisa, AH 1281–85	7	—	—
8	8	Cop	2 Paisa, AH 1281–85	7	—	—

Obverse: *Like Y7*
Reverse: *Mint-date legend, sword, Nagari "Kha"*

Y#	KM#	Metal	Description	VF	EF	Unc
9	9	Silv	1/8 Rupee, AH 1282	10	—	—
10	10	Silv	1/4 Rupee, AH 1274–86	8	—	—
11	11	Silv	1/2 Rupee, AH 1274–86	12	—	—
12	12	Silv	1 Rupee, AH 1274–87	15	—	—

Obverse: *Khande Rao legend in Nagari*
Reverse: *Mint-date legend*

Y#	KM#	Metal	Description	VF	EF	Unc
13	13	Silv	1/2 Rupee, AH 1287 (1870)	350	—	—
14	14	Silv	1 Rupee, AH 1287	275	—	—

MALHAR RAO,
AH 1287–1292 (1870–1875)

Obverse: *Like Y7*
Reverse: *Like Y7 but "Ma Ga," plus ball*

Y#	KM#	Metal	Description	VF	EF	Unc
15	15	Cop	1/2 Paisa, AH 1288, 90 (4 g)	12	—	—
16	16	Cop	1 Paisa, AH 1288–90 (7–9 g)	12	—	—
17	17	Cop	2 Paisa, AH 1288–90 (16 g)	15	—	—

Obverse: *Like Y7*
Reverse: *Like Y11 but "Ma Ga"*

Y#	KM#	Metal	Description	VF	EF	Unc
18	18	Silv	1/8 Rupee, ND AH 129x	17.50	—	—
19	19	Silv	1/4 Rupee, AH 1290	15.00	—	—
20	20	Silv	1/2 Rupee, AH 1287–90	15.00	—	—
21	21–21a	Silv	1 Rupee, AH 1287–90	20.00	—	—
22	22–22A	Silv	2 Rupees, AH 1288	—	—	—

SAYAJI RAO III,
AH 1292–1357 / VS 1932–1996 (1875–1939)

FIRST COINAGE

Obverse: *Nagari "Sa Ga" / ball, scimitar*
Reverse: *Date/value*
Planchets: *Dump*

Y#	KM#	Metal	Description	VF	EF	Unc
A23	A23	Cop	1/4 Paisa, VS 194x	25	—	—
23	23	Cop	1/2 Paisa, VS 1937, 48 (1880, 91)	15	—	—
24	24	Cop	1 Paisa, VS 1937–48	15	—	—
25	25	Cop	2 Paisa, VS 1937–48	20	—	—

Planchets: *Round, struck in collar*

Y#	KM#	Metal	Description	VF	EF	Unc
24a	24a	Cop	1 Paisa, VS 1949 (1892)	15	30	—
25a	25a	Cop	2 Paisa, VS 1949	25	50	—

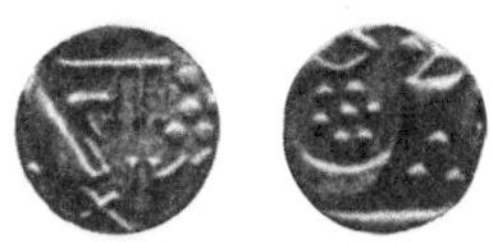

Obverse: *Like Y7*
Reverse: *Like Y11 but "Sa"*

Y#	KM#	Metal	Description	VF	EF	Unc
26	26	Silv	1/8 Rupee, AH 1294–99 (1877–82) (10 mm)	10.00	20	60
27	27	Silv	1/4 Rupee, AH 1292, 99 (13 mm)	12.50	25	75
28	28	Silv	1/2 Rupee, AH 1292–1301 (15–16 mm)	15.00	30	90
29	29	Silv	1 Rupee, AH 1292–1302 (20 mm)	15.00	30	90

SECOND COINAGE

Planchets: *Thick*

Y#	KM#	Metal	Description	VF	EF	Unc
30	30	Cop	1 Pai, VS 1944–47 (1887–90)	4	8	50
31	31	Cop	1 Paisa, VS 1940–47	4	8	50
32	32	Cop	2 Paisa, VS 1940–48	5	10	100

Planchets: *Thin*

Y#	KM#	Metal	Description	VF	EF	Unc
30a	30.2a	Cop	1 Pai, VS 1948–50	4	8	50
31a	31.2a	Cop	1 Paisa, VS 1948–50	4	8	50
32a	32.2a	Cop	2 Paisa, VS 1948–50	5	10	100

Note: Y30–32a have several minor varieties of wreath style and arrangement of legends.

Designs: *Like Y37–39*

Y#	KM#	Metal	Description	VF	EF	Unc
33	33	Silv	2 Annas, VS 1949 (1892) (16 mm)	35	70	—
34	34	Silv	1/4 Rupee, VS 1949 (19 mm)	40	80	—
35	35	Silv	1/2 Rupee, VS 1948–49 (24 mm)	100	200	—
36	36	Silv	1 Rupee, VS 1948–49 (30 mm)	50	100	—

Reduced Size

Y#	KM#	Metal	Description	VF	EF	Unc
33a	33a	Silv	2 Annas, VS 1951–52 (14 mm)	20	60	200
34a	34a	Silv	1/4 Rupee, VS 1951–52 (17 mm)	25	75	250
35a	35a	Silv	1/2 Rupee, VS 1951–52 (22 mm)	75	150	375
36a	36a	Silv	1 Rupee, VS 1951–56 (28 mm)	45	125	300

Y#	KM#	Metal	Description	VF	EF	Unc
37	A37	Gold	1/6 Mohur, VS 1943–59 (1886–1902)	750	1,500	—
38	A38	Gold	1/3 Mohur, VS 1942, 59	750	1,500	—

Y#	KM#	Metal	Description	VF	EF	Unc
39	A39	Gold	1 Mohur, VS 1942–59	1,250	2,500	—

Pratap Singh, *VS 1995–2008 (1939–1951)*

Y#	KM#	Metal	Description	VF	EF	Unc
40	40	Gold	1/3 Mohur, VS 1995 (18 mm)	3,000	6,000	—
41	41	Gold	1 Mohur, VS 1995 (21 mm)	3,500	7,500	—

Note: Offstrikes in silver exist for Y40–41.

Amreli Mint

Khande Rao, AH 1273–1287 (1856–1870)

Design: *Like Y1a*
Planchets: *Dump*

Y#	KM#	Metal	Description	VF	EF	Unc
1	7.2–7.6	Cop	1 Paisa, ND	15	—	—

Obverse: *Nagari "Sri Kha Ga," jhar*
Reverse: *Mint-date legend*
Planchets: *Broad and thin*

Y#	KM#	Metal	Description	VF	EF	Unc
1a	7.1	Cop	1 Paisa, AH 1277 (1861)	15	—	—

Sayaji Rao III, AH 1292–1357 / VS 1932–1996 (1875–1939)

Obverse: *Nagari "Sa Ga," sun, scimitar*
Reverse: *Debased mint-date legend*

Y#	KM#	Metal	Description	VF	EF	Unc
A2	A2	Cop	1/4 Paisa, AH 1312 (1894)	25.00	90	—
2	B23	Cop	1/2 Paisa, AH 1312	12.50	45	—
3	C23	Cop	1 Paisa, AH 1312–13	20.00	135	—
3a	C23a	Cop	1 Paisa, ND, with additional marks Latin "S" on obverse, sword on reverse	35.00	150	—

INDIA–PRINCELY STATES: BHARTPUR

Jaswant Singh, *1852–1893*

Mint: *Braj Indrapur (Bhartpur)*
Designs: *Like Y3*

Y#	KM#	Metal	Description	VF	EF	Unc
1	N/A	Cop	1/2 Paisa, 1858 / VS 1910 (9 g)	—	—	—
2	N/A	Cop	1 Paisa, 1858 / VS 1910 (18 g)	—	—	—

Obverse: *Victoria portrait and legend*
Reverse: *Jaswant Singh legend—Bhartpur*

Y#	KM#	Metal	Description	VF	EF	Unc
3	156–157	Silv	1 Rupee, 1858 / VS 1910 (21–24 mm)	120	175	—

Obverse: ***Victoria portrait and title, no name***
Reverse: ***Jaswant Singh legend—Braj Indrapur***

Y#	KM#	Metal	Description	VF	EF	Unc
4	166.2	Silv	1 Rupee, 1858–65 / VS 1914–22	110	165	—

Mint: ***Dig***
Obverse: ***Like Y4***
Reverse: ***Similar to Y4 but Dig Mint***

Y#	KM#	Metal	Description	VF	EF	Unc
A4	174	Silv	1/4 Rupee, 1858 / VS 1910	150	200	—
B4	N/A	Silv	1/2 Rupee, 1858 / VS 1910	150	200	—
5	176	Silv	1 Rupee, 1858 / VS 1910	100	150	—

Note: For similar issues with a katar at the left of the head, see Bindraban State.

Design: ***Like Y4***

Y#	KM#	Metal	Description	VF	EF	Unc
6	170	Gold	1 Mohur, 1858–62 / VS 1915–19 (21 mm)	15,000	20,000	30,000

INDIA–PRINCELY STATES: BHOPAL

SIKANDAR BEGAM, *AH 1261–1285 (1844–1868)*

SHAH JAHAN BEGAM, *AH 1285–1319 (1868–1901)*

ANONYMOUS ISSUES

Obverse: ***Date / Bhopal legend***
Reverse: ***Value***

Y#	KM#	Metal	Description	VF	EF	Unc
1	1	Cop	1/4 Anna, AH 1266–82 (7–8 gr)	12.50	—	—
2	2	Cop	1/2 Anna, AH 1276–85 (15–16 g)	10.00	—	—
3	3	Cop	1 Anna, AH 1276 (30–32 g)	50.00	—	—

Obverse: ***Persian "Sh/Bhopal"***
Reverse: ***Date/value***

Y#	KM#	Metal	Description	VF	EF	Unc
4	4.1–4.4	Cop	1/4 Anna, AH 1285–1300	12.50	—	—
5	5	Cop	1/2 Anna, AH 1286–1300	10.00	—	—
6	6	Cop	1 Anna, AH 1286–1300	50.00	—	—

Obverse: ***Formal date legend***
Reverse: ***Mint legend***

Y#	KM#	Metal	Description	VF	EF	Unc
7	7	Silv	1/8 Rupee, AH 1271–91	15	40	—
8	8	Silv	1/4 Rupee, AH 1275–88	13	35	—
9	9	Silv	1/2 Rupee, AH 1275–92	15	40	—
10	10	Silv	1 Rupee, AH 1271–93	20	45	—

Obverse and Reverse: ***Rearranged legends both sides***

Y#	KM#	Metal	Description	VF	EF	Unc
11	11	Silv	1/8 Rupee, AH 1294–1306	15	40	—
12	12	Silv	1/4 Rupee, AH 1293–1305	10	35	—
13	13	Silv	1/2 Rupee, AH 1294–1308	15	40	—
14	14	Silv	1 Rupee, AH 1293–1308	20	45	—

Obverse and Reverse: ***Kalima***

Y#	KM#	Metal	Description	VF	EF	Unc
A14	A14	Silv	Nazarana 1 Rupee, AH 1286 (1869)	—	—	—
B14	B14	Silv	Nazarana 1-1/2 Rupees, AH 1286	1,000	1,850	—
C14	C14	Silv	Nazarana 2 Rupees, AH 1286	500	1,000	1,500

Obverse: ***Shah Jahan Begam / value***
Reverse: ***Date / Bhopal legend***

Y#	KM#	Metal	Description	VF	EF	Unc
15	15	Cop	1/2 Paisa, AH 1305–06 (1888)	15	—	—
16	16	Cop	1/4 Anna, AH 1302–06 (7–8 g)	15	—	—
17	17	Cop	1/2 Anna, AH 1302–09 (15 g)	15	—	—
18	18	Cop	1 Anna, AH 1302–06 (30–32 g)	22	—	—

INDIA–PRINCELY STATES: BIKANIR

SARDAR SINGH, *1851–1872*

For pre-Victorian coins of this reign, see Craig, *Coins of the World*.

Design: ***Like Y5***

Y#	KM#	Metal	Description	VF	EF	Unc
1	41	Cop	1 Paisa, 1859 / VS 1916 (7–8 g)	4	8	—

Obverse: *Queen Victoria legend*
Reverse: *Date / regnal symbols*
Planchets: *Dump*

Y#	KM#	Metal	Description	VF	EF	Unc
2	42	Silv	1/8 Rupee, 1859 / VS 1916 (11 mm)	25	—	—
3	43	Silv	1/4 Rupee, 1859 / VS 1916 (15 mm)	10	20	—
4	44	Silv	1/2 Rupee, 1859 / VS 1916 (18 mm)	13	25	—
5	45	Silv	1 Rupee, 1859 / VS 1916 (22 mm)	15	30	—

Planchets: *Broad and thin*

Y#	KM#	Metal	Description	VF	EF	Unc
5a	46	Silv	1 Rupee, 1859 / VS 1916 (30 mm)	—	—	—

Dungar Singh, *1872–1887*

Design: *Like Y10*

Y#	KM#	Metal	Description	VF	EF	Unc
6	50	Cop	1 Paisa, 1859 / VS 1916 (7–8 g)	12.50	—	—

Reverse: *Dungar Singh symbol added*
Planchets: *Dump*

Y#	KM#	Metal	Description	VF	EF	Unc
7	51	Silv	1/8 Rupee, 1859 / VS 1916 (12 mm)	75	125	200
8	52	Silv	1/4 Rupee, 1859 / VS 1916 (14 mm)	100	175	250
9	53	Silv	1/2 Rupee, 1859 / VS 1916 (16–19 mm)	100	175	250
10	54	Silv	1 Rupee, 1859 / VS 1916 (22 mm)	35	50	85

Planchets: *Broad and thin*

Y#	KM#	Metal	Description	VF	EF	Unc
10a	54a	Silv	1 Rupee, 1859 / VS 1916 (30 mm)	100	175	250

Ganga Singh, *1887–1943*

First Coinage

Design: *Like Y15*

Y#	KM#	Metal	Description	VF	EF	Unc
11	61	Cop	1 Paisa, 1859 / VS 1916, VS 1946	7.50	—	—

Planchets: *Broad and thin*

Y#	KM#	Metal	Description	VF	EF	Unc
11a	60	Cop	1 Paisa, 1859 / VS 1916	—	—	—

Reverse: *Ganga Singh symbol added*
Planchets: *Dump*

Y#	KM#	Metal	Description	VF	EF	Unc
12	62	Silv	1/8 Rupee, 1859 / VS 1916 (12 mm)	75	125	200
13	63	Silv	1/4 Rupee, 1859 / VS 1916 (14 mm)	100	175	250
14	64	Silv	1/2 Rupee, 1859 / VS 1916 (16–19 mm)	125	200	300
15	65	Silv	1 Rupee, 1859 / VS 1916, VS 1944 (20–22 mm)	35	45	—

Planchets: *Broad and thin*

Y#	KM#	Metal	Description	VF	EF	Unc
15a	65a	Silv	1 Rupee, 1859 / VS 1916 (30 mm)	200	300	—

Second Coinage

Y#	KM#	Metal	Description	VF	EF	Unc
16	70	Cop	1/2 Pice, 1894	32.50	50	250
17	71	Cop	1/4 Anna, 1895	45.00	85	450

Y#	KM#	Metal	Description	VF	EF	Unc
18	72	Silv	1 Rupee, 1892, 97 *1897, VF $70*	45	100	350

50th Year of Reign

Y#	KM#	Metal	Description	VF	EF	Unc
19	N/A	Silv	1 Rupee, VS 1994	40	60	125

Y#	KM#	Metal	Description	VF	EF	Unc
20	N/A	Gold	1/2 Mohur, VS 1994	750	1,100	1,350
21	N/A	Gold	1 Mohur, VS 1994	700	1,000	1,250

INDIA–PRINCELY STATES: BINDRABAN

Obverse: *Like Bhartpur Y4*
Reverse: *Victoria titles / Bindraban*

Y#	KM#	Metal	Description	VF	EF	Unc
1	16	Silv	1/4 Rupee, 1858–67 / VS 1915–24	130	200	—
2	17	Silv	1/2 Rupee, 1858–67 / VS 1915–25	150	225	—
3	18	Silv	1 Rupee, 1858–59 / VS 1915–16	165	250	—
3a	19	Silv	1 Rupee, 1867	325	—	—

This series is further distinguished from Bhartpur by mintmarks: katar and sword on the obverse, umbrella on the reverse.

INDIA–PRINCELY STATES: BUNDI

IN NAME OF QUEEN VICTORIA

Y1-6 have AD dates on obverse and Samvat dates on reverse. Coins with both dates identifiable usually command higher prices.

Obverse: *Horizontal English legend*

Y#	KM#	Metal	Description	VF	EF	Unc
1	1	Cop	1/2 Paisa, 1867 / VS 1924	10	20	—
2	2	Cop	1 Paisa, 1858, 67 / VS 1915, 24	5	8	—
3	3	Cop	1 Takka, 1859–99 / VS 1915–56	4	8	—

Planchets: *Round*

Y#	KM#	Metal	Description	VF	EF	Unc
4	4	Silv	1/4 Rupee, 1858–79 / VS 1915–36	35	60	—
5	5	Silv	1/2 Rupee, 1858–86 / VS 1915–43	45	75	—
6	6	Silv	1 Rupee, 1858–86 / VS 1915–43	45	85	—

Planchets: *Square*

Y#	KM#	Metal	Description	VF	EF	Unc
6a	6a	Silv	1 Rupee, 1858–77 / VS 1915–34	150	275	—

Planchets: *Round*

Y#	KM#	Metal	Description	VF	EF	Unc
A7	N/A	Gold	1 Mohur, 1860 / VS 1917	17,000	22,500	—

Obverse: *Katar in center*

Y#	KM#	Metal	Description	VF	EF	Unc
B7	N/A	Cop	1/2 Paisa, VS 1963–67 (5 g)	5	8	—

Obverse: *Katar in center*
Planchets: *Round*

Y#	KM#	Metal	Description	VF	EF	Unc
7	7	Silv	1/4 Rupee, VS 1944–55 (1887–98)	70	85	—
8	8	Silv	1/2 Rupee, VS 1945–55	30	50	—
9	9	Silv	1 Rupee, VS 1943–57	35	65	—

Planchets: *Square*

Y#	KM#	Metal	Description	VF	EF	Unc
9a	9a	Silv	1 Rupee, VS 1943–53	150	200	—

Obverse: *Seated figure in center*

Y#	KM#	Metal	Description	VF	EF	Unc
10	10	Silv	1 Rupee, VS 1958 (1901)	125	185	—

Planchets: *Round*

Y#	KM#	Metal	Description	VF	EF	Unc
A10	N/A	Gold	1/2 Mohur, VS 194x	—	—	—

IN NAME OF EDWARD VII

Obverse: *Seated figure in center*

Y#	KM#	Metal	Description	VF	EF	Unc
B11	B11	Silv	1/4 Rupee, VS 1958, 62 (1901, 04)	175	—	—
A11	A11	Silv	1/2 Rupee, VS 1958	250	—	—
11	11	Silv	1 Rupee, VS 1958–63 (21–25 mm)	65	175	—

Obverse: *Katar in center*

Y#	KM#	Metal	Description	VF	EF	Unc
A12	A12	Cop	1/2 Paisa, VS 1963–76 (1906–19) (5 g)	7	—	—

Planchets: ***Small, round***

Y#	KM#	Metal	Description	VF	EF	Unc
12	12	Silv	1/4 Rupee, VS 1963–66 (1906–09)	70	—	—
13	13	Silv	1/2 Rupee, VS 1963–66	70	—	—
14	14	Silv	1 Rupee, VS 1963–69 (18–21 mm)	60	—	—

Planchets: ***Square***

Y#	KM#	Metal	Description	VF	EF	Unc
14a	14a	Silv	1 Rupee, VS 1965–70	150	275	—

Planchets: ***Broad, round***

Y#	KM#	Metal	Description	VF	EF	Unc
14b	14b	Silv	1 Rupee, VS 1966–70 (26 mm)	475	—	—

In Name of GEORGE V

Obverse: ***Katar in center***

Y#	KM#	Metal	Description	VF	EF	Unc
15	15	Cop	1/2 Paisa, VS 1973–92 (1916–35)	7	—	—

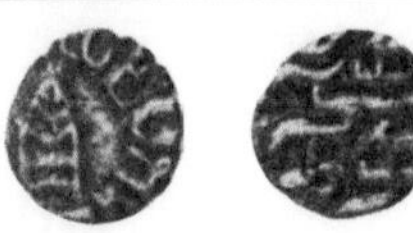

Planchets: ***Round***

Y#	KM#	Metal	Description	VF	EF	Unc
16	16	Silv	1/4 Rupee, VS 1972–82 (1915–25)	40	—	—

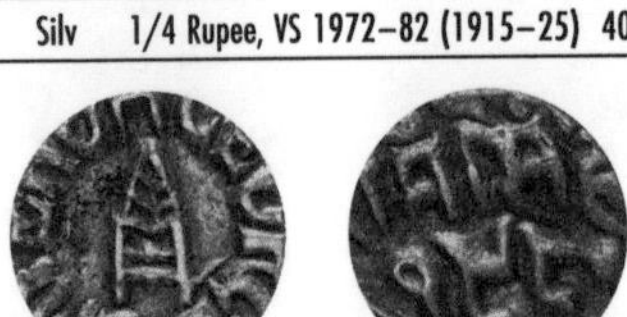

Y#	KM#	Metal	Description	VF	EF	Unc
17	17	Silv	1/2 Rupee, VS 1972–84	30	40	—
18	18	Silv	1 Rupee, VS 1972–89	35	50	—

Planchets: ***Square***

Y#	KM#	Metal	Description	VF	EF	Unc
18a	18a	Silv	1 Rupee, VS 1965–87	250	300	—

Obverse: ***AD date in center***
Planchets: ***Round***

Y#	KM#	Metal	Description	VF	EF	Unc
A19	A19	Silv	1/4 Rupee, 1925	325	—	—
19	19	Silv	1/2 Rupee, 1925	275	375	—
20	20	Silv	1 Rupee, 1925	200	300	—

Planchets: ***Square***

Y#	KM#	Metal	Description	VF	EF	Unc
20a	20a	Silv	1 Rupee, 1925	300	—	—

INDIA–PRINCELY STATES: CAMBAY

Hussain Ja'afar, *AH 1257–1297 (1841–1880)*

Obverse: ***Shah Alam II legend***
Reverse: ***Mint-date legend***

Y#	KM#	Metal	Description	VF	EF	Unc
1	1	Silv	1 Rupee, AH 1282, 93–94 (20 mm)	45	—	—

Ja'afar Ali, *AH 1297–1333 / VS 1937–1972 (1880–1915)*

Obverse: ***Persian "Shah"***
Reverse: ***Date legend***

Y#	KM#	Metal	Description	VF	EF	Unc
2	2	Cop	1/4 Paisa, VS 1962 (1905)	10.00	—	—
3	3	Cop	1/2 Paisa, VS 1962	12.00	—	—
3a	N/A	Cop	1/2 Paisa, VS 1962, square planchet	10.00	—	—
4	4	Cop	1 Paisa, VS 1962	5.00	—	—
4a	N/A	Cop	1 Paisa, VS 1962, square planchet	7.50	—	—

Note: Dates of Y2–4a are rarely on planchets.

Obverse: ***State name***
Reverse: ***Value/date***

Y#	KM#	Metal	Description	VF	EF	Unc
5	5	Cop	1/2 Paisa, VS 1963–64, reverse value in words	25	—	—
5a	5a	Cop	1/2 Paisa, VS 1965–66, value in numerals	15	—	—
6	6	Cop	1 Paisa, VS 1962–70	6	—	—

Obverse: ***Ja'afar Ali legend***
Reverse: ***Mint legend***

Y#	KM#	Metal	Description	VF	EF	Unc
7	7	Silv	1/8 Rupee, AH 1313 (1895) (11 mm)	200	400	—
8	8	Silv	1/4 Rupee, AH 1313 (14 mm)	250	500	—
9	9	Silv	1/2 Rupee, AH 1313, 17 (15–16 mm)	150	325	—
10	10	Silv	1 Rupee, AH 1311–19 (19–20 mm)	35	70	—

INDIA–PRINCELY STATES: CHHOTA UDAIPUR

JITSINGHJI, *SAKA 1773–1803 / VS 1908–1938 (1851–1881)*

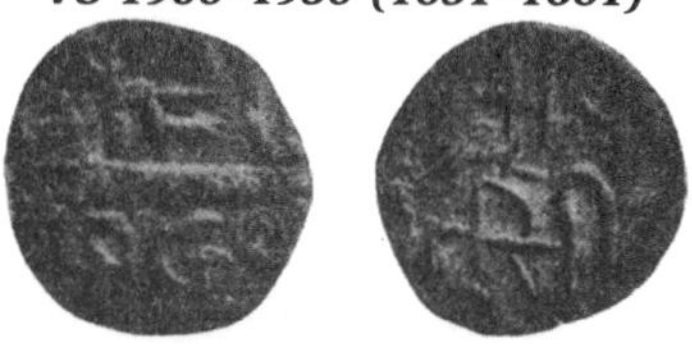

Obverse and Reverse: ***Crude Gujerati legend***

Y#	KM#	Metal	Description	VF	EF	Unc
1	1	Cop	1 Paisa, Saka 1787 (7 g)	12.50	—	—
2	2	Cop	2 Paisa, Saka 1787 (14 g)	13.00	—	—

Obverse: ***Sword and legend***

Y#	KM#	Metal	Description	VF	EF	Unc
3	3	Cop	2 Paisa, VS 1919, 24	15	—	—

MOTISINGHJI, *VS 1938–1962 (1881–1905)*

Obverse: ***Date in circular legend***
Reverse: ***Value / sword in circular legend***

Y#	KM#	Metal	Description	VF	EF	Unc
A4	A4	Cop	1/2 Paisa, VS 1948	100	200	—
4	4	Cop	1 Paisa, VS 1948 (15 mm)	20	40	—
5	5	Cop	2 Paisa, VS 1948–50 (20–22 mm)	25	50	—

INDIA–PRINCELY STATES: COOCH BEHAR

Dating System: Coins of this state are dated in a local era beginning in AD 1510.

NARENDRA NARAYANA, *1847–1863*

Obverse and Reverse: ***Four-line legends on both sides***

Y#	KM#	Metal	Description	VF	EF	Unc
1	141	Silv	1/2 Rupee, ND (20–22 mm)	50	—	—

Y#	KM#	Metal	Description	VF	EF	Unc
2	155	Gold	1 Mohur, ND (9.4 g)	4,000	6,000	—

NRIPENDRA NARAYANA, *1863–1911*

Obverse: ***Nripendra legend (style of Y8)***
Reverse: ***Four-line legend on square***

Y#	KM#	Metal	Description	VF	EF	Unc
3	180	Silv	1/2 Rupee, Yr 354 (1864)	200	400	—

Y#	KM#	Metal	Description	VF	EF	Unc
4	145	Gold	1 Mohur, Yr 354	7,000	10,000	—

RAJENDRA NARAYANA, *1911–1913*

Design: ***Like Y8 but Rajendra legend***

Y#	KM#	Metal	Description	VF	EF	Unc
5	195	Silv	1/2 Rupee, Yr 402 (1912)	150	300	850

Y#	KM#	Metal	Description	VF	EF	Unc
6	200	Gold	1 Mohur, Yr 402	—	—	10,000

JITENDRA NARAYANA, *1913–1922*

Y#	KM#	Metal	Description	VF	EF	Unc
7	215	Silv	1/2 Rupee, Yr 404 (1914)	150	300	850

Obverse: ***Jitendra legend***
Reverse: ***State arms***

Y#	KM#	Metal	Description	VF	EF	Unc
8	230	Gold	1 Mohur, Yr 404	—	—	13,500

JAGADDIPENDRA NARAYANA, *1922–1949*

Design: ***Like Y8 but Jagaddipendra legend***

Y#	KM#	Metal	Description	VF	EF	Unc
9	225	Silv	1/2 Rupee, Yr 413 (1923)	150	300	850

INDIA–PRINCELY STATES: DATIA

GOVIND SINGH, *1907–1948*

Obverse: ***Bust slightly right***
Reverse: ***State arms***

Y#	KM#	Metal	Description	VF	EF	Unc
1	N/A	Gold	1/2 Mohur, ND (5.7 g)	2,800	3,500	—

INDIA–PRINCELY STATES: DEWAS, JUNIOR BRANCH

NARAYAN RAO, *1864–1892*

Reverse: *DEWAS STATE J.B.*

Y#	KM#	Metal	Description	VF	EF	Unc
1	1	Cop	1/12 Anna, 1888	40	125	350
3	3	Cop	1/4 Anna, 1888	60	200	500

INDIA–PRINCELY STATES: DEWAS, SENIOR BRANCH

Krishnaji Rao, *1860–1899*

Obverse: *Bust of Victoria*
Reverse: *DEWAS STATE S.B.*

Y#	KM#	Metal	Description	VF	EF	Unc
1	11	Cop	1/12 Anna, 1888	40	80	200
						Proof: $900
2	12	Cop	1/4 Anna, 1888	50	100	325
						Proof: $1,000

Vikrama Simha Rao, *1937–1948*

Obverse: *Bust of ruler*

Y#	KM#	Metal	Description	VF	EF	Unc
3	13	Cop	1 Paisa, 1944 / VS 2000–01	750	1,200	3,000

INDIA–PRINCELY STATES: DHAR

Anand Rao III, *AH 1276–1316 (1860–1898)*

Obverse: *Hanuman (monkey god)*

Y#	KM#	Metal	Description	VF	EF	Unc
A1	5	Cop	1/2 Paisa, AH 1289 (1872) (16 mm)	25	—	—
B1	6	Cop	1 Paisa, AH 1289 (17–20 mm)	20	—	—

Y#	KM#	Metal	Description	VF	EF	Unc
1	11	Cop	1/12 Anna, 1887	30	70	300
2	12	Cop	1/2 Pice, 1887	35	80	375
3	13	Cop	1/4 Anna, 1887	40	100	475

Anand Rao IV, *1943–1948*

Obverse: *Bust*
Reverse: *State arms*

Y#	KM#	Metal	Description	VF	EF	Unc
4	10	Gold	1 Mohur, 1943	—	—	10,000

INDIA–PRINCELY STATES: DUNGARPUR

Udai Singh, *VS 1901–1955 (1844–1898)*

Obverse: *Date/sword*
Reverse: *State legend*

Y#	KM#	Metal	Description	VF	EF	Unc
C1	1	Cop	1/4 Paisa, VS 1917 (1860)	70	—	—
B1	4	Cop	1/2 Paisa, VS 1917	60	—	—
A1	2	Cop	1 Paisa, VS 1917	25	—	—

Lakshman Singh, *VS 1975–2005 (1918–1948)*

Obverse: *State arms*
Reverse: *State name / value / date*

Y#	KM#	Metal	Description	VF	EF	Unc
1	7–8	Cop	1 Paisa, VS 2001 (1944)	60	90	175

Obverse: *Raj Dungarpur*
Reverse: *Sword and "jhar"*

Y#	KM#	Metal	Description	VF	EF	Unc
1A	9	Gold	1 Mohur, VS 1996 (1939)	—	6,500	—
1C	N/A	Gold	1 Mohur, VS 2000 (1943), milled (10.83 g)	—	5,000	—
1B	N/A	Gold	1/2 Mohur, VS 2000, milled	—	8,500	—

INDIA–PRINCELY STATES: FARIDKOT

Harindar Singh, *1918–1949*

Y#	KM#	Metal	Description	VF	EF	Unc
1	10	Gold	1/3 Mohur, 1941 (20 mm) (3.5–3.8 g)	3,000	5,500	10,000
2	N/A	Gold	2/3 Mohur, 1932 (7.98 g)	2,000	3,600	8,000

INDIA–PRINCELY STATES: GWALIOR

HANDMADE ISSUES

Bhilsa Mint

Mintmarks: Frozen date AH (12)25, bow and arrow

JAYAJI RAO,
AH 1259–1302 (1843–1886)

Obverse: ***Shah Alam II legend, "25"***
Reverse: ***Debased mint legend, bow and arrow, Nagari "Ji" for Jayaji***

Y#	KM#	Metal	Description	VF	EF	Unc
1	23.1/29	Silv	1/8 Rupee, AH (12)25	20	30	200
2	24.1/30	Silv	1/4 Rupee, AH (12)25 (12–14 mm)	20	30	200
3	Several	Silv	1/2 Rupee, AH (12)25 (14–16 mm)	25	40	300
4	27/32	Silv	1 Rupee, AH (12)25 (17–18 mm)	25	40	300

MADHAO RAO II,
AH 1302–1345 (1886–1925)

Obverse: ***Like Y4***
Reverse: ***Similar but Nagari "M" for Madho***

Y#	KM#	Metal	Description	VF	EF	Unc
5	23.2	Silv	1/8 Rupee, AH (12)25 (9–10 mm)	25	40	300
6	24.2	Silv	1/4 Rupee, AH (12)25 (12–13 mm)	25	40	300
7	26.2	Silv	1/2 Rupee, AH (12)25 (14 mm)	25	40	300
8	28	Silv	1 Rupee, AH (12)25 (17–18 mm)	25	40	300

GWALIOR FORT MINT

Mintmarks: Five-petal rosette, bow and arrow, frozen Year 23 (silver), frozen AH 1130 / Year 2 (gold)

JAYAJI RAO,
AH 1259–1302 (1843–1886)

Designs: ***Like Y13a***
Planchets: ***Dump***

Y#	KM#	Metal	Description	VF	EF	Unc
9	77	Silv	1/16 Rupee, Yr 23 (9 mm)	15	25	—
10	78	Silv	1/8 Rupee, Yr 23 (11 mm)	15	25	—
11	79	Silv	1/4 Rupee, Yr 23 (13 mm)	20	30	—
12	80	Silv	1/2 Rupee, Yr 23 (15 mm)	30	40	—
13	81	Silv	1 Rupee, Yr 23 (17–19 mm)	30	40	—

Obverse: ***Muhammad Akbar II legend***
Reverse: ***Mint-date legend, Nagari "Ji"***
Planchets: ***Broad and thin***

Y#	KM#	Metal	Description	VF	EF	Unc
13a	83	Silv	1 Rupee, AH 125x / Yr 23 (25–27 mm)	—	—	—

Obverse: ***Muhammad Shah legend***
Reverse: ***Mint-date legend, Nagari "Ji"***

Y#	KM#	Metal	Description	VF	EF	Unc
14	74	Gold	1/5 Mohur, AH 1130 / Yr 2 (2.21 g)	300	500	—
14a	A75	Gold	1 Mohur, AH 1130 / Yr 2	750	1,000	—

MADHAO RAO II,
AH 1302–1345 (1886–1925)

Obverse: ***Like Y14***
Reverse: ***Similar but Nagari "M" for Madho***

Y#	KM#	Metal	Description	VF	EF	Unc
15	84	Gold	1 Mohur, AH 1130 / Yr 2	1,000	1,500	—

JHANSI MINT

Mintmarks: Figure resembling "99111," Persian (not Nagari) "Ji" for Jayaji

JAYAJI RAO,
AH 1259–1302 (1843–1886)

Y#	KM#	Metal	Description	VF	EF	Unc
A16	111	Cop	1 Paisa, ND (1865–86) (11–15 g)	13	—	—

Obverse: ***Shah Alam II legend***
Reverse: ***Mint-date legend, Persian "Ji"***

Y#	KM#	Metal	Description	VF	EF	Unc
16	112	Silv	1/8 Rupee, ND (1865–86)	85	150	—
19	113	Silv	1 Rupee, AH 1282, 84 (1865, 67)	30	50	—

LASHKAR MINT *(GWALIOR CITY)*

Mintmarks: Bow and arrow, snake, single or double trident, frozen Year 23

JAYAJI RAO,
AH 1259–1302 (1843–1886)

Obverse: ***Shah Alam II legend***
Reverse: ***Degenerate legend, double trident***

Y#	KM#	Metal	Description	VF	EF	Unc
20	N/A	Cop	1/2 Paisa, Yr 23 (5 g)	10	—	—
21	N/A	Cop	1 Paisa, Yr 23 (10 g)	10	—	—
22	N/A	Cop	2 Paisa, Yr 23 (20 g)	15	—	—

Obverse: ***Shah Alam II legend***
Reverse: ***Mintmarks, Najari "Ji"***

Y#	KM#	Metal	Description	VF	EF	Unc
23	N/A	Silv	1/16 Rupee, Yr 23 (8–9 mm)	15	30.00	—
24	120	Silv	1/8 Rupee, Yr 23 (9–11 mm)	18	32.50	—
25	122	Silv	1/4 Rupee, Yr 23 (12–13 mm)	25	45.00	—
26	Several	Silv	1/2 Rupee, Yr 23 (15–16 mm)	30	40.00	—
27	125	Silv	1 Rupee, Yr 23 (18–21 mm)	30	40.00	—

Anonymous Issues

Y#	KM#	Metal	Description	VF	EF	Unc
28	142	Cop	1/2 Paisa, VS 1926 (1869) (3 g)	20	—	—
29	143	Cop	1 Paisa, VS 1926 (6 g)	20	—	—

Note: Y28–29 were struck from 1869–1899 with no change of date.

Madhao Rao II, AH 1302–1345 (1886–1925)

Obverse: ***Like Y27***
Reverse: ***Similar but Nagari "M" for Madho***

Y#	KM#	Metal	Description	VF	EF	Unc
30	156	Silv	1/8 Rupee, Yr 23	18	32.50	—
31	157	Silv	1/4 Rupee, Yr 23	25	45.00	—
32	158	Silv	1/2 Rupee, Yr 23	30	40.00	—
33	159	Silv	1 Rupee, Yr 23	30	40.00	—

Ujjain Mint

Jayaji Rao, AH 1259–1302 (1843–1886)

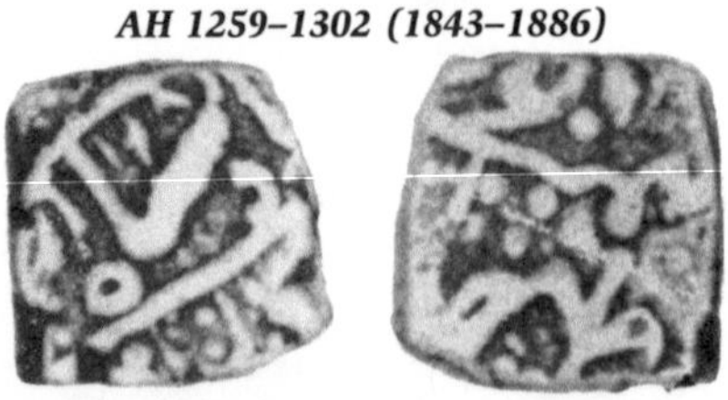

Obverse: ***Shah Alam II legend***

Y#	KM#	Metal	Description	VF	EF	Unc
35	22	Cop	1 Paisa, AH 1272–95	7.50	—	—

Madhao Rao II, AH 1302–1345 (1886–1925)

Obverse: ***Shah Alam II legend***

Y#	KM#	Metal	Description	VF	EF	Unc
36	239	Silv	1/16 Rupee, AH 1312, 13 (8–9 mm)	15	30.00	—
37	240	Silv	1/8 Rupee, AH 1310, 12 (9–10 mm)	18	32.50	—
38	241	Silv	1/4 Rupee, AH 1310–14 (12–13 mm)	25	45.00	—
39	242	Silv	1/2 Rupee, AH 1310–14 (14–15 mm)	30	40.00	—
40	245	Silv	1 Rupee, AH 1310–14 (18–20 mm)	30	40.00	—

MACHINE-STRUCK ISSUES

Madho Rao II, *VS 1943–1982 (1886–1925)*

First Coinage

Y#	KM#	Metal	Description	VF	EF	Unc
41	A161	Cop	1 Pai, VS 1946 (1889) (14 mm)	—	—	—
42	162	Cop	1/2 Paisa, VS 1946 (20 mm)	1,000	—	—
43	165	Cop	1/4 Anna, VS 1944–46 (25 mm)	200	350	—
44	173	Cop	1/2 Anna, VS 1946 (31 mm)	350	450	—

Y#	KM#	Metal	Description	VF	EF	Unc
A45	161	Cop	1 Pai, VS (19)55 (1898)	—	—	—
45	164	Cop	1/2 Paisa, VS 1956–58 (1899–1901)	2.00	4	40
46	169	Cop	1/4 Anna, VS 1953–57	2.50	5	30

Y#	KM#	Metal	Description	VF	EF	Unc
A47	174	Silv	1 Rupee, VS 1954 (1897)	4,000	6,000	—

Obverse: ***Bust to right***
Reverse: ***State arms***

Y#	KM#	Metal	Description	VF	EF	Unc
47	175	Gold	1/3 Mohur, VS 1959 (1902) (3.4 g)	3,000	4,750	6,500

Second Coinage

Y#	KM#	Metal	Description	VF	EF	Unc
48	170	Cop	1/4 Anna, VS 1970 (1913), thick	6.50	15	30
48a	171	Cop	1/4 Anna, VS 1970, 74, thin	6.50	15	30

JIVAJI RAO III,
VS 1982–2005 (1925–1948)

Obverse: ***Young bust***

Y#	KM#	Metal	Description	VF	EF	Unc
49	176.2	Cop	1/4 Anna, VS 1986 (1929), thick	6.50	25	50
49a	177	Cop	1/4 Anna, VS 1986, 99, thin	7.50	30	65

Obverse: ***Older bust***

Y#	KM#	Metal	Description	VF	EF	Unc
50	178	Cop	1/4 Anna, VS 1999 (1942)	6.50	25	50

Y#	KM#	Metal	Description	VF	EF	Unc
51	179	Br	1/2 Anna, VS 1999	6.50	15	30

LOCAL ISSUES
DOHAD *(DAHOD)*

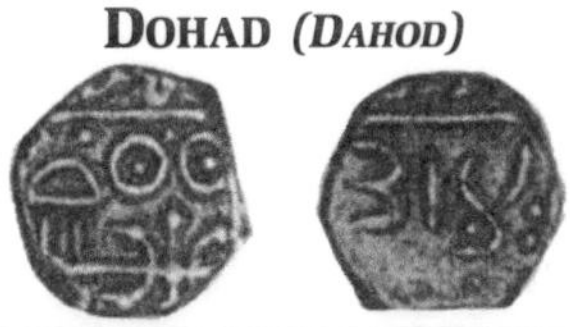

Y#	KM#	Metal	Description	VF	EF	Unc
A1	49	Cop	1/3 Paisa, VS 1912 (1855)	15	30	—
1	50	Cop	1 Paisa, VS 1912 (6.4 g)	25	40	—

JAWAD
JAYAJI RAO,
AH 1259–1302 (1843–1886)

Obverse: ***Snake, other symbols, Nagari "Ji"***

Y#	KM#	Metal	Description	VF	EF	Unc
1	N/A	Cop	1 Paisa, ND	15	35	—

MADHO RAO,
AH 1302–1345 (1886–1925)

Obverse: ***Like Y1 but Nagari "M"***
Reverse: ***Similar to Y1***

Y#	KM#	Metal	Description	VF	EF	Unc
2	110	Cop	1 Paisa, ND	20	45	—

MANDISOR
JAYAJI RAO,
VS 1900–1943 (1843–1886)

Mintmark: ***Trident***

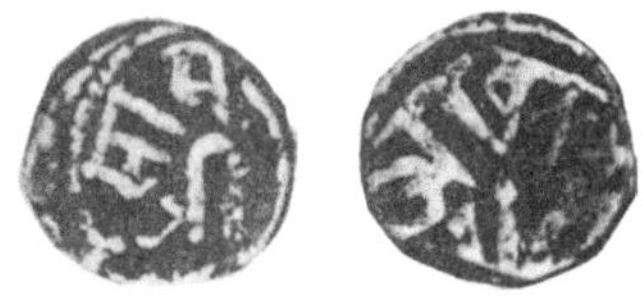

Obverse: ***Nagari "Ji" in circular legend***
Reverse: ***Trisul and date***

Y#	KM#	Metal	Description	VF	EF	Unc
1	180–181	Cop	1 Paisa, VS 1937 (1880)	12	—	—

Note: Varieties exist, sometimes with a retrograde legend.

RAJOD

Mintmarks: Trefoil, yoni (female symbol), or snake at right on obverse

Obverse: ***Hanuman (monkey god), trefoil at right***
Reverse: ***Date/Rajod***

Y#	KM#	Metal	Description	VF	EF	Unc
1	N/A	Cop	1 Paisa, VS 1930 (1873)	35	110	—

Design: ***Like Y1 but obverse yoni at right***

Y#	KM#	Metal	Description	VF	EF	Unc
A2	N/A	Cop	1/2 Paisa, VS 1936 (1879)	17.50	—	—
2	N/A	Cop	1 Paisa, VS 1936 (1879)	25.00	—	—

Design: ***Like Y1 but obverse snake at right***

Y#	KM#	Metal	Description	VF	EF	Unc
3	N/A	Cop	1 Paisa, VS 1940 (1883)	25	—	—

INDIA–PRINCELY STATES: HYDERABAD

AFZAL AD-DAULA,
AH 1273–1285 (1857–1869)

Early issues of this reign are listed in Craig, *Coins of the World*.

Design: ***Like Y11 but crude***

Y#	KM#	Metal	Description	VF	EF	Unc
1	1	Cop	1 Paisa, (Dub) AH 1282–83	15	—	—

Y#	KM#	Metal	Description	VF	EF	Unc
2	2	Silv	1/16 Rupee, AH 1275 (9 mm)	40	80	—
3	3	Silv	1/8 Rupee, AH 1278–79 (11–13 mm)	30	60	—
4	4	Silv	1/4 Rupee, AH 1276–83 (15–16 mm)	35	70	—
5	5	Silv	1/2 Rupee, AH 1275–85 (19–20 mm)	75	150	—
6	6	Silv	1 Rupee, AH 1275–85 (22–25 mm)	20	35	—

Obverse: ***Asaf Jah legend (dynastic founder), Persian "A" (for "Afzal") in center***
Reverse: ***Mint-date legend***

Y#	KM#	Metal	Description	VF	EF	Unc
8	8	Gold	1/8 Mohur, AH 1279–81 (11 mm)	300	500	—
9	9	Gold	1/4 Mohur, AH 1281 (14 mm)	500	750	—
10	10	Gold	1/2 Mohur, AH 1281 (16 mm)	225	350	625
11	11	Gold	1 Mohur, AH 1275–85 (22 mm)	500	850	—

MIR MAHBUB ALI KHAN II, *AH 1285–1329 (1869–1911)*

FIRST COINAGE

Design: ***Like Y16 but crude***

Y#	KM#	Metal	Description	VF	EF	Unc
12	12	Cop	1 Paisa, (Dub) AH 1289–1313 (1872–95)	10	—	—

Designs: ***Like Y11 but Persian "M" for Mahbub in center***

Y#	KM#	Metal	Description	VF	EF	Unc
13	13	Silv	1/16 Rupee, AH 1299–1321 (1882–1903) (7–9 mm)	50.00	100	200
14	14	Silv	1/8 Rupee, AH 1286–1321 (10–13 mm)	12.50	20	75
15	15	Silv	1/4 Rupee, AH 1286–1321 (13–16 mm)	25.00	35	125
16	16	Silv	1/2 Rupee, AH 1286–1317 (17–19 mm)	25.00	35	125
17	17	Silv	1 Rupee, AH 1286–1318 (22–24 mm)	25.00	35	125

Y#	KM#	Metal	Description	VF	EF	Unc
18	18	Gold	1/16 Mohur, AH 1305–21 (7 mm)	400	600	—
19	19	Gold	1/8 Mohur, AH 1293–1321 (10 mm)	350	550	—
20	20	Gold	1/4 Mohur, AH 1301–19 (14 mm)	300	400	—
21	21	Gold	1/2 Mohur, AH 1316–21 (17 mm)	400	600	—
22	22	Gold	1 Mohur, 1 AH 286–1321 (22 mm)	400	550	800

SECOND COINAGE

Machine-struck silver coins dated AH 1305–1307 and copper coins dated 1312–1316 are believed to be patterns.

Obverse: ***Asaf Jah legend***
Reverse: ***Mint-date legend***

Y#	KM#	Metal	Description	VF	EF	Unc
29	29	Silv	2 Annas, AH 1318 (1900) (15 mm)	50	100	—
30	30	Silv	4 Annas, AH 1318 (19 mm)	90	125	—
31	31	Silv	8 Annas, AH 1312, 18 (24 mm)	150	250	—
32	32	Silv	1 Rupee, AH 1312–18 (30 mm)	35	55	175
33	33	Gold	1 Ashrafi (Mohur), AH 1311 / Yr 27 (24 mm)	3,000	4,500	—

THIRD COINAGE

Obverse: ***Persian "M" for Mahbub in loop of toughra***

Y#	KM#	Metal	Description	VF	EF	Unc
34	34	Cop	1 Pai, AH 1326–29 (1908–11)	5	10	35
35	35	Cop	2 Pai, AH 1320–29	6	12	40
36	36	Cop	1/2 Anna, AH 1320–29	8	15	50

Obverse: ***Persian "M" in doorway***

Y#	KM#	Metal	Description	VF	EF	Unc
37	37	Silv	2 Annas, AH 1323 (15 mm)	25	—	—
38	38	Silv	4 Annas, AH 1323–29 (20 mm)	25	—	—
39	39	Silv	8 Annas, AH 1322–29 (24 mm)	75	—	—
40	40	Silv	1 Rupee, AH 1319–29 (30 mm)	20	25	50

Y#	KM#	Metal	Description	VF	EF	Unc
41	41	Gold	1/8 Ashrafi, AH 1325, 29	300	500	750
42	42	Gold	1/4 Ashrafi, AH 1325–29	500	750	1,100
43	43	Gold	1/2 Ashrafi, AH 1325–29	700	1,000	1,500
44	44	Gold	1 Ashrafi, AH 1325–29	1,000	1,500	2,000

MIR USMAN ALI KHAN,
AH 1329–1367 (1911–1948)

FIRST COINAGE

Design: *Like Y46a*
Obverse: *Short initial "Ain" (Persian letter) in loop of toughra*

Y#	KM#	Metal	Description	VF	EF	Unc
46	46	Bz	2 Pai, AH 1329–30	20	—	—

Obverse: *Short initial "Ain" in doorway*

Y#	KM#	Metal	Description	VF	EF	Unc
53	53	Silv	1 Rupee, AH 1330	40	—	—

Obverse: *Short initial "Ain" in loop of toughra*

Y#	KM#	Metal	Description	VF	EF	Unc
54	54.1	Gold	1/8 Ashrafi, AH 1329	—	—	—
56	56.1	Gold	1/2 Ashrafi, AH 1329	1,500	2,000	—
57	57	Gold	1 Ashrafi, AH 1329–30	1,000	1,250	2,750

SECOND COINAGE

Obverse: *Full initial "Ain" in loop of toughra*

Y#	KM#	Metal	Description	VF	EF	Unc
45	45	Bz	1 Pai, AH 1338–53	3.00	7	25
46a	46a	Bz	2 Pai, AH 1330–49	2.50	5	25
47	47	Bz	1/2 Anna, AH 1332–48	5.00	10	34

Y#	KM#	Metal	Description	VF	EF	Unc
48	48	C-N	1 Anna, AH 1338–54	2.50	5	25

Y#	KM#	Metal	Description	VF	EF	Unc
49	49	C-N	1 Anna, AH 1356–61, square	2.50	5	25

Obverse: *Full initial "Ain" in doorway*

Y#	KM#	Metal	Description	VF	EF	Unc
50	50	Silv	2 Annas, AH 1335–55	13	20	—
51	51	Silv	4 Annas, AH 1337–58	13	20	—
52	52	Silv	8 Annas, AH 1337–54	30	50	—
53a	53a	Silv	1 Rupee, AH 1330–43	15	20	30

Obverse: *Full initial "Ain" in doorway*

Y#	KM#	Metal	Description	VF	EF	Unc
54a	54.2	Gold	1/8 Ashrafi, AH 1337–54	300	425	600
55a	55	Gold	1/4 Ashrafi, AH 1337–57	375	600	800
56a	56.2	Gold	1/2 Ashrafi, AH 1337–57	650	975	1,300
57a	57a	Gold	1 Ashrafi, AH 1331–54	750	1,100	1,650

THIRD COINAGE

Y#	KM#	Metal	Description	VF	EF	Unc
58	58	Bz	2 Pai, AH 1362–68 (1943–49)	0.25	—	—

Y#	KM#	Metal	Description	VF	EF	Unc
59	59	Bz	1 Anna, AH 1361–68, square	2.50	5	25

Y#	KM#	Metal	Description	VF	EF	Unc
60	60	Silv	2 Annas, AH 1362 (15 mm)	20.00	30.00	—
61	61	Silv	4 Annas, AH 1362–65 (20 mm)	6.50	12.50	—
62	62	Silv	8 Annas, AH 1363 (24 mm)	20.00	30.00	—
63	63	Silv	1 Rupee, AH 1361–65 (30 mm)	15.00	20.00	20

Y#	KM#	Metal	Description	VF	EF	Unc
64	64	Nick	2 Annas, AH 1366, 68 (1947, 49)	3	7.50	—
65	65	Nick	4 Annas, AH 1366, 68	6	10.00	—
66	66	Nick	8 Annas, AH 1366	20	30.00	—

INDIA–PRINCELY STATES: INDORE

Dating System: Most coins bear Vikrama dates (VS = AD + 57); exceptions use Saka dates (Saka + 78 = AD) or Fasli Era Dates (FE + 590 = AD).

Tukoji Rao II, *VS 1901–1943 (1844–1886)*

First Coinage

Design: ***Like Y3***

Y#	KM#	Metal	Description	VF	EF	Unc
1	10	Cop	1/2 Paisa (1/2 Mudra), Saka 1780, 88 (1858, 66)	350	700	—
2	11	Cop	1 Paisa (Mudra), Saka 1780, 88	525	900	—

Y#	KM#	Metal	Description	VF	EF	Unc
3	15	Silv	1 Rupee, Saka 1780, 88 (1858, 66)	275	550	—

Note: Y1–3 dated Saka 1788 also bear the VS date 1923.

Obverse: ***Like Y3***
Reverse: ***Similar, but sword and lance below surface***

Y#	KM#	Metal	Description	VF	EF	Unc
4	19	Silv	1 Rupee, FE 1287 / VS 1934 (1877)	275	550	—

Obverse: ***Sword and lance / date***

Y#	KM#	Metal	Description	VF	EF	Unc
5	21	Silv	1/2 Rupee, FE 1289	450	—	—
6	24–25	Silv	1 Rupee, FE 1289, 95	65	95	—

Obverse: ***Nagari legend***
Reverse: ***Sun in splendor and date***

Y#	KM#	Metal	Description	VF	EF	Unc
A7	27	Gold	1 Mohur, VS 1941 (1883)	5,000	—	—

Second Coinage

Obverse: ***Bull***
Reverse: ***Sun-face***
Planchets: ***Dump***

Y#	KM#	Metal	Description	VF	EF	Unc
7	12	Cop	1/2 Anna, VS 1942 (1885) (12 g)	1,150	1,875	—

Obverse: ***Seated bull***
Reverse: ***Legend***
Planchets: ***Machine-struck***

Y#	KM#	Metal	Description	VF	EF	Unc
8	13	Cop	1/2 Anna, VS 1942 (1885) (13 g)	2,500	4,850	—

Shivaji Rao, *VS 1943–1960 (1886–1903)*

Obverse: ***Without ruler's name***

Y#	KM#	Metal	Description	VF	EF	Unc
9	30	Cop	1/2 Paisa, VS 1944 (21 mm)	50	75	—
10	32	Cop	1/4 Anna, VS 1943–45 (25 mm)	5	—	—
11	34	Cop	1/2 Anna, VS 1943–44 (31 mm)	6	—	—

Obverse: ***Shivaji Rao legend***

Y#	KM#	Metal	Description	VF	EF	Unc
9a	31	Cop	1/2 Paisa, VS 1946 (1889)	25	—	—
10a	33	Cop	1/4 Anna, VS 1944–59	20	—	—
11a	35	Cop	1/2 Anna, VS 1944–59	15	25	75

Note: Y9–11a occur in several minor varieties, differing in arrangement of legends.

Obverse: ***Shah Alam II legend***
Reverse: ***Like Y4***

Y#	KM#	Metal	Description	VF	EF	Unc
12	37	Silv	1/4 Rupee, FE 1295 / VS 1945 (1888)	40	—	—
13	38	Silv	1/2 Rupee, FE 1295–96 / VS 1946–47	35	—	—
14	39	Silv	1 Rupee, FE 1294–97 / VS 1945–47	33	—	—

Obverse: ***Shah Alam II legend in wreath***
Reverse: ***Sunface***

Y#	KM#	Metal	Description	VF	EF	Unc
15	41	Silv	1/8 Rupee, VS 1947–51 (10 mm)	15	25	—
16	42	Silv	1/4 Rupee, VS 1947–54 (12 mm)	25	35	—
17	43	Silv	1/2 Rupee, VS 1947–54 (16 mm)	15	25	—
18	44	Silv	1 Rupee, VS 1947–55 (22 mm)	25	35	—

Y#	KM#	Metal	Description	VF	EF	Unc
19	47	Silv	1 Rupee, VS 1956, 58 (1889, 1901)	1,250	2,500	—

YESHWANT RAO, *VS 1983–2005 (1926–1948)*

Y#	KM#	Metal	Description	VF	EF	Unc
20	49	Cop	1/4 Anna, VS 1992 (1935)	5	10	50
21	50	Cop	1/2 Anna, VS 1992	10	15	60

INDIA–PRINCELY STATES: JAIPUR

RAM SINGH, *1835–1880*

For pre-Victorian coins of this reign, see Craig, *Coins of the World.*

Obverse: ***Queen Victoria legend***
Reverse: ***Ram Singh legend***
Planchets: ***Dump***

Y#	KM#	Metal	Description	VF	EF	Unc
1	105	Cop	1 Paisa, Yrs 36–45 (17–20 mm) (6 g)	13	—	—

Planchets: ***Broad and thick***

Y#	KM#	Metal	Description	VF	EF	Unc
1a	106	Cop	1 Paisa, 1858–65 / Yrs 23–30 (28 mm)	200	—	—

Planchets: ***Broad and thin***

Y#	KM#	Metal	Description	VF	EF	Unc
1b	107	Cop	1 Paisa, 1872–80 / Yrs 37–45	95	225	—

Designs: ***Like Y1***
Planchets: ***Dump***

Y#	KM#	Metal	Description	VF	EF	Unc
3	110	Silv	1/8 Rupee, Yrs 23–42 (14 mm)	35	65	—
4	111	Silv	1/4 Rupee, Yrs 23–44 (15–17 mm)	25	55	—
5	115	Silv	1/2 Rupee, Yrs 23–45 (18–20 mm)	55	95	—
6	119	Silv	1 Rupee, Yrs 23–45 (21–23 mm)	35	65	—

Planchets: ***Broad and thin***

Y#	KM#	Metal	Description	VF	EF	Unc
6a	120	Silv	1 Rupee, 1858–75 / Yrs 23–40 (27–29 mm)	125	175	—

Y#	KM#	Metal	Description	VF	EF	Unc
A7	N/A	Gold	1/2 Mohur, Yr 23	550	750	—
7	125	Gold	1 Mohur, Yrs 23–45 (18–20 mm)	550	750	—

Planchets: ***Broad and thin***

Y#	KM#	Metal	Description	VF	EF	Unc
7a	N/A	Gold	1 Mohur, 1870 / Yr 35	7,500	—	—

MADHO SINGH II, *1880–1922*

Obverse: ***Queen Victoria legend***
Reverse: ***Madho Singh legend***
Planchets: ***Dump***

Y#	KM#	Metal	Description	VF	EF	Unc
8	130	Cop	1 Paisa, Yrs 2–42 (16–20 mm)	5.50	—	—

Planchets: ***Broad and thin***

Y#	KM#	Metal	Description	VF	EF	Unc
8a	132	Cop	1 Paisa, 1880–1918 / Yrs 1–37 (32–36 mm)	55	90	—

Designs: ***Like Y8***
Planchets: ***Dump***

Y#	KM#	Metal	Description	VF	EF	Unc
9	135	Silv	1/16 Rupee, Yrs 2–33 (10 mm)	30	55	—
10	137	Silv	1/8 Rupee, Yrs 4–42 (13 mm)	30	55	—
11	139	Silv	1/4 Rupee, Yrs 1–42 (16 mm)	25	45	—
12	142	Silv	1/2 Rupee, Yrs 1–37 (18 mm)	25	45	—
13	145	Silv	1 Rupee, Yrs 1–43 (21 mm)	25	45	—

Planchets: ***Broad and thin***

Y#	KM#	Metal	Description	VF	EF	Unc
13a	146	Silv	1 Rupee, Yrs 1–5, plain borders (30–31 mm)	45	70	135
13b	147	Silv	1 Rupee, Yrs 5–42, wreath borders (36–37 mm)	60	100	175

Planchets: ***Dump***

Y#	KM#	Metal	Description	VF	EF	Unc
14	150	Gold	1 Mohur, Yrs 2–41 (18 mm)	475	750	—

Planchets: ***Broad and thin***

Y#	KM#	Metal	Description	VF	EF	Unc
14a	151	Gold	1 Mohur, 1880–91 / Yrs 1–12 (29–36 mm)	—	17,000	—

MAN SINGH II, *1922–1949*

FIRST COINAGE

IN THE NAME OF GEORGE V, 1922–1935

Planchets: ***Round and thin***

Y#	KM#	Metal	Description	VF	EF	Unc
15	155	Cop	1 Paisa, 1922–35 / Yrs 1–14	45	65	—

Planchets: ***Dump***

Y#	KM#	Metal	Description	VF	EF	Unc
A15	158	Silv	1 Rupee, 1922–25 / Yrs 1–4	45	70	150

Planchets: ***Broad and thin***

Y#	KM#	Metal	Description	VF	EF	Unc
B15	159	Silv	1 Rupee, 1922–32 / Yrs 1–11	95	150	275

Planchets: ***Dump***

Y#	KM#	Metal	Description	VF	EF	Unc
C15	163	Gold	1 Mohur, Yrs 2–7	650	850	—

SECOND COINAGE

IN THE NAME OF EDWARD VIII, 1936

Planchets: ***Round and thin***

Y#	KM#	Metal	Description	VF	EF	Unc
D15	167	Cop	1 Paisa, 1936 / Yr 15	100	150	—

Planchets: ***Round and thin***

Y#	KM#	Metal	Description	VF	EF	Unc
E15	170	Silv	1 Rupee, 1936 / Yr 15	—	—	—

THIRD COINAGE

Obverse: ***George VI legend***
Reverse: ***Man Singh legend***
Planchets: ***Round and thin***

Y#	KM#	Metal	Description	VF	EF	Unc
16	175–176	Cop	1/2 Paisa, Yrs 21–23 (17 mm)	2.50	—	—

Planchets: ***Dump***

Y#	KM#	Metal	Description	VF	EF	Unc
17	180	Cop	1 Paisa, 1937–49 / Yrs 16–28 (32 mm)	35	65	—

Y#	KM#	Metal	Description	VF	EF	Unc
18	185–187	Br	1 Anna, 1943–44	5	10	30

Y#	KM#	Metal	Description	VF	EF	Unc
19	188	Br	1 Anna, 1944	15	30	50

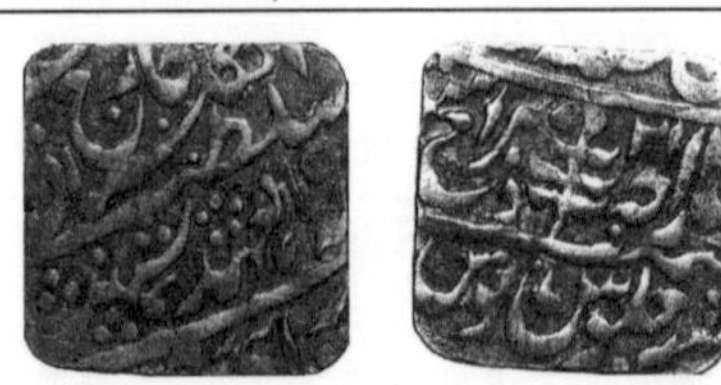

Y#	KM#	Metal	Description	VF	EF	Unc
20	190	Br	2 Annas, 1942 / Yr 21, square	20	45	—

Planchets: ***Broad and thin***

Y#	KM#	Metal	Description	VF	EF	Unc
21	N/A	Silv	1 Rupee, Yrs 17–28, plain borders (27–30 mm)	125	175	—
21a	196	Silv	1 Rupee, Yrs 18–28, borders as Y13b (37–38 mm)	100	150	—

Planchets: ***Dump***

Y#	KM#	Metal	Description	VF	EF	Unc
22	200	Gold	1 Mohur, Yrs 20–28 (19–21 mm)	650	1,000	—

Planchets: ***Broad and thin***

Y#	KM#	Metal	Description	VF	EF	Unc
23	201	Gold	1 Mohur, 1949 / Yr 28	—	—	25,000

INDIA–PRINCELY STATES: JAISALMIR

Obverse: *Queen Victoria legend*
Reverse: *Degenerate mint-date legend*

Y#	KM#	Metal	Description	VF	EF	Unc
1	17	Silv	1/8 Rupee, Yr 22 (12 mm)	15	—	—
2	18	Silv	1/4 Rupee, Yr 22	55	—	—
3	19	Silv	1/2 Rupee, Yr 22 (18 mm)	75	—	—
4	21	Silv	1 Rupee, Yr 22	25	—	—
4a	21b	Silv	1 Rupee, Yr 22, square	125	275	—
A4	22	Silv	1-1/2 Rupee, Yr 22 (40 mm)	800	—	—

Obverse: *Like Y1–4a*
Reverse: *Similar mintmarks, bird and umbrella added*

Y#	KM#	Metal	Description	VF	EF	Unc
5	31	Silv	1/8 Rupee, Yr 22	15	—	—
6	32	Silv	1/4 Rupee, Yr 22 (14–15 mm)	55	—	—
7	33	Silv	1/2 Rupee, Yr 22 (17–19 mm)	50	—	—
8	34	Silv	1 Rupee, Yr 22 (20–23 mm)	25	—	—
8a	34a	Silv	1 Rupee, Yr 22, square	250	375	—
A8	35	Silv	2 Rupees, Yr 22 (40 mm)	900	—	—

Y#	KM#	Metal	Description	VF	EF	Unc
9	37	Gold	1/8 Mohur, Yr 22	200	275	—
10	38	Gold	1/4 Mohur, Yr 22 (reported, not confirmed)			
11	39	Gold	1/2 Mohur, Yr 22 (reported, not confirmed)			
12	40	Gold	1 Mohur, Yr 22	4,000	5,000	—

INDIA–PRINCELY STATES: JAMMU (KASHMIR)

Ranbir Singh, *VS 1914–1942 (1857–1885)*
Pertab Singh, *VS 1942–1982 (1885–1925)*

Obverse: *Mint legend in Persian, leaf mintmark*
Reverse: *Gurmukhi legend*

Y#	KM#	Metal	Description	VF	EF	Unc
1	1.1–1.2	Cop	1 Paisa, VS 1914–22, var, (7 g)	10	—	—

Obverse: *Like Y1*
Reverse: *Takari legend*
Planchets: *Round and machine made*

Y#	KM#	Metal	Description	VF	EF	Unc
2	2	Cop	1/2 Paisa, VS 1935–49 (3 g)	20	—	—

Planchets: *Thin dump*

Y#	KM#	Metal	Description	VF	EF	Unc
2a	2a	Cop	1/2 Paisa, VS 1935–36 (1878–79) (15 mm)	5	—	—

Obverse: *Three-line Gurmukhi legend*
Reverse: *Mint and date in Persian, leaf within wreath*

Y#	KM#	Metal	Description	VF	EF	Unc
3	3	Gold	1/3 Mohur, VS 1921 (1864) (19 mm)	—	27,500	—

INDIA–PRINCELY STATES: JAORA

Muhammad Ismail, *AH 1282–1313 (1865–1895)*

Obverse: *Wheat, pennant / mint legend*
Reverse: *Date / Jaora legend*

Y#	KM#	Metal	Description	VF	EF	Unc
A1	4–5	Cop	1 Paisa, AH 1282–85	30	—	—

Obverse: *Without wheel*

Y#	KM#	Metal	Description	VF	EF	Unc
B1	7	Cop	1 Paisa, AH 1295	15	—	—

Y#	KM#	Metal	Description	VF	EF	Unc
1	10	Cop	1 Paisa, 1893–96	10	20	100
2	12	Cop	2 Paisa, 1893–94	15	30	150

Note: Y1–2 bear dates in three systems: AD dates on obverse, AH and VS dates on reverse. Overlapping dates and incorrect combinations exist.

INDIA–PRINCELY STATES: JHALAWAR

Prithvi Singh, *1847–1875*
Zalim Singh, *1875–1896*

Designs: *Like Y2a*
Planchets: *Rectangular, dump*

Y#	KM#	Metal	Description	VF	EF	Unc
1	1	Cop	1 Paisa, Yrs 2–5 (9 g)	35	—	—
2	2	Cop	1 Takka, Yrs 1–29 (18 g)	25	—	—

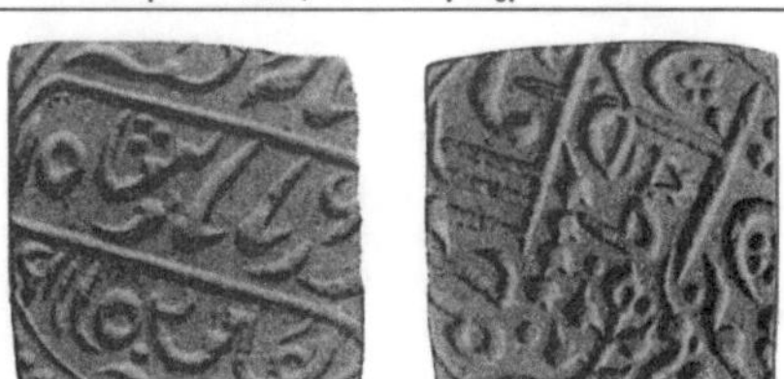

Obverse: *Queen Victoria legend*
Reverse: *Mint-date legend*
Planchets: *Broad and square*

Y#	KM#	Metal	Description	VF	EF	Unc
2a	C21	Cop	1 Takka, Yrs 9, 21	300	—	—

Designs: *Like Y2a*
Planchets: *Round, dump*

Y#	KM#	Metal	Description	VF	EF	Unc
3	3.1–3.2	Silv	1/8 Rupee, Yrs 5–38	65	250	—
4	4.1–4.2	Silv	1/4 Rupee, Yrs 7–38	50	200	—
5	5.1–5.2	Silv	1/2 Rupee, Yrs 1–38	75	300	700
6	6.1–6.2	Silv	1 Rupee, Yrs 1–41	20	30	—

Planchets: *Broad and thin*

Y#	KM#	Metal	Description	VF	EF	Unc
6a	6a/6c	Silv	1 Rupee, Yrs 2–40 (27–28 mm)	75	300	700
6b	6b	Silv	1 Rupee, Yrs 3, 15 (37–38 mm)	1,200	—	—

INDIA–PRINCELY STATES: JIND

Mintmarks: On reverse of Y1. Stylized "Sad" in Persian "S," quatrefoil at lower-right. Compare Maler-Kotla, Nabha, Patiala.

Raghbir Singh, *1864–1887*

Obverse: *Couplet of Ahmad Shah Durrani*
Reverse: *Mint-date legend, stylized "Sad"*
Planchets: *Dump*

Y#	KM#	Metal	Description	VF	EF	Unc
1	5	Silv	1 Rupee	120	200	—

Ranbir Singh, *VS 1943–2005 (1887–1948)*

50th Year of Reign

Obverse: *Like Y1*
Reverse: *Commemorative legend*
Planchets: *Broad and thin*

Y#	KM#	Metal	Description	VF	EF	Unc
2	N/A	Silv	1 Rupee, VS 1993 (1937) (30 mm)	500	750	—

INDIA–PRINCELY STATES: JODHPUR

Takhat Singh, *1843–1873*

First Coinage

Obverse: *Queen Victoria legend*
Reverse: *Takhat Singh legend*
Planchets: *Dump, and broad and thin*

Y#	KM#	Metal	Description	VF	EF	Unc
A1	N/A	Silv	1/4 Rupee	—	—	—
1	46	Silv	1 Rupee, Yrs 16, 22, 52, mint name on obverse	20	50	—
1a	56	Silv	1 Rupee, Yrs 16, 22, 52, mint name on reverse	20	50	—

Note: Y1 and 1a were struck at both Jodhpur and Sujat, but all bear the Jodhpur mint name.

Y#	KM#	Metal	Description	VF	EF	Unc
2	50	Gold	1 Mohur, Yr 22, like Y1	750	1,000	—

Second Coinage

Designs: *Like Y1a*
Reverse: *Nagari legend added*

Y#	KM#	Metal	Description	VF	EF	Unc
3	66	Silv	1 Rupee, Yr 22	25	60	—

Third Coinage

Obverse: *"Queen of India" legend*
Reverse: *Takhat Singh legend, mint name below*

Y#	KM#	Metal	Description	VF	EF	Unc
4	67	Silv	1 Rupee, VS 1926–28	25	60	—

Note: Mint names on Y4 are Jodhpur, Nagore, Pali, and Sujat.

Y#	KM#	Metal	Description	VF	EF	Unc
A4	70	Gold	1 Mohur, VS 1926	3,000	4,500	—

Jaswant Singh, *1873–1895*

Obverse: *Queen Victoria legend*
Reverse: *Victoria-mint legend*

Y#	KM#	Metal	Description	VF	EF	Unc
5	72	Cop	1 Takka, VS 1940–48 (ca 20 g)	10	—	—

Obverse: *Queen Victoria legend*
Reverse: *Jaswant Singh legend*

Y#	KM#	Metal	Description	VF	EF	Unc
6	73	Silv	1/8 Rupee, ND, Yr 22 (11 mm)	60	100	200
7	74	Silv	1/4 Rupee, ND, Yr 22	60	100	200
8	75	Silv	1/2 Rupee, VS 1944 (17 mm)	85	135	250
9	77	Silv	1 Rupee, VS 1929–50, Fasli, FE 1291–93 (19–22 mm)	100	175	300

Note: Mint names on the above coins are Jodhpur, Nagore, Pali, and Sujat.

Y#	KM#	Metal	Description	VF	EF	Unc
10	78	Gold	1/4 Mohur, FE 1293 (1876) (13 mm)	300	400	—
11	79	Gold	1/2 Mohur, FE 1293 (17–18 mm)	500	600	—
12	80	Gold	1 Mohur, FE 1293, VS 1943, 50 (20 mm)	800	1,000	—

Sardar Singh, 1895–1911

First Coinage

Obverse: *Queen Victoria legend*
Reverse: *Sardar Singh legend*

Y#	KM#	Metal	Description	VF	EF	Unc
13	83	Silv	1/8 Rupee, ND	45	—	—
14	84	Silv	1/4 Rupee, ND	45	—	—
15	85	Silv	1/2 Rupee, ND	75	—	—
16	86	Silv	1 Rupee, ND VS 1955–56	35	—	—

Y#	KM#	Metal	Description	VF	EF	Unc
17	88	Gold	1/4 Mohur, VS 1952 (1895) (15 mm)	400	650	—
18	89	Gold	1/2 Mohur, VS 1952 (18 mm)	600	850	—
19	90	Gold	1 Mohur, VS 1952 (21 mm)	850	1,000	—

Second Coinage

Obverse: *Edward VII legend*
Reverse: *Sardar Singh legend*

Y#	KM#	Metal	Description	VF	EF	Unc
20	91.1	Cop	1/4 Anna, 1901–10 (16 mm)	10	—	—
21	92	Cop	1/2 Anna, 1906, 08	20	—	—

Note: Error and blundered dates exist for Y20.

Y#	KM#	Metal	Description	VF	EF	Unc
A22	93	Silv	1/8 Rupee, ND	45	—	—
22	94	Silv	1/4 Rupee, VS 1965 (1908) (19 mm)	50	—	—
A23	95	Silv	1/2 Rupee, ND	75	—	—

Y#	KM#	Metal	Description	VF	EF	Unc
23	98	Gold	1/4 Mohur, 1906 (13 mm)	400	650	—
24	99	Gold	1/2 Mohur, 1906 (18 mm)	600	850	—
25	100	Gold	1 Mohur, 1906 (20 mm)	850	1,000	—

Sumar Singh, 1911–1918

First Coinage

Obverse: *Edward VII legend*
Reverse: *Sumar Singh legend*

Y#	KM#	Metal	Description	VF	EF	Unc
26	119	Gold	1/2 Mohur, ND 1911	600	850	—
A26	120	Gold	1 Mohur, ND 1911	850	1,000	—

Second Coinage

Obverse: *George V legend*
Reverse: *Sumer Singh legend*

Y#	KM#	Metal	Description	VF	EF	Unc
27	110	Cop	1/4 Anna, 1911, 14 (16–18 mm)	15	—	—
28	112	Cop	1/2 Anna, 1914, 18 (25 mm)	50	—	—

Y#	KM#	Metal	Description	VF	EF	Unc
29	113	Silv	1/8 Rupee, ND (13 mm)	50	100	350
30	114	Silv	1/4 Rupee, ND (14 mm)	50	100	350
31	115	Silv	1/2 Rupee, ND (18 mm)	50	100	350
32	116	Silv	1 Rupee, ND (21 mm)	75	150	400

Y#	KM#	Metal	Description	VF	EF	Unc
A33	N/A	Gold	1/4 Mohur, ND	400	650	—
33	120	Gold	1 Mohur, ND (18 mm)	850	1,000	—

Umaid Singh, 1918–1947

First Coinage

Coinage of copper was stopped from 1914 until 1936.

Obverse: *George V legend*
Reverse: *Umaid Singh legend*

Y#	KM#	Metal	Description	VF	EF	Unc
35	124	Silv	1/4 Rupee, ND	175	275	—

Y#	KM#	Metal	Description	VF	EF	Unc
36	127	Gold	1/4 Mohur, ND (16 mm)	350	500	—
37	128	Gold	1/2 Mohur, ND (18 mm)	500	750	—
38	130	Gold	1 Mohur, ND (18–20 mm)	800	1,000	—

Second Coinage

Obverse: *Edward VIII legend*
Reverse: *Umaid Singh legend*

Y#	KM#	Metal	Description	VF	EF	Unc
39	131	Cop	1/4 Anna, 1936	7.50	—	—

Y#	KM#	Metal	Description	VF	EF	Unc
A39	N/A	Gold	1/2 Mohur, ND, 1936	950	1,200	—
B39	140	Gold	1 Mohur, ND, 1936 (reported, not confirmed)			

Third Coinage

Obverse: ***George VI legend***
Reverse: ***Umaid Singh legend***

Y#	KM#	Metal	Description	VF	EF	Unc
40	141	Cop	1/4 Anna, 1937–39, VS 1996, thick (10 g)	5.00	7.50	—
41	143	Cop	1/4 Anna, VS 2000–02, thin (3 g)	2.50	5.00	—

Y#	KM#	Metal	Description	VF	EF	Unc
42	150	Gold	1 Mohur, ND (18 mm)	750	1,100	—

Hanwant Singh, *1947*

Obverse: ***George VI legend***
Reverse: ***Hanwant Singh legend***

Y#	KM#	Metal	Description	VF	EF	Unc
43	152	Cop	1/4 Anna, ND (16 mm)	50	—	—

Y#	KM#	Metal	Description	VF	EF	Unc
A44	158	Gold	1/4 Mohur, ND	1,000	1,350	—
44	160	Gold	1 Mohur, ND (18 mm)	650	900	—

India–Princely States: JUNAGADH

Mahabat Khan II, *1851–1882*

Early issues of this reign are continuations of older anonymous types.

Obverse: ***Mahabat Khan legend***
Reverse: ***Value-mint legend***

Y#	KM#	Metal	Description	VF	EF	Unc
1	27	Cop	1 Dokdo, VS 1931, 35 (1874, 78)	90	150	250

Y#	KM#	Metal	Description	VF	EF	Unc
A2	29	Silv	1/2 Kori, AH 1293–99 / VS 1934–38 (1876–82)	15	25	—
2	30	Silv	1 Kori, AH 1292–99 / VS 1932–38 (1875–82)	15	25	—

Y#	KM#	Metal	Description	VF	EF	Unc
3	34	Gold	1 Kori, AH 1292 / VS 1932 (1875), milled	5,000	7,000	—

Bahadur Khan III, *1882–1891*

Y#	KM#	Metal	Description	VF	EF	Unc
4	39	Gold	1/2 Kori, AH 1309 / VS 1947 (1891)	4,500	5,500	6,500
5	41	Gold	1 Kori, AH 1309 / VS 1947 (18 mm)	3,000	4,000	6,000

Rasal Khan, *1891–1911*

Y#	KM#	Metal	Description	VF	EF	Unc
6	43–45	Cop	1 Dokdo, ND, VS 1963–67 (1906–10) (vars)	5	—	—

Y#	KM#	Metal	Description	VF	EF	Unc
7	48	Cop	2 Dokda, VS 1964	45	65	—

Y#	KM#	Metal	Description	VF	EF	Unc
8	52	Silv	1 Kori, VS 1966 (15 mm)	45	70	—

Y#	KM#	Metal	Description	VF	EF	Unc
A8	56	Gold	1 Kori, AH 1309 / VS 1948 (1891) (4.77 g)	—	—	5,000
A8a	57	Gold	1 Kori, AH 1318 / VS 1956 (1899)	—	—	5,000
A8b	58	Gold	1 Kori, AH 1325 / VS 1963 (1906) (4.62 g)	—	—	7,500
B8	60	Gold	1 Mohur, AH 1325 / VS 1963 (1906) (11.54 g)	—	—	8,000

Mahabat Khan III, *1911–1948*

Y#	KM#	Metal	Description	VF	EF	Unc
9	63	Cop	1 Dokdo, VS 1985, 90	200	—	—

INDIA–PRINCELY STATES: KALAT (QALAT)

Khudadad Khan, Second Reign, *AH 1281–1311 (1864–1893)*

Obverse: *Mahmud Khan legend*
Reverse: *Mint legend*

Y#	KM#	Metal	Description	VF	EF	Unc
1	21	Cop	1 Falus, AH 1186 (error), AH 1281–96	55	—	—

INDIA–PRINCELY STATES: KARAULI

Madan Pal, *1853–1869*

Most coins of this reign are dated 1852 (error for 1859).

Y#	KM#	Metal	Description	VF	EF	Unc
1	36	Cop	1 Paisa, 1852 / Yr 13	20	—	—

Obverse: *Queen Victoria legend*

Y#	KM#	Metal	Description	VF	EF	Unc
2	42	Silv	1/4 Rupee, 1852–59 / Yrs 7–14	30	75	—
3	43	Silv	1/2 Rupee, 1852–59 / Yrs 7–14	100	—	—
4	44	Silv	1 Rupee, 1852–59 / Yrs 7–14	30	75	—

Arjun Pal, *1875–1886*

Y#	KM#	Metal	Description	VF	EF	Unc
5	49	Cop	1/2 Paisa, 1886 / Yr 11 (4.5 g)	25	—	—
6	50	Cop	1 Paisa, 1886 / Yr 11 (9 g)	10	—	—
7	51	Cop	1 Takka, 1881–86 / Yrs 9–11 (18 g)	10	—	—

Obverse: *Empress Victoria legend*
Reverse: *Nagari A (rjun)*

Y#	KM#	Metal	Description	VF	EF	Unc
8	56	Silv	1 Rupee, 1882–86 / Yrs 7–11	30	—	—

Bhanwar Pal, *1886–1927*

Y#	KM#	Metal	Description	VF	EF	Unc
9	61	Cop	1 Paisa, 1886–91 / Yrs 1–5 (9 g)	15	—	—
10	62	Cop	1 Takka, 1886–93 / Yrs 1–8 (18 g)	10	—	—

Obverse: *Like Y8*
Reverse: *Nagari BH (anwar)*

Y#	KM#	Metal	Description	VF	EF	Unc
A11	66	Silv	1/8 Rupee, ND, Yr 5	65	—	—
11	68	Silv	1/4 Rupee, 1893, 96 / Yrs 8, 11	65	—	—
12	69	Silv	1/2 Rupee, 1893, 96 / Yrs 8, 10	80	—	—
13	70	Silv	1 Rupee, 1882–97 / Yrs 1–11	30	60	—

Note: The 1882 date is an error for 1886.

INDIA–PRINCELY STATES: KASHMIR

Mint: *Sringar*

Gulab Singh, *VS 1903–1913 (1846–1856)*

Ranbir Singh, *VS 1914–1942 (1857–1885)*

Pertab Singh, *VS 1942–1979 (1885–1925)*

First Coinage

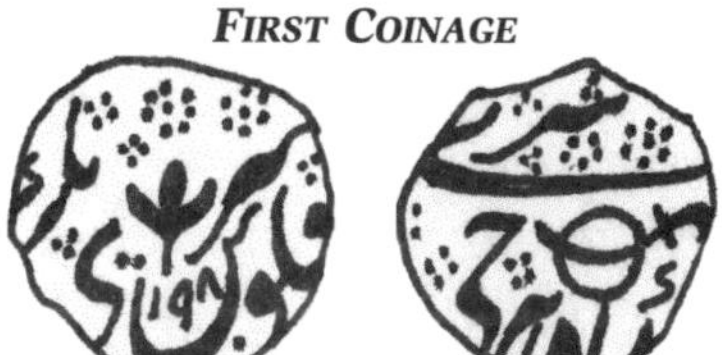

Obverse: *Mint legend, leaf or flower*
Reverse: *Gadadharji legend*

Y#	KM#	Metal	Description	VF	EF	Unc
1	1.2	Cop	1 Falus (Paisa), VS 1904–08 (vars)	10	—	—

Obverse: *Symbols, sword and leaf, no initials*
Reverse: *Mint-date legend*

Y#	KM#	Metal	Description	VF	EF	Unc
2	2	Silv	1/8 Rupee, VS 1903–05 (10–12 mm)	15	—	—
3	3	Silv	1/4 Rupee, VS 1903–04 (13–15 mm)	50	110	—
4	4	Silv	1/2 Rupee, VS 1903–05 (17–19 mm)	20	—	—
5	5	Silv	1 Rupee, VS 1903–06 (20–23 mm)	25	55	—

Second Coinage

Obverse: *Mint legend*
Reverse: *Like Y1, date in frame*

Y#	KM#	Metal	Description	VF	EF	Unc
6	6	Cop	1/2 Paisa, VS 1922–24 (1865–67) (15–18 mm)	8.00	—	—
7	7	Cop	1 Paisa, VS 1920–31 (18–20 mm)	6.50	—	—

Obverse: *Mint legend, sword*
Reverse: *Value, leaf*

Y#	KM#	Metal	Description	VF	EF	Unc
8	8	Cop	1/2 Anna, VS 1920 (19–20 mm)	30	60	—
9	9	Cop	1 Anna, VS 1920, 24 (24 mm)	300	—	—

Obverse: *Persian legends both sides*
Reverse: *Latin JHS added*

Y#	KM#	Metal	Description	VF	EF	Unc
A10	9.1	Silv	1/16 Rupee, ND	250	—	—
10	10	Silv	1/8 Rupee, VS 1914, 25 (1857, 68) (13 mm)	65	—	—
11	11	Silv	1/4 Rupee, VS 1914–25 (14–15 mm)	60	200	—
12	12	Silv	1/2 Rupee, VS 1914, 22 (16–17 mm)	100	475	—
13	13	Silv	1 Rupee, VS 1906–27 (20–22 mm)	35	45	85

Reduced-Weight Silver

Machine-Struck Issues

Obverse: *Persian legend, Latin JHS*
Reverse: *Takari legend*

Y#	KM#	Metal	Description	VF	EF	Unc
16	16	Silv	1 Rupee, VS 1927–28 (1870–71), date at bottom	100	175	—

Hand-Struck Issues

Planchets: *Round*

Y#	KM#	Metal	Description	VF	EF	Unc
14	14	Silv	1/4 Rupee, VS 1928 (15 mm)	30	50	—
15	15	Silv	1/2 Rupee, VS 1928 (17 mm)	30	50	—
16a	16a	Silv	1 Rupee, VS 1927–29, date at top (22 mm)	25	45	—

Planchets: *Dump*

Y#	KM#	Metal	Description	VF	EF	Unc
16b	16b	Silv	1 Rupee, VS 1929–32 (1872–75)	25	45	—

Third Coinage

Obverse: *Persian mint, Raganatha legend, JHS*
Reverse: *Same legend in Takari*

Y#	KM#	Metal	Description	VF	EF	Unc
17	17	Cop	1/4 Paisa, VS 1935–41 (1878–84) (10 mm)	10	—	—
18	18	Cop	1/2 Paisa, VS 1927–41 (14–16 mm)	15	—	—
19	19	Cop	1 Paisa, VS 1937–40 (19 mm)	20	—	—

Obverse: *Persian legend, Latin JHS*
Reverse: *Takari legend*

Y#	KM#	Metal	Description	VF	EF	Unc
20	20	Silv	1/2 Rupee, VS 1946–51 (1889–94) (16 mm)	35	80	—
21	21	Silv	1 Rupee, VS 1931–52 (18–21 mm)	30	55	75

Y#	KM#	Metal	Description	VF	EF	Unc
22	22	Gold	1/4 Mohur, VS 193x (2.3 g)	—	—	1,600

INDIA–PRINCELY STATES: KISHANGARH

Prithvi Singh, *1840–1879*

Obverse: *Queen Victoria legend*
Reverse: *Prithvi Singh legend*

Y#	KM#	Metal	Description	VF	EF	Unc
1	1.1–1.2	Silv	1 Rupee, 1858–59 / Yr 24	30	—	—
B2	B2	Silv	2 Rupees, 1858 / Yr 24	—	—	—

Y#	KM#	Metal	Description	VF	EF	Unc
A1	A1	Gold	1 Mohur, 1858 / Yr 24	1,750	—	—

Sardul Singh, *1879–1900*

Obverse: *Queen Victoria legend*

Y#	KM#	Metal	Description	VF	EF	Unc
A2	A2	Silv	1/2 Rupee, 1880 / Yr 24	60	—	—
2	2	Silv	1 Rupee, 1880 / Yr 24	60	—	—

Y#	KM#	Metal	Description	VF	EF	Unc
C2	C2	Gold	1 Mohur (109 g)	1,750	—	—

Madan Singh, *1900–1926*

First Coinage

Obverse: *Queen Victoria legend*

Y#	KM#	Metal	Description	VF	EF	Unc
A3	A3	Silv	1/2 Rupee, ND, 1900–01	75	—	—
C3	C3	Silv	1 Rupee, 1900 / Yr 60, broad planchet	500	—	—

Y#	KM#	Metal	Description	VF	EF	Unc
D3	D3	Gold	1 Mohur, ND, 1900–01	850	1,150	1,500

Second Coinage

Obverse: *Edward VII legend*

Y#	KM#	Metal	Description	VF	EF	Unc
B3	B3	Silv	1/4 Rupee, ND, 1902	70	—	—
3	3	Silv	1/2 Rupee, 1902 / Yr 24	70	—	—

Third Coinage

Obverse: *George V legend*

Y#	KM#	Metal	Description	VF	EF	Unc
A4	N/A	Silv	1/4 Rupee, ND, 1911–26	75	—	—
A5	N/A	Silv	1/2 Rupee, ND, 1911–26	50	—	—

YAGYANARAIN, *1926–1938*

Obverse: ***George (V or VI) legend***
Reverse: ***Yagyanarain legend***

Y#	KM#	Metal	Description	VF	EF	Unc
4	4	Silv	1/4 Rupee, Yr 24	35	—	—
5	5	Silv	1/2 Rupee, Yr 24	70	—	—
6	6	Silv	1 Rupee, Yr 24	150	—	—
6a	6a	Silv	1 Rupee, Yr 24, broad planchet (26 mm)	350	—	—

Y#	KM#	Metal	Description	VF	EF	Unc
7	7	Gold	1/2 Mohur, Yr 24 (18 mm)	700	—	—
8	8	Gold	1 Mohur, Yr 24 (19 mm)	850	950	1,100

ANONYMOUS ISSUES

Obverse: ***Mint-date legend***
Reverse: ***Nagari word***

Y#	KM#	Metal	Description	VF	EF	Unc
9	9	Silv	1/8 Rupee, Yr 24 (12 mm)	125	—	—
10	10	Silv	1/4 Rupee, Yr 24 (15 mm)	95	—	—
11	11	Silv	1/2 Rupee, Yr 24 (17–18 mm)	40	75	200
12	12	Silv	1 Rupee, Yr 24 (20–24 mm)	40	75	—

Obverse: ***Mint-date legend***
Reverse: ***Value in Hindi/Urdu***

Y#	KM#	Metal	Description	VF	EF	Unc
13	13	Silv	2 Annas, Yr 24 (11 mm)	45	—	—
14	14	Silv	4 Annas, Yr 24 (12–13 mm)	45	—	—
15	15	Silv	8 Annas, Yr 24 (16 mm)	90	165	—

INDIA–PRINCELY STATES: KOTAH

RAM SINGH, *1828–1866*

CHATTAR SAL, *1886–1889*

UMED SINGH, *1889–1945*

Designs: ***Like Y2a***
Rectangular Planchets: ***Dump***

Y#	KM#	Metal	Description	VF	EF	Unc
1	1	Cop	1 Paisa, Yrs 37–40 (9 g)	20	—	—
2	2	Cop	1 Takka, Yrs 1–41 (18 g)	25	—	—

Obverse: ***Queen Victoria legend***
Reverse: ***Date-mint legend***
Planchets: ***Broad and square***

Y#	KM#	Metal	Description	VF	EF	Unc
2a	2a	Cop	1 Paisa, Yrs 15, 28	—	—	—

Planchets: ***Dump***

Y#	KM#	Metal	Description	VF	EF	Unc
3	3	Silv	1/8 Rupee, Yrs 22–38 (9 mm)	60	—	—
4	4	Silv	1/4 Rupee, Yrs 1–38 (12 mm)	50	—	—
5	5	Silv	1/2 Rupee, Yrs 1–38 (13–15 mm)	50	—	—
6	6	Silv	1 Rupee, Yrs 1–44 (18–20 mm)	30	—	—
7	7	Silv	1 Rupee, VS 1956 (1899) (20 mm)	65	—	—

Planchets: ***Broad and thin***

Y#	KM#	Metal	Description	VF	EF	Unc
6a	6a	Silv	1 Nazarana Rupee, Yrs 1–44 (26–30 mm)	225	325	425
7a	7a	Silv	1 Nazarana Rupee, VS 1956 (30 mm)	—	—	—

Y#	KM#	Metal	Description	VF	EF	Unc
A7	A8a	Gold	1/8 Mohur, VS (19)56	700	900	—
B7	C8	Gold	1/2 Mohur, Yr 42	1,250	2,000	—
C7	N/A	Gold	1 Mohur, Yr 15, broad planchet	3,000	4,500	—
8	8	Gold	1 Mohur, Yrs 1–44, dump (18 mm)	950	1,250	—

INDIA–PRINCELY STATES: KUCHAWAN

KESRI SINGH, *1857–1877*

Obverse: ***Queen Victoria legend***
Reverse: ***"Kuchawan, dependency of Jodhpur"***

Y#	KM#	Metal	Description	VF	EF	Unc
1	284	Silv	1/4 Rupee, 1863 (13 mm)	75	—	—
2	285	Silv	1/2 Rupee, 1863 (15–16 mm)	75	—	—
3	286	Silv	1 Rupee, 1863 (19–20 mm)	30	—	—
4	287	Silv	2 Rupees, 1863 (35 mm)	—	—	—

INDIA–PRINCELY STATES: KUTCH

MONETARY SYSTEM

48 trambiyo = 24 dokda = 16 dhingla = 1 kori
100 kori = 1 muhr (mohur)

PRAGMALJI II, *1860–1875*

Obverse: ***Queen Victoria legend***
Reverse: ***Mint / Pragmalji legend***

Y#	KM#	Metal	Description	VF	EF	Unc
1	1	Cop	1 Trambiyo, 1865 (16 mm)	5	10	25

Obverse: *Value/mint in Urdu*
Reverse: *Same in Nagari*

Y#	KM#	Metal	Description	VF	EF	Unc
5	5–5.1	Cop	1 Trambiyo, 1767 (error), 1865–68 (16 mm)	4	8	—
6	6	Cop	1 Dokdo, 1865–69	4	—	—

Y#	KM#	Metal	Description	VF	EF	Unc
8	8	Cop	3 Dokda, 1868	12.50	—	—

Obverse: *Queen Victoria legend*
Reverse: *Pragmalji legend*

Y#	KM#	Metal	Description	VF	EF	Unc
9	9–9.1	Cop	1 Trambiyo, 1869 (14 mm)	4.00	—	—
10	10	Cop	1 Dokdo, 1869–74	4.00	—	—
11	11–11.3	Cop	1-1/2 Dokda, 1869–74 (23 mm)	6.00	—	—
12	12	Cop	3 Dokda, 1863–69 (32 mm)	12.50	—	—

Y#	KM#	Metal	Description	VF	EF	Unc
13	13	Silv	1/2 Kori, 1862–63	5.00	—	—
14	14/A14	Silv	1 Kori, 1860–63	7.50	—	—

Designs: *Similar to Y36–37*

Y#	KM#	Metal	Description	VF	EF	Unc
15	15	Silv	2-1/2 Kori, 1875	30	50	—
16	16–16.1	Silv	5 Kori, 1863–75	25	40	—

Designs: *Like Y14*

Y#	KM#	Metal	Description	VF	EF	Unc
17	17/17a	Gold	25 Kori, 1862–70 (16 mm)	300	400	500

Designs: *Similar to Y36–37*

Y#	KM#	Metal	Description	VF	EF	Unc
18	18	Gold	50 Kori, 1866–74 (24 mm)	600	1,000	1,500
19	19	Gold	100 Kori, 1866 (29 mm)	700	1,250	2,000

KHENGARJI III, *1876–1942*

FIRST COINAGE

Obverse: *Queen Victoria legend*
Reverse: *Khengarji legend*

Y#	KM#	Metal	Description	VF	EF	Unc
22	22	Cop	1 Dokdo, 1878	45.00	—	—
23	23	Cop	1-1/2 Dokda, 1876–78	3.50	25	50

Designs: *Like Y35, 37*

Y#	KM#	Metal	Description	VF	EF	Unc
26	26	Silv	1 Kori, 1876	150	—	—
28	28	Silv	5 Kori, 1876	50	100	—

SECOND COINAGE

Obverse: *Empress Victoria legend*
Reverse: *Khengarji legend*

Y#	KM#	Metal	Description	VF	EF	Unc
30	30–30.1	Cop	1 Trambiyo, 1881–83	2	—	—

Y#	KM#	Metal	Description	VF	EF	Unc
31	31–31.3	Cop	1 Dokdo, 1882–99 (2 vars) (21–22 mm)	1.50	—	—
32	32–32.4	Cop	1-1/2 Dokda, 1882–99 (3 vars) (23–25 mm)	3.00	—	—
33	33–33.1	Cop	3 Dokda, 1883–99 (2 vars) (33–34 mm)	5.00	—	—

Y#	KM#	Metal	Description	VF	EF	Unc
34	34	Silv	1/2 Kori, 1898–1900 (13 mm)	10.00	17.50	35
35	35–35.1	Silv	1 Kori, 1881–1901 (2 vars) (165 mm)	12.50	20.00	40

Y#	KM#	Metal	Description	VF	EF	Unc
36	36	Silv	2-1/2 Kori, 1881–99 (3 vars)	30	45	—

Y#	KM#	Metal	Description	VF	EF	Unc
37	37–37.7	Silv	5 Kori, 1880–1901 (4 vars)	15	25	50

Y#	KM#	Metal	Description	VF	EF	Unc
A37	N/A	Gold	1 Kori, 1888 / VS 1946	—	—	—
B37	N/A	Gold	1/2 Mohur, 1889 / VS 1946	—	—	—
C37	N/A	Gold	1 Mohur, 1889 / VS 1946	—	—	—

THIRD COINAGE

Obverse: *Edward VII legend*
Reverse: *Khengarji legend*

Y#	KM#	Metal	Description	VF	EF	Unc
38	38	Cop	1 Trambiyo, 1908–10 (16 mm)	15	—	—
39	39	Cop	1 Dokdo, 1909 (205 mm)	15	—	—
40	40	Cop	1-1/2 Dokda, 1909	500	—	—
41	41	Cop	3 Dokda, 1909	300	—	—

Y#	KM#	Metal	Description	VF	EF	Unc
45	45	Silv	5 Kori, 1902–09	1,000	2,000	3,250

FOURTH COINAGE

Obverse: *George V legend*
Reverse: *Khengarji legend*

Y#	KM#	Metal	Description	VF	EF	Unc
46	46	Cop	1 Trambiyo, 1919–20 (16 mm)	3.25	5	45
47	47	Cop	1 Dokdo, 1920 (21 mm)	3.25	5	45
48	48	Cop	1-1/2 Dokda, 1926 (235 mm)	3.25	5	45
49	49	Cop	3 Dokda, 1926 (33 mm)	5.00	8	50

Y#	KM#	Metal	Description	VF	EF	Unc
51	51	Silv	1 Kori, 1913–27	10	15	25

Y#	KM#	Metal	Description	VF	EF	Unc
52	52	Silv	2-1/2 Kori, 1916–26	20	40	75
53	53	Silv	5 Kori, 1913–27	25	50	95

Modified Dies

Y#	KM#	Metal	Description	VF	EF	Unc
54	54	Cop	1 Trambiyo, 1928 (16 mm)	3.00	5	25
55	55	Cop	1 Dokdo, 1922–29 (21 mm)	3.50	6	—
56	56	Cop	1-1/2 Dokda, 1926–32 (23 mm)	2.50	5	—
57	57	Cop	3 Dokda, 1928–35 (33 mm)	4.50	9	—

Y#	KM#	Metal	Description	VF	EF	Unc
58	58	Silv	1/2 Kori, 1928 (14 mm)	7.50	—	—
59	59	Silv	1 Kori, 1928–36 (17 mm)	3.00	—	—
52a	52a	Silv	2-1/2 Kori, 1927–35 (25 mm)	12.50	25	50
53a	53a	Silv	5 Kori, 1928–36 (31 mm)	15.00	30	—

FIFTH COINAGE

Obverse: ***Edward VIII legend***
Reverse: ***Khengarji legend***

Y#	KM#	Metal	Description	VF	EF	Unc
63	63	Cop	3 Dokda, 1936	20	—	—

Borders: ***Like Y53***

Y#	KM#	Metal	Description	VF	EF	Unc
65	65	Silv	1 Kori, 1936	20	35	50
66	66	Silv	2-1/2 Kori, 1936	20	35	50
67	67	Silv	5 Kori, 1936	20	35	50

SIXTH COINAGE

Obverse: ***George VI legend***
Reverse: ***Khengarji legend***

Y#	KM#	Metal	Description	VF	EF	Unc
71	71	Cop	3 Dokda, 1937	25	40	100

Y#	KM#	Metal	Description	VF	EF	Unc
73	73	Silv	1 Kori, 1937–40	6.50	10	20
74	74	Silv	2-1/2 Kori, 1937	25.00	35	50
75	75	Silv	5 Kori, 1936–41	25.00	35	50
A75	N/A	Silv	10 Kori, 1941	—	—	—

VIJAYARAJJI, *1942–1947*

Obverse: ***George VI legend***
Reverse: ***Vijayarajji legend***

Y#	KM#	Metal	Description	VF	EF	Unc
76	76	Cop	1 Trambiyo, 1943–44	2	3	30
77	77	Cop	1 Dhinglo (1-1/2 Dokda), 1943–47 (21 mm)	3	4	40

Y#	KM#	Metal	Description	VF	EF	Unc
78	78	Cop	1 Dhabu (3 Dokda), 1943–48 (23 mm)	4	5	35
79	79	Cop	1 Payalo (1/4 Kori), 1943–47 (27 mm)	6	7	40
80	80	Cop	1 Adhio (1/2 Kori), 1943–46 (36 mm)	10	15	75

Y#	KM#	Metal	Description	VF	EF	Unc
81	81	Silv	1 Kori, 1942–44 (2 vars)	5	25	75
82	82	Silv	5 Kori, 1942–43	13	35	100
A82	82A	Silv	10 Kori, 1943	750	—	—

MADANASINHJI, *1947*

Obverse: ***"India Victory" legend***
Reverse: ***Madanasinhji legend***

Y#	KM#	Metal	Description	VF	EF	Unc
83	83	Cop	1 Dhabu, VS 2004	12.50	20	30

Y#	KM#	Metal	Description	VF	EF	Unc
84	84	Silv	1 Kori, VS 2004	15	25	35

Y#	KM#	Metal	Description	VF	EF	Unc
85	85	Silv	5 Kori, VS 2004	500	850	1,750

Y#	KM#	Metal	Description	VF	EF	Unc
A85	N/A	Gold	1 Kori, VS 2004, like Y84	—	—	850
B85	N/A	Gold	1 Mohur, VS 2004, like Y85	—	—	4,000

INDIA–PRINCELY STATES: LADAKH (BOTAAN)

MONETARY SYSTEM

1 timasha (3 masha) = Tibet 1/2 sho
= approximately 1/4 rupee

GULAB SINGH, *VS 1903–1913 (1846–1856)*

Obverse: ***Gulab Singh legend***
Reverse: ***Mint legend***

Y#	KM#	Metal	Description	VF	EF	Unc
1	7.1–7.5	Silv	1 Timasha (3 Masha), ND (1846–56)	75	125	—

RANBIR SINGH, *VS 1914–1942 (1857–1885)*

Obverse: ***Persian legend***
Reverse: ***Nagari legend***

Y#	KM#	Metal	Description	VF	EF	Unc
2	9	Cop	1 Paisa, VS 1923–27	100	125	—

Obverse: ***Persian legend***
Reverse: ***Tibetan legend***

Y#	KM#	Metal	Description	VF	EF	Unc
3	8	Silv	1 Timasha, VS 1928 (1871)	1,500	2,500	—

INDIA–PRINCELY STATES: LUNAVADA

DALAL SINGHJI, *1851–1867*

Y#	KM#	Metal	Description	VF	EF	Unc
A1	N/A	Cop	1 Paisa, ND, "Dalal" in Gujarati	35	—	—
1	5	Cop	1 Paisa, ND, obverse 2 swords	35	—	—
2	6	Cop	1 Paisa, ND, obverse dagger	35	—	—

WAKHAT SINGHJI, *1867–1929*

Obverse: ***Lotus blossom***

Y#	KM#	Metal	Description	VF	EF	Unc
A3	N/A	Cop	1/2 Paisa, ND	25	—	—
3	12	Cop	1 Paisa, ND	15	—	—

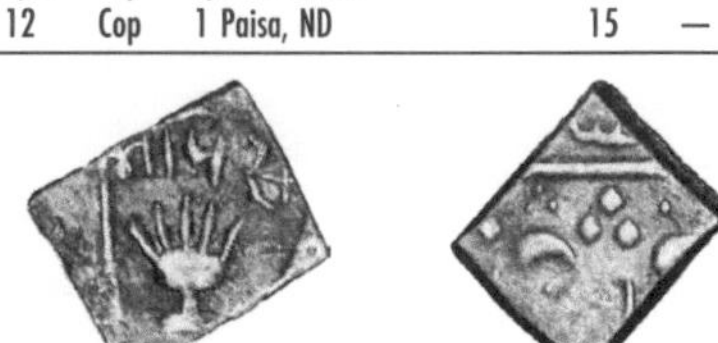

Obverse: ***Hand***

Y#	KM#	Metal	Description	VF	EF	Unc
A4	2.1–2.2	Cop	1/2 Paisa, ND	25	—	—
4	8.1	Cop	1 Paisa, ND	30	—	—

Obverse: *Hand in square*

Y#	KM#	Metal	Description	VF	EF	Unc
7	3	Cop	1/2 Paisa, VS 1942 (1885)	25	—	—
8	9.1	Cop	1 Paisa, VS 1942	18	—	—

Obverse: *Lion to right*

Y#	KM#	Metal	Description	VF	EF	Unc
5	4	Cop	1/2 Paisa, VS 1949 (1892)	25	—	—
6	10	Cop	1 Paisa, VS 1949	25	35	—

Obverse: *Sun symbols*

Y#	KM#	Metal	Description	VF	EF	Unc
9	11	Cop	1 Paisa, ND	20	—	—

Note: Y9 has been attributed to Sunth. Y1–9 are crude and vary greatly in shape and size. Later coins were usually struck over earlier types, often causing two or more designs to show.

INDIA–PRINCELY STATES: MAKRAI

Bharat Singh, *1866–1920*

Obverse: *Katar in lozenge*
Reverse: *Nagari "Makrai"*

Y#	KM#	Metal	Description	VF	EF	Unc
1	1	Cop	1 Paisa, ND (17–22 mm)	30	—	—

INDIA–PRINCELY STATES: MALER-KOTLA

Mintmarks: On reverse. Stylized "Sad" in Persian "S," trefoil at lower-right flower at left (Y7-9 omit trefoil and flower). Ruler's name or initial above "Sad." Compare with coins of Jind, Nabha, Patiala.

Sikandar Ali Khan, *1859–1871*

Obverse: *Couplet of Ahmad Shah Durrani*
Reverse: *Mint-date legend, Persian "S" above "Sad"*

Y#	KM#	Metal	Description	VF	EF	Unc
1	1	Silv	1/4 Rupee, ND	185	—	—
2	2	Silv	1/2 Rupee, ND	450	—	—
3	3.1–3.2	Silv	1 Rupee, ND	65	125	—

Ibrahim Ali Khan, *1871–1908*

Obverse: *Designs like Y3*
Reverse: *Persian "IB" above "Sad"*

Y#	KM#	Metal	Description	VF	EF	Unc
4	4	Silv	1/4 Rupee, ND	70	120	—
5	5	Silv	1/2 Rupee, ND	45	—	—
6	6	Silv	1 Rupee, ND	30	50	—

Ahmad Ali Khan, *1908–1923*

Obverse: *Like Y3*
Reverse: *Ruler's name spelled out above "Sad"*

Y#	KM#	Metal	Description	VF	EF	Unc
7	7	Cop	1/2 Paisa, ND	25	—	—
8	8	Cop	1 Paisa, AH 1326	850	1,750	—

Y#	KM#	Metal	Description	VF	EF	Unc
9	9	Silv	1 Rupee, AH 1326	25	40	—
10	10	Silv	2 Rupees, AH 1326	—	—	—

INDIA–PRINCELY STATES: MEWAR

UDAIPUR MINT

Anonymous Issues

First Coinage

Y#	KM#	Metal	Description	VF	EF	Unc
1	1	Silv	1/16 Rupee, ND (8–9 mm)	6.50	10	—
2	2	Silv	1/8 Rupee, ND (10–11 mm)	6.00	10	—
3	3	Silv	1/4 Rupee, ND (12–14 mm)	8.00	12	—
4	4	Silv	1/2 Rupee, ND (15–17 mm)	10.00	15	—
5	5	Silv	1 Rupee, ND (18–20 mm)	25.00	35	—

Y#	KM#	Metal	Description	VF	EF	Unc
6	6	Gold	2/3 Mohur, ND (17–19 mm) (7.52 g)	550	1,000	—

Note: Y1–6, known as the "New Chandori" series, were struck between 1842 and 1890.

Second Coinage

Y#	KM#	Metal	Description	VF	EF	Unc
7	7.1–7.2	Silv	1/16 Rupee, ND (8–9 mm)	15	—	—
8	8	Silv	1/8 Rupee, ND (11–12 mm)	15	—	—
9	9	Silv	1/4 Rupee, ND (14–15 mm)	10	—	—
10	10	Silv	1/2 Rupee, ND (17–18 mm)	15	—	—

Y#	KM#	Metal	Description	VF	EF	Unc
11	11	Silv	1 Rupee, ND (22–24 mm)	17.50	35	—

Y#	KM#	Metal	Description	VF	EF	Unc
A12	B12	Gold	1/8 Mohur, ND 1851–1930	500	600	—
B12	A12	Gold	1/4 Mohur, ND 1851–1930	700	800	—
C12	C12	Gold	1/2 Mohur, ND 1851–1930	800	1,250	—
12	12	Gold	1 Mohur, ND (23–24 mm)	850	1,500	—

Note: Y7–12, known as the "Swarupshahi" series, were struck between 1851 and 1930.

Provisional Issues

Obverse: ***Nagari "Udaipur"***
Reverse: ***Nagari "Chitor," date***

Y#	KM#	Metal	Description	VF	EF	Unc
13	13	Cop	1 Pai, VS 1975 (1918) (16 mm)	30	—	—

Legends: ***Like Y13, ornamental borders***

Y#	KM#	Metal	Description	VF	EF	Unc
14	14	Cop	1 Pai, VS 1978 (1921)	10	—	—

Third Coinage
Machine-Struck Issues

Y#	KM#	Metal	Description	VF	EF	Unc
15	15	Cop	1/4 Anna, VS 1999 (1942), square	4	12	—

Y#	KM#	Metal	Description	VF	EF	Unc
16	16	Cop	1/2 Anna, VS 1999	3	11	—

Y#	KM#	Metal	Description	VF	EF	Unc
17	17	Cop	1 Anna, VS 2000 (1943), hexagonal	4	12	—

Y#	KM#	Metal	Description	VF	EF	Unc
18	18	Silv	1/16 Rupee (1 Anna), VS 1985 (1928) (12 mm)	7.50	12.50	—
19	19	Silv	1/8 Rupee (2 Annas), VS 1985 (15 mm)	7.50	12.50	—
20	20	Silv	1/4 Rupee, VS 1985 (19 mm)	10.00	15.00	60
21	21	Silv	1/2 Rupee, VS 1985 (24 mm)	10.00	15.00	60
22	22	Silv	1 Rupee, VS 1985 (30 mm)	15.00	20.00	80

Note: Y18–22 were struck in 1931. Other silver coins dated VS 1985, but without city walls on obverse, are believed to be patterns and restrikes.

Local Coinage for Umarda

Design: ***Random lines and dots both sides***
Planchets: ***Thin, dump***

Y#	KM#	Metal	Description	VF	EF	Unc
23	23	Cop	1/2 Paisa, ND (late 19th century?)	10	17.50	—

Designs: ***Like Y23***
Planchets: ***Very thin, square***

Y#	KM#	Metal	Description	VF	EF	Unc
24	24	Cop	1/2 Paisa, ND (ca 1938–41?)	7	15	—

Note: Y23–24 are commonly known as "dhingla paisa."

INDIA–PRINCELY STATES: NABHA

Mintmarks: On reverse; stylized "Sad" in Persian "S"; spiky flower (with or without stem) at lower-right; ruler's symbol at left. Compare with coins from Jind, Maler-Kotla, and Patiala.

Bharpur Singh,
VS 1903–1920 (1846–1863)

Obverse: ***Ahmad Shah Durrani legend***
Reverse: ***As Y2 but leaf to left***

Y#	KM#	Metal	Description	VF	EF	Unc
A1	N/A	Silv	1 Rupee, VS 1907	200	400	—

Obverse: ***Like Y2***
Reverse: ***Similar but leaf at left***

Y#	KM#	Metal	Description	VF	EF	Unc
1	1.1	Silv	1 Rupee, VS 1903–20	60	100	—

Obverse: ***Ahmad Shah Durrani legend***
Reverse: ***Similar to Y1***

Y#	KM#	Metal	Description	VF	EF	Unc
A2	N/A	Gold	1 Mohur, VS 1907, 11	4,000	6,500	—
B2	N/A	Gold	1 Mohur, VS 1907, 11, obverse Govind Singh legend	4,000	6,500	—

Hira Singh, *VS 1927–1968 (1870–1911)*

Obverse: ***Govind Singh (Sikh saint) legend, date***
Reverse: ***Mint-date legend with "Sad," dagger at left***

Y#	KM#	Metal	Description	VF	EF	Unc
2	2	Silv	1 Rupee, VS 1927–29	100	175	—

Y#	KM#	Metal	Description	VF	EF	Unc
3	3	Gold	1 Mohur, VS 1927–29	2,000	3,500	—

INDIA–PRINCELY STATES: NAWANAGAR

Y1–10 are basically degenerate copies of the Gujerati coinage of Muzaffar Shah III (1560–1584). All but Y1 bear the frozen date AH 1178, degenerated from 978 (1570).

Mintmark: Ruler's title, "Sri Jamji," on reverse of Y2–10.

Vibhaji, *VS 1909–1951 (1852–1894)*

First Coinage

Obverse: ***Like Y3***
Reverse: ***Similar but true date replaces legend***
Planchets: ***Thin, dump***

Y#	KM#	Metal	Description	VF	EF	Unc
1	16	Cop	1 Dokdo, VS 1909, 17, 19 (1852, 60, 62)	7.50	—	—

Second Coinage

Y2–8 have relatively fine engraving and thin planchets, and probably date from the mid- to late 19th century. Earlier issues, with heavier engraving and thick dump planchets (style of Y1 but dated AH 1178) are listed in Craig, *Coins of the World*.

Obverse: ***Stylized Persian legend***
Reverse: ***Nagari "Sri Jamji," date***
Planchets: ***Thin***

Y#	KM#	Metal	Description	VF	EF	Unc
2	6	Cop	1 Trambiyo, AH 1178 (14–16 mm) (3.2 g)	4	—	—

Y#	KM#	Metal	Description	VF	EF	Unc
3	7	Cop	1 Dokdo, AH 1178 (17–19 mm) (6.4 g)	3	—	—
4	8	Cop	1 Dhinglo, AH 1178 (20–21 mm) (9.5 g)	4	—	—

Y#	KM#	Metal	Description	VF	EF	Unc
5	9	Silv	1/2 Kori, AH 1178 (12–13 mm)	25	—	—
6	10	Silv	1 Kori, AH 1178 (14–16 mm)	20	—	—

Y#	KM#	Metal	Description	VF	EF	Unc
7	11	Gold	1/2 Kori, AH 1178	800	1,250	1,750
8	12	Gold	1 Kori, AH 1178	1,000	1,500	2,000

Third Coinage

Style Y9–12 were all struck in collars by machine.

Designs: ***Like Y3***

Y#	KM#	Metal	Description	VF	EF	Unc
9	13	Cop	1 Trambiyo, AH 1178 (3.15 g)	5	10	—
10	14	Cop	1 Dokdo, AH 1178 (6.3 g)	5	10	—

Y#	KM#	Metal	Description	VF	EF	Unc
11	17	Cop	3 Dokda, VS 1928 (1871) (19 g)	30	—	—

Y#	KM#	Metal	Description	VF	EF	Unc
12	20	Silv	1 Kori, VS 1934–36 (1877–79)	20	45	95

Fourth Coinage

Coinage on dump planchets resumed.

Y#	KM#	Metal	Description	VF	EF	Unc
13	18	Cop	2 Dokda, VS 1943 (1886)	32.50	—	—

Y#	KM#	Metal	Description	VF	EF	Unc
14	19	Cop	3 Dokda, VS 1942	40	—	—

Y#	KM#	Metal	Description	VF	EF	Unc
15	21	Silv	2-1/2 Kori, VS 1949–50 (1892–93) (17–21 mm)	25	50	250
16	22–23	Silv	5 Kori, VS 1945–50 (22–27 mm)	15	30	175

Jaswant Singh, *VS 1951–1964 (1894–1907)*

Y#	KM#	Metal	Description	VF	EF	Unc
17	24	Cop	1/2 Dokdo, VS 1956 (1899)	45	75	—
18	25	Cop	1 Dokdo, VS 1956	40	60	—
19	26	Cop	1-1/2 Dokda, VS 1956	215	—	—
20	27	Cop	2 Dokda, VS 1956	300	450	—
21	28	Cop	3 Dokda, VS 1956	75	100	—

INDIA–PRINCELY STATES: PARTABGARH (PRATAPGARH)

Udaya Singh, *VS 1921–1947 (1864–1890)*

Obverse: *Sunface with hands*
Reverse: *Nagari legend*

Y#	KM#	Metal	Description	VF	EF	Unc
1	30.1	Cop	1 Paisa, VS 1942 (1885) (7.6–8.1 g)	25	—	—

Obverse: *Sun-face / two swords*
Reverse: *Legend, date in oval*

Y#	KM#	Metal	Description	VF	EF	Unc
2	31	Cop	1 Paisa, VS 1943–48 (1886–91)	15	25	—

Obverse: *Shah of London (Victoria) legend*
Planchets: *Round, dump*

Y#	KM#	Metal	Description	VF	EF	Unc
3	33	Silv	1/8 Rupee, AH 1236 / Yr 45	9	—	—
4	34	Silv	1/4 Rupee, AH 1236 / Yr 45	9	—	—
5	35	Silv	1/2 Rupee, AH 1236 / Yr 45	12	—	—
6	36	Silv	1 Rupee, AH 1236 / Yr 45	20	—	—

Planchets: *Broad*

Y#	KM#	Metal	Description	VF	EF	Unc
A6	38	Silv	2-1/2 Rupee, AH 1236 / Yr 45	—	—	—

Planchets: *Square*

Y#	KM#	Metal	Description	VF	EF	Unc
5a	39a	Silv	1/2 Rupee, AH 1236 / Yr 45	100	175	—
6a	37	Silv	1 Rupee, AH 1236 / Yr 45	85	150	—

Raganath Singh, *VS 1947–1986 (1890–1929)*

Obverse: *Curved legend / ornament*
Reverse: *Four-line legend*

Y#	KM#	Metal	Description	VF	EF	Unc
7	40	Cop	1 Paisa, VS 1953 (1896)	7.50	—	—

INDIA–PRINCELY STATES: PATIALA

Mintmarks: On reverse; stylized "Sad" in Persian "S"; floral ornament at lower right; ruler's symbol at left (these marks occur on silver, but may differ on gold). Compare with coins from Jind, Maler-Kotla, and Nabha.

Narindar Singh, *1845–1862*

Obverse: *Couplet of Ahmad Shah Durrani*
Reverse: *Mint-date legend with "Sad," wide-bladed sword at left*

Y#	KM#	Metal	Description	VF	EF	Unc
B1	B1	Silv	1/4 Rupee, ND	35	60	—
1	1	Silv	1 Rupee, ND	25	40	—
A2	A2	Silv	1 Rupee, VS 1906, Govind Singh legend	1,250	2,000	—

Y#	KM#	Metal	Description	VF	EF	Unc
2	2	Gold	1 Mohur, ND VS 190x	750	1,500	—

Mahindar Singh, *1862–1876*

Obverse: *Like Y1*
Reverse: *Similar but curved knife to left*

Y#	KM#	Metal	Description	VF	EF	Unc
3	3	Silv	1 Rupee, ND	75	—	—

Y#	KM#	Metal	Description	VF	EF	Unc
A4	9	Gold	1 Mohur, ND	1,750	2,500	—

Rajindar Singh,
1876–1900

Obverse: *Like Y1*
Reverse: *Similar but dagger at left*
Planchets: *Dump*

Y#	KM#	Metal	Description	VF	EF	Unc
4	4	Silv	1/4 Rupee, ND	60	120	—
5	5	Silv	1/2 Rupee, ND	60	120	—
6	6	Silv	1 Rupee, VS (19)42–48	50	100	—

Planchets: *Broad and thin*

Y#	KM#	Metal	Description	VF	EF	Unc
6a	6a	Silv	1 Rupee, ND	—	—	—

Y#	KM#	Metal	Description	VF	EF	Unc
7	N/A	Gold	1/3 Mohur, VS (19)50 (3.7 g)	750	1,250	—
9	9	Gold	1 Mohur, VS (19)50 (11 g)	750	1,250	—

Bhupindar Singh,
1900–1938

Obverse: *Like Y1*
Reverse: *Spearhead*

Y#	KM#	Metal	Description	VF	EF	Unc
13	A3	Silv	1 Rupee, VS 1958 (1901)	3,500	4,500	—

Y#	KM#	Metal	Description	VF	EF	Unc
14	14	Gold	1/6 Mohur, VS (19)58 (1901)	600	800	—
15	15	Gold	1/3 Mohur, VS (19)58 (1901)	800	1,000	—
16	16	Gold	2/3 Mohur, VS (19)58 (1901)	900	1,100	—
17	17	Gold	1 Mohur, VS (19)58 (1901)	1,000	1,250	—

Yadavindra Singh,
1938–1948

Obverse: *Like Y1*
Reverse: *Bayoneted rifle at left*

Y#	KM#	Metal	Description	VF	EF	Unc
18	18	Silv	1 Rupee, VS 1994 (1937)	—	—	—

Y#	KM#	Metal	Description	VF	EF	Unc
19	19	Gold	1/6 Mohur, VS (19)94 (1937)	250	500	1,000
20	20	Gold	1/3 Mohur, VS (19)94 (1937)	350	500	1,000
21	21	Gold	2/3 Mohur, VS (19)94 (1937)	450	750	1,500

India–Princely States: Pudukkottai (Pudukota)

Y#	KM#	Metal	Description	VF	EF	Unc
A1	N/A	Cop	1 Amman Cash, ND (ca 1810–90)	5	10	25

Martanda Bhairava,
1886–1928

Rajagopala,
1928–1947

Y#	KM#	Metal	Description	VF	EF	Unc
A2	6	Cop	1 Amman Cash, ND (ca 1886–1947)	5	10	25
1	N/A	Bz	1 Amman Cash, ND (1889–1934)	5	10	25

India–Princely States: Radhanpur

Anonymous Issues

Obverse: *Nagari "Go"*
Reverse: *Blank*

Y#	KM#	Metal	Description	VF	EF	Unc
1	N/A	Cop	1 Paisa, ND	5	—	—

Obverse: *Nagari "Ji"*
Reverse: *Blank*

Y#	KM#	Metal	Description	VF	EF	Unc
2	N/A	Cop	1 Paisa, ND	4	—	—

Note: The meaning of the Nagari initials on Y1–2 is unknown, but it has been suggested that they can be attributed to Zorawar Khan and Bismilla Khan, respectively.

Zorawar Khan,
AH 1240–1291 (1825–1874)

Designs: *Like Y8*

Y#	KM#	Metal	Description	VF	EF	Unc
3	5	Silv	50 Falus, 1867 / AH 1284	125	250	—
4	6	Silv	100 Falus, AH 1284–86	100	225	—

Obverse: *Victoria-mint legend*
Reverse: *Value-Zorawar legend*

Y#	KM#	Metal	Description	VF	EF	Unc
5	8	Silv	2 Annas, 1871 / AH 1288 (15 mm)	300	—	—
6	9	Silv	4 Annas, 1869–72 / AH 1287–88 (18 mm)	150	—	—
7	10	Silv	8 Annas, 1869, 71 / AH 1287–88 (23 mm)	125	—	—
8	11	Silv	1 Rupee, 1871–72 / AH 1287, 89 (28 mm)	100	—	—

Y#	KM#	Metal	Description	VF	EF	Unc
9	15	Gold	1 Mohur, 1860 / AH 1277	4,000	6,000	—

Obverse: *Bust of Queen Victoria*
Reverse: *Zorawar legend*

Y#	KM#	Metal	Description	VF	EF	Unc
A9	N/A	Gold	1 Mohur, 1885 [sic]	7,500	12,000	—

BISMILLA KHAN, *AH 1291–1313 (1874–1895)*

Obverse: ***Empress Victoria legend***

Y#	KM#	Metal	Description	VF	EF	Unc
10	18	Silv	2 Annas, 1880	125	—	—
11	19	Silv	4 Annas, 1880	400	—	—
12	21–25	Silv	8 Annas, 1880–81 / AH 1297, 99	125	—	—
13	27–31	Silv	1 Rupee, 1880–81, 94	125	—	—

INDIA–PRINCELY STATES: RAJKOT

DHARMENDRA SINGHJI, *1930–1948*

Y#	KM#	Metal	Description	VF	EF	Unc
1	N/A	Gold	1 Mohur, 1945	1,500	2,500	3,750

Note: Y1 was struck for presentation only.

Y#	KM#	Metal	Description	VF	EF	Unc
A1	N/A	Gold	1 Mohur, 1945 (1962 restrike)	BV	BV	850

Y#	KM#	Metal	Description	VF	EF	Unc
1a	N/A	Silv	1 Mohur, 1945	100	150	225

Note: Y1a is said to have been struck as a pattern for Y1, but a quantity of restrikes was made for collectors circa 1964. It is sometimes called a 1/2 rupee.

INDIA–PRINCELY STATES: RATLAM (RUTLAM)

RANJIT SINGH, *VS 1921–1950 (1864–1893)*

Y#	KM#	Metal	Description	VF	EF	Unc
1	A21	Cop	1 Paisa, VS 1921 (1864)	25	—	—

Obverse: ***Gujerati "Ratlam" / dagger***
Reverse: ***Date/star***

Y#	KM#	Metal	Description	VF	EF	Unc
2	20	Cop	1 Paisa, VS 1927–28 (1870–71)	22.50	—	—

Y#	KM#	Metal	Description	VF	EF	Unc
3	23	Cop	1 Paisa, 1885	17.50	25	—

Y#	KM#	Metal	Description	VF	EF	Unc
4	24	Cop	1 Paisa, VS 1945, 47–48 (1888, 90–91)	12.50	17.50	—

Y#	KM#	Metal	Description	VF	EF	Unc
4a	25	Cop	1 Paisa, VS 1947 (thin, crude restrike of Y4)	10	15	—

INDIA–PRINCELY STATES: REWAH (REWA)

GULAB SINGH, *VS 1975–2003 (1918–1946)*

Y#	KM#	Metal	Description	VF	EF	Unc
2	29	Silv	1/2 Rupee, VS 1975	600	950	—
3	31	Silv	1 Rupee, VS 1975	400	650	—

Y#	KM#	Metal	Description	VF	EF	Unc
A1	33	Gold	1/2 Mohur, VS 1975 (1918)	2,000	4,000	—
1	35	Gold	1 Mohur, VS 1975–77 (1918–20)	2,000	4,000	—

INDIA–PRINCELY STATES: SAILANA

DULE SINGH, *VS 1907–1947 (1850–1890)*

Obverse: *Banner*
Reverse: *Date/sword*

Y#	KM#	Metal	Description	VF	EF	Unc
1	11	Cop	1/2 Paisa, VS 1937 (1880)	5	—	—

Obverse: *Like Y1*
Reverse: *Date/sword, jhar*

Y#	KM#	Metal	Description	VF	EF	Unc
2	12	Cop	1 Paisa, VS 1940 (1883)	7	—	—

Obverse: *Like Y1*
Reverse: *Persian "Sailana," date*

Y#	KM#	Metal	Description	VF	EF	Unc
3	13	Cop	1 Paisa, VS 1941	7	—	—

Obverse: *Like Y1*
Reverse: *Trident in circular Nagari legend*

Y#	KM#	Metal	Description	VF	EF	Unc
A4	10	Cop	1/2 Paisa, VS 1944 (1887)	5	—	—
4	14	Cop	1 Paisa, VS 1944 (1887)	7	—	—

Jaswant Singh, *1895–1919*

Obverse: *Head of Edward VII*
Reverse: *Like Y6*

Y#	KM#	Metal	Description	VF	EF	Unc
5	15	Bz	1/4 Anna, 1908	25	35	125

Y#	KM#	Metal	Description	VF	EF	Unc
6	16	Bz	1/4 Anna, 1912	20	30	115

INDIA–PRINCELY STATES: SIKKIM

Thotab Namgyel, *VS 1931–1968 (1874–1911)*

Obverse: *Ruler's title, date*
Reverse: *State legend*

Y#	KM#	Metal	Description	VF	EF	Unc
1	N/A	Cop	1 Paisa, VS 1940–42 (1883–85)	135	—	—

INDIA–PRINCELY STATES: SITAMAU

Bahadur Singh, *VS 1942–1956 (1885–1899)*

Y#	KM#	Metal	Description	VF	EF	Unc
1	Several	Cop	1 Paisa, VS 1942, 44, 46, 48	12	—	—

Sardul Singh, *VS 1956–1957 (1899–1900)*

Y#	KM#	Metal	Description	VF	EF	Unc
2	25	Cop	1/2 Paisa, VS 1956 (1889)	15	—	—

INDIA–PRINCELY STATES: SUNTH

Bhawan Singhji, *1835–1871*

Pratap Singhji, *1871–1896*

Obverse: *Various symbols*
Reverse: *Shri Rampur*

Y#	KM#	Metal	Description	VF	EF	Unc
1	1/2	Cop	1/2 Paisa, ND	10	15	—
2	5	Cop	1 Paisa, ND	10	15	—

Note: These coins are often found overstruck by Lunavada, and vice versa.

INDIA–PRINCELY STATES: TONK

Mints: Sironj (to circa 1896), Tonk (1873–1934)

State Symbols: Five-petal flower before AH 1280, fly-whisk (leaf-like symbol) thereafter

Types: The descriptions given are general guides only. Much variation occurs in wording and arrangement of legends, particularly for Y8–28.

Wazir Muhammad Khan, *AH 1250–1280 (1834–1864)*

Designs: *Like Y2*

Y#	KM#	Metal	Description	VF	EF	Unc
1	1	Cop	1 Paisa, AH 1278 (1861)	15	—	—

Obverse: *Victoria-Sironj legend*
Reverse: *Wazir-Muhammad legend*

Y#	KM#	Metal	Description	VF	EF	Unc
2	2	Silv	1 Rupee, AH 1276–80 / Yr 23	25	45	—

MUHAMMAD ALI KHAN,
AH 1280–1284 (1864–1867)

Obverse: *Like Y2*
Reverse: *Muhammad Ali legend*

Y#	KM#	Metal	Description	VF	EF	Unc
3	3	Cop	1 Paisa, AH 1283–89 / Yr 23	10	15	—

Y#	KM#	Metal	Description	VF	EF	Unc
4	4	Silv	1/8 Rupee, ND (12 mm)	20	35	—
5	5	Silv	1/4 Rupee, AH 1289 (14–15 mm)	20	—	—
6	6	Silv	1/2 Rupee, AH 1289 (16–17 mm)	25	—	—
7	7	Silv	1 Rupee, AH 1282–96 / Yr 23 (20–23 mm)	25	40	—

Note: Coins of this series were struck into the following reign to 1879 (AH 1296).

MUHAMMAD IBRAHIM ALI KHAN,
AH 1284–1349 (1868–1930)

FIRST COINAGE

Obverse: *Queen Victoria–Tonk legend*
Reverse: *Md. Ibrahim legend*

Y#	KM#	Metal	Description	VF	EF	Unc
8	8	Cop	1 Paisa, AH 1290 (1873)	15		

Y#	KM#	Metal	Description	VF	EF	Unc
10	10	Silv	1 Rupee, 1873–77 / AH 1290–94	20	—	—

SECOND COINAGE

Sironj Mint

Obverse: *Empress of India–Sironj legend*
Reverse: *Like Y8*

Y#	KM#	Metal	Description	VF	EF	Unc
11	11	Cop	1 Pai, AH 1314 (1896)	37.50	—	—
12	12	Cop	1 Paisa, AH 1298–1308 (1881–90)	30.00	—	—

Y#	KM#	Metal	Description	VF	EF	Unc
A13	A13	Silv	1/8 Rupee, AH 1310 (1893)	30	—	—
13	13	Silv	1/4 Rupee, 1893, 96 / AH 1310, 14	25	—	—
14	14	Silv	1/2 Rupee, 1889, 93, 96 / AH 1306, 10, 14	30	—	—
15	15	Silv	1 Rupee, 1882–93 / AH 1299–1310	75	150	—

Tonk Mint

Obverse: *Ruler of England–Tonk legend*
Reverse: *Like Y8*

Y#	KM#	Metal	Description	VF	EF	Unc
16	16	Cop	1 Paisa, 1876–86 / AH 1290–1303	10	—	—

Obverse: *Like Y12 but Tonk*
Reverse: *Like Y8*
Planchets: *Dump*

Y#	KM#	Metal	Description	VF	EF	Unc
17	17	Silv	1/8 Rupee, 1892, 99 / AH 1309, 17	20	35	—
18	18	Silv	1/4 Rupee, 1888–99 / AH 1305–18	20	35	—
19	19	Silv	1/2 Rupee, 1888–99 / AH 1305–17	20	35	—
20	20	Silv	1 Rupee, 1876–97 / AH 1292–1315	30	50	—

Planchets: *Broad and thin*

Y#	KM#	Metal	Description	VF	EF	Unc
A21	20a	Silv	1 Rupee, 1880 / AH 1297	—	—	—
21	21	Silv	2 Rupees, 1880–81 / AH 1297–98 (32 mm)	—	—	—

Planchets: *Dump*

Y#	KM#	Metal	Description	VF	EF	Unc
22	22	Gold	1 Mohur, 1880 / AH 1297–98 (19 mm)	—	—	—

Planchets: *Broad and thin*

Y#	KM#	Metal	Description	VF	EF	Unc
23	23	Gold	2 Mohurs, 1880 / AH 1297 (31 mm)	—	—	—

THIRD COINAGE

Obverse: *George V legend*
Reverse: *Like Y8*

Y#	KM#	Metal	Description	VF	EF	Unc
24	24	Cop	1 Paisa, 1911–28 / AH 1329–45	5	—	—
A24	A24	Cop	1/4 Anna, 1917 / AH 1335–36	5	—	—

Y#	KM#	Metal	Description	VF	EF	Unc
25	25	Silv	1/8 Rupee, 1928 / AH 1346	25	40	—
26	26	Silv	1/4 Rupee, 1928 / AH 1346	25	40	—
27	27	Silv	1/2 Rupee, 1928 / AH 1346	25	40	—
28	28	Silv	1 Rupee, 1912–30 / AH 1329–48	30	50	—

MUHAMMAD SA'ADAT ALI KHAN,
AH 1349–1368 (1930–1949)

Obverse: *George V legend*
Reverse: *Md. Sa'adat Ali legend*

Y#	KM#	Metal	Description	VF	EF	Unc
29	29	Bz	1 Paisa, 1932 / AH 1350 (26 mm)	4	7	25
29a	29a	Bz	1 Paisa, 1932 / AH 1350 (struck 1934) (21 mm)	4	7	25

Obverse: *George V legend*
Reverse: *Md. Sa'adat Ali legend*
Planchets: *Dump*

Y#	KM#	Metal	Description	VF	EF	Unc
30	30	Silv	1/8 Rupee, 1934 / AH 1351–53	45	65	—

INDIA–PRINCELY STATES: TRAVANCORE

Dates are expressed in the Malabar Era (ME), which began in AD 824. For AD date, add 825 years to ME date.

MONETARY SYSTEM

16 cash = 1 chuckram
4 chuckram = 1 fanam
2 fanam = 1 anantaraya
52-1/2 fanam = 1 pagoda

Martanda Varma II, *1847–1860*

Y#	KM#	Metal	Description	VF	EF	Unc
1	16	Cop	1 Cash, ND (1848–60) (8–10 mm)	1	—	—
2	17	Cop	2 Cash, ND (1848–49) (10–11 mm)	4	—	—
3	18	Cop	4 Cash, ND (13–14 mm)	25	175	300
A3	19	Cop	8 Cash, ND (18–19 mm)	25	—	—

Obverse: ***Three-line legend in beaded circle***
Reverse: ***Blank***

Y#	KM#	Metal	Description	VF	EF	Unc
4	N/A	Gold	1/4 Pagoda, ND (1850) (9 mm, 13 mm) (0.64 g)	150	—	—
5	N/A	Gold	1/2 Pagoda, ND (10 mm, 14.5 mm) (1.27 g)	200	—	—
6	N/A	Gold	1 Pagoda, ND (13 mm, 17 mm) (2.55 g)	250	—	—
7	N/A	Gold	2 Pagodas, ND (15 mm, 20 mm) (5.10 g)	450	—	—

Rama Varma IV, *1860–1880*

Y#	KM#	Metal	Description	VF	EF	Unc
1a	20	Cop	1 Cash, ND (1860–85)	0.40	—	—

Note: Y1a is a slightly degenerate form of Y1, often with no features on face or body.

Obverse: ***Leaf sprays at sides***

Y#	KM#	Metal	Description	VF	EF	Unc
8	21	Silv	1 Chuckram, ND (1860–1901)	7	—	—

Note: Similar coins without leaf sprays are earlier issues.

Y#	KM#	Metal	Description	VF	EF	Unc
9	22	Silv	1 Velli Fanam, ND (1860–61)	45	75	125

Y#	KM#	Metal	Description	VF	EF	Unc
10	24	Silv	1 Velli Fanam, ND (1864)	35	55	—

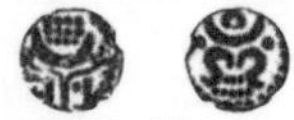

Obverse: ***Leaf sprays at sides***

Y#	KM#	Metal	Description	VF	EF	Unc
11	23	Gold	1 Anantaraya, ND (1860–90)	25	35	—

Note: Similar coins without leaf sprays are earlier issues.

Y#	KM#	Metal	Description	VF	EF	Unc
16	26	Gold	1 Pagoda, 1877 (17 mm)	3,000	4,000	4,500
17	27	Gold	2 Pagodas, 1877 (19 mm)	3,500	4,500	5,500

Rama Varma V, *1880–1885*

Y1a, 8, and 11 were continued through this reign.

Y#	KM#	Metal	Description	VF	EF	Unc
20	31	Gold	1/2 Sovereign, 1881 / ME 1057 (20 mm)	7,000	12,000	16,000
21	32	Gold	1 Sovereign, 1881 / ME 1057 (22 mm)	7,000	12,000	16,000

Note: Y20–21 are presentation coins struck to the British gold standard.

Rama Varma VI, *1885–1924*

First Coinage

Y8 and 11 were continued into this reign.

Y#	KM#	Metal	Description	VF	EF	Unc
1b	34	Cop	1 Cash, ND (1885–95)	4	6	—

Note: Y1b is a yet more degenerate version of Y1.

Y#	KM#	Metal	Description	VF	EF	Unc
22	35	Cop	1/4 Chuckram, ND (1888–89) (13 mm)	30	60	—
23	36	Cop	1/2 Chuckram, ND (17–20 mm)	20	40	—

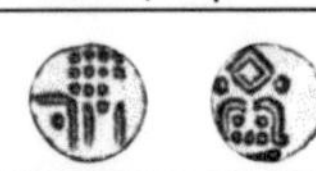

Y#	KM#	Metal	Description	VF	EF	Unc
24	39	Gold	1 Kali Fanam, ND (1890–95)	30	45	—

Second Coinage

Obverse: ***RV monogram***

Y#	KM#	Metal	Description	VF	EF	Unc
29	40	Bz	Cash 1, ND (1901)	1,000.00	1,500.00	—
30	41	Bz	Cash FOUR, ND (1901–10)	6.50	9.00	12
31	42	Bz	Cash EIGHT, ND (1901–10)	7.50	15.00	75
32	43	Bz	CHUCKRAM ONE, ND (1901–10)	7.50	15.00	100
30a	47	Bz	FOUR Cash, ND (1906–35)	7.50	12.50	25
31a	48	Bz	EIGHT Cash, ND (1906–35)	20.00	35.00	55
32a	49	Bz	ONE CHUCKRAM, ND (1906–35)	20.00	35.00	60

Y#	KM#	Metal	Description	VF	EF	Unc
33	44	Silv	CH(uckram)s 2, ND (1901)	30.00	65	115
33a	50	Silv	2 CHS, ND (1906–28)	27.50	50	100
34	54–55	Silv	ONE FANAM, ND (1911)	25.00	35	80
34a	51	Silv	FANAM ONE, ND (1911), ME 1087–1106 (1912–30)	12.00	25	100

Note: The undated variety of Y34a has either plain or reeded edge

Y#	KM#	Metal	Description	VF	EF	Unc
35	37	Silv	1/4 Rupee, 1889, ME 1082–1106 (1903–30)	85	175	400
36	38	Silv	1/2 Rupee, 1889, ME 1084–1107	150	300	—

BALA RAMA VARMA II, *1924–1949*

Y#	KM#	Metal	Description	VF	EF	Unc
41	57	Bz	1 Cash, ND (1938–45)	3.25	6.50	20

Obverse: ***BRV monogram***

Y#	KM#	Metal	Description	VF	EF	Unc
42	58	Bz	4 Cash, ND	7.50	15	25
43	59	Bz	8 Cash, ND	7.50	15	25

Y#	KM#	Metal	Description	VF	EF	Unc
44	60	Bz	1 Chuckram, ME 1114 (1938), ND (1939–45)	15	20	45

Y#	KM#	Metal	Description	VF	EF	Unc
45	61	Silv	1 Fanam, ME 1112 (1937)	25	45	85
45a	65	Silv	1 Fanam, ME 1116–21, modified dies	25	45	85
46	62	Silv	1/4 Rupee, ME 1112	35	55	135
46a	66	Silv	1/4 Rupee, ME 1116–18, modified dies	40	60	125
47	64	Silv	1/2 Rupee, ME 1112	30	50	115
47a	64	Silv	"Chitra" 1/2 Rupee, ME 1114, reeded edge	10	25	75
47b	67	Silv	"Chitra" 1/2 Rupee, ME 1116–21, security edge	40	60	125

Obverse: ***Conch shell within wreath***
Reverse: ***Tamil legend within wreath***

Y#	KM#	Metal	Description	VF	EF	Unc
48	N/A	Gold	1/4 Pagoda, ND (1870–1931) (0.64 g)	1,000	1,500	1,750
49	N/A	Gold	1/2 Pagoda, ND (1870–1931) (1.28 g)	900	1,200	1,500
50	N/A	Gold	1 Pagoda, ND (1870–1931) (2.54 g)	1,500	1,900	2,250
51	N/A	Gold	2 Pagodas, ND (1870–1931) (5.098 g)	2,800	3,800	4,500

INDONESIA

An archipelago of four large and some 6,000 smaller inhabited islands along the equator between Southeast Asia and Australia. The area came under Dutch control in the 17th century, and was known as the Netherlands Indies. Following Japanese occupation in World War II, it declared its independence in 1945 and fought until it was gained in 1949. In the mid-1960s its communist government was overthrown by a military coup. Free parliamentary elections resumed in 1999. *Languages:* Indonesian, English. *Capital:* Jakarta.

MONETARY SYSTEM

100 sen = 1 rupiah

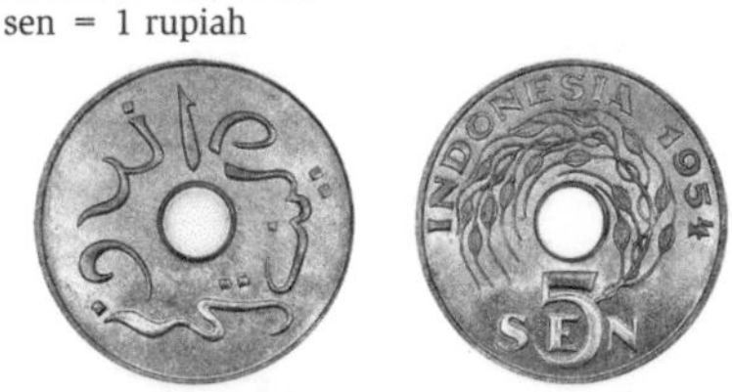

Y#	KM#	Metal	Description	VF	EF	Unc
1	7	Alum	1 Sen, 1952	0.35	0.65	1.50
2	5	Alum	5 Sen, 1951, 54	0.30	0.60	0.75

Y#	KM#	Metal	Description	VF	EF	Unc
3	6	Alum	10 Sen, 1951, 54	0.20	0.35	0.50
4	8	Alum	25 Sen, 1952	0.20	0.35	0.50

Design: ***English inscription INDONESIA over eagle***

Y#	KM#	Metal	Description	VF	EF	Unc
3a	12	Alum	10 Sen, 1957	0.45	0.75	1.25
4a	11	Alum	25 Sen, 1955, 57	0.20	0.35	0.50

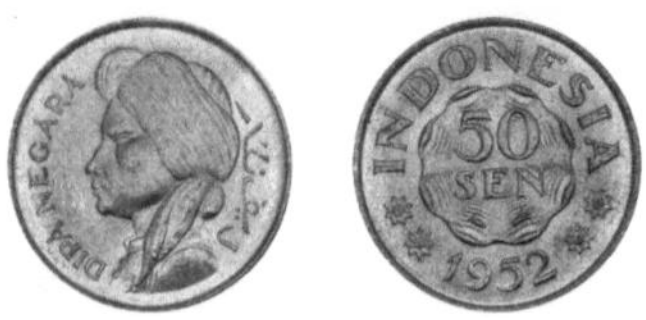

Y#	KM#	Metal	Description	VF	EF	Unc
5	9	C-N	50 Sen, 1952	0.20	0.35	0.75

Design: ***Malayan word behind head omitted***

Y#	KM#	Metal	Description	VF	EF	Unc
5a	10	C-N	50 Sen, 1954–57	0.20	0.35	0.75

Y#	KM#	Metal	Description	VF	EF	Unc
7	13–14	Alum	50 Sen, 1958–61	0.25	0.40	0.75

PROVINCIAL COINAGE

RIAU ARCHIPELAGO

Area comprising small islands between Singapore and Sumatra.

Design: ***KEPULAUAN RIAU inscribed on edge***

Y#	KM#	Metal	Description	VF	EF	Unc
8	5	Alum	1 Sen, 1962	0.50	1.25	2.50
9	6	Alum	5 Sen, 1962	0.50	1.25	2.75
10	7	Alum	10 Sen, 1962	0.50	1.25	3.00
11	8	Alum	25 Sen, 1962	1.00	2.50	5.00
12	9	Alum	50 Sen, 1962	1.25	3.00	6.50

IRIAN BARAT (WEST NEW GUINEA)

Formerly Netherlands New Guinea. Came under administration of Indonesia May 1, 1963.

Design: ***No inscription on edge***

Y#	KM#	Metal	Description	VF	EF	Unc
8a	5	Alum	1 Sen, 1962	0.50	1.25	2
9a	6	Alum	5 Sen, 1962	0.50	1.25	2
10a	7	Alum	10 Sen, 1962	0.50	1.25	2
11a	8	Alum	25 Sen, 1962	1.00	2.50	4
12a	9	Alum	50 Sen, 1962	1.50	3.75	7

Note: Y8–10a have plain edge; Y11a–12a have reeded edge.

IRAN (PERSIA)

Between the Tigris and Indus rivers in southwest Asia, Iran is one of the oldest countries in the world, being mentioned in the Bible as the land of the Persians. Use of the name Iran became widespread in the 1920s. The nation has been ruled by an Islamic theocracy since the monarchy was overthrown in 1979. Reformers and religious conservatives have contended for control since then. *Languages:* Persian, Arabic, Kurdish. *Capital:* Tehran.

MONETARY SYSTEM

50 dinars = 1 shahi
1000 dinars = 20 shahis = 1 qiran (kran)
10 qirans = 1 toman

PRECIOUS METAL CONTENT

Dates	Denomination	Gross Wt (g)	Fineness	Net Wt (g)	Troy Oz.
		SILVER			
1878–1929	3 shahi	0.6908	0.9000	0.6217	0.0200
	1/4 qiran	1.1513	0.9000	1.0362	0.0333
	500 dinar	2.3025	0.9000	2.0723	0.0666
	1,000 dinar	4.6050	0.9000	4.1445	0.1332
	2,000 dinar	9.2100	0.9000	8.2890	0.2665
	5,000 dinar	23.0251	0.9000	20.7226	0.6662
	1 toman	46.0501	0.9000	41.4451	1.3325
1931–36	1/4 rial	1.2500	0.8280	1.0350	0.0333
	1/2 rial	2.5000	0.8280	2.0700	0.0666
	1 rial	5.0000	0.8280	4.1400	0.1331
	2 rial	3.2000	0.6000	1.9200	0.0617
	5 rial	8.0000	0.6000	4.8000	0.1543
1943–51	1 rial	1.6000	0.6000	0.9600	0.0309
	2 rial	3.2000	0.6000	1.9200	0.0617
	5 rial	8.0000	0.6000	4.8000	0.1543
	10 rial	16.0000	0.6000	9.6000	0.3086

Dates	Denomination	Gross Wt (g)	Fineness	Net Wt (g)	Troy Oz.
		GOLD			
1879–1926	1/5 toman / 2,000 dinar	0.5749	0.9000	0.5174	0.0166
	1/2 toman / 5,000 dinar	1.4372	0.9000	1.2935	0.0416
	1 toman	2.8744	0.9000	2.5870	0.0832
	2 toman	5.7488	0.9000	5.1739	0.1663
	5 toman	14.3720	0.9000	12.9348	0.4159
	10 toman	28.7440	0.9000	25.8696	0.8317
1926–29	1 pahlavi	1.9180	0.9000	1.7262	0.0555
	2 pahlavi	3.8360	0.9000	3.4524	0.1110
	5 pahlavi	9.5900	0.9000	8.6310	0.2775
1931–79	1/4 pahlavi	2.0340	0.9000	1.8306	0.0589
	1/2 pahlavi	4.0680	0.9000	3.6612	0.1177
	1 pahlavi	8.1360	0.9000	7.3224	0.2354
	2-1/2 pahlavi	20.3400	0.9000	18.3060	0.5885
	5 pahlavi	40.6799	0.9000	36.6119	1.1771

NASIR AL-DIN SHAH, *AH 1264–1313 (1848–1896)*

Obverse: ***Value in dinar***

Y#	KM#	Metal	Description	VF	EF	Unc
1	881	Cop	12 Dinar, ND, AH 1301 (1884) (15 mm)	135.00	225	—
2	882	Cop	25 Dinar, ND, AH 1293–1307 (20 mm)	17.50	40	85
4	883	Cop	50 Dinar, ND, AH 1293–1305, 1330 (error) (25 mm)	12.50	30	—
5	885	Cop	100 Dinar, ND, AH 1297–1313, 1330 (error) (30 mm)	25.00	50	—

Y#	KM#	Metal	Description	VF	EF	Unc
6	887	Cop	200 Dinar, AH 1300–01 (33 mm)	150	350	—

Obverse: ***Value in Shahi***

Y#	KM#	Metal	Description	VF	EF	Unc
4a	884	Cop	1 Shahi, ND, AH 1305 (25 mm)	85	175	—
5a	886	Cop	2 Shahi, ND, AH 1305 (30 mm)	100	200	—

NEW YEAR ISSUES

These pieces, although having monetary value, were primarily exchanged as New Year tokens among friends. Valued at 3 shahi by weight, they bear only the word "Shahi" and often are known as "Shahi Sefid," or "White Shahi."

Designs: ***Like Y9–12***

Y#	KM#	Metal	Description	VF	EF	Unc
7	888	Silv	(3 Shahi), AH 1296, date in wreath, thin (17 mm)	90	175.00	—
7a	889	Silv	(3) Shahi, ND, AH 1297–1309, date at bottom	10	18.50	—
7b	890	Silv	(3) Shahi, AH 1313, date in lion's legs	75	150.00	—

Obverse: ***Like Y11***
Reverse: ***Like YA25***

Y#	KM#	Metal	Description	VF	EF	Unc
8	891	Silv	(3 Shahi), ND	75	150	—

REGULAR ISSUES

Design: ***Values in qiran and dinar, date at bottom***

Obverse: ***Three-line Nasir legend***

Y#	KM#	Metal	Description	VF	EF	Unc
9	892	Silv	1/4 (Qiran), ND, AH 1296–1311 (1879–94) (15 mm)	30	75	400
10	894.1	Silv	500 Dinar, ND, AH 1296–1311 (18 mm)	100	200	—
11	899	Silv	1,000 Dinar, ND, AH 1296–1306 (23 mm)	15	35	125
12	904	Silv	2,000 Dinar, AH 1296–98 (27 mm)	20	40	150

Obverse: ***Value and date***

Y#	KM#	Metal	Description	VF	EF	Unc
13	914	Silv	5,000 Dinar, AH 1296–97	125	250	925

Obverse: ***Four-line Nasir legend***

Y#	KM#	Metal	Description	VF	EF	Unc
11a	900	Silv	1,000 Dinar, AH 1298–1303	20	45	100
12a	905	Silv	2,000 Dinar, AH 1298–1308	25	50	125

Design: ***Value in qiran, date at bottom***
Obverse: ***Like Y11a***

Y#	KM#	Metal	Description	VF	EF	Unc
12b	908	Silv	2 Qiran, AH 1310	120	350	—

Design: ***Values in shahi and qiran***
Obverse: ***Like Y9–12***
Reverse: ***Like Y10c***

Y#	KM#	Metal	Description	VF	EF	Unc
10b	896	Silv	10 Shahi, AH 1310	100	275	—

Obverse: ***Like Y11a***
Reverse: ***Date in lion's legs***

Y#	KM#	Metal	Description	VF	EF	Unc
10c	897	Silv	10 Shahi, AH 1310–11	125	280	—
11c	901	Silv	1 Qiran, AH 1310–11 (23 mm)	120	275	—
12c	909	Silv	2 Qiran, AH 1310–11 (27 mm)	60	125	—

Obverse: ***Like Y13***

Y#	KM#	Metal	Description	VF	EF	Unc
13c	915	Silv	5 Qiran, AH 1311	2,000	3,500	—

Design: ***Qiran-dinar values resumed, date in lion's legs***

Obverse: ***Like Y9–12***

Y#	KM#	Metal	Description	VF	EF	Unc
9d	893	Silv	1/4 (Qiran), AH 1311–12 (15 mm)	100	200	—
10d	898	Silv	500 Dinar, AH 1311–13	150	250	—

Obverse: ***Like Y11a***

Y#	KM#	Metal	Description	VF	EF	Unc
11d	902	Silv	1,000 Dinar, AH 1311 (23 mm)	150	300	—
12d	911	Silv	2,000 Dinar, AH 1311–12 (27 mm)	85	175	—

Designs: ***Like Y9–12***

Y#	KM#	Metal	Description	VF	EF	Unc
A16	923	Gold	1/5 Toman, AH 1295 (11.5 mm)	300	500	—
B16	Pn17	Gold	1/4 Toman, AH 1295 (14 mm)	—	—	—
C16	Pn16	Gold	5,000 Dinar, AH 1296, 98 (17 mm)	—	—	—
D16	N/A	Gold	1 Toman, AH 1296 (19 mm)	—	—	—

Note: YB16–D16 may be patterns.

Obverse: ***Like Y18 but no legend***
Reverse: ***Like Y18***

Y#	KM#	Metal	Description	VF	EF	Unc
16	924	Gold	1/5 Toman, AH 1297–1301, date on reverse (13 mm)	150	175	—
17	927	Gold	5,000 Dinar, ND, AH 1297–1305, date on obverse (16.5 mm)	150	1,175	—
A18	A932	Gold	1 Toman, ND, AH 1297 (19 mm)	200	350	—

Note: YA18 may be a pattern.

Obverse: ***First portrait with legend***
Reverse: ***Like obverse of Y11a***

Y#	KM#	Metal	Description	VF	EF	Unc
18	933	Gold	1 Toman, AH 1297–1312 (2.9 g) (19 mm)	175	300	—

Y#	KM#	Metal	Description	VF	EF	Unc
19	943	Gold	2 Toman, AH 1297–1309 (5.7 g) (21 mm)	400	900	—

Note: Y18–19 bear accession date AH 1264 at lower right. Actual date (sometimes blundered) appears at upper left, or divided at upper left and upper right.

Y#	KM#	Metal	Description	VF	EF	Unc
21	945	Gold	10 Toman, AH 1296–1311 (28.6 g) (36 mm)	5,000	9,000	—

Obverse: ***Second portrait***

Y#	KM#	Metal	Description	VF	EF	Unc
22	936	Gold	1 Toman, AH 1310, reverse 3-line legend	400	600	—
22a	937	Gold	1 Toman, AH 1311, reverse 4-line legend	225	350	—

Obverse: ***Like Y22a but no legend***
Reverse: ***Like Y21***

Y#	KM#	Metal	Description	VF	EF	Unc
A23	946	Gold	10 Toman, AH 1311	8,000	—	—

LARGESSE ISSUE

Y#	KM#	Metal	Description	VF	EF	Unc
15	917	Silv	1 Toman, (10 Qiran), AH 1301 (1884)	950	1,500	—

Note: Some authorities consider Y15 a medal rather than a coin.

Commemorating Shah's Return from Europe

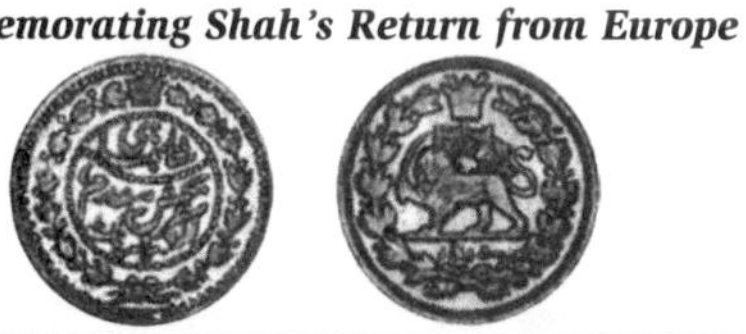

Y#	KM#	Metal	Description	VF	EF	Unc
A15	895	Silv	500 Dinar, AH 1307 (1889)	225	400	—

Obverse: *Like Y18–19*
Reverse: *Like obverse of YA15*

Y#	KM#	Metal	Description	VF	EF	Unc
D15	934	Gold	1 Toman, AH 1307	1,000	2,000	—
B15	943	Gold	2 Toman, AH 1307	1,250	2,500	—

Bank Official's Mint Visit

Obverse: *Like Y19*
Reverse: *Legend in wreath*

Y#	KM#	Metal	Description	VF	EF	Unc
E15	944	Gold	2 Toman, AH 1308	—	—	—

50 Years of Reign

Y#	KM#	Metal	Description	VF	EF	Unc
C15	912	Silv	2,000 Dinar, AH 1313	3,000	5,000	—

Note: YC15 may not have been released to circulation due to the assassination of the shah. Silver and gold pieces dated 1313 with portraits are medals.

GENERAL COINAGE

Y#	KM#	Metal	Description	VF	EF	Unc
23	961	C-N	50 Dinar, AH 1318–37 (1900–19) (19 mm)	2.50	7.50	15
24	962	C-N	100 Dinar, AH 1318–37	2.50	7.50	15

Note: Y23–24 were issued without the name of the ruler through several successive reigns.

MUZAFFAR AL-DIN SHAH, *AH 1314–1324 (1897–1907)*

NEW YEAR ISSUES

Obverse: *Muzaffar legend*
Reverse: *Date in lion's legs*

Y#	KM#	Metal	Description	VF	EF	Unc
25	965	Silv	(3) Shahi, ND, AH 1314–20, thin (16–17 mm)	20	40	85
25a	966	Silv	(3 Shahi), ND, no value below lion	40	85	150

Obverse: *Like Y25*
Reverse: *In name of Sahib al-Zaman*

Y#	KM#	Metal	Description	VF	EF	Unc
A25	967	Silv	(3 Shahi), ND	80	160	280

REGULAR ISSUES

Some coins in this series are characterized by poor dies, weak strikes, blundered dates, and variable date positions.

First Coinage

Obverse: *Muzaffar legend*
Reverse: *Date in lion's legs*

Y#	KM#	Metal	Description	VF	EF	Unc
26	968	Silv	1/4 (Qiran), ND, AH 1316–19 (1898–1901) (15 mm)	17.50	35	65
27	969	Silv	500 Dinar, ND, AH 1313–22 (18–19 mm)	22.50	45	80
A27	N/A	Silv	1,000 Dinar, AH 1313–14 (23 mm)	175.00	325	450
28	973	Silv	2,000 Dinar, AH 1313–14	115.00	200	350

Obverse: ***Crown added at top***

Y#	KM#	Metal	Description	VF	EF	Unc
A27a	972	Silv	1,000 Dinar, AH 1317–22	160.00	240	350
28a	974	Silv	2,000 Dinar, AH 1314–20	22.50	45	160
28b	975	Silv	2 Qiran, AH 1320–22	22.50	35	80

Y#	KM#	Metal	Description	VF	EF	Unc
29	976	Silv	5,000 Dinar, AH 1320	15	30	60

Obverse: ***Like Y26–28***
Reverse: ***Date at bottom***

Y#	KM#	Metal	Description	VF	EF	Unc
A38	986	Gold	1/5 Toman, AH 1309 (error)	200	300	450
38	987	Gold	1/2 Toman, AH 1314–15	250	350	525
39	988	Gold	1 Toman, AH 1314	300	350	550
A39	N/A	Gold	2 Toman, AH 1311 (error)	—	—	—

Note: YA39 is presumably the same size as Y39 but double the weight. Verification of sizes and weights for this series is requested.

Second Coinage

Y#	KM#	Metal	Description	VF	EF	Unc
30	977	Silv	500 Dinar, AH 1319, 23 (1901, 05)	40	100	200
31	978	Silv	1,000 Dinar, AH 1319, 23	40	100	200

Note: Y30–33 dated AH 1319 are probably patterns.

Y#	KM#	Metal	Description	VF	EF	Unc
32	979	Silv	2,000 Dinar, AH 1319, 23	35	75	175
33	981	Silv	5,000 Dinar, AH 1319, 24	2,500	4,500	7,500

Note: Y30–33 dated AH 1319 are probably patterns.

Obverse: ***First portrait, no legend***
Reverse: ***Like obverse of Y26–28***

Y#	KM#	Metal	Description	VF	EF	Unc
A34	991	Gold	1/5 Toman, ND, AH 1317, date on reverse (15 mm)	300	400	700
40	996	Gold	2 Toman, AH 1322, date on obverse (5.7 g) (19 mm)	750	2,000	3,500

Note: Y40 is said to be 1 toman size, but double thick. It bears no value, and may also exist in 1 toman weight (2.9 g).

Reverse: ***Like Y21 but Muzaffar legend***

Y#	KM#	Metal	Description	VF	EF	Unc
B34	998	Gold	10 Toman, AH 1314 (29 g)	5,000	9,000	15,000

Note: YB34 bears value "dah tuman" at top of reverse, but pieces of only 5 toman weight (14.6 g) are said to exist also.

Obverse: ***Value and date added***

Y#	KM#	Metal	Description	VF	EF	Unc
A34a	992	Gold	1/5 Toman, AH 1319	150	200	350

Obverse: ***Second portrait, no legend***

Y#	KM#	Metal	Description	VF	EF	Unc
34	N/A	Gold	1/5 Toman, AH 1323–24	100	200	400
35	994	Gold	1/2 Toman, AH 1316–23	100	150	200
35a	N/A	Gold	1/2 Toman, AH 1323, reverse of YA25 (mule)	—	—	—

Obverse: ***Legend added***

Y#	KM#	Metal	Description	VF	EF	Unc
36	995	Gold	1 Toman, AH 1316–24 (2.9 g) (19 mm)	175	300	450

Commemorating Royal Birthday

Design: ***Like Y33, legend at sides of head***

Y#	KM#	Metal	Description	VF	EF	Unc
A40	980	Silv	5,000 Dinar, AH 1322 (1904)	850	1,500	4,000

Design: *Like Y40, legend at sides of head*

Y#	KM#	Metal	Description	VF	EF	Unc
41	997	Gold	2 Toman, AH 1322 (1904) (5.8 g) (19 mm)	850	1,500	3,000

MUHAMMAD ALI SHAH, *AH 1324–1327 (1907–1909)*

NEW YEAR ISSUES

Obverse: *Muhammad Ali legend*
Reverse: *Date in lion's legs*

Y#	KM#	Metal	Description	VF	EF	Unc
44	1006	Silv	(3) Shahi, AH 1325–27, thin (17 mm)	45	90	175

Obverse: *Like Y44*
Reverse: *Like YA25*

Y#	KM#	Metal	Description	VF	EF	Unc
A44	1008	Silv	(3 Shahi), ND	70	140	200

Obverse: *Like reverse of YA25*
Reverse: *Like reverse of Y44*

Y#	KM#	Metal	Description	VF	EF	Unc
B44	1007	Silv	(3) Shahi, AH 1326	110	160	300

REGULAR ISSUES

First Coinage

Obverse: *Muhammad Ali legend*
Reverse: *Date in lion's legs*

Y#	KM#	Metal	Description	VF	EF	Unc
45	1009	Silv	1/4 (Qiran), AH 1325–27 (15 mm)	23	45	90
46	1010	Silv	500 Dinar, AH 1325–26 (18 mm)	60	120	250
A47	1011	Silv	1,000 Dinar, AH 1325–26 (23 mm)	300	500	750
47	1019	Silv	2 Qiran, AH 1325–27 (28 mm)	12	25	50

Y#	KM#	Metal	Description	VF	EF	Unc
55a		Gold	1/5 Toman, AH 1324 (.56 g)	1,000	1,500	2,000
56	1021	Gold	5,000 Dinar, AH 1324–25 (17 mm)	275	400	600
A56	1022	Gold	1 Toman, AH 1324 (19 mm)	500	800	1,500

Second Coinage

Y#	KM#	Metal	Description	VF	EF	Unc
48	1013	Silv	500 Dinar, AH 1326–27	100	200	350
49	1015	Silv	1,000 Dinar, AH 1326–27	80	175	500
50	1017	Silv	2,000 Dinar, AH 1326	1,000	1,750	3,000
A50	1018	Silv	5,000 Dinar, AH 1327	850	1,500	2,500

Obverse: *Like Y48–A50 but no legend or wreath*
Reverse: *Like obverse of Y45–47*

Y#	KM#	Metal	Description	VF	EF	Unc
53	1025	Gold	1/2 Toman, AH 1327, 62 (error) (1.4 g) (17 mm)	250	450	800
54	1026	Gold	1 Toman, AH 1326–27	400	750	1,500

Note: Similar 1/5 and 2 toman pieces have been reported.

AHMAD SHAH, *AH 1327–1344 (1909–1925)*

FIRST COINAGE

New Year Issue

Obverse: *Ahmad legend*

Y#	KM#	Metal	Description	VF	EF	Unc
64	1031	Silv	(3) Shahi, AH 1328–30 (1910–12), date at bottom	12.50	25	75
A64	1032	Silv	(3) Shahi, AH 1332, date in lion's legs	45.00	80	200

Note: Mules exist from various dies of Y64, A70, and B70.

Regular Issues

Obverse: *Ahmad legend*
Reverse: *Date at bottom*

Y#	KM#	Metal	Description	VF	EF	Unc
65	1035	Silv	1/4 (Qiran), AH 1327–31 (15 mm)	10	20	75
66	1036	Silv	500 Dinar, AH 1327–30 (18 mm)	15	25	85
67	1038	Silv	1,000 Dinar, AH 1327–30 (23 mm)	15	25	100
68	1040	Silv	2 Qiran, AH 1327–29 (28 mm)	15	25	100
68a	1041	Silv	2,000 Dinar, AH 1330	20	45	125

Reverse: ***Date in lion's legs***

Y#	KM#	Metal	Description	VF	EF	Unc
68b	1043	Silv	2,000 Dinar, AH 1330–31	20	45	125

Designs: ***Like Y65–68a***

Y#	KM#	Metal	Description	VF	EF	Unc
75	1066	Gold	1/5 Toman, AH 1329 (14 mm)	Rare		
76	1067	Gold	1/2 Toman, AH 1329	275	375	550
77	1068	Gold	1 Toman, AH 1329	300	500	750

Second Coinage

New Year Issues

Mules exist from various dies of Y64, A70, and B70.

Obverse: ***Ahmad legend, date at bottom***

Y#	KM#	Metal	Description	VF	EF	Unc
A70	1047	Silv	(3) Shahi, AH 1333–42	12.50	25	85

Obverse: ***Like reverse of YA25***
Reverse: ***Date in lion's legs***

Y#	KM#	Metal	Description	VF	EF	Unc
B70	1049	Silv	(3) Shahi, ND, AH 1332–42	25	50	125

Note: YB70 without date cannot be definitely assigned to this reign.

Regular Issues

Obverse: ***Ahmad legend***
Reverse: ***Date in lion's legs***

Y#	KM#	Metal	Description	VF	EF	Unc
C70	1051	Silv	1/4 (Qiran), AH 1327 (error), 32–43 (1914–25)	12.50	25	75

Y#	KM#	Metal	Description	VF	EF	Unc
70	1054	Silv	500 Dinar, AH 1331–43	12.50	25	75
71	1056	Silv	1,000 Dinar, AH 1331–44	15.00	30	100
72	1057	Silv	2,000 Dinar, AH 1330–44	20.00	40	135
69	1058	Silv	5,000 Dinar, AH 1331–44	25.00	50	175

Y#	KM#	Metal	Description	VF	EF	Unc
79	1070	Gold	2,000 Dinar, AH 1335–41 (14 mm)	75	100	150
80	1071	Gold	5,000 Dinar, AH 1333–37 (17 mm)	125	150	200
80a	1072	Gold	5,000 Dinar, AH 1340, 42, reverse of YA25 (mule)	200	300	750
81	1074	Gold	1 Toman, AH 1337–43 (2.9 g) (19 mm)	200	275	350
A81	1073	Gold	2 Toman, AH 1332, size and weight of Y81	600	900	1,250

Note: Gold coins similar to Y70–72, with values of 2, 5, and 15 Ashrafi are believed to be patterns. Other gold pieces larger than 2 toman bear no values, have variable weights, and appear to be medals only.

Tenth-Year-Jubilee Issues

Obverse: ***Legends at sides of head***

Y#	KM#	Metal	Description	VF	EF	Unc
73	1059	Silv	1,000 Dinar, AH 1337 (1919)	100	175	300
74	1060	Silv	2,000 Dinar, AH 1337	125	250	400

Reza Shah Pahlavi, *SH 1304–1320 (1925–1941)*

Solar year adopted S.H. 1304, started March 21, 1925

MONETARY SYSTEM
10,000 dinar = 1 pahlavi, 1926–1930

New Year Issue

Obverse: ***Four-line legend, no wreath***
Reverse: ***Date below lion***

Y#	KM#	Metal	Description	VF	EF	Unc
119	1108	Gold	1 Toman, SH 1305 (1926) (19 mm)	250	375	750

Regular Issues

First Coinage

Y#	KM#	Metal	Description	VF	EF	Unc
95	1091	C-N	50 Dinar, SH 1305, 07 (1926, 28)	30	60	125
96	1092	C-N	100 Dinar, SH 1305, 07	30	60	125

Note: Y95–96 are identical to Y23–24 except for using the solar dating system.

Obverse: ***In the name of Kingdom of Iran***
Reverse: ***Date below lion***

Y#	KM#	Metal	Description	VF	EF	Unc
100	1093	Silv	1/4 (Qiran), SH 1304 (1925) (15 mm)	50	90	175

Y#	KM#	Metal	Description	VF	EF	Unc
A101	1094	Silv	500 Dinar, SH 1304	4,500	—	—
101	1095	Silv	1,000 Dinar, SH 1304–05	20	35	60
102	1096	Silv	2,000 Dinar, SH 1304–05	35	45	80
103	1097	Silv	5,000 Dinar, SH 1304–05	45	80	175

Second Coinage

Obverse: ***In name of Reza***
Reverse: ***Date at bottom***

Y#	KM#	Metal	Description	VF	EF	Unc
105	1098	Silv	500 Dinar, SH 1305	150	300	450
106	1099	Silv	1,000 Dinar, SH 1305–06	10	20	35
107	1100	Silv	2,000 Dinar, SH 1305–06	10	20	35
108	1101	Silv	5,000 Dinar, SH 1305–06	50	100	175

Y#	KM#	Metal	Description	VF	EF	Unc
116	1111	Gold	1 Pahlavi, SH 1305 (1926)	250	375	750
117	1112	Gold	2 Pahlavi, SH 1305	600	122	1,850
118	1113	Gold	5 Pahlavi, SH 1305	2,500	4,500	12,000

Third Coinage

Y#	KM#	Metal	Description	VF	EF	Unc
A109	1102	Silv	500 Dinar, SH 1306–08	17.50	35	60
109	1103	Silv	1,000 Dinar, SH 1306–08	17.50	35	60
110	1104	Silv	2,000 Dinar, SH 1306–08	15.00	25	50
111	1106	Silv	5,000 Dinar, SH 1306–08	35.00	70	150

Y#	KM#	Metal	Description	VF	EF	Unc
120	1114	Gold	1 Pahlavi, SH 1306–08 (1927–29)	200	300	500
121	1115	Gold	2 Pahlavi, SH 1306–08	300	400	650
122	1116	Gold	5 Pahlavi, SH 1306–08	1,250	2,500	5,000

Fourth Coinage

5 dinar = 1 shahi
100 dinar = 1 rial
100 rial = 1 pahlavi

Y#	KM#	Metal	Description	VF	EF	Unc
93	1121	Bz	1 Dinar, SH 1310 (1931)	25	50	125
94	1122	Bz	2 Dinar, SH 1310	28	60	150

Y#	KM#	Metal	Description	VF	EF	Unc
97	1123	C-N	5 Dinar, SH 1310 (18.5 mm)	30	60	175
98	1124	C-N	10 Dinar, SH 1310 (21 mm)	30	60	200
99	1125	C-N	25 Dinar, SH 1310 (24 mm)	40	80	250

Y#	KM#	Metal	Description	VF	EF	Unc
97a	1123a	Cop	5 Dinar, SH 1314	200	300	500
98a	1124a	Cop	10 Dinar, SH 1314	50	100	300
99a	1125a	Cop	25 Dinar, SH 1314	200	300	500
92	1126	Cop	10 Shahi (50 Dinar), SH 1314 (24.5 mm)	5	15	50

Obverse: ***Like Y100***
Reverse: ***Date at bottom***

Y#	KM#	Metal	Description	VF	EF	Unc
104	1127	Silv	1/4 (Rial), SH 1315	5	10	20

Obverse: ***In name of Reza***

Y#	KM#	Metal	Description	VF	EF	Unc
112	1128	Silv	1/2 Rial, SH 1310–15 (1931–36) (18 mm)	6.00	12	30
113	1129	Silv	1 Rial, SH 1310–13 (22.5 mm)	7.50	15	40
114	1130	Silv	2 Rial, SH 1310–13 (26 mm)	7.50	15	50
115	1131	Silv	5 Rial, SH 1310–13 (37 mm)	20.00	35	75

Y#	KM#	Metal	Description	VF	EF	Unc
123	1132	Gold	1/2 Pahlavi, SH 1310–15	450	650	1,200
124	1133	Gold	1 Pahlavi, SH 1310	2,000	2,750	5,500

General Coinage

Y125–128 were issued without the name of the ruler through the last years of Reza Shah and continued into the following reign. The listings have been combined with former YA129–E129.

Y#	KM#	Metal	Description	VF	EF	Unc
125	1138	A-Bz	5 Dinar, SH 1315–21 (1936–42) (16 mm)	1.00	3	7
126	1139	A-Bz	10 Dinar, SH 1315–21 (18 mm)	1.00	3	7
127	1140	A-Bz	25 Dinar, SH 1326–29 (19 mm)	32.50	65	125
128	1142	A-Bz	50 Dinar, SH 1315–32 (20 mm)	2.00	4	12

Y#	KM#	Metal	Description	VF	EF	Unc
128a	1142a	Bz	50 Dinar, SH 1322 (1943)	2	4	10

Mohammad Reza Pahlavi, *1941–1979*

First Coinage

Obverse: ***In the name of Mohammad Reza***
Reverse: ***Lion in full wreath***

Y#	KM#	Metal	Description	VF	EF	Unc
129	1143	Silv	1 Rial, SH 1322–30 (1943–51) (18 mm)	1.50	2.50	6
130	1144	Silv	2 Rial, SH 1322–30 (22 mm)	1.75	3.50	7

Y#	KM#	Metal	Description	VF	EF	Unc
131	1145	Silv	5 Rial, SH 1322–28 (26 mm)	2.00	4.50	10
132	1146	Silv	10 Rial, SH 1323–26 (32 mm)	4.50	9.00	20

Y#	KM#	Metal	Description	VF	EF	Unc
133	1147	Gold	1/2 Pahlavi, SH 1322–23 (1943–44)	BV	BV	275
134	1148	Gold	1 Pahlavi, SH 1322–24	BV	BV	550

Obverse: ***Head in high relief***

Y#	KM#	Metal	Description	VF	EF	Unc
135	1149	Gold	1/2 Pahlavi, SH 1324–30 (1945–51)	BV	BV	BV
136	1150	Gold	1 Pahlavi, SH 1324–30	BV	BV	550

Second Coinage

Design: ***Like Y128***

Y#	KM#	Metal	Description	VF	EF	Unc
137	1156	A-Bz	50 Dinar, SH 1332–54 (1954–76), thin	0.30	0.60	2.50

Obverse: ***No crown at top***
Reverse: ***Lion in small wreath***

Y#	KM#	Metal	Description	VF	EF	Unc
138	1157	C-N	1 Rial, SH (13)31–36 (18.5 mm)	0.75	1.50	4.00
139	1158	C-N	2 Rial, SH 1331–36 (2 vars) (22.5 mm)	1.00	1.75	6.00
140	1159	C-N	5 Rial, SH 1331–36 (26 mm)	1.75	3.50	7.50

Note: Y138 uses only the last two digits of the date.

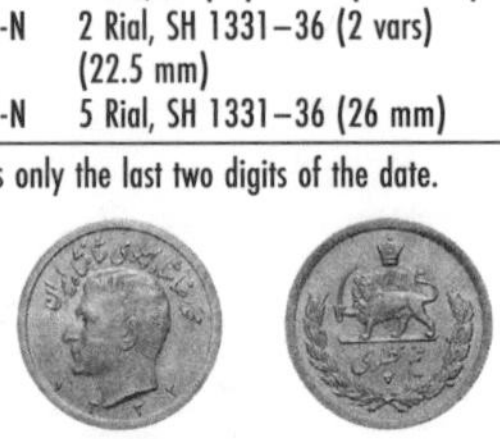

Obverse: ***Head in lower relief***

Y#	KM#	Metal	Description	VF	EF	Unc
141	1160	Gold	1/4 Pahlavi, SH 1332–35 (14 mm)	BV	150	185
141a	Several	Gold	1/4 Pahlavi, SH 1336–55 (16 mm)	BV	BV	185

Y#	KM#	Metal	Description	VF	EF	Unc
142	Several	Gold	1/2 Pahlavi, SH 1333–55	BV	BV	80
143	Several	Gold	1 Pahlavi, SH 1333–55	BV	BV	250
144	Several	Gold	2-1/2 Pahlavi, SH 1339–55	BV	1,375	1,450
145	Several	Gold	5 Pahlavi, SH 1339–55	BV	2,650	3,000

Reduced Weight and Thickness

Y#	KM#	Metal	Description	VF	EF	Unc
A140a	1171a	C-N	1 Rial, SH 1338–54, MS 2536 (1959–77)	0.15	0.20	2.00
B140	1173	C-N	2 Rials, SH 1338–57, MS 2536 (1959–77)	0.15	0.20	3.00
C140a	1175a	C-N	5 Rials, SH 1338–46 (1959–67)	0.40	1.00	3.50
D140a	1177a	C-N	10 Rials, SH 1341–44 (1962–65)	0.75	1.50	4.00

IRAQ

Extending along the Tigris and Euphrates valleys in western Asia, it encompasses the area of the world's oldest known civilization. In modern times it has been held by Turkey, been a British mandate under the League of Nations, and became a sovereign state in 1932. A 1958 military junta ended the monarchy, and the country saw a succession of similar takeovers between the military and the Baath Socialist Party through the 1960s. A U.S.-led deposition of the ruling government in 2003 set the stage for a new government in 2004, though the nation has been in sectarian civil war ever since. *Languages:* Arabic, Kurdish. *Capital:* Baghdad.

MONETARY SYSTEM

50 fils = 1 dirham
200 fils = 1 riyal
1000 fils = 1 dinar (pound)

PRECIOUS METAL CONTENT

Dates	Denomination	Gross Wt (g)	Fineness	Net Wt (g)	Troy Oz.
		SILVER			
1931–53	20 fils	3.6000	0.5000	1.8000	0.0579
	50 fils	9.0000	0.5000	4.5000	0.1447
	1 riyal	20.0000	0.9000	18.0000	0.5787
1959	25 fils	2.5000	0.5000	1.2500	0.0401
	50 fils	0.5000	0.5000	2.5000	0.0802
	100 fils	10.0000	0.5000	5.0000	0.1607

FAISAL I, *1921–1933*

Y#	KM#	Metal	Description	VF	EF	Unc
1	95	Bz	1 Fils, 1931, 33	7.50	15	125
2	96	Bz	2 Fils, 1931, 33	10.00	20	250

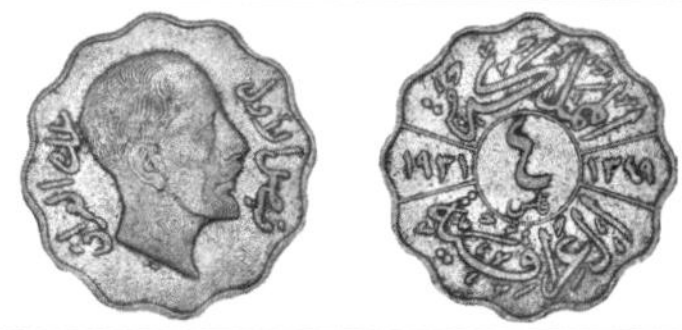

Y#	KM#	Metal	Description	VF	EF	Unc
3	97	Nick	4 Fils, 1931, 33	15	30	400
4	98	Nick	10 Fils, 1931, 33	20	40	500

Y#	KM#	Metal	Description	VF	EF	Unc
5	99	Silv	20 Fils, 1931, 33	60	200	750
6	100	Silv	50 Fils, 1931, 33	75	250	900
7	101	Silv	1 Riyal, 1932	100	300	1,250

GHAZI I, *1933–1939*

Y#	KM#	Metal	Description	VF	EF	Unc
8	102	Bz	1 Fils, 1936, 38	7.50	35	100

Note: Y8 dated 1938 was struck to 1952.

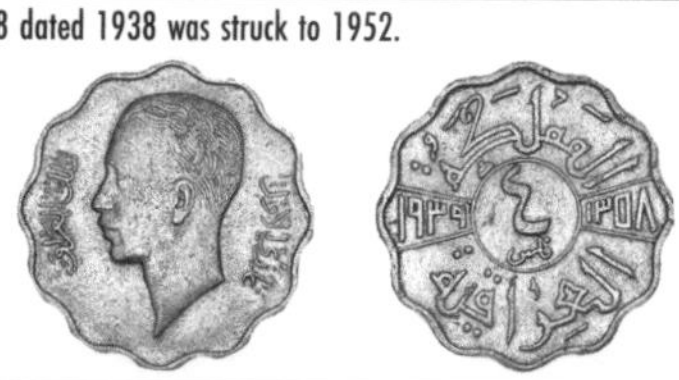

Y#	KM#	Metal	Description	VF	EF	Unc
9	105	Nick	4 Fils, 1938–39	15.00	30	150
10	103	Nick	10 Fils, 1937–38	20.00	40	200
9a	105a	C-N	4 Fils, 1938	7.50	15	30
10a	103a	C-N	10 Fils, 1938	10.00	20	100

Note: Y9a–10a were struck in 1941–1942.

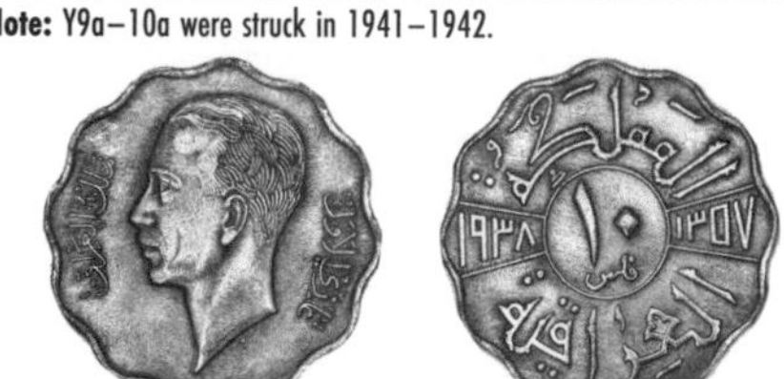

Y#	KM#	Metal	Description	VF	EF	Unc
9b	105b	Bz	4 Fils, 1938	7.50	15	75
10b	103b	Bz	10 Fils, 1938	7.50	15	75

Note: Y9b–10b were struck in 1942–1944.

Y#	KM#	Metal	Description	VF	EF	Unc
11	106	Silv	20 Fils, 1938	5.00	22.50	125
12	104	Silv	50 Fils, 1937–38	7.50	20.00	100

FAISAL II, *1939–1958*

Y#	KM#	Metal	Description	VF	EF	Unc
13	107	Bz	4 Fils, 1943	25	50	200
14	108	Bz	10 Fils, 1943	35	75	500

Y#	KM#	Metal	Description	VF	EF	Unc
15	109	Bz	1 Fils, 1953	1	3	15
16	110	Bz	2 Fils, 1953	60	100	225

Y#	KM#	Metal	Description	VF	EF	Unc
17	111	C-N	4 Fils, 1953	2	4	20
18	112	C-N	10 Fils, 1953	2	4	20

Planchet: ***Round***

Y#	KM#	Metal	Description	VF	EF	Unc
19	113	Silv	20 Fils, 1953	45	70	250
20	114	Silv	50 Fils, 1953	80	120	450
21	115	Silv	100 Fils, 1953	65	100	375

Reverse: ***Redesigned, slightly reduced size***

Y#	KM#	Metal	Description	VF	EF	Unc
22	116	Silv	20 Fils, 1955	7	15	85
23	117	Silv	50 Fils, 1955	7	15	85

Note: The 100 fils 1955 is thought to be a pattern.

REPUBLIC, *1958–*

Y#	KM#	Metal	Description	VF	EF	Unc
24	119	Bz	1 Fils, 1959	0.35	0.65	1.50

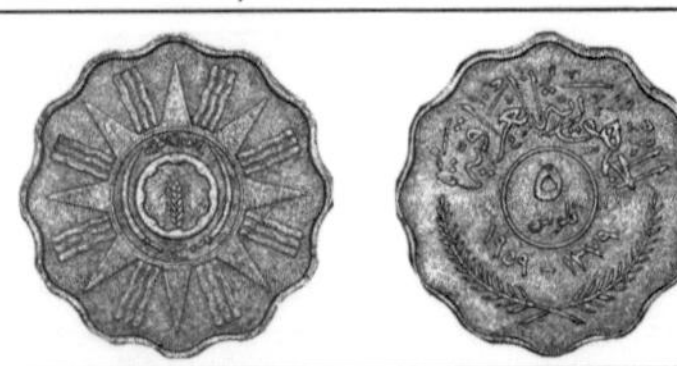

Y#	KM#	Metal	Description	VF	EF	Unc
25	120	C-N	5 Fils, 1959	0.35	0.65	1.50
26	121	C-N	10 Fils, 1959	0.50	1.00	2.50

Y#	KM#	Metal	Description	VF	EF	Unc
27	122	Silv	25 Fils, 1959	1.50	2.50	6.50
28	123	Silv	50 Fils, 1959	3.00	7.50	15.00
29	124	Silv	100 Fils, 1959	5.00	11.00	20.00

Note: Former Y30, the so-called "500 Fils" 1959 bears no denomination and is officially considered a medal.

IRELAND

The island republic sits in the Atlantic, separated from Great Britain by the Irish Sea. Formerly a part of the United Kingdom, it became a self-governing dominion of the British Commonwealth in 1922. It existed as a dominion until December 29, 1937, when a new constitution established an independent Ireland (Eire). A republican form of government was adopted in 1949. *Languages:* English, Gaelic. *Capital:* Dublin.

MONETARY SYSTEM

4 farthings = 1 penny
12 pence = 1 shilling
2 shillings = 1 florin
5 shillings = 1 crown
20 shillings = 1 pound

PRECIOUS METAL CONTENT

Dates	Denomination	Gross Wt (g)	Fineness	Net Wt (g)	Troy Oz.
		SILVER			
1928–43	1 shilling	5.6552	0.7500	4.2414	0.1364
	1 florin	11.3104	0.7500	8.4828	0.2727
	1/2 crown	14.1380	0.7500	10.6035	0.3409

IRISH FREE STATE, *1922–1933*

Legend: ***SAORSTAT EIREANN (in Gaelic)***

Y#	KM#	Metal	Description	VF	EF	Unc
1	1	Bz	1 Farthing, 1928–37	4	7	25
						Proof: $35

Y#	KM#	Metal	Description	VF	EF	Unc
2	2	Bz	1/2 Penny, 1928–37	2	5	25
						Proof: $35

Y#	KM#	Metal	Description	VF	EF	Unc
3	3	Bz	1 Penny, 1928–37	1.25	7.50	30
						Proof: $50

Y#	KM#	Metal	Description	VF	EF	Unc
4	4	Nick	3 Pence, 1928–35	2.50	4.50	22.50
						Proof: $35

Y#	KM#	Metal	Description	VF	EF	Unc
5	5	Nick	6 Pence, 1928–35	0.75	3	30
						Proof: $35

Y#	KM#	Metal	Description	VF	EF	Unc
6	6	Silv	1 Shilling, 1928–37	6.50	12.50	33
						Proof: $35

Y#	KM#	Metal	Description	VF	EF	Unc
7	7	Silv	1 Florin, 1928–37 *1930–33, 35, 37, VF $35;* *1934, VF $85*	5	7.50	45 *Proof: $45*

Y#	KM#	Metal	Description	VF	EF	Unc
8	8	Silv	1/2 Crown, 1928–37 *1937, VF $250*	12	25	55 *Proof: $75*

IRELAND (EIRE), *1937–*

New Obverse Legend: ***EIRE***
Reverses: ***Same as on corresponding denominations, Y1–8***

Y#	KM#	Metal	Description	VF	EF	Unc
9	9	Bz	1 Farthing, 1939–66	2.00	3.50	7.50
						Proof: $350
10	10	Bz	1/2 Penny, 1939–67	0.35	0.50	2.00
						Proof: $450
11	11	Bz	1 Penny, 1940–68	0.25	0.50	2.00
						Proof: $250

Y#	KM#	Metal	Description	VF	EF	Unc
12	12	Nick	3 Pence, 1939–40	1.50	4.50	40
			1940, VF $15			*Proof: $550*
13	13	Nick	6 Pence, 1939–40	2.00	6.00	65
						Proof: $550

Y#	KM#	Metal	Description	VF	EF	Unc
14	14	Silv	1 Shilling, 1939–42	6.50	12.00	37.50
						Proof: $650
15	15	Silv	1 Florin, 1939–43	8.00	17.50	45.00
			1943, VF $7,500			*Proof: $700*
16	16	Silv	1/2 Crown, 1939–43	12.00	16.00	60.00
			1943, VF $375			*Proof: $875*

Note: Y15 has been extensively counterfeited.

Y#	KM#	Metal	Description	VF	EF	Unc
12a	12a	C-N	3 Pence, 1942–68	0.55	0.85	2.50
						Proof: $600
13a	13a	C-N	6 Pence, 1942–69	0.50	0.75	2.50
			1945–47, VF $650			*Proof: $425*
14a	14a	C-N	1 Shilling, 1951–68	0.65	1.00	7.50
						Proof: $425
15a	15a	C-N	1 Florin, 1951–68	0.75	1.00	4.25
						Proof: $500
16a	16a	C-N	1/2 Crown, 1951–67	0.65	1.00	2.50
						Proof: $650

Y#	KM#	Metal	Description	VF	EF	Unc
17	18	Silv	10 Shillings, 1966	9.50	11	22.50
						Proof: $65

ISRAEL

Situated in the Middle East on the eastern end of the Mediterranean Sea, Israel is a republic created by UN resolution in 1948, partitioning traditionally Islamic Palestine. Wars with Arab neighbors added considerably to the original land grant in 1949 and 1967. Continuing religious-based territorial conflicts destabilize the region. *Languages:* Hebrew, Arabic. *Capital:* Jerusalem.

MONETARY SYSTEM

1000 mils = 1 lira (pound)
1000 pruta = 1 pound, to 1960
100 agorot = 1 pound, 1960–1980

PRECIOUS METAL CONTENT

Dates	Denomination	Gross Wt (g)	Fineness	Net Wt (g)	Troy Oz.
		SILVER			
1949	250 pruta	14.4000	0.5000	7.2000	0.2315
	500 pruta	25.5000	0.5000	12.7500	0.4099
1958–67	5 pounds	25.0000	0.9000	22.5000	0.7234
		GOLD			
1960	20 pounds	7.9880	0.9170	7.3250	0.2355
1962–64	50 pounds	13.3400	0.9170	12.2328	0.3933
	100 pounds	26.6800	0.9170	24.4656	0.7866

Hebrew Dates on Israeli Coins

Dates on regular coins are from the ancient Hebrew calendar, and appear only in Hebrew. On commemoratives, the AD date is also included, as are Arabic numerals. The style of date may vary slightly on some denominations.

A.D. Date	Equivalent Hebrew Date	Hebrew Date on Coin
1948	5708	תשח
1949	5709	תשט
1952	5712	תשיב
1954	5714	תשיד
1955	5715	תשטו
1957	5717	תשיז

Y#	KM#	Metal	Description	VF	EF	Unc
1	8	Alum	25 Mils, 5708–09 (1948–49)	12	18	30
			5708, VF $100			

NEW COINAGE SYSTEM

On coins dated 5709, varieties exist with and without a small "pearl" at the bottom of the bar on reverse.

Y#	KM#	Metal	Description	VF	EF	Unc
2	9	Alum	1 Pruta, 5709, with pearl	0.50	1	2
			1 Pruta, 5709, without pearl	2.00	5	15

Y#	KM#	Metal	Description	VF	EF	Unc
3	10	Bz	5 Pruta, 5709, with pearl	0.50	1	2
			5 Pruta, 5709, without pearl	2.00	10	20

Y#	KM#	Metal	Description	VF	EF	Unc
4	11	Bz	10 Pruta, 5709, with pearl	10	15	25
			10 Pruta, 5709, without pearl	1	2	5

Y#	KM#	Metal	Description	VF	EF	Unc
5	17	Alum	10 Pruta, 5712, scalloped	0.50	1	2
5a	20	Alum	10 Pruta, 5717, round	0.50	1	2
5b	20a	AAl	10 Pruta, 5717, round	0.50	1	2

Note: Y5b is copper-plated aluminum.

Y#	KM#	Metal	Description	VF	EF	Unc
6	12	C-N	25 Pruta, 5709, with pearl	0.50	1	2
			25 Pruta, 5709, without pearl	10.00	20	30

Y#	KM#	Metal	Description	VF	EF	Unc
8	13.1	C-N	50 Pruta, 5709, 14, with pearl, reeded edge	10	20.00	40
			50 Pruta, 5709, without pearl	1	1.50	2
			5714, VF $15			
8a	13.2	C-N	50 Pruta, 5714, plain edge	1	1.50	2

Y#	KM#	Metal	Description	VF	EF	Unc
10	14	C-N	100 Pruta, 5709, 15 (28.5 mm)	1	1.50	2

Y#	KM#	Metal	Description	VF	EF	Unc
12	15	C-N	250 Pruta, 5709	5	10	13

Y#	KM#	Metal	Description	VF	EF	Unc
12a	15a	Silv	250 Pruta, 5709	6	10	13

Note: Y12a was issued only in mint sets.

Y#	KM#	Metal	Description	VF	EF	Unc
14	16	Silv	500 Pruta, 5709	10	15	30

Note: Y14 was issued only in mint sets.

Designs: ***Same as Y6, 8, 10***
Edge: ***Plain***

Y#	KM#	Metal	Description	VF	EF	Unc
6a	12a	N-CS	25 Pruta, 5714	1	1.50	2
8b	13.2a	N-CS	50 Pruta, 5714	1	1.50	2
10a	18–19	N-CS	100 Pruta, 5714 (25.6 mm)	1	1.50	2

Y#	KM#	Metal	Description	VF	EF	Unc
22	24	Alum	1 Agora, 5720–40 (1960–80)	0.05	0.10	0.30

Y#	KM#	Metal	Description	VF	EF	Unc
24	25	A-Bz	5 Agorot, 5720–37	0.05	0.10	0.35

Y#	KM#	Metal	Description	VF	EF	Unc
25	26	A-Bz	10 Agorot, 5720–37	0.05	0.10	0.40

Y#	KM#	Metal	Description	VF	EF	Unc
26	27	A-Bz	25 Agorot, 5720–39	0.10	0.15	0.50

Y#	KM#	Metal	Description	VF	EF	Unc
36	36	C-N	1/2 Pound, 5723–39	0.15	0.30	0.75
37	37	C-N	1 Pound, 5723–39	0.25	0.50	1.00

Proofs can be distinguished by the presence of the Hebrew letter "Mem" on all issues except those of 1958, which have no special markings.

10th Anniversary of Republic

Y#	KM#	Metal	Description	VF	EF	Unc
16	21	Silv	5 Pounds, 1958	—	—	10 Proof: $250

Law Is Light (Chanuka)

Y#	KM#	Metal	Description	VF	EF	Unc
17	22	C-N	1 Pound, 1958	—	—	2 Proof: $20

Ingathering of Exiles

Y#	KM#	Metal	Description	VF	EF	Unc
18	23	Silv	5 Pounds, 1959	—	—	15 Proof: $35

Deganya Kibbutz

Y#	KM#	Metal	Description	VF	EF	Unc
19	28	C-N	1 Pound, 1960	—	—	4 Proof: $15

Dr. Theodore Herzl

Y#	KM#	Metal	Description	VF	EF	Unc
20	29	Silv	5 Pounds, 1960	—	—	12 Proof: $35

Reverse: *State emblem of Israel*

Y#	KM#	Metal	Description	VF	EF	Unc
21	30	Gold	20 Pounds, 1960	—	—	165

Henrietta Szold—Hadassah Medical Center

Y#	KM#	Metal	Description	VF	EF	Unc
27	32	C-N	1 Pound, 1960	—	—	10 Proof: $85

Bar Mitzvah

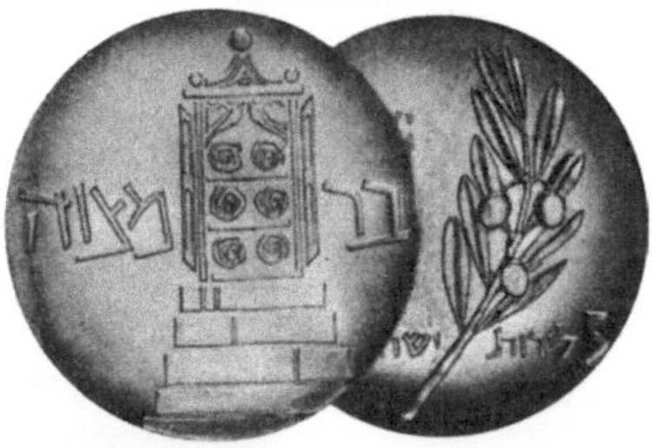

Y#	KM#	Metal	Description	VF	EF	Unc
28	33	Silv	5 Pounds, 1961	—	—	35 Proof: $60

Feast of Purim

Y#	KM#	Metal	Description	VF	EF	Unc
29	31	C-N	1/2 Pound (Half Shekel), 1961–62	—	—	6 Proof: $10

Heroism and Sacrifice

Y#	KM#	Metal	Description	VF	EF	Unc
30	34	C-N	1 Pound, 1961	—	—	6 Proof: $8

Industrialization of the Negev

Y#	KM#	Metal	Description	VF	EF	Unc
31	35	Silv	5 Pounds, 1962	—	—	25 Proof: $35

10th Anniversary, Death of Chaim Weizman

Y#	KM#	Metal	Description	VF	EF	Unc
32	40	Gold	*50 Pounds, 1962, Proof only: $200*			
33	41	Gold	*100 Pounds, 1962, Proof only: $400*			

Chanuka—Italian Lamp

Y#	KM#	Metal	Description	VF	EF	Unc
34	38	C-N	1 Pound, 1962	—	—	13 Proof: $25

Seafaring

Y#	KM#	Metal	Description	VF	EF	Unc
35	39	Silv	5 Pounds, 1963	—	—	200
						Proof: $225

Chanuka—North African Lamp

Y#	KM#	Metal	Description	VF	EF	Unc
38	42	C-N	1 Pound, 1963	—	—	10
						Proof: $25

Israel Museum

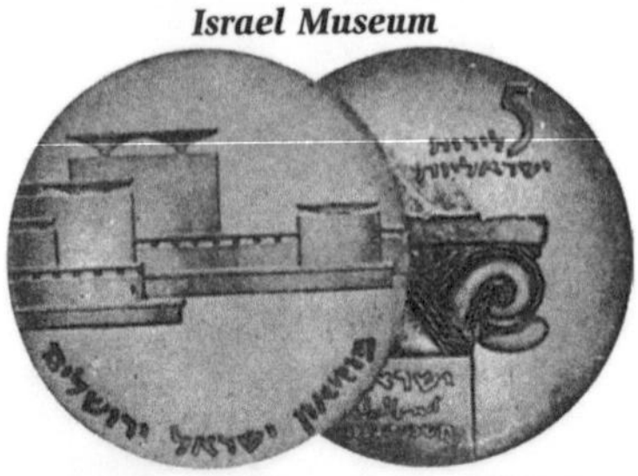

Y#	KM#	Metal	Description	VF	EF	Unc
39	43	Silv	5 Pounds, 1964	—	—	25
						Proof: $45

10th Anniversary, Bank of Israel

Y#	KM#	Metal	Description	VF	EF	Unc
40	44	Gold	50 Pounds, 1964	—	—	250
						Proof: $3,000

ITALIAN SOMALILAND

The southeastern coast of the Somali region, on the eastern "horn" of Africa, became an Italian colony in the late 1800s. It came under British administration during World War II, but was returned to Italy under UN trusteeship in 1950 with 10 years to prepare for independence. In 1960 Italian and British Somaliland joined to form the independent Somali Republic. *Languages:* Somali, Arabic, Italian. *Capital:* Mogadishu.

For later issues, see Somalia.

MONETARY SYSTEM

100 bese (pice) = 1 rupia
100 centesimi = 1 lira

PRECIOUS METAL CONTENT

Dates	Denomination	Gross Wt (g)	Fineness	Net Wt (g)	Troy Oz.
		SILVER			
1910–21	1/4 rupia	2.9160	0.9170	2.6730	0.0859
	1/2 rupia	5.8319	0.9170	5.3459	0.1719
	1 rupia	11.6638	0.9170	10.6918	0.3437
1925	5 lire	6.0000	0.8350	5.0100	0.1611
	10 lire	12.0000	0.8350	10.0200	0.3221

VITTORIO EMANUELE III, *1900–1946*

Y#	KM#	Metal	Description	VF	EF	Unc
1	1	Bz	1 Besa, 1909–21	30	75	250
2	2	Bz	2 Bese, 1909–24	45	130	400
3	3	Bz	4 Bese, 1909–24	85	325	700

Y#	KM#	Metal	Description	VF	EF	Unc
4	4	Silv	1/4 Rupia, 1910, 13	70	150	350
5	5	Silv	1/2 Rupia, 1910–19	70	150	350
6	6	Silv	1 Rupia, 1910–21	90	200	400
			1920, VF $6,000; 21, Rare			

NEW COINAGE SYSTEM

Y#	KM#	Metal	Description	VF	EF	Unc
7	7	Silv	5 Lire, 1925	225	350	650
8	8	Silv	10 Lire, 1925	300	400	750

Note: Y7 and 8 did not circulate and are usually seen in Uncirculated condition.

ITALY

Italy is a boot-shaped European peninsula into the Mediterranean Sea. It was a collection of independent states from the Middle Ages until they gradually unified, 1815–1870. A kingdom was proclaimed in 1861. It became a republic by referendum in 1946. *Language:* Italian. *Capital:* Rome.

MONETARY SYSTEM:
100 centesimi = 1 lira

PRECIOUS METAL CONTENT
Italy was a member of the Latin Monetary Union; see appendix A.

Dates	Denomination	Gross Wt (g)	Fineness	Net Wt (g)	Troy Oz.
		SILVER			
1863–1917	20 centesimi	1.0000	0.8350	0.8350	0.0268
	50 centesimi	2.5000	0.8350	2.0871	0.0671
	1 lira	5.0000	0.8350	4.1750	0.1342
	2 lire	10.0000	0.8350	8.3500	0.2685
	5 lire	25.0000	0.9000	22.5000	0.7234
1926–41	5 lire	5.0000	0.8350	4.1750	0.1342
	10 lire	10.0000	0.8350	8.3500	0.2685
1927–34	20 lire	15.0000	0.8000	12.0000	0.3858
1928	20 lire (commem)	20.0000	0.6000	12.0000	0.3858
1936–41	20 lire	20.0000	0.8000	16.0000	0.5144
1958–2001	500 lire	11.0000	0.8350	9.1850	0.2953
		GOLD			
1861–1927	5 lire	1.6129	0.9000	1.4516	0.0467
	10 lire	3.2258	0.9000	2.9032	0.0933
	20 lire	6.4516	0.9000	5.8064	0.1867
	50 lire	16.1290	0.9000	14.5161	0.4667
	100 lire	32.2581	0.9000	29.0323	0.9334
1931–36	50 lire	4.3995	0.9000	3.9596	0.1273
	100 lire	8.7990	0.9000	7.9191	0.2546
1937	100 lire	5.1966	0.9000	4.6749	0.1504

VITTORIO EMANUELE II, *1861–1878*

Italian Unification

Y#	KM#	Metal	Description	VF	EF	Unc
5	7	Silv	5 Lire, 1861	2,000	4,250	8,000

Y#	KM#	Metal	Description	VF	EF	Unc
6	1	Cop	1 Centesimo, 1861–67 *1867T, VF $50*	2	13.00	40
7	2	Cop	2 Centesimi, 1861–67	2	12.50	45
8	3	Cop	5 Centesimi, 1861–67 *1861B, VF $100*	8	25.00	100
9	11	Cop	10 Centesimi, 1862–67 *1862N, Rare*	11	65.00	350

Y#	KM#	Metal	Description	VF	EF	Unc
10	12	Silv	20 Centesimi, 1863, *EF $6,000*			
11	4	Silv	50 Centesimi, 1861–63 *1861F, VF $175; 1861M, 61T, Rare; 1862N, VF $175; 1862T, VF $475*	40.00	65	135
12	5	Silv	1 Lira, 1861–67 *1861F, 62N, 62T, VF $100; 1861T, VF $2,250; 1867T, VF $500*	22.50	50	200
13	6	Silv	2 Lire, 1861–63 *1861T, VF $3,000: 1862N, VF $1,000*	50.00	225	825
14	8	Silv	5 Lire, 1861–78 *1861, VF $325; 1862, VF $350; 1866N, VF $5,000; 1872R, VF $900; 1873R, VF $1,850*	30.00	60	175

Y#	KM#	Metal	Description	VF	EF	Unc
15	13	Silv	20 Centesimi, 1863–67 *1867T, VF $100*	25	50	135
16	14	Silv	50 Centesimi, 1863–67 *1866M, VF $65; 1867T, VF $375*	40	65	135
17	15	Silv	1 Lira, 1863 *186TT, VF $1.300*	70	350	1,250
18	16	Silv	2 Lire, 1863	100	475	1,250

Y#	KM#	Metal	Description	VF	EF	Unc
A18	17	Gold	5 Lire, 1863, 65	185	275	400
B18	9	Gold	10 Lire, 1861–65 (vars) *1861, VF $5,000*	BV	175	225
19	10	Gold	20 Lire, 1861–78 *1861, 70–71, VF $375; 1870R, VF $1,200; 1873R, VF $5,000*	BV	BV	385
20	18	Gold	50 Lire, 1864 (103 pieces)	125,000	200,000	225,000
21	19	Gold	100 Lire, 1864–78	14,000	20,000	27,500

UMBERTO I,
1878–1900

Y#	KM#	Metal	Description	VF	EF	Unc
22	29	Cop	1 Centesimo, 1895–1900 *1897, VF $55*	3.50	7.00	17.50
23	30	Cop	2 Centesimi, 1895–1900 *1896, VF $65*	1.00	6.50	14.00
24	31	Cop	5 Centesimi, 1895–96	30.00	65.00	175.00
25	27	Cop	10 Centesimi, 1893–94 *1893, VF $25; 1894R, VF $50*	1.00	6.50	65.00

Y#	KM#	Metal	Description	VF	EF	Unc
26	28	C-N	20 Centesimi, 1894–95 *1895R, VF $15*	6.50	20	55

Y#	KM#	Metal	Description	VF	EF	Unc
27	26	Silv	50 Centesimi, 1889, 92 *1892, EF $250*	150	250.00	400
28	24	Silv	1 Lira, 1883–1900 *1883, Rare; 1892, VF $650*	18	35.00	140
29	23	Silv	2 Lire, 1881–99 *1885, 98, VF $100*	15	62.50	250
30	20	Silv	5 Lire, 1878–79 *1878, VF $500*	75	200.00	1,000

Y#	KM#	Metal	Description	VF	EF	Unc
32	21	Gold	20 Lire, 1879–97 *1884, VF $650*	BV	BV	325
33	25	Gold	50 Lire, 1884–91 *1891, EF $6,500*	2,000	4,000	6,000
34	22	Gold	100 Lire, 1880–91 *1880, VF $30,000; 1891, VF $8,000*	2,750	3,500	6,500

VITTORIO EMANUELE III,
1900–1946
FIRST COINAGE

Y#	KM#	Metal	Description	VF	EF	Unc
35	35	Bz	1 Centesimo, 1902–08 *1902, Rare*	8	30	100
36	38	Bz	2 Centesimi, 1903–08 *1905, VF $135*	3	12	35

Y#	KM#	Metal	Description	VF	EF	Unc
37	36	Nick	25 Centesimi, 1902–03	40	75	135

Y#	KM#	Metal	Description	VF	EF	Unc
38	32	Silv	1 Lira, 1901–07 *1905, VF $200*	10	30	100
39	33	Silv	2 Lire, 1901–07 *1901, 04, VF $475; 1903, VF $1,500*	45	185	400
40	35	Silv	5 Lire, 1901, *Rare*			

Note: Y40 has been extensively counterfeited.

Y#	KM#	Metal	Description	VF	EF	Unc
41	37	Gold	20 Lire, 1902–10 *1902, Unc $70,000; 1908, 10, Rare*	900	1,100	1,750
42	39	Gold	100 Lire, 1903, 05	9,000	15,000	37,500

Note: Dates of Y41 after 1905 were not for circulation. In spite of reports to the contrary, no official mint records confirm a 1910-dated Y41, and no genuine specimens are known.

SECOND COINAGE

Y#	KM#	Metal	Description	VF	EF	Unc
43	40	Bz	1 Centesimo, 1908–18 *1908, VF $350; 1911, VF $35; 1918 VF $15*	1.00	4.00	15
44	41	Bz	2 Centesimi, 1908–17 *1908, 10, VF $45; 1912, VF $25; 1915, VF $18*	2.50	6.50	20
45	42	Bz	5 Centesimi, 1908–18	13.50	25.00	150
46	43	Bz	10 Centesimi, 1908, *Rare*			

Y#	KM#	Metal	Description	VF	EF	Unc
47	44	Nick	20 Centesimi, 1908–35 *1914, VF $6; 1919, VF $10; all dates after 1922, Rare*	3	10	40

Note: Dates of Y47 after 1922 were not for circulation and are rare.

Y#	KM#	Metal	Description	VF	EF	Unc
48	45	Silv	1 Lira, 1908–13 *1908–09, VF $40*	5	15	50
49	46	Silv	2 Lire, 1908–12 *1910, VF $100; 1911, VF $200*	25	70	150

Y#	KM#	Metal	Description	VF	EF	Unc
50	57	Silv	1 Lira, 1915–17	12	13.50	40
51	55	Silv	2 Lire, 1914–17	10	20.00	42
52	56	Silv	5 Lire, 1914	3,000	5,000.00	8,000

Note: Y52 has been extensively counterfeited.

Y#	KM#	Metal	Description	VF	EF	Unc
53	47	Gold	10 Lire, 1910–27	2,750	3,500	6,000
54	48	Gold	20 Lire, 1910–27	850	1,250	1,850
55	49	Gold	50 Lire, 1910–27	1,150	1,350	1,850
56	50	Gold	100 Lire, 1910–27	3,250	4,500	7,000

Note: Dates other than 1912 of Y53–56 were not for circulation and are very rare.

50th Anniversary of Kingdom

Y#	KM#	Metal	Description	VF	EF	Unc
57	51	Bz	10 Centesimi, 1911	7	15	32.50

Y#	KM#	Metal	Description	VF	EF	Unc
58	52	Silv	2 Lire, 1911	37.50	65	135
59	53	Silv	5 Lire, 1911	500.00	825	1,750

Y#	KM#	Metal	Description	VF	EF	Unc
60	54	Gold	50 Lire, 1911	1,000	1,200	2,000

THIRD COINAGE

Y#	KM#	Metal	Description	VF	EF	Unc
61	59	Bz	5 Centesimi, 1919–37 *1919, 36, VF $7; 1937, VF $15*	2	5	15

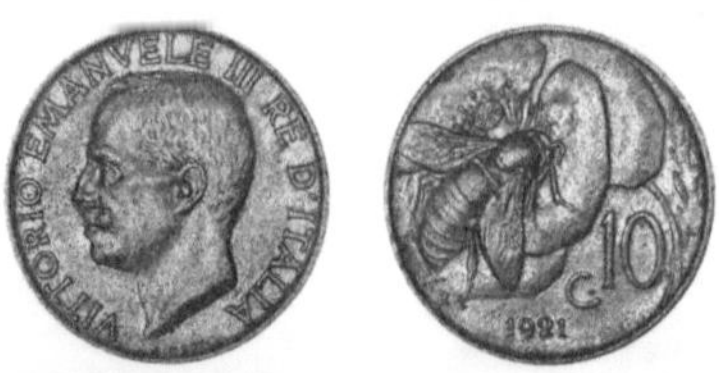

Y#	KM#	Metal	Description	VF	EF	Unc
62	60	Bz	10 Centesimi, 1919–37 *1919, VF $65*	2.50	5	22.50

Y#	KM#	Metal	Description	VF	EF	Unc
63	58	C-N	20 Centesimi, 1918–20, overstruck on Y26 *1920, VF $18*	2.25	25	70

Y#	KM#	Metal	Description	VF	EF	Unc
64	61.1	Nick	50 Centesimi, 1919–28, plain edge *1919, VF $70; 1924, VF $140*	5	20	80
64a	61.2	Nick	50 Centesimi, 1919–35, reeded edge	20	165	1,000

Note: Dates of Y64–64a after 1925 were not for circulation and are rare.

Y#	KM#	Metal	Description	VF	EF	Unc
65	62	Nick	1 Lira, 1922–35 *1926, 27, Rare*	2	14	47.50

Note: 1926, 1927, and 1929–1935 were not for circulation and are rare.

Y#	KM#	Metal	Description	VF	EF	Unc
66	63	Nick	2 Lire, 1923–35 *1925–26, VF $35; 1927, VF $175*	6.50	25	140

Note: Dates of Y66 after 1927 were not for circulation and are rare.

Y#	KM#	Metal	Description	VF	EF	Unc
67	67	Silv	5 Lire, 1926–35	6.50	12.50	20

Note: Dates of Y67 after 1930 were not for circulation and are rare.

Y#	KM#	Metal	Description	VF	EF	Unc
68	68	Silv	10 Lire, 1926–34 *1926, 30, VF $140*	20	45	80

Note: Dates of Y68 after 1930 were not for circulation and are rare.

Y#	KM#	Metal	Description	VF	EF	Unc
69	69	Silv	20 Lire, 1927–34	100	250	375

Note: Dates of Y69 after 1928 were not for circulation and are rare. 1927 Year V is rare and has been extensively counterfeited.

Y#	KM#	Metal	Description	VF	EF	Unc
70	71	Gold	50 Lire, 1931–33 *1933, EF $600*	275	375	450

Y#	KM#	Metal	Description	VF	EF	Unc
71	72	Gold	100 Lire, 1931–33 *1933, EF $800*	400	475	650

First Anniversary, Fascist Government, 1922–1923

Y#	KM#	Metal	Description	VF	EF	Unc
72	64	Gold	20 Lire, 1923	650	850	1,750
73	65	Gold	100 Lire, 1923	2,000	3,000	4,000

25th Anniversary of Reign / 10th Anniversary, Entry Into World War I

Y#	KM#	Metal	Description	VF	EF	Unc
74	66	Gold	100 Lire, 1925	4,250	6,250	9,500

10th Anniversary, End of World War I

Y#	KM#	Metal	Description	VF	EF	Unc
75	70	Silv	20 Lire, 1928	125	200	575

Note: Pieces with Mussolini in this style are not coins.

FOURTH COINAGE

Title: ***RE E IMPERATORE***

Y#	KM#	Metal	Description	VF	EF	Unc
77	73	Bz	5 Centesimi, 1936–39	0.50	1	5

Y#	KM#	Metal	Description	VF	EF	Unc
78	74	Bz	10 Centesimi, 1936–39 *1935, VF $10*	2	3	17.50

Y#	KM#	Metal	Description	VF	EF	Unc
79	75	Nick	20 Centesimi, 1936–38 *1937, Unc $2,500; 1938, Rare*	100	225	475

Y#	KM#	Metal	Description	VF	EF	Unc
80	76	Nick	50 Centesimi, 1936–38 *1937, Unc $2,500; 1938, Rare*	30	65	225
81	77	Nick	1 Lira, 1936–38 *1937, Unc $2,500; 1938, Rare*	45	85	150

Y#	KM#	Metal	Description	VF	EF	Unc
82	78	Nick	2 Lire, 1936–38 *1937, Unc $3,250; 1938, Unc $11,000*	55	135	200

Note: Dates after 1936 of Y79–82 were not made for circulation.

Designs: *Like Y77–78*

Y#	KM#	Metal	Description	VF	EF	Unc
77a	73a	A-Bz	5 Centesimi, 1939–43 *1943, VF $6.50*	2.00	3.50	14
78a	74a	A-Bz	10 Centesimi, 1939–43	2.75	8.50	50

Designs: *Like Y79–82*

Y#	KM#	Metal	Description	VF	EF	Unc
79a	75a	S S	20 Centesimi, 1939–43	2.75	3.75	6.50
80a	76a	S S	50 Centesimi, 1939–43 *1943, VF $55*	1.75	3.00	6.00
81a	77a	S S	1 Lira, 1939–43 *1943, VF $45*	1.75	3.50	7.00
82a	78a	S S	2 Lire, 1939–43 *1942, VF $85; 1943, VF $50*	1.75	5.00	18.00

Note: Two different alloys were used for Y79a–82a: NiOx (non-magnetic) in 1939 and part of 1940, and acmonital (magnetic) in the balance of 1940 through 1943. Coins dated 1937 and 1938 were not for circulation, and are rare.

Y#	KM#	Metal	Description	VF	EF	Unc
89	79	Silv	5 Lire, 1936–41 *1937, VF $50*	4	40	85

Note: Dates of Y89 after 1937 were not for circulation and are rare.

Y#	KM#	Metal	Description	VF	EF	Unc
90	80	Silv	10 Lire, 1936–41	30	50	100

Note: Dates of Y90 after 1936 were not for circulation and are rare.

Y#	KM#	Metal	Description	VF	EF	Unc
91	81	Silv	20 Lire, 1936–41	600	900	1,750

Note: Dates of Y91 after 1936 were not for circulation and are rare. Y91 has been extensively counterfeited.

Y#	KM#	Metal	Description	VF	EF	Unc
92	82	Gold	50 Lire, 1936	3,000	5,000	11,500

Y#	KM#	Metal	Description	VF	EF	Unc
93	83	Gold	100 Lire, 1936 (24 mm)	3,500	5,000	12,000

Reduced Size

Y#	KM#	Metal	Description	VF	EF	Unc
93a	84	Gold	100 Lire, 1937 (21 mm)	16,500	23,000	45,000

REPUBLIC, *1946–*

FIRST COINAGE

Y#	KM#	Metal	Description	VF	EF	Unc
95	87	Alum	1 Lira, 1946–50 *1946, VF $100; 1947, VF $300*	1	3.75	12

Y#	KM#	Metal	Description	VF	EF	Unc
96	88	Alum	2 Lire, 1946–50 *1946, VF $45; 1947, VF $450*	1	3	13

Y#	KM#	Metal	Description	VF	EF	Unc
97	89	Alum	5 Lire, 1946–50 *1946, VF $200; 1947, VF $500*	2	5	17.50

Y#	KM#	Metal	Description	VF	EF	Unc
98	90	Alum	10 Lire, 1946–50 *1946, VF $200; 1947, VF $1,600*	2	5	10

SECOND COINAGE

Y#	KM#	Metal	Description	VF	EF	Unc
99	91	Alum	1 Lira, 1951–2001	1	1.50	4

Y#	KM#	Metal	Description	VF	EF	Unc
100	94	Alum	2 Lire, 1953–2001 *1958, VF $150*	1	2	5

Y#	KM#	Metal	Description	VF	EF	Unc
101	92	Alum	5 Lire, 1951–2001 *1956, VF $130*	1	2	5

Y#	KM#	Metal	Description	VF	EF	Unc
102	93	Alum	10 Lire, 1951–2001	1	2	5

Y#	KM#	Metal	Description	VF	EF	Unc
A102	97	A-Bz	20 Lire, 1957–59	1	2	10

Y#	KM#	Metal	Description	VF	EF	Unc
103	95	S S	50 Lire, 1954–89 *1958, VF $45*	1	2	10

Y#	KM#	Metal	Description	VF	EF	Unc
104	96	S S	100 Lire, 1955–89	1	2	10

Y#	KM#	Metal	Description	VF	EF	Unc
105	98	Silv	500 Lire, 1958–2000, date on edge	5	7	10

Centennial of Italian Unification

Y#	KM#	Metal	Description	VF	EF	Unc
106	99	Silv	500 Lire, ND (1961)	5	7	10

JAMAICA

Discovered by Columbus in 1494, the island was under Spanish rule until the British seized it in 1655. The former colony of the British West Indies lies in the Caribbean Sea, 90 miles south of Cuba. The nation achieved independence and membership in the British Commonwealth in 1962. *Languages:* English, Creole. *Capital:* Kingston.

MONETARY SYSTEM
4 farthings = 1 penny

PRECIOUS METAL CONTENT

Dates	Denomination	Gross Wt (g)	Fineness	Net Wt (g)	Troy Oz.
		SILVER			
1838–62	1-1/2 pence	0.7069	0.9250	0.6539	0.0210

VICTORIA, *1837–1901*

Y#	KM#	Metal	Description	VF	EF	Unc
1	15	C-N	1 Farthing, 1880–1900	2.50	12.50	50 *Proof: $625*
2	16	C-N	1/2 Penny, 1869–1900	3.50	15.00	60 *Proof: $600*
3	17	C-N	1 Penny, 1869–1900 *1882, VF $40*	6.50	25.00	80 *Proof: $175*

Y#	KM#	Metal	Description	VF	EF	Unc
A3	728	Silv	1-1/2 Pence, 1838–62	10	25	175

Note: See Ceylon Y3.

EDWARD VII, *1901–1910*

Reverse: ***Horizontal shading in arms***

Y#	KM#	Metal	Description	VF	EF	Unc
4	18	C-N	1 Farthing, 1902–03	9.50	22.50	45
5	19	C-N	1/2 Penny, 1902–03	9.50	22.50	45
6	20	C-N	1 Penny, 1902–03	12.50	25.00	75

Reverse: ***Vertical shading in arms***

Y#	KM#	Metal	Description	VF	EF	Unc
7	21	C-N	1 Farthing, 1904–10	2.00	7.50	35 *Proof: $1,250*
8	22	C-N	1/2 Penny, 1904–10	2.00	10.00	45
9	23	C-N	1 Penny, 1904–10 *1904, VF $20*	2.50	15.00	50 *Proof: $600*

George V, *1910–1936*

Y#	KM#	Metal	Description	VF	EF	Unc
10	24	C-N	1 Farthing, 1914–34	1.75	9	50
						Proof: $500
11	25	C-N	1/2 Penny, 1914–28	2.50	12	50
						Proof: $500
12	26	C-N	1 Penny, 1914–28	2.00	10	40
			1914, 16, VF $25			*Proof: $500*

George VI, *1936–1952*

Y#	KM#	Metal	Description	VF	EF	Unc
13	27	N-Br	1 Farthing, 1937	1.50	4	20
						Proof: $350
14	28	N-Br	1/2 Penny, 1937	1.50	4	20
						Proof: $350
15	29	N-Br	1 Penny, 1937	2.00	4	20
						Proof: $375

Larger Head

Y#	KM#	Metal	Description	VF	EF	Unc
16	30	N-Br	1 Farthing, 1938–47	0.75	10.00	25.00
						Proof: $125
17	31	N-Br	1/2 Penny, 1938–47	0.60	2.50	22.50
						Proof: $150
18	32	N-Br	1 Penny, 1938–47	0.60	2.50	20.00
						Proof: $175

New Legend: *KING GEORGE THE SIXTH*

Y#	KM#	Metal	Description	VF	EF	Unc
19	33	N-Br	1 Farthing, 1950, 52	0.20	0.45	20.00
						Proof: $350
20	34	N-Br	1/2 Penny, 1950, 52	0.30	0.50	7.50
						Proof: $400
21	35	N-Br	1 Penny, 1950, 52	0.35	2.00	12.50
						Proof: $175

Elizabeth II, *1952–*

Y#	KM#	Metal	Description	VF	EF	Unc
22	36	N-Br	1/2 Penny, 1955–63	0.15	0.45	2.50
						Proof: $450
23	37	N-Br	1 Penny, 1953–63	0.20	0.50	2.50
						Proof: $400

Y#	KM#	Metal	Description	VF	EF	Unc
24	38	N-Br	1/2 Penny, 1964–66	0.15	0.35	1.25
25	39	N-Br	1 Penny, 1964–67	0.15	0.25	1.50

JAPAN

Japan is an archipelago in the North Pacific separated from the coast of China by the Sea of Japan. The country was under shogun (military dictatorship) rule from the 12th through the mid-19th century. The emperor Meiji came to power in 1868 as the nation was exposed to the West. A parliament was established in 1889. A new constitution in 1947 made the emperor a figurehead. *Language:* Japanese. *Capital:* Tokyo.

MONETARY SYSTEM

10 rin = 1 sen
100 sen = 1 yen

PRECIOUS METAL CONTENT

Dates	Denomination	Gross Wt (g)	Fineness	Net Wt (g)	Troy Oz.
		SILVER			
1870–71	5 sen	1.2500	0.8000	1.0000	0.0322
	10 sen	2.5000	0.8000	2.0000	0.0643
	20 sen	5.0000	0.8000	4.0000	0.1286
	50 sen	12.5000	0.8000	10.0000	0.3215
1873–1906	5 sen	1.3479	0.8000	1.0783	0.0347
	10 sen	2.6957	0.8000	2.1566	0.0693
	20 sen	5.3914	0.8000	4.3131	0.1387
	50 sen	13.4785	0.8000	10.7828	0.3467
1870–1914	1 yen	26.9568	0.9000	24.2611	0.7800
	trade dollar	27.2156	0.9000	24.4940	0.7875
1906–1917	10 sen	2.2500	0.7200	1.6200	0.0521
	20 sen	4.0500	0.8000	3.2400	0.1042
	50 sen	10.1250	0.8000	8.1000	0.2604
1922–38	50 sen	4.9500	0.7200	3.5640	0.1146
1957–64	100 yen	4.8000	0.6000	2.8800	0.0926
1964	1,000 yen	20.0000	0.9250	18.5000	0.5948

Dates	Denomination	Gross Wt (g)	Fineness	Net Wt (g)	Troy Oz.
		GOLD			
1870–97	1 yen	1.6667	0.9000	1.5000	0.0482
	2 yen	3.3333	0.9000	3.0000	0.0965
	5 yen	8.3333	0.9000	7.5000	0.2411
	10 yen	16.6667	0.9000	15.0000	0.4823
	20 yen	33.3333	0.9000	30.0000	0.9645
1897–1932	5 yen	4.1667	0.9000	3.7500	0.1206
	10 yen	8.3333	0.9000	7.5000	0.2411
	20 yen	16.6667	0.9000	15.0000	0.4823

MEIJI REIGN,
YEARS 1 TO 45 (1868–1912)
REIGN SYMBOLS 治 明 *ON COINS*
FIRST COINAGE

Y#	KM#	Metal	Description	VF	EF	Unc
1	1	Silv	5 Sen, Yrs 3–4 (1870–71)	320	450	900
2	2	Silv	10 Sen, Yr 3	35	80	275
3	3	Silv	20 Sen, Yrs 3–4	35	75	210
4	4–4a.2	Silv	50 Sen, Yrs 3–4 (31.5 mm) *Yr 4, Early Type, EF $275*	55	120	365
4a	4a.1	Silv	50 Sen, Yr 4 (31 mm) *"Big Dragon" Type, EF $2,100*	75	185	540
5	5	Silv	1 Yen, Yr 3	550	725	1,100

Y#	KM#	Metal	Description	VF	EF	Unc
6	6	Silv	5 Sen, Yr 4	110	185	365

Y#	KM#	Metal	Description	VF	EF	Unc
9	9	Gold	1 Yen, Yr 4	365	635	820
10	10	Gold	2 Yen, Yr 3	900	1,365	1,825
11	11	Gold	5 Yen, Yrs 3–4	1,825	2,450	3,275
12	12	Gold	10 Yen, Yr 4	3,650	5,450	7,275
13	13	Gold	20 Yen, Yr 3 *Yr 4, Early Type, EF $1,635*	36,350	45,450	63,500

SECOND COINAGE

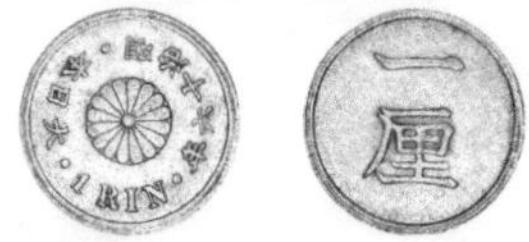

Y#	KM#	Metal	Description	VF	EF	Unc
15	15	Cop	1 Rin, Yrs 6–17 (1873–84) *Yrs 6, 8, Early Type, EF $40; Yr 8, Later Type, EF $725; Yr 9, EF $5,450; Yr 10, EF $900; Yr 13, EF $8,185*	8	15	32.50

Y#	KM#	Metal	Description	VF	EF	Unc
16	16	Cop	1/2 Sen, Yrs 6–21 *Yr 10, VF $350*	2.75	15	42.50
17	17	Cop	1 Sen, Yrs 6–21	2.00	10	110.00
18	18	Cop	2 Sen, Yrs 6–17	4.50	20	225.00

Y#	KM#	Metal	Description	VF	EF	Unc
20	20	Bz	1 Sen, Yrs 31–35 (1898–1902) *Yrs 33, 35, EF $42.50*	7	25	185

Y#	KM#	Metal	Description	VF	EF	Unc
19	19	C-N	5 Sen, Yrs 22–30 (1889–97) *Yr 28, EF $365*	3.50	25	165

Y#	KM#	Metal	Description	VF	EF	Unc
21	21	C-N	5 Sen, Yrs 30–38 (1897–1905) *Yr 36, EF $900*	15	42.50	225

Y#	KM#	Metal	Description	VF	EF	Unc
22	A22	Silv	5 Sen, Yrs 6–13 (1873–80) *Yr 7, EF $450; Yr 13, EF Rare*	30	50	90
23	23	Silv	10 Sen, Yrs 6–39 *Yr 7, EF $90; Yr 13, EF Rare; Yr 34, EF $820; Yr 35, EF $635*	10	15	65
24	24	Silv	20 Sen, Yrs 6–38 *Yr 8, EF $725; Yr 13, EF $31,800; Yr 21, EF $590; Yr 34, EF $725*	16	25	75
25	25	Silv	50 Sen, Yrs 6–38 *Yr 7, EF $22,750; Yr 9, EF $13,650; Yr 10, EF $9,100; Yr 13, EF $41,000; Yr 18, EF $445*	25	50	225
A25	A25	Silv	1 Yen, Yrs 7–45 *Yr 7, EF $3,185; Yr 8, EF $12,750; Yr 11, EF $1,365; Yr 12, EF $4,550*	27	50	225

Reduced Size

Y#	KM#	Metal	Description	VF	EF	Unc
9a	9a	Gold	1 Yen, Yr 7	3,185	4,000	5,450
9a	9a	Gold	1 Yen, Yr 9	12,750	16,350	24,550
9a	9a	Gold	1 Yen, Yr 10	31,800	54,500	100,500
9a	9a	Gold	1 Yen, Yr 13	41,100	68,400	100,500
10a	10a	Gold	2 Yen, Yrs 9, 10, 13	54,500	63,650	90,250
11a	11a	Gold	5 Yen, Yrs 5–30	1,365	1,725	2,450

Same Size, Smaller Design

Y#	KM#	Metal	Description	VF	EF	Unc
12a	12a	Gold	10 Yen, Yr 9	72,750	81,800	122,750
12a	12a	Gold	10 Yen, Yrs 10, 13	81,800	100,400	150,500
13a	13a	Gold	20 Yen, Yr 9	72,750	81,800	140,000
13a	13a	Gold	20 Yen, Yr 10	110,000	136,350	200,800
13a	13a	Gold	20 Yen, Yr 13	90,100	118,000	182,000

THIRD COINAGE

Y#	KM#	Metal	Description	VF	EF	Unc
29	29	Silv	10 Sen, Yrs 40–45 (1907–12)	5	12.50	45
30	30	Silv	20 Sen, Yrs 39–44 *Yr 44, EF $450*	6	17.50	140
31	31	Silv	50 Sen, Yrs 39–45	11	20.00	185

Y#	KM#	Metal	Description	VF	EF	Unc
32	32	Gold	5 Yen, Yrs 30–45 (1897–1912)	820	1,100	1,450
33	33	Gold	10 Yen, Yrs 30–43	635	820	1,100
34	34	Gold	20 Yen, Yrs 30–45	1,635	2,275	3,185

TRADE COINS

Y#	KM#	Metal	Description	VF	EF	Unc
14	14	Silv	Trade Dollar, Yrs 8–10 (1875–77)	1,500	2,275	3,800

Note: Coins dated Year 7 are patterns.

An expanding trade forced Japan to call in the old 1-yen pieces (Y5 and YA25), counterstamp them with a Japanese character "Gin" (meaning "silver") in a small circle, and circulate them, principally in Taiwan.

Y#	KM#	Metal	Description	VF	EF	Unc
28	28	Silv	"Gin" stamp (1870) on Y5	900	1,100	1,450
28a	28a	Silv	"Gin" stamp on YA25, Yrs 7–30	90	145	400
28b	28b	Silv	"Gin" stamp on Y14	1,500	2,365	4,100

Taisho Reign, *Years 1 to 15 (1912–1926)*

Reign Symbols 正大 *on Coins*

First Coinage

Designs: ***Like Y20, A25, and 29–34 except for symbols of Taisho reign***

Y#	KM#	Metal	Description	VF	EF	Unc
35	35	Bz	1 Sen, Yrs 2–4 (1913–15)	5	10	65

Y#	KM#	Metal	Description	VF	EF	Unc
36	36	Silv	10 Sen, Yrs 1–6 (1912–17)	4	7	12
37	37	Silv	50 Sen, Yrs 1–6 (1912–17)	11	21	65
38	38	Silv	1 Yen, Yr 3 (1914)	90	135	320

Y#	KM#	Metal	Description	VF	EF	Unc
39	39	Gold	5 Yen, Yrs 2, 13 (1913, 38)	1,400	2,185	2,900
40	40	Gold	20 Yen, Yrs 1–9 (1913–20)	1,365	1,635	2,275

Second Coinage

Y#	KM#	Metal	Description	VF	EF	Unc
41	41	Bz	5 Rin, Yrs 5–8 (1916–19)	2.50	6	12
42	42	Bz	1 Sen, Yrs 5–13 (1916–24)	0.65	2	9

Y#	KM#	Metal	Description	VF	EF	Unc
43	43	C-N	5 Sen, Yrs 6–9 (1917–20) (20 mm)	13.00	20.00	32.50
44	44	C-N	5 Sen, Yrs 9–12 (1920–23) (18.5 mm)	1.50	2.50	9.00

Y#	KM#	Metal	Description	VF	EF	Unc
45	45	C-N	10 Sen, Yrs 9–15 (1920–26)	1	2.50	6

Y#	KM#	Metal	Description	VF	EF	Unc
46	46	Silv	50 Sen, Yrs 11–15 (1922–26)	4.25	9	25

Showa Reign, *Years 1–64 (1926–1989)*

Reign Symbols 和昭 *on Coins*

First Coinage

Designs: ***Like Y32–34, 39–42, and 44–46 except for symbols of Showa reign***

Y#	KM#	Metal	Description	VF	EF	Unc
47	47	Bz	1 Sen, Yrs 2–13 (1927–38)	0.65	1	6

Y#	KM#	Metal	Description	VF	EF	Unc
48	48	C-N	5 Sen, Yr 7 (1932)	3.50	6.25	25
49	49	C-N	10 Sen, Yrs 2–7 (1927–32)	2.00	3.50	9

Y#	KM#	Metal	Description	VF	EF	Unc
50	50	Silv	50 Sen, Yrs 3–13 (1928–38) *Yr 13, EF $225*	4.25	7	10.50

Y#	KM#	Metal	Description	VF	EF	Unc
51	51	Gold	5 Yen, Yr 5 (1930)	54,500	68,200	81,800
52	52	Gold	20 Yen, Yrs 5–7 (1930–32)	45,450	54,500	72,750

SECOND COINAGE

Y#	KM#	Metal	Description	VF	EF	Unc
53	53	Nick	5 Sen, Yrs 8–12 (1933–37)	2.50	4.50	7

Note: Year 13 was not released to circulation.

Y#	KM#	Metal	Description	VF	EF	Unc
54	54	Nick	10 Sen, Yrs 8–12 (1933–36)	1.50	3.50	7

Y#	KM#	Metal	Description	VF	EF	Unc
55	55	Bz	1 Sen, Yr 13 (1938)	1	2.50	3.25

Y#	KM#	Metal	Description	VF	EF	Unc
56	56	Alum	1 Sen, Yrs 13–15 (1938–40)	0.75	1.50	1.50

Y#	KM#	Metal	Description	VF	EF	Unc
57	57	A-Bz	5 Sen, Yrs 13–15 (1938–40)	1.50	2.50	7

Y#	KM#	Metal	Description	VF	EF	Unc
58	58	A-Bz	10 Sen, Yrs 13–15 (1938–40)	0.75	2	7

WORLD WAR II ISSUES

Y#	KM#	Metal	Description	VF	EF	Unc
59	59	Alum	1 Sen, Yrs 16–18 (1941–43) (0.65 g)	0.50	0.65	1.00
59a	59a	Alum	1 Sen, Yr 18 (1943) (0.55 g)	0.70	1.00	1.50

Y#	KM#	Metal	Description	VF	EF	Unc
60	60	Alum	5 Sen, Yrs 15–16 (1940–41) (1.2 g)	0.50	0.80	2.00
60a	60a	Alum	5 Sen, Yrs 16–17 (1941–42) (1.0 g)	0.50	0.65	1.50
60b	60b	Alum	5 Sen, Yr 18 (1943) (0.8 g)	1.50	2.50	4.50

Y#	KM#	Metal	Description	VF	EF	Unc
61	61	Alum	10 Sen, Yrs 15–16 (1940–41) (1.5 g)	0.50	0.80	2.00
61a	61a	Alum	10 Sen, Yrs 16–17 (1941–42) (1.2 g)	0.50	0.80	1.50
61b	61b	Alum	10 Sen, Yr 18 (1943) (1.0 g)	0.50	0.80	1.50

Y#	KM#	Metal	Description	VF	EF	Unc
62	62	Tin	1 Sen, Yrs 19–20 (1944–45)	0.50	0.70	1

Y#	KM#	Metal	Description	VF	EF	Unc
63	63	Tin	5 Sen, Yr 19 (1944)	1.50	2.00	2.50
64	64	Tin	10 Sen, Yr 19 (1944)	0.50	0.80	1.00

Y#	KM#	Metal	Description	VF	EF	Unc
65	65	Tin	5 Sen, Yrs 20–21 (1945–46)	0.70	1.50	3.50

Y#	KM#	Metal	Description	VF	EF	Unc
68	68	Alum	10 Sen, Yrs 20–21 (1945–46)	0.50	0.80	1

Note: Red fiber 1 sen ND (1945), 5 sen, and 10 sen Year 20 (1945) circulated for only a few days.

Postwar Issues

Y#	KM#	Metal	Description	VF	EF	Unc
67	67	Br	50 Sen, Yr 21 (1946) *Yr 22 (1947), EF $2,450*	1.50	2.25	3.50

Note: Year 22 was not released to circulation.

Y#	KM#	Metal	Description	VF	EF	Unc
69	69	Br	50 Sen, Yrs 22–23 (1947–48)	0.50	0.65	1

Henceforth, numerals in Japanese read from left to right.

Y#	KM#	Metal	Description	VF	EF	Unc
70	70	Br	1 Yen, Yrs 23–25 (1948–50)	0.60	0.80	2

Y#	KM#	Metal	Description	VF	EF	Unc
71	71	Br	5 Yen, Yrs 23–24 (1948–49)	0.50	1	1.25

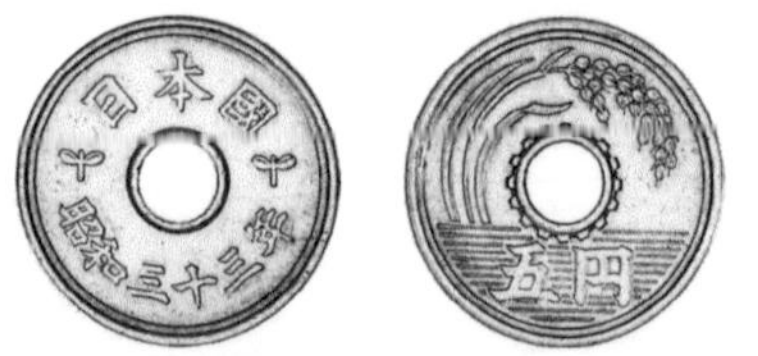

Y#	KM#	Metal	Description	VF	EF	Unc
72	72	Br	5 Yen, Yrs 24–33 (1949–58), script characters	0.50	2.50	9

Y#	KM#	Metal	Description	VF	EF	Unc
72a	72a	Br	5 Yen, Yrs 34–64 (1959–89), block characters	0.25	0.50	2.50

Y#	KM#	Metal	Description	VF	EF	Unc
73	73	Bz	10 Yen, Yrs 26–33 (1951–58), reeded edge	0.50	1.00	85.00
73a	73a	Bz	10 Yen, Yrs 34–64 (1959–89), plain edge *Yrs 25–26, cupro-nickel (1950–51), EF $1,450*	0.10	0.15	1.50

Note: Years 25–26 (1950–51) 10 yen in cupro-nickel were not released to circulation.

Y#	KM#	Metal	Description	VF	EF	Unc
74	74	Alum	1 Yen, Yrs 30–64 (1955–89)	0.05	0.10	0.50

Y#	KM#	Metal	Description	VF	EF	Unc
75	75	Nick	50 Yen, Yrs 30–33 (1955–58)	1	1.50	25

Y#	KM#	Metal	Description	VF	EF	Unc
76	76	Nick	50 Yen, Yrs 34–41 (1959–66) *Yr 35, EF $90*	1	1.50	4

Y#	KM#	Metal	Description	VF	EF	Unc
77	77	Silv	100 Yen, Yrs 32–33 (1957–58)	4	5	9

Y#	KM#	Metal	Description	VF	EF	Unc
78	78	Silv	100 Yen, Yrs 34–41 (1959–66)	4	5	7

1964 Olympic Games

Y#	KM#	Metal	Description	VF	EF	Unc
79	79	Silv	100 Yen, Yr 39 (1964)	4.25	6	7

Y#	KM#	Metal	Description	VF	EF	Unc
80	80	Silv	1,000 Yen, Yr 39 (1964)	25	30	45

JERSEY

The Bailiwick of Jersey is one of Britain's Channel Islands, 12 miles off the northwest coast of France. It has a lieutenant governor appointed by the Crown, and its own legislature and judiciary. *Language:* English. *Capital:* St. Helier.

MONETARY SYSTEM
12 pence = 1 shilling
5 shillings = 1 crown
20 shillings = 1 pound

VICTORIA, *1837–1901*

Y#	KM#	Metal	Description	VF	EF	Unc
1	1	Cop	1/52 Shilling, 1841	40	75	225 *Proof: $600*
2	2	Cop	1/26 Shilling, 1841–61	8	30	110 *Proof: $950*
3	3	Cop	1/13 Shilling, 1841–65 *1865, Proof only: $1,850*	10	50	200 *Proof: $600*

Y#	KM#	Metal	Description	VF	EF	Unc
4	4	Bz	1/26 Shilling, 1866–71	10	30	95
						Proof: $900
5	5	Bz	1/13 Shilling, 1866–71	10	50	150
						Proof: $950

NEW COINAGE SYSTEM

Y#	KM#	Metal	Description	VF	EF	Unc
6	6	Bz	1/48 Shilling, 1877	17.50	75.00	175
						Proof: $1,000
7	7	Bz	1/24 Shilling, 1877–94	4.00	10.00	30
						Proof: $425
8	8	Bz	1/12 Shilling, 1877–94	4.50	12.50	35
						Proof: $500

EDWARD VII, *1901–1910*

Y#	KM#	Metal	Description	VF	EF	Unc
9	9	Bz	1/24 Shilling, 1909	10	20	50
10	10	Bz	1/12 Shilling, 1909	10	20	45

GEORGE V, *1910–1936*

Y#	KM#	Metal	Description	VF	EF	Unc
11	11	Bz	1/24 Shilling, 1911–23	5	10	30
12	12	Bz	1/12 Shilling, 1911–23	5	10	35

Y#	KM#	Metal	Description	VF	EF	Unc
13	13	Bz	1/24 Shilling, 1923, 26	4	12.50	40
						Proof: $950
14	14	Bz	1/12 Shilling, 1923, 26	4	10.00	35

Y#	KM#	Metal	Description	VF	EF	Unc
15	15	Bz	1/24 Shilling, 1931–35	3.50	12	30
						Proof: $675
16	16	Bz	1/12 Shilling, 1931–35	3.50	10	18
						Proof: $600

GEORGE VI, *1936–1952*

Y#	KM#	Metal	Description	VF	EF	Unc
17	17	Bz	1/24 Shilling, 1937–47	2.50	7.50	25
						Proof: $450
18	18	Bz	1/12 Shilling, 1937–47	3.50	10.00	20
						Proof: $300

Commemorating End of German Occupation

Obverse: ***Without IND. IMP.***

Y#	KM#	Metal	Description	VF	EF	Unc
19	19	Bz	1/12 Shilling, 1945 (struck 1949–52)	0.75	1.25	6.50
						Proof: $275

ELIZABETH II, *1952–2022*

Y#	KM#	Metal	Description	VF	EF	Unc
20	20	Bz	1/12 Shilling, 1945 (struck 1954)	0.75	1.25	4.50
						Proof: $300

New Legend: ***BAILIWICK OF JERSEY***

Y#	KM#	Metal	Description	VF	EF	Unc
21	21	Bz	1/12 Shilling, 1957, 64	0.25	0.50	2.50
						Proof: $250

Y#	KM#	Metal	Description	VF	EF	Unc
22	22	N-Br	1/4 Shilling, 1957, 60 *1960 Proof only: $12*	0.25	0.50	1.25
						Proof: $10

300th Anniversary, Accession of Charles II

Y#	KM#	Metal	Description	VF	EF	Unc
23	23	Bz	1/12 Shilling, 1960	0.75	1	3
						Proof: $10

Y#	KM#	Metal	Description	VF	EF	Unc
24	24	N-Br	1/4 Shilling, 1964	0.25	0.50	1.25
						Proof: $12.50

JORDAN

Jordan is a constitutional hereditary monarchy in the Middle East. Under Ottoman Turkish rule from the 16th century through World War I, it was then ruled under British mandate and separated from Palestine in 1920. Its independence was recognized in 1923, and British administration ended in 1946. Parliamentary elections and political liberalization were begun in 1989. *Languages:* Arabic, English. *Capital:* Amman.

MONETARY SYSTEM
1,000 fils = 1 dinar (pound)

ABDULLA IBN AL HUSSEIN, *1946–1951*

Legend: ***KINGDOM OF THE JORDAN***

Y#	KM#	Metal	Description	VF	EF	Unc
1	1	Bz	1 "Fil", 1949 (error)	10.00	25.00	50
2	2	Bz	1 Fils, 1949	8.75	20.00	40
3	3	Bz	5 Fils, 1949	3.50	6.50	30
4	4	Bz	10 Fils, 1949	3.50	6.50	30

Y#	KM#	Metal	Description	VF	EF	Unc
5	5	C-N	20 Fils, 1949	3.50	6.50	30
6	6	C-N	50 Fils, 1949	5.00	15.00	35
7	7	C-N	100 Fils, 1949	7.50	35.00	70
			1949 Proof Set: (25 minted): $3,500			

HUSSEIN I, *1952–1999*

New Legend: *KINGDOM OF JORDAN*

Y#	KM#	Metal	Description	VF	EF	Unc
8	8	Bz	1 Fils, 1955–65	2	4	10
9	9	Bz	5 Fils, 1955–67	2	4	10
10	10	Bz	10 Fils, 1955–67	2	4	10

Y#	KM#	Metal	Description	VF	EF	Unc
A10	13	C-N	20 Fils, 1964–65	1.50	3	10
11	11	C-N	50 Fils, 1955–65	2.00	4	10
12	12	C-N	100 Fils, 1955–65	2.00	4	10

Note: YA10 was not issued to circulation.

KATANGA

Katanga was the southernmost province of the Republic of the Congo, which gained independence from Belgium in June 1960. Katanga seceded from the republic two weeks later and was not reintegrated into the Congo until 1963. *Capital:* Elizabethville.

MONETARY SYSTEM

100 centimes = 1 franc

PRECIOUS METAL CONTENT

Dates	Denomination	Gross Wt (g)	Fineness	Net Wt (g)	Troy Oz.
		GOLD			
1961	5 francs	13.3300	0.9000	11.9970	0.3857

Y#	KM#	Metal	Description	VF	EF	Unc
1	2a	Gold	5 Francs, 1961	BV	550.00	600.00
2	1	Bz	1 Franc, 1961	1.00	4.50	12.50
3	2	Bz	5 Francs, 1961	2.50	5.00	15.00

KIAO CHAU (KIAUTSCHOU)

Between 1898–1914, Kiao Chau was a German-leased territory on the Shantung peninsula in eastern China, under the administration of the Imperial Navy. It is now a district in the People's Republic of China, known as Jiaozhou. *Capital:* Tsingtao.

MONETARY SYSTEM

100 cents = 1 dollar

Y#	KM#	Metal	Description	VF	EF	Unc
1	1	C-N	5 Cents, 1909	300	525	950
2	2	C-N	10 Cents, 1909	300	625	925

KOREA

On a mountainous peninsula in northeastern Asia extending toward the southern tip of Japan, Korea is one of the world's oldest nations. During the latter part of the 19th century Korea became a pawn among China, Russia, and Japan. In 1910 Japan annexed the country, holding it until 1945. Independent since World War II, the country was divided into two zones, North Korea and South Korea, as a result of the Korean War (1950–1953). *Capitals:* Kaesong prior to Korean War; afterward, Pyongyang (North Korea) and Seoul (South Korea).

MONETARY SYSTEMS

1,000 mun = 1 warn, before 1892
100 fun = 1 yang, 1892–1902
5 yang = 1 whan, 1892–1902
100 chon = 1 won, 1902–1910

PRECIOUS METAL CONTENT

Dates	Denomination	Gross Wt (g)	Fineness	Net Wt (g)	Troy Oz.
		SILVER			
1892–98	1 yang	5.2000	0.8000	4.1600	0.1337
	5 yang	26.9500	0.9000	24.2550	0.7798
	1 whan	26.9500	0.9000	24.2550	0.7798
1901–06	10 chon	2.6957	0.8000	2.1566	0.0693
	20 chon	5.3914	0.8000	4.3131	0.1387
	1/2 won	13.4785	0.8000	10.7828	0.3467
1907–10	10 chon	2.2500	0.7200	1.6200	0.0521
	20 chon	4.0500	0.8000	3.2400	0.1042
	1/2 won	10.1250	0.8000	8.1000	0.2604
		GOLD			
1906–10	5 won	4.1667	0.9000	3.7500	0.1206
	10 won	8.3333	0.9000	7.5000	0.2411
	20 won	16.6667	0.9000	15.0000	0.4823

Dating Systems

Dates of Y1–9 are figured from the beginning of Korea's Yi Dynasty in 1392 AD. Y1–3 were actually struck in 1891. Later coins are dated by the year of the current emperor's reign.

EMPEROR KOJONG, *1864–1907*

STRUCK COINAGE

For earlier coinage of the reign see Mandel, *Cast Coinage of Korea,* and Craig, *Coins of the World.*

Y#	KM#	Metal	Description	VF	EF	Unc
A1	1100	Br	5 Mun, ND (1890)	350	500	800

Y#	KM#	Metal	Description	VF	EF	Unc
1	1101	Cop	5 Mun, Yr 497 (1888)	100	200	450
2	1102	Cop	10 Mun, Yr 497	200	400	650
3	1103	Silv	1 Warn, Yr 497	8,000	15,000	25,000

Note: Some authorities claim Y3 is a pattern. Similar coins in silvered or gilt metal, and a 20 mun in copper dated Year 495, are all patterns.

NEW COINAGE SYSTEM, 1892

100 fun = 1 yang

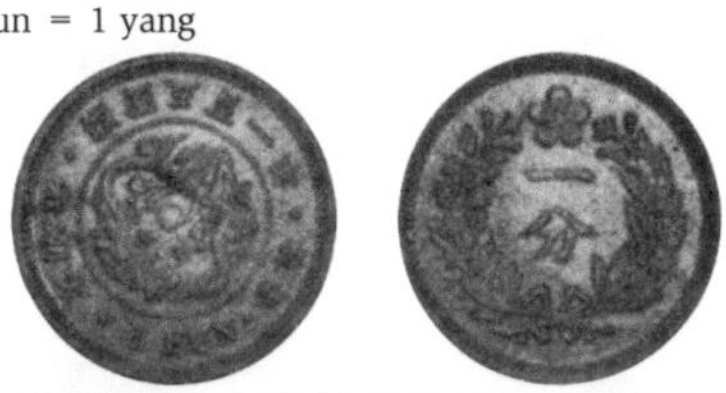

Y#	KM#	Metal	Description	VF	EF	Unc
4	1104	Br	1 Fun, Yrs 501–05 (1892–96)	20	50	100
5	1106	Cop	5 Fun, Yrs 501–05	3	6	80
6	1110	C-N	1/4 Yang, Yrs 501–05	15	25	100

Y#	KM#	Metal	Description	VF	EF	Unc
7	1112	Silv	1 Yang, Yrs 501–02 (1892–93)	60	100	250
8	1114	Silv	5 Yang, Yr 501 (1892)	1,000	1,500	2,500
9	1115	Silv	1 Whan, Yr 502 (1893)	5,000	8,000	15,000

KUANG MU REIGN, *YEARS 1–11 (1897–1907)*

REIGN SYMBOLS 武 光 *ON COINS*

Title assumed by Emperor Kojong in 1897.

FIRST COINAGE

Designs: ***Like Y5–7 except for symbols of Kuang Mu reign***

Y#	KM#	Metal	Description	VF	EF	Unc
A10	1116	Cop	5 Fun, Yrs 2–6 (1898–1902) Yr 3, VF $400	2	5	60

Y#	KM#	Metal	Description	VF	EF	Unc
B10	1117	C-N	1/4 Yang, Yrs 1–5 (1897–1901)	1	3	10
C10	Several	Silv	1 Yang, Yr 1 (1898) (2 vars)	80	120	300

Note: For YB10, all dates but Year 2 are scarce to rare.

SECOND COINAGE

100 chon = 1 won

Y#	KM#	Metal	Description	VF	EF	Unc
10	1121	Bz	1 Chon, Yr 6 (1902)	2,500	4,500	7,500

Y#	KM#	Metal	Description	VF	EF	Unc
11	1122	C-N	5 Chon, Yr 6 (1902)	1,800	3,500	5,000
12	1123	Silv	1/2 Won, Yr 5 (1901)	5,000	8,000	12,000

THIRD COINAGE

Y#	KM#	Metal	Description	VF	EF	Unc
13	1124	Bz	1/2 Chon, Yr 10 (1906)	8	15	40
14	1125	Bz	1 Chon, Yrs 9–10 (1905–06)	10	20	50

Y#	KM#	Metal	Description	VF	EF	Unc
15	1126	C-N	5 Chon, Yrs 9–11 (1905–07)	15	30	80

Y#	KM#	Metal	Description	VF	EF	Unc
16	1127	Silv	10 Chon, Yr 10 (1906)	20	40	80
17	1128	Silv	20 Chon, Yrs 9–10 (1905–06)	40	80	150
18	1129	Silv	1/2 Won, Yr 9–10 (1905–06)	80	140	250

Y#	KM#	Metal	Description	VF	EF	Unc
19	1142	Gold	5 Won, Yr 2 (1898)	30,000	60,000	100,000
20	1130	Gold	10 Won, Yr 10 (1906)	10,000	20,000	35,000
21	1131	Gold	20 Won, Yr 10 (1906)	20,000	40,000	60,000

Fourth Coinage

Y#	KM#	Metal	Description	VF	EF	Unc
B22	1132	Bz	1 Chon, Yr 11 (1907)	5	12	60

Y#	KM#	Metal	Description	VF	EF	Unc
C22	1133	Silv	10 Chon, Yr 11 (1907), thin	20	50	100
D22	1134	Silv	20 Chon, Yr 11 (1907)	30	60	150
E22	1135	Silv	1/2 Won, Yr 11 (1907)	100	200	450

Yung Hi Reign,
Years 1 to 4 (1907–1910)
Reign Symbols 隆熙 *on Coins*

Designs: ***Like YB22–E22 except for reign symbols***

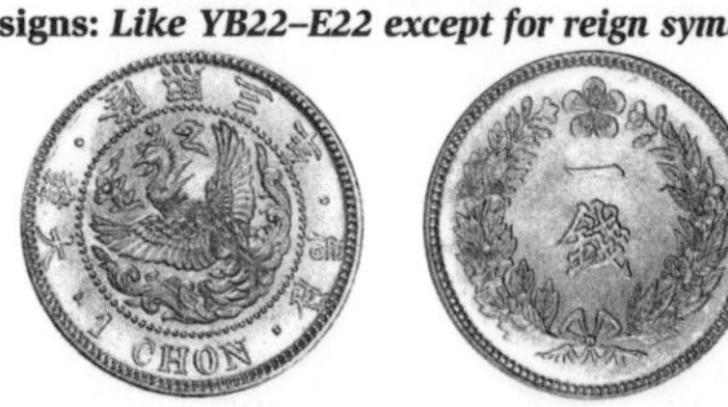

Y#	KM#	Metal	Description	VF	EF	Unc
22	1136	Bz	1/2 Chon, Yrs 1–4 (1907–10) Yr 1 (1907), VF $200	6	12	50
23	1137	Bz	1 Chon, Yrs 1–4 (1907–10)	3	7	25

Note: The cupro-nickel 5 Chon of this reign was not issued to circulation.

Obverse: ***Dragon***

Y#	KM#	Metal	Description	VF	EF	Unc
25	1139	Silv	10 Chon, Yrs 2–4 *Yr 3 (1909), Rare*	15	30	60
26	1140	Silv	20 Chon, Yrs 2–4 (1908–10)	25	50	100
27	1141	Silv	1/2 Won, Yrs 2–3 (1908–09) *Yr 3 (1909), Rare*	100	150	350

KOREA, NORTH

A communist dictatorship, North Korea was established in 1948 with the partitioning of the 600-mile peninsula east of China. *Language:* Korean. *Capital:* Pyongyang.

MONETARY SYSTEM

100 chon = 1 won

Y#	KM#	Metal	Description	VF	EF	Unc
1	1/5/9	Alum	1 Chon, 1959, 70	0.50	0.75	1.50
2	2/6/10	Alum	5 Chon, 1959, 74	1.25	2.00	3.00
3	3/7/11	Alum	10 Chon, 1959	2.00	2.50	4.00

KOREA, SOUTH

South Korea is a republic formed in 1948 when separated from North Korea by compromise in UN negotiation. *Language:* Korean. *Capital:* Seoul.

MONETARY SYSTEM

100 chon = 1 hwan

First Coinage

Dates according to Korean calendar.

Y#	KM#	Metal	Description	VF	EF	Unc
1	1	Bz	10 Hwan, 4292, 94 (1959, 61)	0.75	1.50	3

Y#	KM#	Metal	Description	VF	EF	Unc
2	2	CNZ	50 Hwan, 4292, 94	1	1.75	3.50

Y#	KM#	Metal	Description	VF	EF	Unc
3	3	C-N	100 Hwan, 4292	2.50	5	10

KUWAIT

Kuwait is an independent Arab emirate at the head of the Persian Gulf. An hereditary monarchy was established around Kuwait City on the fringes of the Ottoman Empire by the end of the 18th century. A century later, fearing expansion by the Turks, Kuwait accepted the protection of the British Empire; that protectorate was ended in 1961. *Languages:* Arabic, English. *Capital:* Kuwait City.

MONETARY SYSTEM

1000 fils = 1 dinar

PRECIOUS METAL CONTENT

Dates	Denomination	Gross Wt (g)	Fineness	Net Wt (g)	Troy Oz.
		GOLD			
1961	5 dinar	13.5720	0.9170	12.4455	0.4001

Arabic Legend: *EMIRATE OF KUWAIT*

Y#	KM#	Metal	Description	VF	EF	Unc
1	2	N-Br	1 Fils, 1961	0.50	0.85	1.50
						Proof: $35
2	3	N-Br	5 Fils, 1961	0.60	1.00	2.00
						Proof: $40
3	4	N-Br	10 Fils, 1961	0.60	1.00	2.00
						Proof: $45
4	5	C-N	20 Fils, 1961	0.75	1.50	3.00
						Proof: $50
5	6	C-N	50 Fils, 1961	0.85	1.75	3.25
						Proof: $60
6	7	C-N	100 Fils, 1961	1.00	2.00	6.00
						Proof: $75
7	8	Gold	5 Dinars, 1961	—	—	Rare

New Arabic Legend: *AL KUWAIT*

Y#	KM#	Metal	Description	VF	EF	Unc
8	9	N-Br	1 Fils, 1962–88	0.10	0.15	1.00
						Proof: $55
9	10	N-Br	5 Fils, 1962–97	0.10	0.20	1.00
						Proof: $60
10	11	N-Br	10 Fils, 1962–95	0.15	0.25	1.25
						Proof: $70
11	12	C-N	20 Fils, 1962–97	0.20	0.30	1.50
						Proof: $80
12	13	C-N	50 Fils, 1962–99	0.35	0.50	1.75
						Proof: $95
13	14	C-N	100 Fils, 1962–95	0.75	1.00	3.50
						Proof: $115

LAOS

One of the three former French Indo-Chinese states, Laos lies generally between Thailand and Vietnam. Under French protection since 1893, it became an independent sovereign state in 1949, enduring considerable civil conflict until the communist Pathet Lao seized power and abolished the monarchy in 1975. Since then a socialist regime has led to a gradual return to private enterprise. *Languages:* Lao, French. *Capital:* Vientiane.

MONETARY SYSTEM

100 centimes = 1 kip

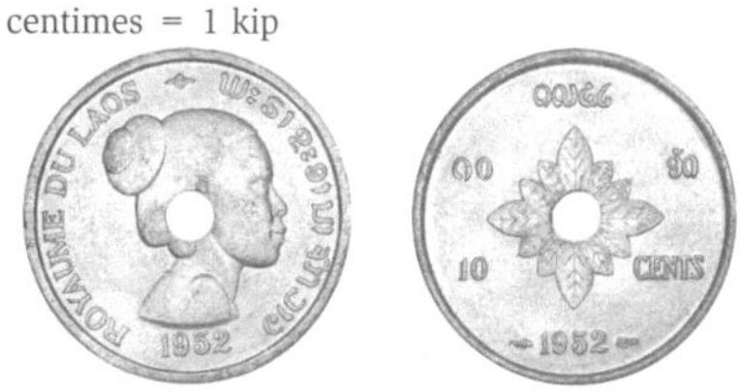

Y#	KM#	Metal	Description	VF	EF	Unc
1	4	Alum	10 Centimes, 1952	0.25	0.50	1.25

Y#	KM#	Metal	Description	VF	EF	Unc
2	5	Alum	20 Centimes, 1952	0.30	0.65	1.75

Y#	KM#	Metal	Description	VF	EF	Unc
3	6	Alum	50 Centimes, 1952	0.50	1.25	2.50

LATVIA

Latvia sits on the Baltic Sea between Lithuania and Estonia. Since passing from Swedish control in 1721, it was a Russian province until 1918 when it became an independent republic. In 1940 Russia incorporated it into the USSR. Independence was declared in 1991 and the country is now a parliamentary democracy. *Language:* Lettish. *Capital:* Riga.

MONETARY SYSTEM

100 santimu = 1 lats

PRECIOUS METAL CONTENT

Dates	Denomination	Gross Wt (g)	Fineness	Net Wt (g)	Troy Oz.
		SILVER			
1924–32	1 lats	5.0000	0.8350	4.1750	0.1342
	2 lati	10.0000	0.8350	8.3500	0.2685
	5 lati	25.0000	0.8350	20.8750	0.6711

Y#	KM#	Metal	Description	VF	EF	Unc
1	1	Bz	1 Santims, 1922–35	5	10	25
2	2	Bz	2 Santimi, 1922–32	5	10	85
3	3	Bz	5 Santimi, 1922	4	8	20
4	4	Nick	10 Santimu, 1922	4	8	20
5	5	Nick	20 Santimu, 1922	6	12	40

Y#	KM#	Metal	Description	VF	EF	Unc
6	6	Nick	50 Santimu, 1922	5	10	25

Y#	KM#	Metal	Description	VF	EF	Unc
7	7	Silv	1 Lats, 1924	10	15	45
8	8	Silv	2 Lati, 1925–26	10	15	45

Y#	KM#	Metal	Description	VF	EF	Unc
9	9	Silv	5 Lati, 1929–32	22.50	45	100

Y#	KM#	Metal	Description	VF	EF	Unc
10	10	Bz	1 Santims, 1937–39	5	10	25
11	11.1	Bz	2 Santimi, 1937 (19 mm)	30	55	100
11a	11.2	Bz	2 Santimi, 1939 (19.5 mm)	5	10	25

LEBANON

A republic on the east coast of the Mediterranean, Lebanon separates Israel and Syria, who along with UN forces, have occupied parts of the country since 1976. It was united with Syria as a single political unit of the Ottoman Empire until 1920 when the League of Nations made it a French mandate, separating the largely Christian nation from Muslim Syria. It was proclaimed independent in 1941, though French troops did not depart until 1946. Civil wars, military occupation, and unresolved borders have destabilized the nation. *Languages:* Arabic, French. *Capital:* Beirut.

MONETARY SYSTEM

100 piastres = 1 lira (pound)

PRECIOUS METAL CONTENT

Dates	Denomination	Gross Wt (g)	Fineness	Net Wt (g)	Troy Oz.
		SILVER			
1929–52	10 piastres	2.0000	0.6800	1.3600	0.0437
	25 piastres	5.0000	0.6800	3.4000	0.1093
	50 piastres	10.0000	0.6800	6.8000	0.2186

FIRST COINAGE

Y#	KM#	Metal	Description	VF	EF	Unc
1	1	A-Bz	2 Piastres, 1924	6.50	13	100
2	2	A-Bz	5 Piastres, 1924	5.00	10	90

SECOND COINAGE

Y#	KM#	Metal	Description	VF	EF	Unc
5	9	C-N	1/2 Piastre, 1934, 36	10	20	100

Y#	KM#	Metal	Description	VF	EF	Unc
6	3	C-N	1 Piastre, 1925–36	4.50	15	100

Y#	KM#	Metal	Description	VF	EF	Unc
3	4	A-Bz	2 Piastres, 1925	10	35	90
4	5	A-Bz	5 Piastres, 1925–40	4	10	65

Y#	KM#	Metal	Description	VF	EF	Unc
8	6	Silv	10 Piastres, 1929	25.00	50	150
9	7	Silv	25 Piastres, 1929–36	17.50	35	125
10	8	Silv	50 Piastres, 1929–36	40.00	80	275

Y#	KM#	Metal	Description	VF	EF	Unc
5a	9a	Zinc	1/2 Piastre, 1941	20	45	100
6a	3a	Zinc	1 Piastre, 1940	20	45	100

Design: *Like Y6*

Y#	KM#	Metal	Description	VF	EF	Unc
7	10	A-Bz	2-1/2 Piastres, 1940	4	10	60

WORLD WAR II PROVISIONAL ISSUES

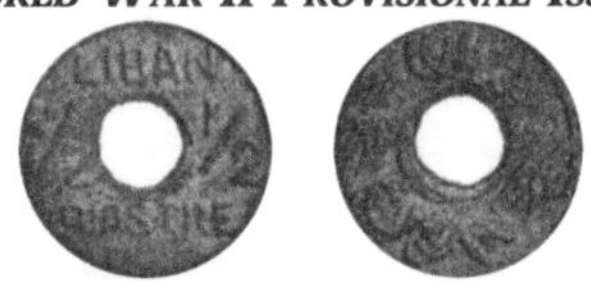

Y#	KM#	Metal	Description	VF	EF	Unc
11	11	Br	1/2 Piastre, ND (1941)	4	10	30

Y#	KM#	Metal	Description	VF	EF	Unc
12	12	Br	1 Piastre, ND (1941)	4	10	60
13	13	Alum	2-1/2 Piastres, ND (1941)	4	10	60

POSTWAR ISSUES

Y#	KM#	Metal	Description	VF	EF	Unc
14	14	Alum	5 Piastres, 1952	1.50	4	10

Y#	KM#	Metal	Description	VF	EF	Unc
15	15	Alum	10 Piastres, 1952	2	4	25

Y#	KM#	Metal	Description	VF	EF	Unc
16	16	A-Bz	25 Piastres, 1952, 61	0.45	0.65	1.25

Y#	KM#	Metal	Description	VF	EF	Unc
17	17	Silv	50 Piastres, 1952	2	4.50	12.50

Y#	KM#	Metal	Description	VF	EF	Unc
18	19	A-Bz	1 Piastre, 1955	0.50	1.00	3.00
19	20	A-Bz	2-1/2 Piastres, 1955	0.25	0.50	1.50

Y#	KM#	Metal	Description	VF	EF	Unc
20	18	Alum	5 Piastres, 1954	0.50	1	7.50

Y#	KM#	Metal	Description	VF	EF	Unc
21	22	A-Bz	10 Piastres, 1955	0.45	0.65	4.50

Y#	KM#	Metal	Description	VF	EF	Unc
22	21	A-Bz	5 Piastres, 1955, 61	0.45	0.65	2

Y#	KM#	Metal	Description	VF	EF	Unc
23	23	A-Bz	10 Piastres, 1955	0.45	0.65	3

Y#	KM#	Metal	Description	VF	EF	Unc
24	24	C-N	10 Piastres, 1961	0.20	0.40	1.75

LIBERIA

Founded in 1822 by the American Colonization Society on the southwest Atlantic coast of Africa, Liberia's first settlers were freed slaves and free persons of color who emigrated from the U.S. The nation became Africa's first independent republic in 1847. During the 19th-century colonial period, Liberia lost much of its territory to Britain and France but was able to maintain its independence. A military coup in 1980 was followed by civil war that lasted until 1997 when free elections returned. *Languages:* English, native tongues. *Capital:* Monrovia.

MONETARY SYSTEM

100 cents = 1 dollar

PRECIOUS METAL CONTENT

Dates	Denomination	Gross Wt (g)	Fineness	Net Wt (g)	Troy Oz.
		SILVER			
1896, 1906	10 cents	2.3200	0.9250	2.1460	0.0690
	25 cents	5.8000	0.9250	5.3650	0.1725
	50 cents	11.6000	0.9250	10.7300	0.3450
1960–62	10 cents	2.0700	0.9000	1.8630	0.0600
	25 cents	5.1800	0.9000	4.6620	0.1500
	50 cents	10.3700	0.9000	9.3330	0.3000
	1 dollar	20.7400	0.9000	18.6660	0.6000
		GOLD			
1964	20 dollars	18.6500	0.9000	16.7850	0.5397

Y#	KM#	Metal	Description	VF	EF	Unc
1	Tn1–Tn2	Cop	1 Cent (token), 1833, issued by American Colonization Society	125	200	300

Y#	KM#	Metal	Description	VF	EF	Unc
2	1/3	Cop	1 Cent, 1847, 62	20	40	250
						Proof: $350
3	2/4	Cop	2 Cents, 1847, 62	30	75	275
						Proof: $350

Y#	KM#	Metal	Description	VF	EF	Unc
4	5	Bz	1 Cent, 1896, 1906	15.00	37.50	75
						Proof: $225
5	6	Bz	2 Cents, 1896, 1906	17.50	42.50	85
						Proof: $250

Y#	KM#	Metal	Description	VF	EF	Unc
6	7	Silv	10 Cents, 1896, 1906	17.50	35	150
						Proof: $550
7	8	Silv	25 Cents, 1896, 1906	45.00	75	250
						Proof: $650
8	9	Silv	50 Cents, 1896, 1906	60.00	120	450
						Proof: $950

Y#	KM#	Metal	Description	VF	EF	Unc
9	10	Br	1/2 Cent, 1937	0.50	1	3.00
10	11	Br	1 Cent, 1937	1.00	2	5.00
11	12	Br	2 Cents, 1937	1.50	3	7.50
9a	10a	C-N	1/2 Cent, 1941	0.45	1	5.00
10a	11a	C-N	1 Cent, 1941	5.00	20	60.00
11a	12a	C-N	2 Cents, 1941	1.00	2	9.50

Y#	KM#	Metal	Description	VF	EF	Unc
12	13	Bz	1 Cent, 1960–84	0.10	0.25	1

Y#	KM#	Metal	Description	VF	EF	Unc
13	14	C-N	5 Cents, 1960–84	0.10	0.25	0.75

Y#	KM#	Metal	Description	VF	EF	Unc
14	15	Silv	10 Cents, 1960–61	1.50	2.75	5
15	16	Silv	25 Cents, 1960–61	2.00	3.00	6
16	17	Silv	50 Cents, 1960–61	4.00	6.00	8
17	18	Silv	1 Dollar, 1961–62	8.00	12.00	15

Y#	KM#	Metal	Description	VF	EF	Unc
27	19	Gold	20 Dollars, 1964	BV	BV	900

LIBYA

Libya, on the northeast coast of Africa, was part of the Ottoman Empire. It was formed as a constitutional monarchy in 1951 from former Italian-occupied territories. The king was deposed in 1969, and the country declared itself an Islamic Socialist Republic under dictator Muammar al-Qaddafi. Today its form of national government is unsettled. *Language:* Arabic. *Capital:* Tripoli.

MONETARY SYSTEM

10 milliemes = 1 piastre 100 piastres = 1 pound

IDRIS I, *1951–1969*

Y#	KM#	Metal	Description	VF	EF	Unc
1	1	Bz	1 Millieme, 1952	0.20	0.40	1.00
2	2	Bz	2 Milliemes, 1952	0.25	0.50	1.25
3	3	Bz	5 Milliemes, 1952	0.30	0.60	1.50

Y#	KM#	Metal	Description	VF	EF	Unc
4	4	C-N	1 Piastre, 1952	0.35	0.75	2.00
5	5	C-N	2 Piastres, 1952	0.50	1.00	2.75
			1952 Proof Set: $2,000			

LIECHTENSTEIN

An independent constitutional principality since 1866, Liechtenstein lies between Austria and Switzerland. The country was tied to the Austrian monetary system until the end of World War I, and to the Swiss thereafter. *Language:* German. *Capital:* Vaduz.

MONETARY SYSTEM

1-1/2 florins = 1 vereinsthaler, 1857–1868
100 heller = 1 krone, 1892–1923
100 rappen = 1 frank, 1924–

PRECIOUS METAL CONTENT

Dates	Denomination	Gross Wt (g)	Fineness	Net Wt (g)	Troy Oz.
		SILVER			
1862	1 thaler	18.5200	0.9000	7.6680	0.5359
1900–15	1 krone	5.0000	0.9000	4.5000	0.1342
	2 kronen	10.0000	0.9000	9.0000	0.2684
	5 kronen	24.0000	0.9000	21.6000	0.6944
	1/2 frank	2.5000	0.8350	2.0875	0.0671
	1 frank	5.0000	0.8350	4.1750	0.1342
	2 franken	10.0000	0.8350	8.3500	0.2685
	5 franken	25.0000	0.9000	22.5000	0.7234
		GOLD			
1898–1900	10 kronen	3.3875	0.9000	3.0488	0.0980
	20 kronen	6.7751	0.9000	6.0976	0.1960
1930–61	10 franken	3.2258	0.9000	2.9032	0.0933
	20 franken	6.4516	0.9000	5.8064	0.1867
	25 franken	8.0645	0.9000	7.2581	0.2333
	50 franken	16.1290	0.9000	14.5161	0.4667
	100 franken	32.2581	0.9000	29.0323	0.9334

Prince Johann II, *1858–1929*

Y#	KM#	Metal	Description	VF	EF	Unc
1	1	Silv	1 Thaler, 1862	1,500	3,000	4,500

Note: Modern restrikes of Y1 have "M" above date.

Values: *In Kronen*

Y#	KM#	Metal	Description	VF	EF	Unc
2	2	Silv	1 Krone, 1900–15	35	50	125
3	3	Silv	2 Kronen, 1912, 15	55	85	150
4	4	Silv	5 Kronen, 1900–15	175	250	425
			1900, VF $300			

Y#	KM#	Metal	Description	VF	EF	Unc
5	5	Gold	10 Kronen, 1900	1,800	2,000	3,000
6	6	Gold	20 Kronen, 1898	1,800	2,000	3,000

Note: Y5 dated 1898 is thought to be a pattern.

Values: *In Franken*

Y#	KM#	Metal	Description	VF	EF	Unc
7	7	Silv	1/2 Frank, 1924	100	225	425
8	8	Silv	1 Frank, 1924	125	275	450
9	9	Silv	2 Franken, 1924	200	350	575
10	10	Silv	5 Franken, 1924	275	425	1,500

Prince Franz I, *1929–1938*

Y#	KM#	Metal	Description	VF	EF	Unc
11	11	Gold	10 Franken, 1930	350	575	750
12	12	Gold	20 Franken, 1930	600	800	1,000

PRINCE FRANZ JOSEF II,
1938–1989

Y#	KM#	Metal	Description	VF	EF	Unc
13	13	Gold	10 Franken, 1946	185	225	275
14	14	Gold	20 Franken, 1946	300	335	375

Y#	KM#	Metal	Description	VF	EF	Unc
15	15	Gold	25 Franken, 1956	300	350	400
16	16	Gold	50 Franken, 1956	550	600	775
17	17	Gold	100 Franken, 1952	1,750	2,000	2,750

National Bank Centennial

Obverse: ***Head to right***
Reverse: ***Arms***

Y#	KM#	Metal	Description	VF	EF	Unc
18	18	Gold	25 Franken, 1961	325	375	450
19	19	Gold	50 Franken, 1961	550	575	600

Note: Y18–19 were not issued to circulation.

LITHUANIA

A Baltic state between Latvia and Poland, Lithuania was united with Poland through marriage in 1386 and came under Russian rule in 1795. It declared independence in 1918 under German protection. It was incorporated into the USSR in 1940. Independence was re-asserted in 1990 and a parliamentary democracy formed. *Languages:* Lithuanian, Russian, Polish. *Capital:* Vilnius.

MONETARY SYSTEM
100 centu = 1 litas

PRECIOUS METAL CONTENT

Dates	Denomination	Gross Wt (g)	Fineness	Net Wt (g)	Troy Oz.
		SILVER			
1925	1 litas	2.7000	0.5000	1.3500	0.0434
	2 litu	5.4000	0.5000	2.7000	0.0868
	5 litai	13.5000	0.5000	6.7500	0.2170
1936–38	5 litai	9.0000	0.7500	6.7500	0.2170
	10 litu	18.0000	0.7500	13.5000	0.4340

FIRST COINAGE

Y#	KM#	Metal	Description	VF	EF	Unc
1	71	A-Bz	1 Centas, 1925	6	12.50	35
2	72	A-Bz	5 Centai, 1925	6	12.50	35

Y#	KM#	Metal	Description	VF	EF	Unc
3	73	A-Bz	10 Centu, 1925	4	10	25
4	74	A-Bz	20 Centu, 1925	5	10	25
5	75	A-Bz	50 Centu, 1925	10	15	40

Y#	KM#	Metal	Description	VF	EF	Unc
6	76	Silv	1 Litas, 1925	5.00	10	25
7	77	Silv	2 Litu, 1925	7.50	15	40
8	78	Silv	5 Litai, 1925	7.50	15	70

SECOND COINAGE

Y#	KM#	Metal	Description	VF	EF	Unc
9	79	Bz	1 Centas, 1936	8	15	40

Y#	KM#	Metal	Description	VF	EF	Unc
10	80	Bz	2 Centai, 1936	8	15	40

Y#	KM#	Metal	Description	VF	EF	Unc
11	81	Bz	5 Centai, 1936	8	15	40

Y#	KM#	Metal	Description	VF	EF	Unc
12	82	Silv	5 Litai, 1936	10	20	45

Y#	KM#	Metal	Description	VF	EF	Unc
13	83	Silv	10 Litu, 1936	20	35	80

20th Anniversary of Independence

Y#	KM#	Metal	Description	VF	EF	Unc
14	84	Silv	10 Litu, 1938	25	50	125

Note: Other coins dated 1938 are patterns.

LUNDY

These "unlawful coins" have created considerable interest among collectors for many years and only for that reason have been included in this volume. Martin Coles Harmon, a London businessman, purchased Lundy Island, off the coast of England, in 1925 for approximately $25,000. He issued the coins listed here in 1929 and was fined by Britain in 1930 for issuing unauthorized coins. They were struck in Birmingham, England. The puffin, a sea bird, is shown on the coins, with Harmon's portrait on obverse. The coins circulated briefly but had no exchange value relative to other currencies. They are not legitimate.

Edge: *LUNDY LIGHTS AND LEADS*

Y#	KM#	Metal	Description	VF	EF	Unc
1	N/A	Bz	1/2 Puffin, 1929	7.50	15	30

Y#	KM#	Metal	Description	VF	EF	Unc
2	N/A	Bz	1 Puffin, 1929	7.50	15	30

LUXEMBOURG (LETZEBURG)

The Grand Duchy of Luxembourg is a constitutional monarchy bordered on the south by France, on the east and north by Germany, and on the west and north by Belgium. It was ceded to the Netherlands in 1815 and achieved autonomy in 1848. *Languages:* Luxembourgish, French, German. *Capital:* Luxembourg.

MONETARY SYSTEM
100 centimes = 1 frang (franc)

PRECIOUS METAL CONTENT

Dates	Denomination	Gross Wt (g)	Fineness	Net Wt (g)	Troy Oz.
		SILVER			
1929	5 francs	8.0000	0.6250	5.0000	0.1608
	10 francs	13.3000	0.7500	9.9750	0.3207
1946	20 francs	8.5000	0.8350	7.0975	0.2282
	50 francs	12.5000	0.8350	10.4375	0.3356
	100 francs	25.0000	0.8350	20.8750	0.6711

GENERAL COINAGE

Y#	KM#	Metal	Description	VF	EF	Unc
1	21	Bz	2-1/2 Centimes, 1854–1908 *1854, 70, VF $20*	8.00	15	35
2	22	Bz	5 Centimes, 1854–70	12.50	65	70
3	23	Bz	10 Centimes, 1854–70	6.00	30	70

Y#	KM#	Metal	Description	VF	EF	Unc
4	27	Zinc	5 Centimes, 1915	5	11	20.00
5	28	Zinc	10 Centimes, 1915	4	8	17.50
6	29	Zinc	25 Centimes, 1916	10	20	40.00

Y#	KM#	Metal	Description	VF	EF	Unc
7	30	Iron	5 Centimes, 1918–22	6	12	40
8	31	Iron	10 Centimes, 1918–23	7	15	45
9	32	Iron	25 Centimes, 1919–22	10	20	45

Issues With Royal Portraits or Monograms

Adolphe, 1890–1905

Y#	KM#	Metal	Description	VF	EF	Unc
10	24	C-N	5 Centimes, 1901	1	6.50	20
11	25	C-N	10 Centimes, 1901	1	6.50	20

Guillaume IV, 1905–1912

Y#	KM#	Metal	Description	VF	EF	Unc
12	26	C-N	5 Centimes, 1908	1.25	7.50	25

Charlotte, 1919–1964

First Coinage

Y#	KM#	Metal	Description	VF	EF	Unc
13	33	C-N	5 Centimes, 1924	1	7.50	20
14	34	C-N	10 Centimes, 1924	1	7.50	20

Y#	KM#	Metal	Description	VF	EF	Unc
15	37	C-N	25 Centimes, 1927 (C TS)	1	7.50	30

Y#	KM#	Metal	Description	VF	EF	Unc
16	43	Nick	50 Centimes, 1930	1.50	8.50	17.50

Y#	KM#	Metal	Description	VF	EF	Unc
17	35	Nick	1 Franc, 1924–35	1.25	9.75	19.50
18	36	Nick	2 Francs, 1924	5.00	15.00	30.00

Y#	KM#	Metal	Description	VF	EF	Unc
19	38	Nick	5 Francs, 1929	9	19.50	39.50
20	39	Nick	10 Francs, 1929	15	25.00	50.00

Y#	KM#	Metal	Description	VF	EF	Unc
21	40	Bz	5 Centimes, 1930	0.75	5	20
22	41	Bz	10 Centimes, 1930	0.75	5	20

Y#	KM#	Metal	Description	VF	EF	Unc
15b	42	Bz	25 Centimes, 1930	1.50	6	20

New Spelling: *LETZEBURG*

Y#	KM#	Metal	Description	VF	EF	Unc
24	44	C-N	1 Franc, 1939	0.85	1.75	5

Second Coinage

Y#	KM#	Metal	Description	VF	EF	Unc
25	45	Bz	25 Centimes, 1946–47	0.25	0.40	1

Y#	KM#	Metal	Description	VF	EF	Unc
25a	45a	Alum	25 Centimes, 1954–72	0.10	0.20	0.65

Y#	KM#	Metal	Description	VF	EF	Unc
26	46.1	C-N	1 Franc, 1946–47 (23 mm)	0.35	0.50	2

Y#	KM#	Metal	Description	VF	EF	Unc
26a	46.2	C-N	1 Franc, 1952 (21 mm)	0.25	0.50	3.00
26b	46.2	C-N	1 Franc, 1953–64, modified reverse die	0.10	0.20	1.50

Y#	KM#	Metal	Description	VF	EF	Unc
27	50	C-N	5 Francs, 1949	0.50	1	6

600th Anniversary, Death of John the Blind

Y#	KM#	Metal	Description	VF	EF	Unc
28	47	Silv	20 Francs, 1946	10	16	27.50
29	48	Silv	50 Francs, 1946	15	20	45.00
30	49	Silv	100 Francs, 1946	20	33	65.00

Note: Y30 without designer's initials on obverse was struck in 1964.

Y#	KM#	Metal	Description	VF	EF	Unc
31	51	C-N	5 Francs, 1962	0.25	0.75	2.25

Y#	KM#	Metal	Description	VF	EF	Unc
32	52	Silv	100 Francs, 1963	10	15	25

Millennium Commemorative

Y#	KM#	Metal	Description	VF	EF	Unc
33	53	Silv	250 Francs, 1963	12.50	20	35

Note: Y33 was struck in both brilliant and antiqued finishes.

GRAND DUKE JEAN, 1964–2000

Y#	KM#	Metal	Description	VF	EF	Unc
38	54	Silv	100 Francs, 1964	10	12	27.50

MACAU

Part of an island at the mouth of the Canton River in China, Macau was colonized by Portugal in the 16th century, the first European settlement in the Far East. It remained a Portuguese overseas province until 1999 when it became a Special Administrative Region of the People's Republic of China with a limited constitution and a high degree of autonomy. *Languages:* Cantonese, Portuguese. *Capital:* Macao.

MONETARY SYSTEM

100 avos = 1 pataca

PRECIOUS METAL CONTENT

Dates	Denomination	Gross Wt (g)	Fineness	Net Wt (g)	Troy Oz.
		SILVER			
1952	1 pataca	3.0000	0.7200	2.1600	0.0694
	5 patacas	15.0000	0.7200	10.8000	0.3472

Y#	KM#	Metal	Description	VF	EF	Unc
1	1	Bz	5 Avos, 1952	7.50	15.00	30
2	2	Bz	10 Avos, 1952	2.00	7.50	13

Y#	KM#	Metal	Description	VF	EF	Unc
3	3	C-N	50 Avos, 1952	1.75	5	15

Y#	KM#	Metal	Description	VF	EF	Unc
4	4	Silv	1 Pataca, 1952	7.50	15	30
5	5	Silv	5 Patacas, 1952	7.50	15	25

MADAGASCAR

The world's fifth-largest island, Madagascar lies in the Indian Ocean off the southeast coast of Africa. It became a French protectorate in 1885. In 1960 it gained independence and, as the Malagasy Republic, remained a member of the French Community. *Languages:* Malagasy, French. *Capital:* Antananarivo.

MONETARY SYSTEM

100 centimes = 1 franc

WORLD WAR II ISSUES

Y#	KM#	Metal	Description	VF	EF	Unc
1	1	Bz	50 Centimes, 1943	4	10	20
2	2	Bz	1 Franc, 1943	6	18	50

POSTWAR ISSUES

Y#	KM#	Metal	Description	VF	EF	Unc
3	3	Alum	1 Franc, 1948, 58	0.30	0.75	5.00
4	4	Alum	2 Francs, 1948	0.35	0.85	6.50
5	5	Alum	5 Francs, 1953	0.55	1.00	6.50

Y#	KM#	Metal	Description	VF	EF	Unc
6	6	A-Bz	10 Francs, 1953	1.25	2.25	12.50
7	7	A-Bz	20 Francs, 1953	2.25	4.00	12.50

MALAWI

In southeast Africa, the nation formerly known as Nyasaland became a British protectorate in 1891. From 1953 to 1963 it was a member of the Federation of Rhodesia and Nyasaland. It achieved full independence in 1964 and is now a republic within the British Commonwealth. *Languages:* English, Chickewa. *Capital:* Lilongwe.

MONETARY SYSTEM
12 pence = 1 shilling
2 shillings = 1 florin
5 shillings = 1 crown
20 shillings = 1 pound

Y#	KM#	Metal	Description	VF	EF	Unc
1	1	CNZ	6 Pence, 1964, 67	0.75	1.50	3

Y#	KM#	Metal	Description	VF	EF	Unc
2	2	CNZ	1 Shilling, 1964, 68	0.75	1.50	3

Y#	KM#	Metal	Description	VF	EF	Unc
3	3	CNZ	1 Florin, 1964	1	1.50	5

Y#	KM#	Metal	Description	VF	EF	Unc
4	4	CNZ	1/2 Crown, 1964	1.50	2	6

MALAYA

Malaya is a peninsula extending into the South China Sea from the southeast tip of Asia. Formerly a federation of states under British suzerainty, it became an independent elective kingdom within the British Commonwealth in 1957. In 1963 it federated with Singapore, Sabah (North Borneo), and Sarawak into Malaysia. *Capital:* Kuala Lumpur.

For earlier issues, see Straits Settlements. For later issues, see Malaya and British Borneo.

MONETARY SYSTEM
100 cents = 1 dollar

GEORGE VI, *1936–1952*

Y#	KM#	Metal	Description	VF	EF	Unc
1	1	Bz	1/2 Cent, 1940, square	3.75	7.50	25
						Proof: $1,750
2	2	Bz	1 Cent, 1939–41, square (22 mm)	0.75	1.25	10
						Proof: $1,750

Y#	KM#	Metal	Description	VF	EF	Unc
2a	6	Bz	1 Cent, 1943, 45, square (19 mm)	0.75	1.25	10
						Proof: $1,500

Y#	KM#	Metal	Description	VF	EF	Unc
3	3	Silv	5 Cents, 1939–45	1.25	2.00	10
						Proof: $2,000
4	4	Silv	10 Cents, 1939–45	2.00	3.50	10
						Proof: $2,000
5	5	Silv	20 Cents, 1939–45	4.50	10.00	25
						Proof: $2,500

New Legend: ***KING GEORGE THE SIXTH***

Y#	KM#	Metal	Description	VF	EF	Unc
7	7	C-N	5 Cents, 1948–50	1	2	10
						Proof: $1,750
8	8	C-N	10 Cents, 1948–50	1	2	10
						Proof: $1,750
9	9	C-N	20 Cents, 1948–50	1	2	10
						Proof: $1,750

MALAYA AND BRITISH BORNEO

Issues for Malaya, Singapore, Sarawak, Brunei, and British North Borneo.

PRECIOUS METAL CONTENT

Dates	Denomination	Gross Wt (g)	Fineness	Net Wt (g)	Troy Oz.
		SILVER			
1939–41	5 cents	1.3577	0.7500	1.0183	0.0327
	10 cents	2.7154	0.7500	2.0365	0.0655
	20 cents	5.4308	0.7500	4.0731	0.1310
1943–45	5 cents	1.3577	0.5000	0.6788	0.0218
	10 cents	2.7154	0.5000	1.3577	0.0437
	20 cents	5.4308	0.5000	2.7154	0.0873

ELIZABETH II, *1952–1963*

Y#	KM#	Metal	Description	VF	EF	Unc
A1	5	Bz	1 Cent, 1956–61, square	0.10	0.20	5
						Proof: $2,000

Y#	KM#	Metal	Description	VF	EF	Unc
1	1	C-N	5 Cents, 1953–61	0.25	1	7.50
						Proof: $650
2	2	C-N	10 Cents, 1953–61	0.25	1	7.50
						Proof: $700
3	3	C-N	20 Cents, 1954–61	0.50	1	10.00
						Proof: $850
4	4	C-N	50 Cents, 1954–61	0.75	2	15.00
						Proof: $1,000

Y#	KM#	Metal	Description	VF	EF	Unc
5	6	Bz	1 Cent, 1962	0.25	0.50	6
						Proof: $1,100

MALDIVES

Formerly a dependency of Ceylon, this group of coral atolls southwest of Sri Lanka became a British Protected State in 1882. It adopted a republican form of government in 1952. The sultanate was restored in 1954 and the country became fully independent in 1965. A republic was re-established as the result of a 1968 referendum. *Languages:* Maldivian Divehi, English. *Capital:* Male.

MONETARY SYSTEM

120 lari (lariat) = 1 rupee, to 1960

IBRAHIM NUR AL-DIN, *AH 1300–1318 (1882–1900)*

Y#	KM#	Metal	Description	VF	EF	Unc
A1	37	Cop	1/4 Larin, AH 1300 (1882) (10–11 mm)	2.50	4	10

MUHAMMAD IMAD AL-DIN V, *AH 1318–1322 (1900–1904)*

Y#	KM#	Metal	Description	VF	EF	Unc
1	38	Cop	1 Larin, AH 1311 (error), AH 1318–19 (0.8–2.7 g) (10–13 mm)	2	7.50	15.00
3	40	Cop	4 Lari, AH 1320 (17 mm)	4	9.00	22.50

Note: Research indicates that former Y2 (2 lari 1319) is actually Y1 struck on heavier planchets. Pieces dated 1319 tend to be heavier and larger than those of 1318. Y1 and 3 have been reported in brass, silver, and gold: all seem to be normal copper pieces unofficially plated for jewelry use.

MUHAMMAD SHAMS AL-DIN III, *AH 1322–1353 (1904–1935)*

Y#	KM#	Metal	Description	VF	EF	Unc
5	41	Cop	1 Larin, AH 1331 (1913)	2	7.50	15

Y#	KM#	Metal	Description	VF	EF	Unc
6	42	Cop	4 Lari, AH 1331	2	3	7.50

AL-AMIR MOHAMMAD FARID DIDI, *1954–1968*

Y#	KM#	Metal	Description	VF	EF	Unc
7	43	Bz	1 Larin, 1960	0.15	0.25	1.00
8	44	Bz	2 Lari, 1960, square	0.20	0.35	0.75

Y#	KM#	Metal	Description	VF	EF	Unc
9	45	N-Br	5 Lari, 1960, scalloped	0.40	0.75	1.25
10	46	N-Br	10 Lari, 1960, scalloped	0.50	0.80	1.50

Y#	KM#	Metal	Description	VF	EF	Unc
11	47	Alum	25 Lari, 1960, 79	1.00	1	2
12	48	Alum	50 Lari, 1960, 79	1.50	2	3

MALTA

Three habitable islands south of Sicily in the Mediterranean Sea, Malta was a British colony from 1814, when it was wrested from Napoleon, until gaining independence as a parliamentary democracy in 1964. It became a republic within the British Commonwealth in 1974, and withdrew from that association in 1979. *Languages:* Maltese, English. *Capital:* Valletta.

MONETARY SYSTEM

English coinage. One-third-farthing coins, called "Granos" (Grains), were struck especially for Malta from 1827 to 1913.

VICTORIA, *1837–1901*

Y#	KM#	Metal	Description	VF	EF	Unc
1	743	Cop	1/3 Farthing, 1844	60	100	250

Y#	KM#	Metal	Description	VF	EF	Unc
2	750	Bz	1/3 Farthing, 1866–85	7.50	20	125

EDWARD VII, *1901–1910*

Y#	KM#	Metal	Description	VF	EF	Unc
3	791	Bz	1/3 Farthing, 1902	5	12.50	75

GEORGE V, *1910–1936*

Y#	KM#	Metal	Description	VF	EF	Unc
4	823	Bz	1/3 Farthing, 1913	5	12.50	75

MANCHUKUO

Japanese forces invaded the Chinese province of Manchuria in 1931, supplanting what had been a strong Russian influence in the area since 1890. Shortly thereafter, it became the nominally independent nation of Manchukuo, though under Japanese control, with a puppet emperor. After World War II the area was returned to China. *Capital:* Hsinking.

MONETARY SYSTEM

10 li (cash) = 1 fen
10 fen = 1 chio

TA-TUNG REIGN, *YEARS 1–3 (1932–1934)* 同 大 *REIGN SYMBOLS ON COINS*

Y#	KM#	Metal	Description	VF	EF	Unc
1	1	Bz	5 Li, Yrs 2–3 (1933–34)	30.00	50	150
2	2	Bz	1 Fen, Yrs 2–3 (1933–34)	12.50	25	75

Y#	KM#	Metal	Description	VF	EF	Unc
3	3	C-N	5 Fen, Yrs 2–3 (1933–34)	5.00	10	40
4	4	C-N	1 Chiao, Yrs 2–3 (1933–34)	7.50	15	50

Kang Teh Reign, *Years 1–12 (1934–1945)*

德康 *Reign Symbols on Coins*

First Coinage

Designs: ***Like Y1–4 except for symbols of Kang Teh reign***

Y#	KM#	Metal	Description	VF	EF	Unc
5	5	Bz	5 Li, Yrs 1–6 (1934–39) *Yr 6 (1939), VF $275*	35	60.00	100
6	6	Bz	1 Fen, Yrs 1–6 (1934–39)	10	17.50	40

Y#	KM#	Metal	Description	VF	EF	Unc
7	7	C-N	5 Fen, Yrs 1–6 (1934–39)	5	10	30
8	8	C-N	1 Chiao, Yrs 1–6 (1934–39)	6	12	35 *Proof: $1,500*

Second Coinage

Y#	KM#	Metal	Description	VF	EF	Unc
9	9	Alum	1 Fen, Yrs 6–10 (1939–43)	3.50	7.50	18.50

Y#	KM#	Metal	Description	VF	EF	Unc
11	11	Alum	5 Fen, Yrs 7–10 (1940–43)	4	8	20
12	12	Alum	10 Fen, Yrs 7–10 (1940–43) *Yr 10, Unc $1,000*	6	12	35

Y#	KM#	Metal	Description	VF	EF	Unc
10	10	C-N	1 Chiao, Yr 7 (1940)	7.50	15	50

Third Coinage

Y#	KM#	Metal	Description	VF	EF	Unc
13	13	Alum	1 Fen, Yrs 10–11 (1943–44)	10	20.00	50
A13	A13	Alum	5 Fen, Yrs 10–11 (1943–44)	12	22.50	55
14	14	Alum	10 Fen, Yr 10 (1943)	12	22.50	55

Y#	KM#	Metal	Description	VF	EF	Unc
13a	13a	Fiber	1 Fen, Yr 12 (1945)	12	25.00	50
A13a	A13a	Fiber	5 Fen, Yr 11 (1944)	10	22.50	45

MARTINIQUE

An island in the West Indies, about 300 miles northeast of Venezuela, Martinique has been a French possession since 1635. It became an Overseas Department of France in 1946. *Languages:* French, Creole. *Capital:* Fort-de-France.

MONETARY SYSTEM
100 centimes = 1 franc

Y#	KM#	Metal	Description	VF	EF	Unc
1	40	C-N	50 Centimes, 1897, 1922	40	150	425
2	41	C-N	1 Franc, 1897, 1922	50	175	450

MAURITIUS

An island east of Madagascar in the Indian Ocean, Mauritius was settled by France in the 18th century. In 1814 it was ceded to the British, who preserved French laws and customs. It became an independent parliamentary democracy within the British Commonwealth in 1968. *Languages:* French, English, Creole, Hindi. *Capital:* Port Louis.

MONETARY SYSTEM
100 cents = 1 rupee

Dates	Denomination	Gross Wt (g)	Fineness	Net Wt (g)	Troy Oz.
		SILVER			
1877–99	10 cents	1.1660	0.8000	0.9328	0.0300
	20 cents	2.3320	0.8000	1.8656	0.0600
1934–38	1/4 rupee	2.9200	0.9160	2.6747	0.0816
	1/2 rupee	5.8300	0.9160	5.3403	0.1717
	1 rupee	11.6600	0.9160	10.6806	0.3434
1946	1/4 rupee	2.9200	0.5000	1.4600	0.0470
	1/2 rupee	5.8300	0.5000	2.9150	0.0937

Victoria, *1837–1901*

Y#	KM#	Metal	Description	VF	EF	Unc
1	7	Bz	1 Cent, 1877–97	4.00	30	125
2	8	Bz	2 Cents, 1877–97	5.00	35	175
3	9	Bz	5 Cents, 1877–97	7.50	40	200
					Proof: $500	

Y#	KM#	Metal	Description	VF	EF	Unc
4	10	Silv	10 Cents, 1877–97	7.50	35	125
					Proof: $300	
5	11	Silv	20 Cents, 1877–99	8.00	25	400
					Proof: $350	

George V, *1910–1936*

Y#	KM#	Metal	Description	VF	EF	Unc
6	12	Bz	1 Cent, 1911–24	2	10	125
7	13	Bz	2 Cents, 1911–24	3	10	125
8	14	Bz	5 Cents, 1917–24	5	25	100

Y#	KM#	Metal	Description	VF	EF	Unc
9	15	Silv	1/4 Rupee, 1934–36	5	30	175

Y#	KM#	Metal	Description	VF	EF	Unc
10	16	Silv	1/2 Rupee, 1934	7	30	150

Y#	KM#	Metal	Description	VF	EF	Unc
11	17	Silv	1 Rupee, 1934	10	35	150

George VI, *1936–1952*

Y#	KM#	Metal	Description	VF	EF	Unc
12	21	Bz	1 Cent, 1943–47	1.25	7.50	25
13	22	Bz	2 Cents, 1943–47	1.25	7.50	25
14	20	Bz	5 Cents, 1942–45	1.75	7.50	40

Y#	KM#	Metal	Description	VF	EF	Unc
15	24	C-N	10 Cents, 1947, scalloped	5	20	100

Reverse: ***Designs similar to Y9–11***

Y#	KM#	Metal	Description	VF	EF	Unc
16	18	Silv	1/4 Rupee, 1938, 46	6	25	175
17	23	Silv	1/2 Rupee, 1946	15	75	350
18	19	Silv	1 Rupee, 1938	13	25	175

New Legend: ***KING GEORGE THE SIXTH***

Y#	KM#	Metal	Description	VF	EF	Unc
23	25	Bz	1 Cent, 1949, 52	1.50	3	12.50
24	26	Bz	2 Cents, 1949, 52	1.50	3	12.50

Planchet: ***Scalloped***
Reverse: ***No circle around denomination***

Y#	KM#	Metal	Description	VF	EF	Unc
19	30	C-N	10 Cents, 1952, scalloped	2	5	30

Y#	KM#	Metal	Description	VF	EF	Unc
20	27	C-N	1/4 Rupee, 1950–51	1.50	2.50	20
21	28	C-N	1/2 Rupee, 1950–51	1.50	3.00	20
22	29	C-N	1 Rupee, 1950–51	1.50	3.00	20

ELIZABETH II, *1952–1968*

Y#	KM#	Metal	Description	VF	EF	Unc
25	31	Bz	1 Cent, 1953–78	0.25	0.50	2
26	32	Bz	2 Cents, 1953–78	0.25	0.50	2
27	34	Bz	5 Cents, 1956–78	0.50	1.00	5

Y#	KM#	Metal	Description	VF	EF	Unc
28	35	C-N	10 Cents, 1954–78	0.25	0.45	1.50

Y#	KM#	Metal	Description	VF	EF	Unc
29	35	C-N	1 Rupee, 1956–78	0.75	1.25	2.25

Y#	KM#	Metal	Description	VF	EF	Unc
30	36	C-N	1/4 Rupee, 1960–78	0.35	0.70	1.50

MEXICO

Conquered from the Aztecs in 1521, Mexico was part of the viceroyalty of New Spain until independence was won in 1821. Over the next 100 years, emperors, dictators, and presidents came and went, along with French and Austrian invaders, revolutions, and civil wars. The nation has been a stable federal republic since the late 1920s. *Language:* Spanish. *Capital:* Mexico City.

Fourteen mints coined silver and gold from 1823 to 1905. Certain issues are much rarer than the values indicated here for a common date and mint. For a detailed listing, refer to any of the numerous specialized catalogs available on Mexican coins.

MONETARY SYSTEM

8 reales = 1 peso
16 reales = 1 escudo
100 centavos = 1 peso

PRECIOUS METAL CONTENT

Dates	Denomination	Gross Wt (g)	Fineness	Net Wt (g)	Troy Oz.
		SILVER			
1822–69	1/4 real	0.8460	0.9027	0.7637	0.0246
	1/2 real	1.6921	0.9027	1.5275	0.0491
	1 real	3.3841	0.9027	3.0548	0.0982
1863–1905	5 centavos	1.3537	0.9027	1.2220	0.0393
	10 centavos	2.7073	0.9027	2.4439	0.0786
	20 centavos	5.4146	0.9027	4.8878	0.1571
1822–1905	2 reales / 25 centavos	6.7683	0.9027	6.1097	0.1964
	4 reales / 50 centavos	13.5365	0.9027	12.2194	0.3929
1822–1914	8 reales / 1 peso	27.0730	0.9027	24.4388	0.7857
1905–18	10 centavos	2.5000	0.8000	2.0000	0.0643
	20 centavos	5.0000	0.8000	4.0000	0.1286
	50 centavos	12.5000	0.8000	10.0000	0.3215
1918–19	10 centavos	1.8125	0.8000	1.4500	0.0466
	20 centavos	3.6250	0.8000	2.9000	0.0932
	50 centavos	9.0625	0.8000	7.2500	0.2331
	1 peso	18.1250	0.8000	14.5000	0.4662
1919–45	10 centavos	1.6667	0.7200	1.2000	0.0386
	20 centavos	3.3333	0.7200	2.4000	0.0772
	50 centavos	8.3333	0.7200	6.0000	0.1929
	1 peso	16.6667	0.7200	12.0000	0.3858
	2 pesos	26.6667	0.9000	24.0000	0.7716
1935	50 centavos	7.9733	0.4200	3.3488	0.1077
1947–49	1 peso	14.0000	0.5000	7.0000	0.2251
	5 pesos	30.0000	0.9000	27.0000	0.8681
1950–54	5 pesos	27.7800	0.7200	20.0016	0.6431
1955–59	5 pesos	18.0500	0.7200	12.9960	0.4170
1955–60	10 pesos	28.8800	0.9000	25.9920	0.8357
1957–67	1 peso	16.0000	0.1000	1.6000	0.0514
		GOLD			
1825–73	1/2 escudo	1.6921	0.8750	1.4805	0.0476
	1 escudo	3.3841	0.8750	2.9611	0.0952
	2 escudos	6.7683	0.8750	5.9222	0.1904
	4 escudos	13.5365	0.8750	11.8444	0.3808
	8 escudos	20.0730	0.8750	23.6889	0.7616
1870–1905	1 peso	1.6921	0.8750	1.4805	0.0476
	2-1/2 pesos	4.2301	0.8750	3.7014	0.1190
	5 pesos	8.4602	0.8750	7.4027	0.2380
	10 pesos	16.9205	0.8750	14.8054	0.4760
	20 pesos	33.8410	0.8750	29.6109	0.9520
1905–59	2 pesos	1.6667	0.9000	1.5000	0.0482
	2-1/2 pesos	2.0833	0.9000	1.8750	0.0603
	5 pesos	4.1667	0.9000	3.7500	0.1206
	10 pesos	8.3333	0.9000	7.0000	0.2411
	20 pesos	16.6667	0.9000	15.0000	0.4823
	50 pesos	41.6667	0.9000	37.5000	1.2056

REPUBLICA MEXICANA, *1823–1905*

Y#	KM#	Metal	Description	VF	EF	Unc
S9	332	Cop	1/8 Real, 1829 (27 mm)	1,500	2,500	12,000
S10	357	Cop	1/4 Real, 1829 (33 mm)	30	100	2,000

Y#	KM#	Metal	Description	VF	EF	Unc
S11	315	Cop	1/16 Real, 1831–33	50	150	600
SA11	333	Cop	1/8 Real, 1829–35 (21 mm)	20	40	900
S12	358	Cop	1/4 Real, 1829–37 (27 mm)	25	75	300

Y#	KM#	Metal	Description	VF	EF	Unc
S14	334	Cop	1/8 Real, 1841–61	50	150	400

Y#	KM#	Metal	Description	VF	EF	Unc
S16	369	Silv	1/2 Real, 1824	75	150	350
S17	371	Silv	1 Real, 1824	5,000	7,500	—
S18	373	Silv	2 Reales, 1824	200	450	1,000
S19	376	Silv	8 Reales, 1823–25	250	900	4,000

Y#	KM#	Metal	Description	VF	EF	Unc
S20	368	Silv	1/4 Real, 1842–63	7	10	75

Y#	KM#	Metal	Description	VF	EF	Unc
S21	370	Silv	1/2 Real, 1825–69	3	5	30
S22	372	Silv	1 Real, 1825–69	4	10	100
S23	374	Silv	2 Reales, 1825–72	7	12	200
S24	375	Silv	4 Reales, 1825–69	25	50	1,000

Y#	KM#	Metal	Description	VF	EF	Unc
S25	377	Silv	8 Reales, 1824–69	15	20	75

Y#	KM#	Metal	Description	VF	EF	Unc
S26	378	Gold	1/2 Escudo, 1825–69	60	100	200
S27	379	Gold	1 Escudo, 1825–70	120	175	350
S28	380	Gold	2 Escudos, 1825–70	275	350	800
S29	381	Gold	4 Escudos, 1825–69	800	1,500	4,000
S30	382	Gold	8 Escudos, 1823, obverse as YS16	6,500	9,000	20,000
S31	383	Gold	8 Escudos, 1825–73	500	600	1,000

EMPEROR MAXIMILIAN, *1864–1867*

Legend: ***IMPERIO MEXICANO***

Y#	KM#	Metal	Description	VF	EF	Unc
S32	384	Cop	1 Centavo, 1864	75	150	1,000

Y#	KM#	Metal	Description	VF	EF	Unc
S33	385	Silv	5 Centavos, 1864–66	40	65	200

Y#	KM#	Metal	Description	VF	EF	Unc
S34	386	Silv	10 Centavos, 1864–66	35	50	200

Y#	KM#	Metal	Description	VF	EF	Unc
S35	387	Silv	50 Centavos, 1866	50	150	800

Y#	KM#	Metal	Description	VF	EF	Unc
S36	388	Silv	1 Peso, 1866–67	40	90	400

Y#	KM#	Metal	Description	VF	EF	Unc
S37	389	Gold	20 Pesos, 1866	1,250	1,600	3,000

REPUBLICA MEXICANA, *1863–1905*

Y#	KM#	Metal	Description	VF	EF	Unc
S15	390	Cop	1 Centavo, 1863	15	25	300

Y#	KM#	Metal	Description	VF	EF	Unc
1	391	Cop	1 Centavo, 1869–97	5	9	20

Obverse: ***Restyled eagle***

Y#	KM#	Metal	Description	VF	EF	Unc
2	393	Cop	1 Centavo, 1898	10	20	50

Y#	KM#	Metal	Description	VF	EF	Unc
3	394	Cop	1 Centavo, 1899–1905	10	20	50

Y#	KM#	Metal	Description	VF	EF	Unc
4	392	C-N	1 Centavo, 1882–83	0.50	1	2
5	395	C-N	2 Centavos, 1882–83	0.50	1	2
6	399	C-N	5 Centavos, 1882–83	0.50	2	5

Y#	KM#	Metal	Description	VF	EF	Unc
7	397	Silv	5 Centavos, 1867–69	70	100	500
8	402	Silv	10 Centavos, 1867–69	70	100	500

Y#	KM#	Metal	Description	VF	EF	Unc
9	396	Silv	5 Centavos, 1863–70	70	100	500
10	401	Silv	10 Centavos, 1863–70	70	100	500

Y#	KM#	Metal	Description	VF	EF	Unc
11	398	Silv	5 Centavos, 1869–97	2	3	15
12	403	Silv	10 Centavos, 1869–97	2	4	35

Y#	KM#	Metal	Description	VF	EF	Unc
11a	398	Silv	5 Centavos, 1878–80, 86, 98, obverse of Y21 (mule)	10	20	75
12a	403.2	Silv	10 Centavos, 1885–86, obverse of Y22 (mule)	100	250	500

Y#	KM#	Metal	Description	VF	EF	Unc
13	406	Silv	25 Centavos, 1869–92	5	10	150
14	407	Silv	50 Centavos, 1869–95	10	25	500
15	408	Silv	1 Peso, 1869–73	15	25	250

Obverse: ***Restyled eagle***

Y#	KM#	Metal	Description	VF	EF	Unc
16	400	Silv	5 Centavos, 1898–1905	4	6	20
17	404	Silv	10 Centavos, 1898–1905	5	10	45
18	405	Silv	20 Centavos, 1898–1905	10	25	100

Y#	KM#	Metal	Description	VF	EF	Unc
19	377	Silv	8 Reales, 1869–97	25	35	150

Y#	KM#	Metal	Description	VF	EF	Unc
20	409	Silv	1 Peso, 1898–1909	40	50	150

Y#	KM#	Metal	Description	VF	EF	Unc
21	410	Gold	1 Peso, 1870–1905	100	125	250

Y#	KM#	Metal	Description	VF	EF	Unc
21a	410.3	Gold	1 Peso, 1898, obverse of Y16 (mule)	160	250	500
22	411	Gold	2-1/2 Pesos, 1870–93	400	600	900

Y#	KM#	Metal	Description	VF	EF	Unc
23	412	Gold	5 Pesos, 1870–1905	450	500	750
24	413	Gold	10 Pesos, 1870–1905	950	1,000	1,600
25	414	Gold	20 Pesos, 1870–1905	1,900	2,250	3,000

ESTADOS UNIDOS MEXICANOS, *1905–*

Y#	KM#	Metal	Description	VF	EF	Unc
27	415	Bz	1 Centavo, 1905–49 (20 mm)	0.25	0.50	2

Y#	KM#	Metal	Description	VF	EF	Unc
28	416	Bz	1 Centavo, 1915 (16 mm)	30	50	85

Note: Considered by many to be a Revolutionary issue minted by Zapata.

Y#	KM#	Metal	Description	VF	EF	Unc
29	419	Bz	2 Centavos, 1905–41 (25 mm)	3	5	20

Y#	KM#	Metal	Description	VF	EF	Unc
30	420	Bz	2 Centavos, 1915 (20 mm)	8.50	20	80

Note: Considered by many to be a Revolutionary issue minted by Zapata.

Y#	KM#	Metal	Description	VF	EF	Unc
31	421	Nick	5 Centavos, 1905–14	2	5	70

Y#	KM#	Metal	Description	VF	EF	Unc
39	428	Silv	10 Centavos, 1905–14 (18 mm)	7.50	15	40
40	435	Silv	20 Centavos, 1905–14 (22 mm)	12.50	25	65
41	445	Silv	50 Centavos, 1905–18 (30 mm)	17.50	35	75

Y#	KM#	Metal	Description	VF	EF	Unc
42	453	Silv	1 Peso, 1910–14 *1914, Unc $2,200*	60	80	300

Y#	KM#	Metal	Description	VF	EF	Unc
55	461	Gold	2 Pesos, 1919–48	BV	BV	140

Y#	KM#	Metal	Description	VF	EF	Unc
56	463	Gold	2-1/2 Pesos, 1918–48 *1947, VF $300*	BV	BV	155
57	464	Gold	5 Pesos, 1905–55 *1905, VF $250*	BV	BV	300
58	473	Gold	10 Pesos, 1905–59 *1920, VF $500*	BV	BV	600

Y#	KM#	Metal	Description	VF	EF	Unc
59	478	Gold	20 Pesos, 1917–59	BV	BV	1,250

Y#	KM#	Metal	Description	VF	EF	Unc
32	422	Bz	5 Centavos, 1914–35	2.50	5	30
33	430	Bz	10 Centavos, 1919–21, 35	15.00	30	125

Y#	KM#	Metal	Description	VF	EF	Unc
34	437	Bz	20 Centavos, 1920, 35	6	10	100

Obverse: ***No fineness shown (.800 fine)***

Y#	KM#	Metal	Description	VF	EF	Unc
43	429	Silv	10 Centavos, 1919 (15 mm)	10	20	90

Y#	KM#	Metal	Description	VF	EF	Unc
44	436	Silv	20 Centavos, 1919 (19 mm)	20	40	200
45	446	Silv	50 Centavos, 1918–19 (27 mm)	10	20	100

Y#	KM#	Metal	Description	VF	EF	Unc
46	454	Silv	1 Peso, 1918–19	20	50	200

Obverse: ***With "0.720" (.720 fine)***

Y#	KM#	Metal	Description	VF	EF	Unc
47	431	Silv	10 Centavos, 1925–35	1	2	10
48	438	Silv	20 Centavos, 1920–43	3	5	12
49	447	Silv	50 Centavos, 1919–45	6	10	50
50	455	Silv	1 Peso, 1920–45 *1920–21, VF $17.50*	9	15	35

Obverse: ***No fineness shown (.420 fine)***

Y#	KM#	Metal	Description	VF	EF	Unc
52	448	Bill	50 Centavos, 1935	3.50	5	10

Independence Centennial

Obverse: ***Date in Roman numerals***

Y#	KM#	Metal	Description	VF	EF	Unc
51	462	Silv	2 Pesos, 1921	40	75	325

Y#	KM#	Metal	Description	VF	EF	Unc
60	481	Gold	50 Pesos, 1921–47 *1921, Unc $3,000*	BV	BV	BV
60a	482	Gold	(50 Pesos), 1943, no value shown	BV	BV	BV

Note: The 1921 date of Y60 is considered a commemorative.

Y#	KM#	Metal	Description	VF	EF	Unc
35	423	C-N	5 Centavos, 1936–42	1	2	10.00
36	432	C-N	10 Centavos, 1936–46	1	2	12.50

Y#	KM#	Metal	Description	VF	EF	Unc
37	424	Bz	5 Centavos, 1942–55 *1942, Unc $200*	0.25	0.40	1

Y#	KM#	Metal	Description	VF	EF	Unc
38	439	Bz	20 Centavos, 1943–55	0.25	0.75	7.50

Y#	KM#	Metal	Description	VF	EF	Unc
53	456	Silv	1 Peso, 1947–49 *1949, Unc $2,000*	6.50	10	15

Y#	KM#	Metal	Description	VF	EF	Unc
54	465	Silv	5 Pesos, 1947–48	18	20	30

Decree of December 29, 1949

Y#	KM#	Metal	Description	VF	EF	Unc
61	417	Br	1 Centavo, 1950–69	0.10	0.20	0.50

Y#	KM#	Metal	Description	VF	EF	Unc
62	425	C-N	5 Centavos, 1950	1	2	6

Y#	KM#	Metal	Description	VF	EF	Unc
63	443	Bill	25 Centavos, 1950–53	1	2	3

Y#	KM#	Metal	Description	VF	EF	Unc
64	449	Bill	50 Centavos, 1950–51	3	4	7

Y#	KM#	Metal	Description	VF	EF	Unc
65	457	Bill	1 Peso, 1950	7	9	13

Y#	KM#	Metal	Description	VF	EF	Unc
67	467	Silv	5 Pesos, 1951–54 *1954, Unc $125*	15	19	25

Completion of Southeastern Railway

Y#	KM#	Metal	Description	VF	EF	Unc
66	466	Silv	5 Pesos, 1950	50	65	100

Bicentennial, Birth of Hidalgo

Y#	KM#	Metal	Description	VF	EF	Unc
68	468	Silv	5 Pesos, 1953	15	19	25

Y#	KM#	Metal	Description	VF	EF	Unc
69	426	Br	5 Centavos, 1954–69	0.10	0.15	0.25

Y#	KM#	Metal	Description	VF	EF	Unc
70	433	Bz	10 Centavos, 1955–67	0.10	0.20	0.40

Y#	KM#	Metal	Description	VF	EF	Unc
71	440	Bz	20 Centavos, 1955–71	0.15	0.30	0.75

Y#	KM#	Metal	Description	VF	EF	Unc
72	450	Bz	50 Centavos, 1955–59	0.20	0.40	1

Y#	KM#	Metal	Description	VF	EF	Unc
A72	459	Silv	1 Peso, 1957–67 (.100 fine)	1.50	2	3

Y#	KM#	Metal	Description	VF	EF	Unc
73	469	Silv	5 Pesos, 1955–57 (.720 fine)	12	15	20
74	474	Silv	10 Pesos, 1955–56 (.900 fine)	20	25	40

Constitution Centennial

Y#	KM#	Metal	Description	VF	EF	Unc
75	458	Silv	1 Peso, 1957 (.100 fine)	5	7	15.00
76	470	Silv	5 Pesos, 1957 (.720 fine)	12	15	23.50
77	475	Silv	10 Pesos, 1957 (.900 fine)	35	45	65.00

Centennial, Birth of Carranza

Y#	KM#	Metal	Description	VF	EF	Unc
78	471	Silv	5 Pesos, 1959	12	15	20

Revolutions of 1810 and 1910

Y#	KM#	Metal	Description	VF	EF	Unc
79	476	Silv	10 Pesos, 1960	20	25	40

Y#	KM#	Metal	Description	VF	EF	Unc
80	444	C-N	25 Centavos, 1964–66	0.10	0.15	0.35

Y#	KM#	Metal	Description	VF	EF	Unc
81	451	C-N	50 Centavos, 1964–69	0.15	0.20	0.50

MEXICAN REVOLUTIONARY COINAGE, 1913–1917

MEXICAN REVOLUTIONARY COINAGE: STATE OF AGUASCALIENTES

Y#	KM#	Metal	Description	VF	EF	Unc
R1	601	Cop	1 Centavo, 1915	100	200	400
R2	602	Cop	2 Centavos, 1915	175	250	500

Y#	KM#	Metal	Description	VF	EF	Unc
R3	604	Cop	5 Centavos, 1915, reverse large 5c	65	125	275

Y#	KM#	Metal	Description	VF	EF	Unc
R4	603	Cop	5 Centavos, 1915	50	90	200
R5	Several	Cop	20 Centavos, 1915 (vars)	50	90	200

Note: YR1–R3 and R5 were also struck in silver for presentation purposes.

MEXICAN REVOLUTIONARY COINAGE: STATE OF CHIHUAHUA

EJERCITO CONSTITUCIONALISTAS
(CONSTITUTIONAL ARMY)

Y#	KM#	Metal	Description	VF	EF	Unc
R11	612/613	Cop	5 Centavos, 1914–15	5	15.00	30
R12	615	Cop	10 Centavos, 1914–15	6	17.50	35

Y#	KM#	Metal	Description	VF	EF	Unc
R11a	613a	Br	5 Centavos, 1914–15	5	15.00	30
R12a	615a	Br	10 Centavos, 1915	6	17.50	35

Note: The 50 centavos and 1 peso with Liberty Cap obverse are considered patterns, as are two types of 5 centavos with eagle obverse.

EJERCITO DEL NORTE
(ARMY OF THE NORTH)

Y#	KM#	Metal	Description	VF	EF	Unc
R16	619	Silv	1 Peso, 1915	75	150	425

PARRAL, *CITY*

Legend: ***FUERZAS CONSTITUCIONALISTAS***

Y#	KM#	Metal	Description	VF	EF	Unc
R7	607	C/Br	2 Centavos, 1913	25	50	100

Y#	KM#	Metal	Description	VF	EF	Unc
R8	608/609	Silv	50 Centavos, 1913	50	100	200

Y#	KM#	Metal	Description	VF	EF	Unc
R9	610	Silv	1 Peso, 1913, reverse with ball in center	3,000	5,000	20,000

Y#	KM#	Metal	Description	VF	EF	Unc
R10	611	Silv	1 Peso, 1913, reverse without ball in center	175	350	750

MEXICAN REVOLUTIONARY COINAGE: STATE OF DURANGO

Y#	KM#	Metal	Description	VF	EF	Unc
R17	625	Cop	1 Centavo, 1914	7.50	15	50
R18	626	Cop	I Centavo, 1914	30.00	60	150
R19	629	Cop	5 Centavos, 1914, ESTADO DE	6.00	12	25
R20	630	Cop	5 Centavos, 1914, E DE	550.00	—	—
R21	632	Cop	V Centavos, 1914	20.00	40	80

Obverse: ***Three stars at bottom***

Y#	KM#	Metal	Description	VF	EF	Unc
R22	627	Cop	1 Centavo, 1914	15	20	40

Y#	KM#	Metal	Description	VF	EF	Unc
R17a	625a	Br	1 Centavo, 1914	100	145	250
R18a	626a	Br	I Centavo, 1914	100	145	250
R20a	631a	Br	5 Centavos, 1914	100	200	600

Y#	KM#	Metal	Description	VF	EF	Unc
R17b	625b	Lead	1 Centavo, 1914	30	60	150
R18b	626b	Lead	I Centavo, 1914	75	150	300
R20b	631b	Lead	5 Centavos, 1914	125	250	700

Note: Some experts consider YR17b, R18b, R21b, and R22b to be die trials or patterns.

Y#	KM#	Metal	Description	VF	EF	Unc
R21b	632a	Lead	V Centavos, 1914	—	—	—
R22b	627a	Lead	1 Centavo, 1914	—	—	—

Note: Some experts consider YR17b, R18b, R21b, and R22b to be die trials or patterns.

Y#	KM#	Metal	Description	VF	EF	Unc
R24	628	Alum	1 Centavo, 1914	3	5	15

Y#	KM#	Metal	Description	VF	EF	Unc
R25	634	Br	5 Centavos, 1914	4	8	20

Obverse: ***Legend MUERA HUERTA ("Death to Huerta")***
Reverse: ***Six stars around lower border***

Y#	KM#	Metal	Description	VF	EF	Unc
R26	620	Silv	1 Peso, 1914	1,250	1,750	3,500

Reverse: *Without stars*

Y#	KM#	Metal	Description	VF	EF	Unc
R27	621	Silv	1 Peso, 1914	550	950	1,500

MEXICAN REVOLUTIONARY COINAGE: STATE OF GUERRERO

Mint towns and mintmarks on coins:

ATLIXTAC; CACALOTEPEC; CAMPO MO(rado), CoMo, C.M.; SURIANA; TAXCO, To; G, Go, GRO, G.R.O. (Guerrero)

Y#	KM#	Metal	Description	VF	EF	Unc
R29	638	Cop	2 Centavos, 1915	400	700	1,500
R30	635	Cop	3 Centavos, 1915	2,250	3,500	—
R31	653	Cop	5 Centavos, 1915, CM	35	60	125
R31a	668	Cop	5 Centavos, 1915, TAXCO GRO	35	65	125
R31b	636	Cop	5 Centavos, 1915, GRO	1,500	3,000	—

Y#	KM#	Metal	Description	VF	EF	Unc
R32	654	Cop	10 Centavos, 1915, CM GRO	15	30.00	50
R32a	669	Cop	10 Centavos, 1915, TAXCO GRO	25	50.00	100
R32b	637	Cop	10 Centavos, 1915, GRO	9	15.00	80
R32c	645	Cop	10 Centavos, 1915, ATLIXTAC GRO	8	12.50	75
R33	655	Cop	20 Centavos, 1915, CM GRO	50	75.00	150
R34	656	Cop	50 Centavos, 1915, CM GRO (vars)	50	75.00	150

Obverse: *Similar to YR32c*
Reverse: *Date on radiant sun*

Y#	KM#	Metal	Description	VF	EF	Unc
R35	670	Cop	50 Centavos, 1915, TAXCO/GRO	50	75	135

Obverse: *Eagle, EDO. DE GRO*
Reverse: *Similar to YR32c*

Y#	KM#	Metal	Description	VF	EF	Unc
RA36	667	Cop	2 Centavos, 1915, To	65	125	250

Design: *Type of Mexico Y32*

Y#	KM#	Metal	Description	VF	EF	Unc
RA37	648	Cop	5 Centavos, 1917, G	35	75	200

Design: *Types of Mexico Y39–40*
Obverse: *MEXICO ESTADO (DE) G.R.O.*

Y#	KM#	Metal	Description	VF	EF	Unc
RA38	663	Silv	10 Centavos, 1914, cast	1,200	—	—
RA39	664	Silv	20 Centavos, 1914, cast	1,200	—	—

Y#	KM#	Metal	Description	VF	EF	Unc
RA40	639	Silv	25 Centavos, 1915, EDG	500	750	950
RA41	640	Silv	50 Centavos, 1915, E deG	2,000	3,000	4,000

Design: *Type of YR35*

Y#	KM#	Metal	Description	VF	EF	Unc
R35a	671	Silv	50 Centavos, 1915, TAXCO/GRO	75	150	300

Y#	KM#	Metal	Description	VF	EF	Unc
R36	641–642	Silv	1 Peso, 1914–15, GRO	100	200	500
R36b	659	Silv	1 Peso, 1914, CAMPO Mo	90	150	400
R36c	672	Silv	1 Peso, 1915, TAXCO GRO	100	200	500

Y#	KM#	Metal	Description	VF	EF	Unc
R37	643	Silv	2 Pesos, 1914–15 GRO	85	150	350
R37a	660	Silv	2 Pesos, 1915, CoMo	95	175	375
R37b	665	Silv	2 Pesos, 1915, SURIANA	12,000	20,000	25,000

Y#	KM#	Metal	Description	VF	EF	Unc
R38	644	Silv	2 Pesos, 1915, CM GRO	175	350	600

Y#	KM#	Metal	Description	VF	EF	Unc
R39	649	Silv	20 Centavos, 1917, CACAHUATEPEC G	250	350	650
R39a	652	Silv	20 Centavos, 1917, CACALOTEPEC/GRO	2,000	2,500	3,000
R40	650	Silv	50 Centavos, 1917, CACAHUATEPEC GRO	175	350	700

Y#	KM#	Metal	Description	VF	EF	Unc
R41	651	Silv	1 Peso, 1917, CACAHUATEPEC Go	17,500	25,000	35,000

MEXICAN REVOLUTIONARY COINAGE: STATE OF JALISCO

Guadalajara, *City*

Y#	KM#	Metal	Description	VF	EF	Unc
R42	675	Cop	1 Centavo, 1915	25	40	80
R43	676	Cop	2 Centavos, 1915	25	40	80
R44	677	Cop	5 Centavos, 1915	25	40	80

Obverse: ***State arms***

Y#	KM#	Metal	Description	VF	EF	Unc
R45	678	Cop	10 Centavos, 1915	2,500	3,500	5,000

MEXICAN REVOLUTIONARY COINAGE: STATE OF MEXICO

Amecameca, *Town*

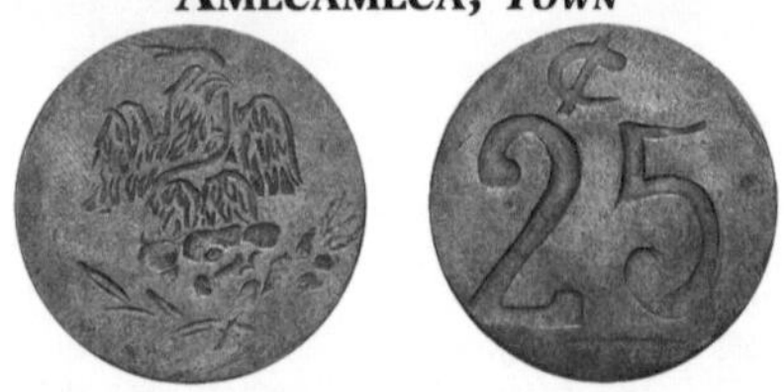

Obverse: ***Incuse eagle***
Reverse: ***Incuse value***

Y#	KM#	Metal	Description	VF	EF	Unc
R47	680	C/Br	5 Centavos, ND (1915–16)	750	1,500	—
R48	681	C/Br	10 Centavos, ND (1915–16)	175	350	—
R49	682	Br	20 Centavos, ND (1915–16) (25 mm)	35	70	350
R50	683	C/Br	20 Centavos, ND (1915–16) (20 mm)	50	100	—
R51	685	C/Br	25 Centavos, ND (1915–16)	30	50	100
R52	686–687	C/Br	50 Centavos, ND (1915–16)	50	100	150

Tenancingo, *Town*

Y#	KM#	Metal	Description	VF	EF	Unc
RA53	688	Cop	2 Centavos, 1915	1,500	—	—
R53	689	Cop	5 Centavos, 1915	50	75	125
R54	690	Cop	10 Centavos, 1916	60	100	200
R55	691	Cop	20 Centavos, 1915	60	100	300

Texcoco, *Town*

Design: ***Type similar to Mexico Y27***

Y#	KM#	Metal	Description	VF	EF	Unc
R56	N/A	Clay	1 Centavo, 1915	4,000	—	—
RA56	N/A	Clay	5 Centavos, 1915 (probably unique)	—	—	—

TOLUCA, *CITY*

Design: ***Counterstamps on Mexico Y27, 29***

Y#	KM#	Metal	Description	VF	EF	Unc
R57	693	Bz	"20 C" in circle on 1 Cent, 1906	75	150	275
R58	694	Bz	"40 C" in circle on 2 Cent, 1906	100	200	350

Y#	KM#	Metal	Description	VF	EF	Unc
R59	692	Card	5 Centavos, 1915	100	200	400

MEXICAN REVOLUTIONARY COINAGE: STATE OF MORELOS

ATLIHUAYAN, *TOWN*

Coins of Atlihuayan, YR60–R72, were struck under Emiliano Zapata.

Design: ***Type similar to YR69***

Y#	KM#	Metal	Description	VF	EF	Unc
R60	698	Cop	10 Centavos, ND, 1915, crude	30	75	150
R62	695	Cop	2 Centavos, 1915	2,500	—	—
R63	696	Cop	5 Centavos, 1915	2,500	—	—
R64	697	Cop	10 Centavos, 1915	2,500	—	—
R65	701	Cop	20 Centavos, 1915	30	75	150
R66	703	Cop	50 Centavos, 1915	25	50	100

Y#	KM#	Metal	Description	VF	EF	Unc
R69	700	Cop	10 Centavos, 1916	25	50	100
R71	704	Cop	50 Centavos, 1916	35	75	150

Design: ***Type similar to YR36***

Y#	KM#	Metal	Description	VF	EF	Unc
R72	708	Silv	1 Peso, 1916	3,000	5,500	—

MEXICAN REVOLUTIONARY COINAGE: STATE OF OAXACA

INDEPENDENT STATE

Y#	KM#	Metal	Description	VF	EF	Unc
R73	709	Cop	1 Centavo, 1915	200	300	450
R74	711	Cop	3 Centavos, 1915	200	300	450

Note: Restrikes or counterfeits of YR73–R74 are known.

Y#	KM#	Metal	Description	VF	EF	Unc
R75	710	Cop	1 Centavo, 1915	25	50	100

Y#	KM#	Metal	Description	VF	EF	Unc
R76	713	Cop	3 Centavos, 1915, large, flat-top 3	20	50	100
R76a	714	Cop	3 Centavos, 1915, small, round-top 3	20	50	100
R77	717–721	Cop	5 Centavos, 1915	5	15	50
R78	722–727	Cop	10 Centavos, 1915	5	15	50
R79	729–733	Cop	20 Centavos, 1915	5	15	50

Design: ***Small bust with long truncation of neck***

Y#	KM#	Metal	Description	VF	EF	Unc
R80	728	Silv	20 Centavos, 1915	2,000	3,000	—
R81	734–737	Silv	50 Centavos, 1915	25	40	175
R82	740–743	Silv	1 Peso, 1915	20	35	125

Note: YR80 is considered to be a pattern.

Y#	KM#	Metal	Description	VF	EF	Unc
R83	744	Silv	2 Pesos, 1915	30	60	125

Y#	KM#	Metal	Description	VF	EF	Unc
R84	746	Silv	2 Pesos, 1915, value as numeral 2	30	60	125
R84a	747–748	Silv	2 Pesos, 1915, value as DOS	30	60	125

Y#	KM#	Metal	Description	VF	EF	Unc
R85	745	Silv	2 Pesos, 1915	45	75	165
R86	751	Silv	5 Pesos, 1915	125	175	300

Y#	KM#	Metal	Description	VF	EF	Unc
R87	750	Gold	5 Pesos, 1915	400	600	1,000
R88	752	Gold	10 Pesos, 1915	500	700	1,200
R89	753–754	Gold	20 Pesos, 1915	750	1,250	2,500

Y#	KM#	Metal	Description	VF	EF	Unc
R90	755	Gold	60 Pesos, 1916	30,000	60,000	80,000

Note: Specimens of YR90 in silver and copper are patterns.

MEXICAN REVOLUTIONARY COINAGE: STATE OF PUEBLA

Chiconcuautla, *Town*

Y#	KM#	Metal	Description	VF	EF	Unc
R91	756	Cop	X Centavos, 1915	20	40	125
R92	758	Cop	20 Centavos, 1915	7	12	25

Tetela del Oro y Ocampo, *Town*

Y#	KM#	Metal	Description	VF	EF	Unc
R93	759	Cop	2 Centavos, 1915 (17 mm)	3	5	15
R94	760–761	Cop	2 Centavos, 1915 (21 mm)	25	35	80
R95	762	Cop	5 Centavos, 1915	200	300	400
R96	TS3	Cop	10 Centavos, 1915	1,000	1,500	2,000
R97	764	Cop	20 Centavos, 1915	175	250	500

Note: Some authorities feel YR95–R97 may be patterns. They also occur in other metals.

MEXICAN REVOLUTIONARY COINAGE: STATE OF SINALOA

Y#	KM#	Metal	Description	VF	EF	Unc
R98	765	Silv	20 Centavos, ND (1913), copy of Y18	600	—	—
R99	766	Silv	50 Centavos, ND (1913), copy of Y41	1,250	—	—
R100	N/A	Silv	8 Reales, ND (1913), copy of Y19	400	—	—
R101	769	Silv	1 Peso, ND (1913), copy of Y20	400	—	—

Note: YR98–R101 are crudely cast copies of earlier national coinage. Legends, when readable, will show dates of various original coins used to make molds.

MOMBASA

Now a seaport in Kenya, this town came under British administration in 1888. It was their first foothold in present-day Kenya.

For later issues, see East Africa.

MONETARY SYSTEM

4 pice = 1 anna
16 annas = 1 rupee

PRECIOUS METAL CONTENT

Dates	Denomination	Gross Wt (g)	Fineness	Net Wt (g)	Troy Oz.
		SILVER			
1888–90	2 annas	1.4580	0.9170	1.3365	0.0430
	1/4 rupee	2.9160	0.9170	2.6730	0.0859
	1/2 rupee	5.8319	0.9170	5.3459	0.1719
	1 rupee	11.6638	0.9170	10.6918	0.3437

Y#	KM#	Metal	Description	VF	EF	Unc
1	1	Bz	1 Pice, 1888 (2 vars)	15	35	85
						Proof: $400

Y#	KM#	Metal	Description	VF	EF	Unc
2	2	Silv	2 Annas, 1890	30	75	175
						Proof: $375
3	3	Silv	1/4 Rupee, 1890	40	100	250
						Proof: $475
4	4	Silv	1/2 Rupee, 1890	50	125	275
						Proof: $500

Y#	KM#	Metal	Description	VF	EF	Unc
5	5	Silv	1 Rupee, 1888	95	185	350
						Proof: $1,250

MONACO

Monaco is a small constitutional monarchy on the Mediterranean coast bounded by France on the west, famous for its resorts and Monte Carlo. *Languages:* French, English, Italian, Monegasque. *Capital:* Monaco-Ville.

MONETARY SYSTEM

100 centimes = 1 franc

PRECIOUS METAL CONTENT

Dates	Denomination	Gross Wt (g)	Fineness	Net Wt (g)	Troy Oz.
		GOLD			
1878–1904	20 francs	6.4516	0.9000	5.8064	0.1867
	100 francs	32.2581	0.9000	29.0323	0.9334

CHARLES III,
1856–1889

Y#	KM#	Metal	Description	VF	EF	Unc
A1	98	Gold	20 Francs, 1878–79	325	400	1,200
B1	99	Gold	100 Francs, 1882–86	BV	BV	2,500
			1882, Rare			

ALBERT I,
1889–1922

Y#	KM#	Metal	Description	VF	EF	Unc
1	105	Gold	100 Francs, 1891–1904	BV	BV	2,500
			1892, Rare			

LOUIS II,
1922–1949

Design: ***Within inner circle: REMB. JUSQU'AU 31 X BRE 1926 (Good Until December 31, 1926)***

Y#	KM#	Metal	Description	VF	EF	Unc
2	110	A-Bz	50 Centimes, 1924	12	25	60
3	111	A-Bz	1 Franc, 1924	12	25	70
4	112	A-Bz	2 Francs, 1924	12	25	75

Reverse: ***Without inner legend***

Y#	KM#	Metal	Description	VF	EF	Unc
5	113	A-Bz	50 Centimes, 1926	12	25	80
6	114	A-Bz	1 Franc, 1926	15	25	80
7	115	A-Bz	2 Francs, 1926	15	20	70

Y#	KM#	Metal	Description	VF	EF	Unc
8	120a	A-Bz	1 Franc, ND (1943)	2	5	15
9	121a	A-Bz	2 Francs, ND (1943)	2	6	18
8a	120	Alum	1 Franc, ND (1943)	3	8	25
9a	121	Alum	2 Francs, ND (1943)	2	7	20

Y#	KM#	Metal	Description	VF	EF	Unc
10	122	Alum	5 Francs, 1945	7.50	15	40

Y#	KM#	Metal	Description	VF	EF	Unc
11	123	C-N	10 Francs, 1946	4	7	20
12	124	C-N	20 Francs, 1947	5	8	25

RAINIER III, *1949–2005*

Y#	KM#	Metal	Description	VF	EF	Unc
13	130	A-Bz	10 Francs, 1950–51	1	4	15
14	131	A-Bz	20 Francs, 1950–51	1	4	12

Y#	KM#	Metal	Description	VF	EF	Unc
15	132	A-Bz	50 Francs, 1950	2.50	5	20
16	133	C-N	100 Francs, 1950	6.50	10	35

Y#	KM#	Metal	Description	VF	EF	Unc
17	134	C-N	100 Francs, 1956	5	8.50	25

Y#	KM#	Metal	Description	VF	EF	Unc
18	140	Nick	1 Franc, 1960–68, 74–95	0.75	1.50	3

Note: All coins of Monaco dated 1995 are found only in sets.

Y#	KM#	Metal	Description	VF	EF	Unc
19	141	Silv	5 Francs, 1960, 66	6.50	10	30

Y#	KM#	Metal	Description	VF	EF	Unc
20	142	A-Bz	10 Centimes, 1962, 74–95	0.50	1	4
21	143	A-Bz	20 Centimes, 1962, 74–95	0.50	1	5
22	144	A-Bz	50 Centimes, 1962	15.00	25	75

MONGOLIA

Mongolia is bounded by Siberia on the north and China to the south. A Chinese province until 1911, it patterned its People's Republic after the Soviet's. It became nominally independent in 1945. Free elections in 1990 created a multi-party parliamentary republic. *Languages:* Mongolian, Russian. *Capital:* Ulaan Baatar.

MONETARY SYSTEM
100 mongo = 1 tukhrik

PRECIOUS METAL CONTENT

Dates	Denomination	Gross Wt (g)	Fineness	Net Wt (g)	Troy Oz.
		SILVER			
1925	10 mongo	1.7996	0.5000	0.8998	0.0289
	15 mongo	2.6994	0.5000	1.3497	0.0434
	20 mongo	3.5592	0.5000	1.7996	0.0579
	50 mongo	10.0000	0.9000	9.0000	0.2893
	1 tukhrik	20.0000	0.9000	18.0000	0.5786

PEOPLE'S REPUBLIC

FIRST COINAGE

Y#	KM#	Metal	Description	VF	EF	Unc
1	1	Cop	1 Mongo, Yr 15 (1925) (21 mm)	10	15	75
2	2	Cop	2 Mongo, Yr 15 (1925) (24 mm)	10	15	75
3	3	Cop	5 Mongo, Yr 15 (1925) (32 mm)	20	50	150

Y#	KM#	Metal	Description	VF	EF	Unc
4	4	Silv	10 Mongo, Yr 15 (1925) (17 mm)	10.00	25	60
5	5	Silv	15 Mongo, Yr 15 (1925) (19 mm)	7.50	15	45
6	6	Silv	20 Mongo, Yr 15 (1925) (22 mm)	10.00	25	60
7	7	Silv	50 Mongo, Yr 15 (1925) (27 mm)	20.00	45	95
8	8	Silv	1 Tukhrik, Yr 15 (1925) (34 mm)	30.00	75	150

SECOND COINAGE

Y#	KM#	Metal	Description	VF	EF	Unc
10	9	A-Bz	1 Mongo, Yr 27 (1937) (18 mm)	5	10.00	22.50
11	10	A-Bz	2 Mongo, Yr 27 (1937) (22 mm)	4	7.50	20.00
12	11	A-Bz	5 Mongo, Yr 27 (1937) (28 mm)	4	10.00	22.50

Y#	KM#	Metal	Description	VF	EF	Unc
13	12	C-N	10 Mongo, Yr 27 (1937) (17 mm)	4.00	7.50	20
14	13	C-N	15 Mongo, Yr 27 (1937) (21 mm)	5.00	10.00	25
15	14	C-N	20 Mongo, Yr 27 (1937) (22 mm)	12.50	25.00	40

THIRD COINAGE

Y#	KM#	Metal	Description	VF	EF	Unc
16	15	A-Bz	1 Mongo, Yr 35 (1945)	5.00	10	25.00
17	16	A-Bz	2 Mongo, Yr 35 (1945)	2.25	4	12.50
18	17	A-Bz	5 Mongo, Yr 35 (1945)	3.50	7	17.50

Y#	KM#	Metal	Description	VF	EF	Unc
19	18	C-N	10 Mongo, Yr 35 (1945)	4.00	8	20.00
20	19	C-N	15 Mongo, Yr 35 (1945)	3.50	7	17.50
21	20	C-N	20 Mongo, Yr 35 (1945)	4.50	9	22.50

FOURTH COINAGE

Y#	KM#	Metal	Description	VF	EF	Unc
22	21	Alum	1 Mongo, 1959	0.75	1.25	3.00
23	22	Alum	2 Mongo, 1959	0.85	1.50	3.50
24	23	Alum	5 Mongo, 1959	1.00	1.75	4.00

Y#	KM#	Metal	Description	VF	EF	Unc
25	24	Alum	10 Mongo, 1959	1.75	3.00	8.00
26	25	Alum	15 Mongo, 1959	1.25	2.25	4.50
27	26	Alum	20 Mongo, 1959	1.50	2.50	5.00

MONTENEGRO

Formerly a principality north of Albania within the Austro-Hungarian Empire, Montenegro declared independence in 1878. It was proclaimed a kingdom in 1910 and was consolidated as part of the Kingdom of the Serbs, Croats, and Slovenes during World War I. The name was changed to Yugoslavia in 1929. When that nation unraveled along ethnic lines in the early 1990s, Montenegro federated with Serbia as the Federal Republic of Yugoslavia. In 2003 the country restructured as two republics and in 2006, by referendum, Montenegro ended the association and established its independence. It joined NATO in 2017. *Languages:* Serbian/Montenegrin. *Capital:* Cetinje/Podgorica.

MONETARY SYSTEM

100 para = 1 perper

PRECIOUS METAL CONTENT

Dates	Denomination	Gross Wt (g)	Fineness	Net Wt (g)	Troy Oz.
		SILVER			
1909–14	1 perper	5.0000	0.8350	4.1750	0.1342
	2 perpera	10.0000	0.8350	8.3500	0.2685
	5 perpera	24.0000	0.9000	21.6000	0.6944
		GOLD			
1910	10 perpera	3.3875	0.9000	3.0488	0.0980
	20 perpera	6.7751	0.9000	6.0976	0.1960
	100 perpera	33.8753	0.9000	30.4878	0.9802

NIKOLA I, *1860–1918*

AS PRINCE, *1860–1910*

Y#	KM#	Metal	Description	VF	EF	Unc
1	1	Bz	1 Para, 1906	7.50	15	50
2	2	Bz	2 Pare, 1906, 08	12.50	20	75

Y#	KM#	Metal	Description	VF	EF	Unc
3	3	Nick	10 Pare, 1906, 08	7.50	15	30
4	4	Nick	20 Pare, 1906, 08	9.50	18	45

Y#	KM#	Metal	Description	VF	EF	Unc
5	5	Silv	1 Perper, 1909	15	35	135
6	7	Silv	2 Perpera, 1910	35	75	225
7	6	Silv	5 Perpera, 1909	200	500	1,100
8	5	Silv	1 Perper, 1909	15	35	700
9	10	Gold	20 Perpera, 1910	400	600	950
10	12	Gold	100 Perpera, 1910	9,500	15,000	18,500
						Proof: $22,000

AS KING, *1910–1918*

Reverse: *New legend*

Y#	KM#	Metal	Description	VF	EF	Unc
11	16	Bz	1 Para, 1913–14	30	65	165
12	17	Bz	2 Pare, 1913–14	6	13	45
13	18	Nick	10 Para, 1913–14	8	15	45
14	19	Nick	20 Para, 1913–14	8	15	45

Y#	KM#	Metal	Description	VF	EF	Unc
15	14	Silv	1 Perper, 1912, 14	17.50	37.50	100
16	20	Silv	2 Perpera, 1914	35.00	60.00	200
17	15	Silv	5 Perpera, 1912, 14	350.00	600.00	1,350

50th Year of Regency

Y#	KM#	Metal	Description	VF	EF	Unc
18	9	Gold	10 Perpera, 1910	300	500	800
19	11	Gold	20 Perpera, 1910	425	650	1,200
20	13	Gold	100 Perpera, 1910	7,500	9,500	15,000
						Proof: $22,000

MOROCCO

A constitutional monarchy on the northwest coast of Africa, Morocco was formerly a French and Spanish protectorate whose independence was recognized in 1956. *Languages:* Moorish-Arabic, Berber, French, and Spanish. *Capital:* Rabat.

MONETARY SYSTEM

500 muzuna = 1 dirham

10 dirham = 1 rial

100 centimes = 1 franc, 1921–1959

PRECIOUS METAL CONTENT

Dates	Denomination	Gross Wt (g)	Fineness	Net Wt (g)	Troy Oz.
		SILVER			
1882–1901	1/2 dirham	1.4558	0.8350	1.2156	0.0391
	1 dirham	2.9116	0.8350	2.4312	0.0782
	2-1/2 dirham	7.2790	0.8350	6.0780	0.1954
	5 dirham	14.5580	0.8350	12.1559	0.3908
	10 dirham	29.1160	0.9000	26.2044	0.8425
1902–18	1/20 rial	1.2500	0.8350	1.0438	0.0336
	1/10 rial	2.5000	0.8350	2.0875	0.0671
	1/4 rial	6.2500	0.8350	5.2188	0.1678
	1/2 rial	12.0000	0.8350	10.4375	0.3356
	1 rial	25.0000	0.9000	22.5000	0.7234
		SILVER			
1929–34	5 francs	5.0000	0.6800	3.4000	0.1093
	10 francs	10.0000	0.6800	6.8000	0.2186
	20 francs	20.0000	0.6800	13.6000	0.4372
1953	100 francs	4.0000	0.7200	2.8800	0.0926
	200 francs	8.0000	0.7200	5.7600	0.1851
1956	500 francs	22.5000	0.9000	20.2500	0.6511
1960	1 dirham	6.0000	0.6000	3.6000	0.1157

Hasan I, *1873–1894*

Y#	KM#	Metal	Description	VF	EF	Unc
C1	C1	Bz	1/2 Muzuna, AH 1310 (1893) (15.5 mm)	300	525	900
B1	B1	Bz	1 Muzuna, AH 1310 (18.5 mm)	200	375	600
1	1	Bz	2-1/2 Muzuna, AH 1310 (23.5 mm)	200	400	650
2	2	Bz	5 Muzuna, AH 1310–11 (28 mm)	100	200	500
3	3	Bz	10 Muzuna, AH 1310–11 (34 mm)	150	250	600

Note: Other machine-struck bronze coins dated AH 1301–1309 are thought to be patterns.

Y#	KM#	Metal	Description	VF	EF	Unc
4	4	Silv	1/2 Dirham, AH 1299–1314 (1882–96) (15 mm)	9.00	20	100
5	5	Silv	1 Dirham, AH 1299–1314 (17 mm)	12.50	30	125

Y#	KM#	Metal	Description	VF	EF	Unc
6	6	Silv	2-1/2 Dirham, AH 1299–1314 (26 mm)	15	50	150
7	7	Silv	5 Dirham, AH 1299–1314 (33 mm)	20	60	200
8	8	Silv	10 Dirham, AH 1299	50	100	250

'Abd al-Aziz, *1896–1908*

First Coinage

Y#	KM#	Metal	Description	VF	EF	Unc
9	9	Silv	1/2 Dirham, AH 1313–19 (1896–1901)	9.00	20	100
10	10	Silv	1 Dirham, AH 1313–18 (1896–1900)	12.50	30	125

Y#	KM#	Metal	Description	VF	EF	Unc
11	11	Silv	2-1/2 Dirham, AH 1313–18 (1896–1900)	15	45	125
12	12	Silv	5 Dirham, AH 1313–18 (1896–1900)	35	85	175
13	13	Silv	10 Dirham, AH 1313 (1896)	225	450	1,000

Note: Y9–22 have variations in Arabic inscriptions, size of numerals, etc., according to the mints, which were Fez, Birmingham, Berlin, and Paris.

Second Coinage

Y#	KM#	Metal	Description	VF	EF	Unc
14	14	Bz	1 Muzuna, AH 1320–21 (1902–03)	8.00	35	100
15	15	Bz	2 Muzuna, AH 1320–23 (1902–05)	12.00	25	70
16	16	Bz	5 Muzuna, AH 1320–22 (1902–04)	6.00	20	60
17	17	Bz	10 Muzuna, AH 1320–23 (1902–05)	7.50	25	95

Note: Y14 dated AH 1319 is probably a pattern.

Y#	KM#	Metal	Description	VF	EF	Unc
18	18	Silv	1/20 Rial, AH 1320–21 (1902–03) (15 mm)	15	45	150
19	19	Silv	1/10 Rial, AH 1320–21 (1902–03) (16.5 mm)	15	45	150

Y#	KM#	Metal	Description	VF	EF	Unc
20	20	Silv	1/4 Rial, AH 1320–21 (1902–03) (25 mm)	8	20	50
21	21	Silv	1/2 Rial, AH 1320–23 (1902–05) (32 mm)	12	45	100
22	22	Silv	1 Rial, AH 1320–21 (1902–03) (37 mm)	30	100	225

Hafiz, *1908–1912*

Y#	KM#	Metal	Description	VF	EF	Unc
23	23	Silv	1/4 Rial, AH 1329 (1911)	12.50	45	35
24	24	Silv	1/2 Rial, AH 1329 (1911)	15.00	60	75
25	25	Silv	1 Rial, AH 1329 (1911)	30.00	90	200

Yusuf, *1912–1927*

First Coinage

Y#	KM#	Metal	Description	VF	EF	Unc
26	26	Bz	1 Muzuna, AH 1330 (1912)	10	25	75
27	27	Bz	2 Muzuna, AH 1330 (1912)	10	25	75
28	28	Bz	5 Muzuna, AH 1330, 40 (1912, 22)	8	20	65
29	29	Bz	10 Muzuna, AH 1330, 40 (1912, 22)	8	20	65

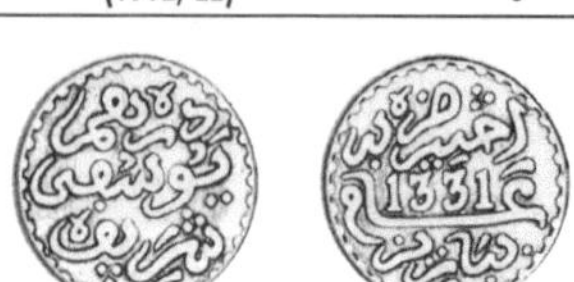

Y#	KM#	Metal	Description	VF	EF	Unc
30	30	Silv	1/10 Rial, AH 1331 (1913)	40	70	175

Y#	KM#	Metal	Description	VF	EF	Unc
31	31	Silv	1/4 Rial, AH 1331 (1913)	35	150	300
32	32	Silv	1/2 Rial, AH 1331, 36 (1913, 18)	25	50	150
33	33	Silv	1 Rial, AH 1331, 36 (1913, 18)	30	60	150

Second Coinage *(French Protectorate)*

100 centimes = 1 franc

Y#	KM#	Metal	Description	VF	EF	Unc
34	34	C-N	25 Centimes, ND (1921–26)	5	17.50	37.50

Y#	KM#	Metal	Description	VF	EF	Unc
35	35	Nick	50 Centimes, ND (1921–24)	2.00	10.00	45
36	36	Nick	1 Franc, ND	3.50	13.50	60

Muhammad bin Yusuf, *AH 1345–1372 (1927–53)*

As Sultan

First Coinage

Y#	KM#	Metal	Description	VF	EF	Unc
37	37	Silv	5 Francs, AH 1347, 52 (1929, 34)	7.50	15	37.50
38	38	Silv	10 Francs, AH 1347, 52 (1929, 34)	10.00	20	65.00
39	39	Silv	20 Francs, AH 1347, 52 (1929, 34)	15.00	30	75.00

Second Coinage

Y#	KM#	Metal	Description	VF	EF	Unc
40	40	A-Bz	50 Centimes, 1945	0.50	1.00	10.00
41	41	A-Bz	1 Franc, 1945	0.50	1.00	10.00
42	42	A-Bz	2 Francs, 1945	0.60	1.50	12.50

Y#	KM#	Metal	Description	VF	EF	Unc
43	43	A-Bz	5 Francs, AH 1365 (1946)	0.75	1.50	12.50

Y#	KM#	Metal	Description	VF	EF	Unc
44	44	C-N	10 Francs, AH 1366 (1947)	1	1.50	12.50
45	45	C-N	20 Francs, AH 1366 (1947)	1	1.50	10.00

Third Coinage

Note: Y46–51 were struck in various years through 1973 with no change of date.

Y#	KM#	Metal	Description	VF	EF	Unc
46	46	Alum	1 Franc, AH 1370 (1951)	0.50	1	3
47	47	Alum	2 Francs, AH 1370 (1951)	0.50	1	3

Y#	KM#	Metal	Description	VF	EF	Unc
48	48	Alum	5 Francs, AH 1370 (1951)	0.75	1.25	4

Y#	KM#	Metal	Description	VF	EF	Unc
49	49	A-Bz	10 Francs, AH 1371 (1952)	0.45	1.25	4.50
50	50	A-Bz	20 Francs, AH 1371 (1952)	0.75	1.50	5.50

Y#	KM#	Metal	Description	VF	EF	Unc
51	51	A-Bz	50 Francs, AH 1371 (1952)	1	1.75	6.50

Y#	KM#	Metal	Description	VF	EF	Unc
A52	A54	Silv	100 Francs, AH 1370 (1951)	—	—	375
52	52	Silv	100 Francs, 1953	4	6	30
53	53	Silv	200 Francs, 1953	6	10	35

As Mohammed V, King, 1955–1961

Y#	KM#	Metal	Description	VF	EF	Unc
54	54	Silv	500 Francs, 1956	10	17.50	50

Monetary Reform, 1959

100 francs = 1 dirham

Y#	KM#	Metal	Description	VF	EF	Unc
55	55	Silv	1 Dirham, 1960	3	4.50	17.50

MOZAMBIQUE

This seacoast country in southeast Africa was colonized by Portugal in 1505 and was formerly known as Portuguese East Africa. After more than a decade of rebellion, Mozambique gained independence in 1975. A second civil war of 16 years' duration ended in 1992 and resulted in a new constitution abrogating the nation's drift to socialism. Free elections were held in 1994 and the country joined the British Commonwealth in in 1995. More recently the nation has been plagued by disputed elections and political turmoil. *Languages:* Portuguese, African tongues. *Capital:* Maputo.

MONETARY SYSTEM

100 centavos = 1 escudo

PRECIOUS METAL CONTENT

Dates	Denomination	Gross Wt (g)	Fineness	Net Wt (g)	Troy Oz.
		SILVER			
1935–51	2-1/2 escudos	3.5000	0.6500	2.2750	0.0731
	5 escudos	7.0000	0.6500	4.5500	0.1463
	10 escudos	12.5000	0.8350	10.4375	0.3356

Counterstamps

Counterstamp Design: ***Crowned "PM" in circle (1889)***

Y#	KM#	Metal	Description	VF	EF	Unc
A1	39–41	Silv	on India Rupee	185	350	—
B1	45–46	Silv	on Austria Y55	350	500	—

Counterstamp Design: ***Large "PM" in oval (ca. 1889–1895)***

Y#	KM#	Metal	Description	VF	EF	Unc
C1	52–54	Silv	on India Rupee	175	325	—
D1	58	Silv	on Austria Y55	350	500	—

Regular Issues

Y#	KM#	Metal	Description	VF	EF	Unc
1	63	Bz	10 Centavos, 1936	5.00	15	50
2	64	Bz	20 Centavos, 1936	8.00	25	75
3	65	C-N	50 Centavos, 1936	12.50	35	115
4	66	C-N	1 Escudo, 1936	10.00	30	150

Y#	KM#	Metal	Description	VF	EF	Unc
5	61	Silv	2-1/2 Escudos, 1935	5	15	75
6	62	Silv	5 Escudos, 1935	7	20	100
7	67	Silv	10 Escudos, 1936	12	40	130

New Reverse Arms

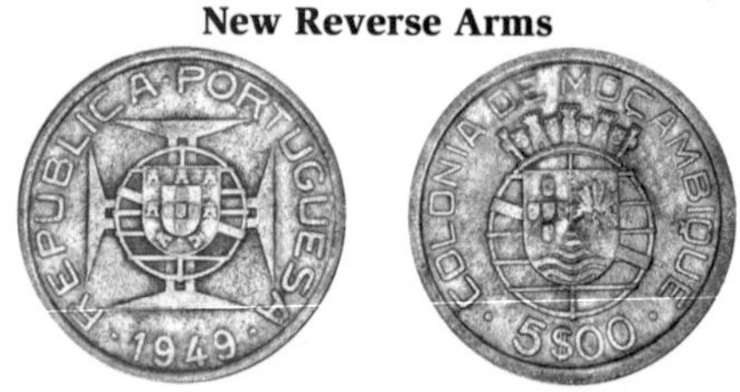

Y#	KM#	Metal	Description	VF	EF	Unc
8	68	Silv	2-1/2 Escudos, 1938–51	3	6	20
9	69	Silv	5 Escudos, 1938, 49	5	15	50
10	70	Silv	10 Escudos, 1938	15	45	125

Y#	KM#	Metal	Description	VF	EF	Unc
11	72	Bz	10 Centavos, 1942	3.00	6.50	20
12	71	Bz	20 Centavos, 1941 (29 mm)	10.00	25.00	100
13	73	Bz	50 Centavos, 1945	1.00	5.00	25
14	74	Bz	1 Escudo, 1945	4.50	15.00	50
15	75	Bz	20 Centavos, 1949–50 (20 mm)	1.00	3.50	10

Y#	KM#	Metal	Description	VF	EF	Unc
16	76	N-Bz	50 Centavos, 1950–51	2	5	20
17	77	N-Bz	1 Escudo, 1950–51	4	15	55

Decree of January 21, 1952

Obverse Design: ***COLONIA DE omitted***

Y#	KM#	Metal	Description	VF	EF	Unc
18	81	Bz	50 Centavos, 1953, 57	0.75	2.50	5
19	82	Bz	1 Escudo, 1953–74	0.50	1.00	4

Y#	KM#	Metal	Description	VF	EF	Unc
20	78	C-N	2-1/2 Escudos, 1952–73	0.50	1	7.50

Y#	KM#	Metal	Description	VF	EF	Unc
21	84	Silv	5 Escudos, 1960	BV	4.00	8
22	79	Silv	10 Escudos, 1952–66	BV	7.50	15
23	80	Silv	20 Escudos, 1952–66	BV	8.00	20

Y#	KM#	Metal	Description	VF	EF	Unc
24	83	Bz	10 Centavos, 1960–61	0.35	1	3.50
25	85	Bz	20 Centavos, 1961	0.35	1	3.00

MUSCAT AND OMAN

A sultanate on the southeast coast of the Arabian peninsula, Muscat and Oman is now known as Oman. Portugal controlled the area from 1508–1659, and the Turks until 1741 when the current royal line was founded. *Language:* Arabic. *Capital:* Muscat.

MONETARY SYSTEM

4 baisah (baizah) = 1 anna
64 baisah = 1 india rupee
200 baisah = 1 riyal = Maria Theresa thaler

PRECIOUS METAL CONTENT

Dates	Denomination	Gross Wt (g)	Fineness	Net Wt (g)	Troy Oz.
		SILVER			
1948–62	1/2 riyal	14.0300	0.5000	7.0150	0.2256
1959	1 riyal	28.0700	0.8330	23.3907	0.7518
		GOLD			
1962	15 riyal	7.9900	0.9160	7.3188	0.2353

Note: Y4-6 and Y11-13 are provincial coinage for Dhofar. Y14-15 are provincial coinage for Muscat.

FESSUL BIN TURKEE, *1888–1913*

Y#	KM#	Metal	Description	VF	EF	Unc
1	1	Cop	1/12 Anna, AH 1311 (1894)	500	900	—
2	2	Cop	1/4 Anna, AH 1311 (1894)	90	175	—

Y#	KM#	Metal	Description	VF	EF	Unc
3	4	C/Br	1/4 Anna, AH 1312–16 (1895–99)	25	45	150

Note: Many variations of Y3 include size and arrangement of lettering and Arabic inscriptions, omission of wreath, etc.

Y#	KM#	Metal	Description	VF	EF	Unc
A3	3	C/Br	1/4 Anna, AH 1315 (1898)	15	45	150

SA'ID BIN TAIMUR, *1932–1970*

Y#	KM#	Metal	Description	VF	EF	Unc
4	22	C-N	10 Baisah, AH 1359 (1940)	12.50	30	75

Y#	KM#	Metal	Description	VF	EF	Unc
5	23	C-N	20 Baisah, AH 1359 (1940), square	15	40	90
6	24	C-N	50 Baisah, AH 1359 (1940), scalloped	20	45	95

Y#	KM#	Metal	Description	VF	EF	Unc
7	25	C-N	2 Baisah, AH 1365 (1946), square	6.25	13.50	22.50

Y#	KM#	Metal	Description	VF	EF	Unc
8	26	C-N	5 Baisah, AH 1365 (1946), scalloped	8.50	17.50	35
10	27	C-N	20 Baisah, AH 1365 (1946), square	12.50	27.50	50

Note: Y4–6 and 11–13 used only in Dhofar Province, Oman.

Y#	KM#	Metal	Description	VF	EF	Unc
11	29	Silv	1/2 Dhufari Riyal, AH 1367 (1948)	25	30	70
						Proof, Restrike: $225

Y#	KM#	Metal	Description	VF	EF	Unc
13	30	Bz	3 Baisah, AH 1378 (1959) (20 mm)	1.50	2.00	3.00

Y#	KM#	Metal	Description	VF	EF	Unc
15	34	Silv	1/2 Riyal, AH 1380–81 (1961–62)	9.50	18	40
12	31	Silv	1 Riyal, AH 1378 (1959)	25.00	40	85

Y#	KM#	Metal	Description	VF	EF	Unc
17	35	Gold	15 Riyal, AH 1381 (1962)	BV	BV	900
						Proof: $3,250

MUSCAT AND OMAN–PROVINCIAL

Design: ***Like Y13***

Y#	KM#	Metal	Description	VF	EF	Unc
14	32	Bz	3 Baisah, AH 1380 (1961) (18 mm)	0.60	0.75	1.50

Y#	KM#	Metal	Description	VF	EF	Unc
16	33	C-N	5 Baisah, AH 1381 (1962)	1	1.50	2

NEJD

Occupying the desert highlands of the Arabian peninsula, Nejd was first unified as a sultanate in the late 18th century. Torn by strife until the early 1900s, it thereafter became the dominant power in the area. It was proclaimed a kingdom in 1927 and was united with the Hejaz in 1932 to form Saudi Arabia. *Language:* Arabic. *Capital:* Riyadh.

For later issues, see Saudi Arabia.

MONETARY SYSTEM

40 para = 1 ghirsh
20 ghirsh = 1 riyal

ABD AL-AZIZ IBN SA'UD, *AS SULTAN AND KING OF NEJD, 1921–1932*

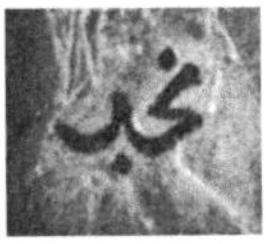

Counterstamp: ***Incuse "Najd" in Arabic***

Y#	KM#	Metal	Description	VF	EF	Unc
1	1–4	Silv	on Turkish or Egyptian 5 Ghirsh	375	750	—
2	9–11/15	Silv	on similar 10 Ghirsh	375	750	—
2a	5–A9	Silv	on India Rupee	225	450	—
3	12–13	Silv	on similar 20 Ghirsh	375	750	—
3a	14	Silv	on Austria Y55	225	375	—

Note: Copies of the Nejd counterstamps on some or all of these silver types were produced in the 1970s.

NEPAL

Situated in the Himalaya Mountains between India and Tibet, Nepal was unified as a kingdom in 1768. A constitutional monarchy was declared in 1951. Amidst a rebellion by communist guerrillas, on-going since the mid-1990s, in 2002 the king dismissed the government and suspended parliament. Representative government was restored by treaty in 2006 after a general strike, and the monarchy was abolished. *Languages:* Nepali, Maithali. *Capital:* Kathmandu.

MONETARY SYSTEM:

32 paisa = 16 dhyak = 8 ani
= 4 do-ani = 2 suka
= 1 mohar

PRECIOUS METAL CONTENT

Dates	Denomination	Gross Wt (g)	Fineness	Net Wt (g)	Troy Oz.
		SILVER			
1932–48	20 paisa	2.2161	0.3330	0.7380	0.0237
	50 paisa	5.5403	0.8000	4.4322	0.1425
	1 rupee	11.0806	0.8000	8.8645	0.2850
1948–53	20 paisa	2.2161	0.3330	0.7380	0.0237
	50 paisa	5.5403	0.3330	1.8449	0.0593
	1 rupee	11.0806	0.3330	3.6898	0.1186

PRITHIVI, *1881–1911*

SAKA DATES, 1803–1833 / SAMVAT DATES, 1938–1968

In the reign of King Prithvi coin dates are expressed in either the Saka or Samvat eras, while only Samvat dates are used in later reigns. In the following listings, the term "Saka" is always spelled out in full, and the abbreviation "S" refers only to Samvat dates.

Y#	KM#	Metal	Description	VF	EF	Unc
1	620	Cop	1/4 Paisa, Saka 1818–19, S 1964 (14 mm)	35	50	100

Legends: ***Circular***

Y#	KM#	Metal	Description	VF	EF	Unc
3	623–627	Cop	1 Paisa, Saka 1810, S 1945–51 (21–24 mm)	3.00	5	—
4	632	Cop	2 Paisa, S 1948–50 (26 mm)	7.50	15	25

Legends: ***In wreaths***

Y#	KM#	Metal	Description	VF	EF	Unc
A3	628	Cop	1 Paisa, S 1949–64	10	25	—

Legends: ***In squares***

Y#	KM#	Metal	Description	VF	EF	Unc
B3	629	Cop	1 Paisa, S 1959–68	3	5	—

Y#	KM#	Metal	Description	VF	EF	Unc
5	621	Cop	1/4 Paisa, S (19)68 (1911) (16 mm)	45	60	75
6	622	Cop	1/2 Paisa, S (19)64, 68b (19 mm)	60	75	100
7	631	Cop	1 Paisa, S 1964, 68 (23 mm)	60	75	100
8	634	Cop	2 Paisa, S 1964, 68 (26.5 mm)	60	75	125

Note: Y5–8 are said to have been issued only in presentation sets.

Reverse: ***Incuse mirror image of obverse***

Y#	KM#	Metal	Description	VF	EF	Unc
9	635–636	Silv	1/64 Mohar, ND	7.50	10	25
10	637–638	Silv	1/32 Mohar, ND (11 mm)	75.00	100	150
11	639	Silv	1/16 Mohar, ND (13 mm)	60.00	75	125

Y#	KM#	Metal	Description	VF	EF	Unc
12	640	Silv	1/8 Mohar, ND	60	75	125
13	641/643	Silv	1/4 Mohar, Saka 1803–27 (18 mm)	10	15	25

Y#	KM#	Metal	Description	VF	EF	Unc
13a	642/644	Silv	1/4 Mohar, Saka 1833 (155 mm)	6	10	10
14	Several	Silv	1/2 Mohar, Saka 1803–29 (21 mm)	10	15	25
14a	646/649	Silv	1/2 Mohar, Saka 1833 (19 mm)	4	6	10

Y#	KM#	Metal	Description	VF	EF	Unc
15	651	Silv	1 Mohar, Saka 1803–33 (5.5 g) (26 mm)	5	10	15
16	653/655	Silv	2 Mohar, Saka 1803–31 (11 g) (26 mm)	15	25	40
16a	654/656	Silv	2 Mohar, Saka 1832–33 (11 g) (29 mm)	10	20	30
17	657–658	Silv	4 Mohar, Saka 1817, 33 (22 g) (29 mm)	150	200	300

Reverse: ***Incuse mirror image of obverse***

Y#	KM#	Metal	Description	VF	EF	Unc
18	659–662	Gold	1/128 Mohar, ND	75	85	125
19	665–666	Gold	1/32 Mohar, ND	80	100	200
20	667–668	Gold	1/16 Mohar, ND, Saka (18)33	175	235	300
21	669–670	Gold	1/8 Mohar, ND, Saka (18)33	180	195	325

Y#	KM#	Metal	Description	VF	EF	Unc
22	671	Gold	1/4 Mohar, Saka 1808–33	100	150	300
23	672	Gold	1/2 Mohar, Saka 1805–33	200	300	400
24	673	Gold	1 Mohar, Saka 1805–33	300	500	800
25	674–675	Gold	1 Asarfi, Saka 1805–33 (12.4 g)	BV	BV	500
26	676–680	Gold	2 Rupees, Saka 1811–33 (23.2 g)	1,000	1,500	2,000

DIVYESWARI LAKSHMI *(REGENT)*

Y#	KM#	Metal	Description	VF	EF	Unc
A26	681	Silv	1/2 Mohar, VS 1971 (1914)	5	8	15

Y#	KM#	Metal	Description	VF	EF	Unc
B26	682	Silv	1 Mohar, VS 1971 (1914)	5	8	15

Y#	KM#	Metal	Description	VF	EF	Unc
C26	683	Gold	1 Mohar, VS 1971 (1914)	350	450	600

TRIBHUVANA, FIRST REIGN, *VS 1968–2007 (1911–1950)*

Y#	KM#	Metal	Description	VF	EF	Unc
27	685	Cop	1 Paisa, VS 1968–77 (1912–20)	1.50	5	13

Y#	KM#	Metal	Description	VF	EF	Unc
28	684	Cop	1/2 Paisa, VS 1978, 85 (1921, 28)	10	30.00	100
29	687–688	Cop	1 Paisa, VS 1975–87 (1918–30)	2	10.00	70
30	689	Cop	2 Paisa, VS 1976–87 (1919–30)	3	10.00	70
31	690	Cop	5 Paisa, VS 1976–88 (1919–31)	4	7.50	30

Reverse: ***Incuse mirror image of obverse***

Y#	KM#	Metal	Description	VF	EF	Unc
A32	691	Silv	1/128 Mohar, ND	30	40	65

Y#	KM#	Metal	Description	VF	EF	Unc
32	692	Silv	1/4 Mohar, VS 1969–70 (16 mm)	12.50	22.50	40
33	693	Silv	1/2 Mohar, VS 1968, 70	15.00	25.00	75

Designs: ***Similar to Y15–17***

Y#	KM#	Metal	Description	VF	EF	Unc
34	694	Silv	1 Mohar, VS 1968–71	20	32.50	50
35	695	Silv	2 Mohar, VS 1968–89 (29 mm)	35	65.00	100
36	696	Silv	4 Mohar, VS 1971	200	300.00	400

Y#	KM#	Metal	Description	VF	EF	Unc
37	701	Gold	1/2 Mohar, VS 1969 (1912)	—	—	—
38	702	Gold	1 Mohar, VS 1969–75	300	450	600
39	703	Gold	1 Asarfi, VS 1969–89 (12.4 g)	450	600	850

Decimal System, VS 1989– (1932–)

100 paisa = 1 rupee

Reverse: ***Trident in center***

Y#	KM#	Metal	Description	VF	EF	Unc
40	706	Cop	1 Paisa, VS 1990–97 (1933–40) (23 mm)	2.00	4	10
41	708	Cop	2 Paisa, VS 1992 (26 mm)	7.50	13	25
42	711	Cop	5 Paisa, VS 1991–97 (30 mm)	2.50	5	10

Reverse: ***Sword in center***

Y#	KM#	Metal	Description	VF	EF	Unc
A41	709.1	Cop	2 Paisa, VS 1992–97 (27 mm)	3	4	8.50
A41a	709.2	Cop	2 Paisa, VS 1992–99 (25 mm)	1	2	3.00

Reduced-Weight Copper

Y#	KM#	Metal	Description	VF	EF	Unc
A42	704	Cop	1 Dam, VS 2000, 04 (14 mm)	20.00	30	100.00
B42	705	Cop	1/2 Paisa, VS 2004 (16 mm)	20.00	30	85.00
43	707	Cop	1 Paisa, VS 2005 (1948) (20 mm)	1.00	2	4.50
44	710	Cop	2 Paisa, VS 1999–2003 (23 mm)	0.50	1	2.00

Y#	KM#	Metal	Description	VF	EF	Unc
43a	707a	Br	1 Paisa, VS 2000–06	0.50	1	1.50
44a	710a	Br	2 Paisa, VS 1999–2010	2.00	3	5.00

Y#	KM#	Metal	Description	VF	EF	Unc
45	712	CNZ	5 Paisa, VS 2000–10 (1943–53)	1.50	3.50	7

Y#	KM#	Metal	Description	VF	EF	Unc
A45	713	Silv	1/16 Rupee, VS (19)96	20	35	50

Y#	KM#	Metal	Description	VF	EF	Unc
46	714	Silv	20 Paisa, VS 1989–2004 (1932–47)	2	4	10

Y#	KM#	Metal	Description	VF	EF	Unc
47	718–719	Silv	50 Paisa, VS 1989–2005	10	15	30
48	723	Silv	1 Rupee, VS 1989–2005	15	20	40

Y#	KM#	Metal	Description	VF	EF	Unc
46a	716	Bill	20 Paisa, VS 2006–10 (1949–53)	2.50	4	8
47a	721	Bill	50 Paisa, VS 2005–10	4.00	6	10
48a	726	Bill	1 Rupee, VS 2005–11	7.50	15	25

Y#	KM#	Metal	Description	VF	EF	Unc
50	717	Gold	1/2 Mohar, VS 1995 (1938)	Rare	—	—
51	702	Gold	1 Mohar, VS 1969–2005	BV	450	550
52	703	Gold	1 Tola Asarfi, VS 1969–2005	400	650	850
53	728	Gold	2 Tola Asarfi, VS 2005	1,000	1,600	2,200

JNANENDRA, *VS 2007 (1950–1951)*

Y#	KM#	Metal	Description	VF	EF	Unc
54	729	Bill	50 Paisa, VS 2007	200	300	450
55	730	Bill	1 Rupee, VS 2007	5	10	20

TRIBHUVANA, *SECOND REIGN, VS 2007–2011 (1951–1955)*

Y43–45 and 46a–48a were resumed during this period.

Y#	KM#	Metal	Description	VF	EF	Unc
56	740	C-N	50 Paisa, VS 2010–11 (1953–54)	0.75	1.75	6.00
57	742–743	C-N	1 Rupee, VS 2010–11 (1953–54)	1.00	2.50	7.50

GENERAL COINAGE, VS 2010–2014 (1953–1957)

Y58–65 do not bear the name of the ruler, and were continued unchanged into the reign of Mahendra.

Y#	KM#	Metal	Description	VF	EF	Unc
58	733–734	Br	1 Paisa, VS 2010–12 (1953–55) (18 mm)	20.00	30	45
59	735	Br	2 Paisa, VS 2010–11 (1953–54) (21 mm)	30.00	50	90
59a	749	Br	2 Paisa, VS 2012–14 (20 mm)	0.50	1	2

Note: Restrikes of Y58 and Y59 dated 2011 exist and are worth $2.00 in Uncirculated.

Y#	KM#	Metal	Description	VF	EF	Unc
61	754	Br	4 Paisa, VS 2012 91955)	1.75	2.50	6

Y#	KM#	Metal	Description	VF	EF	Unc
62	736	Bz	5 Paisa, VS 2010–14 (1953–57)	0.25	0.50	1

Y#	KM#	Metal	Description	VF	EF	Unc
63	737	Bz	10 Paisa, VS 2010–12	0.50	1.00	2
63a			2011, brass restrike	0.30	0.75	1

Designs: *Similar to Y63*

Y#	KM#	Metal	Description	VF	EF	Unc
64	738	C-N	20 Paisa, VS 2010–11 (18 mm)	25	40	60
			Prooflike restrike from mint set, $150			
65	739	C-N	25 Paisa, VS 2010–14 (19 mm)	3	5	9

MAHENDRA, *VS 2012–2028 (1955–1972)*

Coronation Commemoratives

Y#	KM#	Metal	Description	VF	EF	Unc
66	745	Br	1 Paisa, VS 2013 (1956)	0.50	1	1.50

Y#	KM#	Metal	Description	VF	EF	Unc
67	750	Br	2 Paisa, VS 2013 (1956)	0.50	1	1.50

Y#	KM#	Metal	Description	VF	EF	Unc
68	756	Bz	5 Paisa, VS 2013 (1956)	0.75	1.25	2
69	761	Bz	10 Paisa, VS 2013 (1956)	0.75	1.25	2

Y#	KM#	Metal	Description	VF	EF	Unc
70	770	C-N	25 Paisa, VS 2013 (1956)	0.50	0.75	1.25
71	776	C-N	50 Paisa, VS 2013 (1956)	1.00	1.25	2.00
72	790	C-N	1 Rupee, VS 2013 (1956)	1.00	2.00	3.50

Y#	KM#	Metal	Description	VF	EF	Unc
73	767	Gold	1/6 Asarfi, VS 2013 (1956)	125	150	250
76	781	Gold	1/2 Asarfi, VS 2013 (1956)	300	375	500
77	791	Gold	1 Asarfi, VS 2013 (1956)	600	750	1,100

FIRST COINAGE

Y#	KM#	Metal	Description	VF	EF	Unc
78	746	Br	1 Paisa, VS 2014–20 (1957–63) (16 mm)	0.20	0.30	0.50
79	751	Br	2 Paisa, VS 2014–20 (1957–63) (18 mm)	0.20	0.30	0.50

Y#	KM#	Metal	Description	VF	EF	Unc
80	757	Bz	5 Paisa, VS 2014–20 (1957–63) (22 mm)	0.25	0.40	1
81	762	Bz	10 Paisa, VS 2014–20 (1957–63), thick (25 mm)	0.25	0.50	1

Y#	KM#	Metal	Description	VF	EF	Unc
80a	758	A-Bz	5 Paisa, VS 2021 (1964)	1	2	3.50
81a	763	A-Bz	10 Paisa, VS 2021 (1964)	1	2	3.50

Modified Dies

Y#	KM#	Metal	Description	VF	EF	Unc
78a	747	Br	1 Paisa, VS 2021–22 (1964–65)	0.20	0.30	0.50
79a	752	Br	2 Paisa, VS 2021–23 (1964–66)	0.20	0.30	0.50

Y#	KM#	Metal	Description	VF	EF	Unc
80b	758a	Bz	5 Paisa, VS 2021–23 (1964–66) (20.5 mm)	0.20	0.40	0.75
81b	764	Bz	10 Paisa, VS 2021–23 (1964–65), thin (25 mm)	0.20	0.30	0.60

Y#	KM#	Metal	Description	VF	EF	Unc
82	772	C-N	25 Paisa, VS 2015–23 (1958–66) (2 vars) (19 mm)	0.50	0.75	1.25
83	777–778	C-N	50 Paisa, VS 2011–23 (1954–66) (2 vars) (25 mm)	0.50	0.75	1.25
84	784	C-N	1 Rupee, VS 2011–12 (1954–55) (29.5 mm)	2.00	3.00	5.00
84a	785–786	C-N	1 Rupee, VS 2012–23 (1955–66) (2 vars) (28.5 mm)	1.00	2.00	3.00
85	N/A	Gold	1/5 Asarfi, VS 2012 (1955) (23.3 g)	175.00	250.00	350.00
86	775	Gold	1/4 Asarfi, VS 2012 (1955) (29.1 g)	100.00	130.00	180.00
87	782	Gold	1/2 Asarfi, VS 2012, 19 (1955, 62)	325.00	400.00	450.00
88	789/792	Gold	1 Asarfi, VS 2012, 19 (1955, 62)	BV	650.00	775.00
89	793	Gold	2 Asarfi, VS 2012 (1955)	BV	1,200.00	1,800.00

NETHERLANDS, THE

The Netherlands is a constitutional hereditary monarchy in western Europe on the North Sea between Germany and Belgium. Under Spanish rule in the 16th century, Dutch independence was recognized in 1648 and by the end of the century Holland was one of the world's great naval and colonial powers. A liberal constitution was adopted in 1848. *Language:* Dutch. *Capital:* Amsterdam.

MONETARY SYSTEM

100 cents = 1 gulden

PRECIOUS METAL CONTENT

Dates	Denomination	Gross Wt (g)	Fineness	Net Wt (g)	Troy Oz.
		SILVER			
1848–1945	5 cents	0.6850	0.6400	0.4384	0.0141
	10 cents	1.4000	0.6400	0.8960	0.0288
	25 cents	3.5750	0.6400	2.2880	0.0736
1840–1919	1/2 gulden	5.0000	0.9450	4.7250	0.1519
	1 gulden	10.0000	0.9450	9.4500	0.3038
	2-1/2 gulden	25.0000	0.9450	23.6250	0.7595
1921–45	1/2 gulden	5.0000	0.7200	3.6000	0.1157
	1 gulden	10.0000	0.7200	7.2000	0.2315
	2-1/2 gulden	25.0000	0.7200	18.0000	0.5787
1954–67	1 gulden	6.5000	0.7200	4.6800	0.1504
	2-1/2 gulden	15.0000	0.7200	10.8000	0.3472

Dates	Denomination	Gross Wt (g)	Fineness	Net Wt (g)	Troy Oz.
		GOLD			
1849–1975	1 dukaat	3.4940	0.9830	3.4346	0.1104
	2 dukaat	6.9880	0.9830	6.8692	0.2208
1851–53	5 gulden	3.3645	0.9000	3.0281	0.0974
	10 gulden	6.7290	0.9000	6.0561	0.1947
	20 gulden	13.4580	0.9000	12.1122	0.3894
1875–1933	5 gulden	3.3600	0.9000	3.0240	0.0972
	10 gulden	6.7200	0.9000	6.0480	0.1944

GENERAL COINAGE

Y#	KM#	Metal	Description	VF	EF	Unc
1	90	Cop	1/2 Cent, 1850–77 *1855, VF $500*	30	70	125
2	100	Cop	1 Cent, 1860–77	15	25	55

Note: Y1–2 are identical to coins struck 1817–1847 for Willem I and II.

Obverse: *With KONINGRIJK*

Y#	KM#	Metal	Description	VF	EF	Unc
3	109	Bz	1/2 Cent, 1878–1901	10	15	35
4	107/131	Bz	1 Cent, 1877–1901	6	13	35
5	108	Bz	2-1/2 Cents, 1877–98	15	35	85

Obverse: *With KONINKRIJK*

Y#	KM#	Metal	Description	VF	EF	Unc
4a	130	Bz	1 Cent, 1901	10	35	85

Modified Dies

Y#	KM#	Metal	Description	VF	EF	Unc
3c	133	Bz	1/2 Cent, 1903, 06	6.00	12.50	30
4c	132	Bz	1 Cent, 1902–07	8.50	25.00	60
5c	134	Bz	2-1/2 Cents, 1903–06	12.50	35.00	65

WILLEM III, *1849–1890*

Y#	KM#	Metal	Description	VF	EF	Unc
6	91	Silv	5 Cents, 1850–87 *1853, VF $750*	13	20	50
7	80	Silv	10 Cents, 1849–90 *1849–63, VF $145; 1868, VF $750*	40	75	175
8	81	Silv	25 Cents, 1849–90	225	500	900

Y#	KM#	Metal	Description	VF	EF	Unc
9	92	Silv	1/2 Gulden, 1853–68 *1853, VF $4,500*	50	145	325
10	93	Silv	1 Gulden, 1851–66 *1853, VF $750*	40	125	250
11	82	Silv	2-1/2 Gulden, 1849–74 *1849, VF $225; 1853, VF $500; 1856, 60–61, VF $175; 1863, VF $2,000*	40	90	250

Note: Y9–10 dated 1850 are patterns.

Y#	KM#	Metal	Description	VF	EF	Unc
12	94	Gold	5 Gulden, 1851	4,000	5,500	7,500
13	95	Gold	10 Gulden, 1851	4,000	5,500	7,500
14	96	Gold	20 Gulden, 1851, 53 *1853, Unc $25,000*	7,000	11,500	17,500

Note: Y12–14 dated 1850 are patterns.

Reverse: *Date at top*

Y#	KM#	Metal	Description	VF	EF	Unc
B16	105	Gold	10 Gulden, 1875	BV	BV	350

Reverse: *Date at bottom*

Y#	KM#	Metal	Description	VF	EF	Unc
A16	106	Gold	10 Gulden, 1876–89 *1888, VF $500*	BV	BV	350

TRADE COINS

Y#	KM#	Metal	Description	VF	EF	Unc
15	83	Gold	1 Dukaat, 1849–1975	BV	BV	250
16	97	Gold	2 Dukaat, 1854, 67, *Rare*			

Note: Y15 was struck for foreign trade, and was used extensively in the Netherlands East Indies.

WILHELMINA, *1890–1948*

FIRST COINAGE

Note: Y3-5 were continued into this period.

Obverse: ***Child head***

Y#	KM#	Metal	Description	VF	EF	Unc
20	116	Silv	10 Cents, 1892–97	30	55	125
21	115	Silv	25 Cents, 1892–97	135	275	550

Y#	KM#	Metal	Description	VF	EF	Unc
22	117	Silv	1 Gulden, 1892–97 *1896, VF $850*	50	165	325

Y#	KM#	Metal	Description	VF	EF	Unc
28	118	Gold	10 Gulden, 1892–97 *1892, 95, Rare*	BV	BV	400

SECOND COINAGE

Y#	KM#	Metal	Description	VF	EF	Unc
33	137	C-N	5 Cents, 1907–09	15	30	60

Obverse: ***Young head***

Y#	KM#	Metal	Description	VF	EF	Unc
23	119	Silv	10 Cents, 1898, 1901, small head, divided legend	100	200	375
23a	135	Silv	10 Cents, 1903, large head	30	60	125
23b	136	Silv	10 Cents, 1904–06, small head, continuous legend	35	75	125
24	120	Silv	25 Cents, 1898–1906 *1898, VF $400*	50	80	165

Y#	KM#	Metal	Description	VF	EF	Unc
25	121.1	Silv	1/2 Gulden, 1898, "50C" below arms	60	120	225
25a	121.2	Silv	1/2 Gulden, 1904–09, "50C" omitted	28	65	125
26	122.1	Silv	1 Gulden, 1898, 1901, "100C" below arms	75	130	200
26a	122.2	Silv	1 Gulden, 1904–09, "100C" omitted *1906, VF $600*	50	75	235
27	123	Silv	2-1/2 Gulden, 1898	325	600	1,650

Y#	KM#	Metal	Description	VF	EF	Unc
29	124	Gold	10 Gulden, 1898	450	575	700

THIRD COINAGE

Y#	KM#	Metal	Description	VF	EF	Unc
35	138	Bz	1/2 Cent, 1909–40	5	8	13
36	152	Bz	1 Cent, 1913–41 *1924, VF $45*	3	6	9
37	150	Bz	2-1/2 Cents, 1912–41 *1912, 14, VF $35; 1915, 19 VF $20*	6	10	15

Note: For coins like Y36 dated 1942–60, see listings for colonial use following Y52.

Y#	KM#	Metal	Description	VF	EF	Unc
34	153	C-N	5 Cents, 1913–40, square *1932, 34, 36, VF $18; 1933, VF $40*	7.50	13	22.50

Note: For a similar coin dated 1943, see Y34a in listings for colonial use.

Obverse: ***Adult head***

Y#	KM#	Metal	Description	VF	EF	Unc
39	145	Silv	10 Cents, 1910–25 *1911, 13, 14–16, VF $25; 1921, 25, VF $20*	10	20	40
40	146	Silv	25 Cents, 1910–25	20	40	100
41	147	Silv	1/2 Gulden, 1910–19	35	75	200
42	148	Silv	1 Gulden, 1910–17 *1910–11, VF $215; 1916–17, VF $135*	45	85	195

Y#	KM#	Metal	Description	VF	EF	Unc
31	151	Gold	5 Gulden, 1912	185	225	375
30	149	Gold	10 Gulden, 1911–17	BV	BV	350

FOURTH COINAGE

Obverse: ***Older head***

Y#	KM#	Metal	Description	VF	EF	Unc
43	163	Silv	10 Cents, 1926–45 *1926–27, 34, VF $25; 1930, 34, 43, VF $15; 1944D, Rare; 1945P, VF $1,000*	2.50	4.50	7.50
44	164	Silv	25 Cents, 1926–45 *1926, VF $50; 1945P, VF $300*	4.00	7.00	10.00

Note: Y43–44 dated 1941 or 1943 must have a caduceus or acorn mintmark, respectively. For identical 1941–43 coins with a palm tree mintmark, see listings for colonial use.

Y#	KM#	Metal	Description	VF	EF	Unc
45	160	Silv	1/2 Gulden, 1921–30	6.00	15.00	20
46	161	Silv	1 Gulden, 1922–45 *1924, 38, 43, VF $15; 1945, EF $2,500*	8.00	15.00	20
47	165	Silv	2-1/2 Gulden, 1929–40 *1940, 43, VF $40*	22.50	27.50	60

Note: For 1943 coins like Y46–47, but with a palm tree mintmark, see Y46a–47a under listings for colonial use.

Obverse: ***Similar to Y29***
Reverse: ***Similar to Y30***

Y#	KM#	Metal	Description	VF	EF	Unc
32	162	Gold	10 Gulden, 1925–33	BV	BV	325

WORLD WAR II, GERMAN OCCUPATION

Y#	KM#	Metal	Description	VF	EF	Unc
48	170	Zinc	1 Cent, 1941–44 *1941, 44, VF $12*	1.50	4	9.50

Y#	KM#	Metal	Description	VF	EF	Unc
49	171	Zinc	2-1/2 Cents, 1941–42 *1942, Rare*	15	30	60

Y#	KM#	Metal	Description	VF	EF	Unc
50	172	Zinc	5 Cents, 1941–43, square	5.50	10	40

Y#	KM#	Metal	Description	VF	EF	Unc
51	173	Zinc	10 Cents, 1941–43	5	10	25

Y#	KM#	Metal	Description	VF	EF	Unc
52	174	Zinc	25 Cents, 1941–43 *1943, VF $25*	4.25	15	42.50

Netherlands, Types for Colonial Use Only

Coins dated 1941–1943 (except Y34a) must have a palm-tree mintmark to be colonial. For these dates with a caduceus or acorn mintmark, see Y34–36 above.

For Suriname and Curaçao

Y#	KM#	Metal	Description	VF	EF	Unc
36b	39/10a	Bz	1 Cent, 1942, 57–60	2.50	4	7.50

Obverse: *Crowned shield*
Reverse: *Value and stars*

Y#	KM#	Metal	Description	VF	EF	Unc
36a	10	Br	1 Cent, 1943 (for Suriname only)	6	13	20

Y#	KM#	Metal	Description	VF	EF	Unc
34a	172	CNZ	5 Cents, 1941–43, square	1	4	10

Mintmark: *Palm tree*

Y#	KM#	Metal	Description	VF	EF	Unc
43a	9	Silv	10 Cents, 1941–43	10.00	18	40
44a	38	Silv	25 Cents, 1941–43	6.50	13	30

For Netherlands East Indies

Y#	KM#	Metal	Description	VF	EF	Unc
46a	300	Silv	1 Gulden, 1943	10	15.00	27.50
47a	331	Silv	2-1/2 Gulden, 1943	20	27.50	60.00

Postwar Issues

Y#	KM#	Metal	Description	VF	EF	Unc
53	175	Bz	1 Cent, 1948	1.25	2.50	12.50

Y#	KM#	Metal	Description	VF	EF	Unc
54	176	Bz	5 Cents, 1948	1.25	2.50	17.50

Y#	KM#	Metal	Description	VF	EF	Unc
55	177	Nick	10 Cents, 1948	1.25	2.50	22.50
56	178	Nick	25 Cents, 1948	1.25	2.50	25.00

JULIANA, *1948–1980*

Reverse: *Like Y53–54*

Y#	KM#	Metal	Description	VF	EF	Unc
57	180	Bz	1 Cent, 1950–80	0.25	0.50	2 *Proof: $100*
58	181	Bz	5 Cents, 1950–80	0.25	0.75	2 *Proof: $100*

Reverse: *Like Y55–56*

Y#	KM#	Metal	Description	VF	EF	Unc
59	182	Nick	10 Cents, 1950–80	0.25	1	2.25 *Proof: $125*
60	183	Nick	25 Cents, 1950–80	0.25	1	2.50 *Proof: $150*

Y#	KM#	Metal	Description	VF	EF	Unc
61	184	Silv	1 Gulden, 1954–67	4.75	6.75	9.50 *Proof: $250*
62	185	Silv	2-1/2 Gulden, 1959–66	BV	11.00	17.50 *Proof: $300*

NETHERLANDS ANTILLES, THE

Netherlands Antilles is made up of two groups of islands off the coast of Venezuela in the West Indies; the island of Curacao comprises almost half of the country's area. The nation was formed in 1845, then including the island of Aruba. In 1986 Aruba separated from the Netherlands Antilles. The nation voted in 1994 to preserve its federation with the Netherlands. *Languages:* Dutch, Papiamento, English, Spanish. *Capital:* Willemstad.

MONETARY SYSTEM

100 cents = 1 gulden

PRECIOUS METAL CONTENT

Dates	Denomination	Gross Wt (g)	Fineness	Net Wt (g)	Troy Oz.
		SILVER			
1952–70	1/10 gulden	1.4000	0.6400	0.8960	0.0288
	1/4 gulden	3.5750	0.6400	2.2880	0.0736
	1 gulden	10.0000	0.7200	7.2000	0.2315
	2-1/2 gulden	25.0000	0.7200	18.0000	0.5787

Juliana, *1948–1980*

Y#	KM#	Metal	Description	VF	EF	Unc
1	1	Bz	1 Cent, 1952–68	1.00	2.00	4
2	5	Bz	2-1/2 Cents, 1956–65	1.25	2.25	10

Y#	KM#	Metal	Description	VF	EF	Unc
3	6	C-N	5 Cents, 1957–70, square	1.25	2	5

Y#	KM#	Metal	Description	VF	EF	Unc
4	3	Silv	1/10 Gulden, 1954–70	3.00	5.00	12.50
5	4	Silv	1/4 Gulden, 1954–70	3.50	6.50	15.00

Y#	KM#	Metal	Description	VF	EF	Unc
6	2	Silv	1 Gulden, 1952–70	7	11.00	20
7	7	Silv	2-1/2 Gulden, 1964	BV	17.50	25

NETHERLANDS INDIES, THE

The Netherlands Indies is a group of four large and some 3,000 small islands between southeast Asia and Australia. The home of earlier Buddhist and Hindu cultures, it became Islamic after the 12th century and was taken over by the Dutch in the 17th century. Following Japanese occupation during World War II, it became the independent republic of Indonesia in 1945. *Capital:* Batavia (now Jakarta).

MONETARY SYSTEM

100 cents (sen) = 1 gulden (roepiah)

PRECIOUS METAL CONTENT

Dates	Denomination	Gross Wt (g)	Fineness	Net Wt (g)	Troy Oz.
		SILVER			
1854–1945	1/20 gulden	0.6100	0.7200	0.4392	0.0141
	1/10 gulden	1.2500	0.7200	0.9000	0.0289
	1/4 gulden	3.1800	0.7200	2.2896	0.0736

First Coinage

Y#	KM#	Metal	Description	VF	EF	Unc
1	306	Cop	1/2 Cent, 1856–1909	6	12	25
2	307	Cop	1 Cent, 1855–1912 *1855, VF $75*	10	20	70
3	308	Cop	2-1/2 Cents, 1856–1913	30	50	125

Y#	KM#	Metal	Description	VF	EF	Unc
4	N/A	Silv	1/20 Gulden, 1854–55 *1854, VF $200*	12	20	350.00
5	304	Silv	1/10 Gulden, 1854–1901	5	10	37.50
6	305	Silv	1/4 Gulden, 1854–1901	25	50	125.00

Y#	KM#	Metal	Description	VF	EF	Unc
7	309	Silv	1/10 Gulden, 1903–09	3.75	7.50	20
8	310	Silv	1/4 Gulden, 1903–09	25.00	50.00	125

Trade Coin

For Netherlands gold trade ducats, which were used in the Netherlands Indies, see Netherlands Y15-16.

Second Coinage

Rims: ***Wide on both sides***

Y#	KM#	Metal	Description	VF	EF	Unc
14	311	Silv	1/10 Gulden, 1910–30	3	6	12.50
15	312	Silv	1/4 Gulden, 1910–30	5	10	22.50

Rims: ***Narrow on both sides***

Y#	KM#	Metal	Description	VF	EF	Unc
14a	318	Silv	1/10 Gulden, 1937–45	1.00	1.50	40
15a	319	Silv	1/4 Gulden, 1937–45	1.25	2.00	5

Note: 1 and 2-1/2 Gulden types dated 1943 were made for the Netherlands East Indies (see Netherlands Y46a–47a).

Y#	KM#	Metal	Description	VF	EF	Unc
17	313	C-N	5 Cents, 1913–22	3	5	40

Y#	KM#	Metal	Description	VF	EF	Unc
18	314	Bz	1/2 Cent, 1914–45	1.00	1.50	2.50
19	315	Bz	1 Cent, 1914–29	1.25	2.75	15.00
20	316	Bz	2-1/2 Cents, 1914–45	5.00	10.00	45.00

Y#	KM#	Metal	Description	VF	EF	Unc
21	317	Bz	1 Cent, 1936–45	0.35	0.75	2

World War II, Japanese Occupation

Dated in the Japanese calendar. For later issues, see Indonesia.

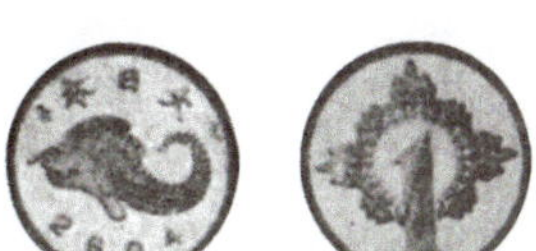

Y#	KM#	Metal	Description	VF	EF	Unc
22	22	Alum	1 Sen, 2603–04 (1943–44)	300	500	900

Y#	KM#	Metal	Description	VF	EF	Unc
23	Pn72	Tin	5 Sen, 2603 (1943)	—	—	22,000

Note: Not issued to circulation.

Y#	KM#	Metal	Description	VF	EF	Unc
24	A24	Tin	10 Sen, 2603–04 (1943–44)	200	300	600

NEW BRUNSWICK

Separated from Nova Scotia in 1784, New Brunswick joined the Canadian federation in 1867. *Capital:* Fredericton.

MONETARY SYSTEM

100 cents = 1 dollar

PRECIOUS METAL CONTENT

Dates	Denomination	Gross Wt (g)	Fineness	Net Wt (g)	Troy Oz.
		SILVER			
1862–64	5 cents	1.1620	0.9250	1.0749	0.0346
	10 cents	2.3240	0.9250	2.1497	0.0691
	20 cents	4.6480	0.9250	4.2994	0.1382

Victoria, *1837–1901*

Y#	KM#	Metal	Description	VF	EF	Unc
1	1	Cop	1/2 Penny, 1843	17.50	75	200
						Proof: $1,500
2	2	Cop	1 Penny, 1843	20.00	80	385
						Proof: $1,650

Y#	KM#	Metal	Description	VF	EF	Unc
3	3	Cop	1/2 Penny, 1854	22.50	57.50	300
						Proof: $750
4	4	Cop	1 Penny, 1854	25.00	75.00	275
						Proof: $650

Y#	KM#	Metal	Description	VF	EF	Unc
5	5	Bz	1/2 Cent, 1861	300.00	350.00	850
						Proof: $2,250
6	6	Bz	1 Cent, 1861, 64	13.50	22.50	165
						Proof: $1,400

Y#	KM#	Metal	Description	VF	EF	Unc
7	7	Silv	5 Cents, 1862, 64	275	625	2,500
8	8	Silv	10 Cents, 1862, 64	275	650	2,500

Y#	KM#	Metal	Description	VF	EF	Unc
9	9	Silv	20 Cents, 1862, 64	125	350	1,750

NEW CALEDONIA

An island halfway between Australia and the Fiji Islands, New Caledonia is one of many French possessions in the South Pacific, having been annexed in 1853. Internal autonomy was granted in 1984, with discussions about independence postponed until 2013. *Languages:* French, Melanesian dialects. *Capital:* Noumea.

MONETARY SYSTEM

100 centimes = 1 franc

Y#	KM#	Metal	Description	VF	EF	Unc
1	1	Alum	50 Centimes, 1949	0.50	1.00	5.00
2	2	Alum	1 Franc, 1949	0.50	1.00	4.00
3	3	Alum	2 Francs, 1949	0.50	1.25	4.50
4	4	Alum	5 Francs, 1952	0.50	1.75	6.00

NEWFOUNDLAND

With its dependency, Labrador, this island was independently administered by the British government. In 1949, by referendum vote, it united with Canada to become the dominion's 10th province. *Capital:* St. John's.

MONETARY SYSTEM

100 cents = 1 dollar

PRECIOUS METAL CONTENT

Dates	Denomination	Gross Wt (g)	Fineness	Net Wt (g)	Troy Oz.
		SILVER			
1865–1912	5 cents	1.1782	0.9250	1.0898	0.0350
	10 cents	2.3564	0.9250	2.1797	0.0701
	20 cents	4.7127	0.9250	4.3592	0.1401
	50 cents	11.7818	0.9250	10.8982	0.3504
1917–44	5 cents	1.1664	0.9250	1.0789	0.0347
	10 cents	2.3328	0.9250	2.1578	0.0694
	25 cents	5.8319	0.9250	5.3945	0.1734
	50 cents	11.6638	0.9250	10.7890	0.3469
1944–45	5 cents	1.1664	0.8000	0.9331	0.0300
	10 cents	2.3328	0.8000	1.8662	0.0600
		GOLD			
1865–88	2 dollars	3.3284	0.9170	3.0510	0.0981

Victoria, *1837–1901*

Y#	KM#	Metal	Description	VF	EF	Unc
1	1	Bz	1 Cent, 1865–96 *1885, 88, VF $150*	12	35	185

Y#	KM#	Metal	Description	VF	EF	Unc
2	2	Silv	5 Cents, 1865–96 *1885, VF $600; 1890, 94, VF $65*	30.00	85	1,450
3	3	Silv	10 Cents, 1865–96 *1865, VF $125; 1870, 85 VF $475; 1873, 76, VF $400; 1880, 88, VF $250*	37.50	150	1,250
4	4	Silv	20 Cents, 1865–1900 *1865, 81, VF $75; 1870, 76, 80, 85, VF $125; 1873, VF $200*	25.00	100	1,250
5	6	Silv	50 Cents, 1870–1900 *1870, 74, 81, VF $145; 1872, 82, 94, VF $95; 1873, 76, 88, VF $220; 1880, VF $325*	50.00	200	1,500

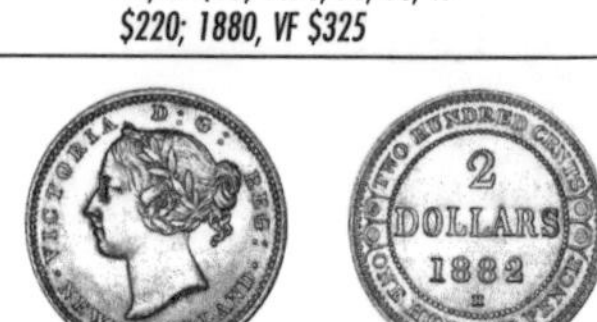

Y#	KM#	Metal	Description	VF	EF	Unc
6	5	Gold	2 Dollars, 1865–88 *1880, VF $1,850*	325	385	600

Edward VII, *1901–1910*

Y#	KM#	Metal	Description	VF	EF	Unc
7	9	Bz	1 Cent, 1904–09 *1904, VF $25; 1907, VF $11*	8.50	22.50	125

Y#	KM#	Metal	Description	VF	EF	Unc
8	7	Silv	5 Cents, 1903–08	22.50	55	225
9	8	Silv	10 Cents, 1903–04	32.50	95	300
10	10	Silv	20 Cents, 1904	45.00	225	2,000
11	11	Silv	50 Cents, 1904–09	16.50	45	300

George V, *1910–1936*

Y#	KM#	Metal	Description	VF	EF	Unc
12	16	Bz	1 Cent, 1913–36	3	5	40

Y#	KM#	Metal	Description	VF	EF	Unc
13	13	Silv	5 Cents, 1912–29 *1917, VF $8; 1919, VF 25*	4.00	16.00	150
14	14	Silv	10 Cents, 1912–19 *1919, VF $ 18.50*	10.00	45.00	275
15	15	Silv	20 Cents, 1912	15.00	65.00	300
16	17	Silv	25 Cents, 1917, 19	10.00	17.50	200
17	12	Silv	50 Cents, 1911–19	12.50	32.50	175

George VI, *1936–1952*

Y#	KM#	Metal	Description	VF	EF	Unc
18	18	Bz	1 Cent, 1938–47 *1944, VF $8.50; 1947, VF $3.25*	1.85	2.50	20

Y#	KM#	Metal	Description	VF	EF	Unc
19	19	Silv	5 Cents, 1938–47 *1946, VF $750; 1947, VF $5*	2.00	3.50	30
20	20	Silv	10 Cents, 1938–47 *1944, VF $ 12.50*	2.75	6.00	50

Note: In 1944, silver fineness was reduced from .925 to .800.

NEW GUINEA

Located on the eastern end of the world's second-largest island, New Guinea is situated north of Australia near the equator. Parts of the region were variously claimed by the Dutch, Germans, French, and British in the 19th century. The League of Nations mandated it to Australia in 1920. After World War II it was united with neighboring Papua as the Australian Territory of Papua New Guinea. Independence came in 1975. *Capital:* Port Moresby.

MONETARY SYSTEM

12 pence = 1 shilling

PRECIOUS METAL CONTENT

Dates	Denomination	Gross Wt (g)	Fineness	Net Wt (g)	Troy Oz.
		SILVER			
1935–45	1 shilling	5.3800	0.9250	4.9765	0.1600

George V, *1910–1936*

Y#	KM#	Metal	Description	VF	EF	Unc
1	1	C-N	1/2 Penny, 1929	150	250	450 *Proof: $450*
2	2	C-N	1 Penny, 1929	150	250	450 *Proof: $550*

Y#	KM#	Metal	Description	VF	EF	Unc
3	3	C-N	3 Pence, 1935	5	10	35
						Proof: $250

Y#	KM#	Metal	Description	VF	EF	Unc
4	4	C-N	6 Pence, 1935	6	9	35
						Proof: $250

Y#	KM#	Metal	Description	VF	EF	Unc
5	5	Silv	1 Shilling, 1935–36	3.50	5	10

Edward VIII, *1936*

Y#	KM#	Metal	Description	VF	EF	Unc
6	6	Bz	1 Penny, 1936	3.50	9	15
						Proof: $375

George VI, *1936–1952*

Y#	KM#	Metal	Description	VF	EF	Unc
7	7	Bz	1 Penny, 1938, 44	4	6	12.50

Y#	KM#	Metal	Description	VF	EF	Unc
8	10	C-N	3 Pence, 1944	3.50	7.50	35
9	9	C-N	6 Pence, 1943	7.00	15.00	45

Y#	KM#	Metal	Description	VF	EF	Unc
10	8	Silv	1 Shilling, 1938, 45	3.50	5	15

NEW ZEALAND

Lying 1,250 miles southeast of Australia, New Zealand comprises two large islands plus many smaller dependencies. Explored by the Dutch in 1642, it was annexed by Britain in 1840. Today New Zealand is a self-governing member of the British Commonwealth. *Languages:* English, Maori. *Capital:* Wellington.

MONETARY SYSTEM

12 pence = 1 shilling
2 shillings = 1 florin
5 shillings = 1 crown
20 shillings = 1 pound

Note: New Zealand converted to a decimal monetary system in 1967.

PRECIOUS METAL CONTENT

Dates	Denomination	Gross Wt (g)	Fineness	Net Wt (g)	Troy Oz.
		SILVER			
1933–49	3 pence	1.1438	0.5000	0.7069	0.0227
	6 pence	2.8276	0.5000	1.4138	0.0455
	1 shilling	5.6552	0.5000	2.8276	0.0909
	1 florin	11.3104	0.5000	5.6552	0.1818
	1/2 crown	14.1380	0.5000	7.0690	0.2273
	1 crown	28.2759	0.5000	14.1380	0.4545

George V, *1910–1936*

Y#	KM#	Metal	Description	VF	EF	Unc
1	1	Silv	3 Pence, 1933–36	5.50	18	45
			1935, VF $95			*Proof: $600*

Y#	KM#	Metal	Description	VF	EF	Unc
2	2	Silv	6 Pence, 1933–36	9.75	45	135
						Proof: $650

Y#	KM#	Metal	Description	VF	EF	Unc
3	3	Silv	1 Shilling, 1933–35	12.50	45	300
					Proof: $700	

Y#	KM#	Metal	Description	VF	EF	Unc
4	4	Silv	1 Florin, 1933–36	17.50	55	375
			1935, VF $30		*Proof: $725*	

Y#	KM#	Metal	Description	VF	EF	Unc
5	5	Silv	1/2 Crown, 1933–35	20	75	465
					Proof: $750	

25th Year of Reign and Waitangi Treaty Commemorative

Y#	KM#	Metal	Description	VF	EF	Unc
6	6	Silv	1 Crown, 1935	2,000	3,300	5,000
					Proof: $5,500	

Y#	KM#	Metal	Description	VF	EF	Unc
1–6	1–6		*1935 Proof Set: $8,000*			

GEORGE VI, *1936–1952*

Y#	KM#	Metal	Description	VF	EF	Unc
7	12	Bz	1/2 Penny, 1940–47	2	8.50	37.50
					Proof: $650	

Y#	KM#	Metal	Description	VF	EF	Unc
8	13	Bz	1 Penny, 1940–47	2.25	15	55
					Proof: $850	

Reverse: ***Designs like Y1–5***

Y#	KM#	Metal	Description	VF	EF	Unc
9	7	Silv	3 Pence, 1937–46	3.75	12.50	35
			1941, VF $35		*Proof: $800*	
10	8	Silv	6 Pence, 1937–46	9.50	32.50	100
			1941–42, VF $55		*Proof: $800*	
11	9	Silv	1 Shilling, 1937–46	12.00	40.00	110
			1941–42, VF $60		*Proof: $1,500*	
12	10	Silv	1 Florin, 1937–46	17.50	55.00	185
			1940,46, VF $60		*Proof: $1,500*	
13	11	Silv	1/2 Crown, 1937–46	18.50	60.00	265
			1944, VF $75		*Proof: $2,000*	

Obverse and Reverse: ***Designs like Y9–13***

Y#	KM#	Metal	Description	VF	EF	Unc
9a	7a	C-N	3 Pence, 1947	2.75	11.50	37.50
					Proof: $900	
10a	8a	C-N	6 Pence, 1947	9.50	30.00	150.00
					Proof: $950	
11a	9a	C-N	1 Shilling, 1947	13.50	50.00	285.00
					Proof: $1,000	
12a	10a	C-N	1 Florin, 1947	13.50	50.00	285.00
					Proof: $1,150	
13a	11a	C-N	1/2 Crown, 1947	10.00	50.00	300.00
					Proof: $1,250	

Centennial of British Settlement

Y#	KM#	Metal	Description	VF	EF	Unc
14	14	Silv	1/2 Crown, 1940	15	32.50	60
						Proof: $5,000

New Legend: ***KING GEORGE THE SIXTH***

Designs: ***Similar to Y7–13***

Y#	KM#	Metal	Description	VF	EF	Unc
20	20	Bz	1/2 Penny, 1949–52	1.00	4.75	10
						Proof: $300
21	21	Bz	1 Penny, 1949–52	0.75	1.50	10
						Proof: $300

Y#	KM#	Metal	Description	VF	EF	Unc
22	15	C-N	3 Pence, 1948–52 *1950, VF $17.50*	1.50	5.50	17.50
						Proof: $700
23	16	C-N	6 Pence, 1948–52 *1948,52, VF $13; 1950, VF $25*	1.50	4.25	8.00
						Proof: $750
24	17	C-N	1 Shilling, 1948–52	12.00	40.00	175.00
						Proof: $950
25	18	C-N	1 Florin, 1948–51 *1948–49, VF $13.50*	4.00	15.00	50.00
						Proof: $1,250
26	19	C-N	1/2 Crown, 1948–51 *1948–49, VF $10*	4.50	20.00	55.00
						Proof: $1,350

Proposed Royal Visit

Y#	KM#	Metal	Description	VF	EF	Unc
27	22	Silv	1 Crown, 1949	15	25	50
						Proof: $13,000

ELIZABETH II, *1952–2022*

Reverse: ***Designs like Y7–13***

Y#	KM#	Metal	Description	VF	EF	Unc
28	23	Bz	1/2 Penny, 1953–65	0.15	0.25	0.45
						Proof: $375
29	24	Bz	1 Penny, 1953–65	0.15	0.30	0.75
						Proof: $375

Y#	KM#	Metal	Description	VF	EF	Unc
30	25	C-N	3 Pence, 1953–65	0.75	1.00	1.75
						Proof: $750
31	26	C-N	6 Pence, 1953–65 *1953–56, VF $3.50*	0.75	1.00	7.00
						Proof: $750
32	27	C-N	1 Shilling, 1953–65 *1953, VF $3; 1955, VF $20*	1.00	1.50	3.00
						Proof: $800
33	28	C-N	1 Florin, 1953, 61–65	1.25	1.75	2.50
						Proof: $950
34	29	C-N	1/2 Crown, 1953, 61–65 *1953,61, VF $8*	2.00	4.50	9.00
						Proof: $1,600

Coronation of Queen Elizabeth II

Y#	KM#	Metal	Description	VF	EF	Unc
35	30	C-N	1 Crown, 1953	7.50	10	13

NICARAGUA

Located in the middle of Central America, Nicaragua is the largest nation in the region. Settled by Spain in 1522, the nation won independence in 1838. During much of the first half of the 20th century, conservative governments were propped up by U.S. Marine Corps occupation forces. A series of Somoza family dictatorships ruled from 1936–1979, when leftist Sandinista guerrillas took power. U.S.-backed contras maintained an armed rebellion through most of the 1980s, and then won control in free elections held in 1990. Power has alternated between liberals and conservatives since then. *Languages:* Spanish, English. *Capital:* Managua.

MONETARY SYSTEM

100 centavos = 1 peso, to 1912
100 centavos = 1 cordoba, since 1912

PRECIOUS METAL CONTENT

Dates	Denomination	Gross Wt (g)	Fineness	Net Wt (g)	Troy Oz.
		SILVER			
1880–1936	5 centavos	1.2500	0.8000	1.0000	0.0322
	10 centavos	2.5000	0.8000	2.0000	0.0643
	20 centavos	5.0000	0.8000	4.0000	0.1286
	25 centavos	6.2500	0.8000	5.0000	0.1608
	50 centavos	12.5000	0.8000	10.0000	0.3215
	1 cordoba	25.0000	0.9000	22.5000	0.7234

Y#	KM#	Metal	Description	VF	EF	Unc
1	1	C-N	1 Centavo, 1878	8	20	90

Y#	KM#	Metal	Description	VF	EF	Unc
2	8	C-N	5 Centavos, 1898 (ESTADO)	5	15	40

Y#	KM#	Metal	Description	VF	EF	Unc
3	9	C-N	5 Centavos, 1899 (REPCA)	5	15	40

Y#	KM#	Metal	Description	VF	EF	Unc
4	2	Silv	5 Centavos, 1880	10	30	150
5	3	Silv	10 Centavos, 1880	10	30	175
6	4	Silv	20 Centavos, 1880	15	35	200

Y#	KM#	Metal	Description	VF	EF	Unc
7	5	Silv	5 Centavos, 1887	8.00	25	60
8	6	Silv	10 Centavos, 1887	10.00	20	75
9	7	Silv	20 Centavos, 1887	12.50	25	115

Y#	KM#	Metal	Description	VF	EF	Unc
10	10	Bz	1/2 Centavo, 1912–37	4.00	25.00	90
			1936–37	1.00	5.00	25
11	11	Bz	1 Centavo, 1912–40	4.00	25.00	100
			1936–40	1.50	7.50	15

Y#	KM#	Metal	Description	VF	EF	Unc
12	12	C-N	5 Centavos, 1912–40	7.50	25	100
			1936–40	3.00	9	25

Y#	KM#	Metal	Description	VF	EF	Unc
13	13	Silv	10 Centavos, 1912–36	4	20	75
14	14	Silv	25 Centavos, 1912–36 *1929–30, EF $70*	10	35	100
15	15	Silv	50 Centavos, 1912, 29	25	85	250
16	16	Silv	1 Cordoba, 1912	70	125	2,000

Edge: ***Lettered "BNN"***

Y#	KM#	Metal	Description	VF	EF	Unc
17	24.1	C-N	5 Centavos, 1946–56 *1946, 52, Unc $15*	0.25	0.50	3
18	17.1	C-N	10 Centavos, 1939–56 *1956, Unc $4.50*	0.50	2.00	15
19	18.1	C-N	25 Centavos, 1939–56 *1939, 46, 52, Unc $15*	0.30	1.00	5
20	19.1	C-N	50 Centavos, 1939–56 *1939, 46, 50, EF $7.5*	1.00	3.00	10

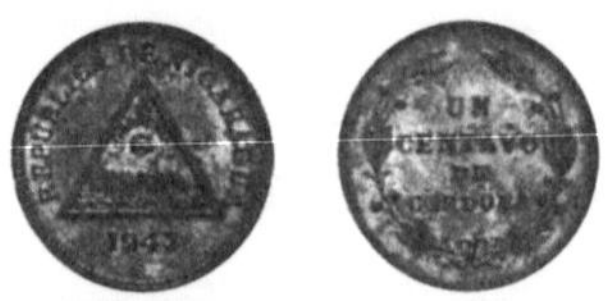

Y#	KM#	Metal	Description	VF	EF	Unc
21	20	Br	1 Centavo, 1943	1	3	20

Designs: ***Similar to Y17–19***
Edge: ***Reeded***

Y#	KM#	Metal	Description	VF	EF	Unc
22	21	Br	5 Centavos, 1943 (21 mm)	3	6	17.50
23	22	Br	10 Centavos, 1943 (24 mm)	4	8	30.00
24	23	Br	25 Centavos, 1943 (27 mm)	4	8	30.00

Banco Central Issues

Edge: ***Lettered "BCN"***

Y#	KM#	Metal	Description	VF	EF	Unc
17a	24.2	C-N	5 Centavos, 1962–65	0.35	0.75	1.50
18a	17.2	C-N	10 Centavos, 1962–65	0.30	0.65	1.25
19a	18.2	C-N	25 Centavos, 1964–65	0.50	1.00	4.00
20a	19.2	C-N	50 Centavos, 1965	1.00	3.00	10.00

NIGERIA

On the Gulf of Guinea, Nigeria came under British control in the late 1800s and was made a colony in 1914. Full independence within the Commonwealth came in 1960, and a republic was proclaimed in 1963. Since then the country has been ruled by military dictatorships and wracked by almost continuous civil war. *Languages:* English, native tongues. *Capital:* Lagos (now Abuja).

MONETARY SYSTEM
12 pence = 1 shilling
20 shillings = 1 pound

Elizabeth II, *1952–1963*

Y#	KM#	Metal	Description	VF	EF	Unc
1	1	Bz	1/2 Penny, 1959	0.25	0.50	1.50
2	2	Bz	1 Penny, 1959	0.25	0.50	1.50

Y#	KM#	Metal	Description	VF	EF	Unc
3	3	N-Br	3 Pence, 1959	0.50	1	3

Reverse: ***Coco beans, date and value below***

Y#	KM#	Metal	Description	VF	EF	Unc
4	4	C-N	6 Pence, 1959, round	0.50	1	4

Y#	KM#	Metal	Description	VF	EF	Unc
5	5	C-N	1 Shilling, 1959–62	0.75	1.50	4.50

Edge: ***Safety edge or reeded***

Y#	KM#	Metal	Description	VF	EF	Unc
6	6	C-N	2 Shillings, 1959	1.50	3	7

Y#	KM#	Metal	Description	VF	EF	Unc
1–6	1–6		*1959 Proof Set: $45*			

NIGERIA– BRITISH WEST AFRICA

This was an administrative grouping of four separate British colonies on the west coast of Africa: The Gambia, Sierra Leone, Gold Coast (now Ghana), and Nigeria. They gained independence between 1957 and 1965.

MONETARY SYSTEM
12 pence = 1 shilling

PRECIOUS METAL CONTENT

Dates	Denomination	Gross Wt (g)	Fineness	Net Wt (g)	Troy Oz.
		SILVER			
1913–20	3 pence	1.4138	0.9250	1.3078	0.0419
	6 pence	2.8276	0.9250	2.6155	0.0838
	1 shilling	5.6552	0.9250	5.2311	0.1689
	2 shillings	11.3104	0.9250	10.4621	0.3364

EDWARD VII, *1901–1910*

Legend: ***NIGERIA – BRITISH WEST AFRICA***

Y#	KM#	Metal	Description	VF	EF	Unc
3	1	Alum	1/10 Penny, 1907–08	3.00	6.00	20.00

Y#	KM#	Metal	Description	VF	EF	Unc
1	3	C-N	1/10 Penny, 1908–10	0.50	1.00	5.50
2	2	C-N	1 Penny, 1907–10	4.00	8.00	25.00

GEORGE V, *1910–1936*

Y#	KM#	Metal	Description	VF	EF	Unc
4	4	C-N	1/10 Penny, 1911	4.50	9.50	25.00
5	5	C-N	1/2 Penny, 1911	10.00	22.50	50.00
6	6	C-N	1 Penny, 1911	30.00	50.00	200.00

NORTH KOREA

SEE KOREA, NORTH

NORTH VIETNAM

SEE VIETNAM, NORTH

NORWAY

Norway lies on the western section of the Scandinavian peninsula in northern Europe and was ruled by the Danes until 1814, when it was united with Sweden. It was separated in 1905, and the Danish prince accepted the throne to begin an hereditary constitutional monarchy. Legislative power has ebbed and flowed between liberal and conservative parties since World War II. *Language:* Norwegian. *Capital:* Oslo.

MONETARY SYSTEM
120 skilling = 1 speciedaler, to 1873
100 ore = 1 krone, since 1873

PRECIOUS METAL CONTENT
Norway was a member of the Scandinavian Monetary Union; see appendix A.

Dates	Denomination	Gross Wt (g)	Fineness	Net Wt (g)	Troy Oz.
		SILVER			
1845–73	12 skilling	2.8900	0.8750	2.5288	0.8130
	24 skilling	5.7800	0.8750	5.0575	0.1626
	1/2 speciedaler	14.4500	0.8750	12.6438	0.4065
	1 speciedaler	28.9000	0.8750	25.2875	0.8127
1874–75	10 ore / 3 skilling	1.5000	0.4000	0.6000	0.0193
	50 ore / 15 skilling	5.0000	0.6000	3.0000	0.0964
	1 krone / 30 skilling	7.5000	0.8000	6.0000	0.1929
1875–1904	10 ore	1.5000	0.4000	0.6000	0.0193
	25 ore	2.4100	0.6000	1.4460	0.0463
	50 ore	5.0000	0.6000	3.0000	0.0964
	1 krone	7.5000	0.8000	6.0000	0.1929
	2 kroner	15.0000	0.8000	12.0000	0.3858
1908–1919	10 ore	1.4500	0.4000	0.5800	0.0185
	25 ore	2.4200	0.6000	1.4520	0.0463
	50 ore	5.0000	0.6000	3.0000	0.0964
	1 krone	7.5000	0.8000	6.0000	0.1929
	2 kroner	15.0000	0.8000	12.0000	0.3852
1964	10 kroner	20.0000	0.9000	18.0000	0.5707
		GOLD			
1874–1910	10 kroner	4.4803	0.9000	4.0323	0.1296
	20 kroner	8.9606	0.9000	8.0645	0.2593

UNION WITH SWEDEN

CARL XV, *1859–1872*

Y#	KM#	Metal	Description	VF	EF	Unc
1	324	Cop	1/2 Skilling, 1863	75	100	650

Y#	KM#	Metal	Description	VF	EF	Unc
2	329	Cop	1/2 Skilling, 1867	22.50	45	200
3	335	Cop	1 Skilling, 1870	50.00	100	400

Y#	KM#	Metal	Description	VF	EF	Unc
4	336	Bill	2 Skilling, 1870–71	22.50	45	125
5	330	Bill	3 Skilling, 1868–69	40.00	75	200
6	337	Bill	4 Skilling, 1871	40.00	80	225

Y#	KM#	Metal	Description	VF	EF	Unc
7	320	Silv	12 Skilling, 1861–62	1,000	2,500	9,500
8	321	Silv	24 Skilling, 1861–62 *1861, Unc $85,000*	4,000	6,500	11,500
9	322	Silv	1/2 Speciedaler, 1861–62 *1861, Rare*	1,200	1,800	3,200
10	323	Silv	1 Speciedaler, 1861–62	1,750	3,000	6,000

Obverse: ***Larger head***

Y#	KM#	Metal	Description	VF	EF	Unc
7a	326	Silv	12 Skilling, 1865	150	250	1,800
8a	327	Silv	24 Skilling, 1865	275	500	2,000
9a	328	Silv	1/2 Speciedaler, 1865	35,000	50,000	—
10a	325	Silv	1 Speciedaler, 1864–69 *1867, VF–EF $10,000*	1,500	2,750	5,000

Oscar II, *1872–1905*

First Coinage

Y#	KM#	Metal	Description	VF	EF	Unc
11	338	Bill	3 Skilling, 1872–73	35	75	165

Y#	KM#	Metal	Description	VF	EF	Unc
12	339	Silv	12 Skilling, 1873	90	180	800
13	340	Silv	1/2 Speciedaler, 1873	13,500	20,000	32,000

Second Coinage (Transition to Decimal System)

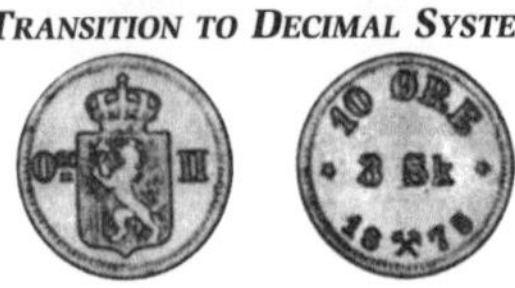

Y#	KM#	Metal	Description	VF	EF	Unc
14	345	Silv	10 Ore / 3 Skilling, 1874–75	75	150	550

Y#	KM#	Metal	Description	VF	EF	Unc
15	346	Silv	50 Ore / 15 Skilling, 1874–75	500	1,300	3,250
16	351	Silv	1 Krone / 30 Skilling, 1875	550	1,350	3,300

Obverse: ***Head facing right***

Y#	KM#	Metal	Description	VF	EF	Unc
17	347	Gold	10 Kroner / 2-1/2 Speciedaler, 1874	1,800	2,500	3,500
18	348	Gold	20 Kroner / 5 Speciedaler, 1874–75	575	700	1,500

Third Coinage (Decimal System)

Y#	KM#	Metal	Description	VF	EF	Unc
19	352	Bz	1 Ore, 1876–1902 *1885, VF $250*	13	35	115
20	353	Bz	2 Ore, 1876–1902	14	40	225
21	349	Bz	5 Ore, 1875–1902 *1875, VF $100; 1878, VF $60*	15	85	450

Y#	KM#	Metal	Description	VF	EF	Unc
22	350	Silv	10 Ore, 1875–1903 *1875, 77–78, VF $200; 1880, 88, VF $95*	35	60	95
23	354	Silv	25 Ore, 1876	60	125	425

Y#	KM#	Metal	Description	VF	EF	Unc
24	360	Silv	25 Ore, 1896–1904 *1896, 98, VF $100*	55	110	225

Y#	KM#	Metal	Description	VF	EF	Unc
25	356	Silv	50 Ore, 1877–1904 *1880, VF $425; 1885, VF $600; 1904, VF $240*	55	235	700
26	357	Silv	1 Krone, 1877–1904 *1878, VF $4,000; 1879, 81, VF $600; 1888, VF $550*	120	250	2,000
27	359	Silv	2 Kroner, 1878–1904 *1885, 87, VF $2,000; 1888, VF $2,500; 1897–98, VF $400*	240	425	1,700

Note: In 1987, gold, silver, and bronze restrikes of Y27, dated 1887, were made.

Y#	KM#	Metal	Description	VF	EF	Unc
28	358	Gold	10 Kroner, 1877, 1902	2,000	2,500	5,000
29	355	Gold	20 Kroner, 1876–1902 *1883, EF $26,500*	450	500	800

INDEPENDENT NORWAY

HAAKON VII, *1905–1957*

FIRST COINAGE

Y#	KM#	Metal	Description	VF	EF	Unc
30	361	Bz	1 Ore, 1906–07	10.00	30	65
31	362	Bz	2 Ore, 1906–07 *1906, VF $35*	12.00	55	325
32	364	Bz	5 Ore, 1907	27.50	125	400

Independence Commemorative

Y#	KM#	Metal	Description	VF	EF	Unc
33	363	Silv	2 Kroner, 1906	60	100	250
33a	365	Silv	2 Kroner, 1907, smaller shield	100	225	350

"Watch on the Border" Commemorative

Y#	KM#	Metal	Description	VF	EF	Unc
34	366	Silv	2 Kroner, 1907	300	750	1,500

SECOND COINAGE

Y#	KM#	Metal	Description	VF	EF	Unc
35	367	Bz	1 Ore, 1908–52 *1908, 15, 21, 23, VF $65; 1912, 27, VF $25; 1913–14, 22, 25–26, 31, VF $7; 1928–29, 30, 32–34, VF $3.50*	0.50	2.50	10.00
36	371	Bz	2 Ore, 1909–52 *1909–12, 15, 19–20, VF $45; 1913–14, 23, 33–34, VF $9; 1921–22, 29, 48, VF $6; 1928, 31, 35–36, 46–47, VF $3.25*	1.00	4.50	14.50
37	368	Bz	5 Ore, 1908–52 *1908–12, 15, 17, VF $65; 1913–14, 22, 30, 32, 35, VF $15; 1916, VF $5; 1921, 33, VF $27.50; 1928–29, 36, 52, VF $7*	2.00	8.00	50.00

Y#	KM#	Metal	Description	VF	EF	Unc
38	372	Silv	10 Ore, 1909–19 *1911, 14, VF $35; 1909, 12–13, 16, VF $17.50; 1915, 18, VF $9.50*	5.50	12	40

Y#	KM#	Metal	Description	VF	EF	Unc
39	373	Silv	25 Ore, 1909–19 *1912, VF $250; 1909, VF $40; 1911, 13–14, 16–17, VF $65*	15	35	190

Y#	KM#	Metal	Description	VF	EF	Unc
40	374	Silv	50 Ore, 1909–19 *1909, 11, 13, 15, VF $75; 1912, VF $125; 1915, VF $25*	12	25	225

Y#	KM#	Metal	Description	VF	EF	Unc
41	369	Silv	1 Krone, 1908–17 *1908, 12–13, VF $95; 1910, VF $200*	45	85	225
42	370	Silv	2 Kroner, 1908–17 *1910, 12, 16, EF $150*	65	95	325

Y#	KM#	Metal	Description	VF	EF	Unc
43	375	Gold	10 Kroner, 1910	600	800	1,500
44	376	Gold	20 Kroner, 1910	550	775	1,300

Constitutional Commemorative

Y#	KM#	Metal	Description	VF	EF	Unc
45	377	Silv	2 Kroner, 1914	35	50	175

World War I Issues

Y#	KM#	Metal	Description	VF	EF	Unc
35a	367a	Iron	1 Ore, 1918–21 *1918, 20, VF $45; 1921, VF $100*	10	20	115
36a	371a	Iron	2 Ore, 1917–20 *1917, VF $275*	40	150	725
37a	368a	Iron	5 Ore, 1917–20 *1918, VF $300*	65	135	400

Third Coinage

Y#	KM#	Metal	Description	VF	EF	Unc
46	378	C-N	10 Ore, 1920–23	35	55	100
47	381	C-N	25 Ore, 1921–23	35	55	100

Y#	KM#	Metal	Description	VF	EF	Unc
48	379	C-N	50 Ore, 1920–23	27.50	55	100

Y#	KM#	Metal	Description	VF	EF	Unc
47a	382	C-N	25 Ore, 1921–23	15.00	65	450
48a	380	C-N	50 Ore, 1920–23 *1920, VF $40*	22.50	175	—

Note: Y47a–48a are Y47–48 reissued with a center hole in 1924.

Fourth Coinage

Y#	KM#	Metal	Description	VF	EF	Unc
49	383	C-N	10 Ore, 1924–51 *1924–26, 38–46, VF $2; 1927, VF $40*	1	4	15

Y#	KM#	Metal	Description	VF	EF	Unc
50	384	C-N	25 Ore, 1924–50 *1924, 27, VF $4.75; 1929, VF $10; 1939, VF $2.50*	1	4	30
51	386	C-N	50 Ore, 1926–49	1	5	15

Y#	KM#	Metal	Description	VF	EF	Unc
52	385	C-N	1 Krone, 1925–51 *1925, 47, VF $8; 1926-27, 37, VF $12; 1936, VF $20*	1.50	15	50

World War II Issues

German Occupation

Y#	KM#	Metal	Description	VF	EF	Unc
53	387	Iron	1 Ore, 1941–45 *1945, VF $20*	1.50	4.50	15
54	394	Iron	2 Ore, 1943–45 *1945, VF $7.50*	2.50	8.00	15
55	388	Iron	5 Ore, 1941–45 *1945, VF $150*	6.00	13.00	50

Y#	KM#	Metal	Description	VF	EF	Unc
56	389	Zinc	10 Ore, 1941–45 *1944, VF $35; 1945, VF $25*	3.50	7	30
57	395	Zinc	25 Ore, 1943–45 *1944, VF $17.50; 1945, VF $40*	5.50	15	50
58	390	Zinc	50 Ore, 1941–45 *1943–44, VF $50; 1945, VF $575*	10.00	30	120

Government in Exile (Struck in London)

Y#	KM#	Metal	Description	VF	EF	Unc
49a	391	N-Br	10 Ore, 1942	150	300	450

Y#	KM#	Metal	Description	VF	EF	Unc
50a	392	N-Br	25 Ore, 1942	175	325	500

Y#	KM#	Metal	Description	VF	EF	Unc
51a	393	N-Br	50 Ore, 1942	200	350	575

Postwar Issues

Y#	KM#	Metal	Description	VF	EF	Unc
59	398	Bz	1 Ore, 1952–57	0.25	1.50	5
60	399	Bz	2 Ore, 1952–57	0.50	2.50	8
61	400	Bz	5 Ore, 1952–57	0.65	3.75	25

Y#	KM#	Metal	Description	VF	EF	Unc
62	396	C-N	10 Ore, 1951–57	0.75	5.00	35
63	401	C-N	25 Ore, 1952–57	0.75	5.50	55

Y#	KM#	Metal	Description	VF	EF	Unc
64	402	C-N	50 Ore, 1953–57 *1954, VF $55*	0.85	8.00	85
65	397	C-N	1 Krone, 1951–57	0.75	7.50	80

OLAV V, *1957–1991*

Y#	KM#	Metal	Description	VF	EF	Unc
66	403	Bz	1 Ore, 1958–72 *1958, 68, VF $1.50*	0.25	0.50	1

Y#	KM#	Metal	Description	VF	EF	Unc
67	404	Bz	2 Ore, 1958	1.50	4.00	25.00
67a	410	Bz	2 Ore, 1959–72, larger letters	0.25	0.50	2.75

Y#	KM#	Metal	Description	VF	EF	Unc
68	405	Bz	5 Ore, 1958–73 *1958, VF $3.25; 1959–61, VF $1*	0.25	0.65	2.50

Y#	KM#	Metal	Description	VF	EF	Unc
69	406	C-N	10 Ore, 1958	3.25	8.00	50.00
69a	411	C-N	10 Ore, 1959–73, larger letters *1959, VF $1.50*	0.35	0.85	2.50

Y#	KM#	Metal	Description	VF	EF	Unc
70	407	C-N	25 Ore, 1958–73 *1958–59, VF $2.25*	0.20	0.50	2.50

Y#	KM#	Metal	Description	VF	EF	Unc
71	408	C-N	50 Ore, 1958–73 *1958, 70, VF $1.50; 1959, VF $7.50*	0.20	0.85	5
72	409	C-N	1 Krone, 1958–73 *1958, VF $17.50*	0.50	1.50	15

Y#	KM#	Metal	Description	VF	EF	Unc
73	412	C-N	5 Kroner, 1963–73 *1970–71, VF $9.50*	2	3	10

Constitution Sesquicentennial

Y#	KM#	Metal	Description	VF	EF	Unc
74	413	Silv	10 Kroner, 1964	16	25	32.50

NOVA SCOTIA

First settled by the French in 1604, control of Nova Scotia passed to England in 1621 with possession being contested by both nations until the Treaty of Utrecht ceded it to Britain in 1713. It joined the dominion in 1867. *Capital:* Halifax.

MONETARY SYSTEM
100 cents = 1 dollar

VICTORIA, *1837–1901*

Y#	KM#	Metal	Description	VF	EF	Unc
3	3	Cop	1/2 Penny, 1840, 43	27.50	80	475
4	4	Cop	1 Penny, 1840, 43	30.00	65	475

Y#	KM#	Metal	Description	VF	EF	Unc
5	5	Cop	1/2 Penny, 1856	2.00	8	60
6	6	Cop	1 Penny, 1856	17.50	45	275

Y#	KM#	Metal	Description	VF	EF	Unc
7	7	Bz	1/2 Cent, 1861, 64	10.00	20.00	100
8	8	Bz	1 Cent, 1861–64 *1862, VF $115*	8.00	17.50	125

PAKISTAN

When India gained its independence in 1947, the two predominantly Muslim regions were separated to form the dominion of Pakistan. It became a republic within the British Commonwealth in 1956, with military rule the norm until the mid-1980s when a measure of representative government was restored. The nation's eastern section broke away in 1971 to form Bangladesh, whereupon West Pakistan left the Commonwealth. *Languages:* Urdu, Bengali. *Capital:* Islamabad.

MONETARY SYSTEM
3 pies = 1 pice
4 pice = 1 anna
16 annas = 1 rupee

Y#	KM#	Metal	Description	VF	EF	Unc
1	1	Bz	1 Pice, 1948–52	0.30	0.50	1.50

Y#	KM#	Metal	Description	VF	EF	Unc
2	2	C-N	1/2 Anna, 1948–51, square	1	2	4

Reverse: ***Crescent to right***

Y#	KM#	Metal	Description	VF	EF	Unc
3	3	C-N	1 Anna, 1948–52, scalloped	0.30	0.50	2.00
4	4	C-N	2 Annas, 1948–51, square	0.30	0.50	2.50

Reverse: ***Crescent to left***

Y#	KM#	Metal	Description	VF	EF	Unc
3a	8	C-N	1 Anna, 1950, scalloped	4.00	6	10
4a	9	C-N	2 Annas, 1950, square	4.50	9	18

Reverse: ***Crescent to right***

Y#	KM#	Metal	Description	VF	EF	Unc
5	5	Nick	1/4 Rupee, 1948–49, 51	0.50	0.50	1.00
6	6	Nick	1/2 Rupee, 1948–49, 51	0.75	0.75	1.50
7	7	Nick	1 Rupee, 1948–49	1.25	2.25	5.00

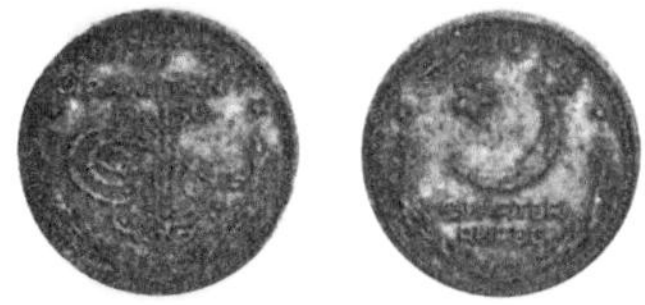

Reverse: ***Crescent to left***

Y#	KM#	Metal	Description	VF	EF	Unc
5a	10	Nick	1/4 Rupee, 1950	6	1.25	25

Y#	KM#	Metal	Description	VF	EF	Unc
8	11	Bz	1 Pie, 1951–56	0.50	0.85	3.50

Y#	KM#	Metal	Description	VF	EF	Unc
9	12	N-Br	1 Pice, 1953–59	0.50	0.85	1.50

Y#	KM#	Metal	Description	VF	EF	Unc
10	13	N-Br	1/2 Anna, 1953–58	0.50	0.80	1.50

Y#	KM#	Metal	Description	VF	EF	Unc
11	14	C-N	1 Anna, 1953–58	0.50	0.80	1.50

Y#	KM#	Metal	Description	VF	EF	Unc
12	15	C-N	2 Annas, 1953–59	0.50	0.80	1.50

Reverse: ***Oat sprigs at sides***

Y#	KM#	Metal	Description	VF	EF	Unc
13	16	Bz	1 Pice, 1961, round	0.30	0.75	1.30

Y#	KM#	Metal	Description	VF	EF	Unc
13a	17	Bz	1 Paisa, 1961–63	0.25	0.40	0.75

Y#	KM#	Metal	Description	VF	EF	Unc
14	18	N-Br	5 Pice, 1961	0.25	0.40	1.00
14a	19	N-Br	5 Paisa, 1961–63	0.40	0.80	1.50

Y#	KM#	Metal	Description	VF	EF	Unc
15	20	C-N	10 Pice, 1961	0.40	0.80	1.25
15a	21	C-N	10 Paisa, 1961–63	0.40	0.80	1.25

Obverse: ***English legend omitted***
Reverse: ***Oat sprigs at sides***

Y#	KM#	Metal	Description	VF	EF	Unc
18	24	Bz	1 Paisa, 1964–65, round	0.25	0.50	1.25

Reverse: ***Value within wreath***

Y#	KM#	Metal	Description	VF	EF	Unc
19	25	Bz	2 Paisa, 1964–66, scalloped	0.25	0.50	1.25

Y#	KM#	Metal	Description	VF	EF	Unc
20	26	N-Br	5 Paisa, 1964–74	0.50	0.80	1.25

Y#	KM#	Metal	Description	VF	EF	Unc
21	27	C-N	10 Paisa, 1964–68	0.35	0.80	1.25

Y#	KM#	Metal	Description	VF	EF	Unc
16	22	Nick	25 Paisa, 1963–67	0.30	0.50	1.25
17	23	Nick	50 Paisa, 1963–69	0.30	0.50	1.25

PALESTINE

From the earliest times Palestine has been the bridge between Asia and Africa. The Turks lost it in 1917 during World War I, and in 1920 the League of Nations placed it under British administration. In 1948 the United Nations divided the country along religious lines with 80 percent becoming the new state of Israel and the remainder split between Jordan and Egypt. *Capital:* Jerusalem.

MONETARY SYSTEM

1,000 mils = 1 pound

PRECIOUS METAL CONTENT

Dates	Denomination	Gross Wt (g)	Fineness	Net Wt (g)	Troy Oz.
		SILVER			
1927–42	50 mils	5.8319	0.7200	4.1990	0.1350
	100 mils	11.6638	0.7200	8.3979	0.2700

Y#	KM#	Metal	Description	VF	EF	Unc
1	1	Bz	1 Mil, 1927–47	1.50	4	15
			1947, Rare			
2	2	Bz	2 Mils, 1927–47	2.00	6	20
			1947, Rare			

Y#	KM#	Metal	Description	VF	EF	Unc
3	3	C-N	5 Mils, 1927–47	1.50	6.00	25
			1947, Rare			
4	4	C-N	10 Mils, 1927–47	4.00	10.00	45
			1947, Rare			
5	5	C-N	20 Mils, 1927–47	8.00	25.00	100
			1934, 41, VF $75			
3a	3a	Bz	5 Mils, 1942–44	1.50	6.50	40
4a	4a	Bz	10 Mils, 1942–43	5.00	15.00	50
5a	5a	Bz	20 Mils, 1942–44	8.00	60.00	160

Y#	KM#	Metal	Description	VF	EF	Unc
6	6	Silv	50 Mils, 1927–42	6	12	40

Y#	KM#	Metal	Description	VF	EF	Unc
7	7	Silv	100 Mils, 1927–42	13	25	110
			1931, 34, VF $125			

PANAMA

The Isthmus of Panama joins Central and South America. It is bisected by the Panama Canal. Panama joined Colombia in seceding from Spain in 1821. It became an independent nation in 1903, often ruled by military dictatorships. *Languages:* English, Spanish. *Capital:* Panama City.

MONETARY SYSTEM

100 centesimos = 1 balboa

PRECIOUS METAL CONTENT

Dates	Denomination	Gross Wt (g)	Fineness	Net Wt (g)	Troy Oz.
		SILVER			
1904–16	2-1/2 centesimos	1.2500	0.9000	1.1250	0.0362
	5 centesimos	2.5000	0.9000	2.2500	0.0723
	10 centesimos	5.0000	0.9000	4.5000	0.1447
	25 centesimos	12.5000	0.9000	11.2500	0.3617
	50 centesimos	25.0000	0.9000	22.5000	0.7234
1930–62	1/10 balboa	2.5000	0.9000	2.2500	0.0723
	1/4 balboa	6.2500	0.9000	5.6250	0.1808
	1/2 balboa	12.5000	0.9000	11.2500	0.3617
	1 balboa	26.7300	0.9000	24.0540	0.7735

Y#	KM#	Metal	Description	VF	EF	Unc
1	6	C-N	1/2 Centesimo, 1907	3	6	10

Y#	KM#	Metal	Description	VF	EF	Unc
2	7.1	C-N	2-1/2 Centesimos, 1907, MEDIOS	15.00	25.00	50
2a	7.2	C-N	2-1/2 Centesimos, 1916, MEDIO	12.50	22.50	70

Y#	KM#	Metal	Description	VF	EF	Unc
3	8	C-N	2-1/2 Centesimos, 1929	5	25	125

Y#	KM#	Metal	Description	VF	EF	Unc
4	9	C-N	5 Centesimos, 1929, 32	7.50	25	80

Y#	KM#	Metal	Description	VF	EF	Unc
5	1	Silv	2-1/2 Centesimos, 1904	13.00	18	25
6	2	Silv	5 Centesimos, 1904, 16	6.50	20	50
			1916	75.00	125	250
7	3	Silv	10 Centesimos, 1904	15.00	50	150
8	4	Silv	25 Centesimos, 1904	20.00	60	200
9	5	Silv	50 Centesimos, 1904–05	65.00	150	275

NEW COINAGE

Y#	KM#	Metal	Description	VF	EF	Unc
10	14	Bz	1 Centesimo, 1935, 37	6.50	17.50	37.50

Y#	KM#	Metal	Description	VF	EF	Unc
11	15	Bz	1-1/4 Centesimos, 1940	2	4	20

Y#	KM#	Metal	Description	VF	EF	Unc
12	16	C-N	2-1/2 Centesimos, 1940	3	7	30

Y#	KM#	Metal	Description	VF	EF	Unc
13	10	Silv	1/10 Balboa, 1930–47, 62	12.50	28.50	75
			1947, EF $12.50; 1962, Unc $10			
14	11	Silv	1/4 Balboa, 1930–47, 62	15.00	50.00	200
			1931, Unc $1,000			
15	12	Silv	1/2 Balboa, 1930–47, 62	20.00	60.00	275
			1962, Unc $25			

Note: Because new dies were cut at the London Mint, design details are more distinct on the 1962 issues of Y13–15.

Y#	KM#	Metal	Description	VF	EF	Unc
16	13	Silv	1 Balboa, 1931–47	25	55	125

50th Anniversary of Independence

Y#	KM#	Metal	Description	VF	EF	Unc
17	17	Bz	1 Centesimo, 1953	1	2.50	6.50

Y#	KM#	Metal	Description	VF	EF	Unc
18	18	Silv	1/10 Balboa, 1953	3	5.00	10
19	19	Silv	1/4 Balboa, 1953	5	7.50	30
20	20	Silv	1/2 Balboa, 1953	10	15.00	30
21	21	Silv	1 Balboa, 1953, reverse similar to Y16	25	45.00	60

Y#	KM#	Metal	Description	VF	EF	Unc
22	22	Bz	1 Centesimo, 1961–87	0.25	0.50	2

Note: 1962 and later dates of Y22 show deeper hairlines.

Y#	KM#	Metal	Description	VF	EF	Unc
23	23.1	C-N	5 Centesimos, 1961	1.50	3	15

Y#	KM#	Metal	Description	VF	EF	Unc
23a	23.2	C-N	5 Centesimos, 1962–93, smaller arms and numeral 5	0.25	1	2.50

Y#	KM#	Metal	Description	VF	EF	Unc
24	24	Silv	1/10 Balboa, 1961	2	4	8
25	25	Silv	1/4 Balboa, 1961	5	7	15
26	26	Silv	1/2 Balboa, 1961	10	14	20

PARAGUAY

An inland country of South America, Paraguay was explored and settled by French Jesuits from 1608–1767 when they were expelled by Spain. In 1811 it declared independence from Spain. For much of its history as a republic, Paraguay has been politically unstable, ruled by a succession of military and civilian dictatorships until a new constitution was adopted and free elections held in the early 1990s. *Languages:* Spanish, Guarani. *Capital:* Asuncion.

MONETARY SYSTEM

100 centesimos (centavos) = 1 peso, to 1944
100 centimos = 1 guarani, since 1944

PRECIOUS METAL CONTENT

Dates	Denomination	Gross Wt (g)	Fineness	Net Wt (g)	Troy Oz.
		SILVER			
1889	1 peso	25.0000	0.9000	22.5000	0.7234

Y#	KM#	Metal	Description	VF	EF	Unc
1	1	Cop	1/12 Real, 1845	25	60	200

Y#	KM#	Metal	Description	VF	EF	Unc
2	2	Cop	1 Centesimo, 1870	6.00	25	75
3	3	Cop	2 Centesimos, 1870	8.50	40	90
4	4.1	Cop	4 Centesimos, 1870	12.50	50	125
4a	4.3	Cop	4 Centesimos, 1870, crude local issue with SAEZ	200.00	350	600

Y#	KM#	Metal	Description	VF	EF	Unc
5	5	Silv	1 Peso, 1889	175	250	500

Y#	KM#	Metal	Description	VF	EF	Unc
6	6	C-N	5 Centavos, 1900, 03	8	25	100
7	7	C-N	10 Centavos, 1900, 03	10	35	150
8	8	C-N	20 Centavos, 1900, 03	5	20	90

Y#	KM#	Metal	Description	VF	EF	Unc
9	9	C-N	5 Centavos, 1908	9.00	25.00	60.00
10	10	C-N	10 Centavos, 1908	6.00	20.00	75.00
11	11	C-N	20 Centavos, 1908	7.00	23.00	80.00
12	12	C-N	50 Centavos, 1925	1.50	4.50	13.00
13	13	C-N	1 Peso, 1925	1.00	4.50	12.00
14	14	C-N	2 Pesos, 1925	1.50	5.50	15.00
15	18	C-N	5 Pesos, 1939	2.00	5.00	10.00
16	19	C-N	10 Pesos, 1939	2.00	6.00	17.50

Y#	KM#	Metal	Description	VF	EF	Unc
17	15	Alum	50 Centavos, 1938	1.00	3.00	7.50
18	16	Alum	1 Peso, 1938	1.00	2.50	7.00
19	17	Alum	2 Pesos, 1938	1.25	3.00	9.00

NEW COINAGE

Y#	KM#	Metal	Description	VF	EF	Unc
20	20	A-Bz	1 Centimo, 1944–50	0.25	0.75	3.00

Y#	KM#	Metal	Description	VF	EF	Unc
21	21	A-Bz	5 Centimos, 1944, 47	0.25	0.75	2.50

Y#	KM#	Metal	Description	VF	EF	Unc
22	22	A-Bz	10 Centimos, 1944, 47	0.25	1.00	3.50

Y#	KM#	Metal	Description	VF	EF	Unc
23	23	A-Bz	25 Centimos, 1944–51	0.50	1.75	5.00

Y#	KM#	Metal	Description	VF	EF	Unc
24	24	A-Bz	50 Centimos, 1944, 51	0.50	1.50	6.00

Y#	KM#	Metal	Description	VF	EF	Unc
25	25	A-Bz	10 Centimos, 1953	0.15	0.30	1.00
26	26	A-Bz	15 Centimos, 1953	0.15	0.30	1.00
27	27	A-Bz	25 Centimos, 1953	0.15	0.30	1.00
28	28	A-Bz	50 Centimos, 1953	0.15	0.30	1.00

PERSIA
SEE IRAN

PERU

On the west coast of South America, Peru, which had been Spain's foremost colony in the New World, won its independence in 1824. A fragile democracy has survived frequent wars, revolutions, dictatorships, and corruption with occasional periods of representative government. *Languages:* Spanish, native tongues. *Capital:* Lima.

MONETARY SYSTEM

16 reales = 1 escudo, to 1863
10 centavos = 1 dinero
100 centavos = 1 sol
10 soles = 1 libra

PRECIOUS METAL CONTENT

Dates	Denomination	Gross Wt (g)	Fineness	Net Wt (g)	Troy Oz.
		SILVER			
1863–1917	1/2 dinero	1.2500	0.9000	1.1250	0.0362
	1 dinero	2.5000	0.9000	2.2500	0.0723
	1/5 sol	5.0000	0.9000	4.5000	0.1447
	1/2 sol	12.5000	0.9000	11.2500	0.3617
	1 sol	25.0000	0.9000	22.5000	0.7234
1880–82	1/2 real	1.2500	0.9000	1.1250	0.0362
	1 peseta	5.0000	0.9000	4.5000	0.1447
	5 pesetas	25.0000	0.9000	22.5000	0.7234
1922–35	1/2 sol	12.5000	0.5000	6.2500	0.2009
	1 sol	25.0000	0.5000	12.5000	0.4019
		GOLD			
1862–63	4 escudos	13.5000	0.8750	11.8125	0.3798
	8 escudos	27.0000	0.8750	23.6250	0.7596
	5 soles	8.0645	0.9000	7.2581	0.2334
	10 soles	16.1290	0.9000	14.5161	0.4667
	20 soles	32.2581	0.9000	29.0322	0.9334
1898–1969	1/5 libra	1.5976	0.9170	1.4645	0.0471
	1/2 libra	3.9940	0.9170	3.6612	0.1177
	1 libra	7.9881	0.9170	7.3224	0.2354
1910	5 soles	2.3404	0.9000	2.1064	0.0677
1930–69	50 soles	33.4363	0.9000	30.0926	0.9675
1950–70	5 soles	2.3404	0.9000	2.1064	0.0677
	10 soles	4.6807	0.9000	4.2126	0.1354
	20 soles	9.3614	0.9000	8.4253	0.2709
	50 soles	23.4036	0.9000	21.0632	0.6772
	100 soles	46.8071	0.9000	42.1264	1.3544

TRANSITION TO DECIMAL SYSTEM, *1858–1863*

Y#	KM#	Metal	Description	VF	EF	Unc
1	177	Silv	1/2 Real, 1858	15	50	100
2	178	Silv	50 Centimos, 1858	40	100	350

Y#	KM#	Metal	Description	VF	EF	Unc
3	180	Silv	1/2 Real, 1859–61	10	25	60
4	181	Silv	1 Real, 1859–61	20	40	100
5	182	Silv	25 Centavos, 1859	45	100	550
6	179	Silv	50 Centavos, 1858–59	75	175	950

Y#	KM#	Metal	Description	VF	EF	Unc
7	184	Gold	4 Escudos, 1863	4,000	10,000	20,000
8	183	Gold	8 Escudos, 1862–63	1,500	1,750	2,500

DECIMAL SYSTEM, *1863–*
FIRST COINAGE

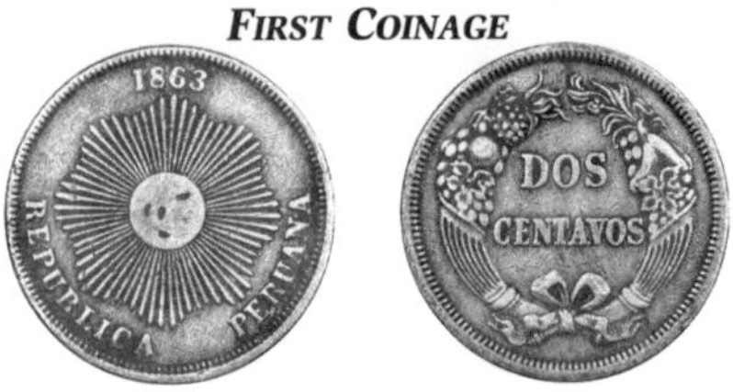

Obverse: ***Date at top***

Y#	KM#	Metal	Description	VF	EF	Unc
9	187.1	C-N	1 Centavo, 1863–64	5	12	25
10	188.1	C-N	2 Centavos, 1863–64	5	15	35

Y#	KM#	Metal	Description	VF	EF	Unc
9a	187.1a	Bz	1 Centavo, 1875–78, 1919 *1878, EF $60; 1919, EF $6*	5	12	25
10a	188	Bz	2 Centavos, 1876–95, 1919 *1878, EF $75; 1919, EF $7.50*	5	15	35

Obverse: ***Date at bottom***
Planchet: ***Thick***

Y#	KM#	Metal	Description	VF	EF	Unc
11	211	Bz	1 Centavo, 1901–39, CENTAVO straight	2.50	7.50	25.00
12	208.2	Bz	1 Centavo, 1909–37, CENTAVO curved	2.00	4.00	20.00
13	212.1	Bz	2 Centavos, 1916–41	2.00	5.00	25.00
			1919	1.00	4.00	10.00

Lima Mint

Y#	KM#	Metal	Description	VF	EF	Unc
14	189/206	Silv	1/2 Dinero, 1863–1917 *1893, EF $150*	3.00	6.00	15.00
15	190/204	Silv	1 Dinero, 1863–1916 *1872, VF $100; 1888, VF $85; 1894, VF $45*	5.00	15.00	40.00
16	191/205	Silv	1/5 Sol, 1863–1917 *1885, EF $7,000; 1915, VF $40*	10.00	20.00	50.00
17	195	Silv	1/2 Sol, 1864–1917 *1908, VF $45*	17.50	27.50	60.00
18	196	Silv	1 Sol, 1864–1916 *1864, VF $300; 1880, VF $70; 1864, DERTEANO in bottom row of coins below cornucopia, EF $2,000*	20.00	35.00	150.00

Note: Y14–18 contain many die varieties.

Branch Mints

Y#	KM#	Metal	Description	VF	EF	Unc
14a	189a	Silv	1/2 Dinero, 1885, Cuzco	350	650	1,150
15a	190a	Silv	1 Dinero, 1886, Cuzco	60	150	600
16a	191a	Silv	1/5 Sol, 1885, Arequipa	5,000	7,000	—

Y#	KM#	Metal	Description	VF	EF	Unc
A19	192	Gold	5 Soles, 1863	BV	700	900
B19	193	Gold	10 Soles, 1863	BV	1,250	2,000
19	194	Gold	20 Soles, 1863	BV	2,250	2,500

Y#	KM#	Metal	Description	VF	EF	Unc
20	210	Gold	1/5 Libra, 1906–69	BV	BV	115
21	209	Gold	1/2 Libra, 1902–69	BV	BV	250
22	207	Gold	1 Libra, 1898–1969	BV	BV	475

Y#	KM#	Metal	Description	VF	EF	Unc
23	Tn1	Silv	1 Sol, 1910	12	25	50

Y#	KM#	Metal	Description	VF	EF	Unc
24	Tn2	Gold	5 Soles, 1910	185	200	350

Provisional Issues

Y#	KM#	Metal	Description	VF	EF	Unc
25	197	C-N	5 Centavos, 1879–80	2	4	10
26	198	C-N	10 Centavos, 1879–80	3	6	20
27	199	C-N	20 Centavos, 1879	10	20	75

Y#	KM#	Metal	Description	VF	EF	Unc
28	202	Silv	1/2 Real, 1882, Ayacucho	800	1,200	2,000
29	200	Silv	1 Peseta, 1880, Lima	20	50	150
30	201	Silv	5 Pesetas, 1880, Lima	45	90	300
30a	201.3	Silv	5 Pesetas, 1881–82, Ayacucho *1881, EF $975*	250	350	1,500

Note: Holed or plugged pieces of Y28 are worth 25% of the listed prices.

SECOND COINAGE

Obverse: ***Dates spelled out***

Y#	KM#	Metal	Description	VF	EF	Unc
31	213	C-N	5 Centavos, 1918–41	1	3	10
32	214	C-N	10 Centavos, 1918–41	2	4	15
33	215	C-N	20 Centavos, 1918–41	3	5	25

Y#	KM#	Metal	Description	VF	EF	Unc
34	216	Silv	1/2 Sol, 1922–35	9.00	15	40
35	217	Silv	1 Sol, 1923, no fineness shown	20.00	80	350
36	218	Silv	1 Sol, 1923–35, fineness 5 Decimos	17.50	30	50

Y#	KM#	Metal	Description	VF	EF	Unc
37	219	Gold	50 Soles, 1930–69	BV	2,000	2,250

THIRD COINAGE

Planchet: ***Thin***

Y#	KM#	Metal	Description	VF	EF	Unc
11a	208a	Bz	1 Centavo, 1941–44, CENTAVO straight *1944, VF $25*	1.00	3	10
12a	211a	Bz	1 Centavo, 1941–49, CENTAVO curved	0.50	1	6
13a	212.2	Bz	2 Centavos, 1941–49	0.50	2	7

Obverse: ***Dates spelled out***

Y#	KM#	Metal	Description	VF	EF	Unc
31a	213.2a	Br	5 Centavos, 1942–44	2	7.50	15
32a	214a	Br	10 Centavos, 1942–44	3	8.00	35
33a	215a	Br	20 Centavos, 1942–44	5	15.00	50

Obverse: ***Dates in numerals***

Y#	KM#	Metal	Description	VF	EF	Unc
38	223	Br	5 Centavos, 1945–51	0.50	2.00	7.00
39	224	Br	10 Centavos, 1945–51	0.50	2.00	7.50
40	221	Br	20 Centavos, 1942–51 (2 vars)	0.50	2.50	8.00

Y#	KM#	Metal	Description	VF	EF	Unc
41	227	Zinc	1 Centavo, 1950–65	0.35	1.00	3
42	228	Zinc	2 Centavos, 1950–58	0.40	1.50	4

Y#	KM#	Metal	Description	VF	EF	Unc
38a	223.2	Br	5 Centavos, 1951–65	0.25	0.50	2.00
39a	224.2	Br	10 Centavos, 1951–65	0.25	0.50	2.50
40a	221.2b	Br	20 Centavos, 1951–65	0.25	0.50	2.50

Central Reserve Bank

Y#	KM#	Metal	Description	VF	EF	Unc
43	220	Br	1/2 Sol, 1943–65	0.20	0.50	1
44	222	Br	1 Sol, 1943–65	0.50	1.00	5

Castilla Commemoratives

Y#	KM#	Metal	Description	VF	EF	Unc
45	232	Br	5 Centavos, 1954	3	6	12.50
46	233	Br	10 Centavos, 1954	4	8	15.00
47	234	Br	20 Centavos, 1954	5	10	20.00

Bullion Issues

Y#	KM#	Metal	Description	VF	EF	Unc
48	235	Gold	5 Soles, 1956–69	BV	BV	175
49	236	Gold	10 Soles, 1956–69	BV	BV	300

Y#	KM#	Metal	Description	VF	EF	Unc
50	229	Gold	20 Soles, 1950–69	BV	BV	550
51	230	Gold	50 Soles, 1950–70	BV	BV	1,000
52	231	Gold	100 Soles, 1950–70 *1952, 58, Unc $3,000*	BV	BV	2,400

PHILIPPINES, THE

A Spanish colony until 1898, the archipelago of more than 7,000 islands lying 500 miles southeast of Asia was ceded to the United States following the Spanish-American War and administered as a territory. Following liberation from Japanese occupiers in World War II, the Philippines' independence was recognized in 1946. The republic has survived bouts of martial law, attempted coups, and separatist guerrilla warfare since then. *Languages:* Filipino, English, Spanish. *Capital:* Manila.

MONETARY SYSTEM

100 centimos = 1 peso, to 1898
100 centavos = 1 peso, 1903–1966

PRECIOUS METAL CONTENT

Dates	Denomination	Gross Wt (g)	Fineness	Net Wt (g)	Troy Oz.
		SILVER			
1864–80	10 centimos	2.5960	0.9000	2.3364	0.0751
	20 centimos	5.1920	0.9000	4.6728	0.1502
	50 centimos	12.9800	0.9000	11.6820	0.3756
1880–85	10 centimos	2.5960	0.8350	2.1677	0.0679
	20 centimos	5.1920	0.8350	4.3353	0.1394
	50 centimos	12.9800	0.8350	10.8383	0.3485
1897	1 peso	25.0000	0.9000	22.5000	0.7234
1903–06	10 centavos	2.6924	0.9000	2.4232	0.0779
	20 centavos	5.3849	0.9000	4.8464	0.1558
	50 centavos	13.4784	0.9000	12.1306	0.3900
	1 peso	26.9568	0.9000	24.2611	0.7800
1907–47	10 centavos	2.0000	0.7500	1.5000	0.0482
	20 centavos	4.0000	0.7500	3.0000	0.0965
	50 centavos	10.0000	0.7500	7.5000	0.2411
	1 peso	20.0000	0.8000	16.0000	0.5144
1961	1/2 peso	12.5000	0.9000	11.2500	0.3617
1961–64	1 peso	26.0000	0.9000	23.4000	0.7523
		GOLD			
1861–85	1 peso	1.6915	0.8750	1.4801	0.0476
	2 pesos	3.3830	0.8750	2.9602	0.0952
	4 pesos	6.7661	0.8750	5.9203	0.1903

SPANISH COLONY, *to 1898*

Isabel II, *1833–1868*

Y#	KM#	Metal	Description	VF	EF	Unc
3	145	Silv	10 Centimos, 1864–68 *1864, EF $550*	15.00	70	225
4	N/A	Silv	20 Centimos, 1864–68 *1864, EF $650*	12.50	30	300
5	N/A	Silv	50 Centimos, 1865–68 *1866–67, VF $300*	35.00	100	700

Y#	KM#	Metal	Description	VF	EF	Unc
6	142	Gold	1 Peso, 1861–68	125	175	500
7	143	Gold	2 Pesos, 1861–68	225	275	600
8	144	Gold	4 Pesos, 1861–68	375	425	800

Alfonso XII, *1875–1885*

Y#	KM#	Metal	Description	VF	EF	Unc
9	148	Silv	10 Centimos, 1880–85 *1880, EF $950; 1884, Unc $5,500*	10.00	15	150
10	N/A	Silv	20 Centimos, 1880–85 *1880–84, Unc $950*	15.00	30	300
11	N/A	Silv	50 Centimos, 1880–85 *1880–84, Unc $300*	27.50	55	85

Y#	KM#	Metal	Description	VF	EF	Unc
12	151	Gold	4 Pesos, 1880–85 *1880–81, 85, Rare*	1,500	2,500	3,750

Alfonso XIII, *1886–1898*

Y#	KM#	Metal	Description	VF	EF	Unc
13	154	Silv	1 Peso, 1897	45	90	400

U.S. TERRITORY, *1898–1935*

Y#	KM#	Metal	Description	VF	EF	Unc
14	162	Bz	1/2 Centavo, 1903–08 *1905–08, Proof only: $550*	1.25	3	30 *Proof: $160*
15	163	Bz	1 Centavo, 1903–36	2.00	5	40 *Proof: $200*

Note: Dates after 1904 of Y14 not for circulation.

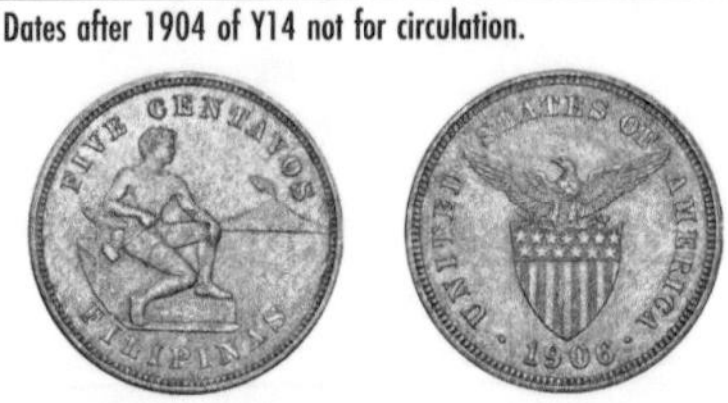

Y#	KM#	Metal	Description	VF	EF	Unc
16	164	C-N	5 Centavos, 1903–28	2.50	6	40 *Proof: $150*

Y#	KM#	Metal	Description	VF	EF	Unc
16a	173	C-N	5 Centavos, 1918, reverse of Y23 (error)	575	1,750	6,500

Size: ***Reduced***

Y#	KM#	Metal	Description	VF	EF	Unc
17	175	C-N	5 Centavos, 1930–35	2.50	8	125

Size: ***Regular***

Y#	KM#	Metal	Description	VF	EF	Unc
18	165	Silv	10 Centavos, 1903–06	4	6.50	60
					Proof: $125	
19	166	Silv	20 Centavos, 1903–06 1905–06, 08, Proof: $325	5	15.00	65
					Proof: $200	
20	167	Silv	50 Centavos, 1903–06	9	12.50	125
					Proof: $250	
21	168	Silv	1 Peso, 1903–06 *1906S, VF $1,500; 1905–06, 08, Proof: $1,000*	35	55.00	350
					Proof: $400	

Size: ***Reduced***

Y#	KM#	Metal	Description	VF	EF	Unc
22	169	Silv	10 Centavos, 1907–35 *1909S, EF $65; 1915S, EF $40*	2	3	40
					Proof: $200	
23	170	Silv	20 Centavos, 1907–29	5	8	85
					Proof: $275	

Size: ***Regular***

Y#	KM#	Metal	Description	VF	EF	Unc
23a	174	Silv	20 Centavos, 1928, reverse of Y16 (error)	15.00	50	1,100
24	171	Silv	50 Centavos, 1907–21	8.50	15	175
					Proof: $450	
25	172	Silv	1 Peso, 1907–12 *1906S, Rare; 1911S, EF $75; 1912S, EF $225*	10.00	20	300
					Proof: $1,000	

COMMONWEALTH, *1935–1946*

Establishment of the Commonwealth

Y#	KM#	Metal	Description	VF	EF	Unc
26	176	Silv	50 Centavos, 1936	30	50	125

Y#	KM#	Metal	Description	VF	EF	Unc
27	177	Silv	1 Peso, 1936	70	85	275

Y#	KM#	Metal	Description	VF	EF	Unc
28	178	Silv	1 Peso, 1936	70	85	250

Y#	KM#	Metal	Description	VF	EF	Unc
29	179	Bz	1 Centavo, 1937–44 *1937–40, EF $3; 1941, EF $7.50*	0.25	0.50	3

Y#	KM#	Metal	Description	VF	EF	Unc
30	180	C-N	5 Centavos, 1937–41 *1937, 41, EF $7.50*	1	2.25	40

Y#	KM#	Metal	Description	VF	EF	Unc
30a	180a	CNZ	5 Centavos, 1944–45	0.25	0.50	1.50

Y#	KM#	Metal	Description	VF	EF	Unc
31	181	Silv	10 Centavos, 1937–45	1.75	2.25	3.50
32	182	Silv	20 Centavos, 1937–45 *1937, 44, Unc $40; 1938, 41, Unc $17.50*	3.00	5.00	8.00
33	183	Silv	50 Centavos, 1944–45	6.00	7.00	10.00

REPUBLIC, *1946–*

MacArthur Commemoratives

Y#	KM#	Metal	Description	VF	EF	Unc
34	184	Silv	50 Centavos, 1947	6.50	10	20

Y#	KM#	Metal	Description	VF	EF	Unc
35	185	Silv	1 Peso, 1947	12.50	20	30

CENTRAL BANK ISSUES, 1958–1966

Y#	KM#	Metal	Description	VF	EF	Unc
36	186	Bz	1 Centavo, 1958–63	0.15	0.25	0.75

Y#	KM#	Metal	Description	VF	EF	Unc
37	187	Br	5 Centavos, 1958–66	0.10	0.20	0.65

Y#	KM#	Metal	Description	VF	EF	Unc
38	188	N-Br	10 Centavos, 1958–66	0.10	0.20	0.65
39	189.1	N-Br	25 Centavos, 1958–66	0.25	0.40	1.00

Y#	KM#	Metal	Description	VF	EF	Unc
40	190	N-Br	50 Centavos, 1958, 64	0.25	0.50	1

Centennial, Birth of Jose Rizal

Y#	KM#	Metal	Description	VF	EF	Unc
41	191	Silv	1/2 Peso, 1961	BV	10	15

Y#	KM#	Metal	Description	VF	EF	Unc
42	192	Silv	1 Peso, 1961	BV	20	30

Centennial, Birth of Andres Bonifacio

Y#	KM#	Metal	Description	VF	EF	Unc
43	193	Silv	1 Peso, 1963	BV	17.50	25

Centennial, Birth of Apolinario Mabini

Y#	KM#	Metal	Description	VF	EF	Unc
44	194	Silv	1 Peso, 1964	BV	17.50	25

POLAND

A central European republic on the Baltic Sea west of Russia, Poland has been controlled by Austria, Germany, Prussia, and Russia. It declared independence after World War I but was taken over by Germany and Russia in 1939. A Soviet-style people's democracy was established in 1952. Trade union recognition in the early 1980s began a move toward greater reforms, and free elections began in 1991. *Language:* Polish. *Capital:* Warsaw.

MONETARY SYSTEM

100 groszy = 1 zloty

PRECIOUS METAL CONTENT

Dates	Denomination	Gross Wt (g)	Fineness	Net Wt (g)	Troy Oz.
		SILVER			
1924–25	1 zloty	5.0000	0.7500	3.7500	0.1206
	2 zlote	10.0000	0.7500	7.5000	0.2411
	5 zlotych	25.0000	0.9000	22.5000	0.7234
1928–32	5 zlotych	18.0000	0.7500	13.5000	0.4340
1932–39	2 zlote	11.0000	0.7500	8.2500	0.2652
	5 zlotych	8.8000	0.7500	6.6000	0.2122
	10 zlotych	22.0000	0.7500	16.5000	0.5305
		GOLD			
1925	10 zlotych	3.2258	0.9000	2.9032	0.0933
	20 zlotych	6.4516	0.9000	5.8064	0.1867

World War I Issues

German Military Coinage

See Germany YA18–C18 for iron 1, 2, and 3 kopeks 1916 used in eastern Poland, Russia, and the Baltic countries.

Regency under Germany and Austria, 1917–1918

MONETARY SYSTEM
100 fenigow (pfennig) = 1 marka

Y#	KM#	Metal	Description	VF	EF	Unc
4	4	Iron	1 Fenig, 1917–18 *1917, F $440, VF $950*	25.00	35.00	60
5	5	Iron	5 Fenigow, 1917–18	15.00	27.50	60
6	6	Iron	10 Fenigow, 1917–18	25.00	50.00	125
7	7	Iron	20 Fenigow, 1917–18 *1917, Unc $145*	22.50	35.00	90

Y#	KM#	Metal	Description	VF	EF	Unc
6a	6a	Zinc	10 Fenigow, 1917 (error planchet)	50	90	150
7a	7a	Zinc	20 Fenigow, 1917 (error planchet)	75	125	250

REPUBLIC, *1919–*

First Coinage

Y#	KM#	Metal	Description	VF	EF	Unc
8	8	Br	1 Grosz, 1923	13.00	20	50.00
9	9	Br	2 Grosze, 1923	1.00	3	7.00
10	10	Br	5 Groszy, 1923	1.00	2	5.00
8a	8a	Bz	1 Grosz, 1923–39	0.50	1	4.50
9a	9a	Bz	2 Grosze, 1923–39	0.50	1	3.50
10a	10a	Bz	5 Groszy, 1923–39 *1923, VF $15*	0.50	1	4.00

Y#	KM#	Metal	Description	VF	EF	Unc
11	11	Nick	10 Groszy, 1923	3	10.00	50
12	12	Nick	20 Groszy, 1923	1	1.50	10
13	13	Nick	50 Groszy, 1923	1	1.50	10

Y#	KM#	Metal	Description	VF	EF	Unc
15	15	Silv	1 Zloty, 1924–25	8	20	120
16	16	Silv	2 Zlote, 1924–25	10	30	150

Obverse: *Like Y15–16*

Y#	KM#	Metal	Description	VF	EF	Unc
17	17	Silv	5 Zlotych, 1925	3,000	4,000	5,000

Note: Y17 was not issued into circulation.

900th Anniversary, Death of Boleslaus I

Y#	KM#	Metal	Description	VF	EF	Unc
32	32	Gold	10 Zlotych, 1925	280	350	400
33	33	Gold	20 Zlotych, 1925	500	580	650

Second Coinage

Y8a–10a were continued through this period.

Y#	KM#	Metal	Description	VF	EF	Unc
14	14	Nick	1 Zloty, 1929	1	10	50

Y#	KM#	Metal	Description	VF	EF	Unc
18	18	Silv	5 Zlotych, 1928–32	25	75	250

Centennial, First Revolt Against Russians

Y#	KM#	Metal	Description	VF	EF	Unc
19	19	Silv	5 Zlotych, 1930	30	120	350

Third Coinage

Y8a–10a were continued through this period.

Y#	KM#	Metal	Description	VF	EF	Unc
20	20	Silv	2 Zlote, 1932–34	2	10	30
21	21	Silv	5 Zlotych, 1932–34	5	15	50
22	22	Silv	10 Zlotych, 1932–33	10	20	75

250th Anniversary, Relief of Vienna

Y#	KM#	Metal	Description	VF	EF	Unc
23	23	Silv	10 Zlotych, 1933	25	40	75

70th Anniversary, Second Revolt Against Russians

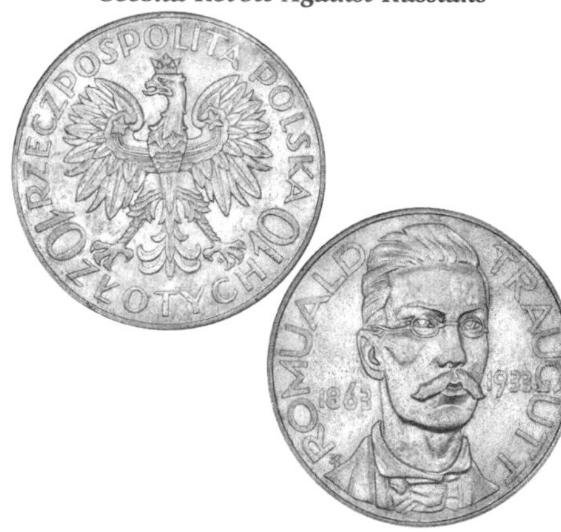

Y#	KM#	Metal	Description	VF	EF	Unc
24	24	Silv	10 Zlotych, 1933	25	45	75

20th Anniversary, Founding of Rifle Corps

Obverse: *Date at right*
Reverse: *Badge below eagle*

Y#	KM#	Metal	Description	VF	EF	Unc
25	25	Silv	5 Zlotych, 1934	10	15	60
26	26	Silv	10 Zlotych, 1934	30	45	95

Reverse: *Date below eagle*

Y#	KM#	Metal	Description	VF	EF	Unc
27	27	Silv	2 Zlote, 1934–36	5	8	15
28	28	Silv	5 Zlotych, 1934–38	5	8	15
29	29	Silv	10 Zlotych, 1934–39	13	20	30

Y#	KM#	Metal	Description	VF	EF	Unc
30	30	Silv	2 Zlote, 1936	2	5	20
31	31	Silv	5 Zlotych, 1936	5	10	30

World War II, German Occupation

Y#	KM#	Metal	Description	VF	EF	Unc
34	34	Zinc	1 Grosz, 1939	7.50	12.50	15
35	35	Zinc	5 Groszy, 1939	12.50	20.00	40

Y#	KM#	Metal	Description	VF	EF	Unc
36	36	Zinc	10 Groszy, 1923	3	10	17.50
37	37	Zinc	20 Groszy, 1923	3	10	25.00

Note: Y36–37 were struck circa 1941–1944.

Obverse: ***Date at bottom***

Y#	KM#	Metal	Description	VF	EF	Unc
38	38	N-Pl	50 Groszy, 1938	2	4	5

Postwar Issues

Y#	KM#	Metal	Description	VF	EF	Unc
39	39	Alum	1 Grosz, 1949	0.10	0.20	0.30

Y#	KM#	Metal	Description	VF	EF	Unc
40	40	Alum	2 Grosze, 1949	0.10	0.20	0.30

Y#	KM#	Metal	Description	VF	EF	Unc
41	41	Bz	5 Groszy, 1949	0.75	1	4

Y#	KM#	Metal	Description	VF	EF	Unc
42	42	C-N	10 Groszy, 1949	1.00	3	8.00
43	43	C-N	20 Groszy, 1949	1.50	5	17.50
44	44	C-N	50 Groszy, 1949	2.00	10	25.00

Y#	KM#	Metal	Description	VF	EF	Unc
45	45	C-N	1 Zloty, 1949	2	3	6

Y#	KM#	Metal	Description	VF	EF	Unc
41a	41a	Alum	5 Groszy, 1949	0.60	0.75	5
42a	42a	Alum	10 Groszy, 1949	0.20	1.00	18
43a	43a	Alum	20 Groszy, 1949	0.30	0.80	30
44a	44a	Alum	50 Groszy, 1949	0.50	1.50	25
45a	45a	Alum	1 Zloty, 1949	0.50	2.00	30

New Legend: ***POLSKA RZECZPOSPOLITA LUDOWA***

Y#	KM#	Metal	Description	VF	EF	Unc
A46	A46	Alum	5 Groszy, 1958–72	0.10	0.50	12

Y#	KM#	Metal	Description	VF	EF	Unc
AA47	AA47	Alum	10 Groszy, 1961–85	0.20	0.50	10
A47	A47	Alum	20 Groszy, 1957–85	0.20	0.50	12
48	48.1	Alum	50 Groszy, 1957–85	0.50	1.00	25

Reverse: ***Like Y45***

Y#	KM#	Metal	Description	VF	EF	Unc
49	49.1	Alum	1 Zloty, 1957–85 *1957, EF $40*	0.15	1	70

Y#	KM#	Metal	Description	VF	EF	Unc
46	46	Alum	2 Zlote, 1958–74	0.20	2	25

Y#	KM#	Metal	Description	VF	EF	Unc
47	47	Alum	5 Zlotych, 1958–74	0.60	3	15

Y#	KM#	Metal	Description	VF	EF	Unc
50	50	C-N	10 Zlotych, 1959–60, 66	0.75	2	7.50

Y#	KM#	Metal	Description	VF	EF	Unc
51	51	C-N	10 Zlotych, 1959–65	0.50	1	5

600th Anniversary, Jagiello University

Y#	KM#	Metal	Description	VF	EF	Unc
52	52	C-N	10 Zlotych, 1964, legend in relief	0.50	1	4
52a	52a	C-N	10 Zlotych, 1964, legend incuse	0.50	1	4

Y#	KM#	Metal	Description	VF	EF	Unc
52b	N/A	C-N	10 Zlotych, 1964, king seated	5	10	15

PORTUGAL

Located on the western section of the Iberian peninsula, Portugal won independence from Moorish Spain in 1143. A kingdom until 1910, a republic was established following a revolution. Power has frequently been held by military dictatorships. Once a great colonial power, most of Portugal's overseas territories were lost in the 1970s. Since the late 1980s, the Portuguese government has tended toward socialism. *Language:* Portuguese. *Capital:* Lisbon.

MONETARY SYSTEM

1000 reis = 1 milreis, to 1910
100 centavos = 1 escudo, since 1912

PRECIOUS METAL CONTENT

Dates	Denomination	Gross Wt (g)	Fineness	Net Wt (g)	Troy Oz.
		SILVER			
1854–1903	50 reis	1.2500	0.9170	1.1458	0.0368
	100 reis	2.5000	0.9170	2.2917	0.0737
	200 reis	5.0000	0.9170	4.5833	0.1474
1908–09	100 reis	2.5000	0.9170	2.0875	0.0671
	200 reis	5.0000	0.8350	4.1750	0.1342
1854–1910	500 reis	12.5000	0.9170	11.4583	0.3684
	1000 reis	25.0000	0.9170	22.9167	0.7368
1912–16	10 centavos	2.5000	0.8350	2.0875	0.0671
	20 centavos	5.0000	0.8350	4.1750	0.1342
	50 centavos	12.5000	0.8350	10.4375	0.3356
	1 escudo	25.0000	0.8350	20.8750	0.6711
1932–60	2-1/2 escudos	3.5000	0.6500	2.2750	0.0731
	5 escudos	7.0000	0.6500	4.5500	0.1463
1928–48	10 escudos	12.5000	0.8350	10.4375	0.3356
		GOLD			
1862–89	2,000 reis	3.5470	0.9170	3.2514	0.1045
	5,000 reis	8.8675	0.9170	8.1285	0.2613
	10,000 reis	17.7350	0.9170	16.2571	0.5227

LUIS I, *1861–1889*

Y#	KM#	Metal	Description	VF	EF	Unc
1	517	Cop	III Reis, 1868–75	7.00	10	40
2	513	Cop	V Reis, 1867–79 *1871, 73, 76–77, VF $50*	6.50	10	40
3	514	Cop	X Reis, 1867–74 *1870, VF $250*	4.00	8	40
4	515	Cop	XX Reis, 1867–74 *1870, VF $200*	25.00	60	120

Note: For related copper coins of 1865–1880, see Azores.

Y#	KM#	Metal	Description	VF	EF	Unc
5	525	Bz	V Reis, 1882–86 *1886, VF $15*	1	3	15
6	526	Bz	X Reis, 1882–86	4	30	60
7	527	Bz	XX Reis, 1882–86	4	30	60

Y#	KM#	Metal	Description	VF	EF	Unc
8	506	Silv	50 Reis, 1862–89 *1888, Extremely Rare*	8	15	50

Y#	KM#	Metal	Description	VF	EF	Unc
9	510	Silv	100 Reis, 1864–89	45	150	250
10	507	Silv	200 Reis, 1862–63	12	23	40

Reverse: *Arms in wreath*

Y#	KM#	Metal	Description	VF	EF	Unc
10a	512	Silv	200 Reis, 1865–88 *1865–68, 71–72, 75–79, EF $100, Unc $250*	25	50	75
11	509	Silv	500 Reis, 1863–89 *1863–65, Rare; 1872, 76, 77, VF $125*	12	23	40

Note: All dates of Y8–9 except 1889 and of Y10a except 1887 are worth considerably more than the listed common-date prices.

Y#	KM#	Metal	Description	VF	EF	Unc
A12	511	Gold	2,000 Reis, 1864–66	185	200	300
A13	508	Gold	5,000 Reis, 1862–63	275	300	500

Reverse: *Mantled arms*

Y#	KM#	Metal	Description	VF	EF	Unc
12	518	Gold	2,000 Reis, 1868–88 *1870–71, 88, Rare*	185	265	400
13	516	Gold	5,000 Reis, 1867–89 *1880, Rare*	275	400	650
14	520	Gold	10,000 Reis, 1878–89	575	850	1,250

CARLOS I,
1889–1908

Y#	KM#	Metal	Description	VF	EF	Unc
15	530	Bz	5 Reis, 1890–1906	3.00	10	30
16	532	Bz	10 Reis, 1891–92	2.25	20	40
17	533	Bz	20 Reis, 1891–92	2.25	18	35
			1892 A (Paris mint)	5.00	30	150

Note: For bronze coins of 1901 with coat of arms replacing portrait, see Azores.

Y#	KM#	Metal	Description	VF	EF	Unc
18	545	C-N	50 Reis, 1900	4.25	18	30
19	546	C-N	100 Reis, 1900	4.25	18	30

Y#	KM#	Metal	Description	VF	EF	Unc
20	536	Silv	50 Reis, 1893	15	20	33

Y#	KM#	Metal	Description	VF	EF	Unc
21	531	Silv	100 Reis, 1890–98 *1894, VF $200*	28	70	115
22	534	Silv	200 Reis, 1891–1903 *1901, VF $125*	18	38	60

Y#	KM#	Metal	Description	VF	EF	Unc
23	535	Silv	500 Reis, 1891–1908 *1894, 1900, Rare*	7	13	18

Obverse: ***Like Y23***

Y#	KM#	Metal	Description	VF	EF	Unc
24	540	Silv	1,000 Reis, 1899	30	45	75

400th Anniversary, Voyages of Discovery

Y#	KM#	Metal	Description	VF	EF	Unc
25	537	Silv	200 Reis, 1898	18	38	60
26	538	Silv	500 Reis, 1898	17	23	35
27	539	Silv	1,000 Reis, 1898	35	45	90

EMANUEL II, *1908–1910*

Y#	KM#	Metal	Description	VF	EF	Unc
28	555	Bz	5 Reis, 1910	2	4	8

Y#	KM#	Metal	Description	VF	EF	Unc
29	548	Silv	100 Reis, 1909–10	2.25	3.50	5
30	549	Silv	200 Reis, 1909	4.75	9.00	15
31	547	Silv	500 Reis, 1908–09	9.50	14.00	20

Peninsular War Centennial

Obverse: ***Like Y29–31***

Y#	KM#	Metal	Description	VF	EF	Unc
32	556	Silv	500 Reis, 1910	100	125	250
33	558	Silv	1,000 Reis, 1910	95	120	225

Marquis de Pombal

Y#	KM#	Metal	Description	VF	EF	Unc
34	557	Silv	500 Reis, 1910	33	45	75

REPUBLIC, *1910–*

FIRST COINAGE

Birth of Republic

Y#	KM#	Metal	Description	VF	EF	Unc
47	560	Silv	1 Escudo, 1910 (struck 1914)	50	100	225

Y#	KM#	Metal	Description	VF	EF	Unc
48	563	Silv	10 Centavos, 1915	3	4	12
49	562	Silv	20 Centavos, 1913–16	50	75	150
50	561	Silv	50 Centavos, 1912–16	13	18	35
51	564	Silv	1 Escudo, 1915–16	25	50	175

World War I, Provisional Issue

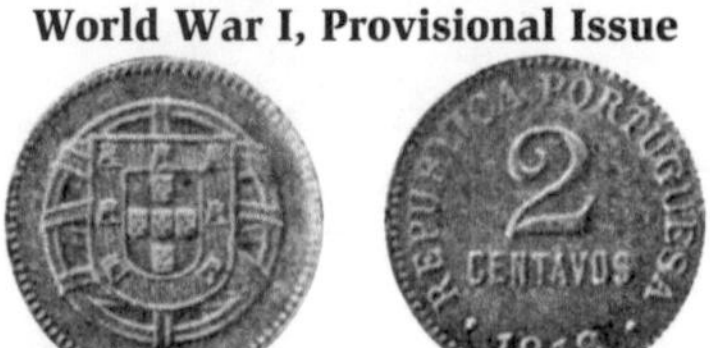

Y#	KM#	Metal	Description	VF	EF	Unc
35	567	Iron	2 Centavos, 1918	200	400	1,250

SECOND COINAGE

Y#	KM#	Metal	Description	VF	EF	Unc
36	565	Bz	1 Centavo, 1917–22 *1921, VF $40; 1922, Extremely Rare*	1	2.50	5
37	568	Bz	2 Centavos, 1918–21 *1921, VF $85*	1	2.50	6
38	569	Bz	5 Centavos, 1920–22 *1920, VF $50; 1922, VF $300*	2	6.00	12

Y#	KM#	Metal	Description	VF	EF	Unc
42	566	C-N	4 Centavos, 1917, 19	1	25	5
43	570	C-N	10 Centavos, 1920–21	18	30	45
44	571	C-N	20 Centavos, 1920–21 *1922, Rare*	18	30	45

THIRD COINAGE

Y#	KM#	Metal	Description	VF	EF	Unc
39	572	Bz	5 Centavos, 1924–27	1.75	7.50	15
40	573	Bz	10 Centavos, 1924–40 *1924, VF $45; 1930, Rare; 1938, VF $60*	3.50	35.00	70
41	574	Bz	20 Centavos, 1924–25	9.00	38.00	90

Y#	KM#	Metal	Description	VF	EF	Unc
45	575	A-Bz	50 Centavos, 1924–26 *1924, VF $300; 1925, Rare*	13	35	70
46	576	A-Bz	1 Escudo, 1924–26 *1926, VF $375*	35	75	150

Y#	KM#	Metal	Description	VF	EF	Unc
60	583	Bz	X Centavos, 1942–69	1.00	18	25
61	584	Bz	XX Centavos, 1942–69	1.25	2	25

Y#	KM#	Metal	Description	VF	EF	Unc
54	577	N-Bz	50 Centavos, 1927–68	0.75	2	30
55	578	N-Bz	1 Escudo, 1927–68 *1935, Rare*	0.75	2	30

Battle of Ourique, 1139

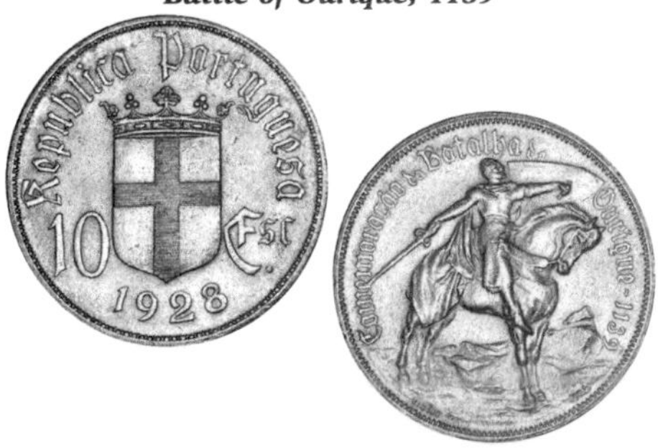

Y#	KM#	Metal	Description	VF	EF	Unc
56	579	Silv	10 Escudos, 1928	35	50	110

Y#	KM#	Metal	Description	VF	EF	Unc
57	580	Silv	2-1/2 Escudos, 1932–51 *1932, 48, VF $45; 1933, VF $90; 1937, Rare*	2.25	6.50	20
58	581	Silv	5 Escudos, 1932–51 *1937, VF $50*	4.00	13.00	25
59	582	Silv	10 Escudos, 1932–48 *1937, VF $300; 1942, Rare*	23.00	50.00	100

Y#	KM#	Metal	Description	VF	EF	Unc
63	586	Silv	10 Escudos, 1954–55	3.50	5.00	10

25 Years of Financial Reform

Y#	KM#	Metal	Description	VF	EF	Unc
62	585	Silv	20 Escudos, 1953	5.00	6.50	15

500th Anniversary, Death of Henry the Navigator

Y#	KM#	Metal	Description	VF	EF	Unc
64	587	Silv	5 Escudos, 1960	1.75	2.25	6
65	588	Silv	10 Escudos, 1960	25.00	30.00	60
66	589	Silv	20 Escudos, 1960	30.00	38.00	75

Y#	KM#	Metal	Description	VF	EF	Unc
67	590	C-N	2-1/2 Escudos, 1963–85	0.50	0.75	1.00
68	591	C-N	5 Escudos, 1963–86	0.75	1.00	1.25

PORTUGUESE GUINEA

This part of West Africa's Guinea coast was claimed by Portugal in 1446, but was little settled by Europeans. Portuguese Guinea became an Overseas Province in 1962 and proclaimed independence in 1973, formally recognized as the Republic of Guinea-Bissau. *Languages:* Portuguese, native tongues. *Capital:* Bolama (to 1941), Bissau (since 1941).

MONETARY SYSTEM

100 centavos = 1 escudo

PRECIOUS METAL CONTENT

Dates	Denomination	Gross Wt (g)	Fineness	Net Wt (g)	Troy Oz.
		SILVER			
1952	10 escudos	5.0000	0.7200	3.6000	0.1157
	20 escudos	10.0000	0.7200	7.2000	0.2315

Y#	KM#	Metal	Description	VF	EF	Unc
1	1	Bz	5 Centavos, 1933	90.00	130	250
2	2	Bz	10 Centavos, 1933	125.00	700	—
3	3	Bz	20 Centavos, 1933	7.50	13	25

Y#	KM#	Metal	Description	VF	EF	Unc
4	4	N-Bz	50 Centavos, 1933	23.00	60	275
5	5	N-Bz	1 Escudo, 1933	8.50	275	—

500th Anniversary of Discovery

Y#	KM#	Metal	Description	VF	EF	Unc
6	6	Bz	50 Centavos, 1946	7.00	28	50
7	7	Bz	1 Escudo, 1946	1.25	6	13

Decree of December 29, 1951

Y#	KM#	Metal	Description	VF	EF	Unc
8	8	Bz	50 Centavos, 1952	0.50	2.50	4.50

Y#	KM#	Metal	Description	VF	EF	Unc
9	9	C-N	2-1/2 Escudos, 1952	1.00	5	9.50

Y#	KM#	Metal	Description	VF	EF	Unc
10	10	Silv	10 Escudos, 1952	30	90	175
11	11	Silv	20 Escudos, 1952	28	80	165

PORTUGUESE INDIA

Three small areas—Goa, Damao, and Diu—on the west coast of India came under Portuguese control in the 16th century. India annexed these enclaves in 1962. *Capital:* Pangim.

MONETARY SYSTEM

50 reis = 1 tanga (Indian anna)   16 tangas = 1 rupia

PRECIOUS METAL CONTENT

Dates	Denomination	Gross Wt (g)	Fineness	Net Wt (g)	Troy Oz.
		SILVER			
1881–82	1/8 rupia	1.4600	0.9170	1.3388	0.0430
	1/4 rupia	2.9200	0.9170	2.6776	0.0860
	1/2 rupia	5.8300	0.9170	5.3461	0.1719
1881–1904	1 rupia	11.6600	0.9170	10.6922	0.3438
1936	1/2 rupia	6.0000	0.8350	5.0100	0.1610
1935	1 rupia	12.0000	0.9170	11.0040	0.3536
1947	1 rupia	12.0000	0.5000	6.0000	0.1929

Luis I, *1861–1889*

Y#	KM#	Metal	Description	VF	EF	Unc
1	301	Cop	3 Reis, 1871	10	20	40
2	302	Cop	5 Reis, 1871	13	20	50
3	303	Cop	10 Reis, 1871	15	20	55

Y#	KM#	Metal	Description	VF	EF	Unc
4	304	Cop	1/4 Tanga / 15 Reis, 1871	25	75	175
5	305	Cop	1/2 Tanga / 30 Reis, 1871	35	85	200
6	306	Cop	1 Tanga / 60 Reis, 1871	65	100	225

Y#	KM#	Metal	Description	VF	EF	Unc
7	307	Cop	1/8 Tanga, 1881–86	10.00	25	55
8	308	Cop	1/4 Tanga, 1881–88 *1888, Rare*	7.50	28	60

Y#	KM#	Metal	Description	VF	EF	Unc
11	309	Silv	1/8 Rupia, 1881	20	38	85
12	310	Silv	1/4 Rupia, 1881	20	38	85
13	311	Silv	1/2 Rupia, 1881–82	20	38	85
14	312	Silv	1 Rupia, 1881–82	18	35	75

CARLOS I, *1889–1908*

Y#	KM#	Metal	Description	VF	EF	Unc
15	13	Bz	1/12 Tanga, 1901, 03	25	40	90
16	14	Bz	1/8 Tanga, 1901, 03	25	40	90
17	15	Bz	1/4 Tanga, 1901, 03	25	40	90
18	16	Bz	1/2 Tanga, 1901, 03	25	40	90

Y#	KM#	Metal	Description	VF	EF	Unc
19	17	Silv	1 Rupia, 1903–04	18	30	75

PORTUGUESE REPUBLIC, *1910–1961*

Y#	KM#	Metal	Description	VF	EF	Unc
20	18	Silv	1 Rupia, 1912	90	125	200

Y#	KM#	Metal	Description	VF	EF	Unc
21	19	Bz	1 Tanga, 1934	100	350	700
22	20	C-N	2 Tangas, 1934	25	250	600
23	21	C-N	4 Tangas, 1934	100	350	750

Y#	KM#	Metal	Description	VF	EF	Unc
24	23	Silv	1/2 Rupia, 1936	25	38	80
25	22	Silv	1 Rupia, 1935	25	32	70

Y#	KM#	Metal	Description	VF	EF	Unc
26	24	Bz	1 Tanga, 1947 (25 mm)	9.50	20	45
26a	28	Bz	1 Tanga, 1952 (20 mm)	9.00	18	45

Y#	KM#	Metal	Description	VF	EF	Unc
27	25	C-N	1/4 Rupia, 1947, 52	13	20	38
28	26	C-N	1/2 Rupia, 1947, 52	15	28	55

Y#	KM#	Metal	Description	VF	EF	Unc
29	27	Silv	1 Rupia, 1947	33	50	85
29a	29	C-N	1 Rupia, 1952	30	45	80

NEW COINAGE SYSTEM

100 centavos = 1 escudo

Y#	KM#	Metal	Description	VF	EF	Unc
34	30	Bz	10 Centavos, 1858–61	3	15	25
35	31	Bz	30 Centavos, 1958–59	4	13	25

Y#	KM#	Metal	Description	VF	EF	Unc
36	32	CNZ	60 Centavos, 1958–59	4.00	13	25
37	33	CNZ	1 Escudo, 1958–59	7.00	13	45
38	34	CNZ	3 Escudos, 1958–59	8.50	14	28
39	35	CNZ	6 Escudos, 1959	8.50	14	28

PRINCE EDWARD ISLAND

Colonized by the French about 1720, PEI became a British possession in 1763 and was united with Canada in 1873. It is the smallest Canadian province. *Capital:* Charlottetown.

MONETARY SYSTEM

100 cents = 1 dollar

Y#	KM#	Metal	Description	VF	EF	Unc
1	4	Bz	1 Cent, 1871	7	17.50	95

PUERTO RICO

Puerto Rico is the farthest east of the Greater Antilles in the Atlantic Ocean. Settled by Spain in 1508, it was ceded to the United States after the Spanish-American War at the turn of the 20th century. It is a self-governing Commonwealth of the United States. *Languages:* Spanish, English. *Capital:* San Juan.

MONETARY SYSTEM

100 centavos = 1 peso

PRECIOUS METAL CONTENT

Dates	Denomination	Gross Wt (g)	Fineness	Net Wt (g)	Troy Oz.
		SILVER			
1895–96	5 centavos	1.2500	0.8350	1.0438	0.0336
	10 centavos	2.5000	0.8350	2.0875	0.0671
	20 centavos	5.0000	0.8350	4.1750	0.1342
	40 centavos	10.0000	0.8350	8.3500	0.2685
	1 peso	25.0000	0.9000	22.5000	0.7234

UNDER SPAIN

ALFONSO XIII, *1886–1898*

Y#	KM#	Metal	Description	VF	EF	Unc
1	20	Silv	5 Centavos, 1896	50	100	200

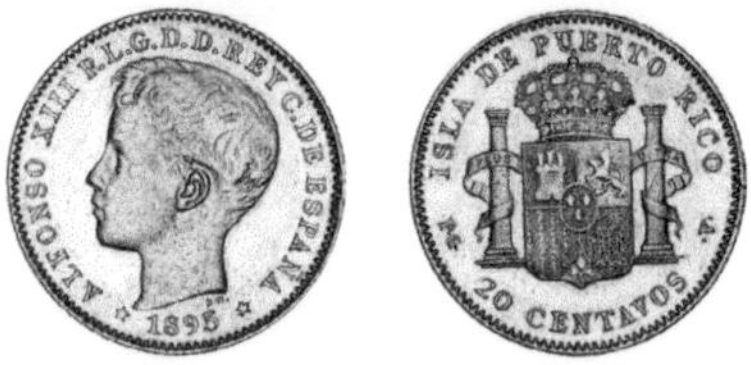

Y#	KM#	Metal	Description	VF	EF	Unc
2	21	Silv	10 Centavos, 1896	85	135	300
3	22	Silv	20 Centavos, 1895	100	135	400
4	23	Silv	40 Centavos, 1896	300	900	2,900
5	24	Silv	1 Peso, 1895	400	950	3,250

REUNION

A French overseas island territory in the Indian Ocean (east of Madagascar) since 1642, Reunion became a French Overseas Department in 1947. *Languages:* French, Creole. *Capital:* St. Denis.

MONETARY SYSTEM

100 centimes = 1 franc

Y#	KM#	Metal	Description	VF	EF	Unc
1	4	C-N	50 Centimes, 1896	60	120	400
2	5	C-N	1 Franc, 1896	100	300	750

BANK TOKENS

Y#	KM#	Metal	Description	VF	EF	Unc
3	Tn1	Alum	5 Centimes, 1920, hexagonal	100	200	550
4	Tn2	Alum	10 Centimes, 1920, hexagonal	225	500	850
5	Tn3	Alum	25 Centimes, 1920, hexagonal	200	400	800

REGULAR ISSUES

Former Y6–7 (50 centimes and 1 franc 1941) have been deleted until their existence can be confirmed.

Y#	KM#	Metal	Description	VF	EF	Unc
8	6	Alum	1 Franc, 1948–73	0.50	0.75	3.25
9	8	Alum	2 Francs, 1948–73	0.65	1.00	5.25
10	9	Alum	5 Francs, 1955–73	0.75	1.25	6.25

Y#	KM#	Metal	Description	VF	EF	Unc
11	10	A-Bz	10 Francs, 1955–73	0.50	1.00	3.50
12	11	A-Bz	20 Francs, 1955–73	1.00	1.75	5.50

Y#	KM#	Metal	Description	VF	EF	Unc
13	12	Nick	50 Francs, 1962–73	1.50	2.50	6
14	13	Nick	100 Francs, 1964–73	1.75	3.50	7

RHODESIA

Explored by Britain in the 1850s and formerly the self-governing colony of Southern Rhodesia (1923–1953), Rhodesia was part of the Federation of Rhodesia and Nyasaland from 1953 to 1963. It declared independence in 1965 and became a republic in 1970, changing its name to Zimbabwe in 1980 after white minority rule was supplanted by black nationalists. *Languages:* English, native tongues. *Capital:* Harare.

For earlier issues, see Southern Rhodesia.

MONETARY SYSTEM

12 pence = 1 shilling
20 shillings = 1 pound

ELIZABETH II, *1952–1970*

Y#	KM#	Metal	Description	VF	EF	Unc
1	1	C-N	6 Pence / 5 Cents, 1964	0.25	0.50	2

Y#	KM#	Metal	Description	VF	EF	Unc
2	2	C-N	1 Shilling / 10 Cents, 1964	0.35	0.65	3

Y#	KM#	Metal	Description	VF	EF	Unc
3	3	C-N	2 Shillings / 20 Cents, 1964	1	2	5

Y#	KM#	Metal	Description	VF	EF	Unc
4	4	C-N	2-1/2 Shillings / 25 Cents, 1964	1	3	7

RHODESIA AND NYASALAND

This federation of the British territories of Nyasaland (now Malawi), Northern Rhodesia (Zambia), and Southern Rhodesia (Zimbabwe) was formed in 1953 and dissolved 10 years later.

For earlier issues, see Southern Rhodesia.

MONETARY SYSTEM

12 pence = 1 shilling
5 shillings = 1 crown

ELIZABETH II, *1952–1964*

Y#	KM#	Metal	Description	VF	EF	Unc
1	1	Bz	1/2 Penny, 1955–64	0.25	0.50	5

Y#	KM#	Metal	Description	VF	EF	Unc
2	2	Bz	1 Penny, 1955–63	0.50	1	2.75

Y#	KM#	Metal	Description	VF	EF	Unc
3	3	C-N	3 Pence, 1955–64	0.50	1	4

Y#	KM#	Metal	Description	VF	EF	Unc
4	4	C-N	6 Pence, 1955–63 *1956, 63, EF $6.50*	0.75	1.50	5

Y#	KM#	Metal	Description	VF	EF	Unc
5	5	C-N	1 Shilling, 1955–57	2	4	7.50

Y#	KM#	Metal	Description	VF	EF	Unc
6	6	C-N	2 Shillings, 1955–57	2.50	5	13

Y#	KM#	Metal	Description	VF	EF	Unc
7	7	C-N	1/2 Crown, 1955–57 *1956, VF $18; 1957, VF $10*	2.50	5	25

Y#	KM#	Metal	Description	VF	EF	Unc
1a–7a	1a–7a	Silv	*1955 Silver Proof Set: $325*			

RHODESIA, SOUTHERN

From 1953 to 1963 a part of the Federation of Rhodesia and Nyasaland in south central Africa, Southern Rhodesia declared independence in 1965 and established the Republic of Rhodesia in 1970. It is now the Republic of Zimbabwe. *Capital:* Salisbury.

See Rhodesia and Nyasaland for later issues.

MONETARY SYSTEM

12 pence = 1 shilling
2 shillings = 1 florin
5 shillings = 1 crown
20 shillings = 1 pound

PRECIOUS METAL CONTENT

Dates	Denomination	Gross Wt (g)	Fineness	Net Wt (g)	Troy Oz.
		SILVER			
1932–42	3 pence	1.4138	0.9250	1.3078	0.0420
	6 pence	2.8276	0.9250	2.6155	0.0841
	1 shilling	5.6552	0.9250	5.2311	0.1682
	2 shillings	11.3104	0.9250	10.4621	0.3364
	1/2 crown	14.1380	0.9250	13.0777	0.4204
1944–46	3 pence	1.1438	0.5000	0.7069	0.0227
	6 pence	2.8276	0.5000	1.4138	0.0455
	1 shilling	5.6552	0.5000	2.8276	0.0909
	2 shillings	11.3104	0.5000	5.6552	0.1818
	1/2 crown	14.1380	0.5000	7.0690	0.2273
1953	1 crown	28.2800	0.5000	14.1400	0.4546

George V, *1910–1936*

Y#	KM#	Metal	Description	VF	EF	Unc
1	6	C-N	1/2 Penny, 1934–36	3	6	30
2	7	C-N	1 Penny, 1934–36	2	5	30

Y#	KM#	Metal	Description	VF	EF	Unc
3	1	Silv	3 Pence, 1932–36	4	15	50

Y#	KM#	Metal	Description	VF	EF	Unc
4	2	Silv	6 Pence, 1932–36	5	20	65

Y#	KM#	Metal	Description	VF	EF	Unc
5	3	Silv	1 Shilling, 1932–36	6	20	80

Y#	KM#	Metal	Description	VF	EF	Unc
6	4	Silv	2 Shillings, 1932–36	13	28	120

Y#	KM#	Metal	Description	VF	EF	Unc
7	5	Silv	1/2 Crown, 1932–36	15	50	175

George VI, *1936–1952*

Y#	KM#	Metal	Description	VF	EF	Unc
8	14	C-N	1/2 Penny, 1938–39	2.00	5.00	30
9	8	C-N	1 Penny, 1937–42	1.50	4.00	25
8a	14a	Bz	1/2 Penny, 1942–44	1.00	3.00	10
9a	8a	Bz	1 Penny, 1942–47	1.00	2.50	15

Obverse: ***EMPEROR to right of head***
Reverse: ***Designs like Y3–7***

Y#	KM#	Metal	Description	VF	EF	Unc
12	9	Silv	3 Pence, 1937	5	13	50
13	10	Silv	6 Pence, 1937	6	15	75
14	11	Silv	1 Shilling, 1937	7	15	75
15	12	Silv	2 Shillings, 1937	15	50	130
16	13	Silv	1/2 Crown, 1937	15	50	150

Obverse: ***KING EMPEROR to right of head***
Reverse: ***Designs like Y3–7***

Y#	KM#	Metal	Description	VF	EF	Unc
17	16–16a	Silv	3 Pence, 1939–46	3.00	15.00	55.00
18	17–17a	Silv	6 Pence, 1939–46	4.00	25.00	80.00
19	18–18a	Silv	1 Shilling, 1939–46	5.00	25.00	85.00
20	19–19a	Silv	2 Shillings, 1939–46 *1946, Unc $800*	15.00	[illegible]	165.00
21	15–15a	Silv	1/2 Crown, 1938–46	15.00	45.00	125.00
17a	16b	C-N	3 Pence, 1947	1.00	7.50	25.00
18a	17b	C-N	6 Pence, 1947	2.00	10.00	27.50
19a	18b	C-N	1 Shilling, 1947	2.50	6.00	40.00
20a	19b	C-N	2 Shillings, 1947	7.00	20.00	60.00
21a	15b	C-N	1/2 Crown, 1947	5.00	10.00	40.00

New Legend: ***KING GEORGE THE SIXTH***

Y#	KM#	Metal	Description	VF	EF	Unc
27	26	Bz	1/2 Penny, 1951–52	1	3	12.50
28	25	Bz	1 Penny, 1949–52	1	3	15.00

Reverse: ***Designs like Y12–16***

Y#	KM#	Metal	Description	VF	EF	Unc
29	20	C-N	3 Pence, 1948–52	0.50	7.50	25
30	21	C-N	6 Pence, 1948–52	1.00	8.50	30
31	22	C-N	1 Shilling, 1948–52	1.50	10.00	35
32	23	C-N	2 Shillings, 1948–52	3.00	15.00	60
33	24	C-N	1/2 Crown, 1948–52	3.00	15.00	60

Elizabeth II, *1952–1965*

Centennial, Birth of Cecil Rhodes

Y#	KM#	Metal	Description	VF	EF	Unc
34	27	C-N	1 Crown, 1953	8	15	30
						Proof: $125

Y#	KM#	Metal	Description	VF	EF	Unc
35	28	Bz	1/2 Penny, 1954	2	15	85
36	29	Bz	1 Penny, 1954	9	45	225

Y#	KM#	Metal	Description	VF	EF	Unc
37	30	C-N	2 Shillings, 1954	75	175	750
38	31	C-N	1/2 Crown, 1954	13	30	100

ROMANIA

This southeastern European republic began with the union of Moldavia and Wallachia in 1859. Romania later gained other territory, including Transylvania, and became a kingdom in 1881. It became a Soviet-style republic in 1947 after communists won post-war elections and King Michael abdicated. An army-assisted rebellion in 1989 restored free elections. *Language:* Romanian. *Capital:* Bucharest.

MONETARY SYSTEM

100 bani = 1 leu

PRECIOUS METAL CONTENT

Dates	Denomination	Gross Wt (g)	Fineness	Net Wt (g)	Troy Oz.
		SILVER			
1870–1914	50 bani	2.5000	0.8350	2.0875	0.0671
	1 leu	5.0000	0.8350	4.1750	0.1342
	2 lei	10.0000	0.8350	8.3500	0.2685
	5 lei	25.0000	0.9000	22.5000	0.7234
1932–35	100 lei	14.0000	0.5000	7.0000	0.2251
	250 lei	13.5000	0.7500	10.1250	0.3255
1939–41	250 lei	12.0000	0.8350	10.0200	0.3222
1941	500 lei	25.0000	0.8350	20.8750	0.6711
1942	200 lei	6.0000	0.8350	5.0100	0.1611
1946	25,000 lei	12.5000	0.7000	8.7500	0.2813
	100,000 lei	25.0000	0.7000	17.5000	0.5626
		GOLD			
1868–1940	12-1/2 lei	4.0323	0.9000	3.6291	0.1167
	20 lei	6.4516	0.9000	5.8064	0.1867
	25 lei	8.0645	0.9000	7.2581	0.2333
	50 lei	16.1290	0.9000	14.5161	0.4667
	100 lei	32.2581	0.9000	29.0323	0.9334

Carol I

As Domnul (Prince), 1866–1881

First Coinage

Y#	KM#	Metal	Description	VF	EF	Unc
1	1	Bz	1 Banu, 1867	15.00	40	135
2	2	Bz	2 Bani, 1867	12.50	35	125
3	3	Bz	5 Bani, 1867	10.00	35	125
4	4	Bz	10 Bani, 1867	10.00	50	150

Obverse: ***Young head, sideburns***

Y#	KM#	Metal	Description	VF	EF	Unc
5	5	Gold	20 Lei, 1868, *Rare*			
			Restrike (2005), Unc $1,750			

Note: 250 restrikes from 2005 exist.

Second Coinage

Obverse: ***Young head, short beard***

Y#	KM#	Metal	Description	VF	EF	Unc
6	6	Silv	1 Leu, 1870	250	1,000	3,500
7	7	Gold	20 Lei, 1870	3,000	4,500	8,000

Third Coinage

Y#	KM#	Metal	Description	VF	EF	Unc
8	9	Silv	50 Bani, 1873, 76	35	85	375

Y#	KM#	Metal	Description	VF	EF	Unc
9	10	Silv	1 Leu, 1873–76 *1876, VF $850*	75	300	750
10	8	Silv	2 Lei, 1872–76	60	150	475

Fourth Coinage

Reverse: ***ROMANIA above arms***

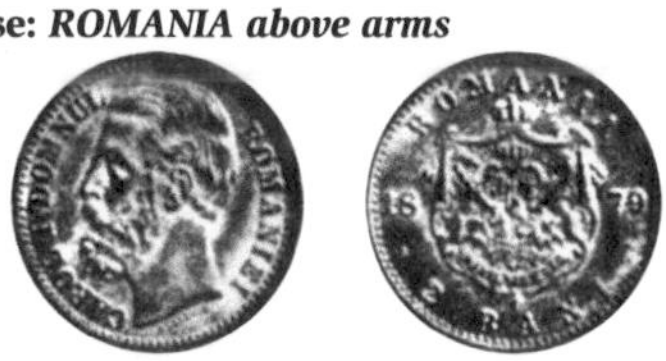

Y#	KM#	Metal	Description	VF	EF	Unc
11	11	Cop	2 Bani, 1879–81 *1881, VF $150*	10	30	100

Y#	KM#	Metal	Description	VF	EF	Unc
13	13	Silv	50 Bani, 1881	40	110	450
14	14	Silv	1 Leu, 1881	70	135	550
15	15	Silv	2 Lei, 1881	100	250	650
16	12	Silv	5 Lei, 1880–81 (2 vars)	80	200	700

As Rege (King), 1881–1914

New Legend: ***REGE replaces DOMNUL***

Y#	KM#	Metal	Description	VF	EF	Unc
27	16	Silv	5 Lei, 1881, reverse of Y16 (with ROMANIA)	80	225	850

Reverse: ***ROMANIA at top removed***

Y#	KM#	Metal	Description	VF	EF	Unc
A17	A18a	Cop	1 Ban, 1888	950	1,250	1,850
17	18	Cop	2 Bani, 1882	15	50	225
18	19	Cop	5 Bani, 1882–85	20	55	275

Note: YA17 was not issued to circulation.

Y#	KM#	Metal	Description	VF	EF	Unc
19	21	Silv	50 Bani, 1884–85 *1885, EF $900*	25	75	300
20	22	Silv	1 Leu, 1884–85 *1885, VF $150*	25	75	300
23	17.1	Silv	5 Lei, 1881–85, lettered edge	50	200	1,100
23a	17.2	Silv	5 Lei, 1901, reeded edge	150	275	1,350

Y#	KM#	Metal	Description	VF	EF	Unc
28	20	Gold	20 Lei, 1883–90	325	350	550

Reverse: ***ROMANIA restored above arms***

Y#	KM#	Metal	Description	VF	EF	Unc
29	26	Cop	1 Ban, 1900	3.00	12.50	45
30	27	Cop	2 Bani, 1900	7.50	15.00	100

Y#	KM#	Metal	Description	VF	EF	Unc
31	28	C-N	5 Bani, 1900	4.50	15	55
32	29	C-N	10 Bani, 1900	4.50	15	65
33	30	C-N	20 Bani, 1900	10.00	35	150

Y#	KM#	Metal	Description	VF	EF	Unc
34	31	C-N	5 Bani, 1905–06	1	3.00	10
35	32	C-N	10 Bani, 1905–06	2	6.00	50
36	33	C-N	20 Bani, 1905–06	10	32.50	125

Y#	KM#	Metal	Description	VF	EF	Unc
24	23	Silv	50 Bani, 1894–1901	12.50	30	100
25	24	Silv	1 Leu, 1894–1901	35.00	125	285
26	25	Silv	2 Lei, 1894–1901	50.00	175	700

40th Anniversary of Reign

Y#	KM#	Metal	Description	VF	EF	Unc
37	34	Silv	1 Leu, 1906	22.50	45	125
38	35	Silv	5 Lei, 1906	75.00	150	350

Y#	KM#	Metal	Description	VF	EF	Unc
39	36	Gold	12-1/2 Lei, 1906	225	400	650
40	38	Gold	25 Lei, 1906	400	700	1,500

Y#	KM#	Metal	Description	VF	EF	Unc
41	37	Gold	20 Lei, 1906	400	600	1,000
42	40	Gold	100 Lei, 1906	2,000	4,000	8,000

Y#	KM#	Metal	Description	VF	EF	Unc
43	39	Gold	50 Lei, 1906	1,700	2,250	4,000

Y#	KM#	Metal	Description	VF	EF	Unc
44	41	Silv	50 Bani, 1910–14	10	20	25

Y#	KM#	Metal	Description	VF	EF	Unc
45	42	Silv	1 Leu, 1910–14	9.00	15	30
46	43	Silv	2 Lei, 1910–14	13.50	25	40

Ferdinand I,
1914–1927

Y#	KM#	Metal	Description	VF	EF	Unc
47	44	Alum	25 Bani, 1921	3	7.50	15
48	45	Alum	50 Bani, 1921	3	7.50	15

Y#	KM#	Metal	Description	VF	EF	Unc
49	46	C-N	1 Leu, 1924	2	4.50	15
50	47	C-N	2 Lei, 1924	3	5.00	20

Note: Gold 20-, 25-, 50-, and 100-lei pieces dated 1922 exist, but their status as official issues is in dispute.

Mihai I

First Reign,
1927–1930

Y#	KM#	Metal	Description	VF	EF	Unc
55	48	N-Br	5 Lei, 1930	4	12.50	35

Y#	KM#	Metal	Description	VF	EF	Unc
56	50	N-Br	20 Lei, 1930	7	18	55

Carol II,
1930–1940

Y#	KM#	Metal	Description	VF	EF	Unc
57	56	N-Br	1 Leu, 1938–41	1	2	5

Y#	KM#	Metal	Description	VF	EF	Unc
58	49	N-Br	10 Lei, 1930	12.50	20	60
59	51	N-Br	20 Lei, 1930	3.00	15	50

Y#	KM#	Metal	Description	VF	EF	Unc
60	55	Nick	50 Lei, 1937–38	5	10	35

Y#	KM#	Metal	Description	VF	EF	Unc
61	54	Nick	100 Lei, 1936, 38	10	20	60

Y#	KM#	Metal	Description	VF	EF	Unc
62	52	Silv	100 Lei, 1932	15	35	75

Y#	KM#	Metal	Description	VF	EF	Unc
63	53	Silv	250 Lei, 1935	65	125	350

Y#	KM#	Metal	Description	VF	EF	Unc
64	57	Silv	250 Lei, 1939–40	20	35	85

Centennial, Birth of King Carol I

Y#	KM#	Metal	Description	VF	EF	Unc
65	Pn266	Gold	20 Lei, 1939 (arms)	1,750	3,000	5,000
66	Pn267	Gold	20 Lei, 1939 (eagle)	2,500	5,000	8,000

Y#	KM#	Metal	Description	VF	EF	Unc
67	Pn270	Gold	100 Lei, 1939	15,000	30,000	55,000

Y#	KM#	Metal	Description	VF	EF	Unc
68	Pn269	Gold	100 Lei, 1939	25,000	40,000	65,000

10th Anniversary, Reign of Carol II

Obverse: ***Large head, ornate border***

Y#	KM#	Metal	Description	VF	EF	Unc
71	Pn272	Gold	20 Lei, 1940	2,000	2,500	3,500

Y#	KM#	Metal	Description	VF	EF	Unc
A71	Pn274	Gold	100 Lei, 1940	7,500	15,000	22,500

Obverse: ***Small head, plain border***

Y#	KM#	Metal	Description	VF	EF	Unc
72	Pn271	Gold	20 Lei, 1940	2,000	2,500	3,500
A72	Pn273	Gold	100 Lei, 1940	7,500	15,000	22,500

MIHAI I

SECOND REIGN, 1940–1947

Y#	KM#	Metal	Description	VF	EF	Unc
73	58	Zinc	2 Lei, 1941	3.50	7	35

Y#	KM#	Metal	Description	VF	EF	Unc
74	61	Zinc	5 Lei, 1942	3.50	8	25

Y#	KM#	Metal	Description	VF	EF	Unc
75	62	Zinc	20 Lei, 1942–44	4	8	22

Y#	KM#	Metal	Description	VF	EF	Unc
76	64	N-CS	100 Lei, 1943–44	3	6	20

Y#	KM#	Metal	Description	VF	EF	Unc
77	63	Silv	200 Lei, 1942	3.50	7	30

Y#	KM#	Metal	Description	VF	EF	Unc
78	59.1	Silv	250 Lei, 1941, edge lettered NIHIL SINE DEO	7	18	30
78a	59.2	Silv	250 Lei, 1941, edge lettered TOTUL PENTRU TARA	20	35	80

Y#	KM#	Metal	Description	VF	EF	Unc
79	60	Silv	500 Lei, 1941	15	30	45

Y#	KM#	Metal	Description	VF	EF	Unc
80	65	Silv	500 Lei, 1944	15	25	40

Note: The 1944 gold piece (size of 20 lei Y71) is considered by some to be a commemorative medal.

SECOND COINAGE

Y#	KM#	Metal	Description	VF	EF	Unc
81	66	Br	200 Lei, 1945	3	5	17.50

Y#	KM#	Metal	Description	VF	EF	Unc
82	67	Br	500 Lei, 1945	3.50	7	35

Y#	KM#	Metal	Description	VF	EF	Unc
83	68	Alum	500 Lei, 1946	3	6	30

Y#	KM#	Metal	Description	VF	EF	Unc
84	69	Br	2,000 Lei, 1946	4	8.50	15

Y#	KM#	Metal	Description	VF	EF	Unc
85	76	Br	10,000 Lei, 1947	4.50	9	20

Y#	KM#	Metal	Description	VF	EF	Unc
86	70	Silv	25,000 Lei, 1946	7.50	12.50	25

Y#	KM#	Metal	Description	VF	EF	Unc
87	71	Silv	100,000 Lei, 1946	13.50	20	40

PEOPLE'S REPUBLIC, *1947–1965*

Currency Reform

Y#	KM#	Metal	Description	VF	EF	Unc
88	72	Br	50 Bani, 1947	3	5	15

Y#	KM#	Metal	Description	VF	EF	Unc
89	73	Br	1 Leu, 1947	5	12.50	30

Y#	KM#	Metal	Description	VF	EF	Unc
90	74	Bz	2 Lei, 1947	5	12.50	30

Y#	KM#	Metal	Description	VF	EF	Unc
91	75	Alum	5 Lei, 1947	5	12.50	30

Y#	KM#	Metal	Description	VF	EF	Unc
92	78	A-Bz	1 Leu, 1949–51	2	3	15

Y#	KM#	Metal	Description	VF	EF	Unc
93	79	A-Bz	2 Lei, 1950–51	2.50	3.50	17.50

Y#	KM#	Metal	Description	VF	EF	Unc
92a	78a	Alum	1 Leu, 1951–52	2.50	3.50	15.00
93a	79a	Alum	2 Lei, 1951–52	2.00	5.00	17.50

Y#	KM#	Metal	Description	VF	EF	Unc
94	77	Alum	5 Lei, 1948–51	3	5	15

Y#	KM#	Metal	Description	VF	EF	Unc
95	80	Alum	20 Lei, 1951	7.40	15	50

CURRENCY REFORM, *1952*

FIRST COINAGE

Obverse: ***No star at top of arms***

Y#	KM#	Metal	Description	VF	EF	Unc
96	81.1	CNZ	1 Ban, 1952	0.25	1.00	12.50
97	82.1	CNZ	3 Bani, 1952	1.25	2.50	20.00
98	83.1	CNZ	5 Bani, 1952	1.25	2.50	20.00

Y#	KM#	Metal	Description	VF	EF	Unc
99	84.1	C-N	10 Bani, 1952	2	5.00	25
100	85.1	C-N	25 Bani, 1952	3	7.50	35

Y#	KM#	Metal	Description	VF	EF	Unc
96a	81.2	CNZ	1 Ban, 1953–54	2.00	5.00	40
97a	82.2	CNZ	3 Bani, 1953–54 *1954, Unc $150*	1.50	3.75	30
98a	83.2	CNZ	5 Bani, 1953–54	2.00	4.00	35

Obverse: ***With star, legend ends ROMANA***

Y#	KM#	Metal	Description	VF	EF	Unc
99a	84.2	C-N	10 Bani, 1954	5	12.50	50
100a	85.2	C-N	25 Bani, 1953–54	4	10.00	40

Obverse: ***Legend ends ROMINA***

Y#	KM#	Metal	Description	VF	EF	Unc
99b	84.3	C-N	10 Bani, 1955–56	3.00	6.00	30
100b	85.3	C-N	25 Bani, 1955	1.50	3.75	30
101	86	C-N	50 Bani, 1955–56	3.50	7.00	45

SECOND COINAGE

Y#	KM#	Metal	Description	VF	EF	Unc
102	89	N-CS	5 Bani, 1963	0.50	0.85	1.75

Y#	KM#	Metal	Description	VF	EF	Unc
103	87	N-CS	15 Bani, 1960	0.30	0.50	2

Y#	KM#	Metal	Description	VF	EF	Unc
104	88	N-CS	25 Bani, 1960	0.50	0.75	4

Obverse: ***ROMANA legend resumed***

Y#	KM#	Metal	Description	VF	EF	Unc
105	90	N-CS	1 Leu, 1963	1	2.50	15

Y#	KM#	Metal	Description	VF	EF	Unc
106	91	N-CS	3 Lei, 1963	0.75	1.25	5

RUSSIA

United by the spread of Christianity in the 10th century, lands were acquired through the late 19th century, making Russia the largest country in the world, occupying most of eastern Europe and northern Asia. The imperial Russia of the Czars, whose modern history began with Ivan the Terrible in the 16th century, was destroyed by the Bolshevik revolution in 1917. The Union of Soviet Socialist Republics was established in 1922 and dissolved in 1991 with Russia joining other former Soviet republics in the Commonwealth of Independent States; see Union of Soviet Socialist Republics for listings. *Languages:* Russian, other languages and dialects. *Capital:* Moscow.

MONETARY SYSTEM

100 kopeks = 1 ruble

PRECIOUS METAL CONTENT

Dates	Denomination	Gross Wt (g)	Fineness	Net Wt (g)	Troy Oz.
		SILVER			
1855–58	5 kopeks	1.0366	0.8680	0.8998	0.0289
	10 kopeks	2.0700	0.8680	1.7968	0.0577
	20 kopeks	4.1463	0.8680	3.5990	0.1157
	25 kopeks	5.1830	0.8680	4.4988	0.1446
	1/2 ruble	10.3600	0.8680	8.9925	0.2892
	1 ruble	20.7300	0.8680	17.9936	0.5785
1859–66	5 kopeks	1.0366	0.7500	0.7775	0.0250
	10 kopeks	2.0732	0.7500	1.5549	0.0500
	15 kopeks	3.1097	0.7500	2.3323	0.1000
	20 kopeks	4.1463	0.7500	3.1097	0.0145
1859–85	25 kopeks	5.1829	0.8680	4.4988	0.1446
	50 kopeks	10.3658	0.8680	8.9975	0.2893
	1 ruble	20.7316	0.8680	17.9950	0.5785
1867–1931	5 kopeks	0.8998	0.5000	0.4499	0.0145
	10 kopeks	1.7996	0.5000	0.8998	0.0289
	15 kopeks	2.6994	0.5000	1.3497	0.0434
	20 kopeks	3.5992	0.5000	1.7996	0.0579
1886–1931	25 kopeks	4.9987	0.9000	4.4988	0.1446
	50 kopeks	9.9979	0.9000	8.9981	0.2893
	1 ruble	10.9957	0.9000	17.9961	0.5786
		GOLD			
1855–85	3 rubles	3.9264	0.9170	3.5992	0.1157
	5 rubles	6.5440	0.9170	5.9987	0.1929
	25 rubles	32.7200	0.9170	29.9933	0.9643
1886–97	5 rubles	6.4519	0.9000	5.8067	0.1867
	10 rubles	12.9039	0.9000	11.6135	0.3734
1896–1908	25 rubles	32.2595	0.9000	29.0336	0.9334
1897–1911	5 rubles	4.3012	0.9000	3.8711	0.1245
	7-1/2 rubles	6.4518	0.9000	5.8066	0.1867
	10 rubles	8.6024	0.9000	7.7422	0.2489
	15 rubles	12.9036	0.9000	11.6132	0.3734
	37-1/2 rubles	32.2590	0.9000	29.0331	0.9334
1923–82	1 chervonetz	8.6024	0.9000	7.7422	0.2489

CZARIST EMPIRE, *to 1917*

GENERAL ISSUES

FIRST COINAGE

Obverse: ***Six coats of arms on wings, no ribbons from crown***

Y#	KM#	Metal	Description	VF	EF	Unc
4	150	Cop	2 Kopeks, 1855–59	20	40	250
5	151	Cop	3 Kopeks, 1855–59	20	40	250
6	152	Cop	5 Kopeks, 1855–59	30	75	400

Y#	KM#	Metal	Description	VF	EF	Unc
13	163	Silv	5 Kopeks, 1855–58	15	30	125
14	164	Silv	10 Kopeks, 1855–58	15	30	125
15	165	Silv	20 Kopeks, 1855–58	20	40	150

Y#	KM#	Metal	Description	VF	EF	Unc
16	166	Silv	25 Kopeks, 1855–58	15	30	100
17	167	Silv	1/2 Ruble, 1855–58	40	100	300
18	168	Silv	1 Ruble, 1855–58	80	150	400

Y#	KM#	Metal	Description	VF	EF	Unc
A26	A26	Gold	5 Rubles, 1855–58	500	750	1,000

SECOND COINAGE

Obverse: ***Eight coats of arms on wings, with ribbons from crown***

Y#	KM#	Metal	Description	VF	EF	Unc
4a	4a	Cop	2 Kopeks, 1859–67	20	40	250
5a	5a	Cop	3 Kopeks, 1859–67 *1865, Rare*	20	40	250
6a	6a	Cop	5 Kopeks, 1859–67	30	75	400

Y#	KM#	Metal	Description	VF	EF	Unc
9	9	Cop	1 Kopek, 1867–1916	5	15	50
10	10	Cop	2 Kopeks, 1867–1916 *1871CPB, Extremely Rare*	5	15	50
11	11	Cop	3 Kopeks, 1867–1916 *1871CPB, Extremely Rare*	5	15	75
12	12	Cop	5 Kopeks, 1867–1916 *1871CPB, Extremely Rare*	15	30	150

Edge: *Engrailed*

Y#	KM#	Metal	Description	VF	EF	Unc
19	19	Silv	5 Kopeks, 1859–66	20	40	100
20	20	Silv	10 Kopeks, 1859–66	15	30	125
21	21	Silv	15 Kopeks, 1860–66	15	30	125
22	22	Silv	20 Kopeks, 1859–66	15	30	150

Edge: *Reeded*

Y#	KM#	Metal	Description	VF	EF	Unc
19a	19a	Silv	5 Kopeks, 1867–1915 *1904, Rare*	20	40	125
20a	20a	Silv	10 Kopeks, 1867–1917	10	25	75
21a	21a	Silv	15 Kopeks, 1867–1917 *1888, Rare*	10	25	75
22a	22a	Silv	20 Kopeks, 1867–1917 *1917, EF $250*	10	25	100

Y#	KM#	Metal	Description	VF	EF	Unc
23	23	Silv	25 Kopeks, 1859–85	25	50	175
24	24	Silv	1/2 Ruble, 1859–85	40	100	200
25	25	Silv	1 Ruble, 1859–85 *1859–62, VF $1,000*	60	125	400

Y#	KM#	Metal	Description	VF	EF	Unc
26	26	Gold	3 Rubles, 1869–85 *1882, Rare*	750	1,250	2,000
B26	B26	Gold	5 Rubles, 1859–85	500	800	1,250 *Proof: $10,000*
27	27	Gold	25 Rubles, 1876	90,000	125,000	200,000 *Proof: $250,000*

Issues With Royal Portraits or Monograms

Alexander II, 1855–1881

Y#	KM#	Metal	Description	VF	EF	Unc
1	1	Cop	1/4 Kopek, 1855–67	20	50	150
2	2	Cop	1/2 Kopek, 1855–67	20	50	150
3	3	Cop	1 Kopek, 1855–67 (3 vars)	20	50	200

Y#	KM#	Metal	Description	VF	EF	Unc
7	7	Cop	1/4 Kopek, 1867–81	25	50	150
8	8	Cop	1/2 Kopek, 1867–81	25	50	150

Dedication of Nikolai I Monument

Y#	KM#	Metal	Description	VF	EF	Unc
28	28	Silv	1 Ruble, 1859	1,000	1,500	4,000
					Proof: $7,500	

Y#	KM#	Metal	Description	VF	EF	Unc
29	29	Cop	1/4 Kopek, 1881–94	25	50	200
					Proof: $1,000	
30	30	Cop	1/2 Kopek, 1881–94	20	40	150
					Proof: $1,000	

Alexander III, 1881–1894

Coronation Commemorative

Y#	KM#	Metal	Description	VF	EF	Unc
43	43	Silv	1 Ruble, 1883	125	300	750

Y#	KM#	Metal	Description	VF	EF	Unc
44	44	Silv	25 Kopeks, 1886–94 *1889, VF $3,000*	100	175	400
45	45	Silv	50 Kopeks, 1886–94 *1889, VF $3,000*	45	100	250
46	46	Silv	1 Ruble, 1886–94 *1889, VF $10,000*	50	250	500
					Proof: $10,000	

Y#	KM#	Metal	Description	VF	EF	Unc
42	42	Gold	5 Rubles, 1886–94	150	250	400
					Proof: $15,000	
A42	A42	Gold	10 Rubles, 1886–94	2,000	4,000	7,500
					Proof: $30,000	

Nikolai II, 1894–1917

Y#	KM#	Metal	Description	VF	EF	Unc
47	47	Cop	1/4 Kopek, 1894–1916 *1894, VF $400*	20	50	100
					Proof: $750	
48	48	Cop	1/2 Kopek, 1894–1916 *1894, VF $300*	10	30	75
					Proof: $750	

Y#	KM#	Metal	Description	VF	EF	Unc
57	57	Silv	25 Kopeks, 1895–1901 *1901, Proof only: $10,000*	40	100	300
58	58	Silv	50 Kopeks, 1895–1914 *1898, 1903, Rare*	30	75	400
					Proof: $4,000	
59	59	Silv	1 Ruble, 1895–1915 *1903–06, VF $750*	75	300	1,000
					Proof: $10,000	

Coronation Commemorative

Y#	KM#	Metal	Description	VF	EF	Unc
60	60	Silv	1 Ruble, 1896	175	350	750
						Proof: $5,000

Dedication of Alexander II Monument

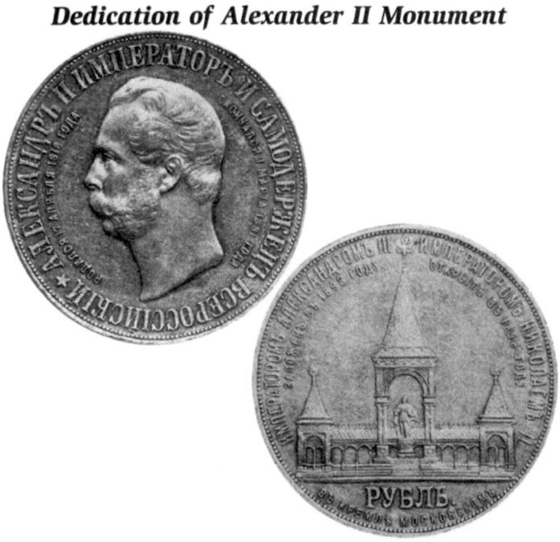

Y#	KM#	Metal	Description	VF	EF	Unc
61	61	Silv	1 Ruble, 1898	1,250	2,500	4,000

Centennial, Defeat of Napoleon

Y#	KM#	Metal	Description	VF	EF	Unc
68	68	Silv	1 Ruble, 1912	800	1,250	2,000

Dedication of Alexander III Monument

Y#	KM#	Metal	Description	VF	EF	Unc
69	69	Silv	1 Ruble, 1912	3,000	6,000	12,500

300th Anniversary of Romanoff Dynasty

Y#	KM#	Metal	Description	VF	EF	Unc
70	70	Silv	1 Ruble, 1913	100	150	300

Note: Early strikes are in low relief.

200th Anniversary, Battle of Gangut

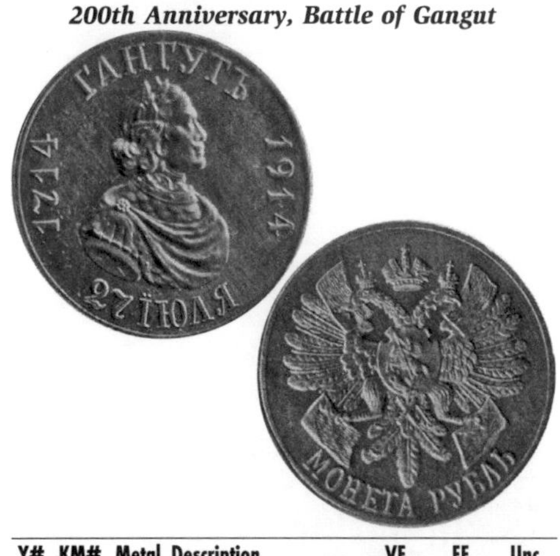

Y#	KM#	Metal	Description	VF	EF	Unc
71	71	Silv	1 Ruble, 1914	7,500	12,500	20,000

Y#	KM#	Metal	Description	VF	EF	Unc
A61	A61	Gold	5 Rubles, 1895–96, *Rare*			
A63	A63	Gold	10 Rubles, 1895–97, *Rare*			
A65	A65	Gold	25 Rubles, 1896, 1908	60,000	100,000	150,000

Note: This series was for presentation only and was not released into circulation.

Reduced-Weight Gold

Y#	KM#	Metal	Description	VF	EF	Unc
62	62	Gold	5 Rubles, 1897–1911	BV	250	300
			1906–07, Rare			*Proof: $10,000*
63	63	Gold	7-1/2 Rubles, 1897	350	500	750

Y#	KM#	Metal	Description	VF	EF	Unc
64	64	Gold	10 Rubles, 1898–1911	BV	450	600
			1906, Rare			*Proof: $10,000*
65	65	Gold	15 Rubles, 1897	BV	500	750
B65	B65	Gold	37-1/2 Rubles, 1902	60,000	100,000	150,000

Note: YB65 was for presentation only.

World War I Issues

For 1, 2, and 3 kopeks 1916 (obverse, German legend; reverse, Russian value in cross) used during German occupation of northwest Russia, see Germany YA18–C18.

RUSSIA–UNION OF SOVIET SOCIALIST REPUBLICS

SEE UNION OF SOVIET SOCIALIST REPUBLICS

RUSSIAN CAUCASIA

Russian Caucasia is the mountainous region that lies just north of Turkey and Iran, between the Black Sea and Caspian Sea. (Note: The Amirate of Daghistan is no longer listed in this volume, as the existence of the coins—which may have been patterns—is unconfirmed. They do not exist in any museum or known collection.)

CITY OF ARMAVIR

A trade center in northwestern Caucasia, Armavir issued provincial coins and notes after coming under Soviet control in early 1918. The coins listed here formerly appeared as Russia, Y72–74.

Y#	KM#	Metal	Description	VF	EF	Unc
1	1	Cop	1 Ruble, 1918 (24 mm)	150	300	500

Y#	KM#	Metal	Description	VF	EF	Unc
2	2	Cop	3 Rubles, 1918 (28 mm)	125	200	300
3	3	Cop	5 Rubles, 1918 (32 mm)	250	300	750

Note: Pieces with larger diameters and/or of different metals are thought to be patterns.

RUSSIAN TURKESTAN

Russian Turkestan is in south central Russia, lying north of Iran and Afghanistan, and stretching from Sinkiang in the east to the Caspian Sea in the west. One of the earliest centers of civilization, it served traders and conquerors as the bridge between Eastern and Western worlds.

KHANATE OF KHIVA *(Khwarezm)*

A former Islamic state between Iran and the Aral Sea. It was independent until becoming a Russian protectorate in 1873, regaining independence in 1918. In 1920, it became the Khwarezm Soviet People's Republic. *Capital:* Khiva.

Sayyid Muhammad Khan, *AH 1272–1282 (1856–1865)*

Y#	KM#	Metal	Description	VF	EF	Unc
1	1	Cop	1 Pul, AH 1274 (1857) (15 mm)	30	75	—

Y#	KM#	Metal	Description	VF	EF	Unc
2	2	Silv	1 Tenga, AH 1275–81 (1858–64) (2 vars)	30	75	—

SAYYID MUHAMMAD RAHIM, *AH 1282–1328 (1865–1910)*

Y#	KM#	Metal	Description	VF	EF	Unc
3	3	Cop	1 Pul, AH 1302–11 (1884–93) (17 mm)	30	75	—

Y#	KM#	Metal	Description	VF	EF	Unc
6	6	Silv	1 Tenga, AH 1284–1313 (1867–95)	30	50	—

SAYYID ABDULLAH KHAN AND DJUNAID KHAN, *AH 1337–1338 (1918–1920)*

Y#	KM#	Metal	Description	VF	EF	Unc
8	8	Silv	1 Tenga, AH 1337 (1918)	100	200	—
A9	A9	Cop	1 Tenga, AH 1337 (1918)	250	500	—
9	9	Cop	2-1/2 Tenga, AH 1337 (1918) (21 mm)	50	100	—
10	10	Cop	5 Tenga, AH 1337 (1918) (28 mm)	50	100	—
11	11	Cop	15 Tenga, AH 1338 (1919)	250	400	—

KHWAREZM SOVIET PEOPLE'S REPUBLIC

The successor to the Khanate of Khiva was formed by Bolshevik factions early in 1920. Four years later it was divided between the Uzbek and Turkmen Soviet Socialist Republics.

Y#	KM#	Metal	Description	VF	EF	Unc
1	15	Bz/Br	20 Rubles, AH 1338–40 (1920–22)	50	80	—

Y#	KM#	Metal	Description	VF	EF	Unc
2	16	Bz/Br	25 Rubles, AH 1339 (1921)	40	75	—

Y#	KM#	Metal	Description	VF	EF	Unc
3	17	Bz/Br	100 Rubles, AH 1339 (1921)	50	80	—

Y#	KM#	Metal	Description	VF	EF	Unc
4	18	Bz/Br	500 Rubles, AH 1339 (1921) (25 mm)	200	350	—
4a	19	Bz/Br	500 Rubles, AH 1339–40 (1921–22) (19 mm)	40	75	—

EMIRATE OF BUKHARA

A former Islamic state situated north of Afghanistan and east of Khiva. Falling under Russian protection in 1868, it was again briefly independent from 1920 to 1924. In the latter year it was divided between the Uzbek, Turkmen, and Tadzhik Soviet Socialist Republics. *Capital:* Bukhara.

SAYYID ABDUL AHAD, *AH 1303–1329 (1885–1911)*

Y#	KM#	Metal	Description	VF	EF	Unc
1	87	Cop	1 Falus, AH 1322, 24 (1904, 06) (15 mm)	25	40	—

Y#	KM#	Metal	Description	VF	EF	Unc
2	63	Silv	1 Tenga, AH 1304–22 (1886–1904) (2 vars)	25	40	—

Y#	KM#	Metal	Description	VF	EF	Unc
3	65	Gold	1 Tilla, AH 1303–28 (1885–1910) (21–23 mm)	250	400	—

ALIM IBN SAYYID MIR AMIN, *AH 1329–1338 (1911–1920)*

Y#	KM#	Metal	Description	VF	EF	Unc
4	42	Bz	1 Falus, AH 1331–36 (1913–18) (15–16 mm)	20	35	—
5	44	Bz	4 Falus, AH 1333–34 (1915–16) (15 mm)	20	35	—
A5	45	Bz	8 Falus, AH 1335 (1917) (16 mm)	30	50	—

Y#	KM#	Metal	Description	VF	EF	Unc
6	46.1	Bz	1 Tenga, AH 1336 (1918) (15 mm)	30	50	—

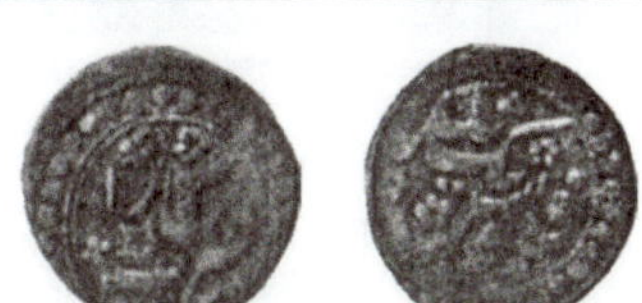

Y#	KM#	Metal	Description	VF	EF	Unc
6a	46.2	Bz	1 Tenga, AH 1336–37 (1918–19) (17–18 mm)	20	35	—

Y#	KM#	Metal	Description	VF	EF	Unc
7	47	Bz/Br	2 Tenga, AH 1337 (1919)	25	50	—

Y#	KM#	Metal	Description	VF	EF	Unc
8	48	Bz/Br	3 Tenga, AH 1336–37 (1918–19)	25	50	—
9	49	Bz/Br	4 Tenga, AH 1336 (1918) (30 mm)	125	200	—
10	50	Bz/Br	5 Tenga, AH 1336–37 (1918–19) (27 mm)	65	100	—

Y#	KM#	Metal	Description	VF	EF	Unc
11	53	Bz/Br	10 Tenga, AH (1919) 1337	25	40	—

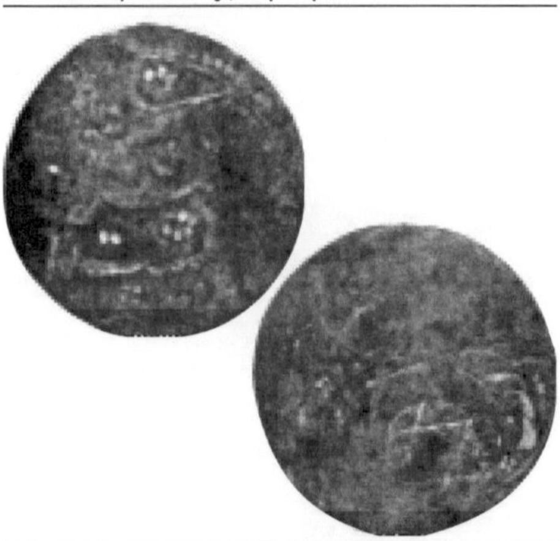

Y#	KM#	Metal	Description	VF	EF	Unc
12	51	Bz/Br	20 Tenga, AH 1336–37 (1918–19)	50	125	—

RWANDA

Formerly part of German East Africa, a post–World War I League of Nations mandate placed Ruanda-Urundi (in east-central Africa) under Belgian trusteeship. It was later united administratively with the Belgian Congo as a UN trust territory. These districts were renamed in 1960 and became independent in 1962. In the 1990s civil war, genocide, and border wars with the Congo wracked the nation until the 21st century when a new constitution instituted an uneasy balance of political power. Rwanda joined the Commonwealth of Nations in 2009. *Languages:* Kinyarwanda, French, English, Kiswahili. *Capital:* Kigali.

MONETARY SYSTEM
100 centimes = 1 franc

Y#	KM#	Metal	Description	VF	EF	Unc
1	5	C-N	1 Franc, 1964–65	0.50	1.00	2.50
2	6	Bz	5 Francs, 1964–65	0.35	0.70	3.50
3	7	C-N	10 Francs, 1964	1.25	2.50	7.00

RWANDA AND BURUNDI

Formerly part of German East Africa, a post–World War I League of Nations mandate placed Ruanda-Urundi in east-central Africa under Belgian trusteeship. It was later united administratively with the Belgian Congo as a UN trust territory. These districts were renamed in 1960 and became independent in 1962.

MONETARY SYSTEM
100 centimes = 1 franc

Legend: *B.E.R.B. (Banque d'Emission du Rwanda et du Burundi)*

Y#	KM#	Metal	Description	VF	EF	Unc
1	1	Br	1 Franc, 1960–64	0.75	2	6

SAARLAND

An important mining region between France and Germany, Saarland was taken from Germany and united economically to France as reparations after both World Wars. In 1935 and again in 1957, the inhabitants (mostly Germans) voted to return to Germany.

MONETARY SYSTEM
100 centimen = 1 frank

Y#	KM#	Metal	Description	VF	EF	Unc
1	1	A-Bz	10 Franken, 1954	4	8.00	15.00
2	2	A-Bz	20 Franken, 1954	5	9.00	16.50
3	3	A-Bz	50 Franken, 1954	25	32.50	55.00

Y#	KM#	Metal	Description	VF	EF	Unc
4	4	C-N	100 Franken, 1955	7.50	15	30

ST. PIERRE AND MIQUELON

These barren islands 10 miles off the southwest coast of Newfoundland are the last North American remnant of the French colonial empire. *Language:* French. *Capital:* St. Pierre.

MONETARY SYSTEM
100 centimes = 1 franc

Y#	KM#	Metal	Description	VF	EF	Unc
1	1	Alum	1 Franc, 1948	1	4	25
2	2	Alum	2 Francs, 1948	2	6	30

ST. THOMAS AND PRINCE

Two islands in the Gulf of Guinea off the west coast of Africa, St. Thomas and Prince was colonized by Portugal in the 15th century. Its independence was granted in 1975. *Language:* Portuguese. *Capital:* Sao Tome.

MONETARY SYSTEM
100 centavos = 1 escudo

PRECIOUS METAL CONTENT

Dates	Denomination	Gross Wt (g)	Fineness	Net Wt (g)	Troy Oz.
		SILVER			
1939–51	2-1/2 escudos	3.5000	0.6500	2.2750	0.0731
	5 escudos	7.0000	0.6500	4.5500	0.1463
1939	10 escudos	12.5000	0.8350	10.4375	0.3356
1951	10 escudos	12.5000	0.7200	9.0000	0.2894

Y#	KM#	Metal	Description	VF	EF	Unc
1	2	N-Bz	10 Centavos, 1929	3	15.00	45
2	3	N-Bz	20 Centavos, 1929	4	17.50	50
3	1	N-Bz	50 Centavos, 1928–29 *1928, VF $85*	35	75.00	225

Y#	KM#	Metal	Description	VF	EF	Unc
4	4	C-N	1 Escudo, 1939	20	50	250

Y#	KM#	Metal	Description	VF	EF	Unc
5	8	N-Bz	50 Centavos, 1948	15	50	175
6	9	N-Bz	1 Escudo, 1948	20	60	225

Y#	KM#	Metal	Description	VF	EF	Unc
7	5	Silv	2-1/2 Escudos, 1939, 48	15	40	150
8	6	Silv	5 Escudos, 1939, 48	20	50	175
9	7	Silv	10 Escudos, 1939	30	75	350

Obverse: ***COLONIA DE omitted***

Y#	KM#	Metal	Description	VF	EF	Unc
10	10	C-N	50 Centavos, 1951	7	15	50
11	11	C-N	1 Escudo, 1951	10	40	150

Y#	KM#	Metal	Description	VF	EF	Unc
12	12	Silv	2-1/2 Escudos, 1951	8	25	75
13	13	Silv	5 Escudos, 1951	5	16	45
14	14	Silv	10 Escudos, 1951	7	15	30

Y#	KM#	Metal	Description	VF	EF	Unc
15	15	Bz	10 Centavos, 1962	1.00	2.00	10
16	16.1	Bz	20 Centavos, 1962	1.00	2.50	12
17	17.1	Bz	50 Centavos, 1962	1.00	2.00	10
18	18	Bz	1 Escudo, 1962, 71	0.50	2.00	4

Y#	KM#	Metal	Description	VF	EF	Unc
19	19	C-N	2-1/2 Escudos, 1962, 71	1.00	2.50	7.50
20	20	Silv	5 Escudos, 1962	1.50	4.00	9.00

SAN MARINO

The world's smallest and oldest republic, San Marino is said to have been founded at the beginning of the 4th century. It is completely surrounded by Italy, but managed to survive intact the Napoleonic Wars, the unification of Italy, and both World Wars. *Language:* Italian. *Capital:* San Marino.

MONETARY SYSTEM
100 centesimi = 1 lira

PRECIOUS METAL CONTENT

Dates	Denomination	Gross Wt (g)	Fineness	Net Wt (g)	Troy Oz.
		SILVER			
1898–1906	50 centesimi	2.5000	0.8350	2.0875	0.0671
	1 lira	5.0000	0.8350	4.1750	0.1342
	2 lire	10.0000	0.8350	8.3500	0.2685
	5 lire	25.0000	0.9000	22.5000	0.7234
1931–38	5 lire	5.0000	0.8350	4.1750	0.1342
	10 lire	10.0000	0.8350	8.3500	0.2685
1931–36	20 lire	15.0000	0.8000	12.0000	0.3858
1935–38	20 lire	20.0000	0.6000	12.0000	0.3858
		GOLD			
1925	10 lire	3.2258	0.9000	2.9032	0.0933
	20 lire	6.4516	0.9000	5.8064	0.1867

FIRST COINAGE

Y#	KM#	Metal	Description	VF	EF	Unc
1	1	Cop	5 Centesimi, 1864–94	20	45	115
2	2	Cop	10 Centesimi, 1875–94	20	65	135

Y#	KM#	Metal	Description	VF	EF	Unc
3	3	Silv	50 Centesimi, 1898	22.50	35	65
4	4	Silv	1 Lira, 1898, 1906	25.00	50	135
5	5	Silv	2 Lire, 1898, 1906	35.00	85	165

Y#	KM#	Metal	Description	VF	EF	Unc
6	6	Silv	5 Lire, 1898	115	175	500

SECOND COINAGE

Y#	KM#	Metal	Description	VF	EF	Unc
14	12	Bz	5 Centesimi, 1935–38	3.25	5.00	10
15	13	Bz	10 Centesimi, 1935–38	3.25	6.50	15

Y#	KM#	Metal	Description	VF	EF	Unc
9	9	Silv	5 Lire, 1931–38	6.50	10	22.50

Y#	KM#	Metal	Description	VF	EF	Unc
10	10	Silv	10 Lire, 1931–38	22.50	32.50	85

Y#	KM#	Metal	Description	VF	EF	Unc
11	11	Silv	20 Lire, 1931–36 (15 g, .800 fine)	40	100	225
11a	11a	Silv	20 Lire, 1935, 37–38 (20 g, .600 fine)	175	300	650

Y#	KM#	Metal	Description	VF	EF	Unc
12	7	Gold	10 Lire, 1925	350	475	950
13	8	Gold	20 Lire, 1925	1,000	1,500	2,000

SARAWAK

A territory on the northwest coast of Borneo, Sarawak was given by the sultan of Brunei to an Englishman, James Brooke, in 1841. Brooke and his descendants were known as the "White Rajahs." Following World War II, Sarawak became a British colony. In 1963 it joined Malaya, Sabah, and Singapore to form Malaysia. *Languages:* Malay and Chinese dialects. *Capital:* Kuching.

MONETARY SYSTEM

100 cents = 1 dollar

PRECIOUS METAL CONTENT

Dates	Denomination	Gross Wt (g)	Fineness	Net Wt (g)	Troy Oz.
		SILVER			
1900–15	5 cents	1.3500	0.8000	1.0800	0.0347
	10 cents	2.7100	0.8000	2.1680	0.0697
	20 cents	5.4300	0.8000	4.3440	0.1396
	50 cents	13.5700	0.8000	10.8560	0.3490
1920	5 cents	1.3500	0.4000	0.5400	0.0174
	10 cents	2.7100	0.4000	1.0840	0.0349
	20 cents	5.4300	0.4000	2.1720	0.0699
1927	20 cents	5.0800	0.4000	2.0320	0.0653
	50 cents	10.3000	0.5000	5.1500	0.1656

J. BROOKE, RAJAH, *1841–1868*

Y#	KM#	Metal	Description	VF	EF	Unc
1	Tn1	C/Br	1 Doit, Sept 24, 1841	5,000	7,000	10,000

Regular Coinage

Y#	KM#	Metal	Description	VF	EF	Unc
2	1	Cop	1/4 Cent, 1863	125	250	500
						Proof: $3,500
3	2	Cop	1/2 Cent, 1863	100	175	300
						Proof: $3,500
4	3	Cop	1 Cent, 1863	15	80	200
						Proof: $1,500

C. BROOKE, RAJAH, *1868–1917*

Y#	KM#	Metal	Description	VF	EF	Unc
5	4	Cop	1/4 Cent, 1870, 96	45	75	200
						Proof: $3,500
6	5	Cop	1/2 Cent, 1870–96	30	60	200
						Proof: $3,500
7	6	Cop	1 Cent, 1870–91	25	55	200
						Proof: $3,500

Y#	KM#	Metal	Description	VF	EF	Unc
8	7	Cop	1 Cent, 1892–97	25	55	250
						Proof: $3,500

Y#	KM#	Metal	Description	VF	EF	Unc
9	8	Silv	5 Cents, 1900–15	45	80	275
					Proof: $3,500	
10	9	Silv	10 Cents, 1900–15	35	55	175
					Proof: $4,500	
11	10	Silv	20 Cents, 1900–15	60	175	500
			1915, EF $500		*Proof: $4,500*	
12	11	Silv	50 Cents, 1900, 06	250	500	2,000
					Proof: $15,000	

Note: Most Sarawak silver has been mounted and repaired (examine the edge). Values shown are for original examples. Repaired coins are worth less than half these values.

C.V. Brooke, Rajah, *1917–1946*

Y#	KM#	Metal	Description	VF	EF	Unc
13	20	Bz	1/2 Cent, 1933	10	20	40
14	18	Bz	1 Cent, 1927–41	1	2	25
			1941, VF $600		*Proof: $350*	

Y#	KM#	Metal	Description	VF	EF	Unc
15	12	C-N	1 Cent, 1920	10	20	95
16	14	C-N	5 Cents, 1920, 27	7	25	125
17	16	C-N	10 Cents, 1920–34	5	10	25

Y#	KM#	Metal	Description	VF	EF	Unc
18	13	Silv	5 Cents, 1920	100	200	500
19	15	Silv	10 Cents, 1920	90	175	350
20	17	Silv	20 Cents, 1920, 27	60	95	200
			1920	125	225	900
21	19	Silv	50 Cents, 1927	65	125	750

SAUDI ARABIA

An absolute monarchy until the country's first constitution was adopted in 1992, Saudi Arabia covers most of the Arabian peninsula. The country was formed from the sultanate of Nejd and the kingdom of Hejaz, captured from the Turks and established as the United Kingdom of Saudi Arabia in 1932. *Language:* Arabic. *Capital:* Riyadh.

MONETARY SYSTEM

20 ghirsh = 1 riyal
40 riyals, silver = 1 guinea, gold (1959)

PRECIOUS METAL CONTENT

Dates	Denomination	Gross Wt (g)	Fineness	Net Wt (g)	Troy Oz.
		SILVER			
1928–30	1/4 riyal	6.0500	0.9170	5.5479	0.1783
	1/2 riyal	12.1000	0.9170	11.0957	0.3567
	1 riyal	24.1000	0.9170	22.0997	0.7105
1935	1/4 riyal	3.1000	0.9170	2.8427	0.0913
	1/2 riyal	5.8500	0.9170	5.3645	0.1724
1935–50	1 riyal	11.6000	0.9170	10.6372	0.3419
1955	1/4 riyal	2.9500	0.9170	2.7052	0.0869
	1/2 riyal	5.9500	0.9170	5.4562	0.1754
		GOLD			
1945–47	1 sovereign	7.9881	0.9170	7.3224	0.2354
	4 sovereigns	31.9522	0.9170	29.2895	0.9417
1951, 57	1 guinea	7.9881	0.9170	7.3224	0.2354

Abd al-Aziz ibn Sa'ud, *AH 1344–1371 (1926–1953)*

Y#	KM#	Metal	Description	VF	EF	Unc
1	1	Cop	1/4 Ghirsh, AH 1343 (1925)	125	200	—
2	2	Cop	1/2 Ghirsh, AH 1343 (1925)	95	150	350

Note: These copper coins were struck in occupied Mecca at the Hejaz Mint in 1925 by Ibn Sa'ud while establishing his dual kingdom.

Y#	KM#	Metal	Description	VF	EF	Unc
A3	A3	Bz	1/2 Ghirsh, AH 1344 (1926)	35	65	125

Title: King of Hejaz and Sultan of Nejd

Y#	KM#	Metal	Description	VF	EF	Unc
3	4	C-N	1/4 Ghirsh, AH 1344 (1926)	15	35	—
4	5	C-N	1/2 Ghirsh, AH 1344 (1926)	30	65	—
5	6	C-N	1 Ghirsh, AH 1344 (1926)	35	70	—

TITLE: KING OF HEJAZ AND NEJD AND DEPENDENCIES

Y#	KM#	Metal	Description	VF	EF	Unc
6	7	C-N	1/4 Ghirsh, AH 1346 (1928)	25	50	—
7	8	C-N	1/2 Ghirsh, AH 1346 (1928)	25	50	—
8	9	C-N	1 Ghirsh, AH 1346 (1928)	30	60	—

Modified Dies

Y#	KM#	Metal	Description	VF	EF	Unc
6a	13	C-N	1/4 Ghirsh, AH 1348 (1930)	45	95	—
7a	14	C-N	1/2 Ghirsh, AH 1348 (1930)	45	95	—
8a	15	C-N	1 Ghirsh, AH 1348 (1930)	50	100	—

Y#	KM#	Metal	Description	VF	EF	Unc
12	10	Silv	1/4 Riyal, AH 1346, 48 (1928, 30) (24 mm)	160	285	—
13	11	Silv	1/2 Riyal, AH 1346, 48 (1928, 30) (27 mm)	400	800	—
14	12	Silv	1 Riyal, AH 1346, 48 (1928, 30) (37 mm)	150	250	—

TITLE: KING OF SAUDI ARABIA

Edge: ***Plain***

Y#	KM#	Metal	Description	VF	EF	Unc
9	19.1	C-N	1/4 Ghirsh, AH 1356 (1937)	10	40	65
10	20.1	C-N	1/2 Ghirsh, AH 1356 (1937)	10	40	65
11	21.1	C-N	1 Ghirsh, AH 1356 (1937)	8	35	60

Edge: ***Reeded***

Y#	KM#	Metal	Description	VF	EF	Unc
9a	19.2	C-N	1/4 Ghirsh, AH 1356 (1937)	1.00	2.50	7.50
10a	20.2	C-N	1/2 Ghirsh, AH 1356 (1937)	1.50	3.00	10.00
11a	21.2	C-N	1 Ghirsh, AH 1356 (1937)	2.50	5.00	13.00

Y#	KM#	Metal	Description	VF	EF	Unc
18	16	Silv	1/4 Riyal, AH 1354 (1935)	5.00	10	17.50
19	17	Silv	1/2 Riyal, AH 1354 (1935)	6.00	15	30.00
20	18	Silv	1 Riyal, AH 1354–70 (1935–51)	7.50	20	35.00

Y#	KM#	Metal	Description	VF	EF	Unc
A21	22–25	C-N	1/4 Ghirsh, counterstamped with Arabic "65" in AH 1365 (1946)	30	—	—
B21	26–29	C-N	1/2 Ghirsh, counterstamped with Arabic "65" in AH 1365 (1946)	40	—	—
C21	30–33	C-N	1 Ghirsh, counterstamped with Arabic "65" in AH 1365 (1946)	45	—	—

Y#	KM#	Metal	Description	VF	EF	Unc
21	35	Gold	USA (1 Sovereign), ND (1947) .2354 Troy ounces fine gold	1,350	1,750	2,250
22	34	Gold	USA (4 Sovereigns), ND (1945–46), gross weight 493.1 grains	1,500	1,900	2,500

Note: Y21–22 were struck at Philadelphia, and although often considered bullion pieces only, are said to have circulated briefly. Counterfeits exist.

Y#	KM#	Metal	Description	VF	EF	Unc
23	36	Gold	1 Guinea, AH 1370 (1951)	400	425	475

SA'UD IBN ABDUL AZIZ, *AH 1371–1382 (1953–1964)*

Y#	KM#	Metal	Description	VF	EF	Unc
30	44	Bz	1 Halala, AH 1383 (1964)	0.60	1	3

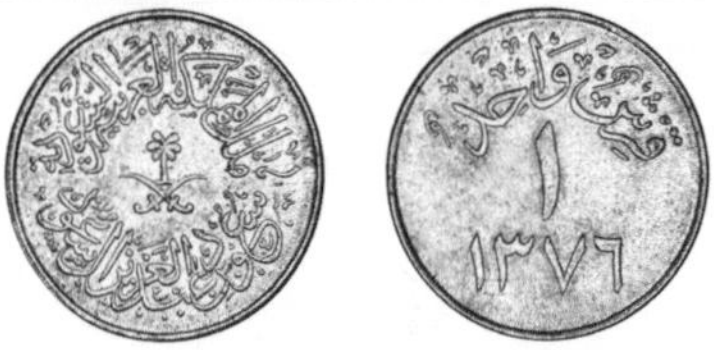

Y#	KM#	Metal	Description	VF	EF	Unc
A23	40	C-N	1 Ghirsh, AH 1376, 78 (1957, 59)	2	4	6
24	41	C-N	2 Ghirsh, AH 1376, 79 (1957, 60)	2	4	6
25	42	C-N	4 Ghirsh, AH 1376, 78 (1957, 59)	1	3	5

Y#	KM#	Metal	Description	VF	EF	Unc
26	37	Silv	1/4 Riyal, AH 1374 (1955)	3	6	10
27	38	Silv	1/2 Riyal, AH 1374 (1955)	6	10	30
28	39	Silv	1 Riyal, AH 1374 (1955)	10	20	40

Y#	KM#	Metal	Description	VF	EF	Unc
29	43	Gold	1 Guinea, AH 1377 (1957–58)	BV	385	475

SERBIA

For 500 years Serbia was a vassal principality of Turkey. It gained its freedom in 1878. After World War I it joined other Slavic states to form Yugoslavia. When that federation dissolved in the early 1990s, Serbia joined with Montenegro as the Federal Republic of Yugoslavia. The federation restructured as two republics in 2003 and separated in 2006 by a Montenegrin referendum. *Languages:* Serbian, Romanian, Hungarian, Slovak, Croatian. *Capital:* Belgrade.

MONETARY SYSTEM

100 para = 1 dinar

PRECIOUS METAL CONTENT

Dates	Denomination	Gross Wt (g)	Fineness	Net Wt (g)	Troy Oz.
		SILVER			
1875–1915	50 para	2.5000	0.8350	2.0875	0.0671
	1 dinar	5.0000	0.8350	4.1750	0.1342
	2 dinara	10.0000	0.8350	8.3500	0.2685
	5 dinara	25.0000	0.9000	22.5000	0.7234
		GOLD			
1879–82	10 dinara	3.2258	0.9000	2.9032	0.0933
	20 dinara	6.4516	0.9000	5.8064	0.1867

MICHAEL, OBRENOVICH III,
1839–1842, 1860–1868

Y#	KM#	Metal	Description	VF	EF	Unc
1	1	Bz	1 Para, 1868	20.00	45	125
2	2	Bz	5 Para, 1868	25.00	50	165
3	3	Bz	10 Para, 1868	27.50	60	200

MILAN, OBRENOVICH IV
AS PRINCE, 1868–1882

Y#	KM#	Metal	Description	VF	EF	Unc
4	4	Silv	50 Para, 1875	25	65	175
5	5	Silv	1 Dinar, 1875	30	75	250
6	6	Silv	2 Dinara, 1875	75	200	650

Y#	KM#	Metal	Description	VF	EF	Unc
7	7	Bz	5 Para, 1879	25	50	175
8	8	Bz	10 Para, 1879	25	50	225

Y#	KM#	Metal	Description	VF	EF	Unc
4a	9	Silv	50 Para, 1879	25	60	400
5a	10	Silv	1 Dinar, 1879	25	60	450
6a	11	Silv	2 Dinara, 1879	30	75	550
9	12–13	Silv	5 Dinara, 1879	75	165	600
						Proof: $2,000

Y#	KM#	Metal	Description	VF	EF	Unc
10	14	Gold	20 Dinara, 1879	345	375	900

As King Milan I, 1882–1889

Y#	KM#	Metal	Description	VF	EF	Unc
11	16	Gold	10 Dinara, 1882	200	275	450
12	17	Gold	20 Dinara, 1882	325	375	650

General Coinage

Y13–16 were issued without the name of the ruler through successive reigns.

Y#	KM#	Metal	Description	VF	EF	Unc
13	23	Bz	2 Pare, 1904	3	15	40

Y#	KM#	Metal	Description	VF	EF	Unc
14	18	C-N	5 Para, 1883–1917	4.00	17.50	50
15	19	C-N	10 Para, 1883–1917	3.50	10.00	30
16	20	C-N	20 Para, 1883–1917	3.50	10.00	30

Alexander I, *1889–1902*

Y#	KM#	Metal	Description	VF	EF	Unc
17	21	Silv	1 Dinar, 1897	15	35	100
18	22	Silv	2 Dinara, 1897	20	55	125

Petar I, *1903–1918*

Obverse: ***Designer's name SCHWARTZ below neck***

Y#	KM#	Metal	Description	VF	EF	Unc
19	24.1	Silv	50 Para, 1904–15	3	7.50	17.50
20	25.1	Silv	1 Dinar, 1904–15	5	10.00	25.00
21	26.1	Silv	2 Dinara, 1904–15	10	18.00	40.00

Obverse: ***Without name below neck***

Y#	KM#	Metal	Description	VF	EF	Unc
19a	24.2	Silv	50 Para, 1915	15.00	30	65
20a	25.2	Silv	1 Dinar, 1915	13.00	25	70
21a	26.2	Silv	2 Dinara, 1915	22.50	50	125

Centennial, First Uprising Against Turks

Y#	KM#	Metal	Description	VF	EF	Unc
22	27	Silv	5 Dinara, 1904	65	160	525

World War II
German-Formed State

Y#	KM#	Metal	Description	VF	EF	Unc
23	30	Zinc	50 Para, 1942	3	10	30
24	31	Zinc	1 Dinar, 1942	3	10	30
25	32	Zinc	2 Dinara, 1942	3	10	30

Y#	KM#	Metal	Description	VF	EF	Unc
26	33	Zinc	10 Dinara, 1943	5	15	25

SEYCHELLES

Seychelles is a tropical 100-island archipelago in the Indian Ocean, some 1,000 miles east of Africa. Formerly a British colony, it became independent within the Commonwealth in 1976 and has evolved into a socialist multi-party republic. *Languages:* English, Creole. *Capital:* Victoria.

MONETARY SYSTEM:
100 cents = 1 rupee

PRECIOUS METAL CONTENT

Dates	Denomination	Gross Wt (g)	Fineness	Net Wt (g)	Troy Oz.
		SILVER			
1939–44	25 cents	2.9160	0.5000	1.4800	0.0469
	1/2 rupee	5.8319	0.5000	2.9160	0.0937
	1 rupee	11.6638	0.5000	5.8319	0.1875

GEORGE VI,
1936–1952

Y#	KM#	Metal	Description	VF	EF	Unc
1	1	C-N	10 Cents, 1939–44	12.50	20	80

Y#	KM#	Metal	Description	VF	EF	Unc
2	2	Silv	25 Cents, 1939–44	5	15	90
3	3	Silv	1/2 Rupee, 1939	15	25	100
4	4	Silv	1 Rupee, 1939	20	65	165

New Legend: ***KING GEORGE THE SIXTH***

Y#	KM#	Metal	Description	VF	EF	Unc
5	5	Bz	1 Cent, 1948	0.50	2.50	12.50
6	6	Bz	2 Cents, 1948	0.50	2.50	15.00
7	7	Bz	5 Cents, 1948	0.75	3.00	20.00

Y#	KM#	Metal	Description	VF	EF	Unc
8	8	C-N	10 Cents, 1951	3	8	25

Y#	KM#	Metal	Description	VF	EF	Unc
9	9	C-N	25 Cents, 1951	3	10	25

ELIZABETH II,
1952–1976

Y#	KM#	Metal	Description	VF	EF	Unc
14	14	Bz	1 Cent, 1959–69	0.50	1	4
15	15	Bz	2 Cents, 1959–69	1.00	2	6
16	16	Bz	5 Cents, 1964–71	0.50	1	4

Y#	KM#	Metal	Description	VF	EF	Unc
10	10	N-Br	10 Cents, 1953–74, 12-sided	0.25	0.50	1

Y#	KM#	Metal	Description	VF	EF	Unc
11	11	C-N	25 Cents, 1954–74	0.50	1	2
12	12	C-N	1/2 Rupee, 1954–74	0.50	1	2
13	13	C-N	1 Rupee, 1954–74	0.50	1	3

SIAM
SEE THAILAND

SIERRA LEONE

Sierra Leone is nominally a constitutional democracy on the Atlantic Ocean in west Africa. It became a British colony in the 19th century and gained independence within the British Commonwealth in 1961, declaring itself a republic in 1971. An era of military coups and civil war has been followed by more peaceful and democratic government. *Languages:* English, Mende, Temne, Krio. *Capital:* Freetown.

MONETARY SYSTEM
100 cents = 1 leone

ELIZABETH II, *1952–1971*

Y#	KM#	Metal	Description	VF	EF	Unc
1	16	Bz	1/2 Cent, 1964	0.10	0.25	1

Y#	KM#	Metal	Description	VF	EF	Unc
2	17	Bz	1 Cent, 1964	0.10	0.25	1

Y#	KM#	Metal	Description	VF	EF	Unc
3	18	C-N	5 Cents, 1964	0.20	0.50	1

Y#	KM#	Metal	Description	VF	EF	Unc
4	19	C-N	10 Cents, 1964, 78	0.25	0.50	1

Y#	KM#	Metal	Description	VF	EF	Unc
5	20	C-N	20 Cents, 1964	0.30	0.80	1.25

Y#	KM#	Metal	Description	VF	EF	Unc
6	21	C-N	*1 Leone, 1964, Proof only: $12*			
6a	21a	Silv	*1 Leone, 1964, Proof only: $1,250*			

Y#	KM#	Metal	Description	VF	EF	Unc
1–6	16–21		*Proof Set: $30*			
1–6a	16–21a	Silv	*Silver Proof Set: $5,500*			

SLOVAKIA

In 1939, Nazi Germany annexed the historical regions of Bohemia and Moravia in Czechoslovakia, declaring them a protectorate of Germany on behalf of their large populations of ethnic Germans. In reality, Germany needed the arms-manufacturing capabilities of the region to prepare for the coming war. From 1939 until 1945, ethnic Germans in the protectorate were subject to German law, while the remainder of the population was ruled by a puppet Czech government. After Germany surrendered to the Allies in 1945, the region returned to Czechoslovakia, and its ethnic Germans were expelled to Austria and Germany. *Languages:* Czech, German. *Capital:* Prague.

MONETARY SYSTEM
100 haleru = 1 koruna

GERMAN PROTECTORATE, *1939–1945*

MONETARY SYSTEM
100 halierov = 1 koruna

Y#	KM#	Metal	Description	VF	EF	Unc
S19b	8	Zinc	5 Halierov, 1942	10	20	40

Y#	KM#	Metal	Description	VF	EF	Unc
S20	1	Bz	10 Halierov, 1939, 42	2	5	15

Y#	KM#	Metal	Description	VF	EF	Unc
S21	4	Bz	20 Halierov, 1940–42 *1942, EF $55*	3	7.50	17.50

Y#	KM#	Metal	Description	VF	EF	Unc
S22	5	C-N	50 Halierov, 1940–41 *1940, VF $40*	2	3	7

Y#	KM#	Metal	Description	VF	EF	Unc
S23	6	C-N	1 Koruna, 1940–45	1.50	2.50	6.50
S21a	4a	Alum	20 Halierov, 1942–43	1.75	3.50	8.00
S22b	5a	Alum	50 Halierov, 1943–44	1.75	3.50	6.50

Y#	KM#	Metal	Description	VF	EF	Unc
S24	2	Nick	5 Korun, 1939	3	5	12

Y#	KM#	Metal	Description	VF	EF	Unc
S25	9	Silv	10 Korun, 1944	4	7	12.50

Election of President Tiso

Y#	KM#	Metal	Description	VF	EF	Unc
S26	3	Silv	20 Korun, 1939	10	17.50	40

Y#	KM#	Metal	Description	VF	EF	Unc
S27	7	Silv	20 Korun, 1941	10	13	20

Fifth Anniversary of Independent Slovakia

Y#	KM#	Metal	Description	VF	EF	Unc
S28	10	Silv	50 Korun, 1944	11	15	30

SOMALIA

On the Horn of Africa, this independent republic was established in 1960 with the union of the former British Somaliland protectorate and the former Italian trust territory of Somalia. The army seized power in 1969 and renamed the country Somali Democratic Republic. Decades of civil war and famine were followed by several transitional governments and, eventually, a federal parliamentary republic that began in 2012. *Languages:* Somali, Arabic, English, Italian. *Capital:* Mogadishu.

MONETARY SYSTEM
100 centesimi = 1 somalo

Italian Trust Territory Issues

Y#	KM#	Metal	Description	VF	EF	Unc
1	1	Bz	1 Centesimo, 1950	1.50	4.00	8
2	2	Bz	5 Centesimi, 1950	1.50	4.00	8
3	3	Bz	10 Centesimi, 1950	0.85	2.25	8

Y#	KM#	Metal	Description	VF	EF	Unc
4	4	Bill	50 Centesimi, 1950	5	12.50	22.50
5	5	Bill	1 Somalo, 1950	4	10.00	20.00

SOUTH AFRICAN REPUBLIC

This Boer republic in the Transvaal was independent between 1857–1877 and 1881–1900, each period ending with annexation by Great Britain. It is now part of the Republic of South Africa. *Capital:* Pretoria.

MONETARY SYSTEM

12 pence = 1 shilling
20 shillings = 1 pond

PRECIOUS METAL CONTENT

Dates	Denomination	Gross Wt (g)	Fineness	Net Wt (g)	Troy Oz.
		SILVER			
1892–97	3 pence	1.4138	0.9250	1.3078	0.0420
	6 pence	2.8276	0.9250	2.6155	0.0841
	1 shilling	5.6552	0.9250	5.2311	0.1682
	2 shillings	11.3104	0.9250	10.4621	0.3364
	2-1/2 shillings	14.1380	0.9250	13.0777	0.4205
	5 shillings	28.2759	0.9250	26.1552	0.8409
1961–64	2-1/2 cents	1.4100	0.5000	0.7050	0.0226
	5 cents	2.8300	0.5000	1.4150	0.0454
	10 cents	5.6600	0.5000	2.8300	0.0909
	20 cents	11.3100	0.5000	5.6550	0.1818
	50 cents	28.2800	0.5000	14.1400	0.4546
		GOLD			
1874–1902	1/2 pond	3.9940	0.9170	3.6612	0.1177
	1 pond	7.9881	0.9170	7.3224	0.2354
1961–64	1 rand	3.9940	0.9170	3.6612	0.1177
	2 rand	7.9881	0.9170	7.3224	0.2354

THOMAS FRANCOIS BURGERS, PRESIDENT, *1872–1877*

Y#	KM#	Metal	Description	VF	EF	Unc
A1	1.1	Gold	1 Pond, 1874, coarse beard	2,750	30,000	54,000
A2	1.2	Gold	1 Pond, 1874, fine beard	4,300	16,000	32,000

PAUL KRUGER, PRESIDENT, *1883–1902*

Y#	KM#	Metal	Description	VF	EF	Unc
1	2	Bz	1 Penny, 1892–98 *1893, VF $50*	2	10	45

Y#	KM#	Metal	Description	VF	EF	Unc
2	3	Silv	3 Pence, 1892–95	5	170	1,000
2	3	Silv	3 Pence, 1896–97	5	20	100
3	4	Silv	6 Pence, 1892–95	4	200	900
3	4	Silv	6 Pence, 1896	4	20	150
3	4	Silv	6 Pence, 1897	5	20	100

Y#	KM#	Metal	Description	VF	EF	Unc
4	5	Silv	1 Shilling, 1892, 94, 95, 96	30	250	1,150
4	5	Silv	1 Shilling, 1893	600	1,300	6,500
4	5	Silv	1 Shilling, 1897	5	20	100

Y#	KM#	Metal	Description	VF	EF	Unc
5	6	Silv	2 Shillings, 1892, 94, 95	10	400	1,300
5	6	Silv	2 Shillings, 1893	250	2,000	9,000
5	6	Silv	2 Shillings, 1896, 97	10	50	250

Y#	KM#	Metal	Description	VF	EF	Unc
6	7	Silv	2-1/2 Shillings, 1892, 94–95	15	60	1,300
6	7	Silv	1-1/2 Shillings, 1893	185	1,800	4,000
6	7	Silv	2-1/2 Shillings, 1896–97	10	50	250
7	8.1	Silv	5 Shillings, 1892, single shaft on wagon	150	500	2,200
7a	8.2	Silv	5 Shillings, 1892, double shaft on wagon	250	750	3,500

Reverse: ***Single shaft on wagon***

Y#	KM#	Metal	Description	VF	EF	Unc
8	9.2	Gold	1/2 Pond, 1893	1,200	4,000	18,000
8	9.2	Gold	1/2 Pond, 1894–97	125	300	2,500
9	10.2	Gold	1 Pond, 1892, 98–99, 1900	400	800	1,400
9	10.2	Gold	1 Pond, 1892	1,000	6,500	15,000
9	10.2	Gold	1 Pond, 1893–1897	400	1,200	3,300

Reverse: ***Double shaft on wagon***

Y#	KM#	Metal	Description	VF	EF	Unc
8a	9.1	Gold	1/2 Pond, 1892	175	400	2,500
9a	10.1	Gold	1 Pond, 1892	400	600	3,500

The Veld Pond

Y#	KM#	Metal	Description	VF	EF	Unc
10	11	Gold	1 Pond, 1902	3,000	5,500	15,000

Note: Many deceptive counterfeits exist.

SOUTH AFRICA, UNION OF

The nation was formed on the continent's southern tip by Britain in 1910, after the Boer War. Settled in the 1800s by the Dutch, the country became a republic, left the Commonwealth, and changed its name to Republic of South Africa in 1961. A new constitution in 1993 dismantled the Boer-descended Afrikaaner apartheid rule and provided for a multi-racial democracy with majority rule. *Languages:* English, Afrikaans. *Capital:* Pretoria.

MONETARY SYSTEM

12 pence = 1 shilling
20 shillings = 1 pound
2 shillings = 1 florin

PRECIOUS METAL CONTENT

Dates	Denomination	Gross Wt (g)	Fineness	Net Wt (g)	Troy Oz.
		SILVER			
1923–51	3 pence	1.4138	0.8000	1.1310	0.0364
	6 pence	2.8276	0.8000	2.2621	0.0727
	1 shilling	5.6552	0.8000	4.5241	0.1454
	1 florin	11.3104	0.8000	9.0483	0.2909
	2-1/2 shillings	14.1380	0.8000	11.3104	0.3636
	5 shillings	28.2759	0.8000	22.6207	0.7273
1951–60	3 pence	1.1438	0.5000	0.7069	0.0227
	6 pence	2.8276	0.5000	1.4138	0.0455
	1 shilling	5.6552	0.5000	2.8276	0.0909
	2 shillings	11.3104	0.5000	5.6552	0.1818
	2-1/2 shillings	14.1380	0.5000	7.0690	0.2273
	5 shillings	28.2759	0.5000	14.1380	0.4545
		GOLD			
1923–32	1/2 sovereign	3.9940	0.9170	3.6612	0.1177
	1 sovereign	7.9881	0.9170	7.3224	0.2354
1952–60	1/2 pound	3.9940	0.9170	3.6612	0.1177
	1 pound	7.9881	0.9170	7.3224	0.2354

George V, *1910–1936*

Legend: ***ZUID-AFRIKA***

Y#	KM#	Metal	Description	VF	EF	Unc
11	12.1	Bz	1/4 Penny, 1923–24 (1/4 Penny 1/4)	3	7	15
11a	12.2	Bz	1/4 Penny, 1928, 30, 31 (1/4 Penny)	2	5	15
			1926, Proof only: $22,000			

Y#	KM#	Metal	Description	VF	EF	Unc
12	13.1	Bz	1/2 Penny, 1923–26 (1/2 Penny 1/2)	10	30	75
12a	13.2	Bz	1/2 Penny, 1928–31 (1/2 Penny)	12	20	50
13	14.1	Bz	1 Penny, 1923–24 (1 Penny 1)	10	23	45
13a	14.2	Bz	1 Penny, 1926–30 (Penny)	5	15	80

Y#	KM#	Metal	Description	VF	EF	Unc
15	15.1	Silv	3 Pence, 1923–25	10	30	100
16	16.1	Silv	6 Pence, 1923–24	15	40	125

Y#	KM#	Metal	Description	VF	EF	Unc
17	15.2	Silv	3 Pence, 1925–30	5	20	130
18	16.2	Silv	6 Pence, 1925–30	10	25	200

Y#	KM#	Metal	Description	VF	EF	Unc
19	17.1	Silv	1 Shilling, 1923–24 (1 Shilling 1)	15	43	250
19a	17.2	Silv	1 Shilling, 1926–30 (Shilling)	20	50	1,300

Y#	KM#	Metal	Description	VF	EF	Unc
20	18	Silv	1 Florin, 1923–30 *1925, VF $400, EF $2,000, Unc $5,000*	50	110	1,000
21	19.1	Silv	2-1/2 Shillings, 1923–25 (2-1/2 Shillings 2-1/2)	15	50	300
21a	19.2	Silv	2-1/2 Shillings, 1926–30 (2-1/2 Shillings)	25	125	1,500

Design: ***Same as British Sovereign, but with Pretoria mintmark, "SA"***

Y#	KM#	Metal	Description	VF	EF	Unc
A21	20	Gold	1/2 Sovereign, 1923–26 *1923, Proof only: $1,000*	BV	100	175
22	21	Gold	1 Sovereign, 1923–32 *1924, VF $1,500*	BV	BV	350

New Legend: ***SUID-AFRIKA***
Designs: ***Similar to Y11–21***
Reverse: ***"D" for penny/pence***

Y#	KM#	Metal	Description	VF	EF	Unc
23	12.3	Bz	1/4 Penny, 1931–36 *1933–34, 36, VF $2,500*	2	5	15
24	13.3	Bz	1/2 Penny, 1931–36 *1931, Proof only: $2,000*	8	30	60
25	14.3	Bz	1 Penny, 1931–36	2	18	60

Y#	KM#	Metal	Description	VF	EF	Unc
26	15.3	Silv	3 Pence, 1931–36 *1931, VF $2,000*	3	12	60
27	16.3	Silv	6 Pence, 1931–36 *1931, VF $250*	5	15	200
28	17.3	Silv	1 Shilling, 1931–36 *1931, VF $300*	8	35	250
29	22	Silv	2 Shillings, 1931–36 *1931, VF $800*	10	35	350
30	19.3	Silv	2-1/2 Shillings, 32, 34, 35, 36 *1931, VF $1,200, EF $1,800, Unc $4,000; 1933, Unc $2,500*	12	100	1,100

GEORGE VI, *1936–1952*

Reverse: ***Designs like Y23–30***

Y#	KM#	Metal	Description	VF	EF	Unc
31	23	Bz	1/4 Penny, 1937–47	1	3	7
32	24	Bz	1/2 Penny, 1937–47	1	5	8
33	25	Bz	1 Penny, 1937–47	1	5	35

Y#	KM#	Metal	Description	VF	EF	Unc
34	26	Silv	3 Pence, 1937–47	1	5	18
35	27	Silv	6 Pence, 1937–47 *1939, Proof only: $7,000*	2	10	30
36	28	Silv	1 Shilling, 1937–47 *1939, Proof only: $7,000*	2	10	45
37	29	Silv	2 Shillings, 1937–47	4	10	50
38	30	Silv	2-1/2 Shillings, 1937–47	5	20	60

Royal Visit Commemorative

Y#	KM#	Metal	Description	VF	EF	Unc
39	31	Silv	5 Shillings, 1947	BV	10	25

New Legend: ***GEORGIUS SEXTUS REX***
Designs: ***Similar to Y31–39***
Reverse: ***SOUTH AFRICA – SUID-AFRIKA***

Y#	KM#	Metal	Description	VF	EF	Unc
40	32.1	Bz	1/4 Penny, 1948–50	0.35	0.50	2.00
41	33	Bz	1/2 Penny, 1948–52	0.50	1.50	4.00
42	34.1	Bz	1 Penny, 1948–50	0.50	2.00	7.50

Y#	KM#	Metal	Description	VF	EF	Unc
43	35.1	Silv	3 Pence, 1948–50	1.00	2.50	8
43a	35.2	Silv	3 Pence, 1951–52	1.00	1.50	4
44	36.1	Silv	6 Pence, 1948–50	1.50	2.00	7

Y#	KM#	Metal	Description	VF	EF	Unc
45	37.1	Silv	1 Shilling, 1948–50 (value spelled out) *1949, Proof only: $300*	3.00	7.50	60
45a	37.2	Silv	1 Shilling, 1951–52 (value 1 S)	1.50	3.00	5
46	38.1	Silv	2 Shillings, 1948–50	8.00	50.00	200
47	39.1	Silv	2-1/2 Shillings, 1948–50 (value spelled out)	50.00	90.00	225
47a	39.2	Silv	2-1/2 Shillings, 1951–52 (value 2-1/2 S)	5.00	7.00	15

Note: Silver fineness of Y43a, 45a, and 47a was reduced from .800 to .500.

Y#	KM#	Metal	Description	VF	EF	Unc
48	40.1	Silv	5 Shillings, 1948–50	BV	10	25

Y#	KM#	Metal	Description	VF	EF	Unc
57	42	Gold	*1/2 Pound, 1952, Proof only: $225*			

All Values Abbreviated

Beginning in 1951, the following denominations used the transposed reverse legend, while the other denominations continued to place the English name first. The change was intended to give the Afrikaans language equal status with English.

Reverse: ***SUID-AFRIKA – SOUTH AFRICA***

Y#	KM#	Metal	Description	VF	EF	Unc
49	32.2	Bz	1/4 Penny, 1951–52	0.35	0.50	2
50	34.2	Bz	1 Penny, 1951–52	0.50	1.00	3

Y#	KM#	Metal	Description	VF	EF	Unc
51	36.2	Silv	6 Pence, 1951–52	1.00	2	4
52	38.2	Silv	2 Shillings, 1951–52	2.50	4	8
53	40.2	Silv	5 Shillings, 1951	6.00	8	25

Third Centennial, Founding of Capetown

Y#	KM#	Metal	Description	VF	EF	Unc
56	41	Silv	5 Shillings, 1952	6	8	15

Y#	KM#	Metal	Description	VF	EF	Unc
58	43	Gold	*1 Pound, 1952, Proof only: $450*			

ELIZABETH II, *1952–1961*

Legends: ***SOUTH AFRICA – SUID-AFRIKA on Y60, 62, 64, 66 and 68; SUID-AFRIKA – SOUTH AFRICA on all other coins Y59–70***
Reverse: ***Designs similar to Y31–39***

Y#	KM#	Metal	Description	VF	EF	Unc
59	44	Bz	1/4 Penny, 1953–60	0.35	0.50	1.00
60	45	Bz	1/2 Penny, 1953–60	0.35	0.50	2.00
61	46	Bz	1 Penny, 1953–60	0.35	0.50	2.50

Y#	KM#	Metal	Description	VF	EF	Unc
62	47	Silv	3 Pence, 1953–60	0.50	1.00	3
63	48	Silv	6 Pence, 1953–60	0.75	1.50	3
64	49	Silv	1 Shilling, 1953–60	1.50	2.00	4
65	50	Silv	2 Shillings, 1953–60	3.00	4.00	8
66	51	Silv	2-1/2 Shillings, 1953–60	4.00	5.00	10
67	52	Silv	5 Shillings, 1953–59 *1959, Unc $110*	6.00	7.50	15

Y#	KM#	Metal	Description	VF	EF	Unc
68	53	Gold	*1/2 Pound, 1953–60, Proof only: $225*			
69	54	Gold	*1 Pound, 1953–60, Proof only: $450*			

50th Anniversary of Union

Y#	KM#	Metal	Description	VF	EF	Unc
70	55	Silv	5 Shillings, 1960	6.50	7.50	12

REPUBLIC, *1961–* *Decimal System*

100 cents = 1 rand

Y#	KM#	Metal	Description	VF	EF	Unc
71	56	Br	1/2 Cent, 1961–64	0.25	0.50	0.85

Y#	KM#	Metal	Description	VF	EF	Unc
72	57	Br	1 Cent, 1961–64	0.35	0.50	1

Y#	KM#	Metal	Description	VF	EF	Unc
73	58	Silv	2-1/2 Cents, 1961–64	0.50	1	3

Y#	KM#	Metal	Description	VF	EF	Unc
74	59	Silv	5 Cents, 1961–64	0.50	0.75	2

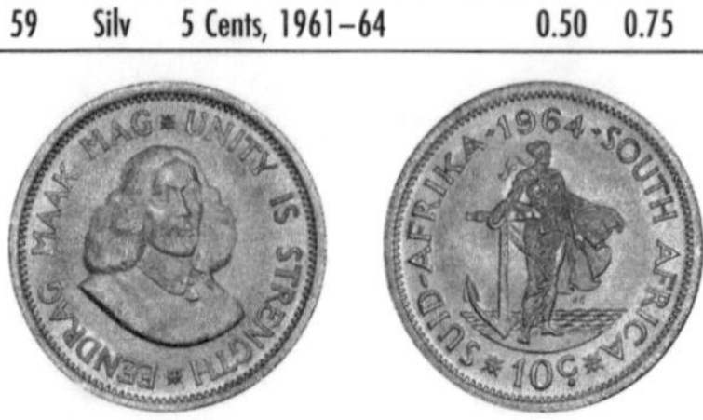

Y#	KM#	Metal	Description	VF	EF	Unc
75	60	Silv	10 Cents, 1961–64	BV	1.50	3

Y#	KM#	Metal	Description	VF	EF	Unc
76	61	Silv	20 Cents, 1961–64	BV	3	5

Y#	KM#	Metal	Description	VF	EF	Unc
77	62	Silv	50 Cents, 1961–64	BV	7	10

Y#	KM#	Metal	Description	VF	EF	Unc
78	63	Gold	1 Rand, 1961–83	BV	BV	BV
79	64	Gold	2 Rand, 1961–83	BV	BV	BV

SOUTH KOREA

SEE KOREA, SOUTH

SOUTH VIETNAM

SEE VIETNAM, SOUTH

SPAIN

A monarchy covering most of the Iberian peninsula in southwest Europe, Spain was essentially united by the marriage of Isabella of Castille and Ferdinand of Aragon in 1469, with the last Muslims expelled in 1502. In the mid-16th century it was the most powerful monarchy in the world. Spain lost its empire in the old and new worlds in wars and revolutions throughout the 18th and 19th centuries. A new constitution declared Spain a republic in 1931. Following a civil war (1936-39), fascist Francisco Franco Bahamonde effectively became dictator for life. The monarchial line was nominally restored in 1947. A peaceful transition to democracy followed Franco's death in 1975. *Languages:* Spanish, Catalan, Basque. *Capital:* Madrid.

MONETARY SYSTEM

100 centimos = 10 decimos = 1 real

PRECIOUS METAL CONTENT

Dates	Denomination	Gross Wt (g)	Fineness	Net Wt (g)	Troy Oz.
		SILVER			
1850–65	1 real	1.3146	0.9000	1.1831	0.0380
	2 reales	2.6291	0.9000	2.3662	0.0761
	4 reales	5.2582	0.9000	4.7324	0.1521
	10 reales	13.1455	0.9000	11.8310	0.3804
	20 reales	26.2910	0.9000	23.6619	0.7607
1864–68	10 centimos	1.2980	0.8100	1.0514	0.0338
	20 centimos	2.5960	0.8100	2.1028	0.0676
	40 centimos	5.1920	0.8100	4.2055	0.1352
	1 escudo	12.9800	0.9000	11.6820	0.3756
	2 escudos	25.9600	0.9000	23.3640	0.7512
1869–1934	20 centimos	1.0000	0.8350	0.8350	0.0268
	50 centimos	2.5000	0.8350	2.0875	0.0671
	1 peseta	5.0000	0.8350	4.1750	0.1342
	2 pesetas	10.0000	0.8350	8.3500	0.2685
	5 pesetas	25.0000	0.9000	22.5000	0.7234
		GOLD			
1850–64	20 reales	1.6674	0.9000	1.5007	0.0482
	40 reales	3.3349	0.9000	3.0014	0.0965
	100 reales / 1 doblon	8.3371	0.9000	7.5034	0.2412
1865–68	2 escudos	1.6774	0.9000	1.5097	0.0485
	4 escudos	3.3548	0.9000	3.0193	0.0971
	10 escudos	8.3870	0.9000	7.5483	0.2427
1876–1962	10 pesetas	3.2258	0.9000	2.9032	0.0933
	20 pesetas	6.4516	0.9000	5.8064	0.1867
	25 pesetas	8.0645	0.9000	7.2581	0.2333
	100 pesetas	32.2581	0.9000	29.0323	0.9334

ISABEL II, *1833–1868*

FIRST DECIMAL COINAGE

10 decimas = 1 real, 1848–1855

Reverse: ***Arms in order chain***

Y#	KM#	Metal	Description	VF	EF	Unc
13	592	Silv	20 Reales, 1850	175	400	900

Y#	KM#	Metal	Description	VF	EF	Unc
15	597	Cop	Media Decima (= 1/20) de Real, 1852–53	35	75	175
16	590	Cop	Decima (= 1/10) de Real, 1850–53	15	30	100
17	601	Cop	Doble Decima (= 1/5) de Real, 1853	60	125	375
18	591	Cop	1/2 Real, 1848–53	45	100	350

Reverse: ***Arms without pillars***

Y#	KM#	Metal	Description	VF	EF	Unc
19	598	Silv	1 Real, 1852–55	20	45	135
20	599	Silv	2 Reales, 1852–55	35	95	200
21	600	Silv	4 Reales, 1852–55	45	150	475

Reverse: ***Arms flanked by pillars***

Y#	KM#	Metal	Description	VF	EF	Unc
22	595	Silv	10 Reales, 1851–56	375	425	875
23	593	Silv	20 Reales, 1850–55	125	225	475

Y#	KM#	Metal	Description	VF	EF	Unc
A23	594	Gold	1 Doblon (100 Reales), 1850–51	225	325	475

Y#	KM#	Metal	Description	VF	EF	Unc
B23	596	Gold	100 Reales, 1851–55	225	325	500

SECOND DECIMAL COINAGE

100 centimos = 1 real, 1854–1864

Y#	KM#	Metal	Description	VF	EF	Unc
24	602	Cop	5 Centimos de Real, 1854–64	12.50	35	65
25	603	Cop	10 Centimos, 1854–64	20.00	65	125
26	615	Cop	25 Centimos, 1854–64	20.00	65	125

Note: Y24–25 dated 1854 are believed to be patterns.

Reverse: ***Arms without pillars***

Y#	KM#	Metal	Description	VF	EF	Unc
27	606	Silv	1 Real, 1857–64	17.50	35	125
28	607	Silv	2 Reales, 1857–64	25.00	70	225
29	608	Silv	4 Reales, 1856–64	50.00	100	275

Reverse: ***Arms flanked by pillars***

Y#	KM#	Metal	Description	VF	EF	Unc
30	611	Silv	10 Reales, 1857–64	50	100	350
31	609	Silv	20 Reales, 1856–64	125	250	500

Reverse: ***Oval arms on cartouche***

Y#	KM#	Metal	Description	VF	EF	Unc
32	610	Gold	20 Reales, 1861–63	175	285	350
33	616	Gold	40 Reales, 1861–63	175	250	325
35	605	Gold	100 Reales, 1856–62	BV	400	500

Reverse: ***Mantled arms***

Y#	KM#	Metal	Description	VF	EF	Unc
A35	618	Gold	40 Reales, 1864	175	200	300
B35	617	Gold	100 Reales, 1863–64	BV	400	500

THIRD DECIMAL COINAGE

100 centimos = 1 escudo, 1864–1868

Y#	KM#	Metal	Description	VF	EF	Unc
36	632	Bz	1/2 Centimo de Escudo, 1866–68	12.50	25	60
37	633	Bz	1 Centimo, 1866–68	15.00	25	50
38	634	Bz	2-1/2 Centimos, 1866–68	15.00	30	75
39	635	Bz	5 Centimos, 1866–68	20.00	40	100

Note: Y37–39 dated 1865 are patterns.

Reverse: ***Arms without pillars***

Y#	KM#	Metal	Description	VF	EF	Unc
40	627	Silv	10 Centimos, 1864–68	15	35	75
41	625	Silv	20 Centimos, 1865–68	25	50	125
42	628	Silv	40 Centimos, 1864–68	35	65	150

Reverse: ***Arms flanked by pillars***

Y#	KM#	Metal	Description	VF	EF	Unc
43	626	Silv	1 Escudo, 1865–68	50	90	200
44	629	Silv	2 Escudos, 1865–68	150	225	500
			1865–66, Rare			

Note: For similar silver coins 1864–1868 with values in centimos de peso, see the Philippines.

Y#	KM#	Metal	Description	VF	EF	Unc
45	630	Gold	2 Escudos, 1865	125	225	300
46	631	Gold	4 Escudos, 1865–68	175	200	300
47	636	Gold	10 Escudos, 1865–68	385	425	500

PROVISIONAL ISSUES,
1868–1870

Battle of Alcolea Bridge

Y#	KM#	Metal	Description	VF	EF	Unc
A50	645	Bz	25 Milesimas de Escudo, 1868	300	425	700

Dates on Spanish Coins

Beginning in 1868 (starting with 1868 dates of Y41–47), most Spanish coins bear two dates. The large, obvious date is the year of authorization, and does not necessarily correspond to the year of coinage. True dates of coinage appear as tiny incuse numerals on the six-pointed stars found on most types. In the following listings the large dates are shown in normal fashion. Coinage dates are indicated by * within parentheses. Coins in this catalog which do not have stars with small incuse dates are YA50–54, 63–67, 69–70, 100–107, 103–106, and 109–112.

NEW MONETARY SYSTEM
100 centimos = 1 peseta, 1869–

Y#	KM#	Metal	Description	VF	EF	Unc
51	660	Bz	1 Centimo, 1870	2.00	10	22.50
52	661	Bz	2 Centimos, 1870	2.25	10	30.00
53	662	Bz	5 Centimos, 1870	10.00	65	185.00
54	663	Bz	10 Centimos, 1870	12.00	85	200.00

Obverse Legend: ***GOBIERNO PROVISIONAL***

Y#	KM#	Metal	Description	VF	EF	Unc
A55	652	Silv	1 Peseta, 1869 (*69)	50	225	550

New Legend: ***ESPAÑA***

Y#	KM#	Metal	Description	VF	EF	Unc
55	650	Silv	20 Centimos, 1869–70 (*69–70)	625	1,100	2,000
56	651	Silv	50 Centimos, 1869–70 (*69–70)	100	300	600
58	653	Silv	1 Peseta, 1869–70 (*69–73)	70	250	550
59	654	Silv	2 Pesetas, 1869–70 (*69–75)	35	100	400
60	655	Silv	5 Pesetas, 1869–70 (*69–71) *1869, Rare*	70	275	850

AMADEO I,
1871–1873

Y#	KM#	Metal	Description	VF	EF	Unc
61	666	Silv	5 Pesetas, 1871 (*71–75)	35	125	475

REPUBLIC,
1873–1874

Mint: ***Cartagena***

Y#	KM#	Metal	Description	VF	EF	Unc
64	715	Silv	10 Reales (2-1/2 Pesetas), 1873	550	750	1,500
63	716	Silv	5 Pesetas, 1873	225	425	750

Note: Former Y62, 2 Pesetas 1873, is a fantasy struck later for collectors.

Carlos VII, Pretender, *1872–1876, 1885*

Y#	KM#	Metal	Description	VF	EF	Unc
66	669	Bz	5 Centimos, 1875	50	100	175
67	670	Bz	10 Centimos, 1875	60	120	200

Note: Silver coins of Carlos VII, 1874–1885, are fantasies struck for collectors.

Alfonso XII, *1875–1885*

First Coinage

Obverse Legend: ***REY DE ESPAÑA***

Y#	KM#	Metal	Description	VF	EF	Unc
74	671	Silv	5 Pesetas, 1875–76 (*75–76)	40	175	450

Second Coinage

Obverse Legend: ***POR LA GRATIA DE DIOS***

Y#	KM#	Metal	Description	VF	EF	Unc
69	674	Bz	5 Centimos, 1877–79	12.50	60	175
70	675	Bz	10 Centimos, 1877–79	20.00	75	185

Obverse Legend: ***POR LA G. DE DIOS***

Y#	KM#	Metal	Description	VF	EF	Unc
B75	672	Silv	1 Peseta, 1876 (*76)	20	90	200
75	676	Silv	5 Pesetas, 1877–82 (*77–82)	25	90	200

Y#	KM#	Metal	Description	VF	EF	Unc
77	677	Gold	10 Pesetas, 1878–79 (*78–79, 1961–62) *1961–62, Unc $165; 1879, VF $1,000*	250	325	385
78	673	Gold	25 Pesetas, 1876–81 (*76–81, 1961–62) *1876 (*19–61), $1,100*	365	385	415

THIRD COINAGE

Obverse: ***Head with sideburns, moustache***

Y#	KM#	Metal	Description	VF	EF	Unc
A76	685	Silv	50 Centimos, 1880–85 (*80–86)	11	45	135
B76	686	Silv	1 Peseta, 1881–85 (*81–86)	30	175	750
C76	678	Silv	2 Pesetas, 1879–84 (*79–84)	20	45	200
76	688	Silv	5 Pesetas, 1882–85 (*82–87)	25	150	450

Y#	KM#	Metal	Description	VF	EF	Unc
A78	687	Gold	25 Pesetas, 1881–85 (*81–86) *(*85), VF $1,000, (*86), VF $4,000*	350	375	400

ALFONSO XIII,
1886–1931

FIRST COINAGE

Y#	KM#	Metal	Description	VF	EF	Unc
79	690	Silv	50 Centimos, 1889, 92 (*89, 92) *1889 (*18–89), VF $25*	7.50	12.50	85
80	691	Silv	1 Peseta, 1889, 91 (*89, 91) *1891 (*18–91), EF $285*	40.00	60.00	300
81	692	Silv	2 Pesetas, 1889–92 (*89–92)	40.00	375.00	1,250
82	689	Silv	5 Pesetas, 1888–92 (*88–92) *1888MSM, VF $1,350*	25.00	115.00	650

Y#	KM#	Metal	Description	VF	EF	Unc
A82	693	Gold	20 Pesetas, 1887–90 (*89–90, 1961–62)	285	335	365

SECOND COINAGE

Y#	KM#	Metal	Description	VF	EF	Unc
83	703	Silv	50 Centimos, 1894 (*94)	30	50	155
84	702	Silv	1 Peseta, 1893–94 (*93–94)	55	275	850
85	704	Silv	2 Pesetas, 1894 (*94)	125	250	900
86	700	Silv	5 Pesetas, 1892–94 (*92–94)	30	130	350

Y#	KM#	Metal	Description	VF	EF	Unc
A86	701	Gold	20 Pesetas, 1892 (*92)	1,250	2,250	4,500

THIRD COINAGE

Y#	KM#	Metal	Description	VF	EF	Unc
87	705	Silv	50 Centimos, 1896, 1900 (*96, 1900)	12.50	30	75
88	706	Silv	1 Peseta, 1896–1902 (*96–02)	15.00	40	80
89	707	Silv	5 Pesetas, 1896–99 (*96–99) *1895 (*18–95), EF $1,750*	25.00	40	90

Y#	KM#	Metal	Description	VF	EF	Unc
A89	709	Gold	20 Pesetas, 1896, 99 (*99, 1961–62)	300	325	550

Y#	KM#	Metal	Description	VF	EF	Unc
90	708	Gold	100 Pesetas, 1897 (*97, 1961–62)	BV	1,850	2,650

Fourth Coinage

Y#	KM#	Metal	Description	VF	EF	Unc
96	726	Bz	1 Centimo, 1906 (*6)	1	3	6
97	722	Bz	2 Centimos, 1904–05 (*04–05)	3	6	20

Y#	KM#	Metal	Description	VF	EF	Unc
92	723	Silv	50 Centimos, 1904 (*04, 10)	4.00	10	20
94	721	Silv	1 Peseta, 1903–05 (*03, 05)	15.00	40	100
95	725	Silv	2 Pesetas, 1905 (*05)	12.50	25	65

Y#	KM#	Metal	Description	VF	EF	Unc
91	724	Gold	20 Pesetas, 1904 (*04)	2,250	4,000	5,250

Fifth Coinage

Y#	KM#	Metal	Description	VF	EF	Unc
98	731	Bz	1 Centimo, 1911–13 (*11–13)	4	8	15.00
99	732	Bz	2 Centimos, 1911–12 (*11–12)	4	8	18.50

Y#	KM#	Metal	Description	VF	EF	Unc
93	730	Silv	50 Centimos, 1910 (*10)	7.50	11.50	35

Sixth Coinage

Y#	KM#	Metal	Description	VF	EF	Unc
100	740	N-Br	25 Centimos, 1925	3.75	28.50	70

Y#	KM#	Metal	Description	VF	EF	Unc
101	742	C-N	25 Centimos, 1927	2.50	25	65

Y#	KM#	Metal	Description	VF	EF	Unc
102	741	Silv	50 Centimos, 1926	6.75	9	15

REPUBLIC, *1931–1938*

First Coinage

Y#	KM#	Metal	Description	VF	EF	Unc
107	751	N-Bz	25 Centimos, 1934	1.25	6	25

Y#	KM#	Metal	Description	VF	EF	Unc
108	750	Silv	1 Peseta, 1933 (*34)	7	22.50	40

Second Coinage

Y#	KM#	Metal	Description	VF	EF	Unc
103	752	Iron	5 Centimos, 1937	4.75	11	17.50
A104	756	Iron	10 Centimos, 1938	1,000.00	1,600	2,250.00

Y#	KM#	Metal	Description	VF	EF	Unc
104	757	Cop	25 Centimos, 1938	4	12	20

Y#	KM#	Metal	Description	VF	EF	Unc
105	754	Cop	50 Centimos, 1937 (*34, 36)	6.75	13.50	30

Y#	KM#	Metal	Description	VF	EF	Unc
106	755	Br	1 Peseta, 1937	2.50	5	11.50

NATIONALIST GOVERNMENT, *1937–1947*

Monarchy declared under regency of Franco, 1947.

FIRST COINAGE

Y#	KM#	Metal	Description	VF	EF	Unc
109	753	C-N	25 Centimos, 1937	0.50	1.50	5

Y#	KM#	Metal	Description	VF	EF	Unc
110	765	Alum	5 Centimos, 1940–53 *1940, Unc $40; 1953, Unc $100*	0.50	3	18.50
111	766	Alum	10 Centimos, 1940–53	0.65	3	6.50

Y#	KM#	Metal	Description	VF	EF	Unc
112	767	A-Bz	1 Peseta, 1944	0.80	7	25

SECOND COINAGE

Reverse: ***Arrows pointing down***

Y#	KM#	Metal	Description	VF	EF	Unc
115	776	C-N	50 Centimos, 1949 (*51)	5	10	32.50

Reverse: ***Arrows pointing up***

Y#	KM#	Metal	Description	VF	EF	Unc
116	777	C-N	50 Centimos, 1949, 63 (*51–65)	0.50	3	8

Y#	KM#	Metal	Description	VF	EF	Unc
113	775	A-Bz	1 Peseta, 1947–63 (*48–67)	0.60	3	10
114	785	A-Bz	2-1/2 Pesetas, 1953 (*54–71) *(*68) (*69), Unc $650*	1. 00	4	15

Note: All dates of Y113 before 1962 are valued much higher in Unc.

Y#	KM#	Metal	Description	VF	EF	Unc
117	778	Nick	5 Pesetas, 1949 (*49–50) *(*51), Unc $4,000; (*52), Unc $23,000*	2	5	15

FRANCISCO FRANCO, REGENT, *1947–1975*

Y#	KM#	Metal	Description	VF	EF	Unc
118	786	C-N	5 Pesetas, 1957 (*58–75)	0.25	1.00	2.50
119	787	C-N	25 Pesetas, 1957 (*58–75)	0.35	1.75	4.00
120	788	C-N	50 Pesetas, 1957 (*58–75)	0.50	2.00	5.00

Note: Y118–120 with the mintmark BA replacing the six-pointed star on reverse commemorate the 1958 Barcelona numismatic exposition.

Y#	KM#	Metal	Description	VF	EF	Unc
121	790	Alum	10 Centimos, 1959	0.05	0.10	1

VISCAYAN REPUBLIC *(Euzkadi)*

Located in Spain on the Bay of Biscay, the Viscayan Republic was autonomous in 1936 and 1937. *Capital:* Bilbao.

Y#	KM#	Metal	Description	VF	EF	Unc
1	1	Nick	1 Peseta, 1937	3	10	20
2	2	Nick	2 Pesetas, 1937	3	10	20

STRAITS SETTLEMENTS

A British Crown Colony until 1946, the Straits Settlements was dissolved to form the Malay Federation. *Capital:* Singapore.

MONETARY SYSTEM

100 cents = 1 dollar

PRECIOUS METAL CONTENT

Dates	Denomination	Gross Wt (g)	Fineness	Net Wt (g)	Troy Oz.
		SILVER			
1871–1905	5 cents	1.3577	0.8000	1.0862	0.0349
	10 cents	2.7154	0.8000	2.1723	0.0698
	20 cents	5.4308	0.8000	4.3446	0.1397
	50 cents	13.4784	0.9000	12.1306	0.3900
1907–17	5 cents	1.3577	0.6000	0.8146	0.0262
	10 cents	2.7154	0.6000	1.6292	0.0524
	20 cents	5.4308	0.6000	3.2585	0.1048
	50 cents	10.1088	0.9000	9.0979	0.2925
	1 dollar	20.2176	0.9000	18.1958	0.5850
1918–21	5 cents	1.3577	0.4000	0.5431	0.0175
	10 cents	2.7154	0.4000	1.0862	0.0349
	20 cents	5.4308	0.4000	2.1723	0.0698
	50 cents	8.4240	0.5000	4.2120	0.1354
1919–26	1 dollar	16.8480	0.5000	8.4240	0.2708
1926–35	5 cents	1.3577	0.6000	0.8146	0.0262
	10 cents	2.7154	0.6000	1.6292	0.0524
	20 cents	5.4308	0.6000	3.2585	0.1048

VICTORIA, *1837–1901*

Legend: ***EAST INDIA COMPANY***

Y#	KM#	Metal	Description	VF	EF	Unc
1	1	Cop	1/4 Cent, 1845	20.00	65	300
2	2	Cop	1/2 Cent, 1845	22.50	70	300
3	3	Cop	1 Cent, 1845	25.00	75	300

New Legend: ***INDIA STRAITS***

Y#	KM#	Metal	Description	VF	EF	Unc
4	4	Cop	1/4 Cent, 1862	250	500	1,500
					Proof: $4,500	
5	5	Cop	1/2 Cent, 1862	90	250	1,000
					Proof: $6,000	
6	6	Cop	1 Cent, 1862	50	150	700
					Proof: $8,000	

New Legend: ***STRAITS SETTLEMENTS***

Edge: ***Plain***

Y#	KM#	Metal	Description	VF	EF	Unc
7	7	Cop	1/4 Cent, 1872–84 *1873, EF $60; 1883, VF $600*	50	100 *Proof: $3,500*	250
8	8	Cop	1/2 Cent, 1872–84 *1883, VF $150*	100	200 *Proof: $3,000*	450
9	9	Cop	1 Cent, 1872–86 *1878, EF $1,250*	50	100 *Proof: Rare*	150

Edge: ***Reeded***

Y#	KM#	Metal	Description	VF	EF	Unc
7a	14	Cop	1/4 Cent, 1889–1901	25.00	65	150
			1898, Proof only: $3,500			
8a	15	Cop	1/2 Cent, 1889–91	20.00	60	150
			1890–91, Proof only: $4,500			
9a	16	Cop	1 Cent, 1887–1901	17.50	100	500
						Proof: $6,000

Y#	KM#	Metal	Description	VF	EF	Unc
13	10	Silv	5 Cents, 1871–1901	20	60	200
						Proof: $3,500
14	11	Silv	10 Cents, 1871–1901	15	55	150
						Proof: $4,500
15	12	Silv	20 Cents, 1871–1901	35	100	200
						Proof: $7,000
16	13	Silv	50 Cents, 1886–1901	100	175	750

Edward VII, *1901–1910*

Reverse: ***Designs like Y10–12***

Y#	KM#	Metal	Description	VF	EF	Unc
17	17	Cop	1/4 Cent, 1904–08	27.50	65	200
			1904, Proof only: Rare			
18	18	Cop	1/2 Cent, 1904, 08	35.00	85	235
			1904, Proof only: Rare			
19	19	Cop	1 Cent, 1903–08	20.00	50	150
						Proof: Rare

Y#	KM#	Metal	Description	VF	EF	Unc
20	20	Silv	5 Cents, 1902–10	10	22.50	100
						Proof: $3,500
21	21	Silv	10 Cents, 1902–10	15	60.00	300
						Proof: $4,000
22	22	Silv	20 Cents, 1902–10	25	85.00	350
						Proof: $5,000
23	23	Silv	50 Cents, 1902–05 (31 mm)	125	350.00	2,000
						Proof: $8,500

Note: In 1909 the fineness of Y20–22 was reduced from .800 to .600.

Y#	KM#	Metal	Description	VF	EF	Unc
24	24	Silv	50 Cents, / 1/2 Dollar, 1907–08 (28 mm)	25	85	350
						Proof: $5,000

Y#	KM#	Metal	Description	VF	EF	Unc
25	25	Silv	1 Dollar, 1903–04 (37 mm)	65	100	250
						Proof: $12,000
25a	26	Silv	1 Dollar, 1907–09 (34 mm)	45	70	225
						Proof: $12,000

George V, *1910–1936*

For later issues, see Malaya.

Y#	KM#	Metal	Description	VF	EF	Unc
27	27	Cop	1/4 Cent, 1916	10	20	65
						Proof: $3,500
28	28	Cop	1/2 Cent, 1916	10	20	65
						Proof: $4,500

Y#	KM#	Metal	Description	VF	EF	Unc
29	37	Bz	1/2 Cent, 1932, square	8.50	15	60
						Proof: $300
30	32	Bz	1 Cent, 1919–26, square	12.50	25	95
						Proof: $400

Y#	KM#	Metal	Description	VF	EF	Unc
31	34	C-N	5 Cents, 1920	10	35	75
						Proof: Rare

Y#	KM#	Metal	Description	VF	EF	Unc
32	31	Silv	5 Cents, 1918–20 *1920, Unc $1,750*	4.00	10.00	40
32a	36	Silv	5 Cents, 1926, 35, smaller bust	2.50	6.00	20 *Proof: $5,500*
34	29	Silv	10 Cents, 1916–27 *1920, EF $150*	5.00	17.50	75 *Proof: $7,500*
35	30	Silv	20 Cents, 1916–35	6.00	20.00	95 *Proof: Rare*
36	35	Silv	50 Cents, 1920–21	7.50	20.00	60 *Proof: Rare*

Note: Y34–35 were struck in both .600 and .400 silver.

Y#	KM#	Metal	Description	VF	EF	Unc
37	33	Silv	1 Dollar, 1919–26 *1919–20, Proof restrike: $300; 1925–26, Proof only: Rare*	40	85	200

Note: Modern restrikes exist.

SUDAN

Sudan, located along the Nile River in northeastern Africa, is the continent's largest country. First conquered and unified by Egypt in the early 19th century, the people of Sudan revolted in 1881. The country was retaken in 1898 and made part of a joint British-Egyptian protectorate. Full independence came for Sudan in 1956. It has been ruled since by unstable parliamentary governments and military regimes, and civil wars have raged since the early 1980s. *Languages:* Arabic, native dialects. *Capital:* Khartoum.

MONETARY SYSTEM

40 para = 1 ghirsh (piastre), 1885-1898
10 millim = 1 ghirsh, 1956–

El Mahdi, *1881–1885*

Y#	KM#	Metal	Description	VF	EF	Unc
1	1	Silv	10 Ghirsh, AH 1302 (1885), *Rare*			
2	2	Silv	20 Ghirsh (Piastres), AH 1302 (1885)	750	1,500	—

Note: Y1 was reliably reported in 1894, but its existence today is unconfirmed.

Y#	KM#	Metal	Description	VF	EF	Unc
3	3	Gold	100 Ghirsh, AH 1255, Yr 2 (1840)	8,500	—	—

Note: Y3 is a crude copy, including date, of the same Egyptian coin.

Khalifa Abdullah, *1885–1898*

Y#	KM#	Metal	Description	VF	EF	Unc
A4	A8	Cop	5 Para, AH 1308 (1891)	—	—	—
4	8	Cop	10 Para, AH 1308 (1891)	—	—	—

Note: YA4–4 are now thought to be patterns.

Borders: ***Double crescents***

Y#	KM#	Metal	Description	VF	EF	Unc
6	5.1	S/B	5 Ghirsh, AH 1304, 11 (1887, 94)	150	225	—
7	6	S/B	10 Ghirsh, AH 1304, 11 (1887, 94)	400	600	—
8	7.1	S/B	20 Ghirsh, AH 1304, 09 (1887, 92)	125	200	—

Borders: ***Plain***

Y#	KM#	Metal	Description	VF	EF	Unc
9	4	S/B	1 Ghirsh, AH 1304, 11 (1897, 94)	225	—	—
10	9	S/B	2 Ghirsh, AH 1310–11 (1893– 94)	500	—	—
11	10	S/B	4 Ghirsh, AH 1310 (1893)	1,000	—	—
12	11	S/B	5 Ghirsh, AH 1310 (1893)	200	—	—
13	12	S/B	10 Ghirsh, AH 1310 (1893)	350	—	—
15	22.2	S/B	2 Ghirsh, AH 1312 (1895)	250	—	—

Borders: ***Crescents, stars, and roses***

Y#	KM#	Metal	Description	VF	EF	Unc
16	23.1	S/B	2-1/2 Ghirsh, AH 1312 (1895)	150	275	—
17	19	S/B	5 Ghirsh, AH 1311 (1894)	175	350	—
19	14	S/B	20 Ghirsh, AH 1310 (?)–12	30	—	—

Borders: ***Crescents only***

Y#	KM#	Metal	Description	VF	EF	Unc
22	24	S/B	2-1/2 Ghirsh, AH 1312 (1895)	300	—	—
23	20	S/B	5 Ghirsh, AH 1311 (1894)	275	—	—
24	21	S/B	20 Ghirsh, AH 1311–12 (1894–95), reverse legend as Y19	75	125	—
25	25	S/B	20 Ghirsh, AH 1312 (1895), reverse legend as Y12	30	75	—

Y#	KM#	Metal	Description	VF	EF	Unc
27	22.1	S/B	2 Ghirsh, AH 1311	200	—	—

Y#	KM#	Metal	Description	VF	EF	Unc
30	13	S/B	10 Ghirsh, AH 1310 (1893)	750	—	—
31	15	S/B	20 Ghirsh, AH 1310–15 (1893–98), spears on reverse	55	90	—
32	16	S/B	20 Ghirsh, AH 1312–15 (1895–98), spears on obverse	25	60	—

REPUBLIC,
1956–1969

Y#	KM#	Metal	Description	VF	EF	Unc
34	29	Bz	1 Millim, 1956–69	0.50	1	2

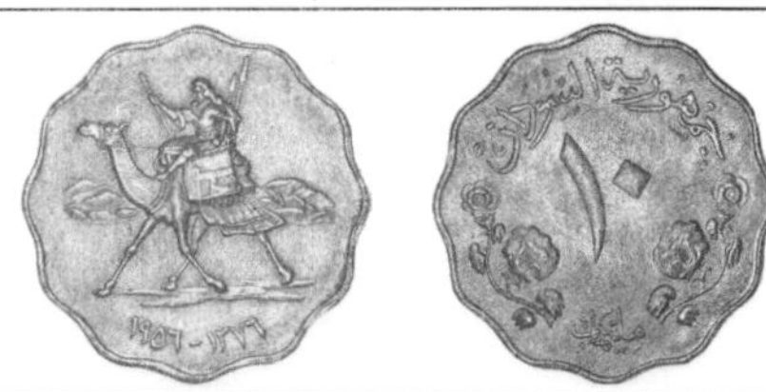

Y#	KM#	Metal	Description	VF	EF	Unc
35	30	Bz	2 Millim, 1956–69	0.50	1	2
36	31	Bz	5 Millim, 1956–69	0.50	1	2
37	32	Bz	10 Millim, 1956–96	0.50	1	2

Y#	KM#	Metal	Description	VF	EF	Unc
38	33	C-N	2 Ghirsh, 1956 (175 mm)	0.75	1.50	3.50
38a	36	C-N	2 Ghirsh, 1963–69 (20 mm)	0.75	1.50	3.50
39	34	C-N	5 Ghirsh, 1956–69	0.75	1.50	3.50
40	35	C-N	10 Ghirsh, 1956–69	0.75	1.50	3.50

SURINAME

Formerly Dutch Guiana on the north coast of South America, Suriname was raised to equality with the homeland by the revised Netherlands charter of 1954; this included internal autonomy and a voice in the government of the Netherlands. It was proclaimed an independent republic in 1975. Under military rule through the 1980s, free elections were restored in 1991. *Language:* Dutch. *Capital:* Paramaribo.

MONETARY SYSTEM

100 cents = 1 gulden

PRECIOUS METAL CONTENT

Dates	Denomination	Gross Wt (g)	Fineness	Net Wt (g)	Troy Oz.
		SILVER			
1962–66	1 gulden	10.0000	0.7200	7.2000	0.2315

JULIANA, *1948–1975*

For Netherlands coins struck for Suriname, see the Netherlands Y36a, Y36b, and Y43a.

Y#	KM#	Metal	Description	VF	EF	Unc
2	11	Bz	1 Cent, 1962–72	0.20	0.50	2
						Proof: $20

Y#	KM#	Metal	Description	VF	EF	Unc
3	12	N-Br	5 Cents, 1962–72	0.40	0.85	3.50
						Proof: $20

Y#	KM#	Metal	Description	VF	EF	Unc
4	13	C-N	10 Cents, 1962–86	0.25	0.50	2.00
						Proof: $20
5	14	C-N	25 Cents, 1962–86	0.30	0.50	3.00
						Proof: $20

Y#	KM#	Metal	Description	VF	EF	Unc
6	15	Silv	1 Gulden, 1962, 66	10.00	13.50	25.00

SWEDEN (SVERIGE)

A constitutional monarchy in the eastern part of the Scandinavia peninsula, Sweden broke away from its Danish conquerors in the mid-16th century but lost much of its territory to Russia, Poland, and Denmark in 1721. It was united with Norway from early in the 19th century to 1905. Its government is now dominated by social democrats. *Language:* Swedish. *Capital:* Stockholm.

MONETARY SYSTEM

100 ore = 1 riksdaler riksmynt, to 1873
100 ore = 1 krona, 1873–

PRECIOUS METAL CONTENT

Sweden was a member of the Scandinavian Monetary Union; see appendix A.

Dates	Denomination	Gross Wt (g)	Fineness	Net Wt (g)	Troy Oz.
		SILVER			
1860–72	10 ore	0.8500	0.7500	0.6375	0.0240
	25 ore	2.1300	0.7500	1.5975	0.0513
	50 ore	4.2500	0.7500	3.1875	0.1024
	1 riksdaler riksmynt	8.5000	0.7500	6.3750	0.2049
	2 riksdaler riksmynt	17.0000	0.7500	12.7500	0.4099
	4 riksdaler riksmynt	34.0061	0.7500	25.5046	0.8201
1874–1942	10 ore	1.4500	0.4000	0.5800	0.0185
	25 ore	2.4200	0.6000	1.4520	0.0463
	50 ore	5.0000	0.6000	3.0000	0.0964
	1 krona	7.5000	0.8000	6.0000	0.1929
	2 kronor	15.0000	0.8000	12.0000	0.3852
1935	5 kronor	25.0000	0.9000	22.5000	0.7234
1942–68	10 ore	1.4400	0.4000	0.5760	0.0185
	25 ore	2.3200	0.4000	0.9280	0.0298
	50 ore	4.8000	0.4000	1.9200	0.0617
	1 krona	7.0000	0.4000	2.8000	0.0900
	2 kronor	14.0000	0.4000	5.6000	0.1800
1952	5 kronor	22.7000	0.4000	9.0800	0.2920
1954–71	5 kronor	18.0000	0.4000	7.2000	0.2315
		GOLD			
1860–72	1 dukat	3.4856	0.9760	3.4019	0.1094
	1 carolin / 10 francs	3.2258	0.9000	2.9032	0.0933
1873–1925	5 kronor	2.2402	0.9000	2.0162	0.0648
	10 kronor	4.4803	0.9000	4.0323	0.1296
	20 kronor	8.9606	0.9000	8.0645	0.2593

CARL XV, *1859–1872*

Y#	KM#	Metal	Description	VF	EF	Unc
1	715	Bz	1/2 Ore, 1867	15	30	60

Y#	KM#	Metal	Description	VF	EF	Unc
2	705	Bz	1 Ore, 1860–72	4	13	30
3	706	Bz	2 Ore, 1860–72	6	18	40
4	707	Bz	5 Ore, 1860–72	10	28	75

Y#	KM#	Metal	Description	VF	EF	Unc
5	710	Silv	10 Ore, 1861–71 *1862, VF $1,600*	12	25	45
6	712	Silv	25 Ore, 1862–71 *1862, VF $1,800*	30	70	140
7	713	Silv	50 Ore, 1862	1,200	2,000	3,200

Y#	KM#	Metal	Description	VF	EF	Unc
8	708	Silv	1 Riksdaler Riksmynt, 1860–71 *1862, VF $1,700*	80	170	325
9	714/725	Silv	2 Riksdaler Riksmynt, 1862–71 *1862, VF $2,000*	275	550	900
10	711/726	Silv	4 Riksdaler Riksmynt, 1861–71	250	400	800

Reverse: *Crowned arms with mantle*

Y#	KM#	Metal	Description	VF	EF	Unc
B10	709	Gold	1 Dukat, 1860–68	700	1,200	2,000

Y#	KM#	Metal	Description	VF	EF	Unc
A10	716	Gold	1 Carolin / 10 Francs, 1868–72	250	400	800

OSCAR II,
1872–1907
FIRST COINAGE

Y#	KM#	Metal	Description	VF	EF	Unc
11	728	Bz	1 Ore, 1873	10	20	40
12	729	Bz	2 Ore, 1873	20	45	70
13	730	Bz	5 Ore, 1873	35	70	140

Y#	KM#	Metal	Description	VF	EF	Unc
17	727	Silv	10 Ore, 1872–73	50	75	150
18	731	Silv	1 Riksdaler Riksmynt, 1873	500	1,000	1,750

SECOND COINAGE

Y#	KM#	Metal	Description	VF	EF	Unc
14	734	Bz	1 Ore, 1874–77, small letters	15.00	35	75
14a	745	Bz	1 Ore, 1877–79, medium letters	15.00	35	75
14b	750	Bz	1 Ore, 1879–1905, large letters *1879, VF $600*	2.50	10	20
15	735	Bz	2 Ore, 1874–78, small letters obverse	10.00	40	100
15a	746	Bz	2 Ore, 1877–1905, large letters obverse	4.00	10	30
16	736	Bz	5 Ore, 1874–89, small letters obverse	25.00	60	150
16a	757	Bz	5 Ore, 1888–1905, large letters obverse *1888, VF $1,000 long text*	6.00	20	60

Y#	KM#	Metal	Description	VF	EF	Unc
19	737	Silv	10 Ore, 1874–76	40	70	150
20	738	Silv	25 Ore, 1874–78	35	90	250
21	740	Silv	50 Ore, 1875–99	35	90	250

Y#	KM#	Metal	Description	VF	EF	Unc
A27	755	Silv	10 Ore, 1880–1904	5	13	50

Y#	KM#	Metal	Description	VF	EF	Unc
28	739	Silv	25 Ore, 1880–1905	8	25	70

Obverse Legend: ***SVERIGES O. NORGES***

Y#	KM#	Metal	Description	VF	EF	Unc
22	741	Silv	1 Krona, 1875–76	60	180	500
23	742	Silv	2 Kronor, 1876–80	95	350	825

Y#	KM#	Metal	Description	VF	EF	Unc
25	732	Gold	10 Kronor, 1873–76	BV	200	300
26	733	Gold	20 Kronor, 1873–76 *1876, VF $800*	BV	400	500
27	744	Gold	20 Kronor, 1876–77, modified arms	BV	400	500

Obverse Legend: ***SVERIGES OCH NORGES***

Y#	KM#	Metal	Description	VF	EF	Unc
22a	747	Silv	1 Krona, 1877–89	100	350	800
23a	749	Silv	2 Kronor, 1878, 80 *1878, VF $1,000*	145	500	1,200

Y#	KM#	Metal	Description	VF	EF	Unc
24	756	Gold	5 Kronor, 1881–99	75	125	190

Y#	KM#	Metal	Description	VF	EF	Unc
25a	743	Gold	10 Kronor, 1876–95	BV	200	300
26a	748	Gold	20 Kronor, 1877–99 *1885, VF $1,750*	BV	400	500

Obverse: ***Older head***

Y#	KM#	Metal	Description	VF	EF	Unc
29	760	Silv	1 Krona, 1890–1904	35	110	300
30	761	Silv	2 Kronor, 1890–1904	50	180	350

Reverse: ***Denomination and three crowns in wreath***

Y#	KM#	Metal	Description	VF	EF	Unc
24a	766	Gold	5 Kronor, 1901	75	125	190

Y#	KM#	Metal	Description	VF	EF	Unc
25b	767	Gold	10 Kronor, 1901	BV	125	175
26b	765	Gold	20 Kronor, 1900–02	BV	400	500

25th Year of Reign

Y#	KM#	Metal	Description	VF	EF	Unc
31	762	Silv	2 Kronor, 1897	8.50	15	50

THIRD COINAGE

Y#	KM#	Metal	Description	VF	EF	Unc
32	768	Bz	1 Ore, 1906–07	1	3	12
33	769	Bz	2 Ore, 1906–07	1	8	25
34	770	Bz	5 Ore, 1906–07	3	15	50

Y#	KM#	Metal	Description	VF	EF	Unc
35	774	Bill	10 Ore, 1907	2.50	9	25

Y#	KM#	Metal	Description	VF	EF	Unc
36	775	Silv	25 Ore, 1907	3.50	15	45
37	771	Silv	50 Ore, 1906–07	20.00	50	125

Y#	KM#	Metal	Description	VF	EF	Unc
38	772	Silv	1 Krona, 1906–07	25	70	200
39	773	Silv	2 Kronor, 1906–07	25	95	250

Golden Wedding Anniversary

Y#	KM#	Metal	Description	VF	EF	Unc
40	776	Silv	2 Kronor, 1907	8.50	15	40

GUSTAF V, *1907–1950*

Y#	KM#	Metal	Description	VF	EF	Unc
44	777	Bz	1 Ore, 1909–50	0.50	1.00	5
45	778	Bz	2 Ore, 1909–50	0.50	2.50	6
46	779	Bz	5 Ore, 1909–50	1.00	5.00	15
			1910, VF $300; 1927, VF $200			

Y#	KM#	Metal	Description	VF	EF	Unc
47	780	Bill	10 Ore, 1909–19, 27–42	1	1.50	7

Y#	KM#	Metal	Description	VF	EF	Unc
48	785	Silv	25 Ore, 1910–19, 27–41	1	2	9
49	788	Silv	50 Ore, 1911–19, 27–39	5	8	23

Y#	KM#	Metal	Description	VF	EF	Unc
55	795	N-Bz	10 Ore, 1920–47	0.50	2	9

Y#	KM#	Metal	Description	VF	EF	Unc
56	798	N-Bz	25 Ore, 1921–47	0.75	5	20
57	796	N-Bz	50 Ore, 1920–47	1.50	6	30

Y#	KM#	Metal	Description	VF	EF	Unc
50	786	Silv	1 Krona, 1910–42	3.50	6.00	13
51	787	Silv	2 Kronor, 1910–40	6.50	7.50	14

Y#	KM#	Metal	Description	VF	EF	Unc
62	797	Gold	5 Kronor, 1920	75	100	150

Y#	KM#	Metal	Description	VF	EF	Unc
63	800	Gold	20 Kronor, 1925	650	1,000	1,500

400th Anniversary of Political Liberty

Y#	KM#	Metal	Description	VF	EF	Unc
58	799	Silv	2 Kronor, 1921	7	11	20

300th Anniversary, Death of Gustaf II Adolf

Y#	KM#	Metal	Description	VF	EF	Unc
59	805	Silv	2 Kronor, 1932	8	12	25

500th Anniversary of the Riksdag

Y#	KM#	Metal	Description	VF	EF	Unc
60	806	Silv	5 Kronor, 1935	12	15	25

300th Anniversary of Delaware Settlement

Y#	KM#	Metal	Description	VF	EF	Unc
61	807	Silv	2 Kronor, 1938	6.50	9	18

World War I Issues

Designs: *Like Y44–46*

Y#	KM#	Metal	Description	VF	EF	Unc
52	789	Iron	1 Ore, 1917–19	2.50	5	12
53	790	Iron	2 Ore, 1917–19	3.00	10	25
54	791	Iron	5 Ore, 1917–19	15.00	30	70

Regular Issues

Y#	KM#	Metal	Description	VF	EF	Unc
64	813	Bill	10 Ore, 1942–50	0.50	1.25	5
65	816	Bill	25 Ore, 1943–50	0.50	1.25	5
66	817	Bill	50 Ore, 1943–50	1.00	3.50	15

Y#	KM#	Metal	Description	VF	EF	Unc
67	814	Bill	1 Krona, 1942–50	1.50	2.50	10
68	815	Bill	2 Kronor, 1942–50	2.50	3.50	12

World War II Issues

Y#	KM#	Metal	Description	VF	EF	Unc
69	810	Iron	1 Ore, 1942–50	0.25	1.00	4.50
70	811	Iron	2 Ore, 1942–50	0.50	2.00	10.00
71	812	Iron	5 Ore, 1942–50	1.00	4.50	15.00

GUSTAF VI ADOLF, *1950–1973*

Y#	KM#	Metal	Description	VF	EF	Unc
72	820	Bz	1 Ore, 1952–71	0.10	0.15	0.50
73	821	Bz	2 Ore, 1952–71	0.10	0.15	0.50
74	822	Bz	5 Ore, 1952–71	0.10	0.25	0.50

Y#	KM#	Metal	Description	VF	EF	Unc
75	823	Bill	10 Ore, 1952–62	0.50	1	4.50
76	824	Bill	25 Ore, 1952–61	0.50	1	6.00
77	825	Bill	50 Ore, 1952–61	1.00	5	18.00

Y#	KM#	Metal	Description	VF	EF	Unc
78	826	Silv	1 Krona, 1952–68	1.50	2	4.50
79	827	Silv	2 Kronor, 1952–66	3.00	4	10.00

Y#	KM#	Metal	Description	VF	EF	Unc
80	829	Silv	5 Kronor, 1954–71	4	5	10

King's 70th Birthday

Y#	KM#	Metal	Description	VF	EF	Unc
81	828	Silv	5 Kronor, 1952	15	20	30

Sesquicentennial, Constitution of 1809

Y#	KM#	Metal	Description	VF	EF	Unc
82	830	Silv	5 Kronor, 1959	5	10	15

Y#	KM#	Metal	Description	VF	EF	Unc
83	835	C-N	10 Ore, 1962–73	0.05	0.10	0.25
84	836	C-N	25 Ore, 1962–73	0.10	0.15	0.45
85	837	C-N	50 Ore, 1962–73	0.15	0.20	0.50

King's 80th Birthday

Y#	KM#	Metal	Description	VF	EF	Unc
86	838	Bill	5 Kronor, 1962	9.50	18	35

SWITZERLAND
(HELVETIA, CONFOEDERATIO HELVETICA)

Located in central Europe, Switzerland forms no military alliances and did not join the United Nations until 2002. It gained independence from the Holy Roman Empire in 1648, and its constitution of 1848 established the nation as a federated republic of cantons. *Languages:* German, French, Italian. *Capital:* Berne.

MONETARY SYSTEM

100 rappen (centimes) = 1 franc

PRECIOUS METAL CONTENT

Switzerland was a member of the Scandinavian Monetary Union; see appendix A.

Dates	Denomination	Gross Wt (g)	Fineness	Net Wt (g)	Troy Oz.
		SILVER			
1850–57	1/2 franc	2.5000	0.9000	2.2500	0.0723
	1 franc	5.0000	0.9000	4.5000	0.1447
	2 francs	10.0000	0.9000	9.0000	0.2894
1850–1928	5 francs	25.0000	0.9000	22.5000	0.7234
1860–61	1/2 franc	5.0000	0.8000	4.0000	0.1286
	1 franc	10.0000	0.8000	8.0000	0.2572
1874–1967	1/2 franc	2.5000	0.8350	2.0875	0.0671
	1 franc	5.0000	0.8350	4.1750	0.1342
	2 francs	10.0000	0.8350	8.3500	0.2685
1931–69	5 francs	15.0000	0.8350	12.5250	0.4027
		GOLD			
1883–1949	10 francs	3.2258	0.9000	2.9032	0.0933
	20 francs	6.4516	0.9000	5.8064	0.1867
	100 francs	32.2581	0.9000	29.0323	0.9334
1934	100 francs	25.9000	0.9000	23.3100	0.7494
1939	100 francs	17.5000	0.9000	15.7500	0.5064

Shooting Festival Coins

Y#	KM#	Metal	Description	VF	EF	Unc
1-S	17	Silv	4 Franken, 1842, Chur	500	775	1,450

Y#	KM#	Metal	Description	VF	EF	Unc
2-S	20	Silv	40 Batzen, 1847, Glarus	1,500	2,250	4,000

Y#	KM#	Metal	Description	VF	EF	Unc
3-S	S3	Silv	5 Franken, 1855, Solothurn (design as Y29)	1,200	2,000	5,000

Y#	KM#	Metal	Description	VF	EF	Unc
4-S	S4	Silv	5 Franken, 1857, Bern	300	450	1,250

Y#	KM#	Metal	Description	VF	EF	Unc
5-S	S5	Silv	5 Franken, 1859, Zurich	200	325	850

Y#	KM#	Metal	Description	VF	EF	Unc
6-S	S6	Silv	5 Franken, 1861, Nidwalden	200	500	900
7-S	S7	Silv	5 Franken, 1863, La Chaux-de-Fonds	200	325	1,200
8-S	S8	Silv	5 Franken, 1865, Schaffhausen	85	150	450
9-S	S9	Silv	5 Franken, 1867, Schwyz	125	225	525
10-S	S10	Silv	5 Franken, 1869, Zug	150	275	1,000
11-S	S11	Silv	5 Franken, 1872, Zurich	65	100	425
12-S	S12	Silv	5 Franken, 1874, St Gallen	65	125	325
13-S	S13	Silv	5 Franken, 1876, Lausanne	65	125	325
14-S	S14	Silv	5 Franken, 1879, Basel	50	80	235

Y#	KM#	Metal	Description	VF	EF	Unc
15-S	S15	Silv	5 Francs, 1881, Fribourg	50	80	325
16-S	S16	Silv	5 Franken, 1883, Lugano	50	80	275
17-S	S17	Silv	5 Franken, 1885, Bern	60	100	300

MODERN SERIES

Y#	KM#	Metal	Description	VF	EF	Unc
44	S18	Silv	5 Francs, 1934, Fribourg	20	40	80

Y#	KM#	Metal	Description	VF	EF	Unc
47	S20	Silv	5 Francs, 1939, Luzern	20	40	70

Y#	KM#	Metal	Description	VF	EF	Unc
45	S19	Gold	100 Francs, 1934, Fribourg	1,200	2,250	3,000

Y#	KM#	Metal	Description	VF	EF	Unc
48	521	Gold	100 Franken, 1939, Luzern	500	700	950

Y#	KM#	Metal	Description	VF	EF	Unc
18	3.1–3.2	Bz	1 Rappen, 1850–1941 *1850, VF $200*	2	6.00	13
18	3.1–3.2	Bz	1851–1894 *1855, VF $475; 1863–64, VF $400; 1876–82, VF $125; 1896, Rare*	30	50.00	125
19	4.1–4.2	Bz	2 Rappen, 1850–1941 *1870, 88, VF $55; 1896, Rare; 1902–06, VF $60; 1941, VF $2, EF $4, Unc $10*	8	12.50	20

Y#	KM#	Metal	Description	VF	EF	Unc
18a	3a	Zinc	1 Rappen, 1942–46 *1945, VF $22*	2.50	8.50	18
19a	4a	Zinc	2 Rappen, 1942–46 *1945, VF $12; 1946, VF $45*	4.50	10.00	23

Y#	KM#	Metal	Description	VF	EF	Unc
20	5	Bill	5 Rappen, 1850–77 *1851, VF $400*	30	65	175
21	6	Bill	10 Rappen, 1850–76 *1875, VF $850*	35	75	185
22	7	Bill	20 Rappen, 1850–59 *1851, VF $275; 1858, VF $60*	35	75	175

Y#	KM#	Metal	Description	VF	EF	Unc
23	26	C-N	5 Rappen, 1879–1931, 1940–80 *1879–19, VF $5; 1887, 89, VF $75; 1896, Rare; 1920–62, VF $1*	0.25	1.00	5.00
24	27	C-N	10 Rappen, 1879–1931, 1940–2000 *1896, Rare*	0.20	0.50	1.00
25	29a	C-N	20 Rappen, 1939–2000	0.25	0.60	1.25

Y#	KM#	Metal	Description	VF	EF	Unc
23a	26b	Nick	5 Rappen, 1932–41	1.25	3	15
24a	27b	Nick	10 Rappen, 1932–39	1.25	3	20
25a	29	Nick	20 Rappen, 1881–1938 *1881, 83, 87, 94–99, 03, 27, VF $11*	2.00	10	60

Y#	KM#	Metal	Description	VF	EF	Unc
23b	26a	Br	5 Rappen, 1918	15	25	50
24b	27a	Br	10 Rappen, 1918–19 *1919, VF $95*	23	33	65

Y#	KM#	Metal	Description	VF	EF	Unc
26	8	Silv	1/2 Franc, 1850–51	125	250	750
27	9–9a	Silv	1 Franc, 1850–61 *1857, Rare; 1860, VF $275; 1861, VF $50, EF $150, Unc $500*	200	325	750
28	10–10a	Silv	2 Francs, 1850–63 *1850, 63, VF $350; 1857, Rare; 1860 VF $1,500*	85	375	1,250
29	11	Silv	5 Francs, 1850–74 *1850, VF $475; 1855, VF $1,500; 1873, VF $2,250*	275	500	1,250

Y#	KM#	Metal	Description	VF	EF	Unc
30	23	Silv	1/2 Franc, 1875–1967 *1875, 77–78, VF $150; 1879–94, VF $65; 1896, Rare; 1898–1900, 03–13, VF $15; 1901, VF $100*	3.00	5.00	8.00
31	24	Silv	1 Franc, 1875–1967 *1875, 77, 80, VF $80; 1876, 1900–01, 04, VF $45; 1896, Rare; 1903, 05, 07–14, 31–37, VF $11*	7.50	9.00	14.50
32	21	Silv	2 Francs, 1874–1967 *1896, Rare; 1901, VF $135; 1908, VF $60*	11.50	13.50	18.00

Y#	KM#	Metal	Description	VF	EF	Unc
33	34	Silv	5 Francs, 1888–1916 *1896, 1912, Rare; 1916, VF $1,350*	200	475	1,250

Y#	KM#	Metal	Description	VF	EF	Unc
34	37	Silv	5 Fr(ancs), 1922–23	55	110	225
34a	38	Silv	5 FR(ancs), 1924–28 *1924, VF $350; 1928, Rare*	100	150	350

Y#	KM#	Metal	Description	VF	EF	Unc
36	40	Silv	5 Francs, 1931–69, smaller size	11	13	18

Y#	KM#	Metal	Description	VF	EF	Unc
40	31.1	Gold	20 Francs, 1883, reeded edge	125	145	200
40a	31.3	Gold	20 Francs, 1886–96, lettered edge	125	145	200

Y#	KM#	Metal	Description	VF	EF	Unc
41	35.1	Gold	20 Francs, 1897–1935, stars on edge	BV	BV	130
41a	35.2	Gold	20 Francs, 1947, 49, lettered edge	BV	BV	130

Y#	KM#	Metal	Description	VF	EF	Unc
42	36	Gold	10 Francs, 1911–22	90	110	140
43	39	Gold	100 Francs, 1925	5,000	7,000	8,500

Armament Fund

Y#	KM#	Metal	Description	VF	EF	Unc
46	41	Silv	5 Francs, 1936	13	25	50

600th Anniversary, Battle of Laupen

Y#	KM#	Metal	Description	VF	EF	Unc
49	42	Silv	5 Francs, 1939	300	500	650

Zurich Exposition

Y#	KM#	Metal	Description	VF	EF	Unc
50	43	Silv	5 Francs, 1939	50	75	125

650th Anniversary of Confederation

Y#	KM#	Metal	Description	VF	EF	Unc
51	44	Silv	5 Francs, 1941	35	50	85

500 Anniversary, Battle of St. Jakob an der Birs

Y#	KM#	Metal	Description	VF	EF	Unc
52	45	Silv	5 Francs, 1944	25	40	85

Centennial of Swiss Confederation

Y#	KM#	Metal	Description	VF	EF	Unc
53	48	Silv	5 Francs, 1948	8.50	13	20

Y#	KM#	Metal	Description	VF	EF	Unc
54	46	Bz	1 Rappen, 1948–2000	0.20	0.30	0.50
55	47	Bz	2 Rappen, 1948–74	0.30	0.60	1.00

Red Cross Centennial

Y#	KM#	Metal	Description	VF	EF	Unc
56	51	Silv	5 Francs, 1963	6.50	8	15

SYRIA

In western Asia, bordered by Turkey to the north, Syria was part of the Ottoman Empire until 1920, when it was made an independent state under French mandate. In 1944 it was granted complete independence and was proclaimed a republic. In 1958 Syria joined Egypt as the United Arab Republic. It broke away and declared itself independent again in 1961. Since 1963 the country has been ruled by military dictatorship. *Languages:* Arabic, French. *Capital:* Damascus.

MONETARY SYSTEM

100 ghirsh (piastres) = 1 lira (pound)

PRECIOUS METAL CONTENT

Dates	Denomination	Gross Wt (g)	Fineness	Net Wt (g)	Troy Oz.
		SILVER			
1929–37	10 piastres	2.0000	0.6800	1.3600	0.0437
	25 piastres	5.0000	0.6800	3.4000	0.1093
	50 piastres	10.0000	0.6800	6.8000	0.2186
1947–50	25 piastres	2.5000	0.6000	1.5000	0.0482
	50 piastres	5.0000	0.6000	3.0000	0.0965
	1 lira	10.0000	0.6800	6.8000	0.2186
		GOLD			
1950	1/2 pound	3.3793	0.9000	3.0414	0.0978
	1 pound	6.7586	0.9000	6.0827	0.1956

FIRST COINAGE

Y#	KM#	Metal	Description	VF	EF	Unc
1	68	C-N	1/2 Piastre, 1921	10	32.50	65

SECOND COINAGE

Y#	KM#	Metal	Description	VF	EF	Unc
4	75	N-Bz	1/2 Piastre, 1935–36	15	50	95

Y#	KM#	Metal	Description	VF	EF	Unc
5	71	N-Bz	1 Piastre, 1929–36	10	25	60

Y#	KM#	Metal	Description	VF	EF	Unc
5a	71a	Zinc	1 Piastre, 1940	25	50	100

Y#	KM#	Metal	Description	VF	EF	Unc
2	69	A-Bz	2 Piastres, 1926	25.00	50	100
3	70	A-Bz	5 Piastres, 1926–40	5.00	20	50
6	76	A-Bz	2-1/2 Piastres, 1940, like Y5	7.50	25	60

Y#	KM#	Metal	Description	VF	EF	Unc
7	72	Silv	10 Piastres, 1929	15.00	60	125
8	73	Silv	25 Piastres, 1929–37	20.00	65	125
9	74	Silv	50 Piastres, 1929–37	22.50	75	175

WORLD WAR II ISSUES

Y#	KM#	Metal	Description	VF	EF	Unc
10	77	Br	1 Piastre, ND	10	20	50

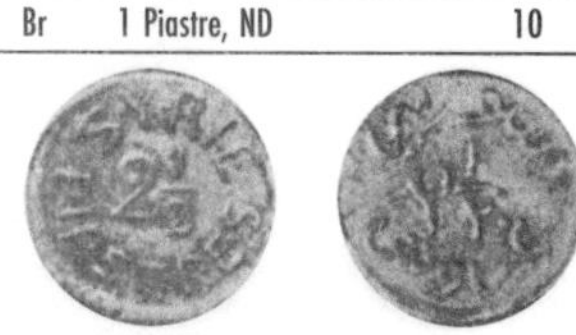

Y#	KM#	Metal	Description	VF	EF	Unc
11	78	Alum	2-1/2 Piastres, ND	40	65	125

REPUBLIC, *1944–1958*

Y#	KM#	Metal	Description	VF	EF	Unc
12	81	C-N	2-1/2 Piastres, 1948, 56	1	3	7.50

Y#	KM#	Metal	Description	VF	EF	Unc
13	82	C-N	5 Piastres, 1948, 56	1	2	6

Y#	KM#	Metal	Description	VF	EF	Unc
14	83	C-N	10 Piastres, 1948, 56	1	2	6

Y#	KM#	Metal	Description	VF	EF	Unc
15	79	Silv	25 Piastres, 1947	2.25	5.00	18
16	80	Silv	50 Piastres, 1947	3.50	7.50	20

Y#	KM#	Metal	Description	VF	EF	Unc
17	85	Silv	1 Lira (Pound), 1950	10	15	25

Y#	KM#	Metal	Description	VF	EF	Unc
18	84	Gold	1/2 Pound, 1950	BV	350	450
19	86	Gold	1 Pound, 1950	BV	500	650

SYRIAN ARAB REPUBLIC, *1961–*

Y#	KM#	Metal	Description	VF	EF	Unc
24	93	A-Bz	2-1/2 Ghirsh, 1962, 65	0.25	0.50	1

Y#	KM#	Metal	Description	VF	EF	Unc
25	104	A-Bz	5 Ghirsh, 1962, 65	0.25	0.50	1

Y#	KM#	Metal	Description	VF	EF	Unc
26	95	A-Bz	10 Ghirsh, 1962, 65	0.25	0.50	1

SYRIA–UNITED ARAB REPUBLIC

SEE UNDER UNITED ARAB REPUBLIC

TANNU TUVA

Located north of Mongolia and south of Siberia near the geographic center of Asia, Tannu Tuva broke away from the Chinese Empire in 1911 and later became a Russian protectorate. An independent People's Republic was proclaimed in 1921 and the country was annexed by the USSR as an autonomous region in 1944. A republican constitution was adopted in 1993 and the nation officially changed its name to Tyva. *Language:* Tuvan. *Capital:* Kyzyl.

MONETARY SYSTEM
100 kopejek = 1 aksha

Y#	KM#	Metal	Description	VF	EF	Unc
1	1	A-Bz	1 Kopejek, 1934	165	325	—
2	2	A-Bz	2 Kopejek, 1934	185	375	—
3	3	A-Bz	3 Kopejek, 1934	165	325	—
4	4	A-Bz	5 Kopejek, 1934	185	375	—

Y#	KM#	Metal	Description	VF	EF	Unc
5	5	C-N	10 Kopejek, 1934	165	325	—
6	6	C-N	15 Kopejek, 1934	185	375	—
7	7	C-N	20 Kopejek, 1934	200	400	—

THAILAND (SIAM)

A constitutional monarchy in southeast Asia, Thailand occupies the western half of the Malay peninsula. The monarchy was relegated to titular status in a 1932 coup, when representative government was established. The name of the country was officially changed from Siam to Thailand in 1939. *Languages:* Thai, English. *Capital:* Bangkok.

MONETARY SYSTEM

To 1908:	After 1908:
8 att = 1 fuang	100 satang = 1 baht
2 fuang = 1 salung	
4 salung = 1 baht (tical)	

PRECIOUS METAL CONTENT

Dates	Denomination	Gross Wt (g)	Fineness	Net Wt (g)	Troy Oz.
		SILVER			
1908–25	1 salung	3.7500	0.8000	3.0000	0.0965
	2 salung	7.5000	0.8000	6.0000	0.1929
	1 baht	15.0000	0.9000	13.5000	0.4340
1929	25 satang	3.7500	0.6500	2.4375	0.0784
	50 satang	7.5000	0.6500	4.8750	0.1567
1941	5 satang	1.5000	0.6500	0.9750	0.0313
	10 satang	2.5000	0.6500	1.6250	0.0522
	20 satang	3.0000	0.6500	1.9500	0.0627
1963	20 baht	19.6000	0.7500	14.7000	0.4726

THAI NUMERALS

Western	1	2	3	4	5
Thai	๑	๒	๓	๔	๕

6	7	8	9	0	10
๖	๗	๘	๙	๐	๑๐

For details of dating system, see the introduction to this book.

MODERN COINS OF THE BANGKOK DYNASTY

PHRA CHOM KLAO, RAMA IV *(MONGKUT), 1851–1868*

Y#	KM#	Metal	Description	VF	EF	Unc
5	5	Tin	1/16 Fuang (Solot), ND (1862) (23 mm)	60	150	500
6	6.1–6.4	Tin	1/8 Fuang (Att), ND (29 mm)	50	100	350

Note: Contemporary counterfeits of Y5–6 are common and are usually heavier than the originals.

Planchet: ***Cast, thick flan (3 mm)***

Y#	KM#	Metal	Description	VF	EF	Unc
1	1	Cop	1/4 Fuang, ND (1865) (22 mm)	85	135	400
2	2	Cop	1/2 Fuang, ND (28 mm)	60	125	375

Planchet: ***Cast, thin flan (1.5 mm)***

Y#	KM#	Metal	Description	VF	EF	Unc
3	3	Cop	1/4 Fuang, ND (1865) (22 mm)	75	125	400
4	4	Cop	1/2 Fuang, ND	85	150	375

Y#	KM#	Metal	Description	VF	EF	Unc
7	7.1–7.2	Silv	1/16 Baht, ND (1860) (13 mm)	35	140	425
8	8	Silv	1/8 Baht, ND (15 mm)	15	65	225
9	9	Silv	1/4 Baht, ND (20 mm)	30	135	400
10	10.1	Silv	1/2 Baht, ND (27 mm)	150	250	600
11	11	Silv	1 Baht, ND (31 mm)	100	200	850
12	12	Silv	2 Baht, ND (37 mm)	650	1,350	3,500
A12	A12	Silv	4 Baht, ND, reverse Chinese inscription, *Rare*			
13	13	Gold	2-1/2 Baht, ND (1863, 95), as Y8	1,500	3,000	4,500

Y#	KM#	Metal	Description	VF	EF	Unc
14	14/14.5	Gold	4 Baht, ND (1863, 95)	2,000	4,000	5,500
15	15–15.1	Gold	8 Baht, ND (1863, 95)	2,500	5,000	6,500

Note: Y13–15 have reeded edges. Similar gold pieces with plain edges are presentation strikings of Y7–A12. Contemporary counterfeits of Y7–15, A34, and 39 were made primarily to be worn as religious charms.

PHRA MAHA CHULALONGKORN, RAMA V *1868–1910*

FIRST COINAGE

Y#	KM#	Metal	Description	VF	EF	Unc
16	16	Tin	1/16 Fuang, ND (1868)	20	50	250

Y#	KM#	Metal	Description	VF	EF	Unc
28	28	Silv	1 Fuang, ND (1868)	30	150	350
29	29	Silv	1 Salung, ND	45	185	500
31	31	Silv	1 Baht, ND	35	175	350

Second Coinage

Y#	KM#	Metal	Description	VF	EF	Unc
17	17	Cop	1/2 Att, CS 1236, 44 (1874, 82)	5	15	100
18	18	Cop	1 Att, CS 1236–44 (1874–82)	8	20	150
19	19	Cop	2 Att, CS 1236–44 (1874–82)	15	40	300
20	20	Cop	4 Att, CS 1238 (1876)	100	250	950

Y#	KM#	Metal	Description	VF	EF	Unc
21	21	Bz	1/2 Att, CS 1249, RS 109–124 (1897–1905)	5	25	125
22	22	Bz	1 Att, CS 1249, RS 109–124 (1897–1905)	10	50	225
23	23	Bz	2 Att, CS 1249, RS 109–124 (1897–1905)	20	100	350

Y#	KM#	Metal	Description	VF	EF	Unc
24	24	C-N	2-1/2 Satang, RS 116 (1897)	4	10	50
25	25	C-N	5 Satang, RS 116 (1897)	10	20	150
26	26	C-N	10 Satang, RS 116 (1897)	20	95	300
27	27	C-N	20 Satang, RS 116 (1897)	15	30	250

Y#	KM#	Metal	Description	VF	EF	Unc
32	32	Silv	1 Fuang, ND (1876–1902)	15	40	175
33	33	Silv	1 Salung, ND	20	50	200
34	34	Silv	1 Baht, ND	30	75	300

Reverse: ***Date at bottom***

Y#	KM#	Metal	Description	VF	EF	Unc
32a	32a	Silv	1 Fuang, RS 121–127 (1902–08)	20	50	225
33a	33a	Silv	1 Salung, RS 120–127 (1901–08)	25	55	250
34a	34a	Silv	1 Baht, RS 120–126 (1901–07)	30	75	350

Design: ***Like Y32–34***

Y#	KM#	Metal	Description	VF	EF	Unc
A34	N/A	Gold	2 Baht, ND (1876)	–	–	–

Third Coinage

Y#	KM#	Metal	Description	VF	EF	Unc
39	39	Silv	1 Baht, RS 127 (1908)	2,500	4,000	8,000

Note: Smaller coins of this design are patterns.

General Coinage

Y35–37 were struck during four reigns without regal identification.

Y#	KM#	Metal	Description	VF	EF	Unc
50	50	Bz	1/2 Satang, BE 2480 (1937)	1	5	15

Y#	KM#	Metal	Description	VF	EF	Unc
35	35	Bz	1 Satang, RS 127–130, BE 2456–80 (1908–37)	0.60	1	2.75

Note: Coins with RS dates are worth many times more in EF and above.

Y#	KM#	Metal	Description	VF	EF	Unc
36	36	Nick	5 Satang, RS 127–31, BE 2456–80 (1908–38)	0.80	1.50	4.00
37	37	Nick	10 Satang, RS 127–31, BE 2456–80 (1908–38)	1.00	1.50	4.50

Note: Coins with RS dates are worth many times more in EF and above.

VAJIRAVUDH, RAMA VI, *1910–1925*

Y#	KM#	Metal	Description	VF	EF	Unc
43	43	Silv	1 Salung, BE 2458–68 (1915–25)	3.50	7	40
44	44	Silv	2 Salung, BE 2458–64 (1915–21)	6.00	15	125
45	45	Silv	1 Baht, BE 2456–61 (1913–18)	12.00	18	135

PRAJADHIPOK, RAMA VII, *1925–1936*

Y#	KM#	Metal	Description	VF	EF	Unc
48	48	Silv	25 Satang, BE 2472 (1929)	5.00	10	100
49	49	Silv	50 Satang, BE 2472 (1929)	7.50	15	125

ANANDA MAHIDOL, RAMA VIII, *1935–1946*

Beginning with Y51, coins bear a longer legend because of the change in name from Siam to Thailand.

Y#	KM#	Metal	Description	VF	EF	Unc
51	51	Bz	1 Satang, BE 2482 (1939)	1	3	7

Y#	KM#	Metal	Description	VF	EF	Unc
54	54	Bz	1 Satang, BE 2484 (1941)	0.50	1	3.50

Y#	KM#	Metal	Description	VF	EF	Unc
55	55	Silv	5 Satang, BE 2484 (1941)	2	3	5
56	56	Silv	10 Satang, BE 2484 (1941)	3	5	9
A56	A56	Silv	20 Satang, BE 2485 (1942)	5	8	14

Y#	KM#	Metal	Description	VF	EF	Unc
57	57	Tin	1 Satang, BE 2485 (1942) (not holed)	0.25	0.50	1

Note: Y57 was restruck for circulation in 1969–1971.

Y#	KM#	Metal	Description	VF	EF	Unc
58	58	Tin	5 Satang, BE 2485 (1942)	0.75	1.50	3
59	59	Tin	10 Satang, BE 2485 (1942)	1.00	2.00	5

Design: ***Values and B.E. dates in "Western" numerals***

Y#	KM#	Metal	Description	VF	EF	Unc
60	60	Tin	1 Satang, BE 2487 (1944) (not holed)	0.15	0.30	0.60

Planchet: ***Thick***

Y#	KM#	Metal	Description	VF	EF	Unc
61	61	Tin	5 Satang, BE 2487–88 (1944–45)	0.60	1.50	4
62	62	Tin	10 Satang, BE 2487 (1944)	1.25	2.50	5

Planchet: ***Thin***

Y#	KM#	Metal	Description	VF	EF	Unc
61a	61a	Tin	5 Satang, BE 2488 (1945)	0.75	1.50	3.75
62a	62a	Tin	10 Satang, BE 2488 (1945)	1.25	2.75	5.00
63	63	Tin	20 Satang, BE 2488 (1945)	1.25	3.00	6.25

Obverse: ***Child bust***

Y#	KM#	Metal	Description	VF	EF	Unc
64	64	Tin	5 Satang, BE 2489 (1946)	0.50	1.00	2.00
65	65	Tin	10 Satang, BE 2489 (1946)	0.60	1.25	2.50
66	66	Tin	25 Satang, BE 2489 (1946)	3.00	6.00	15.00
67	67	Tin	50 Satang, BE 2489 (1946)	35.00	70.00	200.00

Obverse: ***Older bust***

Y#	KM#	Metal	Description	VF	EF	Unc
68	68	Tin	5 Satang, BE 2489 (1946)	0.25	0.60	1.25
69	69	Tin	10 Satang, BE 2489 (1946)	0.60	1.25	2.00
70	70	Tin	25 Satang, BE 2489 (1946)	0.25	0.60	1.25
71	71	Tin	50 Satang, BE 2489 (1946)	1.00	1.50	3.25

Phumiphol Adulyadet, Rama IX, *1946–2016*

Obverse: ***Large bust, one medal on uniform***

Y#	KM#	Metal	Description	VF	EF	Unc
72	72	Tin	5 Satang, BE 2493 (1950)	0.50	1.00	2.00
73	73	Tin	10 Satang, BE 2493 (1950)	0.50	1.00	1.50

Y#	KM#	Metal	Description	VF	EF	Unc
72a	72a	A-Bz	5 Satang, BE 2493	0.25	1.00	2.00
73a	73a	A-Bz	10 Satang, BE 2493	0.75	1.50	2.50
76	76	A-Bz	25 Satang, BE 2493	1.50	3.00	5.25
77	77	A-Bz	50 Satang, BE 2493	3.00	6.00	25.00

Obverse: ***Small bust, three medals on uniform***

Y#	KM#	Metal	Description	VF	EF	Unc
78	78	A-Bz	5 Satang, BE 2500 (1957)	0.10	0.20	0.35
79	79	A-Bz	10 Satang, BE 2500 (1957)	0.10	0.25	0.50

Y#	KM#	Metal	Description	VF	EF	Unc
78a	78a	Bz	5 Satang, BE 2500 (1957)	0.50	1.50	2.00
79a	79a	Bz	10 Satang, BE 2500 (1957)	0.25	0.75	1.25

Y#	KM#	Metal	Description	VF	EF	Unc
80	80	A-Bz	25 Satang, BE 2500 (1957)	0.25	0.75	1.25
81	81	A-Bz	50 Satang, BE 2500 (1957)	0.35	0.85	2.50
82	82.1	CNS	1 Baht, BE 2500 (1957)	0.60	1.00	5.00

Y#	KM#	Metal	Description	VF	EF	Unc
83	83	C-N	1 Baht, BE 2504 (1961)	0.60	0.85	2

Y#	KM#	Metal	Description	VF	EF	Unc
84	84	C-N	1 Baht, BE 2505 (1962)	0.25	0.35	0.65

King's 36th Birthday

Y#	KM#	Metal	Description	VF	EF	Unc
85	85	C-N	1 Baht, ND (1963)	0.25	0.75	2

Y#	KM#	Metal	Description	VF	EF	Unc
86	86	Silv	20 Baht, ND (1963)	10	15	30

TIBET

High in the mountains of central Asia, Tibet was an independent kingdom until the 13th century, when it was incorporated into the Chinese Empire. It enjoyed brief periods of independence until it was annexed by the Republic of China in 1911. Civil war in China and the two world wars allowed Tibet to exercise virtual autonomy until the Red Army occupied the nation in 1950 and set up a province-level government as the Tibet Autonomous Region of the People's Republic of China. *Languages:* Lhasa, local dialects. *Capital:* Lhasa.

MONETARY SYSTEM

10 skar = 1 shokang
15 skar = 1 tangka
10 sho = 1 srang
3 tangka = 1 Indian rupee

In the Lhasa dialect, "srang" is pronounced "sang" and "skar" is pronounced "kar" or "karma."

Most earlier issues are seldom encountered in grades above Very Fine. When found, they command substantial premiums.

CHINESE ISSUES

KUANG HSU, *1875–1908*

Struck in Szechuan Province for Tibet.

Y#	KM#	Metal	Description	VF	EF	Unc
1	1	Silv	1/4 Rupee, ND (ca 1903) (19 mm)	400	800	3,250
2	2	Silv	1/2 Rupee, ND (ca 1903) (24 mm)	400	900	3,500
3	3.2	Silv	1 Rupee, ND (ca 1903), bust within collar	150	350	600
3a	3–3.1	Silv	1 Rupee, ND, no collar	175	400	750
3b	3.3	Silv	1 Rupee, ND, larger, wider head	150	375	700

HSUAN T'UNG, *1908–1911*

Y#	KM#	Metal	Description	VF	EF	Unc
A4	A4	Cop	1/2 Skar, ND (1908), as Y5	1,750	—	—
4	4	Cop	1 Skar, ND, similar (27 mm)	500	1,000	—

Y#	KM#	Metal	Description	VF	EF	Unc
5	5	Silv	1 Sho, ND (1908) (22 mm)	300	500	—
6	6	Silv	2 Sho, ND (25 mm)	300	500	—

Y#	KM#	Metal	Description	VF	EF	Unc
A7	A7	Cop	1/8 Sho, Yr 1 (1909), as Y9 (22 mm)	375	—	—
B7	B7	Cop	1/4 Sho, Yr 1, as Y9 (26 mm)	350	—	—

Y#	KM#	Metal	Description	VF	EF	Unc
8	8	Silv	5 Sho, Yr 1 (1909)	4,500	—	—
9	9	Silv	1 Srang Yr 1 (1909), reeded edge	1,250	2,000	5,000

Note: Varieties of Y9 with a plain edge are thought to be counterfeit.

TANGKA SYSTEM

Y#	KM#	Metal	Description	VF	EF	Unc
A13	A13	Silv	1 Tangka (1890–91)	30	60	120

Y#	KM#	Metal	Description	VF	EF	Unc
13	13	Silv	1 Tangka ND (ca 1840–1925)	20	35	50

Note: Many varieties exist of Y13. They average about 4.4 grams.

Y#	KM#	Metal	Description	VF	EF	Unc
14	14	Silv	1 Tangka ND (1909)	65	115	200
15	15	Silv	2 Tangka ND (1912), as Y13, (9.3 g)	1,500	2,000	3,500

SRANG SYSTEM

FIRST COINAGE

Y#	KM#	Metal	Description	VF	EF	Unc
10	10	Cop	2-1/2 Skar (1909) (22 mm)	650	1,100	2,200
A10	A10	Cop	5 Skar (1909) (25 mm)	750	1,300	2,500
11	11	Cop	7-1/2 Skar (1909) (28 mm)	750	1,300	2,500

Y#	KM#	Metal	Description	VF	EF	Unc
12	12	Silv	1 Srang (1909), plain edge	1,250	2,000	4,000

Second Coinage

Y#	KM#	Metal	Description	VF	EF	Unc
16	16	Cop	2-1/2 Skar, (1913–18)	85	175	—
17	17	Cop	5 Skar, (1913–18)	60	125	—

Y#	KM#	Metal	Description	VF	EF	Unc
18	18	Silv	5 Sho, (1913–27), as Y12, (3 vars)	150	225	500
A18	A18	Silv	1 Srang (1914–19), as Y12, reeded edge	4,000	7,000	12,000

Third Coinage

Y#	KM#	Metal	Description	VF	EF	Unc
A19	A19	Cop	2-1/2 Skar, (1918–21)	325	450	—

Y#	KM#	Metal	Description	VF	EF	Unc
19	19	Cop	5 Skar, (1918–25)	12.50	22.50	—

Y#	KM#	Metal	Description	VF	EF	Unc
20	20	Cop	7 1/2 Skar, (1918–25)	15	30	100

Y#	KM#	Metal	Description	VF	EF	Unc
21	21	Cop	1 Sho (1918–28), central legend horizontal on reverse	7.50	15	40

Y#	KM#	Metal	Description	VF	EF	Unc
21a	21a	Cop	1 Sho (1918–23), central legend vertical on reverse	6	12	35

Y#	KM#	Metal	Description	VF	EF	Unc
32	32	Silv	5 Sho, ND (ca 1928–29) (27 mm)	—	—	9,000

Note: Believed to be a pattern.

Y#	KM#	Metal	Description	VF	EF	Unc
22	22	Gold	20 Srang (1918–21)	3,000	4,500	6,000

FOURTH COINAGE

Y#	KM#	Metal	Description	VF	EF	Unc
23	23	Cop	1 Sho (1932–38)	10	20	50

Y#	KM#	Metal	Description	VF	EF	Unc
27	27	Cop	3 Sho (1946)	60	100	700

Y#	KM#	Metal	Description	VF	EF	Unc
24	24	Silv	1-1/2 Srang (1935–46)	20	60	100

Y#	KM#	Metal	Description	VF	EF	Unc
25	25	Silv	3 Srang (1933–34)	30	60	200

Y#	KM#	Metal	Description	VF	EF	Unc
26	26	Silv	3 Srang (1935–46)	20	45	125

FIFTH COINAGE

Y#	KM#	Metal	Description	VF	EF	Unc
28	28–28.2	Cop	5 Sho (1947–50), 2 suns on obverse (minor vars)	8	20	12
28a	28a	Cop	5 Sho (1949–53), moon and sun (minor vars)	8	20	12

Y#	KM#	Metal	Description	VF	EF	Unc
29	29–29.1	Bill	10 Srang (1948–49), 2 suns on obverse (2 vars)	20	40	150
29a	29a	Bill	10 Srang (1950–52), moon and sun (2 vars)	20	40	150

Note: Modern copies exist in gold, silver, and cupro-nickel.

Y#	KM#	Metal	Description	VF	EF	Unc
30	30	Bill	10 Srang (1950–51)	15	30	150

Y#	KM#	Metal	Description	VF	EF	Unc
31	N/A	Bill	5 Srang, ND (ca 1947–48)	25	50	150

Y#	KM#	Metal	Description	VF	EF	Unc
A32	Pn20–21	Cop	5 Srang (1953), similar to Y24 (26 mm)	1,500	2,500	10,000

TIMOR

An island 400 miles northwest of Australia, Timor was a Portuguese colony from the 16th century until 1859, when the western portion was ceded to the Netherlands and joined Indonesia when that nation was formed in 1959. The eastern portion was held by Portugal until 1975 when East Timor declared its independence. It was invaded and occupied by Indonesia days later but after protracted rebellion, won its independence in 2002 as the Democratic Republic of Timor-Leste. *Capital:* Dili.

MONETARY SYSTEM

100 avos = 1 pataca, to 1958
100 centavos = 1 escudo, 1958–

PRECIOUS METAL CONTENT

Dates	Denomination	Gross Wt (g)	Fineness	Net Wt (g)	Troy Oz.
		SILVER			
1945–51	50 avos	3.5000	0.6500	2.2750	0.0731
1958	3 escudos	3.5000	0.6500	2.2750	0.0731
	6 escudos	7.0000	0.6500	4.5500	0.1463
1964	10 escudos	7.0000	0.6500	4.5500	0.1463

Y#	KM#	Metal	Description	VF	EF	Unc
1	5	Bz	10 Avos, 1945–51 *1945, Unc $300*	10	18	35

Y#	KM#	Metal	Description	VF	EF	Unc
2	6	N-Bz	20 Avos, 1945	40	80	175

Y#	KM#	Metal	Description	VF	EF	Unc
3	7	Silv	50 Avos, 1945–51 *1945, EF $90*	7.50	13	25

Y#	KM#	Metal	Description	VF	EF	Unc
4	10	Bz	10 Centavos, 1958	5	20	45
5	11	Bz	30 Centavos, 1958	5	15	40

Y#	KM#	Metal	Description	VF	EF	Unc
6	12	C-N	60 Centavos, 1958	7.50	15	40
7	13	C-N	1 Escudo, 1958	7.50	20	50

Y#	KM#	Metal	Description	VF	EF	Unc
8	14	Silv	3 Escudos, 1958	12	15	40
9	15	Silv	6 Escudos, 1958	10	11	30
10	16	Silv	10 Escudos, 1964	10	11	30

TOGO

After World War I the German colony of Togoland in west Africa was split up and administered by Britain and France. The British section became part of Ghana. The coinage here is that of the French section, which became an independent republic in 1960. Since 1963 the country has been ruled by a succession of military dictatorships. *Languages:* French, native dialects. *Capital:* Lome.

See French West Africa for integrated coinage (1957).

MONETARY SYSTEM
100 centimes = 1 franc

Y#	KM#	Metal	Description	VF	EF	Unc
1	1	A-Bz	50 Centimes, 1924–26	4	15	100
2	2	A-Bz	1 Franc, 1924–25	5	20	125
3	3	A-Bz	2 Francs, 1924–25	8	30	150

Y#	KM#	Metal	Description	VF	EF	Unc
4	4	Alum	1 Franc, 1948	5	15	45
5	5	Alum	2 Francs, 1948	6	20	80

Y#	KM#	Metal	Description	VF	EF	Unc
6	6	A-Bz	5 Francs, 1956	2.50	5	15

TONGA

Located east of Fiji in the South Pacific, the nation of Tonga consists of about 150 islands, 36 of which are populated. The area had been settled by Polynesians for at least 3,000 years before Dutch and British explorers landed there in the 17th and 18th centuries. Part of the British Commonwealth since 1900, it declared independence in 1970. The nation is an hereditary constitutional monarchy largely controlled by the king, his appointees, and a nobility class, though demands for social and economic reforms by average citizens have lately become more strident. *Languages:* Tongan, English. *Capital:* Nuku'alofa.

MONETARY SYSTEM
1 koula = 16 British pounds

PRECIOUS METAL CONTENT

Dates	Denomination	Gross Wt (g)	Fineness	Net Wt (g)	Troy Oz.
		GOLD			
1962	1/4 koula	8.1250	0.9170	7.4506	0.2395
	1/2 koula	16.2500	0.9170	14.9010	0.4791
	1 koula	32.5000	0.9170	29.8025	0.9582

SALOTE TUPOU III, *1918–1965*

Y#	KM#	Metal	Description	VF	EF	Unc
1	1	Gold	1/4 Koula, 1962	BV	BV	450
						Proof: $550

Obverse: ***Full-length portrait***
Reverse: ***Arms***

Y#	KM#	Metal	Description	VF	EF	Unc
2	2	Gold	1/2 Koula, 1962	BV	BV	875
						Proof: $900
3	3	Gold	1 Koula, 1962	BV	BV	1,750
						Proof: $2,000

Y#	KM#	Metal	Description	VF	EF	Unc
1a–3a	1a–3a		*Platinum Proof Set: $5,500*			

TONKIN

Formerly a French protectorate in Indo-China, Tonkin is now a part of Vietnam. *Capital:* Hanoi.

Y#	KM#	Metal	Description	VF	EF	Unc
1	1	Zinc	1/600 Piastre, 1905	30	60	150

Note: Counterfeits are common, but most are cast rather than struck.

TUNISIA

Formerly a monarchy on the Mediterranean coast of Africa, Tunisia was a French protectorate from 1881 to 1956. An independent kingdom was proclaimed in 1956, but was changed to a nominal republic in 1957 under a constituent assembly. It has been ruled by dictatorships since. *Languages:* Arabic, French. *Capital:* Tunis.

MONETARY SYSTEM
16 kharubs = 1 piastre (sebili), to 1891
100 centimes = 1 franc, 1891–1957
100 millim = 1 dinar, 1957–

PRECIOUS METAL CONTENT

Dates	Denomination	Gross Wt (g)	Fineness	Net Wt (g)	Troy Oz.
		SILVER			
1891–1928	50 centimes	2.5000	0.8350	2.0875	0.0671
	1 franc	5.0000	0.8350	4.1750	0.1342
	2 francs	10.0000	0.8350	8.3500	0.2685
1930–39	5 francs	5.0000	0.6800	3.4000	0.1093
	10 francs	10.0000	0.6800	6.8000	0.2186
	20 francs	20.0000	0.6800	13.6000	0.4372
		GOLD			
1881–91	25 piastres	4.9200	0.9000	4.4280	0.1424
	50 piastres	9.8400	0.9000	8.8560	0.2847
	100 piastres	19.6800	0.9000	17.7120	0.5694
1891–1928	10 francs	3.2258	0.9000	2.9032	0.0933
	20 francs	6.4516	0.9000	5.8064	0.1867
1930–37	100 francs	6.5500	0.9000	5.8950	0.1895

Muhammad al-Sadiq Bey, *1859–1882*

Under French Protectorate, 1881–1882.

Designs: ***Similar to Y5–9***

Y#	KM#	Metal	Description	VF	EF	Unc
1	201	Silv	8 Kharubs, AH 1299 (1882)	300	500	800
2	202	Silv	1 Piastre, AH 1299 (1882)	350	700	1,000
3	203	Silv	2 Piastres, AH 1299 (1882)	375	750	1,200

Y#	KM#	Metal	Description	VF	EF	Unc
4	200	Gold	25 Piastres, AH 1298, 1300 (1881, 83)	350	450	700
A4	204	Gold	50 Piastres, AH 1299 (1882)	500	550	950

Ali Bey, *1882–1902*

First Coinage

Y#	KM#	Metal	Description	VF	EF	Unc
5	205	Silv	8 Kharubs, AH 1301–07 (1884–90) (17.5 mm)	20	40	90
6	206/215	Silv	1 Piastre, AH 1303–08 (1886–91) (22.5 mm)	30	60	125
7	207/210	Silv	2 Piastres, AH 1307–08 (1890–91) (27 mm)	65	125	200
8	208/216	Silv	4 Piastres, AH 1305–08 (1888–91) (31 mm)	75	150	300
9	209	Gold	25 Piastres, AH 1300, 02 (1883, 85)	350	450	750
A10	213	Gold	50 Piastres, AH 1304 (1887)	—	—	—
B10	211	Gold	100 Piastres, AH 1303 (1886)	—	—	—
10	212/214	Gold	25 Piastres / 15 Fr, AH 1304–08 (1887–91)	350	650	950

Second Coinage

All current silver and gold denominations were coined annually from 1891 to the late 1930s. In years when large quantities were not needed for circulation, limited numbers (20 to 1,000 pieces) of each denomination were struck, probably to be used as gifts by the Bey.

Y#	KM#	Metal	Description	VF	EF	Unc
11	219	Bz	1 Centime, 1891	10	25.00	50
12	220	Bz	2 Centimes, 1891	9	20.00	40
13	221	Bz	5 Centimes, 1891–93	8	17.50	35
14	222	Bz	10 Centimes, 1891–93	8	17.50	35

Y#	KM#	Metal	Description	VF	EF	Unc
15	223	Silv	50 Centimes, 1891–1902	8	15	35
16	224	Silv	1 Franc, 1891–1902	20	40	60
17	225	Silv	2 Francs, 1891–1902	20	40	75

Note: Dates after 1891 of Y15 and after 1892 of Y16–17 were not struck for circulation.

Y#	KM#	Metal	Description	VF	EF	Unc
18	226	Gold	10 Francs, 1891–1902	185	200	250
19	227	Gold	20 Francs, 1891–1902	BV	325	375

Note: Dates after 1891 of Y18 and after 1901 of Y19 were not struck for circulation.

Muhammad al-Hadi Bey, *1902–1906*

Y#	KM#	Metal	Description	VF	EF	Unc
20	228	Bz	5 Centimes, 1903–04	3	10	20
21	229	Bz	10 Centimes, 1903–04	3	10	25

Y#	KM#	Metal	Description	VF	EF	Unc
22	230	Silv	50 Centimes, 1903–06	250	375	700
23	231	Silv	1 Franc, 1903–06	60	125	250
24	232	Silv	2 Francs, 1903–06	75	150	350

Note: Y22 and dates other than 1904 of Y23–24 were not struck for circulation.

Y#	KM#	Metal	Description	VF	EF	Unc
25	233	Gold	10 Francs, 1903–06, *Rare*			
26	234	Gold	20 Francs, 1903–06	BV	325	375

Note: Y25 and dates 1905–1906 of Y26 were not struck for circulation.

MUHAMMAD AL-NASR BEY, *1906–1922*

FIRST COINAGE

Y#	KM#	Metal	Description	VF	EF	Unc
27	235	Bz	5 Centimes, 1907–17	1	4	15.00
28	236	Bz	10 Centimes, 1907–17	2	5	17.50

Y#	KM#	Metal	Description	VF	EF	Unc
29	237	Silv	50 Centimes, 1907–21	5	9	25
30	238	Silv	1 Franc, 1907–21	5	10	30
31	239	Silv	2 Francs, 1907–21	15	30	65

Note: Dates after 1917, 1918, and 1916 of Y29, 30, and 31, respectively, were not struck for circulation.

Y#	KM#	Metal	Description	VF	EF	Unc
32	240	Gold	10 Francs, 1907–21, *Rare*			
33	241	Gold	20 Francs, 1907–21, *Rare*			

Note: Y32–33 were not struck for circulation.

SECOND COINAGE

Y#	KM#	Metal	Description	VF	EF	Unc
34	242	C-N	5 Centimes, 1918–20 (19 mm)	1	5	20
34a	245	C-N	5 Centimes, 1920 (17 mm)	15	25	100
35	243	C-N	10 Centimes, 1918–20	1	5	20
36	244	C-N	25 Centimes, 1918–20	1	5	25

GENERAL COINAGE

Issued without name of ruler through successive reigns.

Y#	KM#	Metal	Description	VF	EF	Unc
37	246	A-Bz	50 Centimes, 1921–45	1	2	9
38	247	A-Bz	1 Franc, 1921–45	1	3	10
39	248	A-Bz	2 Francs, 1921–45	3	5	15

MUHAMMAD AL-HABIB BEY, *1922–1929*

Y#	KM#	Metal	Description	VF	EF	Unc
40	254	C-N	10 Centimes, 1926	20	50	125

Y#	KM#	Metal	Description	VF	EF	Unc
41	249	Silv	50 Centimes, 1922–28	45	90	250
42	250	Silv	1 Franc, 1922–28	50	100	300
43	251	Silv	2 Francs, 1922–28	75	150	375

Note: Y41–43 were not struck for circulation.

Y#	KM#	Metal	Description	VF	EF	Unc
44	252	Gold	10 Francs, 1922–28, *Rare*			
45	253	Gold	20 Francs, 1922–28, *Rare*			

Note: Y44–45 were not struck for circulation.

AHMED BEY, *1929–1942*

Y#	KM#	Metal	Description	VF	EF	Unc
46	258	C-N	5 Centimes, 1931–38	1.00	6	15
47	259	C-N	10 Centimes, 1931–38	1.50	10	20
48	260	C-N	25 Centimes, 1931–38	2.50	10	30

Y#	KM#	Metal	Description	VF	EF	Unc
49	255	Silv	10 Francs, 1930–34	40	80	125
50	256	Silv	20 Francs, 1930–34	50	100	250

Y#	KM#	Metal	Description	VF	EF	Unc
51	261	Silv	5 Francs, AH 1353–57 (1934–38)	7	15	50
52	262	Silv	10 Francs, AH 1353–57 (1934–38)	10	20	100
53	263	Silv	20 Francs, AH 1353–57 (1934–38)	12	25	150

Note: Dates after AH 1355 of Y51, and after AH 1353 of Y52–53 were not struck for circulation.

Y#	KM#	Metal	Description	VF	EF	Unc
54	264	Silv	5 Francs, 1939	7.50	15	50
55	265	Silv	10 Francs, 1939	10.00	20	100
56	266	Silv	20 Francs, 1939	20.00	40	150

Y#	KM#	Metal	Description	VF	EF	Unc
57	257	Gold	100 Francs, 1930–37 *1931, 33, 36–37, EF $1,750*	BV	365	400

Note: Dates after 1934 or 1935 of Y57 were not struck for circulation.

Y#	KM#	Metal	Description	VF	EF	Unc
58	267	Zinc	10 Centimes, 1941–42	6	12	30
59	268	Zinc	20 Centimes, 1942	15	30	60

MUHAMMAD AL-AMIN BEY, *1943–1957*

Y#	KM#	Metal	Description	VF	EF	Unc
60	271	Zinc	10 Centimes, 1945	30	60	150
61	272	Zinc	20 Centimes, 1945	50	90	200

Y#	KM#	Metal	Description	VF	EF	Unc
62	273	A-Bz	5 Francs, 1946	1.25	4	10

Y#	KM#	Metal	Description	VF	EF	Unc
63	277	C-N	5 Francs, 1954, 57	0.50	1.00	3
64	274	C-N	20 Francs, 1950, 57	0.75	1.00	4
65	275	C-N	50 Francs, 1950, 57	1.00	1.50	5
66	276	C-N	100 Francs, 1950, 57	1.25	3.00	10

REPUBLIC, *1957–*

Y#	KM#	Metal	Description	VF	EF	Unc
67	280	Alum	1 Millim, 1960, 83	0.05	0.10	0.25
68	281	Alum	2 Millim, 1960, 83	0.10	0.15	0.30
69	282	Alum	5 Millim, 1960–96	0.10	0.15	0.35

Y#	KM#	Metal	Description	VF	EF	Unc
70	306	Br	10 Millim, 1960–97	0.15	0.25	0.50
71	307	Br	20 Millim, 1960–97	0.20	0.40	0.65
72	308	Br	50 Millim, 1960–97	0.30	0.80	1.25
73	309	Br	100 Millim, 1960–2000	0.45	1.00	1.75

TURKEY

Once the cornerstone of the Ottoman Empire, Turkey is a republican parliamentary democracy bridging Europe and Asia between the Mediterranean and Black Seas. The 600-year-old Ottoman Empire was dismantled after World War I and reduced in size by more than half. The republic was formed in 1923. *Languages:* Turkish, Kurdish. *Capital:* Ankara.

MONETARY SYSTEM

40 paras = 1 kurus (kurush, piastre) 100 kurus = 1 lira

PRECIOUS METAL CONTENT

Dates	Denomination	Gross Wt (g)	Fineness	Net Wt (g)	Troy Oz.
		SILVER			
1844–1919	20 para	0.6013	0.8300	0.4491	0.0160
	1 kurus	1.2027	0.8300	0.9982	0.0321
	2 kurus	2.4055	0.8300	1.9966	0.0642
	5 kurus	6.0130	0.8300	4.9908	0.1605
	10 kurus	12.0270	0.8300	9.9824	0.3209
	20 kurus	24.0550	0.8300	19.9657	0.6419
1899–1904	5 para	1.0023	0.1000	0.1002	0.0032
	10 para	2.0046	0.1000	0.2005	0.0064
1934–41	25 kurus	3.0000	0.8300	2.4900	0.0801
	50 kurus	6.0000	0.8300	4.9800	0.1601
	100 kurus	12.0000	0.8300	9.9600	0.3202
1947–48	50 kurus	4.0000	0.6000	2.4000	0.0772
	1 lira	7.5000	0.6000	4.5000	0.1447
		GOLD			
1861–1993	25 kurus	1.8041	0.9170	1.6538	0.0532
	50 kurus	3.6083	0.9170	3.3076	0.1063
	100 kurus	7.2166	0.9170	6.6152	0.2127
	250 kurus	18.0414	0.9170	16.5380	0.5317
	500 kurus	36.0828	0.9170	33.0759	1.0634
Monnaies de Luxe					
1876–1909	12-1/2 kurus	0.8770	0.9170	0.8042	0.0258
1909–18	12-1/2 kurus	0.9020	0.9170	0.8271	0.0266
1876–1980	25 kurus	1.7540	0.9170	1.6078	0.0517
	50 kurus	3.5080	0.9170	3.2157	0.1034
	100 kurus	7.0160	0.9170	6.4313	0.2068
	250 kurus	17.5400	0.9170	16.0783	0.5169
	500 kurus	35.0800	0.9170	32.1567	1.0338

The accession date of the ruler appears in Arabic numerals on the lower reverse of each coin. The regnal year (year of issue), also in Arabic, is usually found below the toughra (monogram of the ruler).

ABDUL AZIZ, *1861–1876*

ACCESSION DATE AH 1277 ON COINS

Y#	KM#	Metal	Description	VF	EF	Unc
1	685	Cop	5 Para, Yr 1 (1861)	15	25	50
2	686	Cop	10 Para, Yr 1 (1861)	15	25	40
3	687	Cop	20 Para, Yr 1 (1861)	15	30	60

Y#	KM#	Metal	Description	VF	EF	Unc
4	699	Cop	5 Para, Yr 4 (1864)	3.00	6.00	15
5	700	Cop	10 Para, Yr 4 (1864)	3.00	6.00	15
6	701	Cop	20 Para, Yr 4 (1864)	3.50	7.50	20
7	702	Cop	40 Para, Yr 4 (1864)	10.00	20.00	100

Y#	KM#	Metal	Description	VF	EF	Unc
8	688	Silv	20 Para, Yrs 1–7 (1861–67)	20.00	40	125
9	689	Silv	1 Kurus, Yrs 1–7 (1861–67)	12.50	25	75
10	690	Silv	2 Kurus, Yrs 1–5 (1861–65)	75.00	150	250

Y#	KM#	Metal	Description	VF	EF	Unc
11	691	Silv	5 Kurus, Yrs 1–15 (1861–75)	12.50	25	—
12	692	Silv	10 Kurus, Yrs 1–2 (1861–62)	100.00	200	—
13	693	Silv	20 Kurus, Yrs 1–15 (1861–75)	30.00	60	—

Y#	KM#	Metal	Description	VF	EF	Unc
16	694	Gold	25 Kurus, Yrs 1–12 (1861–72)	100	120	150
A16	695	Gold	50 Kurus, Yrs 1–9 (1861–69)	475	525	—
17	696	Gold	100 Kurus, Yrs 1–14 (1861–74)	400	425	500
A17	698	Gold	250 Kurus, Yrs 1–9 (1861–69)	850	1,200	—
B17	697	Gold	500 Kurus, Yrs 1–13 (1861–73)	BV	1,750	2,300

MURAD V, *1876*

ACCESSION DATE AH 1293 ON COINS

Designs: ***Similar to Y9–17***
Obverse: ***No flower to right of toughra***

Y#	KM#	Metal	Description	VF	EF	Unc
18	710	Silv	1 Kurus, Yr 1 (1876)	145	250	—

Y#	KM#	Metal	Description	VF	EF	Unc
20	711	Silv	5 Kurus, Yr 1 (1876)	325	525	—
22	712	Silv	20 Kurus, Yr 1 (1876)	85	175	600

Y#	KM#	Metal	Description	VF	EF	Unc
A22	713	Gold	25 Kurus, Yr 1 (1876)	250	375	425
B22	714	Gold	50 Kurus, Yr 1 (1876)	625	1,050	—
C22	715	Gold	100 Kurus, Yr 1 (1876)	375	400	450

ABDUL HAMID II, *1876–1909*

ACCESSION DATE AH 1293 ON COINS

FIRST COINAGE

Obverse: ***Flower at right of toughra***

Y#	KM#	Metal	Description	VF	EF	Unc
23	728	Cop	5 Para, Yrs 2–4 (1877–79) *Yr 2, VF $250*	3	10	30

Y#	KM#	Metal	Description	VF	EF	Unc
26	717	Silv	20 Para, Yrs 1, 4 (1876, 79)	100	225	—

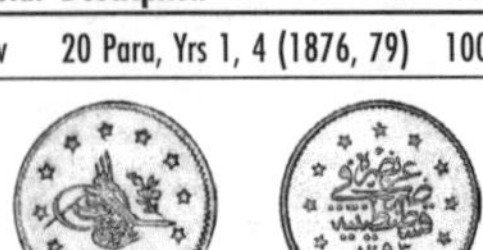

Y#	KM#	Metal	Description	VF	EF	Unc
27	718	Silv	1 Kurus, Yrs 1–4 (1876–79)	150	275	600
28	719	Silv	2 Kurus, Yr 1 (1876)	750	1,500	—

Y#	KM#	Metal	Description	VF	EF	Unc
29	720	Silv	5 Kurus, Yrs 1–4 (1876–79)	35	75	—
30	721	Silv	10 Kurus, Yrs 1, 3 (1876, 78)	75	150	—
31	722	Silv	20 Kurus, Yrs 1–3 (1876–78)	75	150	—

Y#	KM#	Metal	Description	VF	EF	Unc
A31	723	Gold	25 Kurus, Yrs 3–6 (1878–81)	135	200	—
B31	724	Gold	50 Kurus, Yrs 1–6 (1876–81)	200	400	—
C31	725	Gold	100 Kurus, Yrs 1–6 (1876–81)	375	475	—
D31	726	Gold	250 Kurus, Yrs 1–2 (1876–77)	2,000	4,000	—
E31	727	Gold	500 Kurus, Yrs 1–2 (1876–77)	1,700	2,200	—

SECOND COINAGE

Obverse: ***"El-Ghazi" (the Victorious) at right of toughra***

Y#	KM#	Metal	Description	VF	EF	Unc
24	743	Bill	5 Para, Yrs 25–30 (1900–05)	1.00	3.50	—
25	744	Bill	10 Para, Yrs 25–30 (1900–05)	1.50	5.00	—

Y#	KM#	Metal	Description	VF	EF	Unc
F31	734	Silv	20 Para, Yr 8 (1883)	25	50	100

Y#	KM#	Metal	Description	VF	EF	Unc
32	735	Silv	1 Kurus, Yrs 8–34 (1883–1909)	4	7.50	25
33	736	Silv	2 Kurus, Yrs 8–34 (1883–1909)	5	9.00	35

Y#	KM#	Metal	Description	VF	EF	Unc
34	737	Silv	5 Kurus, Yrs 8–34 (1883–1909)	7.50	15	60
35	738	Silv	10 Kurus, Yrs 12–33 (1887–1908)	25.00	45	150

Y#	KM#	Metal	Description	VF	EF	Unc
36	729	Gold	25 Kurus, Yrs 7–32 (1882–1907)	100	150	185
37	731	Gold	50 Kurus, Yrs 7–34 (1882–1909)	200	400	450
38	730	Gold	100 Kurus, Yrs 6–34 (1881–1909)	375	425	500
39	732	Gold	250 Kurus, Yrs 7–32 (1882–1907)	800	975	1,100
40	733	Gold	500 Kurus, Yrs 7–32 (1882–1907)	1,700	2,200	2,800

GOLD PRESENTATION PIECES

(MONNAIES DE LUXE)

Y#	KM#	Metal	Description	VF	EF	Unc
A40	745	Gold	12-1/2 Kurus, Yrs 25, 30 (1900, 05)	200	350	900
B40	739	Gold	25 Kurus, Yrs 26–34 (1901–1909)	135	175	200
C40	740	Gold	50 Kurus, Yrs 25–33 (1900–1908)	BV	250	400
D40	741	Gold	100 Kurus, Yrs 23–33 (1898–1908)	BV	500	900
41	742	Gold	250 Kurus, Yrs 24–33 (1899–1908)	BV	1,250	1,850
42	746	Gold	500 Kurus, Yrs 26–33 (1901–08)	BV	1,950	2,500

MOHAMMED RESHAT V, *1909–1918*

ACCESSION DATE AH 1327 ON COINS

FIRST COINAGE

Obverse: ***"Reshat" at right of toughra***

Y#	KM#	Metal	Description	VF	EF	Unc
43	759	Nick	5 Para, Yrs 2–7 (1910–15)	2.00	4	45
44	760	Nick	10 Para, Yrs 2–7 (1910–15)	1.25	3	20
45	761	Nick	20 Para, Yrs 2–6 (1910–14)	2.25	5	65
46	766	Nick	40 Para, Yrs 3–5 (1911–13)	2.25	5	65

Y#	KM#	Metal	Description	VF	EF	Unc
47	748	Silv	1 Kurus, Yrs 1–3 (1909–11)	3.50	7.50	25
48	749	Silv	2 Kurus, Yrs 1–6 (1909–14)	4.00	8.50	35

Y#	KM#	Metal	Description	VF	EF	Unc
49	750	Silv	5 Kurus, Yrs 1–7 (1909–15)	3.75	7	30
50	751	Silv	10 Kurus, Yrs 1–7 (1909–15) *Yr 3, VF $2,000*	13.00	23	75

Y#	KM#	Metal	Description	VF	EF	Unc
A51	752	Gold	25 Kurus, Yrs 1–6 (1909–14)	125	165	235
B51	753	Gold	50 Kurus, Yrs 1–6 (1909–14)	165	225	450
C51	755	Gold	100 Kurus, Yrs 1–7 (1909–15)	375	400	450
D51	756	Gold	250 Kurus, Yrs 1–6 (1909–14)	800	1,250	1,500
E51	758	Gold	500 Kurus, Yrs 1–6 (1909–14)	1,600	2,000	2,500

Note: Some gold and silver coins struck in 1910 and 1911 have names of cities visited by Mohammed V. Some are rare. Monnaies de luxe were also issued during this reign.

SECOND COINAGE

Obverse: ***"El-Ghazi" (the Victorious) at right of toughra***

Y#	KM#	Metal	Description	VF	EF	Unc
43a	767	Nick	5 Para, Yr 7 (1915)	40	60	150
44a	769	Nick	10 Para, Yrs 7–8 (1915–16)	2	5	25

Y#	KM#	Metal	Description	VF	EF	Unc
46a	779	C-N	40 Para, Yrs 8–9 (1916–17)	2	5	60

Y#	KM#	Metal	Description	VF	EF	Unc
A50	770	Silv	2 Kurus, Yrs 7–9 (1915–17) *Yr 9, EF $800*	35	70	—
B50	771	Silv	5 Kurus, Yrs 7–9 (1915–17) *Yr 9, VF $200*	15	30	—
C50	772	Silv	10 Kurus, Yrs 7–10 (1915–18)	20	40	—
51	780	Silv	20 Kurus, Yrs 8–10 (1916–18)	25	50	—

Obverse: ***"El-Ghazi" at right of toughra***

Y#	KM#	Metal	Description	VF	EF	Unc
53	773	Gold	25 Kurus, Yrs 7–10 (1915–18)	100	165	235
54	775	Gold	50 Kurus, Yrs 7–9 (1915–17)	200	300	350
55	776	Gold	100 Kurus, Yrs 7–10 (1915–18)	375	450	475
56	777	Gold	250 Kurus, Yrs 7–10 (1915–18)	4,500	6,000	—
57	784	Gold	500 Kurus, Yrs 7–10 (1915–18)	4,000	5,500	—

MOHAMMED VI, *1918–1922*

ACCESSION DATE AH 1336 ON COINS

Designs: ***Similar to Y43–57***

Y#	KM#	Metal	Description	VF	EF	Unc
58	828	C-N	40 Para, Yr 4 (1921)	7.50	15	—

Y#	KM#	Metal	Description	VF	EF	Unc
59	815	Silv	2 Kurus, Yrs 1–2 (1918–19)	150	275	475
60	816	Silv	5 Kurus, Yrs 1–2 (1918–19)	175	275	650
61	817	Silv	10 Kurus, Yrs 1–2 (1918–19)	650	1,500	4,500
62	818	Silv	20 Kurus, Yrs 1–2 (1918–19)	250	375	750

Y#	KM#	Metal	Description	VF	EF	Unc
63	819	Gold	25 Kurus, Yrs 1–2 (1918–19)	125	250	300
64	820	Gold	50 Kurus, Yrs 1–5 (1918–22)	200	400	475
65	821	Gold	100 Kurus, Yrs 1–5 (1918–22)	400	500	600
66	822	Gold	250 Kurus, Yrs 1–5 (1918–22)	15,000	25,000	—
67	823	Gold	500 Kurus, Yrs 1–5 (1918–22)	5,000	7,500	—

Note: Gold monnaies de luxe also struck.

REPUBLIC, *1923–*

A.H. DATING SYSTEM

Y#	KM#	Metal	Description	VF	EF	Unc
68	830	A-Bz	100 Para, AH 1340–41 (1922–24)	3	6	65
69	831	A-Bz	5 Kurus, AH 1340–41 (1922–24)	3	8	35
70	832	A-Bz	10 Kurus, AH 1340–41 (1922–24)	3	8	35

Y#	KM#	Metal	Description	VF	EF	Unc
71	833	Nick	25 Kurus, AH 1341 (1924)	4.50	9	45

WESTERN DATING SYSTEM

Y#	KM#	Metal	Description	VF	EF	Unc
68a	834	A-Bz	100 Para, 1926	4.50	9	65
69a	835	A-Bz	5 Kurus, 1926	4.50	9	65
70a	836	A-Bz	10 Kurus, 1926	5.00	10	75

Note: Y68a–70a dated 1928 are rare.

Y#	KM#	Metal	Description	VF	EF	Unc
71a	837	Nick	25 Kurus, 1926, 28 *1926, VF $250*	5	10	75

Y#	KM#	Metal	Description	VF	EF	Unc
72	840	Gold	25 Kurus, 1926–29	150	275	450
73	841	Gold	50 Kurus, 1926–28	200	300	600
74	842	Gold	100 Kurus, 1926–29	375	500	1,000
75	843	Gold	250 Kurus, 1926–28	975	1,500	3,000
76	839	Gold	500 Kurus, 1926–29	1,750	2,000	4,000

MONNAIES DE LUXE

Y#	KM#	Metal	Description	VF	EF	Unc
77	844	Gold	25 Kurus, 1927–28 (23 mm)	200	350	750
78	845	Gold	50 Kurus, 1927–28 (28 mm)	400	600	1,200
79	846	Gold	100 Kurus, 1927–28 (35 mm)	BV	750	1,500
80	847	Gold	250 Kurus, 1927–28 (45 mm)	850	1,000	1,850
81	848	Gold	500 Kurus, 1927–28 (49 mm)	3,000	5,000	7,500

DECIMAL COINAGE, *1933–*

100 kurus = 1 lira

WESTERN DATES AND NUMERALS

Y#	KM#	Metal	Description	VF	EF	Unc
82	860	Silv	100 Kurus, 1934	60	90	150

Y#	KM#	Metal	Description	VF	EF	Unc
87	861	C-N	1 Kurus, 1935–37	4.50	10.00	50
88	862	C-N	5 Kurus, 1935–43	1.00	5.00	20
89	863	C-N	10 Kurus, 1935–40	2.00	7.50	30

Y#	KM#	Metal	Description	VF	EF	Unc
83	864	Silv	25 Kurus, 1935–37	6	15	40
84	865	Silv	50 Kurus, 1935–37	7	20	45
85	866	Silv	1 Lira, 1937–39	13	28	55

Y#	KM#	Metal	Description	VF	EF	Unc
86	869	Silv	1 Lira, 1940–41	14	25	100

Y#	KM#	Metal	Description	VF	EF	Unc
90	867	C-N	1 Kurus, 1938–44, scalloped	1.25	4.50	15

Y#	KM#	Metal	Description	VF	EF	Unc
91	868	A-Bz	10 Para, 1940–42	1.50	3	10

Y#	KM#	Metal	Description	VF	EF	Unc
92	880	N-Br	25 Kurus, 1944–46	0.75	2	8.50

NEW COINAGE

Y#	KM#	Metal	Description	VF	EF	Unc
A92	884	Br	1/2 Kurus, 1948	350.00	600.00	950.00
93	881	Br	1 Kurus, 1947–51	0.35	0.65	1.00
94	885	Br	2-1/2 Kurus, 1948–51	0.45	0.75	1.75

Note: YA92 was not issued to circulation.

Y#	KM#	Metal	Description	VF	EF	Unc
95	887	Br	5 Kurus, 1949–57	0.35	0.75	1.75
96	888	Br	10 Kurus, 1949–56	0.40	0.80	2.00
97	886	Br	25 Kurus, 1948–56	0.20	0.40	1.25

Y#	KM#	Metal	Description	VF	EF	Unc
98	882	Silv	50 Kurus, 1947–48	2.75	4.00	10.00
99	883	Silv	1 Lira, 1947–48	3.00	4.25	12.50

Obverse: ***President Inonu (1938–1950)***

Y#	KM#	Metal	Description	VF	EF	Unc
A99	850	Gold	25 Kurus, Yrs 20–25 (1943–49) (15 mm)	100	120	200
B99	852	Gold	50 Kurus, Yrs 20–27 (1943–51) (18 mm)	150	180	210
C99	854	Gold	100 Kurus, Yrs 20–27 (1943–51) (22 mm)	BV	325	365
D99	856	Gold	250 Kurus, Yrs 20–23 (1943–47) (27 mm)	BV	850	1,500
E99	858	Gold	500 Kurus, Yrs 20–24 (1943–48) (35 mm)	BV	1,650	1,900

Obverse: ***President Ataturk (1923–1938)***

Y#	KM#	Metal	Description	VF	EF	Unc
100	851	Gold	25 Kurus, Yrs 20–66 (1943–89)	BV	100	165
101	853	Gold	50 Kurus, Yrs 20–66 (1943–89)	BV	200	375
102	855	Gold	100 Kurus, Yrs 20–65 (1943–88)	BV	375	450
103	857	Gold	250 Kurus, Yrs 20–70 (1943–93)	BV	800	7,000
104	859	Gold	500 Kurus, Yrs 20–69 (1943–92)	BV	1,600	1,850

Note: Gold monnaies de luxe with portraits of Inonu and Ataturk were issued in the same denominations as above.

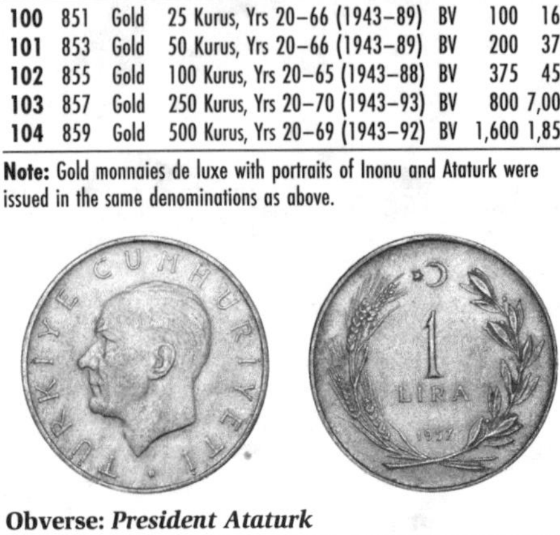

Obverse: ***President Ataturk***

Y#	KM#	Metal	Description	VF	EF	Unc
110	889	C-N	1 Lira, 1957	0.75	1.25	3

Y#	KM#	Metal	Description	VF	EF	Unc
111	890.1	Bz	5 Kurus, 1958–68	0.05	0.10	0.25

Y#	KM#	Metal	Description	VF	EF	Unc
112	891.1	Bz	10 Kurus, 1958–68	0.10	0.15	0.40

Y#	KM#	Metal	Description	VF	EF	Unc
113	892	S S	25 Kurus, 1959–66	0.15	0.25	0.75

Designs: ***Similar to Y110; rough ground under figure's feet, 1960 and later***

Y#	KM#	Metal	Description	VF	EF	Unc
114	889a.1	S S	1 Lira, 1959–67	0.10	0.20	0.65

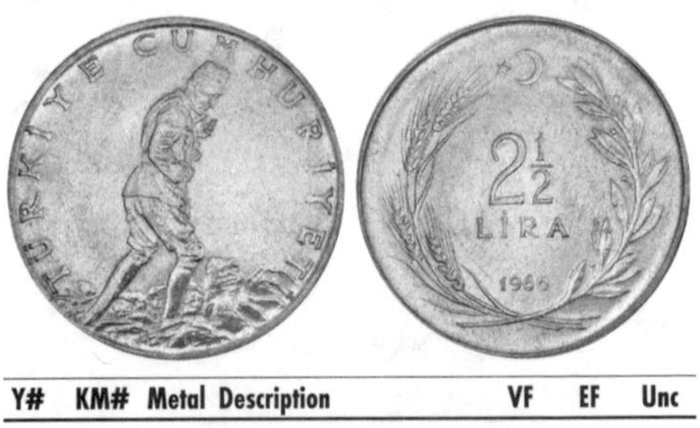

Y#	KM#	Metal	Description	VF	EF	Unc
115	893.1	S S	2-1/2 Lira, 1960–68	0.25	1	3

May 27, 1960, Revolution

Y#	KM#	Metal	Description	VF	EF	Unc
116	894	Silv	10 Lira, 1960	10	15	20
116a	894	Silv	*Circa 1970 Prooflike restrike, $22.50*			

Y#	KM#	Metal	Description	VF	EF	Unc
117	895	Br	1 Kurus, 1961–63	0.25	0.75	3
117a	895a	Bz	1 Kurus, 1963–74	0.25	0.50	3

UIGHURISTAN REPUBLIC

A breakaway Islamic republic in East Turkestan, Uighuristan (also called the First East Turkestan Republic) existed only two short years, from 1933 to 1934. See East Turkestan for more information.

Y#	KM#	Metal	Description	VF	EF	Unc
D38	D38	Cop	10 Wen, AH 1352 (1933)	250	500	—

UNION OF SOVIET SOCIALIST REPUBLICS (USSR)

A former confederacy of Soviet republics in Eastern Europe and Asia that resulted from the overthrow of the Czarist regime in 1917. The Soviet Union became a superpower through intensified development of its vast resources. The federation was dissolved in 1991. *Capital:* Moscow.

MONETARY SYSTEM
100 kopeks = 1 ruble

FIRST COINAGE

Legend: *PCOCP*

Y#	KM#	Metal	Description	VF	EF	Unc
80	80	Silv	10 Kopeks, 1921–23	5	15	75
					Proof: $1,000	
81	81	Silv	15 Kopeks, 1921–23	5	15	75
					Proof: $1,000	
82	82	Silv	20 Kopeks, 1921–23	5	15	75
					Proof: $1,000	

Y#	KM#	Metal	Description	VF	EF	Unc
83	83	Silv	50 Kopeks, 1921–22	10	25	100
					Proof: $2,000	
84	84	Silv	1 Ruble, 1921–22	25	100	250
					Proof: $4,000	

Y#	KM#	Metal	Description	VF	EF	Unc
85	85	Gold	1 Chervonetz (10 Rubles)			
			a 1923	1,000	2,000	3,000
			b 1975–80	BV	BV	500

SECOND COINAGE

New Legend: *CCCP*

Y#	KM#	Metal	Description	VF	EF	Unc
75	75	Bz	1/2 Kopek, 1925–28	10	30	150

Y#	KM#	Metal	Description	VF	EF	Unc
76	76	Bz	1 Kopek, 1924–25	10	50	250
					Proof: $2,000	
77	77	Bz	2 Kopeks, 1924–25	10	50	250
			1925, VF $1,000			
78	78	Bz	3 Kopeks, 1924	15	50	250
					Proof: $2,000	
79	79	Bz	5 Kopeks, 1924	25	75	500
					Proof: $3,000	

Y#	KM#	Metal	Description	VF	EF	Unc
86	86	Silv	10 Kopeks, 1924–31	5	15	100
			1931, Rare		*Proof: $1,000*	
87	87	Silv	15 Kopeks, 1924–31	5	15	100
			1931, Rare		*Proof: $1,000*	
88	88	Silv	20 Kopeks, 1924–31	5	15	100
			1931, Rare		*Proof: $1,000*	

Y#	KM#	Metal	Description	VF	EF	Unc
89	89	Silv	50 Kopeks, 1924–27	15	30	150
					Proof: $2,000	

Y#	KM#	Metal	Description	VF	EF	Unc
90	90	Silv	1 Ruble, 1924	30	60	125
					Proof: $4,000	

THIRD COINAGE

Y#	KM#	Metal	Description	VF	EF	Unc
91	91	A-Bz	1 Kopek, 1926–35	5	20	75
92	92	A-Bz	2 Kopeks, 1926–35	5	20	75
			1927, Rare			
93	93	A-Bz	3 Kopeks, 1926–35	5	20	75
			1927, VF $50			
94	94	A-Bz	5 Kopeks, 1926–35	25	50	150

Y#	KM#	Metal	Description	VF	EF	Unc
95	95	C-N	10 Kopeks, 1931–34	5	25	100
96	96	C-N	15 Kopeks, 1931–34	5	25	100
97	97	C-N	20 Kopeks, 1931–34	5	25	100
			1934, Rare			

FOURTH COINAGE

Obverse: ***Three ribbons on each side of wreath***

Y#	KM#	Metal	Description	VF	EF	Unc
98	98	A-Bz	1 Kopek, 1935–36	5	10	75
99	99	A-Bz	2 Kopeks, 1935–36	5	10	75
100	100	A-Bz	3 Kopeks, 1935–36	5	30	75
101	101	A-Bz	5 Kopeks, 1935–36	25	75	200

Y#	KM#	Metal	Description	VF	EF	Unc
102	102	C-N	10 Kopeks, 1935–36	5	25	75
103	103	C-N	15 Kopeks, 1935–36	5	25	75
104	104	C-N	20 Kopeks, 1935–36	5	25	75

FIFTH COINAGE

Obverse: ***Five ribbons on each side of wreath***

Y#	KM#	Metal	Description	VF	EF	Unc
105	105	A-Bz	1 Kopek, 1937–46	3	10	25
106	106	A-Bz	2 Kopeks, 1937–46	3	10	30
107	107	A-Bz	3 Kopeks, 1937–46	3	10	40
108	108	A-Bz	5 Kopeks, 1937–46	5	25	75

Y#	KM#	Metal	Description	VF	EF	Unc
109	109	C-N	10 Kopeks, 1937–46	3	10	25
110	110	C-N	15 Kopeks, 1937–46	3	10	25
111	111	C-N	20 Kopeks, 1937–46	3	10	25

SIXTH COINAGE

Obverse: ***8 and 7 ribbons on wreath***

Y#	KM#	Metal	Description	VF	EF	Unc
112	112	A-Bz	1 Kopek, 1948–56	3	10	25
113	113	A-Bz	2 Kopeks, 1948–56	3	10	25
114	114	A-Bz	3 Kopeks, 1948–56	3	10	25
115	115	A-Bz	5 Kopeks, 1948–56	5	25	75

Y#	KM#	Metal	Description	VF	EF	Unc
116	116	C-N	10 Kopeks, 1948–56	3	10	25
117	117	C-N	15 Kopeks, 1948–56	3	10	25
118	118	C-N	20 Kopeks, 1948–56	3	10	25

SEVENTH COINAGE

Obverse: ***Seven ribbons on each side of wreath***

Y#	KM#	Metal	Description	VF	EF	Unc
119	119	A-Bz	1 Kopek, 1957	3	10	25
120	120	A-Bz	2 Kopeks, 1957	3	10	25
121	121	A-Bz	3 Kopeks, 1957	3	10	25
122	122	A-Bz	5 Kopeks, 1957	5	25	75

Reverse: ***Denomination on square cartouche***

Y#	KM#	Metal	Description	VF	EF	Unc
123	123	C-N	10 Kopeks, 1957	3	10	25
124	124	C-N	15 Kopeks, 1957	3	10	25
125	125	C-N	20 Kopeks, 1957	3	10	25

Currency Revaluation

New ruble equal to 10 old rubles, January 1, 1961.

Y#	KM#	Metal	Description	VF	EF	Unc
126	126a	A-Bz	1 Kopek, 1961–91	0.50	1	5
127	127a	A-Bz	2 Kopeks, 1961–91	0.50	1	5
128	128a	A-Bz	3 Kopeks, 1961–91	0.50	1	5
129	129a	A-Bz	5 Kopeks, 1961–91	0.50	2	10

Y#	KM#	Metal	Description	VF	EF	Unc
130	130	CNZ	10 Kopeks, 1961–91	0.50	1	3
131	131	CNZ	15 Kopeks, 1961–91	0.50	1	3
132	132	CNZ	20 Kopeks, 1961–91	0.50	1	3
133	133a.1	CNZ	50 Kopeks, 1961	3.00	6	15
133a	133a.2	CNZ	50 Kopeks, 1964–91, lettered edge	1.00	3	10

Y#	KM#	Metal	Description	VF	EF	Unc
134	134a.1	CNZ	1 Ruble, 1961	3	5	20
134a	134a.2	CNZ	1 Ruble, 1964–91, lettered edge	1	2	5

UNITED ARAB REPUBLIC

The United Arab Republic was established on February 1, 1958, merging Syria and Egypt under one rule. The UAR was intended to develop into a broader, pan-Arab state, but tensions between the two political entities ultimately led Syria to withdraw in 1961. Egypt kept the name "United Arab Republic" until a merger with Libya and Syria in 1972 created the Federation of Arab Republics.

During their brief time together as the UAR, Egypt and Syria maintained separate coinages.

MONETARY SYSTEM

Egypt
10 milliemes (millim) = 1 ghirsh (piastre)
100 ghirsh = 1 jiniah (pound)

Syria
100 ghirsh (piastres) = 1 lira (pound)

PRECIOUS METAL CONTENT

Dates	Denomination	Gross Wt (g)	Fineness	Net Wt (g)	Troy Oz.
		SILVER			
Egypt					
1959–60	5 ghirsh	3.5000	0.7200	2.5200	0.0810
	10 ghirsh	7.0000	0.7200	5.0400	0.1620
	25 ghirsh	17.5000	0.7200	12.6000	0.4051
1964	5 ghirsh	2.5000	0.7200	1.8000	0.0578
	10 ghirsh	5.0000	0.7200	3.6000	0.1157
	25 ghirsh	10.0000	0.7200	7.2000	0.2315
	50 ghirsh	20.0000	0.7200	14.4000	0.4630
Syria					
1958–59	25 ghirsh	2.5000	0.6000	1.5000	0.0482
	50 ghirsh	5.0000	0.6000	3.0000	0.0965
		GOLD			
Egypt					
1958–60	1/2 pound	4.2500	0.8750	3.7188	0.1195
	1 pound	8.5000	0.8750	7.4375	0.2391
	5 pounds	42.5000	0.8750	37.1875	1.1957
1964	5 pounds	26.0000	0.8750	22.7500	0.7315
	10 pounds	52.0000	0.8750	45.5000	1.4630

UNITED ARAB REPUBLIC—EGYPT, *1958–1971*

Agriculture and Industry Fair

Y#	KM#	Metal	Description	VF	EF	Unc
105	390	A-Bz	20 Milliemes, 1958	1.75	2.75	6.50

Founding of the UAR

Y#	KM#	Metal	Description	VF	EF	Unc
106	391	Gold	1/2 Pound, 1958	BV	BV	275

Y#	KM#	Metal	Description	VF	EF	Unc
107	392	Silv	10 Ghirsh, 1959	3.50	6	15

Aswan Dam

Y#	KM#	Metal	Description	VF	EF	Unc
108	401	Gold	1 Pound, 1960	BV	BV	550
109	402	Gold	5 Pounds, 1960	BV	BV	2,350

National Assembly

Y#	KM#	Metal	Description	VF	EF	Unc
110	400	Silv	25 Ghirsh, 1960	10	15	20

Y#	KM#	Metal	Description	VF	EF	Unc
111	393	A-Bz	1 Millieme, 1960, 66	0.10	0.15	0.75
112	403	A-Bz	2 Milliemes, 1962, 66	0.20	0.35	1.00
113	394	A-Bz	5 Milliemes, 1960, 66	0.20	0.40	1.00
B113	396	A-Bz	10 Milliemes, 1958, without "Misr" (Egypt) above denomination	15.00	25.00	60.00
A113	395	A-Bz	10 Milliemes, 1960,66	0.25	0.50	1.25

Y#	KM#	Metal	Description	VF	EF	Unc
114	397	Silv	5 Ghirsh, 1960, 66	2.25	2.75	6.50
115	398	Silv	10 Ghirsh, 1960, 66	3.00	4.00	9.50
116	399	Silv	20 Ghirsh, 1960, 66 *1966 Proof Set, $135*	10.00	12.00	22.00

Note: 1966 dates are Proof only.

Diversion of the Nile

Y#	KM#	Metal	Description	VF	EF	Unc
117	404	Silv	5 Ghirsh, 1964	2.00	3	6.00
118	405	Silv	10 Ghirsh, 1964	4.00	6	8.00
119	406	Silv	25 Ghirsh, 1964	5.00	9	12.50
120	407	Silv	50 Ghirsh, 1964	12.50	16	22.50
121	408	Gold	5 Pounds, 1964	BV	1,250	1,500.00
122	409	Gold	10 Pounds, 1964	BV	2,500	2,850.00

UNITED ARAB REPUBLIC—SYRIA, *1958–1961*

Y#	KM#	Metal	Description	VF	EF	Unc
A19	87	Silv	25 Ghirsh, 1958	1.50	2	5

Y#	KM#	Metal	Description	VF	EF	Unc
B19	88	Silv	50 Ghirsh, 1958	2.50	5	12

Founding of the Republic

Y#	KM#	Metal	Description	VF	EF	Unc
20	89	Silv	50 Ghirsh, 1959	2	4	10

Y#	KM#	Metal	Description	VF	EF	Unc
21	90	A-Bz	2-1/2 Ghirsh, 1960	0.25	0.50	1

Y#	KM#	Metal	Description	VF	EF	Unc
22	91	A-Bz	5 Ghirsh, 1960	0.25	0.50	1

Y#	KM#	Metal	Description	VF	EF	Unc
23	92	A-Bz	10 Ghirsh, 1960	0.25	0.50	1

UNITED STATES OF AMERICA

Settled in the late 16th and early 17th centuries—and contested over for the next 200 years—by the Spanish, British, French, and Dutch, the USA declared independence as a republic in 1776 and constituted itself as a federation of states in 1789. Throughout the 19th century, the nation expanded westward through territorial acquisitions from indigenous peoples, France, Spain, and Russia. *Language:* English. *Capital:* Washington, DC.

MONETARY SYSTEM

10 cents = 1 dime
100 cents = 1 dollar

PRECIOUS METAL CONTENT

Dates	Denomination	Gross Wt (g)	Fineness	Net Wt (g)	Troy Oz.
		SILVER			
1851–53	3 cents	0.8019	0.7500	0.6014	0.0193
1853–73	3 cents	0.7465	0.9000	0.6719	0.0216
	1/2 dime	1.2442	0.9000	1.1197	0.0360
	1 dime	2.4883	0.9000	2.2395	0.0720
	1/4 dollar	6.2208	0.9000	5.5987	0.1800
	1/2 dollar	12.4416	0.9000	11.1974	0.3600
1873–1964	1 dime	2.5000	0.9000	2.2500	0.0723
	20 cents	5.0000	0.9000	4.5000	0.1447
	1/4 dollar	6.2500	0.9000	5.6250	0.1808
	1/2 dollar	12.5000	0.9000	11.2500	0.3617
1840–1935	1 dollar	26.7296	0.9000	24.0566	0.7734
1873–85	trade dollar	27.2156	0.9000	24.4940	0.7875
1942–45	5 cents	5.0000	0.3500	1.7500	0.0563
		GOLD			
1837–1933	1 dollar	1.6718	0.9000	1.5046	0.0484
	2-1/2 dollars	4.1795	0.9000	3.7616	0.1209
	3 dollars	5.0154	0.9000	4.5139	0.1451
	5 dollars	8.3591	0.9000	7.5232	0.2419
	10 dollars	16.7181	0.9000	15.0463	0.4837
	20 dollars	33.4363	0.9000	30.0962	0.9675
	50 dollars	83.5906	0.9000	75.2316	2.4187

The prices shown are for the commonest date and mint. For a detailed catalog of all dates, mint marks, and principal varieties of each coin type, *A Guide Book of United States Coins* by R.S. Yeoman, which is revised annually, is recommended. With respect to conditions, Uncirculated and Proof issues are priced for typical pieces in MS-60 or PF-60 states of preservation.

Y#	KM#	Metal	Description	VF	EF	Unc
1	85	C-N	1 Cent, 1856–58	60	150	1,000
						Proof: $8,200

Y#	KM#	Metal	Description	VF	EF	Unc
2	87	C-N	1 Cent, 1859	55	110	700
						Proof: $2,500

Y#	KM#	Metal	Description	VF	EF	Unc
2a	90	C-N	1 Cent, 1860–64	35	55	200
						Proof: $1,250
2b	90a	Bz	1 Cent, 1864–1909	6	10	60
						Proof: $200

Y#	KM#	Metal	Description	VF	EF	Unc
3	94	Bz	2 Cents, 1864–73	30	55	250
						Proof: $550

Obverse: ***No lines around star***

Y#	KM#	Metal	Description	VF	EF	Unc
4	75	Silv	3 Cents, 1851–53	65	80	275

Obverse: ***Three outlines to star***

Y#	KM#	Metal	Description	VF	EF	Unc
4a	80	Silv	3 Cents, 1854–58	70	125	800
						Proof: $5,000

Obverse: ***Two outlines to star***

Y#	KM#	Metal	Description	VF	EF	Unc
4b	88	C-N	3 Cents, 1859–73	60	95	300
						Proof: $1,100

Y#	KM#	Metal	Description	VF	EF	Unc
5	95	C-N	3 Cents, 1865–89	30	40	200
						Proof: $325

Y#	KM#	Metal	Description	VF	EF	Unc
6	96	C-N	5 Cents, 1866–67	90	175	500
						Proof: $3,000

Y#	KM#	Metal	Description	VF	EF	Unc
6a	97	C-N	5 Cents, 1867–83	45	65	225
						Proof: $325

LIBERTY SEATED SERIES

Y#	KM#	Metal	Description	VF	EF	Unc
7	60	Silv	1/2 Dime, 1837–38	145	250	950
						Proof: $16,500
8	61	Silv	1 Dime, 1837	300	500	1,800
						Proof: $8,500

Y#	KM#	Metal	Description	VF	EF	Unc
7a	62	Silv	1/2 Dime, 1838–59	40	80	350
						Proof: $4,000
8a	63	Silv	1 Dime, 1838–60	35	55	550
						Proof: $2,000

Y#	KM#	Metal	Description	VF	EF	Unc
9	64–A64	Silv	1/4 Dollar, 1838–65	55	85	625
						Proof: $1,850
10	68–A68	Silv	1/2 Dollar, 1839–66	150	250	1,750
						Proof: $1,500
11	71	Silv	1 Dollar, 1840–65	550	700	4,250
						Proof: $5,000

Obverse: ***Arrows at date***
Reverse: ***Rays around eagle***

Y#	KM#	Metal	Description	VF	EF	Unc
9a	78	Silv	1/4 Dollar, 1853	55	200	2,000
					Proof:	*$45,000*
10a	79	Silv	1/2 Dollar, 1853	150	300	3,500
					Proof:	*$57,500*

Obverse: ***Arrows at date***

Y#	KM#	Metal	Description	VF	EF	Unc
7b	76	Silv	1/2 Dime, 1853–55	35	70	325
					Proof:	*$8,200*
8b	77	Silv	1 Dime, 1853–55	30	50	650
					Proof:	*$8,500*
9b	81	Silv	1/4 Dollar, 1854–55	45	85	1,200
					Proof:	*$15,000*
10b	82	Silv	1/2 Dollar, 1854–55	140	200	1,500
					Proof:	*$13,500*

Obverse: ***Legend replaces stars***

Y#	KM#	Metal	Description	VF	EF	Unc
7c	91	Silv	1/2 Dime, 1860–73	45	80	250
					Proof:	*$625*
8c	92–A92	Silv	1 Dime, 1860–91	25	35	425
					Proof:	*$600*

Obverse: ***Arrows removed at date***
Reverse: ***Motto on ribbon above eagle***

Y#	KM#	Metal	Description	VF	EF	Unc
9c	98–A98	Silv	1/4 Dollar, 1866–91	45	65	550
					Proof:	*$750*
10c	99–A99	Silv	1/2 Dollar, 1866–91	80	120	800
					Proof:	*$1,150*
11a	100	Silv	1 Dollar, 1866–73	500	625	4,500
					Proof:	*$4,000*

Obverse: ***Arrows at date***

Y#	KM#	Metal	Description	VF	EF	Unc
8d	105	Silv	1 Dime, 1873–74	55	150	900
					Proof:	*$1,200*
9d	106	Silv	1/4 Dollar, 1873–74	65	200	1,100
					Proof:	*$1,500*
10d	107	Silv	1/2 Dollar, 1873–74	100	250	950
					Proof:	*$2,150*

Y#	KM#	Metal	Description	VF	EF	Unc
12	109	Silv	20 Cents, 1875–78	150	250	1,100
					Proof:	*$2,750*

Note: Dates after 1876 were not for circulation.

Trade Dollar

Though legal tender, trade dollars were struck for circulation in the Orient only.

Y#	KM#	Metal	Description	VF	EF	Unc
13	108	Silv	1 Dollar, 1873–85	200	275	1,600
						Proof: $3,000

Note: Dates after 1878 were not for circulation.

Liberty Head Series

Reverse: ***Without CENTS***

Y#	KM#	Metal	Description	VF	EF	Unc
14	111	C-N	V (Cents), 1883	11	15	50
						Proof: $450

Reverse: ***CENTS below wreath***

Y#	KM#	Metal	Description	VF	EF	Unc
14a	112	C-N	V Cents, 1883–1912	15	30	125
						Proof: $350

Y#	KM#	Metal	Description	VF	EF	Unc
15	113	Silv	1 Dime, 1892–1916	10	25	225
						Proof: $500

Y#	KM#	Metal	Description	VF	EF	Unc
16	114	Silv	1/4 Dollar, 1892–1916	40	70	375
						Proof: $650
17	116	Silv	1/2 Dollar, 1892–1915	95	200	950
						Proof: $1,100

Y#	KM#	Metal	Description	VF	EF	Unc
18	110	Silv	1 Dollar, 1878–1921	28	30	125
						Proof: $3,000

Y#	KM#	Metal	Description	VF	EF	Unc
19	73	Gold	1 Dollar, 1849–54	200	225	500

Y#	KM#	Metal	Description	VF	EF	Unc
20	83	Gold	1 Dollar, 1854–56, small head	350	450	5,000
20a	86	Gold	1 Dollar, 1856–89, large head	250	300	900
						Proof: $5,000

Y#	KM#	Metal	Description	VF	EF	Unc
21	84	Gold	3 Dollars, 1854–89	850	1,150	3,500
						Proof: $12,500

Y#	KM#	Metal	Description	VF	EF	Unc
22	72	Gold	2-1/2 Dollars, 1840–1907	295	375	550
						Proof: $7,500
23	69	Gold	5 Dollars, 1839–66	450	475	6,000
						Proof: $35,000
24	66	Gold	10 Dollars, 1838–66	950	1,000	7,500
						Proof: $47,500

Y#	KM#	Metal	Description	VF	EF	Unc
25	74–A74	Gold	20 Dollars, 1849–66	2,250	2,600	8,500
						Proof: $200,000

Reverse: ***Motto above eagle***

Y#	KM#	Metal	Description	VF	EF	Unc
23a	101	Gold	5 Dollars, 1866–1908	435	450	700
						Proof: $15,000
24a	102	Gold	10 Dollars, 1866–1907	BV	BV	1,250
						Proof: $12,500

Reverse: ***TWENTY D.***

Y#	KM#	Metal	Description	VF	EF	Unc
25a	74.2	Gold	20 Dollars, 1866–76	BV	BV	7,500
						Proof: $67,500

Reverse: ***TWENTY DOLLARS***

Y#	KM#	Metal	Description	VF	EF	Unc
25b	74.3	Gold	20 Dollars, 1877–1907	BV	BV	2,600
						Proof: $37,500

20TH-CENTURY DESIGNS

Y#	KM#	Metal	Description	VF	EF	Unc
26	132	Bz	1 Cent, 1909–58	0.10	0.15	0.35
						Proof: $10
26a	132a	Z-CS	1 Cent, 1943	0.40	0.50	3.00

Y#	KM#	Metal	Description	VF	EF	Unc
36	201	Bz	1 Cent, 1959–82	—	—	0.15
						Proof: $1

Reverse: ***Value below mound***

Y#	KM#	Metal	Description	VF	EF	Unc
27	133	C-N	5 Cents, 1913	20	25	65
						Proof: $1,900

Reverse: ***Value below line***

Y#	KM#	Metal	Description	VF	EF	Unc
27a	134	C-N	5 Cents, 1913–38	2	4	40
						Proof: $1,000

Y#	KM#	Metal	Description	VF	EF	Unc
37	192	C-N	5 Cents, 1938–41, 1946–2003	—	—	0.50
						Proof: $3

Y#	KM#	Metal	Description	VF	EF	Unc
37a	192a	Bill	5 Cents, 1942–45	2.25	2.75	8
						Proof: $100

Y#	KM#	Metal	Description	VF	EF	Unc
28	140	Silv	1 Dime, 1916–45	3	3.50	12.50
						Proof: $180

Y#	KM#	Metal	Description	VF	EF	Unc
38	195	Silv	1 Dime, 1946–64	BV	2	3
						Proof: $5

Obverse: ***Bared right breast***
Reverse: ***No stars below eagle***

Y#	KM#	Metal	Description	VF	EF	Unc
29	141	Silv	1/4 Dollar, 1916–17	125	175	375

Obverse: ***Mailed right breast***
Reverse: ***Three stars below eagle***

Y#	KM#	Metal	Description	VF	EF	Unc
29a	145	Silv	1/4 Dollar, 1917–30	17.50	35	175

Y#	KM#	Metal	Description	VF	EF	Unc
39	164	Silv	1/4 Dollar, 1932–64	BV	5	10
						Proof: $10

Y#	KM#	Metal	Description	VF	EF	Unc
30	142	Silv	1/2 Dollar, 1916–47	17.50	20	55
						Proof: $450

Y#	KM#	Metal	Description	VF	EF	Unc
40	199	Silv	1/2 Dollar, 1948–63	BV	10	20
						Proof: $20

Y#	KM#	Metal	Description	VF	EF	Unc
41	202	Silv	1/2 Dollar, 1964	BV	BV	12
						Proof: $20

Y#	KM#	Metal	Description	VF	EF	Unc
31	150	Silv	1 Dollar, 1921–35	26	29	35
						Proof: $30,000

Y#	KM#	Metal	Description	VF	EF	Unc
32	128	Gold	2-1/2 Dollars, 1908–29	300	325	550
						Proof: $9,500
33	129	Gold	5 Dollars, 1908–29	475	500	1,250
						Proof: $16,000

Reverse: ***No motto***

Y#	KM#	Metal	Description	VF	EF	Unc
34	125	Gold	10 Dollars, 1907–08	900	925	2,250

Reverse: ***Motto added***

Y#	KM#	Metal	Description	VF	EF	Unc
34a	130	Gold	10 Dollars, 1908–33	900	925	1,250
						Proof: $20,000

Design: ***In high relief***

Y#	KM#	Metal	Description	VF	EF	Unc
35	126	Gold	20 Dollars, MCMVII (1907)	9,500	11,500	23,000
						Proof: $42,500

Design: ***In low relief***

Y#	KM#	Metal	Description	VF	EF	Unc
35a	127	Gold	20 Dollars, 1907–08	BV	BV	2,350

Reverse: ***Motto added above sun***

Y#	KM#	Metal	Description	VF	EF	Unc
35b	131	Gold	20 Dollars, 1908–32	BV	BV	2,350
						Proof: $45,000

COMMEMORATIVE COINS

Listed alphabetically by subject.

Y#	KM#	Metal	Description	VF	EF	Unc
C1	N/A	Silv	1/4 Dollar, 1893 Columbian Exposition (Isabella Quarter)	—	—	685

Y#	KM#	Metal	Description	VF	EF	Unc
C2	N/A	Silv	1 Dollar, 1900 Lafayette Memorial	—	—	1,500

Y#	KM#	Metal	Description	VF	EF	Unc
C4	148	Silv	1921 Alabama Centennial	—	—	400
C5	173	Silv	1936 Albany, NY Charter	—	—	250
C6	190	Silv	1937 Battle of Antietam	—	—	625
C7	168	Silv	1935–39 Arkansas Centennial	—	—	150
C8	174	Silv	1936S San Francisco–Oakland Bay Bridge	—	—	180
C9	165	Silv	1934–38 Daniel Boone Bicentennial	—	—	155
C10	175	Silv	1936 Bridgeport, Conn Centennial	—	—	140
C11	155	Silv	1925S California Diamond Jubilee	—	—	225
C12	176	Silv	1936 Cincinnati Musical Center	—	—	375
C13	177	Silv	1936 Cleveland, Great Lakes Exposition	—	—	130
C14	178	Silv	1936 Columbia, SC Sesquicentennial	—	—	250
C16	N/A	Silv	1892–93 Columbian Exposition	—	—	75
C17	169	Silv	1935 Connecticut Tercentenary	—	—	245
C18	179	Silv	1936 Delaware Tercentenary	—	—	235
C19	180	Silv	1936 Elgin, Ill Centennial	—	—	210
C20	181	Silv	1936 Gettysburg Memorial	—	—	525
C22	151	Silv	1922 Grant Memorial	—	—	200
C23	163	Silv	1928 Hawaii Sesquicentennial	—	—	2,650
C24	170	Silv	1935 Hudson, NY Sesquicentennial	—	—	850
C25	154	Silv	1924 Huguenot–Walloon Tercentenary	—	—	170
C26	197	Silv	1946 Iowa Centennial	—	—	105
C27	156	Silv	1925 Lexington–Concord Sesquicentennial	—	—	120
C28	143	Silv	1918 Lincoln–Illinois Centennial	—	—	200
C29	182	Silv	1936 Long Island Tercentenary	—	—	110
C30	183	Silv	1936 Lynchburg, Va Sesquicentennial	—	—	250
C31	146	Silv	1920 Maine Centennial	—	—	175
C32	166	Silv	1934 Maryland Tercentenary	—	—	170
C34	149	Silv	1921 Missouri Centennial	—	—	750
C35	153	Silv	1923S Monroe Doctrine Centennial	—	—	165
C36	191	Silv	1938 New Rochelle, NY	—	—	345
C37	184	Silv	1936 Norfolk, Va Bicentennial	—	—	310
C38	159	Silv	1926–39 Oregon Trail Memorial	—	—	200
C39	135	Silv	1915S Panama–Pacific Exposition	—	—	800
C40	147	Silv	1920–21 Pilgrim Tercentenary	—	—	110
C42	185	Silv	1936 Providence, RI Tercentenary	—	—	125
C43	186	Silv	1937 Roanoke Island, NC 350th Anniversary	—	—	200
C44	187	Silv	1936 Robinson–Arkansas	—	—	145
C45	171	Silv	1935–36 San Diego, Calif Pacific Exposition	—	—	120
C46	160	Silv	1926 US Independence Sesquicentennial	—	—	150
C47	172	Silv	1935 Old Spanish Trail	—	—	1,200
C48	157	Silv	1925 Stone Mountain Memorial	—	—	100
C49	167	Silv	1934–38 Texas Centennial	—	—	160
C50	158	Silv	1925 Fort Vancouver Centennial	—	—	400
C51	162	Silv	1927 Vermont Sesquicentennial	—	—	300
C52	198	Silv	1946–51 Booker T Washington Memorial	—	—	30
C53	200	Silv	1951–54 Washington–Carver	—	—	40
C54	188	Silv	1936 Wisconsin Territorial Centennial	—	—	200
C55	189	Silv	1936 York County, Maine Tercentenary	—	—	175

Y#	KM#	Metal	Description	VF	EF	Unc
C56	152	Gold	1 Dollar, 1922 Grant Memorial	—	—	1,800
C58	121	Gold	1 Dollar, 1904–05 Lewis and Clark Exposition	—	—	1,500
C59	119	Gold	1 Dollar, 1903 Louisiana Purchase–Jefferson	—	—	865
C60	120	Gold	1 Dollar, 1903 Louisiana Purchase–McKinley	—	—	865
C61	144	Gold	1 Dollar, 1916–17 McKinley Memorial	—	—	675
C62	136	Gold	1 Dollar, 1915S Panama–Pacific Exposition	—	—	700

Y#	KM#	Metal	Description	VF	EF	Unc
C63	137	Gold	2-1/2 Dollars, 1915S Panama–Pacific Exposition	—	—	4,000

Y#	KM#	Metal	Description	VF	EF	Unc
C64	138	Gold	50 Dollars, 1915S Panama–Pacific Exposition, round	—	—	110,000
C65	139	Gold	50 Dollars, 1915S Panama–Pacific Exposition, octagonal	—	—	100,000

Y#	KM#	Metal	Description	VF	EF	Unc
C66	161	Gold	2-1/2 Dollars, 1926 Philadelphia Sesquicentennial	—	—	525

URUGUAY

The smallest republic in South America, Uruguay was settled by the Portuguese in 1680 and taken by Spain a century later. The nation revolted in 1811 and was conquered by Brazil in 1817. It declared independence in 1825 and established a republic in 1828. The civilian government was ousted by a repressive military coup in 1973. Representative government was restored in 1984. *Language:* Spanish. *Capital:* Montevideo.

MONETARY SYSTEM

100 centesimos = 1 real, to 1862
100 centesimos = 1 peso, 1862–

PRECIOUS METAL CONTENT

Dates	Denomination	Gross Wt (g)	Fineness	Net Wt (g)	Troy Oz.
		SILVER			
1877–1917	10 centesimos	2.5000	0.9000	2.2500	0.0723
	20 centesimos	5.0000	0.9000	4.5000	0.1447
	50 centesimos	12.5000	0.9000	11.2500	0.3617
	1 peso	25.0000	0.9000	22.5000	0.7234
1920–30	20 centesimos	5.0000	0.8000	4.0000	0.1286
1942–54	20 centesimos	3.0000	0.7200	2.1600	0.0694
	50 centesimos	7.0000	0.7200	5.0400	0.1620
	1 peso	9.0000	0.7200	6.4800	0.2083
1961	10 pesos	12.5000	0.9000	11.2500	0.3617
		GOLD			
1930	5 pesos	8.4850	0.9170	7.7779	0.2501

First Coinage

Y#	KM#	Metal	Description	VF	EF	Unc
1	1/6	Cop	5 Centesimos, 1840–55 *1840, 44, EF $3,000; 1855, Unc $2,750*	80	200	—
2	2/7	Cop	20 Centesimos, 1840–55	100	325	—
3	3–4	Cop	40 Centesimos, 1844	300	450	—

Note: Y1–3 occur in several minor varieties.

Y#	KM#	Metal	Description	VF	EF	Unc
4	8	Cop	5 Centesimos, 1857	15	50	—
5	9	Cop	20 Centesimos, 1857	25	55	—
6	10	Cop	40 Centesimos, 1857	20	40	—

Montevideo Peso

Y#	KM#	Metal	Description	VF	EF	Unc
10	5	Silv	1 Peso, 1844	550	1,100	2,500

Second Coinage

Y#	KM#	Metal	Description	VF	EF	Unc
7	11	Bz	1 Centesimo, 1869	5.00	25.00	50
8	12	Bz	2 Centesimos, 1869	7.50	27.50	55
9	13	Bz	4 Centesimos, 1869	12.50	35.00	80

Y#	KM#	Metal	Description	VF	EF	Unc
11	14	Silv	10 Centesimos, 1877, 93	10	20	75
12	15	Silv	20 Centesimos, 1877, 93	15	25	85
13	16	Silv	50 Centesimos, 1877–94	25	65	125
14	17	Silv	1 Peso, 1877–95 *1878, EF $1,750*	50	90	325

Third Coinage

Y#	KM#	Metal	Description	VF	EF	Unc
15	19	C-N	1 Centesimo, 1901–36	2.00	7.00	20.00
16	20	C-N	2 Centesimos, 1901–41	2.00	7.00	20.00
17	21	C-N	5 Centesimos, 1901–41	2.00	6.00	15.00
16a	20a	Cop	2 Centesimos, 1943–51	0.75	1.00	5.00
17a	21a	Cop	5 Centesimos, 1944–51	0.75	2.50	7.50

Y#	KM#	Metal	Description	VF	EF	Unc
20	24	Silv	20 Centesimos, 1920	10	20	85
22	22	Silv	50 Centesimos, 1916–17	25	50	150
23	23	Silv	1 Peso, 1917	25	85	200

Constitution Centennial

Y#	KM#	Metal	Description	VF	EF	Unc
18	25	A-Bz	10 Centesimos, 1930	5	10	30

Y#	KM#	Metal	Description	VF	EF	Unc
21	26	Silv	20 Centesimos, 1930	5	10	30

Y#	KM#	Metal	Description	VF	EF	Unc
24	27	Gold	5 Pesos, 1930	BV	400	500

FOURTH COINAGE

Y#	KM#	Metal	Description	VF	EF	Unc
19	28	A-Bz	10 Centesimos, 1936	4	8	40

Y#	KM#	Metal	Description	VF	EF	Unc
25	29	Silv	20 Centesimos, 1942	2	4	7.50

Y#	KM#	Metal	Description	VF	EF	Unc
26	31	Silv	50 Centesimos, 1943	6	8	20

Y#	KM#	Metal	Description	VF	EF	Unc
27	30	Silv	1 Peso, 1942	6.50	13.50	50

FIFTH COINAGE

Y#	KM#	Metal	Description	VF	EF	Unc
28	32	C-N	1 Centesimo, 1953	0.20	0.30	1.00
29	33	C-N	2 Centesimos, 1953	0.20	0.30	1.25
30	34	C-N	5 Centesimos, 1953	0.20	0.30	1.50
31	35	C-N	10 Centesimos, 1953, 59	0.20	0.30	1.50

Y#	KM#	Metal	Description	VF	EF	Unc
32	36	Silv	20 Centesimos, 1954	2	4	7.50

SIXTH COINAGE

Y#	KM#	Metal	Description	VF	EF	Unc
33	37	CNZ	2 Centesimos, 1960	0.10	0.20	0.50
34	38	CNZ	5 Centesimos, 1960	0.10	0.20	0.50
35	39	CNZ	10 Centesimos, 1960	0.20	0.30	0.50

Y#	KM#	Metal	Description	VF	EF	Unc
36	40	C-N	25 Centesimos, 1960	0.30	0.40	0.75
37	41	C-N	50 Centesimos, 1960	0.40	0.50	1.00
38	42	C-N	1 Peso, 1960	0.50	0.75	1.50

Sesquicentennial, Gaucho Heroes

Y#	KM#	Metal	Description	VF	EF	Unc
39	43	Silv	10 Pesos, 1961	6.50	9	15

VATICAN CITY

The Papal States covered some 16,000 square miles in the mid-19th century. In 1871 the territory became part of the unified kingdom of Italy. In 1929 Vatican City was established as an independent state within the city of Rome with the Pope holding full executive and judicial power. Its present area is 108.7 acres (.17 square miles). *Population:* 932. *Languages:* Italian, Latin.

MONETARY SYSTEM

100 centesimi = 1 lira

PRECIOUS METAL CONTENT

Dates	Denomination	Gross Wt (g)	Fineness	Net Wt (g)	Troy Oz.
		SILVER			
1929–46	5 lire	5.0000	0.8350	4.1750	0.1342
	10 lire	10.0000	0.8350	8.3500	0.2685
1958–65	500 lire	11.0000	0.8350	9.1850	0.2953
		GOLD			
1929–35	100 lire	8.7990	0.9000	7.9191	0.2546
1936–59	100 lire	5.1966	0.9000	4.6749	0.1504

Pius XI,
1922–1939

Y#	KM#	Metal	Description	VF	EF	Unc
1	1	Bz	5 Centesimi, 1929–38 *1938, Rare*	6.50	16	30

Y#	KM#	Metal	Description	VF	EF	Unc
2	2	Bz	10 Centesimi, 1929–38 *1938, VF $1,450*	6.50	16	30

Y#	KM#	Metal	Description	VF	EF	Unc
3	3	Nick	20 Centesimi, 1929–37 *1935, VF $100*	6.50	13	20

Y#	KM#	Metal	Description	VF	EF	Unc
4	4	Nick	50 Centesimi, 1929–37 *1935, VF $40*	6.50	13	20
5	5	Nick	1 Lira, 1929–37	6.50	13	20

Y#	KM#	Metal	Description	VF	EF	Unc
6	6	Nick	2 Lire, 1929–37	5.00	13	17.50

Y#	KM#	Metal	Description	VF	EF	Unc
7	7	Silv	5 Lire, 1929–37	9.50	13.50	22.50

Y#	KM#	Metal	Description	VF	EF	Unc
8	8	Silv	10 Lire, 1929–37	16.50	32.50	50

Y#	KM#	Metal	Description	VF	EF	Unc
9	9	Gold	100 Lire, 1929–35 (24 mm)	BV	285	600
9a	10	Gold	100 Lire, 1936–37 (21 mm) *1937, VF $2,500*	BV	300	400

Jubilee Issues, 1933

These coins are similar to the 1929–1937 types and are dated "1933–1934."

Obverse: ***Crowned arms***

Y#	KM#	Metal	Description	VF	EF	Unc
11	11	Bz	5 Centesimi	6.50	22.50	35
12	12	Bz	10 Centesimi	6.50	22.50	35

Y#	KM#	Metal	Description	VF	EF	Unc
13	13	Nick	20 Centesimi	6.50	13.00	20.00
14	14	Nick	50 Centesimi	6.50	13.00	20.00
15	15	Nick	1 Lira	8.25	12.50	22.50
16	16	Nick	2 Lire	5.25	13.00	26.00

Obverse: ***Bust facing left***

Y#	KM#	Metal	Description	VF	EF	Unc
17	17	Silv	5 Lire	9.50	13.50	22.50
18	18	Silv	10 Lire	20.00	40.00	50.00

Obverse: ***Bust facing right***

Y#	KM#	Metal	Description	VF	EF	Unc
19	19	Gold	100 Lire	BV	275	575

SEDE VACANTE, *1939*

Y#	KM#	Metal	Description	VF	EF	Unc
20	20	Silv	5 Lire, 1939	10.00	17.50	45
21	21	Silv	10 Lire, 1939	17.50	32.50	65

PIUS XII, *1939–1958*

First Coinage

Designs: ***Like Y1–6***

Y#	KM#	Metal	Description	VF	EF	Unc
22	22	Bz	5 Centesimi, 1939–41 *1941, VF $20*	10	15	20.00
23	23	Bz	10 Centesimi, 1939–41 *1941, VF $12.50*	5	10	17.50

Y#	KM#	Metal	Description	VF	EF	Unc
24	24	Nick	20 Centesimi, 1939	6.50	12.50	20.00
25	25	Nick	50 Centesimi, 1939	6.50	12.50	22.50
26	26	Nick	1 Lira, 1939	5.00	11.00	20.00
27	27	Nick	2 Lire, 1939	6.50	12.50	22.50
24a	24a	S S	20 Centesimi, 1940–41	3.25	9.50	13.00
25a	25a	S S	50 Centesimi, 1940–41	3.25	9.50	13.00
26a	26a	S S	1 Lira, 1940–41	3.25	11.00	17.50
27a	27a	S S	2 Lire, 1940–41	5.00	6.50	13.00

Reverse: ***Designs like Y7–10***

Y#	KM#	Metal	Description	VF	EF	Unc
28	28	Silv	5 Lire, 1939–41	9.50	13.50	25
29	29	Silv	10 Lire, 1939–41	20.00	37.50	65

Y#	KM#	Metal	Description	VF	EF	Unc
30	30	Gold	100 Lire, 1939–41	300	325	450

Second Coinage

Y#	KM#	Metal	Description	VF	EF	Unc
31	31	A-Bz	5 Centesimi, 1942–46 *1943–46, VF $50*	17.50	40	65
32	32	A-Bz	10 Centesimi, 1942–46 *1943–46, VF $50*	17.50	40	80

Y#	KM#	Metal	Description	VF	EF	Unc
33	33	S S	20 Centesimi, 1942–46 *1943–46, VF $50*	6.50	12.50	22.50
34	34	S S	50 Centesimi, 1942–46 *1943–46, VF $50*	6.50	12.50	22.50
35	35	S S	1 Lira, 1942–46 *1943–46, VF $50*	6.50	12.50	22.50
36	36	S S	2 Lire, 1942–46 *1943–46, VF $50*	9.50	17.50	30.00

Y#	KM#	Metal	Description	VF	EF	Unc
37	37	Silv	5 Lire, 1942–46 *1943–46, VF $70*	25	50	100
38	38	Silv	10 Lire, 1942–46 *1943–46, VF $80*	50	100	145

Y#	KM#	Metal	Description	VF	EF	Unc
39	39	Gold	100 Lire, 1942–49	245	275	425

Third Coinage

Y#	KM#	Metal	Description	VF	EF	Unc
40	40	Alum	1 Lira, 1947–49	6.50	20	42.00
41	41	Alum	2 Lire, 1947–49	11.50	25	47.50

Y#	KM#	Metal	Description	VF	EF	Unc
42	42	Alum	5 Lire, 1947–49	8.25	20.00	40
43	43	Alum	10 Lire, 1947–49	4.50	22.50	50

Holy Year Commemoratives

Y#	KM#	Metal	Description	VF	EF	Unc
44	44	Alum	1 Lira, MCML (1950)	6.50	12.50	17.50

Y#	KM#	Metal	Description	VF	EF	Unc
45	45	Alum	2 Lire, MCML	6.50	13.50	22.50

Y#	KM#	Metal	Description	VF	EF	Unc
46	46	Alum	5 Lire, MCML	6.50	17.50	30.00
47	47	Alum	10 Lire, MCML	6.50	17.50	32.50

Y#	KM#	Metal	Description	VF	EF	Unc
48	48	Gold	100 Lire, MCML	245	275	425

Fourth Coinage

Y#	KM#	Metal	Description	VF	EF	Unc
49	49	Alum	1 Lira, 1951–58 *1955-56, VF $6.00; 1957-58, VF $4*	1.25	2.75	6.50
50	50	Alum	2 Lire, 1951–58 *1955-56, VF $12.50*	1.25	8.00	12.00

Y#	KM#	Metal	Description	VF	EF	Unc
51	51	Alum	5 Lire, 1951–58 *1955-58, VF $6.00*	2.50	6.50	12

Y#	KM#	Metal	Description	VF	EF	Unc
52	52	Alum	10 Lire, 1951–58	1.75	4.75	13

Y#	KM#	Metal	Description	VF	EF	Unc
A52	A52	A-Bz	20 Lire, 1957–58	1.75	5.75	16.50

Y#	KM#	Metal	Description	VF	EF	Unc
54	54	S S	50 Lire, 1955–58	3	6	20

Y#	KM#	Metal	Description	VF	EF	Unc
55	55	S S	100 Lire, 1955–58	3	6	20

Y#	KM#	Metal	Description	VF	EF	Unc
56	56	Silv	500 Lire, 1958	12.50	25	42.50

Y#	KM#	Metal	Description	VF	EF	Unc
53	53	Gold	100 Lire, 1951–56	350	375	750

Reverse: ***Papal arms***

Y#	KM#	Metal	Description	VF	EF	Unc
A53	A53	Gold	100 Lire, 1957–58	BV	245	325

SEDE VACANTE, 1958

Y#	KM#	Metal	Description	VF	EF	Unc
57	57	Silv	500 Lire, 1958	13.50	18	35

JOHN XXIII, 1958–1963

Y#	KM#	Metal	Description	VF	EF	Unc
58	58	Alum	1 Lira, 1959–62	1.25	2.50	6

Y#	KM#	Metal	Description	VF	EF	Unc
59	59	Alum	2 Lire, 1959–62	1.50	3.50	7

Y#	KM#	Metal	Description	VF	EF	Unc
60	60	Alum	5 Lire, 1959–62	1	2	4
61	61	Alum	10 Lire, 1959–62	1	2	4

Y#	KM#	Metal	Description	VF	EF	Unc
62	62	A-Bz	20 Lire, 1959–62	0.85	1.50	3.75

Y#	KM#	Metal	Description	VF	EF	Unc
63	63	S S	50 Lire, 1959–62	1.00	2.00	5.00
64	64	S S	100 Lire, 1959–62	0.85	1.50	3.75

Note: Issues of 50, 100, and 500 lire of 1959 have A-I or AN-I (year one and later) upside down under bust. Coins minted in 1960 and later have AN-II, etc., right side up.

Y#	KM#	Metal	Description	VF	EF	Unc
65	65	Silv	500 Lire, 1959–62	6	11	25

Note: Coins dated 1960 to 1962 have the date under the bust on the obverse.

Y#	KM#	Metal	Description	VF	EF	Unc
66	66	Gold	100 Lire, 1959	550	700	1,000

Ecumenical Council Commemoratives

Y#	KM#	Metal	Description	VF	EF	Unc
67	67	Alum	1 Lira, 1962	1.25	2	4
68	68	Alum	2 Lire, 1962	1.25	2	4

Y#	KM#	Metal	Description	VF	EF	Unc
69	69	Alum	5 Lire, 1962	0.50	1.00	2.00
70	70	Alum	10 Lire, 1962	1.00	1.75	3.25

Y#	KM#	Metal	Description	VF	EF	Unc
71	71	A-Bz	20 Lire, 1962	1	1.75	3.50

Y#	KM#	Metal	Description	VF	EF	Unc
72	72	S S	50 Lire, 1962	0.50	1.50	2.50

Y#	KM#	Metal	Description	VF	EF	Unc
73	73	S S	100 Lire, 1962	0.45	0.90	2.50

Y#	KM#	Metal	Description	VF	EF	Unc
74	74	Silv	500 Lire, 1962	9	11	25

SEDE VACANTE, 1963

Y#	KM#	Metal	Description	VF	EF	Unc
75	75	Silv	500 Lire, 1963	9	11	22.50

PAUL VI, 1963–1978

First Coinage

Reverses: ***Similar to Y49–55***

Y#	KM#	Metal	Description	VF	EF	Unc
76	76	Alum	1 Lira, 1963–65	0.50	1.00	2.00
77	77	Alum	2 Lire, 1963–65	0.65	1.50	2.50
78	78	Alum	5 Lire, 1963–65	0.75	1.50	3.00
79	79	Alum	10 Lire, 1963–65	0.75	1.50	3.00

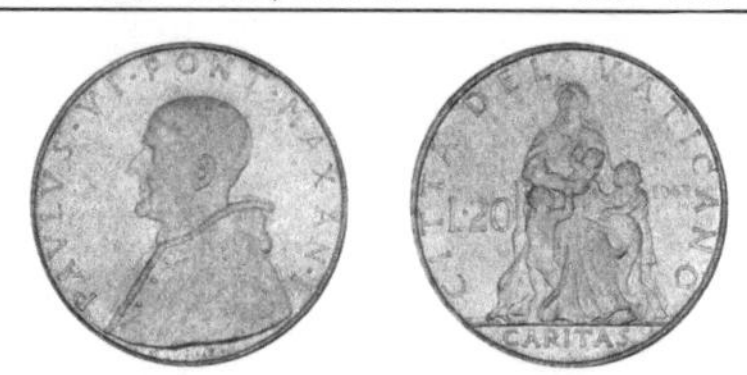

Y#	KM#	Metal	Description	VF	EF	Unc
80	80	A-Bz	20 Lire, 1963–65	0.75	1	3

Y#	KM#	Metal	Description	VF	EF	Unc
81	81	S S	50 Lire, 1963–65	0.75	1	3
82	82	S S	100 Lire, 1963–65	0.75	1	3

Y#	KM#	Metal	Description	VF	EF	Unc
83	83	Silv	500 Lire, 1963–65	8.50	11	22.50

VENEZUELA

Venezuela is a republic on the Caribbean coast in northern South America. Venezuela won its independence from Spain in 1826 and in 1830 broke away from the "Gran Colombia" federation it had established with New Granada (Colombia) and Ecuador. The nation was ruled by civilian and military dictatorships until 1959. Since then it has been one of the continent's most stable democracies. *Languages:* Spanish, Indian dialects. *Capital:* Caracas.

MONETARY SYSTEM

100 centavos = 10 reales = 1 peso, to 1865
100 centavos = 1 venezolano, 1865–1879
100 centimos = 1 bolivar, 1879–

PRECIOUS METAL CONTENT

Dates	Denomination	Gross Wt (g)	Fineness	Net Wt (g)	Troy Oz.
		SILVER			
1858	1/2 real	1.1500	0.9000	1.0350	0.0333
	1 real	2.3000	0.9000	2.0700	0.0666
	2 reales	4.6000	0.9000	4.1400	0.1331
	5 reales	11.5000	0.9000	10.3500	0.3328
1873–1945	1/5 bolivar	1.0000	0.8350	0.8350	0.0268
	1/4 bolivar / 5 centavos	1.2500	0.8350	1.0438	0.0336
	1/2 bolivar / 10 centavos	2.5000	0.8350	2.0875	0.0671
	1 bolivar / 20 centavos	5.0000	0.8350	4.1750	0.1342
	2 bolivares	10.0000	0.8350	8.3500	0.2685
	50 centavos	12.5000	0.8350	10.4375	0.3356
	5 bolivares / 1 venezolano	25.0000	0.9000	22.5000	0.7234
1954–65	25 centimos	1.2500	0.8350	1.0438	0.0336
	50 centimos	2.5000	0.8350	2.0875	0.0671
	1 bolivar	5.0000	0.8350	4.1750	0.1342
	2 bolivares	10.0000	0.8350	8.3500	0.2685
		GOLD			
1875	5 venezolanos	8.0645	0.9000	7.2581	0.2333
1879–1930	10 bolivares	3.2258	0.9000	2.9032	0.0933
	20 bolivares	6.4516	0.9000	5.8064	0.1867
	100 bolivares	32.2581	0.9000	29.0323	0.9334

REPUBLICA DE VENEZUELA, *1830–1863*

Y#	KM#	Metal	Description	VF	EF	Unc
1	1	Cop	1/4 Centavo, 1843, 52 (19 mm)	20	50	200
2	2	Cop	1/2 Centavo, 1843, 52 (24 mm)	30	60	300
3	3	Cop	1 Centavo, 1843, 52 (32 mm)	75	150	650

Size: ***Reduced***

Y#	KM#	Metal	Description	VF	EF	Unc
4	4	Cop	1/4 Centavo, 1852 (18 mm)	20	50	200
5	5	Cop	1/2 Centavo, 1852 (22 mm)	50	100	400
6	6	Cop	1 Centavo, 1852 (30 mm)	25	85	400

Size: ***Further reduced***

Y#	KM#	Metal	Description	VF	EF	Unc
7	7	Cop	1 Centavo, 1858–63 (26 mm)	15	60	400

Designs: ***LIBERTAD incuse 1858, raised 1858–1863***

Y#	KM#	Metal	Description	VF	EF	Unc
8	8	Silv	"1-1/2" (= 1/2) Real, 1858	500	1,000	5,000
9	9	Silv	1 Real, 1858	450	950	3,000
10	10	Silv	2 Reales, 1858	500	2,000	7,000
11	11	Silv	5 Reales, 1858	1,000	4,500	12,000

Obverse: ***President José A. Paez***
Reverse: ***Value in wreath***

Y#	KM#	Metal	Description	VF	EF	Unc
A11	A11	Silv	10 Reales, 1863	10,000	20,000	40,000

Note: YA11 was not issued to circulation. Smaller silver coins are probably patterns; copper denominations are believed to be fantasies produced later.

ESTADOS UNIDOS DE VENEZUELA, *1864–1953*

FIRST COINAGE

Y#	KM#	Metal	Description	VF	EF	Unc
25	25	C-N	1 Centavo, 1876–77	15	50	300
26	26	C-N	2-1/2 Centavos, 1876–77	40	150	600

Y#	KM#	Metal	Description	VF	EF	Unc
12	12	Silv	GR.1,250 (5 Centavos), 1874, 76	35	100	400

Y#	KM#	Metal	Description	VF	EF	Unc
13	13	Silv	GR.2.500 (10 Centavos), 1874, 76	35	125	450
14	14	Silv	GRAM,5 (20 Centavos), 1874, 76	60	175	1,000
15	15	Silv	G.12,500 (50 Centavos), 1873–76	225	700	2,500
16	16	Silv	GRAM.25 (1 Venezolano), 1876	200	1,250	10,000

Note: Y12–17 bear no denominations, but have their weights stated in grams. Silver coins are identical to Y20–24, as only the legal names of denominations were changed in 1879.

Y#	KM#	Metal	Description	VF	EF	Unc
17	17	Gold	GR.8,0645 (5 Venezolanos), 1875	400	475	1,000

SECOND COINAGE

100 centimos = 1 bolivar

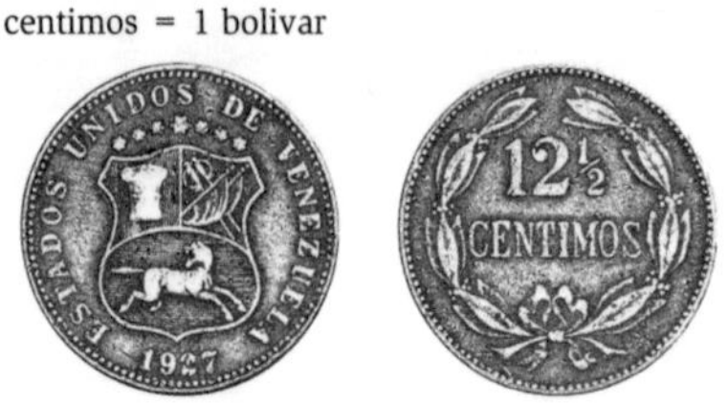

Y#	KM#	Metal	Description	VF	EF	Unc
27	27	C-N	5 Centimos, 1896–1938	1	4.00	30
28	28	C-N	12-1/2 Centimos, 1896–1938	2	7.50	60

Note: Higher grades of all dates before 1936 are worth more.

Y#	KM#	Metal	Description	VF	EF	Unc
19	19	Silv	GRAM.1 (1/5 Bolivar), 1879	550.00	1,100	3,500
20	20	Silv	GR.1.250 (1/4 Bolivar), 1894–1948	0.75	1	2
			1901, 03, VF $25			

Note: Higher grades of all dates before 1929 are worth more.

Y#	KM#	Metal	Description	VF	EF	Unc
21	21	Silv	GR.2.500 (1/2 Bolivar), 1879–1936	4	10	25
			1879, 1903, 11, VF $200; 1887–88, VF $550; 1889, EF $25,000			
22	22	Silv	GRAM.5 (1 Bolivar), 1879–1936	3	6	15
23	23	Silv	GRAM.10 (2 Bolivares), 1879–1936	10	20	75
			1886, 88–89, VF $200			
24	24	Silv	GRAM.25 (5 Bolivares), 1879–1936			
			1879	250	1,500	5,000
			1886–1905	65	250	2,500
			1910–19	35	50	1,500
			1921–29	30	45	500
			1935–36	20	35	150

Note: All dates of Y21 and Y22 before 1929 are worth more, as are all dates of Y23 before 1911. See also note on denominations following Y16.

Y#	KM#	Metal	Description	VF	EF	Unc
31	31	Gold	GR.3,2258 (10 Bolivares), 1930	BV	175	250
32	32	Gold	GR.6.4516 (20 Bolivares), 1879–1912	BV	300	350
33	34	Gold	GR.32,2580 (100 Bolivares), 1886–89	BV	2,000	3,500

Obverse: ***Modified shield***

Y#	KM#	Metal	Description	VF	EF	Unc
29	29	Br	5 Centimos, 1944	4.00	8	50
30	30	Br	12-1/2 Centimos, 1944	10.00	20	225
29a	29a	C-N	5 Centimos, 1945–48	0.20	1	10
30a	30a	C-N	12-1/2 Centimos, 1945–48	0.20	2	20

Reverse: ***Modified arms***

Y#	KM#	Metal	Description	VF	EF	Unc
21a	21a	Silv	GR.2.500 (1/2 Bolivar), 1944–46 *1944, Unc $30*	2	3	15
22a	22a	Silv	*GRAM.5 (1 Bolivar), 1945*	2	3	6
23a	23a	Silv	GRAM.10 (2 Bolivares), 1945	3	5	10

Y#	KM#	Metal	Description	VF	EF	Unc
35	35	Silv	25 Centimos, 1954	0.20	1.00	2
36	36	Silv	50 Centimos, 1954	0.50	1.50	3

Reverse: ***Smaller shield***

Y#	KM#	Metal	Description	VF	EF	Unc
35a	35a	Silv	25 Centimos, 1960	0.20	1.00	1.75
36a	36a	Silv	50 Centimos, 1960	0.40	1.50	2.75

Y#	KM#	Metal	Description	VF	EF	Unc
37	37	Silv	1 Bolivar, 1954	1.50	2	6

Obverse: ***Smaller head and legend***

Y#	KM#	Metal	Description	VF	EF	Unc
37a	37a	Silv	1 Bolivar, 1960, 65	BV	BV	5

Y#	KM#	Metal	Description	VF	EF	Unc
A37	A37	Silv	2 Bolivares, 1960, 65	BV	BV	10

Y#	KM#	Metal	Description	VF	EF	Unc
38	38.1	C-N	5 Centimos, 1958	0.10	0.20	1.00
39	39	C-N	12-1/2 Centimos, 1958	0.10	0.20	1.50

Design: ***Restyled letters, numbers***

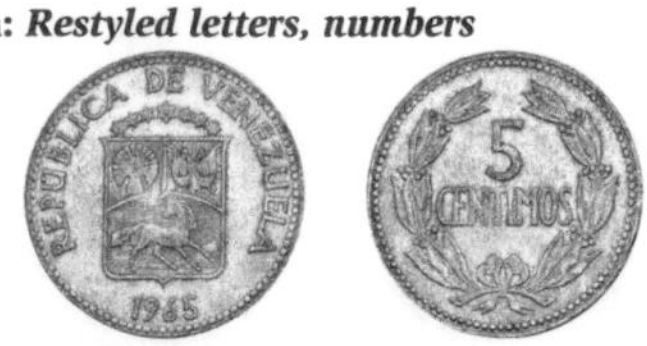

Y#	KM#	Metal	Description	VF	EF	Unc
38a	38.2	C-N	5 Centimos, 1964–65	0.10	0.15	1

VIETNAM

Formerly part of French Indo-China, Vietnam was formed after World War II of Annam, Tonkin, and Cochin China. A provisional communist government was formed in 1945, while a French-sponsored monarchy was established in 1949. After the French were driven out in 1954 the country was partitioned between the two rival factions. Following decades of warfare, the country was unified under communist rule in 1975. *Language:* Vietnamese. *Capital:* Hanoi.

MONETARY SYSTEM

10 xu = 1 hao
100 xu = 1 dong

PROVISIONAL GOVERNMENT, *1945–1946*

Y#	KM#	Metal	Description	VF	EF	Unc
1	1	Alum	20 Xu, 1945	125	275	550

Y#	KM#	Metal	Description	VF	EF	Unc
2	2.1	Alum	5 Hao 1946, value incused	25	50	95
2a	2.2	Alum	5 Hao 1946, value raised	30	60	120

Y#	KM#	Metal	Description	VF	EF	Unc
3	3	Alum	1 Dong, 1946	35	75	135

Y#	KM#	Metal	Description	VF	EF	Unc
4	4	Bz	2 Dong, 1946	30	60	150

VIETNAM, NORTH

A part of former French Indo-China largely composed of the former Tonkin. A 1954 Geneva accord separated Vietnam at the 17th parallel into North and South Vietnam. After 20 years of warfare, the communist North conquered South Vietnam and the nation was re-unified. *Capital:* Hanoi.

MONETARY SYSTEM

10 xu = 1 hao
100 xu = 1 dong

Y#	KM#	Metal	Description	VF	EF	Unc
5	5	Alum	1 Xu, 1958	2.25	5.00	10
6	6	Alum	2 Xu, 1958	2.50	5.50	11
7	7	Alum	5 Xu, 1958	3.00	6.50	15

VIETNAM, SOUTH

South Vietnam, formerly a part of French Indo-China, was established below the 17th parallel by a Geneva accord in 1954. After 20 years of civil war, the country was conquered by North Vietnam and became part of a re-unified Vietnam in 1975. *Capital:* Saigon (now Ho Chi Minh City).

MONETARY SYSTEM

100 su (xu) = 1 dong

Y#	KM#	Metal	Description	VF	EF	Unc
1	1	Alum	10 Su, 1953	1	1.75	4
2	2	Alum	20 Su, 1953	1	1.75	3

Y#	KM#	Metal	Description	VF	EF	Unc
3	3	Alum	50 Xu, 1953	5	10	25

Y#	KM#	Metal	Description	VF	EF	Unc
4	4	Alum	50 Su, 1960	2	4	10

Y#	KM#	Metal	Description	VF	EF	Unc
5	5	C-N	1 Dong, 1960	0.75	1.25	4

Y#	KM#	Metal	Description	VF	EF	Unc
6	6	Alum	50 Xu, 1963	1	2	5

Y#	KM#	Metal	Description	VF	EF	Unc
7	7	C-N	1 Dong, 1964	0.35	0.50	1
8	8	C-N	5 Dong, 1966, scalloped	0.75	1.25	5
9	9	C-N	10 Dong, 1964	0.75	3.00	6

WEST AFRICAN STATES

A former federation of eight French colonial territories on the northwest coast of Africa, the West African States was composed of the autonomous (since 1958) republics of Dahomey, Ivory Coast, Mali, Mauritania, Niger, Senegal, Togo, and Upper Volta. Many of the countries reformed in 1975 as the Economic Community of West African States.

MONETARY SYSTEM
100 centimes = 1 franc

Y#	KM#	Metal	Description	VF	EF	Unc
1	3.1	Alum	1 Franc, 1961–75	0.20	0.40	0.75
2	2	A-Bz	5 Francs, 1960	0.25	0.50	1.00
3	1	A-Bz	10 Francs, 1959, 64	0.25	0.50	1.00

YEMEN

Yemen is situated in the southwest tip of the Arabian peninsula. Formerly an independent feudal kingdom, North Yemen became a Marxist republic (Yemen Arab Republic) in 1962 after a military coup. South Yemen, with its important port city of Aden, was under British control from 1839 until 1967, when the People's Democratic Republic of Southern Yemen was established. The two countries merged in 1990 to form a parliamentary republic. Since the late 1990s the country has been under attack by militant internal and foreign Muslims attempting to overthrow the government and create an Islamic state.

MONETARY SYSTEM
2 halala = 1 buqsha (bogach)
2 buqsha = 1 ghirsh (piastre)
40 buqsha = 1 imadi, ahmadi, ryal, or Maria Theresa thaler

IMAM YAHYA BIN MOHAMMED HAMID AL-DIN

AS REBEL, AH 1321 (1903–1904)

Y#	KM#	Metal	Description	VF	EF	Unc
A1	410	Silv	1 Ghirsh, AH 1321 (1903)	175	—	—

AS IMAM AND KING, AH 1322–1367 (1904–1948)

Y#	KM#	Metal	Description	VF	EF	Unc
B1	B1	Bz	1/2 Halala, AH 1322 (1904)	185	—	—

Note: Date 1322 is the accession date, not the issue date.

Y#	KM#	Metal	Description	VF	EF	Unc
1	1.4	Bz	1/2 Halala, AH 1342 (1923), crescents, type	900	—	—

Y#	KM#	Metal	Description	VF	EF	Unc
1a	1.1–1.2	Bz	1/2 Halala, AH 1342–46, (1924–28) plain type	40	80	—
2	C1	Bz	1 Halala, AH 1322 (1904)	550	—	—

Y#	KM#	Metal	Description	VF	EF	Unc
2a	2.1–2.8	Bz	1 Halala, AH 1330–61 (1912–43)	25	85	—
3	3.1–3.3	Bz	1 Bogach, AH 1341–67 (1923–49)	20	60	—

Note: There are at least five distinct varieties of Y3.

Y#	KM#	Metal	Description	VF	EF	Unc
4	4.1	Silv	1/20 Imadi, AH 1337–66 (1919–48)	20	40	75
5	5.1–5.4	Silv	1/10 Imadi, AH 1337–42 (1919–28)	125	250	—
5a	5.5	Silv	1/10 Imadi, AH 1343–66 (1925–48)	25	50	85
8	8	Silv	1/8 Imadi, AH 1339 (1921)	800	1,200	—
6	6	Silv	1/4 Imadi, AH 1341–43 (1923–25)	50	100	200
7	7	Silv	1 Imadi, 1 AH 344 (1926)	15	28	—

Y#	KM#	Metal	Description	VF	EF	Unc
10	10	Silv	1/4 Imadi, AH 1344–66 (1926–48)	35	50	100

Ahmed Hamid al-Din, *1948–1962*

Y#	KM#	Metal	Description	VF	EF	Unc
11	11.1	Bz	1 Halala, AH 1368–86 (1949–67)	1.00	3.00	10
12	12	Bz	1 Bogach, AH 1368–79 (1949–60)	1.75	3.75	15

Y#	KM#	Metal	Description	VF	EF	Unc
11a	11a	Alum	1 Halala, AH 1374–78 (1955–59)	1.50	3.00	10
12a	12a	Alum	1 Bogach, AH 1374–77 (1955–58)	2.75	5.50	15

Y#	KM#	Metal	Description	VF	EF	Unc
13	13–13.1	Silv	1/16 Imadi, AH 1367–74 (1948–55), pentagonal	15	30	60
A14	A14	Silv	1/10 Imadi, AH 1370 (1951)	1,500	2,500	—
14	14	Silv	1/8 Imadi, AH 1367–80 (1948–61), pentagonal	4	4	50

Y#	KM#	Metal	Description	VF	EF	Unc
14a	14a	Silv	1/8 Ahmadi, AH 1368, hexagonal	1,250	2,000	—

Y#	KM#	Metal	Description	VF	EF	Unc
15	15	Silv	1/4 Ahmadi, AH 1367–80 (1948–61)	7	12	20

Y#	KM#	Metal	Description	VF	EF	Unc
16	16	Silv	1/2 Ahmadi, AH 1367–82 (1948–63)	13	20	30

Y#	KM#	Metal	Description	VF	EF	Unc
17	17	Silv	1 Ahmadi (Ryal), AH 1367–80 (1948–61)	25	38	90

Y#	KM#	Metal	Description	VF	EF	Unc
18	18	Alum	1 Halala, ND (1956)	0.60	0.90	2.25
19	19	Alum	1 Bogach, ND (1956)	0.75	1.00	2.50

Note: Date AH 1367 on Y18–19 is the accession date, not the issue date.

Y#	KM#	Metal	Description	VF	EF	Unc
G15	G15	Gold	1/4 Ahmadi, "(1)"	1,000	1,250	2,500
G16	G16	Gold	1/2 Ahmadi, "(2)"	2,500	3,000	4,000
G17	G17.2	Gold	1 Ahmadi, "(4)"	3,500	4,500	5,500

YEMEN ARAB REPUBLIC, *1962–1990*

Y#	KM#	Metal	Description	VF	EF	Unc
20	20	Bz/Br	1 Halala, AH 1382 (1963)	1	1.50	4
22	22	Bz/Br	1 Bogach, AH 1382–84 (1963–65)	1	1.50	4

Y#	KM#	Metal	Description	VF	EF	Unc
21	21	Bz/Br	1 Halala, AH 1382 (1963), value spelled out	2	5.00	20
32	32	Bz/Br	1/2 Bogach (1 Halala), AH 1382 (1963), value as fraction	1	1.50	4

Y#	KM#	Metal	Description	VF	EF	Unc
23	23	Silv	1/20 Ryal, AH 1382 (1963)	20.00	40	75
24	24	Silv	1/10 Ryal, AH 1382 (1963)	3.50	10	20
25	25	Silv	1/5 Ryal, AH 1382 (1963)	25.00	50	150
A25	A25	Silv	1/4 Ryal, AH 1382 (1963)	175.00	550	975

Note: Thick and thin varieties exist of Y23–24 and A25.

Y#	KM#	Metal	Description	VF	EF	Unc
26	26	A-Bz	1/2 Bogach, AH 1382 (1963)	0.15	0.20	0.50
27	27	A-Bz	1 Bogach, AH 1382 (1963)	0.20	0.40	1.00
A27	A27	A-Bz	2 Bogach, AH 1383 (1964)	0.25	0.40	1.25

Y#	KM#	Metal	Description	VF	EF	Unc
28	28	Silv	5 Bogach, AH 1382 (1963)	1.25	1.75	3.50
29	29	Silv	10 Bogach, AH 1382 (1963)	2.25	2.75	5.00
30	30	Silv	20 Bogach, AH 1382 (1963)	4.50	5.00	10.00
31	31	Silv	1 Ryal, AH 1382 (1963)	8.50	12.50	25.00

YUGOSLAVIA

On the east shore of the Adriatic Sea, south of Hungary, this former part of the Ottoman Empire was formed after World War I by uniting to the Kingdom of Serbia, several Austro-Hungarian provinces, and the Kingdom of Montenegro as the Kingdom of the Serbs, Croats, and Slovenes. The name Yugoslavia was adopted in 1929. Following the Second World War, Josip Tito won a federal election and abolished the monarchy, creating a communist state. He kept ethnic and nationalistic differences under control, but after his death in 1980 tensions mounted. The federation was dissolved by civil war and the separation into independent republics beginning in 1991. In 2002, Yugoslavia was officially replaced by the federation of Serbia and Montenegro.

MONETARY SYSTEM

100 para = 1 dinar

PRECIOUS METAL CONTENT

Dates	Denomination	Gross Wt (g)	Fineness	Net Wt (g)	Troy Oz.
		SILVER			
1931–32	10 dinara	7.0000	0.5000	3.5000	0.1125
	20 dinara	14.0000	0.5000	7.0000	0.2251
	50 dinara	22.0000	0.7500	16.5000	0.5305
1938	20 dinara	9.0000	0.7500	6.7500	0.2170
	50 dinara	15.0000	0.7500	11.2500	0.3617
		GOLD			
1925	20 dinara	6.4516	0.9000	5.8064	0.1867
1931–33	1 dukat	3.4909	0.9861	3.4424	0.1107
	4 dukata	13.9636	0.9861	13.7695	0.4427

Petar I,
1918–1921
(Previously King of Serbia)

Y#	KM#	Metal	Description	VF	EF	Unc
1	1	Zinc	5 Para, 1920	5	10	60
2	2	Zinc	10 Para, 1920	3	7	20

Y#	KM#	Metal	Description	VF	EF	Unc
3	3	N-Bz	25 Para, 1920	3	6	20

Alexander I,
1921–1934
First Coinage

Y#	KM#	Metal	Description	VF	EF	Unc
4	4	C-N	50 Para, 1925	2.00	4	12.50
5	5	C-N	1 Dinar, 1925	2.00	4	12.50
6	6	C-N	2 Dinara, 1925	4.50	9	25.00

Y#	KM#	Metal	Description	VF	EF	Unc
10	7	Gold	20 Dinara, 1925	BV	375	475

Second Coinage

Y#	KM#	Metal	Description	VF	EF	Unc
7	10	Silv	10 Dinara, 1931	7	15	35
8	11	Silv	20 Dinara, 1931	7	15	35
9	16	Silv	50 Dinara, 1932	10	25	110

Note: There are two varieties of Y9: with and without name below truncation of neck.

Trade Coins

Y#	KM#	Metal	Description	VF	EF	Unc
A11	12	Gold	1 Dukat, 1931–33	175	285	325

Note: YA11 has a small official counterstamp on obverse near rim.

Y#	KM#	Metal	Description	VF	EF	Unc
12	14.1	Gold	4 Dukata, 1931–32	750	1,200	1,750

Note: Y12 has a small official counterstamp on obverse near rim.

Petar II,
1934–1945

Y#	KM#	Metal	Description	VF	EF	Unc
13	17	Bz	25 Para, 1938	2	5.50	13

Y#	KM#	Metal	Description	VF	EF	Unc
14	18	A-Bz	50 Para, 1938	1.00	3	8.50
15	19	A-Bz	1 Dinar, 1938	1.00	2	7.00
16	20	A-Bz	2 Dinara, 1938, large crown	1.25	3	9.00

Y#	KM#	Metal	Description	VF	EF	Unc
17	21	A-Bz	2 Dinara, 1938, small crown	10	20	40

Y#	KM#	Metal	Description	VF	EF	Unc
18	22	Nick	10 Dinara, 1938	1	3	10

Y#	KM#	Metal	Description	VF	EF	Unc
19	23	Silv	20 Dinara, 1938	7.50	15	45

Y#	KM#	Metal	Description	VF	EF	Unc
20	24	Silv	50 Dinara, 1938	12	15	27.50

CROATIA

German-Formed State, *1941–1944*

See Serbia for other World War II issues from this area.

Y#	KM#	Metal	Description	VF	EF	Unc
1	2	Zinc	2 Kune, 1941	5	15	30

FEDERATED REPUBLIC, *1945–1952*

Y#	KM#	Metal	Description	VF	EF	Unc
21	25	Zinc	50 Para, 1945	0.75	2.75	8
22	26	Zinc	1 Dinar, 1945	0.50	1.50	7
23	27	Zinc	2 Dinara, 1945	1.00	2.75	8
24	28	Zinc	5 Dinara, 1945	2.00	4.00	10

FEDERATED PEOPLE'S REPUBLIC, *1953–1962*

Legend: ***FEDERATIVNA NARODNA REPUBLIKA JUGOSLAVIJA***

Y#	KM#	Metal	Description	VF	EF	Unc
25	29	Alum	50 Para, 1953	0.10	0.20	0.50
26	30	Alum	1 Dinar, 1953	0.10	0.20	0.50
27	31	Alum	2 Dinara, 1953	0.20	0.30	0.75
28	32	Alum	5 Dinara, 1953	0.30	0.50	1.00

Y#	KM#	Metal	Description	VF	EF	Unc
29	33	A-Bz	10 Dinara, 1955	0.50	1	1.50

Y#	KM#	Metal	Description	VF	EF	Unc
30	34	A-Bz	20 Dinara, 1955	1	1.50	2.50

Y#	KM#	Metal	Description	VF	EF	Unc
31	35	A-Bz	50 Dinara, 1955	2	3	6

SOCIALIST FEDERATED REPUBLIC, *1963–1991*

New Legend: *SOCIJALISTICKA FEDERATIVNA REPUBLIKA JUGOSLAVIJA*

Y#	KM#	Metal	Description	VF	EF	Unc
32	36	Alum	1 Dinar, 1963	0.05	0.10	0.30
33	37	Alum	2 Dinara, 1963	0.10	0.20	0.50
34	38	Alum	5 Dinara, 1963	0.20	0.30	0.75

Y#	KM#	Metal	Description	VF	EF	Unc
35	39	A-Bz	10 Dinara, 1963	0.50	0.75	2

Y#	KM#	Metal	Description	VF	EF	Unc
A35	40	A-Bz	20 Dinara, 1963	1	1.50	3

Y#	KM#	Metal	Description	VF	EF	Unc
B35	41	A-Bz	50 Dinara, 1963	2	5	12.50

ZAMBIA

Located in south-central Africa, Zambia was formerly known as Northern Rhodesia. Between 1953–1963 it was part of the Federation of Rhodesia and Nyasaland. It became an independent republic in 1964. *Languages:* English and native tongues. *Capital:* Lusaka.

MONETARY SYSTEM

12 pence = 1 shilling
20 shillings = 1 pound

FIRST COINAGE

Y#	KM#	Metal	Description	VF	EF	Unc
1	1	CNZ	6 Pence, 1964	0.35	0.65	1.25

Y#	KM#	Metal	Description	VF	EF	Unc
2	2	CNZ	1 Shilling, 1964	0.60	1.25	2.50

Y#	KM#	Metal	Description	VF	EF	Unc
3	3	CNZ	2 Shillings, 1964, 75	0.75	1.50	3.25

ZANZIBAR

The Arab Sultanate of Zanzibar and Pemba was a group of islands off the east African coast plus a narrow strip of mainland. It was a possession of Muscat and Oman until becoming independent in the mid-19th century. In 1890 it became a British protectorate. In 1964 Zanzibar united with Tanganyika to form Tanzania.

For later issues, see East Africa.

MONETARY SYSTEM

64 pysa (pice) = 1 Indian rupee
136 pysa = 1 ryal, to 1908
100 cents = 1 rupee, 1908–1909

PRECIOUS METAL CONTENT

Dates	Denomination	Gross Wt (g)	Fineness	Net Wt (g)	Troy Oz.
		SILVER			
1882	1 ryal	27.2156	0.9000	24.4940	0.7875
		GOLD			
1882	2-1/2 ryals	4.1795	0.9000	3.7616	0.1209

SULTAN BARGHASH BIN SA'ID, *1870–1888*

Y#	KM#	Metal	Description	VF	EF	Unc
1	1	Cop	1 Pysa, AH 1299 (1882)	10	50	200
						Proof: $650

Y#	KM#	Metal	Description	VF	EF	Unc
2	7	Cop	1 Pysa, AH 1304 (1887)	15	75	350
						Proof: $800

Y#	KM#	Metal	Description	VF	EF	Unc
5	4	Silv	1 Ryal, AH 1299	350	550	1,250

Y#	KM#	Metal	Description	VF	EF	Unc
7	6	Gold	5 Ryals, AH 1299	25,000	45,000	95,000

Note: Other silver and gold coins dated AH 1299 (former Y3–4, 6) are patterns.

SULTAN ALI BIN HAMUD, *1902–1911*

Y#	KM#	Metal	Description	VF	EF	Unc
8	8	Bz	1 Cent, 1908	650	1,200	1,850
9	9	Bz	10 Cents, 1908	975	2,250	3,000

Y#	KM#	Metal	Description	VF	EF	Unc
10	10	Nick	20 Cents, 1908	1,200	2,250	4,000

Note: Y8–10 were not released to circulation.

APPENDIX A

PRECIOUS METAL CONTENT OF WORLD COINAGE, 1850–1964

Nearly all modern coins are composed of a mixture of two or more metals. This mixture, called an alloy, may be simply the traditional 90% silver and 10% copper, or something as complex as 50% silver, 40% copper, 5% zinc and 5% tin. Usually it is not important to know the exact composition of a coin; therefore the listings in the body of this catalog indicate only the principal metals used. The heading "Silver," for instance, is used for coins containing from 40% to 99.9% silver (those with less than about 50% silver may also be termed "Billon"), and "Gold" is applied to any coin containing enough gold to have a yellow color, from as low as 17.5% to as high as 99.9%.

Normally it is only in the case of precious metals that the exact proportions of a coin's alloy become significant to the collector. Such information can be used to determine the genuineness of a given coin, or to compute its intrinsic value based on its bullion content of gold or silver. In addition, some coins are now valued more for their metal content than as numismatic items. In the main body of the catalog, such coins are indicated by the abbreviation "BV" (Bullion Value) in the appropriate price guide columns. To determine the current bullion value of a coin, multiply the net troy ounce figure by the daily price quotation for the metal involved. As an example, if the day's fixed price of gold is $1,750 per ounce, the bullion value of a British sovereign is determined by multiplying $1,750 times .2354 ounce, giving $411.95 as the value of the gold in that coin.

In the previous edition of this book, this appendix listed Holland Wallace's compilation of the gross weights, finenesses, and net metal contents of every country's silver and gold coins, 1850–1964, expressed in both grams and troy ounces. For the 15th edition, this information has been moved to the country listings (the Latin and Scandinavian Monetary Unions remain below, for general reference). The weights and finenesses are those specified by law, and do not take into account any tolerances or fluctuations caused by the manufacturing process. Such tolerances range from a fraction of a percent up to many percentage points, depending on the technical ability and the willingness of the coining authority to adhere to its legal standards. Weights shown are, of course, for coins in substantially original condition that have not lost noticeable weight through wear.

In almost every case the weights and finenesses have been taken from official sources such as mint reports and other publications of various governments. Unofficial statistics have been used only where they seem to be highly reliable. Material from supposedly authoritative sources has sometimes been disregarded when it seemed questionable. Certain coinage, for the most part that of more irregular manufacture (most often issued in Asia or Mideast), has been omitted due to lack of any precise official data whatever. Other coinage, which may have been struck to less-strict standards, is included on the basis of gross weight in an observed range.

Because of the large volume of statistical material involved in the preparation of these tables, errors are possible. Further information that will increase the accuracy of the listings is invited.

Latin Monetary Union

The Latin Monetary Union was formed by treaties standardizing the silver and gold coinage of Belgium, France, Greece, Italy, and Switzerland. Derived from the French coinage system established in 1803, the union was formed in 1865 and dissolved in 1926. Many other countries, although not union members, struck coinage to identical standards both earlier and later. Other denominations shown below were struck prior to the union or by nonmember nations; these values have proportional weights and are included here for ease of reference.

Dates	Denomination	Gross Wt (g)	Fineness	Net Wt (g)	Troy Oz.
		SILVER			
1865–1926	20 centimes	1.0000	0.8350	0.8350	0.0268
	50 centimes / 1/2 franc	2.5000	0.8350	2.0875	0.0671
	1 franc	5.0000	0.8350	4.1750	0.1342
	2 francs	10.0000	0.8350	8.3500	0.2685
	5 francs	25.0000	0.9000	22.5000	0.7234
		GOLD			
1865–1926	5 francs	1.6129	0.9000	1.4516	0.0467
	10 francs	3.2258	0.9000	2.9032	0.0933
	20 francs	6.4516	0.9000	5.8064	0.1867
	50 francs	16.1290	0.9000	14.5161	0.4667
	100 francs	32.2581	0.9000	29.0323	0.9334
		GOLD			
Other	12-1/2 francs	4.0323	0.9000	3.6291	0.1167
	25 francs	8.0645	0.9000	7.2581	0.2333
	40 francs	12.9032	0.9000	11.6129	0.3734

Scandinavian Monetary Union

This union was formed by treaties between Denmark, Sweden, and Norway to standardize their monetary systems. Although never formally terminated, it was gradually abandoned following World War I. The only issues on this standard after World War II were Danish 2-kroner commemoratives to 1958.

Dates	Denomination	Gross Wt (g)	Fineness	Net Wt (g)	Troy Oz.
		SILVER			
1874–1958	10 ore	1.4500	0.4000	0.5800	0.0185
	25 ore	2.4200	0.6000	1.4520	0.0463
	50 ore	5.0000	0.6000	3.0000	0.0964
	1 krone / krona	7.5000	0.8000	6.0000	0.1929
	2 kroner / kronor	15.0000	0.8000	12.0000	0.3852
		GOLD			
1873–1931	5 kroner / kronor	2.2402	0.9000	2.0162	0.0648
	10 kroner / kronor	4.4803	0.9000	4.0323	0.1296
	20 kroner / kronor	8.9606	0.9000	8.0645	0.2593

APPENDIX B

ALPHABETICAL INDEX OF WORLD COIN DENOMINATIONS

abbasi—Afghanistan

adhio—Kutch

afghani—Afghanistan

agora (agorot)—Israel

ahmadi—Afghanistan

amani—Afghanistan

amman cash—Pudukkottai

anantaraya—Travancore

anna—Burma, India, India Princely States, Mombasa, Muscat and Oman, Pakistan

argentino—Argentina

asarfi—Nepal

ashrafi—Bahawalpur, Hyderabad, Nepal

att—Thailand

aurar—Iceland

avo—Macao, Timor

baht—Thailand

baisah—Muscat and Oman

balboa—Panama

ban (bani, banu)—Romania

belga—Belgium

birr—Ethiopia

besa (bese)—Ethiopia, Italian Somaliland

bit—Danish West Indies

bogach (buqsha)—Yemen

bolivar—Venezuela

boliviano—Bolivia

carolin—Sweden

cash—China, Pudukkattai, Travancore

cen—China

cent—British Caribbean Territories, British Honduras, British North Borneo, Brunei, Canada, Ceylon, China, Curacao, Danish West Indies, East Africa, Ethiopia, Hawaii, Hong Kong, Kiao Chau, Liberia, Malaya, Mauritius, the Netherlands, the Netherlands Indies, New Brunswick, Newfoundland, Nova Scotia, Prince Edward Island, Sarawak, Seychelles, Sierra Leone, South Africa, Straits Settlements, Suriname, United States, Zanzibar

centas (centai, centu)—Lithuania

centavo—Angola, Argentina, Bolivia, Brazil, Cape Verde, Chile, Colombia, Costa Rica, Cuba, Dominican Republic, Ecuador, El Salvador, Guatemala, Honduras, Mexico, Mozambique, Nicaragua, Paraguay, Peru, the Philippines, Portugal, Portuguese Guinea, Portuguese India, Puerto Rico, St. Thomas and Prince, Timor, Venezuela

centecimo—Bolivia

centesimo (centesimi)—Eritrea, Italy, San Marino, Somalia, Vatican City

centesimo (centesimos)—Chile, Dominican Republic, Panama, Paraguay, Uruguay

centime—Belgian Congo, Belgium, Cambodia, Cameroon, Comoro Islands, France, French Cochin China, French Equatorial Africa, French Indo-China, French Oceania, French West Africa, Guadeloupe, Haiti, Laos, Luxembourg, Madagascar, Martinique, Monaco, Morocco, New Caledonia, Reunion, Switzerland, Togo, Tunisia

centimo—Costa Rica, Guatemala, Paraguay, the Philippines, Spain, Venezuela

chervonetz—U.S.S.R.

ch'ien—China

chio—China, Manchukuo

chomsih—Mukalla, Quaiti, Tarim and Ghurfah

chon—Korea, North Korea

Christian d'Or—Denmark

chuckram—Travancore

colon (colones)—Costa Rica, El Salvador

condor—Chile, Ecuador

cordoba—Nicaragua

crown—Australia, Bermuda, Great Britain, Ireland, Malawi, New Zealand, Rhodesia and Nyasaland, Southern Rhodesia

cruzeiro—Brazil

dala—Hawaii

daler—Danish West Indies

decima—Spain

decimo—Chile, Colombia, Ecuador

dhabu—Kutch

dhinglo—Kutch, Travancore

dhyak—Nepal

dime—Hawaii, United States

dinar—Afghanistan, Hejaz, Iran, Kuwait

dinar (dinara)—Serbia, Yugoslavia

dinero—Peru

dirham—Iraq, Morocco

doblon—Spain

dokdo (dokda)—Junagadh, Kutch, Navanagar

dollar—Canada, China, Great Britain, Hawaii, Hong Kong, Liberia, Newfoundland, Straits Settlements, United States

dong—South Vietnam, Vietnam

double—Guernsey

drachma (drachmai)—Crete, Greece

dub—Hyderabad

dukaat—the Netherlands

dukat—Sweden

dukat (dukata)—Yugoslavia

dukat (dukaten)—Austria, Hungary

eagle—United States

escudo—Angola, Cape Verde, Chile, Costa Rica, Ecuador, Mexico, Mozambique, Portugal, Portuguese Guinea, Portuguese India, St. Thomas and Prince, Spain, Timor

eyrir (aurar)—Iceland

falus—Bukhara, Indian Princely States

fanam—Travancore

farthing—Ceylon, Great Britain, Ireland, Jamaica, Malta

fen—China, Chinese Turkestan, Manchukuo

fenig (fenigow)—Poland

filler—Hungary

fils—Iraq, Jordan, Kuwait, Saudi Arabia

florin—Australia, Austria, East Africa, Fiji, Great Britain, Ireland, Malawi, New Zealand, South Africa

forint—Hungary

franc—Algeria, Austria, Belgian Congo, Belgium, Cambodia, Cameroon, Comoro Islands, Danish West Indies, Ecuador, France, French Equatorial Africa, French Oceania, French Somaliland, French West Africa, Guadeloupe, Guinea, Hungary, Katanga, Luxembourg, Madagascar, Martinique, Monaco, Morocco, New Caledonia, Reunion, Rwanda and Burundi, St. Pierre and Miquelon, Sweden, Switzerland, Togo, Tunisia, West African States

franco—Dominican Republic

frang—Albania, Luxembourg

frank (franken)—Belgium, Liechtenstein, Saarland, Switzerland

fuang—Thailand

fun—Korea

gersh—Ethiopia

ghirsh—Egypt, Hejaz, Nejd, Saudi Arabia, Sudan, Syria, Yemen

gourde—Haiti

groat—Great Britain

groschen—Austria

grosz (grosze, groszy)—Poland

guarni—Paraguay

guinea—Saudi Arabia

gulden—Austria, Curacao, Danzig, the Netherlands, the Netherlands Indies, Suriname

habibi—Afghanistan

halala—Saudi Arabia, Yemen

haler (halere, haleru, halierov)—Bohemia-Moravia, Czechoslovakia, Slovakia

hao—China, Vietnam

heller—Austria, German East Africa

hsien—China

hwan—South Korea

imadi—Yemen

jinia—Egypt, Saudi Arabia

kapang—Sarawak

kharub—Tunisia

kopejek—Tanna Tuva

kopek—Germany, Russia

kori—Junagadh, Kutch

korona—Hungary

koruna (korun, koruny)—Bohemia-Moravia, Czechoslovakia, Slovakia

krajczar—Hungary

kreuzer—Austria

krona (kronor)—Sweden

krona (kronur)—Iceland

krone (kronen)—Austria, Liechtenstein

krone (kroner)—Denmark, Greenland, Norway

kroon (krooni)—Estonia

kuna (kune)—Croatia

kurus—Turkey

kyat—Burma

larin (lari)—Maldives

lats (lati)—Latvia

lek (leke, leku)—Albania

lempira—Honduras

leone—Sierra Leone

lepton (lepta)—Crete, Greece

leu (lei)—Romania

lev (leva) bulgaria—

li—China, Chinese Turkestan, Manchukuo

liang—China, Chinese Turkestan

libra—Peru

lira (lire)—Eritrea, Italian Somaliland, Italy, San Marino, Syria, Turkey, Vatican City

litas (litai, litu)—Lithuania

mace—China, Chinese Turkestan

macuta—Angola

mahalek—Ethiopia

maravedis—Spain

mark—Estonia, German New Guinea, German States, Germany

markka (markkaa)—Finland

matona—Ethiopia

mazuna—Morocco

mei—China

melgarejo—Bolivia

mil—Cyprus, Hong Kong, Israel, Palestine

milesima—Spain

millieme (millim)—Egypt, Libya

millim—Sudan, Tunisia

milreis—Brazil, Portugal

misqal—Chinese Turkestan

mohar—Nepal

mohur—Burma, India, India Princely States

mongo—Mongolia

mun—Korea

muzuna—Morocco

naye paise—India

onza—Costa Rica

ore—Denmark, Faeroe Islands, Greenland, Norway, Sweden

pagoda—Travancore

pahlavi—Iran

pai—Baroda, Hyderabad

paisa (paise)—Afghanistan, India, India Princely States, Nepal

para—Egypt, Hejaz, Sudan, Turkey

para (pare)—Montenegro, Serbia, Yugoslavia

pataca—Macao, Timor

payalo—Kutch

pengo—Hungary

penni (pennia)—Finland

penny (pence)—Australia, British Guinea, British West Africa, Ceylon, Fiji, Ghana, Great Britain, Guernsey, Ireland, Jamaica, Malawi, New Brunswick, New Guinea, New Zealand, Nigeria, Nova Scotia, Rhodesia and Nyasaland, Rhodesia, South Africa, Southern Rhodesia, Zambia

perper (perpera)—Montenegro

pesa—German East Africa

peseta—Peru, Puerto Rico, Spain, Viscayan Republic

pessa—Lahej

peso—Argentina, Cambodia, Chile, Colombia, Costa Rica, Cuba, Dominican Republic, El Salvador, Guatemala, Honduras, Mexico, Paraguay, the Philippines, Puerto Rico, Uruguay

peso bolivano—Bolivia

pfennig—Danzig, German New Guinea, Germany

piastre—Cambodia, Cyprus, Egypt, French Cochin China, French Indo-China, Lebanon, Libya, Sudan, Syria, Tonkin, Tunisia, Turkey

pice—Bhutan, East Africa, India, India Princely States, Mombasa, Pakistan

pie—India Princely States, Pakistan

pond—South African Republic

pound—Great Britain, Israel, Rhodesia, South Africa

pruta (prutah)—Israel

puffin—Lundy

pul—Afghanistan, Khiva

pya—Burma

pysa—Zanzibar

qindar ari—Albania

qindar leku—Albania

qiran—Afghanistan, Iran

quetzal—Guatemala

rand—South Africa

rappen—Switzerland

real (reales)—Chile, Colombia, Dominican Republic, Ecuador, El Salvador, Guatemala, Honduras, Mexico, Paraguay, Peru, Spain, Venezuela

reichsmark—Germany

reichspfennig—Germany

reis—Azores, Brazil, Portugal, Portuguese India

rentenpfennig—Germany

rial—Iran, Morocco

riel—Cambodia

rigsdaler—Denmark

riksdaler—Sweden

rin—Japan

riyal—Iraq, Muscat and Oman, Saudi Arabia

ruble—Armavir, Khiva, Khwarezm, Russia, U.S.S.R.

rupee—Afghanistan, Bhutan, Burma, Ceylon, India, India Princely States, Mauritius, Mombasa, Nepal, Pakistan, Seychelles, Tibet

rupia—Italian Somaliland, Portuguese India

rupie (rupien)—German East Africa

ryal—Hejaz, Muscat and Oman, Nejd, Yemen, Zanzibar

salung—Thailand

sanar—Afghanistan

santeem—Ethiopia

santims (santimi, santimu)—Latvia

sapeque—Annam, French Cochin China, French Indo-China

satang—Thailand

schilling—Austria

scudo—Bolivia, Peru

sen—Cambodia, China, Indonesia, Japan, the Netherlands Indies

sent (senti)—Estonia

shahi—Afghanistan, Iran

shilling—Australia, British West Africa, Cyprus, East Africa, Fiji, Ghana, Great Britain, Guernsey, Ireland, Jamaica, Jersey, Malawi, New Guinea, New Zealand, Nigeria, Rhodesia and Nyasaland, Rhodesia, South Africa, Southern Rhodesia, Zambia

sho—Tibet

skarung (skar)—Tibet

skilling—Demark, Norway

sol (soles)—Bolivia, Peru

somalo—Somalia

sovereign—Australia, Canada, Great Britain, India, South Africa

speciedaler—Norway

srang—Tibet

stotinka (stotinki)—Bulgaria

su—South Vietnam

sucre—Ecuador

sueldo—Bolivia

tael—China, Chinese Turkestan

takka—India Princely States

talari—Ethiopia

tallero—Eritrea

tanga—Portuguese India

tangka—Tibet

tenga—Bukhara, Khiva

thaler—Austria

tical—Thailand

tilla—Afghanistan, Bukhara

timasha—Ladakh

toman—Daghistan, Iran

trade dollar—Japan, United States

trambiyo—Kutch, Navanagar

tukhrik—Mongolia

venezolano—Venezuela

vereinsthaler—Austria, Liechtenstein

wark—Ethiopia

warn—Korea

wen—China, Chinese Turkestan

whan—Korea

won—Korea

xu—North Vietnam, South Vietnam, Vietnam

yang—Korea

yen—Japan

yuan—China

zloty (zlote, zlotych)—Poland

About the Editor

Arthur Friedberg has been a professional numismatist for more than 30 years. His firm, The Coin & Currency Institute, Inc., co-owned with his brother Ira, is a founding member of the elite International Association of Professional Numismatists (IAPN).

In June 2001, in Rome, Italy, Friedberg was elected president of the Association, marking the first time in the 50-year history of the organization that an American has occupied that office. He is also a life member of the American Numismatic Association and has been a member of the prestigious Professional Numismatists Guild since 1977.

Friedberg joined Coin & Currency (a family firm) after college. He graduated in 1972 with a BA in history from The George Washington University in Washington, DC, later earning an MBA from New York University, in 1976. Within a short time he and Ira co-authored revisions of *Gold Coins of the World* and *Paper Money of the United States*. They also wrote the new editions of *Appraising and Selling Your Coins*, which has more than a quarter of a million copies in print. The brothers are coauthors of the *Guide Book of United States Paper Money* (Whitman Publishing). Arthur is a contributor to the *Standard Catalog of World Coins* and has written numerous articles for *Numismatist*, the journal of the American Numismatic Association.

He has been a consultant to the Money and Medal Programme of the Food and Agriculture Organization of the United Nations in Rome, Italy, and has testified as an expert on commemorative coin matters before the United States Senate Banking Committee. He has also been retained by advertising agencies, law firms, insurance companies, and others to provide advice on coins and on international and domestic numismatic marketing.

In 1993 the Friedbergs were awarded the Prix d'Honneur of the IAPN for *Gold Coins of the World* as the best book of the preceding year. They have also been presented the Medal of Merit of the American Numismatic Association (1992) for "distinguished service to the hobby." Arthur Friedberg received the first-place Heath Literary Award (1994) as author of the article judged best in *The Numismatist* during 1993, and the Swiss Vrenelli Prize (1999) for "outstanding contributions to numismatics."

Credits and Acknowledgments

Contributors

Antonio Allessandrini
Jan Olav Aamlid
Garry Charman
Miguel Costa
Roberto Delzanno
Paolo Esteves
Stephen C. Fenton
David L. Ganz
A. J. Gatlin
Michael Hardmeier
Terez Horvath
Dariusz Jasek
Arne Kirsch
J.C. Lee
Nirat Lertchitvikul
Gary Levitan
Jan Lingen
Dmitry Markov
Tom Michael
Masahiro Oka
Federico Pastrone
Francesco Pastrone
Theo Peters
Ian Pitt
Michael Pitt
Kent Ponterio
Richard Ponterio
Tony Raymond
Marco Rinaldi
William M. Rosenblum
Albert Scheffers
Daniel Frank Sedwick
Scott Semans
M. Louis Teller
Gunnar Thesen
Antonio Miguel Trigueiros
Jean-Luc van der Schueren
Randy Weir
Zhou Shou Yuan
Jeffrey S. Zarit

Images

Cabinet des Medailles, Brussels
Coin & Currency Institute
Daniel Frank Sedwick, LLC
Fritz Rudolf Künker Münzenhandlung
Goldberg Rare Coins
Heritage Auctions
Numismatik Lanz München
Hess-Divo AG
Hungarian Mint, Ltd.
Ponterio & Associates, Inc.
Teller Numismatic Enterprises
Royal Belgian Mint
Spink & Son, Ltd.
Stack's Bowers Galleries
UBS Gold & Numismatics

Cliff Tsuboi provided coins for photography and assisted with image cataloging.

We also wish to acknowledge the contributions of the following individuals who were instrumental in the previous editions of *A Catalog of Modern World Coins*.

Stephen Album
Alain Baron
Alex Basok
Aubrey E. Bebee
Lauren Benson
Kenneth E. Bressett
Colin R. Bruce II
Adolfo Cayon
Juan R. Cayon
Pavel Cerny
Daniel K.E. Ching
William B. Christensen
Samuel T. Clements
Courtney L. Coffing
Scott Cordry
Filipe Correia
Freeman L. Craig Jr.
William D. Craig
William Cross
Eddie J. Cummings
Jean-Paul Divo
Augusto Dragoni
Sanford J. Durst
James F. Elmen
Steve Eyer
Dennis Gill
Ira M. Goldberg
Bruce R. Hagen
Thomas B. Hamilton
Lee E. Harvey
Wade Hinderling
Patrick D. Hogan
Clyde Hubbard
Granvyl G. Hulse
Thomas Ikins
Norman Jacobs
R.W. Julian
Art Kagin
Don Kagin
Paul Kagin
Ernst Kraus
Chester L. Krause
Samuel Lachman
Lars O. Lagerqvist
Donald Lorimer
Enrico Manara
Walter L. Mason Jr.
Balazs Meekesh
Johan Mevius
Robert Mish
Clifford Mishler
Charles Moore
Bill Noyes
Laszlo Nudelman
Masamichi Oka
Charles K. Panish
Mathias Paoletti
William A. Pettit
Ronald Posner
Bill Randel
Mary Anne Randel
Ed Reiter
Joseph Rose
William M. Rosenblum
Russell Rulau
Remy Said
Hans M.F. Schulman
Neil Shafer
Edward Smith
Scott Semans
R.C. Soxman
William F. Spengler
Harvey Stack
Robert L. Steinberg
Karl Stephens
Maurice A. Storck
Richard D. Thompsen
Albert A. Tom
Robert van Bebber
Didier Vanoverbeek
Cliff van Rensburg
E.D.J. van Roekel
Ruben W. Vergara
I.V. Victorov
Holland Wallace
J.B. Westergaard
R.B. White
Nelson M. Whitman
Gus Wing
Jeffrey Young
Charles E. Wyatt
Chin Lin Yao

INDEX